'*Oasis of Imagination* offers a refreshing and much-needed vision for the church to engage with the wider culture in a way that is neither shrill nor shallow. Ted Turnau's passionate call to cherish the creative arts as God himself does provides fresh, compelling ways for the church to connect with and bless the world. Whether you consider yourself a creative or not, his insights will inspire you to imagine a church faithful to its own imaginative calling and show you how you can play your own part in offering hospitality and hope to a weary world. This book is a must-read for anyone seeking to deepen their relationships and influence beyond the walls of the church.'
Peter Dray, Director of Creative Evangelism, The Universities and Colleges Christian Fellowship (UK)

'This is a wonderful book. Above all it is full of . . . imagination. It combines solid theoretical foundations with lively examples. It's all very rich, but Part 4 holds a special interest for me. I have been personally invested in several of the personages here. Few if any studies that I know of join together this company under the theme "subversive, hopeful protest". The section on Blind Willie Johnson is worth the price of the book. Non-Christians ought to read this book, if only to disabuse them of the bromides about evangelicals. Christians must read this book in order greatly to enhance their lives.'
William Edgar, Professor Emeritus of Apologetics, Westminster Theological Seminary

'We have waited a long time for a biblical theology of the imagination, and Ted Turnau has given us a deep, thirst-quenching drink. Here you will find a sure-footed guide, who avoids both cultural indifference and culture wars, plants a dagger in heart of Christian kitsch, and then encourages us onwards, without nostalgia, not to be satisfied with merely consuming, or even intelligently critiquing our culture, but to decide to contribute. You'll be taken into territory that is unfamiliar, thrilling and occasionally disturbing. You'll be shown how the gospel is provocative, unsettling and yet deeply compelling to a lost world. Above all, Ted has laid down a challenge for artists, churches, pastors, creatives of all kinds, to "plant oases", where we can begin to imagine what it's like to inhabit

the glory of the kingdom-yet-to-come, and make it so attractive that, even as we worship here, we long to be home, bringing many others with us.'
Chris Green, vicar of St James, Muswell Hill

'I don't know of a more comprehensive, more inviting or more compelling case for a Christian understanding of the imagination than the one offered in this book. *Oasis of Imagination* belongs in every church library, every seminary, every Christian classroom and on every believer's shelf. I wish I'd had this book years ago. I will be using it for years to come.'
Karen Swallow Prior, author of *The Evangelical Imagination: How stories, images, and metaphors created a culture in crisis*

OASIS OF IMAGINATION

Ted Turnau is Chair of Literature and Culture at Anglo-American University, Prague, Czech Republic, where he also teaches on popular culture, the media, religion and social theory. He is the author of *Popologetics: Popular culture in Christian perspective* (P&R, 2012), *The Pop Culture Parent: Helping kids to engage their world for Christ*, with co-authors E. Stephen Burnett and Jared Moore (New Growth, 2020), and *Imagination Manifesto: A call to plant oases of imagination* (IVP, 2023). He speaks widely on popular culture, the media and Christian cultural engagement. He and his wife Carolyn have three adult children, three cats and a rabbit.

OASIS OF IMAGINATION

Engaging our world through a better creativity

Ted Turnau

INTER-VARSITY PRESS
SPCK Group, RH101, The Record Hall, 16–16A Baldwin's Gardens, London EC1N 7RJ, England
Email: ivp@ivpbooks.com
Website: www.ivpbooks.com

First published 2023

British Library Cataloguing-in-Publication Data
A catalogue record for this book is available from the British Library.

ISBN: 978–1–78974–475–0
eBook ISBN: 978–1–78974–477–4

Set in Minion Pro 11.5/15pt
Typeset in Great Britain by CRB Associates, Potterhanworth, Lincolnshire
Printed in Great Britain by Clays Ltd

Produced on paper from sustainable sources

Inter-Varsity Press publishes Christian books that are true to the Bible and that communicate the gospel, develop discipleship and strengthen the church for its mission in the world.

IVP originated within the Inter-Varsity Fellowship, now the Universities and Colleges Christian Fellowship, a student movement connecting Christian Unions in universities and colleges throughout Great Britain, and a member movement of the International Fellowship of Evangelical Students. Website: www.uccf.org.uk. That historic association is maintained, and all senior IVP staff and committee members subscribe to the UCCF Basis of Faith.

For my father, Roger William Turnau (1938–96),
whose faith and passion for truth profoundly shaped my own

For Bill Edgar,
a friend and mentor who has been like a second father to me,
and one of the most insightful and eirenic people I have ever met.
Thank you for opening my mind to the wonders of culture
and imagination

For my daughter, Claire Elise Turnau Ward – a beautiful, artistic soul.
I didn't know until the very end that I was writing this for you

Contents

Plates

Acknowledgments

First and foremost, I thank my wife, Carolyn. She is my alpha-reader – the one who is in my head but with enough distance to catch my mistakes. Her encouragement and patient, loving service made this book possible.

I want to thank those who read early drafts of parts of this book: Bill Edgar, Reverend Wade Bradshaw, Dan Strange, Reverend Randy Edwards and Alastair Gordon. Iron sharpening iron, they gave much encouragement and helpful (sometimes hard, but welcome) suggestions. (By the way, Wade, you win. I owe you $50. See the discussion of kitsch in chapter 8.)

I want to thank the artists who spared time to be interviewed by me, giving me glimpses of truly creative hearts and minds: Ruth Naomi Floyd, Ryan and Amy Green, Josh Larson, and Sho Baraka. To the two Hollywood creatives, the actress and the filmmaker I interviewed for chapter 4, who wish to remain anonymous: thank you for giving of yourselves so selflessly. And a warm thank you to Ally Gordon, David 'Cully' McCulloch, Nate Orr and Sarah White of Morphē Arts for giving me insight into the challenges and opportunities facing Christian creatives today.

Thanks also to Jennifer Schneider, Tereza Radostova and George Shortess for advice and suggestions regarding cognitive science. I should note that Dr Shortess does not agree with my conclusions, so chapter 6 represents my views, not his.

I would like to thank Bruce Barron for his editing suggestions. Also my agent Pieter Kwant, who believed in this work, gave many great suggestions and guided it to the right publisher. Deep gratitude is due to my editor and dear friend Caleb Woodbridge and the rest of the team at IVP in the UK (Joshua Wells, Rima Devereaux, Michelle Clark and Richard Augustus, to name but four). Their patient attention and guidance helped this project of more than ten years come to fruition.

A huge debt of gratitude is owed to my dear friend Jason Ramasami, whose illustrations breathe life and clarity into many of the ideas in this book. His selfless work has made this book richer and more approachable.

I would like to thank God for his good gift of tasty pour-over coffee, without which none of this would have been possible.

Finally, I want to thank an editor who shall remain nameless . . . because I've lost his rejection letter. Back in 2011, he told me that there was no way anyone would publish a 550-page book by a first-time author. Further, he said, my manuscript actually contained *two* books, so I would be wise to split them up. This book was originally meant to be part 2 of my first book, *Popologetics* (P&R, 2012), but that editor was absolutely right. Because of his prompting, here we are. Thanks.

Introduction

The parable of the oasis that was really a portal to another universe

Once upon a time, there was a traveller who habitually trekked throughout a dry and hostile land. It didn't bother him much, for it was all he knew. One day he saw in the distance a patch of greenery. That much colour in a land of unbroken dust-brown enticed him, and he set out for it. As he drew closer, the patch of green revealed more detail to him. This was a place of tall trees, lush undergrowth, and wild flowers.

He entered into the shade. In the centre of the oasis, he found a still pool of crystal clear water.

But he found he was not alone, for there was a man across the pool from him, staring intently down into the water.

The traveller enquired why the man was staring so. Perhaps he had seen a fish? 'No,' the man replied. 'No fish. Something more remarkable. See for yourself.'

The traveller stared intently, too, and saw something glimmering at the bottom of the pool.[1] It might have been simply the shimmering sunlight refracted on to the rocks below. But no, it was something more. He couldn't see it clearly, but he found the light mesmerizing. It fascinated him in a way that he could not put into words.

He cautiously asked the man across the pool about the glimmering light, what he thought it was. They talked about it until the sky grew dark and it was time for the traveller to move on.

But he was so intrigued that he came back the next day, both to gaze into the pool and to continue his conversation with the stranger.

[1] See page 1 in plate section.

The stranger had brought food, so they shared a meal together as they continued talking, sharing ideas and theories about the mysterious light at the bottom of the pool. The traveller resolved to return again the next day. And so he did. This became his habit for some time.

Gradually, he found that he had become more and more dissatisfied with the dry and hostile land. He much preferred the cool shade of the oasis and the company offered there. Eventually, the stranger lost his strangeness and became a trusted friend and discussion partner.

And all the while, the light at the bottom of the pool came more and more into focus, as if someone were adjusting a hidden lens. Whole cities full of light and life began to take shape before his unbelieving eyes. The traveller knew it was impossible, for cities do not reside at the bottom of ordinary pools. Nevertheless, he continued to study the image. He sensed in it a piercing beauty that entranced and drew him magnetically, almost more than he could bear. He loved his time gazing into the pool. And yet he felt a profound sadness, for the light stirred in him deep grief as well as deep gladness.

It became increasingly obvious that this was no ordinary pool. It was, rather, a doorway to another world, another way of being. It also became clear that the man who had been a stranger and was now his friend had, in effect, become his guide. It was only a matter of time before the traveller would take the plunge to the bottom of the pool to begin the most improbable, miraculous journey he could have ever imagined.

Why we need oases

How are we to relate and contribute to a culture largely estranged from Christ? How do we invite in those who have grown accustomed to the desert?

Culture is a conversation. This book is about how creative culture-making can help the Christian church enter into and contribute to this conversation in ways that build bridges, ways that heal rifts, even in a world that might no longer welcome Christian commitments.

Christian cultural creativity done well creates oases for the imagination. Oases are open, porous spaces that invite the stranger in; spaces that refresh the soul, provoke conversation, challenge assumptions and lead the imagination to a new place. The landscape today is littered with false oases – spiritual paths that lead to shallow, toxic pools to nowhere.[2] Most in the West are no longer enchanted by the gospel. They are enchanted by something – anything – else.

Our world needs Christian creatives who can plant true oases.

Our world needs church communities to understand and draw alongside their creatives to support and encourage those planting oases.

Theologically conservative Christians have spent too much time and energy fighting non-Christian culture (culture warring), withdrawing into safe spaces (the 'Christian bubble') or just trying to keep their heads above water spiritually. There is more going on, a deeper, wider drama, and every Christian – artistically gifted or not – has a part to play.

Have we played our part? If culture is a shared conversation that runs between and through us, many Christians simply try to opt out or else force the conversation one way or another. If culture is a piece of music, some Christians seem tone-deaf. Our musical ear for culture-making shapes how the surrounding culture sees the Christian faith – as beautiful or ugly. The Christian church in the post-Christian West is in danger of defaulting on its aesthetic calling. You might never have thought of the church as having an 'aesthetic calling', a responsibility not only to proclaim truth but also to show its beauty. That's part of the problem. But don't worry, we'll explore what that means and why it matters.

Thomas à Kempis, the medieval writer of *The Imitation of Christ,* wrote, 'All men desire peace, but very few desire those things that make for peace.'[3] Similarly, we all long for the Christian faith to be seen as beautiful. We all desire oases for the imagination. Too few in the church are willing

[2] I recommend two fascinating studies of America's current spiritual landscape. Tara Isabella Burton presents a landscape dominated by intuition-driven made-to-order spiritualities (what she calls the 'Religious Remixed') in *Strange Rites: New religions for a godless world* (New York: Public Affairs, 2020). She argues persuasively that the decline in American institutional religions does not mean that religion per se is disappearing. Rather, that faith commitment is being displaced into other outlets. Religion isn't something that evaporates from human life; it shape-shifts into more culturally acceptable forms. Pastor David Zahl in *Seculosity: How career, parenting, politics, and romance became our new religion and what to do about it* (Minneapolis, MN: Fortress Press, 2019) argues that even secular pursuits can be invested with a religious weight – that, by them, we hope to achieve 'enoughness', a sense that our existence means something. But these secular religions simply place us on hamster wheels of achievement anxiety without end.

[3] Thomas à Kempis, *The Imitation of Christ*, book 3, chapter 25.

to do the things that would help to make it happen. This book seeks to encourage those things that make for oases, that make for a powerful and beautiful aesthetic witness.

Oases engage cultural hopes and fears, building bridges into the inner lives of those far from Christ, as well as those struggling with their faith in Christ. I teach university classes on culture, media, world view and religion. I hear the questions and struggles of my students. University is an odd time of life, a dress rehearsal for adulthood. Many students wrestle with questions like, 'How much may I hope? What childhood dreams must I release? What, realistically, can I expect out of life? What will my desires – for myself, my loved ones, my world – come to?' The answers the world has to offer often prove empty.

These questions linger far beyond graduation. I am old enough to understand the midlife crisis. I didn't really want the expensive sports car or extramarital affair that stereotypically accompany a midlife crisis, but I do understand the restlessness that comes with catching sight of one's own death. Life is so brief. What is left for me, now that I'm closer to the grave than to the cradle? What have my life and aspirations amounted to? Has it all been worth it? In what may I still hope? Where does my true home lie?

This is the human condition – chained to desires we cannot fulfil in the present, unsure if we may realistically hope they ever will be. The Germans call this 'Sehnsucht', a yearning for an unknown far-off country that is our truest home.[4] Well-made, well-planted oases raise questions, summon hopes and reveal possible paths to take us home. They stir desire for something else, something better.

And desire is the engine that shapes what I call the 'imaginary landscape' – the aspirations and anxieties that underlie cultural works.[5]

4 On Sehnsucht and the longing for home that drove the younger brother in Jesus' parable and drives us, see Timothy Keller, *The Prodigal God: Recovering the heart of the Christian faith* (New York: Dutton, 2008), pp. 92–95.

5 Readers may notice a similarity to Charles Taylor's concept of 'social imaginary' – that is, broadly shared background assumptions about reality that make beliefs plausible or implausible. 'Imaginary landscape' is more focused on how individual creative cultural works penetrate our shared (and fragmented) cultural consciousness. See Charles Taylor, *Modern Social Imaginaries* (Durham, NC, and London: Duke University Press, 2003), pp. 23–25. For a good summary of the concept of social imaginary, see James K. A. Smith, *Desiring the Kingdom: Worship, worldview, and cultural formation* (Grand Rapids, MI: Baker Academic, 2009), pp. 65–68.

Oases can set up resonances within the musical conversation of culture, giving people ears for something richer than the tired old tunes they are used to.

The things that make for oases: imagination

So what are the 'things that make for oases', that lead to positive contributions to the cultural conversation? The key ingredient is imagination. We will explore imagination more in part 2 but, for now, here is a brief working definition:

> The imagination is a human power that orientates us – mind and body – in the world, through which we perceive and create. It orientates us both individually and collectively, so we can speak of a 'collective imagination' or 'imaginary landscape'. The imagination inspires us to create, *and* it colours our experience of the world and our assumptions about reality. The imagination mediates: we shape our world through it, and through it our world shapes us.

Think of the imagination as a permeable filter between us and the world. But unlike, say, a coffee filter, this filter is active, dynamic, flowing. It shapes our sense of place in the world, our identities, who we are or think we are. It can shape oases, true and false. And it is shaped by oases, true and false.

Imagination is always in conversation with faith (or unfaith).[6] Each informs the other. The playground of the imagination is the place where issues of belief and unbelief are decided. Faith struggles are often less intellectual, more aesthetic and imaginative; less about arguments and evidence, more about imaginary horizons inherited from culture. We dwell within those horizons, and what lies beyond feels, literally, beyond belief. For this reason alone, the imaginative and aesthetic witness of Christians matters greatly.

[6] That is, imagination informs and inflects the various types of atheism, New Age paganism and varieties of 'other enchantment', as I called it above.

The aim of this book is to help Christians to develop a better understanding of the imagination and what it does so that our communities can live robust, imaginative lives as they encourage and support those who plant oases. These creative cultural works form imaginary worlds that welcome in both Christians and non-Christians for refreshment, recalibration and conversation. Creative cultural involvement is all about using the imagination to construct worlds for both the church and the common good, reversing the spiritual confusion and 'desertification' of our post-Christian world.[7]

The plan of the book

The imagination is a hard subject to pin down. It skitters all over the place like a chihuahua on espresso. We will approach it carefully, in stages.

- Part 1 asks if we should even engage culture and, if so, how? Spoiler alert: the answer is 'Yes, and we ought to pay attention to the imagination.'
- Part 2 asks, what is the imagination and why does it matter? It presents a theory of the imagination by exploring the testimony of God's 'two books', Scripture and nature, especially *human* nature, as revealed in selected works of cognitive science, philosophy and literary theory.
- Part 3 sharpens our focus to ask, what makes the *Christian* imagination distinctive and resonant in a post-Christian world? What makes for good or bad Christian art and entertainment?
- Part 4 explores examples of the Christian imagination done well in a variety of media and genres. What might an oasis of the imagination look like, whether in film, music, video games, literature or other media?
- Part 5 examines the resources that Christians need to reform, refresh and sustain the Christian imagination: worship and the artist-within-community. Why does the church need artists, and what do artists need from the church?

7 As mentioned in note 1, when a society becomes disenchanted with the gospel, it becomes enchanted with other things. For a detailed study of what this looks like in the West, see Jason A. Josephson-Storm, *The Myth of Disenchantment: Magic, modernity, and the birth of the human sciences* (Chicago, IL: University of Chicago Press, 2017).

The book's overall arc explores questions such as, 'How can we, in this day and age, best enter the cultural conversation for the common good? What kinds of imagination are best suited to expressing creatively the multifaceted glory of Christian faith in a culture that is both suspicious and tired of it? How can we set creatives free by encouraging and supporting those who plant oases?'

Christian cultural creativity could become a game-changer and a productive step away from complacency, divisive culture wars and the self-protective bubble Christianity that have become so common. We can create communities of imaginative flourishing that radiate healing light out into the broader culture.

How to use this book

I hope that this book attracts different types of readers with different interests, concerns and attention spans concerning the Christian imagination and creative cultural involvement (what I call the church's 'aesthetic witness'). I hate it when authors assert stuff without sharing the reasoning *behind* their assertions, so I have organized the book in the form of a logical argument – A leads to B leads to C and so on. But you don't have to use it that way. Think of it as a 'make your own adventure' book and dip in where you're most interested, meandering back to things you missed if you want to. For example, if you:

- are convinced that we ought to engage culture through creativity, but want to know what that looks like in practice, skip to the artists I showcase in part 4;
- want clarity about what makes a Christian imagination resonate in a post-Christian world (the stuff that ties the case studies in part 4 together), go to part 3;
- want practical guidance on how the church can feed its own imaginative life and treat its creatives better, skip straight to part 5;
- are a nerd like me and have questions about how to define the imagination in general, go to part 2, where we get into the technical, nitty-gritty details of a Christian theory of imagination;

- are really unsure about whether or not Christians *should* involve themselves in this cultural conversation at all, or why culture warring or cultural withdrawal aren't the ways to go, then you probably need the whole enchilada, starting with part 1.

The choices are yours.

Becoming a part of the cultural conversation in a way that builds bridges rather than erects walls is necessary work.[8] This conversation shapes our shared imaginary landscape, our shared cultural narratives, hopes, fears and desires. If we do not enter in and contribute in a meaningful, healing way that resonates past our own communities, we have no right to complain when the imaginary landscape becomes a desert or choked with weeds that tangle people, will-o'-the-wisps and enchantments that lead away from God into quicksand. Like nature, the imaginary landscape abhors a vacuum. In the absence of a winsome, honest Christian creativity, it will inevitably become enchanted by other things, other visions of the world.[9] Like Jesus' parable about the formerly demon-possessed man whose house is 'swept clean' (Luke 11:24–26), the collective imagination never stays unoccupied for long.

Consider the call to contribute imaginatively to the cultural conversation as part of the privilege of serving as ambassadors for Christ (2 Corinthians 5:14–21). For Christ's love compels us to rethink how we use and enjoy the imagination so that we might connect with non-Christian friends and neighbours at a deeper level, enabling the gospel to shine all the brighter. We will also learn how to love and serve our Christian brothers and sisters more fully. Along the way, we become richly blessed, surrounded by imaginatively robust Christian communities. Contributing creative cultural works that resonate in our shared culture (oasis planting) isn't just about loving and serving others. It is about being

[8] Of course, the gospel will remain a stumbling block and foolishness for many (see 1 Corinthians 1:23). But cultural insensitivity makes the stumbling block worse, and makes the gospel look *more* foolish and repugnant. That does not honour Christ.

[9] Because our current cultures are so fragmented, it would be more accurate to talk in terms of competing imaginary *landscapes*, plural. For the sake of convenience, however, I will continue to speak in terms of a mainstream imaginary landscape rather than mapping the multitudes of intersecting post-Christian landscapes. In both cases, the calling of the Christian imagination remains the same: engage in a way that refreshes, encourages, challenges and creates space for conversation.

fully and joyfully human, alive to all the wonder that God has woven into this world around us.

Starting positions

Imagination is a huge topic. It encompasses our whole personalities and applies to all areas of life: leadership, science, parenting, engineering, business, architecture, education, urban planning and so on. We cannot possibly cover all of that. This book is concerned with the area that has the most direct impact on the aesthetic witness of the church: arts and entertainment. We will be particularly interested in imaginative works intended for life *outside* the sanctuary or fellowship hall[10] – the places where non-Christians live and where Christians spend most of their time.

I bring a number of starting assumptions to this task that my readers may or may not share.

1. The Christian Bible is trustworthy, our ultimate authority for belief and practice, including about the topic of the imagination.
2. God also speaks truth through his creation. The Bible is not a textbook on every subject. It doesn't address quantum mechanics, contemporary literary theory, nor how to write a sitcom. To understand the dynamics and patterns of God's creation, we must listen to God's voice by studying creation. Scientists, philosophers and thinkers of all stripes will prove helpful here.
3. Nevertheless, the Bible gives us our foundational framework for understanding the *meaning* of creation. We should be attentive to sympathetic resonances between what we read in the Bible and what we find in creation (via scientists, philosophers and others). That is where I shall try to position my own understanding of the imagination.
4. Finally, we are interested in a certain kind of Christian imagination: one that resonates and invites with the other-enchanted in a

10 Though we will explore worship in part 5, we will steer clear of the 'worship wars'. Others have written well on that topic. See, for example, Mike Cosper's *Rhythms of Grace: How the Church's worship tells the story of the gospel* (Wheaton, IL: Crossway, 2013).

post-Christian world. That is, we must contextualize our investigation for the world we live in.[11]

Who is this book for?

This book is for Christian creatives who seek clarity about the imagination and how to avoid pitfalls that ensnare some artists. It's for Christian leaders who long for their churches to adopt a less defensive posture and, instead, explore more positive ways to engage the world around them, those who wish to understand the creatives in their midst better and how best to pastor them. It's for everyday Christians who are not artists by profession but want to learn about art and imagination to better support the creatives in their communities.

This is *not* a 'how to' book. I will not explain how to plant an oasis. Artists and other creatives know that territory better than I. For those who want a shorter, more direct dive into practical stuff, I have co-written a shorter book with the jazz vocalist, art photographer and social activist Ruth Naomi Floyd called *Imagination Manifesto.* In this book, however, we will delve into a bit more theory and theology, seeking to explore important questions. In a time when the gospel has lost credibility, how can the imagination help us move forwards? How can we restore the aesthetic witness of Christ's church in a post-Christian world? How can we re-enter the cultural conversation and start making music rather than being satisfied with tone-deafness?

This is a call to action, in your Christian community and beyond. But I do not wish to 'tie up heavy burdens, hard to bear, and lay them on people's shoulders' (Matthew 23:4). Instead, this is more than a call to action; it is a call to wonder, a call to open your imagination to the beauty of God's grace revealed in Christ to the dark world through the power of the Spirit. To hear the call of imagination, you will have to use *your* imagination. May God enlighten the eyes of your heart to open you to that wonder, so you may walk in it.

---

11 Contextualization does not mean compromising the gospel, selling out to the world. It means letting Christian truth shine in wavelengths our post-Christian friends can actually see. For an excellent introduction to contextualization, see Tim Keller's talk on YouTube, 'Tim Keller – Center Church: What is contextualization?', Redeemer City to City, YouTube (28 February 2013), <www.youtube.com/watch?v=3eUvwzmV0P8>, accessed January 2023. See also Keller's book, *Center Church: Doing balanced, gospel-centered ministry in your city* (Grand Rapids, MI: Zondervan, 2012), especially part 3, 'Gospel contextualization'.

Part 1
THE CASE FOR OASES

1

Why engage culture? Calling, holiness and the new creation

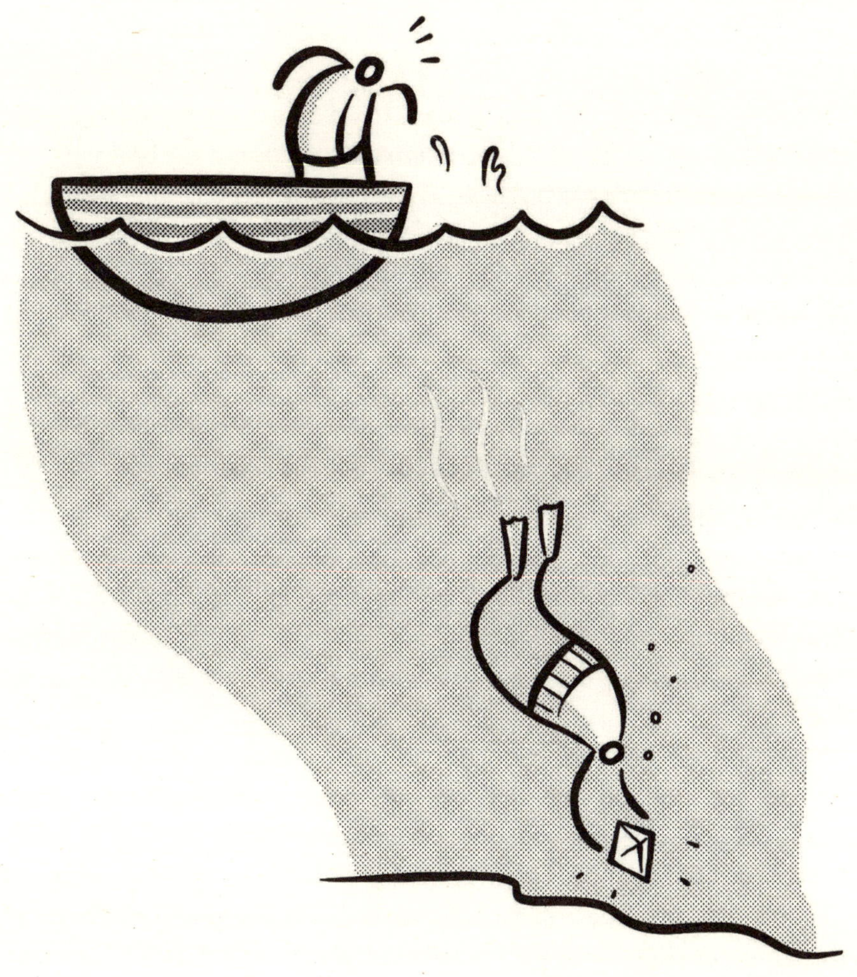

Introduction: plight of the DJ

Years ago, after I finished a talk on creative cultural engagement at a Christian conference, a young man approached me with a dilemma. He was thin, blonde, earnest and looked to be about 19. He said:

> I'm a DJ and I'm doing pretty well. I just signed with a major label. The thing is, I can't tell the people in my church what I do for a living. When I've tried, they say, 'Why are you playing music for druggies?' What should I do?

My heart broke for this young man. I had an answer for him (see the introduction to part 2), but his question burrowed into my brain and sat there for years. In fact, his predicament inspired this book: that image left in my mind of the isolation of a Christian creative trying to make a difference in a post-Christian world, *often against the wishes of his brothers and sisters in Christ*. My theological instincts tell me that this is wrong and I want to set it right. We can start by asking whether or not cultural engagement is a good idea.

Concerning the phrase 'cultural engagement'

For many, the phrase 'cultural engagement' triggers images of endless nasty public debates, culture warriors yelling past one another and the thousands of emotionally wounded people left in their wake. Or the phrase can summon images of smug Christians in the grip of the 'hipness unto death', their cultural savvy overriding love for others. This is *not* what I mean.

To my mind, 'cultural engagement' means, broadly, that Christians ought to be concerned enough about the culture we live in to understand it and involve ourselves with it because we want to make the world a better place for everyone. Think not of engaging in battle so much as engaging in conversation for the common good. William Temple, Archbishop of Canterbury during the 1940s, is supposed to have said that the Christian church is 'the only society that exists for the benefit of those who are not its members'.[1] German theologian Dietrich Bonhoeffer was even more pointed, writing from a Nazi prison: 'The Church is the Church only when it exists for others . . . not dominating, but helping and serving. It must tell men of every calling what it means to live for Christ, to exist for others.'[2] The church is called primarily to *serve*. That is what I mean by 'engaging'.

The opposite of being engaged is being *dis*engaged. Too often the church seems to be disengaged, strangely detached from the world, either withdrawing from it or fighting against it. Too often Christians also don't seem to *want* to serve the common good. This feels obvious – of course we want to make the world a better place – yet many Christians remain suspicious of the idea that Christians should be involved with culture.

This suspicion stems from two attitudes:

- 'Culture won't last, so why bother?'
- 'Culture (the world) stains and undermines holiness.'

Let us address each of these in turn.

Is engaging culture worth it? Will culture last?

Culture as calling

'Culture' is a complicated term. Culture is the call God has given for us to use, care for, develop and reconfigure his creation wisely for his glory, and to love and serve those around us. Culture begins in Genesis 1:26–28 with the creation of the first man and woman:

> Then God said, 'Let us make man in our image, after our likeness. And let them have dominion over the fish of the sea and over the

[1] The quotation seems to be a simplified summary of this statement by Temple: 'Only in His own gift of Himself is it reasonable to expect that all men will find what they need; only in a Church which is the vehicle of this gift, and is known to be this, and not a mutual benefit society organised by its own members for their several and collective advantage – only in a Church expressive of Divine transcendence can all nations find a home.' From his 'Lecture on church and state', in *Church and Nation: The Bishop Paddock Lectures for 1914–15* (London: Macmillan and Co., 1915), <www.gutenberg.org/ebooks/43896>, accessed January 2023.

[2] Dietrich Bonhoeffer, *Letters and Papers from Prison*, tr. Reginald Fuller, Frank Clark, et. al., ed. Eberhard Bethge (New York: Touchstone, 1997), p. 382.

birds of the heavens and over the livestock and over all the earth and over every creeping thing that creeps on the earth.'

So God created man in his own image,
in the image of God he created him;
male and female he created them.

And God blessed them. And God said to them, 'Be fruitful and multiply and fill the earth and subdue it, and have dominion over the fish of the sea and over the birds of the heavens and over every living thing that moves on the earth.'

Theologians call this the 'Cultural Mandate', God's call for us to *image* him as Creator, to reflect his creativity. Unlike God, we cannot create ex nihilo. Rather, we create *a Dei creatura*, from God's creation. We take his creation and rule over its resources wisely in imitation of God. That call remains even after the fall. Though culture is now bent by sin, God's grace still runs along cultural channels, lightening an otherwise sin-darkened world, so it still merits our active involvement. Theologian William Edgar puts it this way:

Cultural engagement is the human response to the divine call to enjoy and develop the world that God has generously given to his image-bearers. Culture includes the symbols, the tools, the conventions, the social ties, and all else contributing to this call. Cultural activity occurs in a historical setting, and is meant to improve the human condition. Because of the fall, culture can and has become sinister. Christ's redeeming grace moves culture in the right direction, ennobles it, and allows it to extend the realm of God's shalom, his goodness, his justice, his love.[3]

Further, culture becomes home, a lived context for experience, shaping the lens through which we see the world around us, the imaginary

[3] William Edgar, *Created and Creating: A biblical theology of culture* (Downers Grove, IL: InterVarsity Press, 2016), pp. 176–177. For another helpful summary of the Cultural Mandate, see chapter 2 of William D. Romanowski's *Cinematic Faith: A Christian perspective on movies and meaning* (Grand Rapids, MI: Baker Academic, 2019).

landscape that forms our hopes, fears, dreams and anxieties.[4] In other words, culture is not just 'out there', it lives *in and through* us. We are called to involve ourselves actively with this creational gift that shapes our lived experience of reality.

The Cultural Mandate versus the Great Commission?

Some have accused the Cultural Mandate of being a distraction from the Great Commission, Jesus' command to go and make disciples of all nations (Matthew 28:16–20). Some worry that if Christians focus too much on culture, evangelism will be neglected.[5] This is a red herring; they are not really opposed. The Great Commission includes, but goes far beyond, evangelism. Jesus calls us to 'go and make disciples'. More than simply evangelizing, making disciples includes training people into a whole way of life. It is an inescapably *cultural* thing.

Both William Edgar[6] and New Testament scholar Richard Middleton[7] argue that the Cultural Mandate and Great Commission dovetail. They both lead us to involve ourselves with the world in the hope that 'the earth will be filled with the knowledge of the glory of the LORD as the waters cover the sea' (Habakkuk 2:14), enabling people to flourish and find 'life to the full' (John 10:10, NIV). Properly understood, both the Cultural Mandate and the Great Commission work towards the same end: making the world a better place for God's glory and for the shalom of his image-bearers.

---

4 Some call this 'world view'. I prefer 'imaginary landscape' to highlight the affective and imaginative aspect of our perspectives and postures in the world.

5 This is a criticism that is characteristic of the Reformed Two Kingdoms theology (or R2K). While I appreciate R2K's robust doctrine of the church, word and sacraments, R2K cordons off a 'secular' kingdom that is neatly detached from the spiritual concerns of the church. Such dualism effectively undermines Christ's universal lordship over all of creation. Theologian David VanDrunen is considered the major proponent of this dualistic perspective. See his *Living in God's Two Kingdoms: A biblical vision for Christianity and culture* (Wheaton, IL: Crossway, 2010). For an accessible critique of R2K, see Keith Mathison, '2K or not 2K? That is the question: A review of David VanDrunen's *Living in God's Two Kingdoms*, part 1', Ligonier Ministries (9 December 2010), <www.ligonier.org/learn/articles/2k-or-not-2k-question-review-david-vandrunens-living-gods-two-kingdoms>, and part 2, <www.ligonier.org/learn/articles/2k-or-not-2k-question-review-david-vandrunens-living-gods-two-kingdoms-part-2>, both accessed January 2023. See also David T. Koyzis, 'Two kingdoms and cultural obedience', *Comment* (1 March 2010), <https://comment.org/two-kingdoms-and-cultural-obedience>, accessed January 2023.

6 Edgar, *Created and Creating*, pp. 125 and 186.

7 Richard Middleton, *A New Heaven and a New Earth: Reclaiming biblical eschatology* (Grand Rapids, MI: Baker Academic, 2014), pp. 68–70.

That is why there should be no tension between those who insist that Christians share the good news and those who insist that the gospel must result in social justice, mercy ministries and a creative cultural life. It's not an either/or but a both/and. Sharing the gospel means more than just saving an individual soul here or there. It introduces people to a new creation where sin and social oppression shall be no more, a remaking of the whole cosmos. Both the Cultural Mandate and the Great Commission call us to engage culture in a project of remaking the world for the glory of God and the love of others.

Does it matter in the long run?

In Ridley Scott's classic sci-fi film *Blade Runner* (1982), a 'replicant' (an artificially made human, designed for dangerous off-world work) named Roy Batty returns to earth to seek his maker, demanding that he lengthen his lifespan beyond the usual four years. Late in the film he realizes that he cannot change his fate. Feeling death taking hold, he reflects on his life and the things that he's seen and done, that all his life's moments and memories will be lost, 'like tears in the rain'. He then quietly bows his head and falls silent. Death comes for us all, but the question lingers: will all *our* moments be lost like tears in the rain? Death brings with it a horrible futility, a crashing down of all our hopes.

We *want* our lives to have a lasting impact, to mean something in the long term. God has made us with 'eternity in our hearts' (see Ecclesiastes 3:11). Does what we do with our lives matter, when all is said and done, or does it all just go away?

For atheists who have no hope beyond death, the answer is simple: 'Yes, all our moments *are* lost. We are a doomed species caught in an absurd situation, and death gets the final word.'[8] They see this as integrity, facing up to hard truths that Christians simply won't accept. Christians, however, have a hope that extends beyond death. But does what we invest most of our time and energy in now – our jobs, our family life, our free time – simply evaporate when Jesus returns? Do they *mean* anything in the new creation or will they all be lost in time, like tears in the rain?

[8] That is, if atheists are consistent. Some atheists will try to avoid this conclusion by means of more positive sentiments, such as a parent telling a child that a deceased grandparent 'lives on in our hearts'.

Many Christians believe that once Jesus returns, the world and everything in it will be destroyed. Our souls will be saved and go to heaven, but all that once occupied us will be gone, forgotten. Why, then, invest time and energy in this world? Famous American radio preacher J. Vernon McGee asserted, 'You don't polish the brass on a sinking ship!'[9] Better to spend your energy getting people *off* the ship into lifeboats. Likewise, many Christians see this world as a doomed, sinking ship. Why try to improve a doomed planet? Instead, try to save as many souls as you can before the world goes up in flames. So, yes, all our moments, our jobs, everything that *seems* important here, will be lost like tears in the rain when Jesus comes again. Or so these Christians believe.

Clues that the old creation survives into the new

However, there are tantalizing clues that suggest continuity between the old and new creation, that God intends not the destruction of the old world but, rather, its cleansing, renewing and glorifying.

The first clue is that the Bible portrays God as one who genuinely cares for his creation, even protecting it against his own people. The people of Judah are exiled because they refused to let the land rest (2 Chronicles 36:21) and polluted the land with idolatry and social injustice (Ezekiel 36:17–18). Habakkuk predicts that the terror and destruction the Chaldeans visited on trees and animals will be revisited on them (Habakkuk 2:17). Revelation 11:18 is most explicit: the day of the Lord is a time 'for destroying the destroyers of the earth'. God is *invested* in his non-human creation. He cares about what happens to it when it is victimized. Wouldn't it be odd if he then chooses to destroy it?

The second clue is that God will set creation free. In Romans 8:19–21, Paul presents creation as a groaning prisoner eagerly awaiting the liberation of God's people when Jesus returns. That will liberate all

[9] This popularly attributed quote is derived from a longer story about the Morro Castle, a luxury liner that caught fire and went down. The point remains the same. McGee asserts, 'God says that He has no intention of saving this civilization, marvellous though it is. It is godless, and God has judged it. The torch will be put to it one of these days.' J. Vernon McGee, 'From the top of the Mount of Olives you can see forever', a pamphlet published by his Thru the Bible Radio Network, 1984, <www.ttb.org/resources/electronic-booklets>, see under 'Additional booklets', accessed January 2023. McGee may have been borrowing from famous nineteenth-century evangelist Dwight L. Moody's quote, 'I look upon this world as a wrecked vessel. God has given me a lifeboat and said, "Moody, save all you can."', quoted in George Marsden, *Understanding Fundamentalism and Evangelicalism* (Grand Rapids, MI: Eerdmans, 1991), p. 21.

creation. 'Liberation' and 'destruction' are two *very* different concepts. You don't liberate people by executing them, unless you work for some evil totalitarian regime that uses Orwellian double-speak: 'You are scheduled for "liberation" at 12 noon today. Here's your last meal.' God doesn't set his creation free by destroying it.[10]

In fact, the Bible's understanding of redemption is stubbornly material and cosmic in scope. God will be satisfied with nothing less than the redemption, renewal and transformation of all creation. Romans 8:19–23 extends redemption beyond God's people to every created thing. Biblical salvation encompasses not just individual souls but also bodies (1 Corinthians 15:35–54) and the whole cosmos![11] As theologian Anthony Hoekema puts it:

> Christ is involved in redemption as the one through whom and for whom all things were created, and as the one who is therefore deeply concerned with the entire creation. Nothing short of the total deliverance of creation from its 'bondage to decay' (Rom. 8:21) will satisfy the redemptive purposes of God.[12]

Anti-clues: doesn't the Bible predict creation's total destruction?

But what about other passages that seem to point to cosmic destruction? Both the Old and New Testaments contain destruction imagery associated with the day of the Lord, the time when God himself will come to judge the earth. The Bible presents images of fires (Isaiah 10:16), mighty storms (Jeremiah 25:32), earthquakes (Ezekiel 38:19; Revelation 8:5), stars falling from the sky (Mark 13:24–26; Revelation 6:13) and the sky being rolled back as a scroll (Revelation 6:14, quoting Isaiah 34:4).[13] Some cataclysm is

---

10 This Orwellian scenario actually comes very close to David VanDrunen's reading of Romans 8:19–23: creation is set free from its groaning by being annihilated. It is, quite literally, 'redeeming' creation through a mercy killing. See VanDrunen, *Living in God's Two Kingdoms*, pp. 65–66.

11 Other passages Richard Middleton examines that point to a creation-wide salvation include Acts 3:19–21; Ephesians 1:9–10; Colossians 1:19–20; 2 Peter 3:10–13. See Middleton, *A New Heaven and a New Earth*, pp. 156–158 and 160–163.

12 Anthony Hoekema, *The Bible and the Future* (Grand Rapids, MI: Eerdmans, 1979), p. 33.

13 For a more complete list of biblical imagery associated with the day of the Lord, see Leland Ryken, James C. Wilhoit and Tremper Longman III (eds), 'Day, Day of the Lord', *Dictionary of Biblical Imagery* (Downers Grove, IL: InterVarsity Press, 1998).

surely in view, but does it result in the utter annihilation of the old creation, so that God must create the new creation from scratch?

It is helpful to keep in mind the structure of creation as the ancient Hebrews saw it. Creation consisted of layers. From the lowest layer upwards, they are:

- the depths – the seas and all that is under the earth;
- the earth – the realm of humans, plants and land animals;
- the sky – seen as a dome, the 'firmament' or 'expanse', where the sun, moon and stars dwell;
- the highest heavens – beyond the sky, the dwelling place of God.[14]

The vivid imagery associated with the day of the Lord has more to do with God approaching from the highest heavens to judge the evil powers of the world (and the world reacting to his presence) than it does with the annihilation of creation. Descriptions of earthquakes indicate that the earth itself is trembling as God draws near (Isaiah 24:1–3, 18–21; Revelation 6:12).[15] Stars falling from the firmament means that there is disruption in the heavens (the layer separating the highest heaven from earth) as God approaches – God even is said to roll it back like a scroll to clear a way for himself. As Isaiah pleaded when he longed for God to judge the world, 'Oh that you would rend the heavens and come down!' (Isaiah 64:1).[16] Further, stars were often associated with rebellious spirits, and they are described as falling as God judges them. Recall the famous passage where God casts down the Morning Star ('Lucifer' in Latin) in Isaiah 14:12, echoed by Jesus in Luke 10:18 ('I saw Satan fall like lightning') and by John, who foresaw stars falling like ripe figs (Revelation 6:13). The tumult on

---

14 See E. C. Lucas, 'Cosmology' in T. Desmond Alexander and David W. Baker (eds), *Dictionary of the Old Testament: Pentateuch* (Downers Grove, IL: InterVarsity Press, 2003), pp. 137–138. See also John R. Roberts, 'Biblical cosmology: Implications for Bible translation', *Journal of Translation*, vol. 9, no. 2 (2013), pp. 1–53, especially 'Picture of biblical cosmology', p.6, <www.sil.org/system/files/reapdata/12/43/41/124341128276351405827628859265062803872/siljot2013_2_01.pdf>, accessed January 2023.

15 Middleton (*A New Heaven and a New Earth*, pp. 109–114) notes that earthquakes have been part of the rhetoric of theophany (the appearance of God) since Sinai (Exodus 19:18), especially when God comes in judgment. See also Judges 5:4–5; Psalms 29; 97:4–5; Isaiah 29:6; 30:30; Micah 1:3–4; Habakkuk 3:6.

16 Middleton, *A New Heaven and a New Earth*, pp. 187–189. See also Psalm 18:9 (NIV), 'He parted the heavens and came down.' The whole psalm is full of prophetic divine judgment imagery.

earth and in the heavens does not describe the destruction of creation. It foretells the crushing defeat of demonic forces as they are cast down from their lofty positions. God wins; they lose.

Another indication of the survival of the old creation is its connection with our resurrection bodies. Middleton sees an interesting parallel between what will happen to our bodies (as reported by Paul in 1 Corinthians 15:35–58) and what will happen to the world.[17] There will surely be a change, as from seed to flower, the perishable 'putting on' the imperishable, but the seed and the flower are not completely different. So, too, there will be continuity between our present perishable bodies and our glorified imperishable bodies. God will not destroy the one and replace it with something completely new, just as Jesus' raised body was not destroyed and replaced. You could still see the nail marks! But it was different, too, with all sorts of wonderful abilities.[18] Middleton's argument is that the way God treats our physical bodies indicates how he will treat creation as a whole. It will be different, but there will be continuity as well. We live in the seed form of the new creation that groans and waits to be renewed and glorified into its full flowering.[19]

But surely a passage like 2 Peter 3:10–13 promises a fiery end to this present creation, right? Not really. Let's take a closer look.

> But the day of the Lord will come like a thief, and then the heavens will pass away with a roar, and the heavenly bodies [*stoicheia*] will be burned up and dissolved [*lythēsetai*], and the earth and the works that are done on it will be exposed [*heurethēsetai*]. Since all these things are thus to be dissolved [*lyomenōn*], what sort of people ought you to be in lives of holiness and godliness, waiting for and hastening the coming of the day of God, because of which the heavens will be set on fire and dissolved [*lythēsetai*], and the heavenly bodies [*stoicheia*] will melt as they burn! But according to his promise we are waiting for new heavens and a new earth in which righteousness dwells.

---

17 This paragraph summarizes Middleton, *A New Heaven and a New Earth*, pp. 201–204.

18 I am *not* saying that we will necessarily share all those abilities. The Bible doesn't say anything about that.

19 This is a specific instance of a much wider theme in the New Testament: the already/not yet nature of the kingdom of God.

This is a difficult passage, but the deeper you dig into it, the less it points to the annihilation of creation and the more it points to judgment against the evil powers and *their* destruction. First, unfortunately the King James Version's translators used an unreliable manuscript for this passage. Verse 10 does *not* say that the earth will be 'burned up', κατακαήσεται (*katakaēsetai*). The word used in older and more reliable manuscripts is εὑρεθήσεται (*heurethēsetai*), which means will be 'exposed' (literally, 'found'). That is, the works done on the earth will be revealed for what they are in the searching heat of God's judgment.[20]

Still, there are things that are described as 'passing away with a roar', 'dissolving' and being 'set on fire'. But what precisely are they? The heavens – that is, the layer separating God's throne room and the earth. God will burn his way through that as he approaches in judgment, as we saw in Isaiah 64:1. There is another object that dissolves and melts: the *stoicheia*. Some translate this word as 'elements', following Stoic philosophers who used it to refer to the four elements (fire, earth, air, water).[21] It occurs only three other times in the New Testament (Galatians 4:3, 9; Hebrews 5:12), to refer to elementary teachings.[22] Biblical scholar Clifford Winters suggests that *stoicheia* in 2 Peter 3 means that God will burn up the heretical principles and teachings that have plagued his people.[23] Most modern translators draw on the context of the heavens in 2 Peter 3:10 and 12 to translate it as 'heavenly bodies', which, as mentioned, were often associated with demonic or rebellious spirits.[24] In any case, unless Peter was following the Stoic philosophers, he is talking about God judging evil powers, not annihilating the earth.

Finally, notice the word Peter uses three times in our passage: *lythēsetai*, translated as 'dissolved', from the verb λύω (*lúō*), 'dissolving'. It is often

---

20 The King James Version relies on the Textus Receptus, a manuscript of the Greek New Testament used widely in the sixteenth century. Though it was the best available manuscript at the time, older and more reliable manuscripts have since been discovered. For further discussion, see Middleton, *A New Heaven and a New Earth*, pp. 161–162, and Douglas J. Moo, 'Nature in the new creation: New Testament eschatology and the environment', *Journal of the Evangelical Theological Society*, vol. 49, no. 3 (September 2006), p. 468.

21 See Middleton, *A New Heaven and a New Earth*, p. 190.

22 Euclid uses the word in his treatise on the basic principles of geometry.

23 Clifford Winters, 'A strange death: Cosmic conflagration as conceptual metaphor in 2 Peter 3:6–13', *Conversations with the Biblical World*, vol. 33 (2013), pp. 147–161, cited in Middleton, *A New Heaven and a New Earth*, pp. 197–199.

24 These spirits might have led people astray with false teaching about fundamental principles, so perhaps Peter has both meanings in view.

taken to mean 'destroy',[25] but is better translated as 'loosing' or 'releasing'. The same verb is used when Jesus asks Lazarus to be released from his bandages in John 11:44. Here it means not destruction but transformation, a radical change of nature.[26] Further, biblical scholar Albert Wolters argues that, in fact, Peter here is drawing on the vocabulary of metalworking found in Malachi 3:2–3, describing fire that refines rather than destroys.[27] The evidence is fairly conclusive: even here, the Bible predicts not the destruction of creation but, rather, its cleansing, by judging evil powers (the *stoicheia*) and its radical transformation for his glory into the new heavens and new earth.

God will come in judgment against evil, not against creation. In the process, God will reclaim, purify, heal, renew and glorify creation by his own presence. No wonder creation groans with eager expectation (Romans 8:19, 22)!

Will culture survive? When the kings come marching in

Does this mean that the new creation will include culture or only nature? Will the new creation be somehow a-cultural or will some cultural works survive into the new creation?

Notice that the biblical story begins in a garden and ends in a city.[28] Apparently God's plan for the new creation involves cultural development.

There is a third clue about the continuity between the old and the new creation (and cultures). John draws a fascinating picture that gives us a partial answer to this question. Pagan kings, drawn by the light of God and of the Lamb, march into the new Jerusalem bearing treasures – the 'glory and honour' of their nations (Revelation 21:24–26). John borrows this image from Isaiah 60. Theologian Richard Mouw wrote a whole book

25 Note that the verb used here, *lúō*, is unusual and different from the verb and related noun used in 3:6–7, ἀπώλετο (*apōleto*), generally translated as 'to perish' or 'to be destroyed'. That makes sense – Peter is describing the flood – but verses 10–12 are different. *Lúō* does *not* mean 'to destroy' here.

26 Moo, 'Nature in the new creation', p. 468.

27 Albert Wolters, 'Worldview and textual criticism in 2 Peter 3:10', *Westminster Theological Journal*, vol. 49 (1987), pp. 405–413, <www.allofliferedeemed.co.uk/Wolters/AMW2Peter3.pdf>, accessed January 2023. See also Middleton, *A New Heaven and a New Earth*, pp. 194–195.

28 See, for example, Andy Crouch, *Culture Making: Recovering our creative calling* (Downers Grove, IL: InterVarsity Press, 2008), chapter 6.

on this one chapter alone.[29] These are not necessarily converted, Christian kings. They certainly were not in Isaiah 60 – they were nations that had been hostile to and oppressed Israel. But now, God has won a great victory and their roles are reversed. Submissive pagan kings bring their treasures to serve God's people. The same is likely to be the case in Revelation 21:24–26. These 'kings' may or may not trust in Christ individually. Regardless, they submissively bring treasures for God's glory and to serve God's people in a cultural role.[30]

The role of 'king' here is significant. In the ancient world, kings weren't merely political; they were the patrons and representatives of their whole cultures:

> The king of a given nation could bear, singly, a far-reaching authority that is today divided among many different kinds of leaders: the captains of industry; the moulders of public opinion in art, entertainment and sexuality; educational leaders; representatives of family interests; and so on. This is why Isaiah and John could link the entrance of the kings into the City with the gathering in of the 'wealth of the nations'.[31]

Who are the 'kings' of today? What might they bring to the new Jerusalem? Not gold in treasure chests, probably, but the 'glory and honour' of their cultures – the very best, presented to glorify the King of Kings, adorn his city and nourish his people. Perhaps the cultural 'kings' of the UK (not only the monarch but also, perhaps, the BBC's executives) will bear episodes of *Doctor Who* or David Attenborough's nature documentaries (updated to acknowledge nature's Lord). Maybe America's 'kings' (Hollywood executives), will bear their music, films and video games. China's cultural leaders might arrive with their millennia-old traditions of visual art, drama, music and the martial arts. Africa could contribute its rich storytelling, singing and polyrhythmic musical

---

[29] Richard Mouw, *When the Kings Come Marching In: Isaiah and the new Jerusalem* (Grand Rapids, MI: Eerdmans, rev. edn, Kindle edn, 2002).

[30] See Mouw, *When the Kings Come Marching In*, loc. 430.

[31] Mouw, *When the Kings Come Marching In*, loc. 457–461. This eschatological ingathering of treasure from Gentile peoples may well be prefigured in the appearance of the gift-bearing Magi in Matthew 2:1–12. Thanks to my wife Carolyn for pointing this out.

treasures. There is so much richness that these and other 'kings' could bring to *the* King.

Whatever the future may hold, Revelation 21:24–26 points to a reality: cultural works play a role in the new creation. What, specifically, *will* endure into the new creation, to be carried by our 'kings' into the new Jerusalem? And how does this cultural ingathering fit with the prohibition against any unclean thing or person entering the new city (Revelation 21:27)? John gives us no details as to how that tension is to be resolved.[32] At the very least, Isaiah 60 and Revelation 21 offer intriguing clues that even in the new creation, culture will continue to matter.

Though it is hard to discern now, King Jesus reigns over the culture of even the pagan kings, and their works will also find a place in glorifying him in his city. Anthony Hoekema notes:

> With respect to non-Christian culture . . . we must remember that Christ's sovereign power is so great that he can rule in the midst of his enemies, and cause those who do not know him to make contributions in art and science which serve his cause. The powers awakened by the resurrection of Jesus Christ are active in the world today! The sovereign rule of Christ over history is so marvellous that he can make even his enemies praise him, though they do so involuntarily.[33]

That promise of the flow of culture towards the new creation should encourage us to enter the cultural conversation happening all around us *now*.

The fourth clue is that Christian salvation is wide. One unfortunate legacy of modern evangelicalism is that it individualizes and spiritualizes salvation to 'Jesus died to save my soul from hell so I can escape this

32 Perhaps only exceptional cultural works enter the new Jerusalem. Perhaps non-Christian cultural works will themselves be cleansed and glorified. Perhaps we will perceive culture from the old creation with new, glorified senses so that they no longer have the power to defile. We cannot be dogmatic here. Thanks to E. Stephen Burnett for suggesting the third option.

33 Hoekema, *The Bible and the Future*, p. 74. This irresistible reign of Christ, he says, should give us no reasons for cultural or historical pessimism. Far from it. The Christian posture towards culture and history should be infused with hope because of the promise of the new creation, where our (and non-Christian) current cultural efforts may well find a home (see pp. 38–40, 73–75 and 285–287).

wicked world and go to heaven.' The New Testament, by contrast, paints a picture of Jesus' living, dying and rising to give us new life for a purpose: not merely to save individual souls *from* the world but, rather, to save our souls (and our bodies) *for* the world. Christ came to save *all* of his creation, and he saved us specifically so that we could become his agents of healing within this broken world, not only through evangelism and acts of charity, but through how we live our ordinary cultural lives. What we do in our everyday lives counts as a contribution to the shalom of the new creation. What if *that* is part of the treasure of the nations set before the King to enrich the life of the new Jerusalem?[34]

If that is true, our cultural contributions now will matter *then*. Our current cultural efforts point forwards towards the new creation, witnessing to it in the still broken and rebellious world of the present. Jesus reminds us that we are not of this world (John 17:14). Rather, we are to live as beacons of the *next* world, the new creation, while in *this* world.

Paul uses the language of citizenship in Philippians to press the point home. Our citizenship is in heaven, Paul says (Philippians 3:20), so live like it in the here and now, knowing that Christ will bring everything 'under his control' and transform us into something utterly new. As Middleton asserts about this passage, 'The text is talking not about going to heaven, but rather about the source of our confidence to live on earth in a manner different from (and in tension with) the present fallen world, until Christ's return.'[35] That is to say, heaven is not a 'where' but a 'when'. 'Heaven' will be realized on earth when God comes to judge, renew, heal and live with us for ever – a truly new creation. Until then, we are to live in this world as a people in tune with the new creation and its coming King. That's the point of engaging with the current cultural conversation: to bring healing, shalom and witness to what God has in store for his cosmos. Our lives and cultural endeavours are to be a preview of coming attractions. As theologian N. T. Wright put it, 'Jesus' resurrection is the

34 Artist Makoto Fujimura notes how Jesus' wounds persisted in his glorified body. He takes it as a sign that *our* wounds are precious to the Father and will last into the new creation. He connects this to the Japanese aesthetic of *wabi-sabi*, finding an enduring beauty in the worn, used and passing away. It is worth pondering the ramifications of this sort of hope – an enduring beauty in those things that we once considered worn out – for the continuity of culture in the new creation. See Makoto Fujimura, *Art and Faith: A theology of making* (New Haven, CT, and London: Yale University Press, 2020), pp. 101–104.

35 Middleton, *A New Heaven and a New Earth*, p. 218.

beginning of God's new project not to snatch people away from earth to heaven but to colonize earth with the life of heaven. That, after all, is what the Lord's Prayer is about.'[36]

Cultural engagement is a key part of that project.

'Will cultural engagement stain us and make us worldly?'

At the beginning of this chapter, I asserted that Christians are suspicious of cultural engagement because they believe culture will not last, and that culture will lead us into sin and worldliness. Let us turn our attention to that latter suspicion. Some readers might respond to the clues that culture persists into the new creation by saying, 'Yeah, yeah, that all sounds fine, but the Bible is definite about this – we are to steer clear of the world. It undermines our holiness before God and compromises our witness. Cultural engagement will only serve to make us worldly.' This is a serious charge. Is it correct?

What is 'the world'?

When concerned Christians talk about worldliness, they usually have in mind a verse such as 1 John 2:15: 'Do not love the world or the things in the world. If anyone loves the world, the love of the Father is not in him.'

What does John mean by 'the world' here? It is not as obvious as you might suppose. When John 3:16 says, 'For God so loved *the world* that he gave his one and only Son' (NIV), is that the same world we're *not* supposed to love according to 1 John 2:15? How is that fair? Does God love something we're forbidden to love?

It turns out that John uses the word 'world' (*kósmos*) in (at least) two very different senses – one positive and one negative.

- When using the positive sense, he means the world God created, including the world of human beings and their cultures. Not just planet earth, but the world of men and women and children. The idea of John 3:16 is that Jesus came to save us humans, not only trees and animals. He came to renew his creation as a whole. Primarily, he came for us because he loved *us*, the human world.

[36] N. T. Wright, *Surprised by Hope: Rethinking heaven, the resurrection, and the mission of the church* (New York: HarperOne, 2008), p. 293.

- When using the negative sense, John means an organized system of rebellion against God, all the ways in which humans and demons try to defy God and cast him from his throne, even in our minds.[37] That is what John tells us *not* to love in 1 John 2:15. In the next verse, John defines what he means by 'worldly': the lust of the flesh, the lust of the eyes and the boastful pride of life – a grasping, greedy, boastful existence. The 'world' strives to find life in creatures rather than in the Creator. It dishonours God through sheer ingratitude. It seeks to dethrone him. Multiply that idolatrous attitude by billions of people, as a collective resistance to God's reign, and you understand what John means by 'the world' in a negative sense.

Keep these two meanings of 'world' in mind. It is right and good to love the world (positive sense), but not to love the world (negative sense). It is OK to love God's creation, including much of what we have done with his creation (culture). Enjoy people, enjoy culture, enjoy the world as a great succession of gifts from the Father, *but* do not seek ultimate meaning and fulfilment there. Don't be grasping, greedy and boastful with them, as though they weren't gifts but the Giver himself, as though they could save you. They cannot. That idolatrous attitude pushes the things of this world from the positive to the negative sense of 'world'.

We are allowed, even *invited,* to enjoy God's gifts with gratitude. It honours God when we do so. Culture, too, is a gift, a reworking of God's good creation to be enjoyed gratefully. However, when culture expresses rebellion *against* God (which it does as well), the other sense of 'world' emerges. Loving *that* is the 'worldliness' we are to avoid.

Culture, therefore, is a mixed bag, so cultural engagement can be tricky. Keeping these two senses of 'world' separate brings clarity.

Jesus calls us *into* the world

To complicate things further, Jesus explicitly *calls us into the world*. There is a slogan that conservative Christians like: 'In the world, but not of it.' It summarizes Jesus' prayer in John 17:14–19:

37 For more on this second sense of 'world' and worldliness, see F. F. Bruce, *The Epistles of John* (Grand Rapids, MI: Eerdmans, 1970), pp. 60–64.

> I have given them your word, and the world has hated them because they are not of the world, just as I am not of the world. I do not ask that you take them out of the world, but that you keep them from the evil one. They are not of the world, just as I am not of the world. Sanctify them in the truth; your word is truth. As you sent me into the world, so I have sent them into the world. And for their sake I consecrate myself, that they also may be sanctified in truth.

Jesus here has in mind the second understanding of 'world' – a system hostile to God's kingship – though the first sense isn't wholly hidden from view.

Let us explore ideas from this passage that should inform Christian cultural engagement.[38]

- In verse 14, Jesus says that we are not to be 'of the world'. Our deepest affections and loyalties must lie not with the world, but with our King. We are not to be part of that systemic rebellion against God . . . except when we are. Then we need to repent. In ordinary Christian life, though, we are called to be different, in tune with the new creation, rooted in a different 'world'.
- What marks us as different – not 'of the world' – is that we have been given the Word. John likely means both the Word incarnate (Jesus himself, John 1:1) and the Word inscribed (the Bible). What sets us apart is our connection with the Word (the 'truth' in v. 17), *not* our separation from the world.
- Being different/set apart will inevitably put us at cross purposes with 'the world' in its negative sense, those set against God's rule. Some hostility from the world is unavoidable.
- Nevertheless, Jesus sends us precisely into *this* world (v. 18), not another one. Why? Because God loves this world of lost human beings despite its ongoing rebellion (we can see both meanings of 'world' here).
- That is why the popular phrase 'In, but not of, the world' falls short. It gives the impression of resignation: 'Guess we're stuck here in this

38 For a helpful treatment of this passage and its application to culture, see Arturo Azurdia, *Connected Christianity: Engaging culture without compromise* (Fearn, Ross-shire, Scotland, and Bridgend, Wales: Christian Focus with Bryntirion Press, 2009).

dark and nasty place. We'd best keep to ourselves and soldier on until Jesus calls us home.' No. We are not stuck in this world; God *put* us here, and Christ *calls us further into it.* We are called to live *pro mundi beneficio* – that is, for the sake or benefit of this world, for the ultimate good of those who *are* of the world. As dark and messed up as it is, this is our mission field.

Is this world worth fighting for? Yes, because God loved it so. Is withdrawal from engagement with the world an option? Not really, because we've been *called* into this world. That inevitably includes *culture.*

Some might say, 'I'll engage the *people* around me, but not their culture.' Nonsense. If you are not engaging their culture, you're not *really* engaging *them.* As any missionary or ambassador will tell you, you don't truly relate to people without understanding their cultural context, their language and life-world. We are called into the world, which means that we are called to engage the network of cultural works that make up this world.

Christians, understandably, balk at this. 'Can we do that without compromising our holiness?' The short answer is, 'Yes!' John 17 affirms as much. Simply stay connected to the truth that sanctifies. Stay connected to Jesus, who 'consecrated' (in Greek, this is the same word as 'sanctified') himself for us. As Jesus said in John 15:1–11, you are a branch that needs to stay connected to the vine. Abiding in him is the key to cultural engagement with holiness.

Two kinds of holiness

You can see this play out in the way the Pharisees pursued holiness versus the way Jesus pursued holiness. The Pharisees saw sin as a contagion that you could catch from being around sinners or ritually unclean objects. They washed their hands when they returned from the market (Mark 7:3–4) not to practise good hygiene; people back then knew nothing of germs. Rather, it was a ritual way to remove the residue of sin picked up from others, a way to mark oneself as being holier than your average Jew.[39]

[39] Ritual handwashing before eating was an expansion of earlier traditions meant to protect the eating of holy food, such as temple sacrifices. In essence, the Pharisees brought temple regulations into everyday life to set themselves off as especially observant, especially holy. See Eli Rosencruft's answer to the question, 'Are the Rabbinic rules of hand washing before eating bread related to their ruling that the scriptures were unclean?', Biblical Hermeneutics

Their understanding of holiness was rooted in fear of contamination and desire for religious prestige.

Jesus showed precious little regard for such rituals. Instead, he made it a point to spend time with notoriously sinful people. Love drove him to seek their company. As he put it, he didn't come for the healthy, but for the sick, for sinners (Mark 2:17; Luke 5:32). His type of holiness, rooted in God's grace, did not fear contamination. Rather, it was almost as though his righteousness *decontaminated* the sinful, making them whole, 'infecting' them with new, holy desires to please God. He didn't fear being defiled by leprosy; leprosy had better fear *him* (Mark 1:40–45)!

Jesus' attitude reveals a very different understanding of 'clean' and 'unclean' from that of the Pharisees, as Mark 7:1–23 makes clear. The Pharisees believed that sin could be caught from external things; Jesus saw sin as internal, emerging from the warped desires of the heart. Uncleanness comes from within, not without. Rules – such as ritual washing or separation from mainstream culture – do nothing to make one clean (see Colossians 2:21–23). Holiness concerns not separation but motivation. To be holy, our 'affections'[40] must change through a renewed apprehension and appreciation of God's grace. As Scottish pastor-theologian Thomas Chalmers said in his 1855 sermon, 'The expulsive power of a new affection':

> The love of God and the love of the world are two affections, not merely in a state of rivalship, but in a state of enmity and that so irreconcilable, that they cannot dwell together in the same bosom. The heart is not so constituted; and the only way to dispossess it of an old affection, is by the expulsive power of a new one.[41]

For this reason, a change of heart does not occur until our desires are reordered. Current desires must be unseated by a stronger, better desire.

(note 39 *cont.*) Stack Exchange (6 August 2012), <https://hermeneutics.stackexchange.com/questions/2262/are-the-rabbinic-rules-of-hand-washing-before-eating-bread-related-to-their-uli>, accessed January 2023.

40 The Puritans considered the affections to be the core desires that direct emotion, intellect and will.

41 The whole sermon is available online at: <www.monergism.com/thethreshold/sdg/Chalmers,%20Thomas%20-%20The%20Exlpulsive%20Power%20of%20a%20New%20Af.pdf>, accessed January 2023.

We therefore need not separation from the world; rather, we need to be gripped by a new desire for God's lordship over our lives, a new affection to be enthroned in our hearts. Jesus' heart, rooted in his deep affection for the Father, shone bright and drew others to God.

But what about us? Jesus' heart was pure. Ours are not. Isn't there still a danger that we will be compromised by the world? This is a genuine concern, so let me close this chapter with a few pieces of advice.

Some practical pointers concerning cultural engagement and holiness

Of course, we must not engage cultural works carelessly. There are things in the world to avoid, places where hearts are weak in resisting the world's temptations. Here are a few things to bear in mind.

- **It's about your heart** Soak your head and heart in Scripture enough to know where you fall short and be cautious about anything that might tap into or exploit those weaknesses. Remember, sin lies not in the things out there. Those things become sinful and worldly as they interact with the desires of your heart. Understand what interacts badly and refrain from those things. That takes time, experience, repeated repentance and a mature self-understanding.
- **Remember Christian liberty and avoid one-size-fits-all rules** I remember in one of my seminary classes, William Edgar summed up Paul's discussion of weak and strong consciences in Romans 14. He said that the strong must avoid flaunting their strength and causing the weak to stumble. But we must also avoid a dictatorship of the weak, forcing everyone else to follow the rules of those with weak consciences. For example, perhaps you are tempted by films with scenes of violence or adult themes. You may not therefore demand that no good Christian ever watch such films. The things that cause your heart to stumble may not be the same things that cause your brothers and sisters to stumble. Not every weakness or path to personal holiness is the same. Different hearts struggle differently. Don't become your local Pharisee.
- **Remember the gospel and the grace available to you** In your attempt to engage wisely with the world around you, you will mess up. You may watch something that, on reflection, you realize you

shouldn't have. Or you may realize that you've refrained from engaging something you really should have. Remember who God is and who you are. God is not some cruel, Dickensian teacher waiting to dish out corporal punishment for misbehaving. When you sin – which each of us does multiple times every day – be quick to repent (1 John 1:5, 10) and remember your identity. You are a son or daughter of the King, safe in your Father's arms, no-one can snatch you from him (John 10:28–30). Jesus, your older brother, died to bring you into this relationship. Rejoice: you are safe! Mike Cosper, discussing Christians engaging films and television, writes:

> It's the promise of grace that propels us out into the world without . . . . fear . . . While our stories are indeed shaping our hearts and imaginations, they cannot do any permanent damage to those who are in Christ. In other words, you're not going to watch a film that will steal your soul; the world can't really hurt you. Instead, you can take comfort in knowing that you're forever secure in the hands of Jesus.
>
> The last thing our knowledge of our security in Christ should do, though, is call us to some kind of indiscriminate license in our viewing. Shall we go on watching porn, so that grace might increase? As Paul would say, 'Of course not! That's ridiculous! In the light of the gospel, nothing could sound more absurd.'
>
> Grace shapes our encounters with the world by first promising that nothing will ever harm us eternally and second, by motivating us to better things, better standards, better ways of thinking about the things we encounter. Where the law motivates with the threat of punishment, grace motivates with the promise of joy. We can step into the world with a sense of invitation. This is our Father's world. What do we want to explore today?[42]

The generous salvation we have in Jesus should make us fearless, not foolish. Spiritual maturity results not in amnesia about our idols,

[42] Mike Cosper, *The Stories We Tell: How TV and movies long for and echo the truth* (Wheaton, IL: Crossway, 2014, Kindle edn), loc. 675–681.

nor recklessness but, rather, a confidence that comes from knowing a holiness established not by our work but by Christ's. This will keep you from self-righteousness when you *don't* make mistakes as well. Engaging the cultural conversation happens in the context of grace, so relax a little.

- **Stay connected to your local church** Are we really the best judges of our own hearts, of how well we are balancing our desire to please God through holy living versus pleasing God through engaging his world? Not really. We need to have our hearts repeatedly exposed to the Word of God that sanctifies us (John 17:17). And we need people who know us and will hold us accountable. This should be the job of the local church. Sit under the preaching of the Word, let the Spirit do his work on your heart. Pay attention when he alerts you to where you've gone off the rails. Pursue relationships with Christian friends with whom you can be vulnerable about your struggles, friends who can hold your feet to the fire.[43]

  From the perspective of our individualistic culture, this will sound incredibly invasive, but it is the best way to stay sane. Our calling – gospel-motivated engagement with the world – only works if we're grounded in the Word as applied to our hearts by pastors and friends at our local church. Untethered from the ministry of the church, cultural engagement can go wrong. In those cases where someone has been compromised by the world and 'gone rogue', there is usually a disconnect from the local church and lack of accountability.

Conclusion: stalking the borders

Let us return to the Christian DJ, engaging his culture by working the clubs. His is a difficult mission field, and he will surely face temptation. Writer and painter Makoto Fujimura calls such artists *mearcstapa*, an Old English word used in *Beowulf* for those who stalk the borderlands, the guardians and explorers – think of Aragorn when he was known as Strider the Ranger in *The Lord of the Rings*. For Fujimura, artists are those who

[43] The painful truth is that not everyone who needs support can find it in their local church. If that is the case, seek other organizations or networks where you could find a trusted friend, someone who could be a prayer and accountability partner. But your local church should be the first place you look – that's why God has given us the church. Do not assume that they are too unconcerned or out of touch to love you in this way.

move between the spheres of church and the wider culture, between their own tribe and others:

> *Mearcstapa* is not a comfortable role. Life on the borders of a group – and in the space between groups – is prone to dangers literal and figurative, with people both at 'home' and among the 'other' likely to misunderstand or mistrust the motivations, piety, and loyalty of the border-stalker. But *mearcstapa* can be a role of cultural leadership in a new mode, serving functions including empathy, memory, warning, guidance, mediation, and reconciliation. Those who journey to the borders of their group and beyond will encounter new vistas and knowledge that can enrich the group.[44]

Where is the support for this DJ *mearcstapa*? Who knows him well enough to keep him accountable, to speak gospel encouragement into his life, to call him to repentance when necessary? Who has his back if his church neither understands nor accepts his creative engagement with culture?

If he does stumble and fall, and it becomes known, those in his church community might respond with, 'I told you so. I saw it coming. Nothing good ever comes from a Christian going into places like that!' But then his church would also be implicated if that happened. By failing to comprehend its calling to cultural engagement, they set up him up to fall. They would be complicit because they were absent. Christian creatives, those on the frontiers of cultural engagement, need brothers and sisters who, instead, step up and lend support, get to know, understand and treat them like the cultural emissaries they are.

Failing to support our *mearcstapas* means failing to be the church God wants us to be. Consequences include alienated artists and a deepening chasm between the surrounding culture and the church that is supposed to be a light to it.[45] Sort of the way things are now, come to think of it. I hope to change our image of the church from one of a fortress or walled

---

44 Makoto Fujimura, *Culture Care: Reconnecting with beauty for our common life* (Downers Grove, IL: InterVarsity Press, Kindle edn, 2017), loc. 674. The term was suggested to him by fellow painter Bruce Herman.

45 Bridging and healing that alienation is the focus of chapter 17.

resort to one more like a home, a base for imaginative outreach to our cultures. We are not only *permitted* to engage culture, it is also our *calling*, as we are beckoned to live in tune with the coming new creation.

2
How not to engage post-Christian culture: the path of culture warring

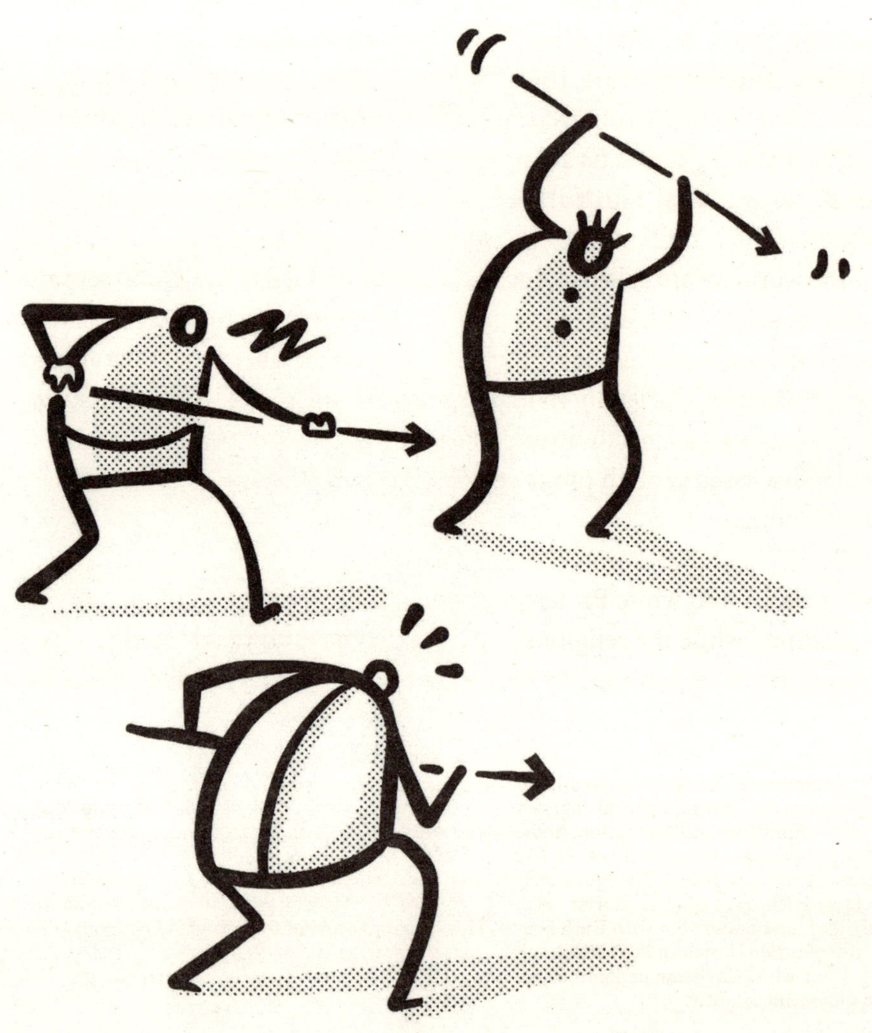

Introduction: welcome to the post-Christian West[1]

Why engage culture? For the sake of evangelism, so that people might be saved. To serve the common good. To change social structures to better reflect the justice, mercy and shalom of the kingdom. To engage imaginations, to attune them to the magnificent reality of God and the coming new creation. In short, to change the world.

The real question is, how can we engage the world to change it? Changing the world around you is unlike changing anything else – your mind, a lightbulb, a nappy. Changing the world, even taking modest steps in that direction, is more complex, requires more nuance and more time than they do. Your approach depends on what *kind* of world you are trying to change. Understanding the cultural obstacles helps us to understand which paths of engagement might prove most fruitful and which simply leave us spinning our wheels.

The world we are called to engage is deeply divided, pluralistic, sceptical about absolute truth and enchanted by everything *except* the gospel. Let us not delude ourselves: our cultures are no longer Christian. They are, on the whole, post-Christian, inoculated against the gospel. Non-Christians get just enough gospel to dismiss it as irrelevant. Consider the recent and much discussed growth of the religious 'nones' (those who claim to have no religion).

- Catholics and white Protestant populations in the USA are in decline,[2] while the religiously unaffiliated have climbed rapidly, from 6 per cent in 1991 to 26 per cent in surveys conducted between

[1] Chapters 2, 3 and 4 are available as an imaginary screenplay in my two-part essay, 'Dialogues concerning cultural engagement', parts 1 and 2, *Foundations*, vol. 70 (Spring 2016), <www.affinity.org.uk/foundations/issue-70/issue-70-article-2-dialogues-concerning-cultural-engagement-part-one>, and vol. 71 (Autumn 2016), and <www.affinity.org.uk/foundations-issues/issue-71-article-1-dialogues-concerning-cultural-engagement-part-two>, respectively, accessed February 2023. A shorter version of the dialogues can be found in chapters 2 and 3 of a book I have co-written with Ruth Naomi Floyd, *Imagination Manifesto: A call to plant oases of imagination* (London: IVP, 2023).

[2] Non-white Christian denominations and non-Christian religions have been holding steady or increasing slightly.

2018 and 2019.[3] A 2020 poll showed that the number of those who belong to a church, mosque or synagogue has dipped below 50 per cent for the first time ever (47 per cent), continuing an eight-decade decline.[4]

- The youngest are most disaffected with religion: an unprecedented 4 in 10 of those under 40 claim no religion at all, making the 'nones' the fastest-growing religious category in America.[5]
- Parallel trends can be seen in the UK and Australia.[6]

But the decline in numbers is not the most important storyline. The centres of cultural influence – the media and entertainment, government, the judiciary and education – have shifted. They often treat the Christian faith with indifference or hostility. The overall flow of the cultures in the West is *away* from traditional Christian moral norms, as illustrated by the legalization of gay marriage in the USA and of abortion in Ireland.[7]

---

3 Betsy Cooper, Daniel Cox, Rachel Lienesch and Robert P. Jones, 'Exodus: Why Americans are leaving religion – and why they're unlikely to come back', PRRI.org (22 September 2016), <www.prri.org/research/prri-rns-poll-nones-atheist-leaving-religion>, accessed February 2023; Pew Research Center, 'In US, decline of Christianity continues at rapid pace: An update on America's changing religious landscape', Pew Research Center (17 October 2019), <www.pewresearch.org/religion/2019/10/17/in-u-s-decline-of-christianity-continues-at-rapid-pace/#:~:text=The%20religious%20landscape%20of%20the,points%20over%20the%20past%20decade>, accessed February 2023.

4 Jeffrey M. Jones, 'US church membership falls below majority for first time', Gallup (29 March 2021), <https://news.gallup.com/poll/341963/church-membership-falls-below-majority-first-time.aspx>, accessed February 2023.

5 Jana Riess, 'Why millennials are really leaving religion (it's not just politics, folks)', *Religion and Ethics Newsweekly* (16 July 2018), <www.pbs.org/wnet/religionandethics/2018/07/16/millennials-really-leaving-religion-not-just-politics-folks/34880>; Jana Riess, 'Religious "nones" are gaining ground in America, and they're worried about the economy', Religion News Service (16 November 2016), <https://religionnews.com/2017/11/16/religious-nones-are-gaining-ground-in-america-and-theyre-worried-about-the-economy-says-new-study>, both accessed February 2023.

6 Harriet Sherwood, 'UK secularism on rise as more than half say they have no religion', *The Guardian* (11 July 2019), <www.theguardian.com/world/2019/jul/11/uk-secularism-on-rise-as-more-than-half-say-they-have-no-religion#:~:text=UK%20secularism%20on%20rise%20as%20more%20than%20half%20say%20they%20have%20no%20religion,-This%20article%20is&text=The%20growth%20of%20secularism%20in,religious%20to%20declare%20themselves%20atheist>; Australian Bureau of Statistics, '1301.0 – Year Book Australia 2006: Religious affiliation', Australian Bureau of Statistics (20 January 2006), <www.abs.gov.au/ausstats/abs@.nsf/bb8db737e2af84b8ca2571780015701e/bfdda1ca506d6cfaca2570de0014496e!OpenDocument>; Australian Bureau of Statistics, 'Religion in Australia: 2016 census data summary', Australian Bureau of Statistics (28 June 2017), <www.abs.gov.au/ausstats/abs@.nsf/Lookup/by+Subject/2071.0~2016~Main+Features~Religion+Data+Summary~70>, all accessed February 2023.

7 Tara Isabella Burton points to changes in social structure, family and technology (especially the rise of the Internet) as the reasons for the shift from institutional religions, such as Christianity, to 'intuitional' religions of made-to-order spirituality. See her book *Strange Rites: New religions for a godless world* (New York: Public Affairs, 2020), especially chapters 2 and 3.

Even when the Christian side wins a victory – such as the overturning of *Roe* v. *Wade* in the USA – it comes at the expense of resentment in mainstream culture. The majority of people in the USA remain unconvinced and society remains deeply divided. Why? Because the world we are trying to engage is markedly post-Christian.[8]

Christian cultural influence has waned. To borrow pastor and author Vermon Pierre's vivid image, Christians are the kid who always gets chosen last for games at school or in the park, if at all. Christians are irrelevant to the game that's being played.[9] Sociologist James Davison Hunter sees a twofold challenge facing Christians: difference (Christians dwell in a pluralistic society, so it's one perspective among many) and dissolution (we no longer share a common 'language' – definitions of words like 'goodness', 'freedom' and 'justice' are fragmented, making cultural debates tortured and endless).[10] Christians find themselves in a world where simply being heard about things that matter is complex and difficult. *That* is what I mean by 'post-Christian'.

The sky is not falling. It's too soon to write the church's epitaph. As G. K. Chesterton famously quipped, 'At least five times . . . the Faith has to all appearance gone to the dogs. In each of these five cases it was the dog that died.'[11] Yet we must learn to see today's world with eyes unclouded. The imaginary landscape of the West – its values, hopes and

---

On the shift away from Christian norms, see Hunter Baker, 'Can Christians change the world after *Obergefell*?' in Collin Hansen (ed.), *Revisiting 'Faithful Presence'*: To Change the World *five years later* (Deerfield, IL: The Gospel Coalition Press, Kindle edn, 2015), e-book available online at <www.thegospelcoalition.org/article/revisiting-faithful-presence-to-change-the-world-five-years-later>, accessed February 2023. Baker asserts that in the case of *Obergefell* v. *Hodges* (the Supreme Court's decision to legalize same-sex marriage in all 50 states), 'public Christianity in America suffered what might be its greatest defeat in the nation's history' (Kindle edn, 2015), loc. 786. For more on the gay rights debate, see chapter 4.

8 The Global East and South have seen spiritual revival, while the secularized Global North and West are, as a whole, moving away from the gospel.

9 Vermon Pierre, 'Faithful presence needs prophets' in Hansen, *Revisiting Faithful Presence*, loc. 1177–1183. Even when Hollywood gets the religion bug (in TV programmes such as *The Good Place* or *God Friended Me*), it's always a watered-down, God-optional perspective similar to moralistic therapeutic deism rather than anything distinctly Christian.

10 James Davison Hunter, 'The challenge of faithfulness' in *To Change the World: The irony, tragedy, and possibility of Christianity in the late modern world* (Oxford and New York: Oxford University Press, 2010), pp. 200–210.

11 G. K. Chesterton, 'The five deaths of the faith', *The Everlasting Man* (San Francisco, CA: Ignatius Press, 1993 [1925]), part 2, chapter 6, <www.worldinvisible.com/library/chesterton/everlasting/part2c6.htm>, accessed February 2023. The five occasions, according to Chesterton, had to do with the Arian heresy, the Albigensians, humanist scepticism, Voltaire and Darwinism.

fears – has become disenchanted with the Christian gospel and enchanted by other things: sexual liberation, wellness, political tribalism, the list is endless.[12] Rather than being in the driver's seat of culture, we have become 'exilic disciples',[13] ambassadors to our own cultures. Yet Christians *still* want to make the world a better place, still long to see God's shalom (peace, flourishing, justice) brought to bear. We want to see truth proclaimed and broken lives and social systems healed. But we now must reckon with creating change from a position of relative cultural powerlessness.

Can politics save the day?

There are large numbers of Christians – particularly in the USA – who want to fight this cultural shift tooth and nail, primarily by political means. They insist that if we elect people who will fight for us (even if they are not models of virtue themselves) and the right judicial appointments are made, we will be able to force a cultural change, 'recapturing' the culture for Christ. Committed Christians, they believe, must become culture warriors. The motivations of such culture warriors are noble: they want to change whole societies into ones that honour God and are healthy for all involved. But is politics really the best path forwards?

While political engagement in itself is not wrong, there are signs that the culture-warring path does more harm than good to the cause of the gospel. At its core, politics is about the use and distribution of power. Lawmakers use the power of the law to steer culture this way or that. You can be sure that in a pluralistic, divided society, this use of power *will* involve coercion. Of course, governments must use some coercion to prevent murder, corruption, abuse, to get us to pay taxes for the public good and so on (and Christians agree that this is good – see Romans 13:1–6). But where governments, particularly Christian-influenced governments, form laws and make judicial decisions that go against the will of most of the population, it will inspire resentment among those who

[12] Burton's *Strange Rites* explores the varieties of 'intuitional religion' that have displaced traditional institutional religions such as Christianity. They span the lifestyle and political spectrums.

[13] Timothy Keller, *Every Good Endeavor* (New York: Dutton, 2012), p. 242.

feel that they have been coerced. There will be an eventual, inevitable backlash. History shows us that the end result will *not* be a better culture, one more open to the gospel.

A cautionary tale from the culture wars[14]

The way the Reagan Revolution of 1980–88 played out serves as a good example of what can go wrong when leaning into the political path.

During his presidential campaign, Ronald Reagan extended an olive branch to evangelicals and said that if they helped him to win the election, then he would further their agenda (principally, by eliminating or restricting abortion and reintroducing prayer in state-run schools). He did win and for a while, things went according to plan. Abortion rates were temporarily lowered because federal funding for abortions was cut. Family values were front and centre on the national agenda. Even if you didn't agree with the Christian Right, you had to deal with them.

But something else happened as well. The alliance between evangelicals and the Republican Party changed the character of American evangelicalism, and it deepened the suspicion and hatred inherent in an already polarized society.[15] Conservative Christians became defined not by their love for one another and those alienated from Christ, but by their conservative politics. Because the Republican Party offered evangelical Christians a degree of influence, evangelicals felt obliged to defend whatever Republicans were for and attack whatever Democrats were for (because the Democrats were now the enemy).

Besides producing some weird admixtures (pro-gun Christians, anti-environmentalist Christians), a culture-war mentality developed that raged throughout the 1990s and into the new millennium. Theologically conservative Christians became defined in American culture by what we were against, and by our perpetual censorious outrage at those who live differently from how we do. As a result, currently evangelical Christians

---

14 For a more thorough and nuanced account of the rise of the Religious Right in the USA, see Paul D. Miller, *The Religion of American Greatness: What's wrong with Christian nationalism* (Downers Grove, IL: IVP Academic, 2022), chapter 7. He provides a balanced and insightful critique of American Christian nationalism, but much applies elsewhere too.

15 See Elizabeth Bruenig, 'Why evangelicals aren't what they used to be', *New York Times* (6 November 2020), <www.nytimes.com/2020/11/06/opinion/evangelicals-republicans.html>, accessed February 2023.

in America are not known as humble, loving people. Far from it. They are now commonly considered judgmental, even hateful.

Further, as the culture wars have played out in the USA, it is far from clear what remains of the gains won by evangelicals during the Reagan–Bush years. Gay marriage is now a legal institution. Though a conservative Supreme Court majority overturned *Roe* v. *Wade*, there remains no cultural consensus regarding abortion. A handful of states have banned it outright but, for many, abortion remains a go-to option for women with crisis pregnancies. A massive backlash inspired by progressive, secular culture-makers (university professors, journalists, the media and entertainment producers) has largely erased any shifts towards a Christian consensus. The political victories of the 1980s never persuaded the core culture-makers. Even the overturning of *Roe* has only galvanized the culture-makers. Their imagination, their vision of how the world should be, remained untouched and unchanged. If anything, they are more progressive than ever. And they are the ones who have the power to influence the shape of the collective imagination of American society in the long run.[16] They believed their country had been hijacked by a conservative Christian agenda and desperately needed a change of direction. A backlash was inevitable. The New Atheism and a new hostility towards conservative Christianity (and religion in general) are part of that backlash movement, as is the rapid growth in numbers of the religious 'nones'.[17]

Has evangelical political influence caused cultural reform in a Godwards direction? No. And, short of a spiritual revival that sweeps the nation, it will not. At present America (and the UK) are simply too divided and too deeply relativistic to return wholesale to past traditional values. The path of political engagement has not made things better; it has only further deepened divisions in an already divided country. And the reputation of Christ has been stained because of it.

---

16 There are obvious parallels with the UK: a turn towards cultural conservatism in the 1980s, followed by a backlash powered, at least in part, by culture-makers. I have used an example from the situation in the USA simply because I know it better, having grown up within it.

17 The New Atheism has had markedly greater staying power in the USA than it has in the UK precisely because of this resentment. It would not surprise me if, in the next generation or two (enough time for the present conservative Supreme Court justices to retire), some form of *Roe* v. *Wade* were reinstated. That conservative Christian cultural victory will likely be temporary.

The political path remains a temptation, however, where Christians make up the majority or a significant minority. It seems reasonable to try to legislate ourselves into a position of cultural power and legitimacy. But given the world that we live in – divided, pluralistic, sceptical, relativistic, inoculated, post-Christian – culture warring is a strategic misstep. It is running back into the arms of the Emperor Constantine without realizing that the Constantinian solution is at least partly responsible for our current predicament, the current inoculation against Christianity.[18]

How the church assisted in sidelining itself

There is no doubt that the Christian faith has left an indelible mark on the West. Historian Tom Holland asserts that Christianity has shaped us more than we know: 'To live in a Western country is to live in a society still utterly saturated by Christian concepts and assumptions.'[19] Even atheist objections to the Christian faith are coloured by Christian concerns for justice, mercy and the dignity of every human being. That shaping of cultures and their institutions took centuries, and change flowed through many channels: preaching, sacrificial love of the poor and vulnerable, standing up in protest against those in power, art and storytelling that captured the imagination and, occasionally, it flowed through political leaders. But it was never simply about political influence, never simply Constantine laying down the law. Whenever the church has relied primarily on political influence to change society, things have gone wrong.

Though he does not use the term 'Constantinian', sociologist David Martin points to church–state dynamics as an important player in the decline of the cultural influence of the Christian church. His landmark book *A General Theory of Secularization* is a complex and nuanced work.

---

[18] Emperor Constantine the Great (AD 280–337) famously converted to Christianity and became a patron of the early Christian church. His Edict of Milan (AD 313) made persecution of Christians illegal and paved the way for his grandson, Theodosius I, to make Nicene Christianity the official state religion of the Roman Empire in AD 381. 'Constantinianism', a term popularized by the late Mennonite theologian John H. Yoder, refers to an arrangement whereby the state supports and protects the Christian church. For a helpful critique of Constantinianism, see Craig A. Carter, *Rethinking Christ and Culture: A post-Christendom perspective* (Grand Rapids, MI: Brazos, 2006), especially chapter 4. For more on the debate, see John D. Roth (ed.), *Constantine Revisited: Leithart, Yoder, and the Constantinian debate* (Eugene, OR: Pickwick Publications, 2013).

[19] Tom Holland, *Dominion: How the Christian revolution remade the world* (New York: Basic Books, 2019, Kindle edn), loc. 13.

One part of his argument focuses on how, wherever church and state power have mixed, it is invariably the church that has ended up the loser, in terms of social legitimacy and plausibility over time.[20] The closer the ties between church and state, the more decisive the secularization that invariably follows.

In France, where the church was a de facto tool of foreign policy for the state, secularization was quick and violent. 'Strangle the last king with the guts of the last priest!' was Diderot's (attributed) slogan during the French Revolution, and France remains deeply secular to this day. In Scandinavia, Protestant Germany and England and Wales, where the connection was looser but still present (a state-sponsored church), secularization was experienced as a gradual loss of relevance and legitimacy, which has continued to this day.

In the USA, where there had been fairly strict separation between church and state (at least in principle), religion had fared rather better, until relatively recently. The Reagan, Bush and Trump presidencies were perceived by many as an informal state sponsorship of the evangelical church. In the predictable backlash, evangelicals have lost cultural influence and people (especially young people) have left their churches.

The takeaway? Whenever the church becomes too cosy with the powers that be, it always ends up ceding social influence and legitimacy. In the eyes of the common people, the church loses its right to speak prophetically to those in power *for* the powerless when it becomes a resident *in* the halls

20 David Martin, *A General Theory of Secularization* (New York: Harper & Row, 1978). 'Secularization' refers to the process of uncoupling religion from other social spheres that, it is argued, led to the decline of religion in the West. From the 1930s until the 1970s, sociologists treated it as an established fact. Secularization theory was undermined by the resurgence of the public impact of religion in the 1980s (the Religious Right, the Iranian revolution and so on). Even Peter Berger, a major proponent of secularization theory, changed course, editing a collection of essays entitled *The Desecularization of the World: Resurgent religion and world politics* (Grand Rapids, MI: Eerdmans, 1999). Although religion as a social force remains, given the most recent statistics, traditional religious institutions are definitely in decline in the West. For a thorough overview of the debate on secularization in sociology, see Michael Hainz, 'In favour, against and beyond secularization: Contemporary sociological disputes on a core concept of the sociology of religion', conference paper delivered at Eurojess, Lviv, Ukraine (August 2013), <www.researchgate.net/publication/271699405_In_Favour_Against_and_Beyond_Secularization_-_Contemporary_Sociological_Disputes_on_a_Core_Concept_of_the_Sociology_of_Religion>, accessed February 2023. For a more general discussion of secularization, listen to the podcast of David G. Robertson interviewing Professor Linda Woodhead, 'The secularisation thesis', *The Religious Studies Project* (16 April 2012), <www.religiousstudiesproject.com/podcast/podcast-linda-woodhead-on-the-secularisation-thesis>, accessed February 2023.

of power. Wherever Christians have sought to impose their will on society through political coercion, even in subtle ways, they end up paying for it in the currency of the resentment of the next generation. This has been a major part of the story of the rapid or gradual decline of Christian fervour in Europe and, more recently, in North America. When the Christian faith or social order is imposed, it simply inoculates the next generation against the Christian faith, and that inoculation is notoriously difficult to overcome.

What's worse, the lure of political influence is like a drug: addictive and soul-deforming over time. According to Christian philosopher and culture critic James K. A. Smith, politics easily becomes a type of worship, complete with its own type of 'discipleship', its own set of spiritually formative practices.[21] The ways in which we practise politics have the power to bend us away from what is true and biblical, and towards other ends, other goals, even other gods. Smith, therefore, advises Christians not to eschew politics but to be ambivalent and circumspect in our political allegiances, lest Christians end up practising a secularized, sub-biblical form of politics, ignoring their own most deeply held biblical beliefs to support whomever they think will further their interests. We can (and too often do) reach a point where we don't care about the quality (or lack thereof) of our political hero's character or principles. It doesn't matter what that person has done or does now – he or she is still *our* hero! It's too easy for power politics to become a new golden calf. That undercuts and distorts our cultural witness.[22] Many evangelicals have sold their souls for political gain, and everyone knows it.

Please understand: when I argue against the political path of cultural change, I am not claiming that Christians should avoid politics altogether

21 James K. A. Smith, *Awaiting the King: Reforming public theology*, Cultural Liturgies, Volume 3 (Grand Rapids, MI: Baker Academic, Kindle edn, 2017). Interestingly (in light of Martin's thesis), Smith argues for an established church that avoids the temptations of political self-interest, genuinely serving the common good by forming habits and virtues essential to a pluralist democracy (tolerance, love, patience). He makes a good case, but this is not often what happens when the church wades into politics. Rather, churches become co-opted by secular political ideals (and idols), which distorts the worship and spiritual formation that happens through these compromised churches.

22 It will take generations to undo the damage that the white evangelical church has already done to its own witness in the USA because of their allegiance to Donald Trump. For a helpful survey of the historical forces that led to this unhappy liaison between Trump and evangelicals, see Michael Gerson's 'The last temptation', *The Atlantic* (April 2018), <www.theatlantic.com/magazine/archive/2018/04/the-last-temptation/554066>, accessed February 2023.

(as if that were possible) or that no Christian should ever run for political office or seek to build coalitions for change. Christians *should* be represented and their voices *should* be heard. But we need to do so with a watchful eye towards the common good, lest we become just one more self-focused political interest group. We need to learn how to practise our politics with humility and empathy, loving those with whom we differ – politics without enemies. We need a more imaginative approach to politics, one that unveils the possibilities for beauty and depth in our common life – politics as oasis.

The political dynamics we have now feel like a predictable film – we all know who's going to do what. It's tedious and too easily turns toxic. We need politicians with an eye for unexpected plot twists, for doing what's right in unexpected ways. We need Christian politicians with the hearts of poets, poets who yearn for political shalom. As Percy Bysshe Shelley famously put it, 'Poets are the unacknowledged legislators of the world.'[23]

For those of us who are not called to politics, we need to pray for those Christians who are, because they need a ton of wisdom, patience and creativity. They operate now in a culture that is fragmented and post-Christian. Many of the definitions that used to provide common ground – 'freedom', 'happiness', 'healthy', 'family' – are now endlessly contested and contestable. We must see past our current frustration and remember that in our political debates we are dealing with human beings, not just representatives of agendas. We must learn how to love and serve even our political adversaries.

Love does not mean agreeing with everything and everyone. Else why would Jesus tell us to love our enemies in Matthew 5:43–46? Rather, it means being willing to enter into their worlds and listen, even as we seek change in the imaginary landscape that informs these post-Christian cultural narratives.

Once we see cultural engagement as an act of love and service, we will understand that cultural influence is not a zero-sum, winner-takes-all game. Evangelicals have lived too long with an 'us versus them' mindset.

[23] Percy Bysshe Shelley, 'A defence of poetry' in Mary Wollstonecraft Shelley (ed.), *Essays, Letters from Abroad, Translations and Fragments* (London: Edward Moxton, 1840), <www.poetryfoundation.org/articles/69388/a-defence-of-poetry>, accessed February 2023. Thanks to Caleb Woodbridge for suggesting this reference.

Instead, we need a 'we are for you, even if we disagree' mindset. Without erasing the antithesis between our respective core commitments, we *can* enter into a loving dialogue with those with whom we disagree. We can disagree with people without making them the 'other', moral pariahs and lepers, lesser beings in our eyes. In the light of grace, we recognize that we are *all* moral pariahs and lepers. We *all* need a Saviour. That is the gospel. We can bring healing by taking the low road of humility and love.

Humble, healing engagement: the story of Dan Cathy and Shane Windmeyer

Take, for example, the reconciliation between Dan Cathy, president of Chick-fil-A (an American chicken sandwich fast-food restaurant chain), and Shane Windmeyer, a gay rights activist. In 2012, in an interview for a Baptist magazine Cathy was asked if he supported the traditional view of marriage and family. Cathy responded, 'Guilty as charged.' He elaborated:

> We [at Chick-fil-A] are very much supportive of the family – the biblical definition of the family unit. We are a family-owned business, a family-led business, and we are married to our first wives. We give God thanks for that . . . We want to do anything we possibly can to strengthen families. We are very much committed to that . . . We intend to stay the course. We know that it might not be popular with everyone, but thank the Lord, we live in a country where we can share our values and operate on biblical principles.[24]

Those comments, plus his company's financial support of groups that supported a pro-traditional family agenda, caused him to be labelled 'anti-gay' and 'homophobic'. There was a media outcry, despite the fact that he is the president of a fast-food chain who has little or no political influence, he is not a culture warrior to be feared. The LGBTQI+ community fumed and boycotted. Christians took umbrage on Cathy's behalf, snarled right back and started anti-boycott campaigns, making sure that they ate more

[24] K. Allen Blume/Biblical Recorder, '"Guilty as Charged," Cathy says of Chick-fil-A's stand on biblical and family values', *Baptist Press* (16 July 2012), <www.bpnews.net/38271>, accessed February 2023.

Chick-fil-A products than ever. But, very quietly, something else was happening behind the scenes.

Months later, a *Huffington Post* article came out authored by Shane Windmeyer, head of Campus Pride, a university-based gay rights organization, one of the groups calling for people to boycott Chick-fil-A.[25] Windmeyer relates how Cathy contacted him, seeking a meeting shortly after the calls for boycotting began. Windmeyer, suspecting a trap, hesitated, but Dan Cathy was relentless. He texted Windmeyer, emailed him, called him, invited him to football games and family meals. Windmeyer finally did meet with Cathy, and met repeatedly. Not once during all this time did Cathy ask for Campus Pride to stop boycotting. He simply wanted to get to know Windmeyer as a human being. Over the months, the hostility and distrust melted and a friendship formed. Cathy listened to Windmeyer's complaints and compromises were reached. Chick-fil-A would no longer fund groups that Campus Pride considered anti-gay. Windmeyer, for his part, showed exceptional bravery in writing a very public essay that spoke well of a man that his community would rather vilify.[26] Both men took enormous heat over their friendship, but both showed courage, openness and humility. Neither compromised his principles, but each discovered a new-found respect for the other and common ground on which to meet. That is cultural engagement done in love.

Some might object that Cathy's friendship with Windmeyer accomplished very little in terms of the pro-family agenda, but consider what *was* accomplished. Did Cathy's relationship with Windmeyer somehow make Windmeyer less vocal in his advocacy of LGBTQI+ rights? No. Is there still a deep divergence between their moral visions of what America should be? Yes. So was nothing accomplished? Not at all.

Through a difficult process of listening and dialogue, both men had their imaginary landscapes broadened to accept the other as a human being worth listening to, worthy of respect and love. Whatever else Windmeyer chooses to say about Cathy, he can no longer call him a

25 Shane Windmeyer, 'Dan and me: My coming out as a friend of Dan Cathy and Chick-fil-A', *HuffPost* (28 January 2013; updated 6 December 2017), <www.huffpost.com/entry/dan-cathy-chick-fil-a_b_2564379>, accessed February 2023.

26 The comments on the original *HuffPost* blog post (which have now been deleted) were full of harsh criticism of Windmeyer for fraternizing with the enemy.

homophobe, a bigot, an idiot who just doesn't understand. He now calls him 'friend'. Cathy listened and loved well. That is a crucial part of engagement if we are going to be minority partners in the broader cultural conversation. These two men will not agree on everything, but they have come to trust each other's integrity and good will. They resisted the cultural default mode of 'cancelling' and dehumanizing those on the other side of the issue. That is a huge step in the right direction. That kind of bridge-building has potential to yield enormous practical benefits in the long term for the good of the whole of society, not only this or that particular interest group.

Conclusion: farewell to dreams of empire

This type of winsome cultural engagement relinquishes claims of conquest over land in the name of God. Christians need to wake up to the fact that we are not a moral majority. We are a minority voice in a society full of competing moral perspectives, all clamouring for attention. Some of those voices are deeply disconcerting to us, and it is understandable that we feel threatened. But they are *human* voices, voices worth engaging in conversation lovingly and respectfully.

Our success or failure should not be judged by how well we have wrested the reins of power from our opponents to 'recapture the culture'. Our success should be judged by the humility with which we treat our opponents, how charitably we articulate our agendas, how gracefully we accept setbacks, how well we love our fellow citizens and how well we demonstrate that we are *for* them, that we long to call them 'friends'. By taking the low road, we may find that we have more of an impact on the culture in the long run than we could by trying to coerce change through politics or by withdrawing into a safe zone. We are not cultural conquistadors. We are now the loyal, loving opposition.

The moral? Naked power politics that does not love our political opponents will not succeed. Lasting change comes only when we intentionally address the whole person, including the cultural and imaginative contexts of those across the cultural/political divide from us. The key lies not in forcing agendas on others, but in building bridges.

3

How not to engage post-Christian culture (when you should): the path of pietistic withdrawal

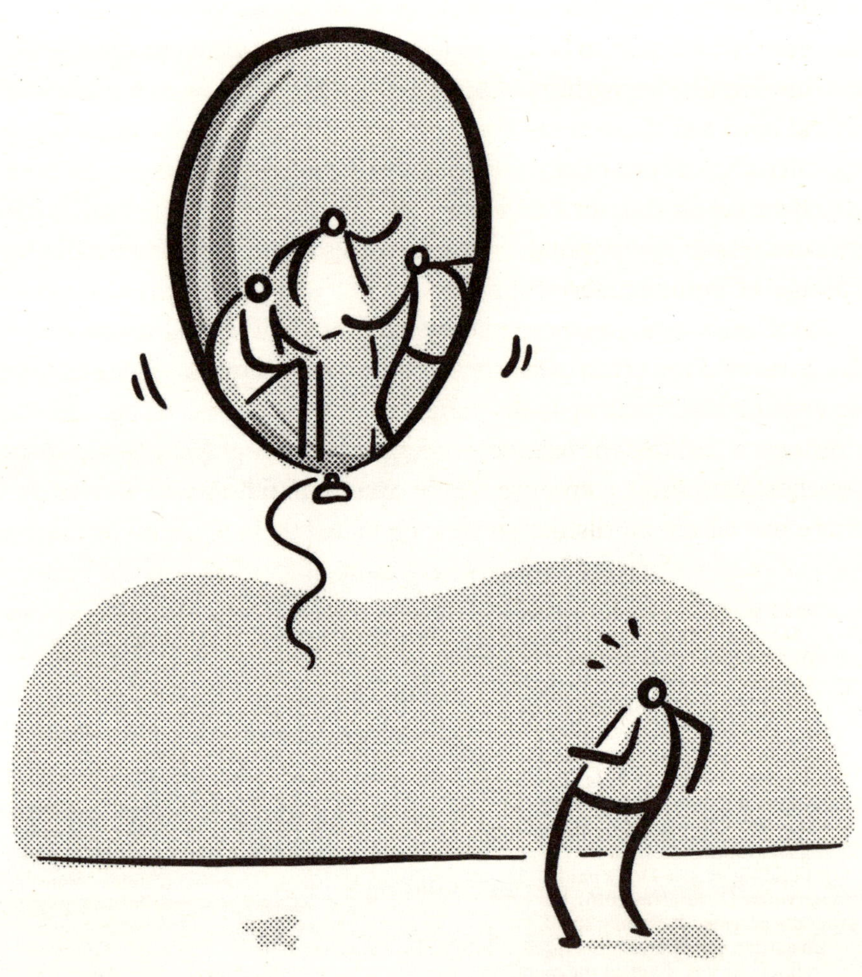

Introduction: 'strategic withdrawal' from the 'deluge' of modern culture

Some Christians react to the culture wars and excesses of the political path with, 'Yuck! I don't want any part of that! Just leave me alone to live a quiet life of Christian obedience.' These tend to be good, salt-of-the-earth Christian people who feel that if the world is going to the dogs, they would be better off staying out of the kennel. When the dogs run wild, stay off the street.

This path seeks withdrawal into a Christian subculture that insulates us from the wider culture, the so-called 'Christian bubble'. The heart-motivation behind this is often noble: we need to be a *distinctive* community, we need to be different and uncompromised by the world.

This impulse to withdraw, to preserve Christian distinctiveness, is stated most forcefully (and, for some, most persuasively) by Rod Dreher, a writer and editor of the *American Conservative* magazine, in his book *The Benedict Option.*[1] In it, Dreher calls for a 'strategic withdrawal' [2] from culture (especially popular culture) to escape from what he calls the 'deluge' of 'liquid modernity', because the 'strongly anti-Christian nature of contemporary popular culture occludes the meaning of the gospel, and hides from us the kinds of habits and practices we need to engage in to be truly faithful to what we have been given'.[3]

Modern culture, he argues, is relativistic, obsessively self-centred and hostile to those committed to the Christian faith. If we wish to preserve our Christian distinctiveness – which is key to eventually saving

[1] Rod Dreher, *The Benedict Option: A strategy for Christians in a post-Christian nation* (New York: Sentinel, 2017). For a fuller critique of the book, see my review, 'Book reviews: The Benedict Option', *Foundations*, vol. 73 (Autumn 2017), <www.affinity.org.uk/foundations-issues/issue-73-book-review-4>, accessed February 2023.

[2] See Dreher, *The Benedict Option*, p. 2, and his article, 'The accidental Benedict option', *American Conservative* (19 April 2015), <www.theamericanconservative.com/dreher/accidental-benedict-option>, accessed February 2023. Dreher denies that he is calling for isolationism (see, for example, 'Critics of the Benedict Option', *American Conservative* (8 July 2015), <www.theamericanconservative.com/dreher/critics-of-the-benedict-option>, accessed February 2023). But he also calls for readers to 'head for the hills': 'If you aren't going to head for higher ground, whatever that might mean, then you and your Christian neighbors had better start building an ark. Don't panic. *Prepare*', in his article 'Head for higher ground', *American Conservative* (21 January 2016), <www.theamericanconservative.com/dreher/head-for-higher-ground>, accessed February 2023).

[3] In earlier *American Conservative* columns, Dreher referred to the 'acid bath' of modernity. In his book, he has changed the metaphors used to focus on flood imagery.

society – we should detach from the secular onslaught so that we may remain a light for the world. Just as St Benedict withdrew into an intentional community as civilization fell apart around him, so Dreher urges conservative Christians to withdraw from our present toxic culture into intentional communities and focus on spiritual formation and preserving our Christian roots.[4] The goal: to survive this present darkness and chaos to emerge much later as the stewards and heralds of true civilization.

Do 'thick communities' mean that we are no longer called *into* the world?

To maintain Christian distinctiveness, Dreher asserts, we must build 'thick communities'. Such communities educate and train their members into habits that form a 'thick culture', which fosters holy living.[5] They demand high levels of commitment and deep relationships. By forming these quasi-monastic communities, he argues, we can preserve the faith so that it survives past the deluge threatening all Western culture. If we fail to preserve our Christian roots, if we become compromised by the world, then there will be nothing sane left to return to once society, presumably, falls apart. We need to do better than the thin communities and culture that characterize the church now.

Dreher's not wrong. The Christian church *has* become rather thin and threadbare around its cultural edges.[6] We are in desperate need of intentional communities that pass on Christian knowledge, traditions and cultural patterns. Dreher's position, however, seems to depend on the idea that Christian culture can somehow exist in isolation from the culture that surrounds it. That's not really how culture works. As I said in the introduction, culture is a conversation. Even when we attempt to cloister ourselves in thick communities, some exchange is inevitable, in the form

4 Dreher, *The Benedict Option*, pp. 12–15 and 'FAQ'.

5 Dreher, *The Benedict Option*, chapters 5 and 6.

6 According to one survey, US white evangelical Protestants' knowledge of the Bible and their own tradition was not particularly impressive. Out of 32 questions, they got an average of 17.6 right. See Pew Research Center's 'US Religious Knowledge Survey: Executive summary', Pew Research Center (28 September 2010), <www.pewforum.org/2010/09/28/u-s-religious-knowledge-survey>, accessed February 2023. Another more recent survey found that over half of all US church attendees had not heard of Jesus' command to go and make disciples of people from all nations (Matthew 28:16–20). See Barna, '51% of churchgoers do not know of the great commission', Barna (27 March 2018), <www.barna.com/research/half-churchgoers-not-heard-great-commission>, accessed February 2023.

of laws, the electricity that powers our appliances, language, architecture, systems of musical notation, groceries and so on. Dreher seems to draw the line at 'arts and entertainment' as that which we should shield ourselves from. That is what we must not engage and enjoy.

So, the real question is, are 'thick community' and cultural engagement mutually exclusive options? Is it possible to be involved with culture without compromising our faith?[7]

As we discussed in chapter 1, it is indeed possible. In fact, thick communities and loving cultural engagement *need* each other. On the one hand, you cannot really have gospel-centred cultural engagement without staying grounded in thick relationships in the church. On the other hand, you cannot really have a gospel-centred community without engaging the culture around you (and not simply by 'being the church' but also by moving out into *their* cultural spaces).[8] A church saved by grace will *necessarily* want to be actively involved with the world, with the culture outside its doors. Mission is the natural response to the gospel. We simply do not have the right to ignore Jesus' call that sends us out *into* the world (John 17:14–19). We may not be called overseas, but we are all missionaries nonetheless, sent into the world. Jesus' command mentions no exemptions for personal or family safety or holiness. Christ said it is our connection with the Word that keeps us safe, not our separation from the world.

An approach that seeks to withdraw from the world until the dark ages are past (so that we may then reclaim our rightful place in the world) withholds love from a hurting world. Although Dreher claims that the path of withdrawal is to enable the church 'to be for the world as Christ meant us to be', he places such a sharp emphasis on the disconnect between the church and our post-Christian culture that, in effect, he treats it as an unbridgeable gulf. What Dreher commends is, finally, unbiblically insular and motivated by self-protection rather than love for those around

---

[7] To be clear, Dreher is not against evangelism. But he does believe that engaging and enjoying the surrounding culture (especially popular culture and entertainment) necessarily undermines Christian culture and commitment. That drastically narrows the scope of what counts as 'cultural engagement'.

[8] Dreher, *The Benedict Option*, p. 101. The full quote is, 'The best witness Christians can offer to post-Christian America is simply to be the church, as fiercely and creatively a minority as we can manage.' When all is said and done, cultural engagement for Dreher means being a distinctive Christian community. What it can *not* mean is moving out into secular cultural spaces, bringing our (sometimes unwelcome) distinctiveness into conversation with the broader cultural community.

us. A bunker mentality simply does not fit with the Christian gospel of love and grace. The church does not exist to be our refuge, to keep us and ours safe. Rather, it is to be our equipping station, preparing us as we move out into the world to love and serve those around us.

Other problems with the path of withdrawal

Another problem: Dreher (and many other culturally bubble-bound Christians) see nothing but darkness and corruption in post-Christian culture. There is no recognition that there are places of light, blessing and common grace in the world. In other words, a biblically guided assessment of culture will find traces of grace, reasons for hope in our engagement with the world. Do not overlook these, for they are gifts from God.[9] It is precisely the existence of common grace that allows us to engage mainstream, post-Christian culture from *within* the centres of cultural production, such as Hollywood. As we shall see in the next chapter, Christians can be a winsome and healing influence in the very streams of culture that many Christians withdraw and recoil from.

Finally, the path of cultural withdrawal lacks confidence in God's control over history, his grace and providence for his people, even his ability to save. Dreher's 'doctrine of salvation', if we could put it that way, is *sola fides in bulla* – salvation comes by faith . . . in the bubble. Trust the conservative community's ability to save rather than trust in God's power and grace.

In reality, God alone saves. It may often be through church communities, but conservative communities, in and of themselves, cannot save. Indeed, when people do pin their hopes on them to save, they often become toxic and smothering. But God can and does save: *he* is our ultimate hope. We can risk engagement with the world around us not only because we are called to it by the love of Christ but also because we *are finally safe.* Our safety lies precisely in the power of a loving God, not our own ability to wall ourselves off from a scary world, hiding lights under bushel baskets (Matthew 5:15). We can be courageous because, ultimately, we are covered by the blood of the Lamb and safe in our Father's hands.

[9] On common grace in culture, see Richard Mouw, *He Shines in All That's Fair: Culture and common grace* (Grand Rapids, MI, and Cambridge: Eerdmans, 2001) and my book, *Popologetics: Popular culture in Christian perspective* (Phillipsburg, NJ: P&R, 2012), pp. 65–72.

The path of pietistic withdrawal (particularly the Benedict Option) is not really a viable or biblical path for Christians whom God has called into the world. That is not to say Dreher's book is without merit; we do need to work on building thick communities. Further, Dreher rightly emphasizes the need for beauty in our forms of liturgy and Christian life together. But we are not called to community for the sake of community. We are called to community to pursue God, one another and those who need Christ, which inevitably will lead us from community out into the wider world.

Conclusion: finding a way forwards

Both paths we have considered – political activism and pietistic withdrawal – fall short of biblical and effective strategies for effective involvement with post-Christian culture. Not that either is totally mistaken. Christians ought to have a political voice, if we can engage politically with humility and love for our opponents. Christians also should pursue intentional community, if we can do so without withdrawing from the world to which Christ called us. Is there another option, a path that avoids both the coercion and backlash involved in the culture war mindset on the one hand *and* the quietism and insularity of pietistic withdrawal on the other? Can we find a way to build bridges out into the culture around us in constructive ways?

There are, of course, several. Some are obvious. We can perform acts of sacrificial service to the surrounding community, such as feeding the poor, housing the homeless, advocating on social justice issues, speaking up for the voiceless, living out the biblical injunction to care for the foreigner, orphans and widows, the poor, the disadvantaged, the dispossessed. Acts of love and service are the bread and butter of compassionate churches. Another is church-initiated habits of hospitality and community that aim to eradicate the cultural pandemic of loneliness and isolation inherent in an age of social media by providing something, well, thicker. Again, this can have a profound impact on the local culture, giving shelter to many who are recovering from broken families and relationships and who are looking for a home.

But there is one more path that is less obvious and receives less attention than these two. It is the path of creative engagement with the post-Christian imagination.

4

How to engage post-Christian culture: the path of cultural creativity (exploring oasis planting)

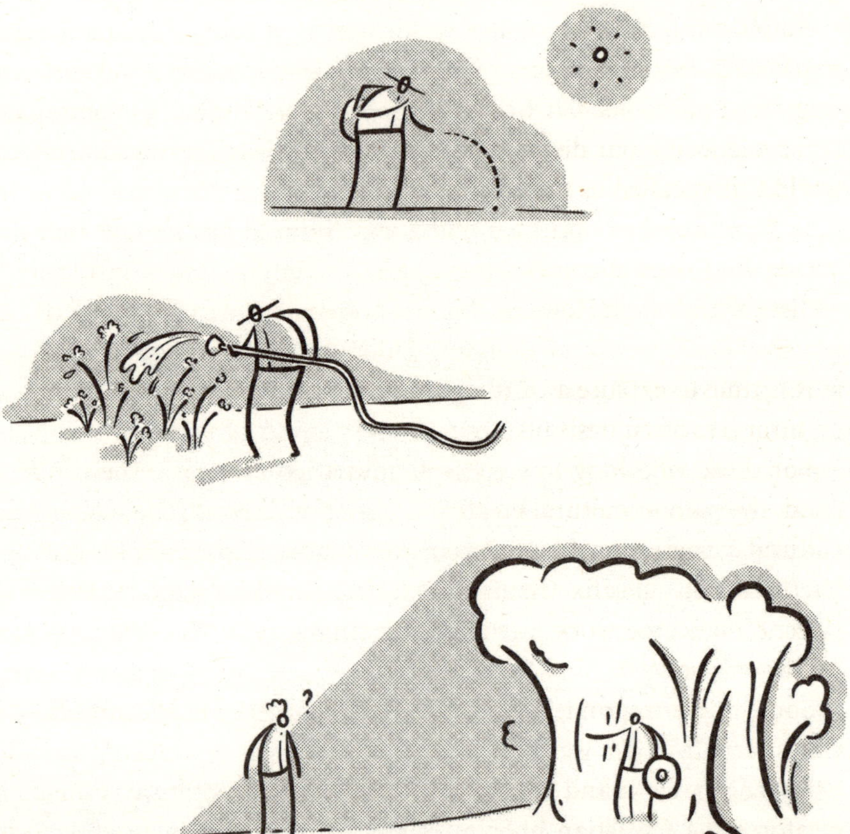

Introduction: a creative, bridge-building path

We have explored two possible paths for engaging post-Christian culture. Each has positive elements, but also aspects that undermine entering into that cultural conversation in a healthy and biblical way.

The political/culture warring path shows strong conviction and a desire for society to be changed for the better. Compromises made in pursuit of power, however – often involving resorting to unloving, coercive tactics – end up creating resentment and a cultural backlash.

The path of withdrawal shows the need for deeply rooted intentional communities and may recognize the value of Christians nurturing their own culture and creativity. This path, however, elevates self-protection above missional engagement, causing us to default on the calling Christ gave us.

Both these paths do have legitimate aspects to them. Christians ought to have a political voice, but only if we can speak humbly and with love with our opponents. Christians should pursue intentional community and avoid losing our distinctiveness, but without withdrawing from the world Christ called us into.

Is there another option, a path that avoids both the coercion and backlash of the culture war model and the quietism and insularity of pietistic withdrawal? How can we build bridges into culture in constructive ways?

It is time to explore a third option – the path of engagement through cultural creativity, oasis planting.

For those who long to see Christ honoured and serve the common good, the path of cultural creativity that contributes to the mainstream cultural conversation – building bridges, planting oases – holds promise, but there is no quick fix. Changing the imaginary landscape requires slow, patient, dedicated work, perhaps spanning generations before positive results will be seen.

Some might respond, 'Creative cultural engagement? We already *have* Christian films!' As we shall see, the Christian film industry does not really engage with and contribute to our common culture so much as reinforce the Christian bubble. True creative engagement enters into the ongoing cultural conversation in the world through Christian involvement in mainstream creative industries, creating works that build bridges and plant oases.

This chapter explores the creative, bridge-building path to be found in such centres of cultural influence, using Hollywood as a case study.[1]

Is creative cultural engagement biblical?

So, what makes the path of cultural creativity (oasis planting) better in principle than either the path of culture warring or the path of pietistic withdrawal? Not only more effective strategically but also better in the sense of inherent goodness, sound theologically, in harmony with biblical principles?

The case for creative cultural engagement hangs on the doctrine of common grace – namely, that God's grace is so vast, it spills over the boundaries of his chosen people (his church) into the lives of others who care nothing for God. God is so generous that he shows goodness even to his enemies (see, for example, Acts 14:17) by giving them governments that render justice, journalists who hunger after and print the truth, artists who create beauty, people who show real kindness to one another, marriages that last and so on. Not perfectly, but mostly. These good things we enjoy aren't due to our inherent goodness. Rather, they are gifts from God.[2]

Some Christians are suspicious of the concept of common grace, seeing in it a slippery slope that leads to ever greater compromises with worldliness and undermining Christian distinctiveness. Such criticisms have a point – a badly defined doctrine of common grace can lead to Christianity lite, a pale imitationof the faith. But it need not be if it is properly articulated.

Common grace is not undifferentiated generosity from God. It has a point. Or, rather, it points; it is a signpost indicating his being and character. It provides the necessary context for God's reaching out in saving grace. Common grace must always be seen as correlating with two other

---

[1] Later chapters explore other cultural forms.

[2] For a more expansive treatment of common grace, see John Murray, 'Common grace', *Collected Writings of John Murray: Volume 2: Systematic theology* (Edinburgh, Scotland, and Carlisle, PA: Banner of Truth, 1991 [1982]), pp. 93–122, <www.sounddoctrine.net/Modern_Day_Reform_Teaching/John%20Murray/Common_Grace.htm>, accessed February 2023. A briefer treatment, but one orientated towards cultural interpretation, can be found in my book, *Popologetics*, pp. 66–71.

doctrines: the image of God and general revelation. Because God is generous, the fall into sin did not extinguish the image of God in human beings. Though distorted, it remains, to restrain sin and enable non-Christians to produce real good and real truth – a grace common to all humanity. Note how Dutch theologian Herman Bavinck sees common grace and the image of God as virtually dovetailing:

> God did not leave sin alone to do its destructive work. He had and, after the fall, continued to have a purpose for his creation; he interposed common grace between sin and the creation – a grace that, while it does not inwardly renew, nevertheless restrains and compels. All that is good and true has its origin in this grace, including the good we see in fallen man. The light still does shine in the darkness. The spirit of God makes its home and works in all creation.
>
> Consequently, traces of the image of God continue in mankind. Understanding and reason remain, and he possesses all sorts of natural gifts. In him dwells a feeling, a notion of the Godhead, a seed of religion. Reason is a precious gift of God and philosophy . . . Music too is God's gift. The arts and sciences are good, useful, and of great value. The state is an institution of God. The goods of life do not just serve to provide for man's needs in the strict sense; they also serve to make life pleasant. They are not purely *ad necessitatem* [for necessity]; they are also *ad oblectamentum* [for delight]. Men still have a sense of the truth and of right and wrong; we see natural love that binds parents and children together. In the things that appertain to this earthly life, man can still accomplish much good.[3]

And because we carry the (common) grace of being created in the image of God, common grace is necessarily revelational. Our very selves reveal something of God's glory. Common grace reveals God's generosity, love of beauty, justice and mercy. As such, it leads naturally towards God

[3] Herman Bavinck, 'Common grace', rectoral address, Theological University Kampen (December 1894), in R. C. Van Leeuwen (tr.), *Calvin Theological Journal*, vol. 24, no. 1 (April 1989), p. 51.

himself – or would do, had our own sin not distorted and suppressed our perception of God's signposts in the world (see Romans 1:18–25). Bavinck points out that the grace of God being spread to everyone is God's way of revealing himself to all people:

> There is . . . a rich revelation of God even among the heathen – not only in nature but also in their heart and conscience, in their life and history, among their statesmen and artists, their philosophers and reformers. There exists no reason at all to denigrate or diminish this divine revelation.[4]

Common grace, then, is an expression of the image of God and functions as general revelation. It is the hinge on which any sort of cultural engagement turns, giving us a divinely instituted point of contact between the church and those who care nothing for God.

Generally, the doctrine of common grace is employed to help us interpret non-Christian cultural works, to lawfully appreciate the goodness and truth in them (as Bavinck does in the first quote). But in the case of creative cultural engagement, we can picture common grace as a bridge that allows traffic to flow *both* ways. Common grace is not found only in non-Christian works that are received and enjoyed by Christians but also in the hearts of non-Christians, allowing them to receive, enjoy and appreciate works made by Christians. If a Christian cultural work is compelling and accessible, the goodness, beauty and truth will connect and resonate with the God-given (but non-saving) goodness, beauty and truth that dwell within the hearts of non-Christians.

We must be intentional, therefore, about creating works that invite non-Christians in, that are accessible to them (versus, say, trying to shape culture through strong-arm tactics or withdrawing and making works that speak only to other Christians). In other words, we must become skilled in the art of imaginative hospitality.[5]

---

4 Bavinck, 'Common grace', p. 41. Bavinck here is surely riffing on a similar warning given by Calvin: 'If we regard the Spirit of God as the sole fountain of truth, we shall neither reject the truth itself, nor despise it wherever it shall appear, unless we wish to dishonour the Spirit of God', *Institutes of the Christian Religion*, ed. John T. MacNeill, tr. Ford Lewis Battles (Philadelphia, PA: Westminster Press, 1960), 2.2.15.

5 Credit to Caleb Woodbridge for suggesting the fantastic phrase 'imaginative hospitality'.

Picture yourself preparing for guests you've invited to supper. Assuming that they will take off their shoes, you pick up any Lego bricks scattered on the rug, so your guests won't step on them.[6] You tidy up, vacuum, plump up the cushions, all in the name of making your guests feel as welcome as possible. Creative cultural engagement is a way of doing the same. Jesus did this when he told parables using common situations (seeds growing in fields) and the latest news (about a tower that fell on some hapless people). He started where his audience felt at home, though his stories undoubtedly took them into uncharted territory.

The point is, if our engagement with post-Christian culture is to be guided by love (the way Jesus engaged his pre-Christian culture), then we would be well advised to invite people with all the skill and winsomeness and power we can. This will take time. It will also take a change of attitude, from one of cultural conquest, saying 'God is on our side', to one of humility and charity, taking care that we are on *God's* side.

These are the theological and biblical principles upon which creative cultural engagement rests. But we also need to explore the practical, strategic value of this approach. Let us begin our exploration by considering a cultural minority that has had a tremendous impact on popular culture.

Changing the tide: learning from the LGBTQI+ community's impact on popular culture and the same-sex marriage debate

One of the most striking cultural success stories of the twenty-first century is the shift in opinions regarding LGBTQI+ rights, particularly same-sex marriage. The LGBTQI+ community made a concerted, sustained, creative effort to engage with a hostile culture. Christians can learn something here.

Gay marriage is a difficult subject. Christians debate whether God blesses same-sex unions or not. I believe the Bible is clear: homosexual behaviour is a sin, and unrepentance will have devastating results (1 Cornthians 6:9–10).[7] But conservative Christians are likewise guilty of

[6] As the Internet has taught us, stepping on Lego bricks barefoot or in stockinged feet is one of the most extreme forms of torture known to humankind.

[7] The Greek words that describe same-sex activity in 1 Corinthians 6:9 are fairly explicit and leave little room for doubt.

sin, for we have not loved LGBTQI+ people well (or at all), violating an equally clear biblical mandate to love those whose lifestyles depart from God's will (Matthew 5:43–48).[8]

Though I have concerns about some of the content that comes to us from LGBTQI+ creatives, I admire their inventiveness and sheer tenacity. Their creative contributions to mainstream culture have had a tremendous impact. Just look at the numbers. Attitudes regarding same-sex marriage in the USA shifted dramatically from those recorded in 2004 to those held in 2019 (see Figure 4.2). In 2004, 60 per cent were opposed to it and 31 per cent in favour; in 2019, those numbers flipped almost exactly, with 61 per cent in favour, 31 per cent opposed.[9]

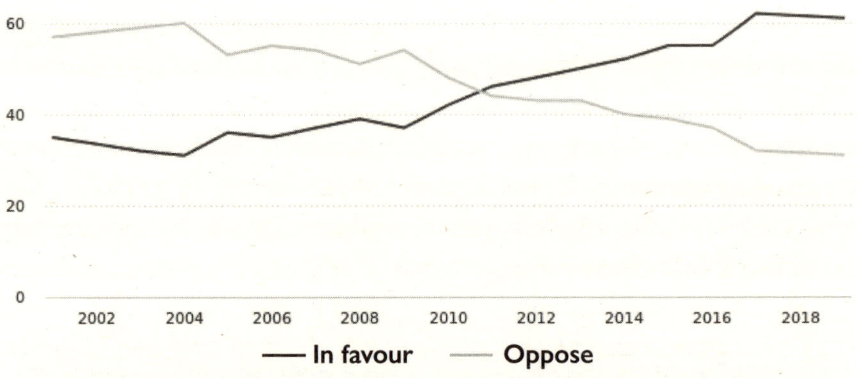

Figure 4.2 **Percentages of adults in the USA who are in favour of or oppose same-sex marriage from 2001 to 2019** (Pew Research Center, 2019, reproduced with permission)

A similar shift has occurred in the UK, from 37 per cent giving their approval in 2004 to 66 per cent in 2018.[10] This sea change in attitudes happened in 14 years – too fast for a simple generational shift.

One reason for this change could well be a commitment by the gay community to long-term involvement in the entertainment industry. By

8 Sam Allberry's *Is God Anti-Gay?* (Epsom, Surrey: The Good Book Company, 2013) strikes a fine, biblical balance between clarity and compassion on the issue of same-sex attraction.

9 Statistics and the graph in Figure 4.2 are from Pew Research Center, 'Attitudes on same-sex marriage: Public opinion on same-sex marriage', Pew Research Center (14 May 2019), <www.pewresearch.org/religion/fact-sheet/changing-attitudes-on-gay-marriage>, accessed February 2023.

10 See Nancy Kelley, 'Over the rainbow?', NatCen Social Research (11 July 2019), <http://natcen.ac.uk/blog/over-the-rainbow>, accessed February 2023.

telling compelling stories, they have been able to change the imaginary landscape of Western society, particularly in the USA. Sociologist James Davison Hunter acknowledges, 'At most 3 percent of the American population, their influence has become enormous . . . far disproportionate to their size.'[11]

It was not always so. From the 1980s into the early 1990s, both the USA and UK were politically and culturally conservative. It was a time of 'family values' and a resurgent Religious Right.[12] Homosexuals were a marginalized minority in Hollywood and in the media in the UK, including the BBC.[13] Gay characters were routinely portrayed in film and on television as two-dimensional caricatures: the effeminate, over-the-top camp comic relief (Mr Humphries in the BBC's *Are You Being Served?*, the homeless cabaret singer in Terry Gilliam's *Fisher King*) or the terrifying lesbian killer whore (*Basic Instinct*). From the end of the 1990s to the present, however, new gay characters were being written that were complex, serious, smart, playful, witty, supportive and, above all, relatable and sympathetic: Colin Russell (*EastEnders*), Will Truman (*Will and Grace*), rodeo cowboy Jack Twist (*Brokeback Mountain*), San Franciscan councilman Harvey Milk (*Milk*), Captain Jack Harkness (*Doctor Who*), talented high-school singer Blaine Anderson (*Glee*), numerous characters in *Queer as Folk*, ethically grounded armed robber Omar Little (*The Wire*) and self-conflicted black drug dealer Chiron (*Moonlight*). These characters were three-dimensional, flawed, relatable people caught up in compelling plotlines that had viewers rooting for them and identifying with them. This change in representation led to a change in social attitudes.[14]

---

11 James Davison Hunter, *To Change the World: The irony, tragedy, and possibility of Christianity in the late modern world* (Oxford and New York: Oxford University Press, 2010), p. 20.

12 The Religious Right is a peculiarly American phenomenon. The UK, however, was also experiencing a period of cultural and political resurgence of conservativism while Margaret Thatcher was prime minister.

13 For an interesting, behind-the-scenes look at the resistance to introducing gay characters into TV programmes in the UK, see Emma Powys Maurice's interview with lead writer and executive producer of *Doctor Who* and creator, writer and co-producer of *Queer as Folk*, 'Russell T. Davies on queer representation on TV, time loop anomalies and homophobic folk dancers. Yes, really', *Pink News* (5 January 2020), <www.pinknews.co.uk/2020/01/05/russell-t-davies-john-barrowman-doctor-who-queer-as-folk-lgbt-television>, accessed February 2023. Thanks to Caleb Woodbridge for suggesting this article.

14 See Angela Wattercutter, 'How pop culture changed the face of the same-sex marriage debate', *Wired* (27 June 2013), <www.wired.com/2013/06/pop-culture-same-sex-marriage>,

These characters did not leap on to the screen fully formed. They had to be created, written and given the green light by producers. Creating an influential TV series or film with a sympathetic character is a long process that requires many people who wield varying levels of creative influence, from directors or producers of films and those who commission TV programmes down. Those people needed to sign off on the ideas presented to them. Writers needed to agree on what worked and what didn't. The LGBTQI+ community and allies worked to gain positions of creative influence within the entertainment industry that enabled all this to happen.[15] They now consistently provide a pool of talented actors, writers, directors, commissioners and producers, people who are known and trusted by the heavy hitters of the industry.

The promise and perils of Christian involvement in Hollywood

Could Christians do the same? Perhaps. Christians face significant hurdles when working in Hollywood, for example. It is tempting to see them as a marginalized, closeted minority, just as LGBTQI+ people once were. And just as Hollywood once caricatured LGBTQI+ people, Hollywood has a history of trafficking in caricatures of conservative Christians. Consider the itinerant evangelist and lascivious, conniving con man Elmer Gantry (*Elmer Gantry,* 1960) or the sadistic faux-pious Warden Norton (*Shawshank Redemption,* 1994) or the killjoy Catholic mayor Comte de Reynaud (*Chocolat,* 2000), the rigid and censorious book-banning Kitty Farmer (*Donnie Darko,* 2001) or the sanctimonious Mrs Hunt, who rejects her own grandchild when her son gets his girlfriend pregnant (*If Beale Street Could Talk,* 2018). It's a real rogues' gallery of the judgmental, pious hypocrites, fanatical religiously driven sadists, devious and/or deluded.[16]

(note 14 *cont.*) accessed February 2023. A graph featured in the article (and provided by the Gay and Lesbian Alliance Against Defamation, GLAAD) showed a steady increase in the numbers of gay characters on television, from 26 in 2003 to 111 in 2012. Approval ratings for same-sex marriage mirrored this rise.

15 See, for example, Michael O'Connell and Degen Pener, 'The 50 most powerful LGBTQ players in Hollywood', *The Hollywood Reporter* (3 June 2020), <www.hollywoodreporter.com/lists/pride-2020-50-powerful-lgbtq-players-hollywood-1295933>, accessed February 2023.

16 There are, of course, exceptions, such as Ned Flanders from *The Simpsons*.

Hollywood certainly *seems* like hostile territory for Christians. Perhaps if Christians could get their act together and have some coherent creative agenda, like those in the LGBTQI+ community have done, we could change things for the better. But we haven't. The trend is for the conservative (Protestant) Christian community to underinvest in developing culturally creative talent for mainstream arts and entertainment (as well as education and publishing).[17]

Some Christians have found success and influence in Tinseltown – Denzel Washington, Chris Pratt, Scott Derrickson (director of *Doctor Strange*) and others. But they are a minority, and the history between Christians and Hollywood has been fraught. Almost from its inception, Christians have tried to influence Hollywood to include more pious content, with mixed results.[18] That history, plus the current political climate, has left many Hollywood power players decidedly cool, even antagonistic, towards conservative Christians.

To get an insider's perspective, I interviewed two Christians who work in Hollywood. One is a talented film and television actress. Though not an 'A-lister', she has worked steadily over the years, both in mainstream and Christian film, building an impressive resumé of creative work. The other is a filmmaker with a passion for storytelling. Making short films since childhood, he went to film school, graduated and now has a couple of feature-length films to his credit. Both prefer to remain anonymous – talking openly about Christian faith in Hollywood, the heart of 'cancel culture', can be risky. Though they have differing perspectives, each gave a more nuanced view of the cultural landscape of America's (and the world's) dream factory from the perspective of a practising Christian.[19]

---

17 James Davison Hunter, *To Change the World*, pp. 81–88. Hunter isn't interested in the entertainment industry per se, but he does document an overall failure of faith groups to invest in cultural talent in general.

18 See William Romanowski's *Reforming Hollywood: How American Protestants fought for freedom at the movies* (Oxford and New York: Oxford University Press, 2012). It is interesting to note that Catholics and liberal Protestants led the effort. More conservative Protestants mostly chose the path of pietistic withdrawal (see chapter 3).

19 The quotes included in the next sections are from telephone interviews with the actress on 8 January and 29 June, 2020, and with the filmmaker on 6 July 2020. I quote verbatim from the interviews, except for minor corrections for the sake of grammar or clarity.

Looking for fresh perspectives, but not too fresh

One would hope that Hollywood would be open to Christians. After all, it is obsessed with finding the Next Big Thing, something that will resonate with audiences and turn a profit. The filmmaker told me, 'One thing that Hollywood says they value is fresh voices and new perspectives', such as the voices of sexual or gender minorities. For instance, studio executives actively search for those who claim 'two-spirit' gender identity.[20] Such openness to alternative perspectives would seem to create room for Christian creatives to bring imaginative new takes on faith, culture and life. But there's a catch: a 'fresh' perspective must not threaten widely accepted cultural values, especially those dear to Hollywood. According to media scholar William Romanowski, popular culture is popular precisely because it resonates with and reiterates the audience's beliefs rather than challenges them:

> Typically, then, the popular arts do not introduce new beliefs, but reinforce already existing ones; people generally want to be entertained while also being affirmed in what they already believe.[21]

Christian values often run counter to mainstream secular culture. Perhaps Christian perspectives are a little *too* 'fresh' (or too ancient) for Hollywood to feature regularly.[22]

There is interest, however, in Christian values that blend seamlessly with wider culture, a sort of Christianity lite. The actress said that studios are interested in stories about:

---

20 'Two-spirit' is a Native American term for a third gender for those born male or female who identify as the opposite sex. See <www.dictionary.com/e/gender-sexuality/two-spirit>, accessed February 2023.

21 William D. Romanowski, *Eyes Wide Open: Finding God in popular culture* (Grand Rapids, MI: Brazos Press, rev. exp. edn 2007 [2001]), p. 93. It is also true that finding such resonance can create space for the introduction of new values. That's what LGBTQI+ filmmakers, producers, directors and others have done so successfully.

22 Hollywood's track record regarding Christian themes is uneven; it ebbs and flows with public taste. During the 1950s and 1960s, Hollywood loved sweeping biblical epics such as *The Ten Commandments* (1956) and *The Greatest Story Ever Told* (1965), because they were proven moneymakers. But then epics went out of style, biblical epics along with them. More recently, Mel Gibson's film *The Passion of the Christ* (2004) became an unexpected box office hit. In response, Hollywood gave the green light to a series of biblical dramas, such as *Nativity Story* (2006), *Noah* (2014), *Exodus: Gods and Kings* (2014) and *Risen* (2016), with varying financial returns. Beyond biblical stories, Hollywood remains reluctant to make films that bring a Christian perspective and experience into everyday life. There are isolated exceptions, such as *Chariots of Fire* (1981), *The Mission* (1986), *Dead Man Walking* (1995) and *The Apostle* (1997).

> faithfulness, courage, redemption, hope, all of the things that we would say, 'Whatever is good, whatever is true, whatever is noble, think on these things' (Philippians 4:8). They are looking for that content, but they specifically don't want it to be explicit because they want it to have a wider audience.

Hollywood wants stories about the good things Christians can bring to community life, but without naming the source; stories that resonate without alienating non-Christians. Hollywood seeks a Christianity shorn of its narrative specifics, bankable fruits safely detached from their historical roots. Why? Because the specifics of the faith can challenge accepted cultural beliefs, disturb rather than comfort, and that's bad for business.[23]

Further contributing to anti-Christian bias, Hollywood detests the political positions held by many Christians. They assume that Christians denigrate and oppress racial and sexual minorities (too often with good reason). And they associate the claim that salvation can be found in Christ alone with rank intolerance.

The impact of such assumptions on Christians in Hollywood can be severe. According to the filmmaker, taking a stand that 'doesn't fit Hollywood's current cultural narrative' concerning LGBTQI+ rights could result in a career being 'cancelled'. The actress pointed to the danger of publicly saying anything about the exclusive claims of Christ:

[23] I suspect one source of Hollywood's aversion to the details of specific religions is the long American tradition of 'civil religion'. The term was coined by sociologist Robert Bellah in his 1967 article, 'Civil religion in America', *Daedalus*, vol. 96, no. 1 (Winter 1967), pp. 1–21, <www.robertbellah.com/articles_5.htm>, accessed February 2023. He argues that America was not founded as a Christian nation. Rather, America's religious self-understanding, its civil religion, 'is a collection of beliefs, symbols, and rituals with respect to sacred things and institutionalized in a collectivity. This religion – there seems no other word for it – while not antithetical to and indeed sharing much in common with Christianity, was neither sectarian nor in any specific sense Christian.' Peter Gardella, in his detailed exploration of the symbols, artifacts and rituals of American civil religion (and the controversies that surround them), identifies four key values that define America's national religion: personal freedom, political democracy, world peace and tolerance. See also his book *American Civil Religion: What Americans hold sacred* (Oxford and New York: Oxford University Press, 2014), p. 3. Likely Hollywood executives have internalized the sacred nature of tolerance (or, at least, they suspect ticket-buyers hold it sacred), so want to avoid challenging, offending or excluding anyone.

> To be honest, if you say from a public platform, 'Jesus saves, and Jesus is the only way', you're just done. You're done! You can't say that. That's a thing that immediately is called bigotry of some sort.

For entertainment industry executives, a Christian perspective is dangerously out of step with the American mainstream (as they see it).

There are quite a few Christians working in Hollywood, according to both the filmmaker and the actress. But if Christians want to survive, they must keep a low profile, often hiding that part of their identity.

Biases melt when you form relationships and live with integrity

While Hollywood is extra-sensitive about bias against race, gender or sexual orientation, most are blind to bias against Christians. As the filmmaker put it:

> In Hollywood, people often do not understand that they have an underlying belief system that's very negative towards Christianity, toward Christians. And that drives their behaviour [regarding] wanting to work with believers, to hire believers. But they often don't even realize it, because it's just working so deeply within their psyche.

But much of that bias evaporates once a personal relationship is established. Then the Christian is no longer an abstract concept but becomes a real person. Even so, the filmmaker avoids the term 'Christian' because of its negative connotations:

> People will have a blanket feeling about Christians, about believers. But once they're actually able to have a relationship with someone who's a believer, it's amazing seeing how people's opinions change, and how they start to warm up to what faith is, and who Jesus is. But as long as they are kept at a distance, it's easier in general to despise that particular belief system. So what I've found is that when you are really caring for people and loving people where they are, and coming alongside them, and you start to share your own belief system, you don't hit the same kind of resistance. I find it helpful

> not to use words like 'Christian' . . . So instead, I'll say, 'I'm a follower of Jesus' or 'I'm a believer.' Once you start changing the terminology, they don't have preconceived expectations, or baggage attached to that new terminology that you are using, and therefore you can engage with them more on a human level.

For this filmmaker, Hollywood industry culture changes one relationship at a time.

For her part, the actress is trying to change Hollywood industry culture by maintaining personal and professional integrity within a culture that rewards bad behaviour and regularly abuses power:

> One of the greatest challenges in being a person who wants to live out the gospel in their lives in an environment like this is simply to live with integrity, to do your job excellently, to show up and have actually done your work and know your lines, even though everyone around you doesn't. And then once you're handed some power, to actually use that with integrity and for good, to make sure people are treated fairly, to make sure crews are not being abused. What I would like for Christians in leadership positions in Hollywood to do is to start *there*. Just to start . . . to live the gospel out with integrity, because it comes with great sacrifice. You lose money and you lose opportunities often if you are not going along with the flow of 'normalcy'. And I'm sure that is true in every industry because of how broken our world is, how easy it is for power to become abusive.

For her, it's not so much about theology as it is about the witness of a consistent life.

Does working in Hollywood change Christians?

Hollywood culture pressures people to conform to its own ideology and lifestyle. That is what concerns parents when a child shows talent and wants to find a job in Hollywood. How do Christians handle the cultural pressure to conform? Some adapt, and some resist.

The actress was brought up in a conservative Protestant Christian home. She found that her theological views regarding alternative sexualities and other religions have changed to become more affirming. Cultural pressure likely contributed, but she sees it more as a product of her maturing faith that has come about, especially as she worked alongside and got to know gay creatives. They befriended her and she wants to defend them. For her, love weighs far more heavily than the specifics of the theological system she was brought up with. In this sense, Hollywood has changed her perspective.

The filmmaker came to faith as an adult. He considers theological integrity as equally important as lived integrity. He is keenly aware not only of controversial issues, like homosexuality and transgender identity, but also of local cultural idols, such as pinning personal worth to appearance and career success. He says being grounded in a 'core community' is key to ongoing Christian faithfulness. He takes a more self-consciously missional approach, resisting the prevailing cultural narratives of Hollywood (about sexuality, appearance and so on), while reaching out to those who disagree with his perspective.

For both, however, there is a deep cultural divide between Hollywood and Christianity that they are seeking to bridge. That cultural chasm is at least partly the fault of the conservative Christian reaction to Hollywood, particularly the divisive influence of the Christian film industry. Let us consider its role in Hollywood's imaginary landscape.

Notes from the mirror world: Hollywood and the Christian film industry

Outspoken Christians, feeling unwelcome in mainstream Hollywood, have built a parallel film industry with studios such as Sherwood Pictures (*Facing the Giants*, 2006, and *Fireproof*, 2008) and Pure Flix Entertainment (*God's Not Dead*, 2014).[24]

The Christian film industry: rooting for the home team

Though they bill themselves as evangelistic, their main audience is other conservative Protestant Christians. The filmmaker I interviewed calls

24 For a detailed history of faith-based films, see Terry Lindvall's *Sanctuary Cinema: Origins of the Christian film industry* (New York: NYU Press, 2011) and William D. Romanowski's *Reforming Hollywood: How American Protestants fought for freedom at the movies* (Oxford and New York: Oxford University Press, 2012).

these films 'hit them over the head'-type films, more sermon than film. They tend to feature unrealistic plots that heavily favour Christian characters, serving mainly to comfort believers:

> If you look at films that are more pointed in terms of [Christian belief], [films that] would say, 'These are *Christian* movies', they would feel more like propaganda, because they're not seeing both sides of it. You're just seeing that the Christians win in the end, and anyone who did not believe in Jesus, bad things happen to them. And I think that doesn't ring true to people as they're watching it. But if you're a believer, you're watching it and thinking in the back of your mind, 'I *am* pretty good.' You're feeling sort of better about yourself. I think that's the danger of stories like that: they're appealing to the people whose belief-set matches [the film's], but it's not challenging beyond that. As Scripture tells us, 'It rains on the righteous and unrighteous' (Matthew 5:45). If we're just creating stories where it [only] rains on the unrighteous, that's just not reality. Jesus was executed on a cross. It just doesn't get worse than that. Yet there are Christian stories being told where, ultimately, just really good things happen to the Christians.

Not surprisingly, non-Christians find such films nearly unwatchable. The actress, familiar with both Christian and mainstream film industries, believes that these films make the cultural divide in Hollywood worse:

> If you're making content that very specifically preaches to the choir – of which there's a growing number of films that are being made right now – you will be marginalized [in Hollywood]. Because a lot of those films – and I've seen a couple of them – some of them are great, and some come across as extremely offensive.

I suggested *God's Not Dead* as an example. She responded:

> Yes, that's exactly what I'm talking about. That movie for me was extremely offensive, to me, and to any non-believer that would potentially see this movie. I mean, it painted a very black-and-white

> picture about 'Christians are good, and everybody else is bad.' I mean *truly* bad. And the only value to their life is if they accept Jesus while they're dying in a car accident. It's just, that narrative, nobody wants to hear [it], outside of a very specific community of people who are not well-loved (certainly on the coasts) right now.

Perhaps it's no accident that Pure Flix's headquarters is not in Hollywood but in Scottsdale, Arizona, well away from both coasts.[25]

Why explicitly Christian films offend non-Christians

What makes these Christian films so offensive to non-Christians? It's a combination of several factors.

Let us return to the popular and financially successful *God's Not Dead* as an example.[26] First, the film presents a simplistic universe populated with black hats and white hats. The villains (non-Christians) are two-dimensional, spiteful, smug, self-centred and utterly detestable, while the heroes (Christians) are sweet, loving, victimized and without character flaws.[27] It's tailor-made to help Christians feel good about themselves and to demonize those with different beliefs and lifestyles. In other words, the film presents a tribal mentality, dividing the world into the good (our tribe, the Christians) and the bad (their tribe, the non-Christians), the Saved and the Lost. Those tribal affiliations are fairly locked . . . until the main non-Christian villain repents as he's dying. How could that *not* offend non-Christians?

---

25 James Davison Hunter says that Christian lack of influence can be seen in how the centres of Christian culture-making are almost always *outside* the centres of mainstream cultural power, such as New York and Los Angeles. See *To Change the World*, pp. 88–92.

26 Its success allowed Pure Flix to give the green light to not one but two sequels.

27 On *God's Not Dead*, see Josh Keefe's video 'Why Christian movies are BAD', Josh Keefe, YouTube (14 August 2017), <www.youtube.com/watch?v=50_3J6Go5Ng>, 8:44. Concerning Christians without character flaws, don't (necessarily) blame the writers. Screenwriter Sean Paul Murphy blogged about his script for *Hidden Secrets* (2006), a comedy that features a graceless, legalistic Christian alongside other more merciful Christians. He says that he was explicitly told by executives at Pure Flix that the Christian characters were *not* to have any character flaws – that would hurt the film's profits. Further, those projects in the Christian film industry that are given the go ahead have no interest in exploring serious problems in the church (racism, legalism, sexual abuse and so on). The self-protective cultural dynamics of conservative Protestantism – its aversion to self-reflection and self-criticism – have made honest Christian storytelling financially unattractive for Christian film studios. See 'Building the faith-based film ghetto', SeanPaulMurphyVille.com (29 September 2017), <https://seanpaulmurphyville.blogspot.com/2017/09/building-faith-based-film-ghetto.html>, accessed February 2023.

Second – just as true, but less obvious – the Christian gospel contains an offensive theological truth: all humans have offended God and the cross of Christ is in fact the only remedy. Jesus is indeed the only way to God and life, both now and for ever. The biblical witness is clear: to reject Christ is to reject life and to embrace a path of self-destruction. This is not a message that is easy for anyone to hear. Being labelled a sinner is humiliating. Learning that you cannot make it right but must rely on God's undeserved grace is more humiliating still! The message is stark and deeply uncomfortable. Who wants to hear that? And yet, this *is* a central tenet of biblical Christian faith, as attested to by passages such as John 14:6, 'I am the way, and the truth, and the life. No one comes to the Father except through me'[28] and Peter's bold statement in Acts 4:12 (NIV), 'Salvation is found in no one else, for there is no other name under heaven given to mankind by which we must be saved.' Historically, it is attested to by the blood of thousands on thousands of Christians, past and present, who preferred a violent death over demoting Jesus to being one god among many.

Mainstream Hollywood takes offence at Christian films because of their cultural style (insensitive, tone-deaf and arrogant) *and* they are an expression of non-negotiable theological exclusivity.[29]

But there is a third reason for Hollywood's animosity towards blatantly Christian films: the harsh social reality of the Christian subculture.

A mirror world of duelling cancel cultures

Conservative Christian subculture routinely punishes dissent as viciously as secular culture does. As the actress put it, 'the conservative Christian community can be very powerful in immediately smooshing people to the ground if they don't get in line.' The damage caused by Christian cancel culture is real, and the resentment it causes lingers. Hollywood has more than its fair share of 'exvangelicals' who carry stories and wounds of collective Christian bullying. This trait – more than humility or loving

[28] The writings of John are especially clear in identifying Christ with light, eternal life and the Father. For example, John 3:36 (NIV), 'Whoever believes in the Son has eternal life, but whoever rejects the Son will not see life, for God's wrath remains on them.' See also John 17:3 and 1 John 2:23.

[29] Hollywood's animosity to the Christian film industry never overrides its instinct for business opportunities – it is happy to distribute Christian films, for a price.

one's enemy – has become characteristic of conservative Protestant subculture. Instead of living out the gospel with a generosity of spirit to those who disagree, too many conservative Protestants are concerned about enforcing their values, policing their borders and keeping the tribe pure.

The result is a bizarre mirror world, a cultural polarization in which each side's intolerance is mirrored by the other: duelling cancel cultures. Two cultures have emerged; each committed to culture war purity, each a photo-negative of the other. Conservative Christians long for a world of sexual purity, a world free of abortions and same-sex relationships, free from evolution taught in schools (the only social issues that seem to consistently attract the ire of conservative Christian subculture).[30] Secular Hollywood prides itself on its openness and tolerance, but it, too, is committed to a form of doctrinal purity, longing for a world free of any anti-LGBTQI+ sentiment, free from any opposition to a woman's right to choose and free from (ironically) anyone who would judge another as unworthy, a sinner needing salvation.

There is a major difference between these mirror images, however. One is better funded and has more cultural influence than the other. As the filmmaker put it, 'Hollywood is doing an amazing job of discipling the world.' Hollywood's cultural dominance fuels a victim mentality within the culturally weaker Christian film industry, the reach of which rarely extends beyond its own subculture. The hostility between them runs deep, and the alienation seems all but complete.

Christian cultural witness in Hollywood: building bridges through brokenness

It's tough to work as a Christian in Hollywood, caught between two antagonistic cultures. Put yourself in the shoes of a talented, creatively trained Christian. What would you do if you wanted your stories to reach a mainstream audience?

[30] It seems as though conservative Protestant subcultures are hesitant to speak out on issues that are championed by those more theologically and politically liberal, such as racial justice, justice for the poor and migrants, as well as confronting the sexual abuse that can happen in churches and is too often covered up. To their credit, Catholic (or Catholic background) filmmakers have addressed the issue of sexual abuse in films such as *Doubt* (2008), *Calvary* (2014) and *The Two Popes* (2019).

Some simply give up on the faith. The actress has adapted her theology to fit Hollywood's ethos better and focuses on expressing the gospel through a commitment to professional integrity and justice in a culture that downplays both. The filmmaker has taken the stance of quiet resistance, seeking to build personal relationships that melt biases and allow the gospel to flow. Even so, it is difficult to navigate duelling cancel cultures. Both actress and filmmaker must keep a low profile if they wish to remain as creative witnesses in this centre of cultural influence.

One other ingredient is necessary to bring change to Hollywood's culture and, through it, to mainstream post-Christian culture: brokenness, the polar opposite of cancel culture. Christians *can* make a difference through humility, meeting those who are different on the very human ground of shared weakness, failure, darkness and suffering. Lasting, imagination-shaping connections are made not on the basis of heroic purity but, rather, stumbling imperfection.

Both my interview subjects reflect this in their own ways. The actress often chooses to play flawed characters, bringing an emotional vulnerability to her performances that appeals to flawed humans. The filmmaker's films feature characters who are out of their depth, struggling to grasp what's going on, as we all do. By bringing faith to bear in brokenness, bridges can be built that can have a lasting impact, even among the cultural cross-pressures that Christian creatives face.

Christians in Hollywood and Japan's 'hidden Christians'

The pressures that the actress and filmmaker endure remind me of artist Makoto Fujimura's description of Kakure Kirishitan, the 'hidden Christians', who were driven underground during the brutal persecution of Christians in Japan during the Tokugawa era (1603–1868).[31]

During those dark years, Japan closed itself off from outside influences. Japanese citizens suspected of Christian sympathies were compelled to step on a bronze bas-relief image of Christ on the cross or of Mary holding the deceased Christ (the pietà). These images were called *fumi-e*, literally, 'stepping images'. One by one, these citizens were ordered to step

[31] Makoto Fujimura, *Silence and Beauty: Hidden faith born of suffering* (Downers Grove, IL: InterVarsity Press, 2016), especially chapter 3.

on the *fumi-e*, visually desecrating those held sacred and beloved by Christians. Any hesitation would be noted, and that person and the other members of the family would be interrogated and likely executed. Fujimura therefore calls a culture that bullies people into conformity, forcing them to trample underfoot that which is most precious to them, a '*fumi-e* culture'.[32] The hidden Christians of Japan learnt to go through the motions of apostasy, stepping on the *fumi-e* while adopting certain Buddhist rites and beliefs to disguise their hidden faith. They clung to Christ in a defeated, hidden, decidedly unheroic and untriumphant way, yet survived for 200 years. Though broken, they remained participants in a hidden grace.

My point is not that Christian creatives in Hollywood have endured anything like the persecution of Japanese Christians of the Tokugawa period. It is possible to be a professing Christian *and* live and work in Hollywood. However, listening to the actress and filmmaker, and recalling Fujimura's book, I was struck by four ideas.

- Post-Christian society in the USA is inhabited by (at least) two *fumi-e* cultures. Secular Hollywood banishes as intolerant anyone who insists on the uniqueness of Christ, and conservative Protestantism banishes as unfaithful anyone who deviates from its chosen beliefs and practices. Duelling *fumi-e* cultures make bridge-building difficult, providing little space for Christian creatives trying to navigate both cultures.
- It is understandable that Christian creatives would hide the more provocative aspects of their faith to survive in a duelling *fumi-e* society, using the forms and rhetoric of secular Hollywood to blend in but without wholly denying Christ.[33] Their faith will look different from that of ordinary conservative Protestants who don't face those pressures, and that difference will inspire suspicion, just as the Buddhist-infused hidden Christians were objects of suspicion for the

32 Fujimura, *Silence and Beauty*, chapter 5. This book is Fujimura's prolonged meditation on Shusako Endo's novel *Silence*, translated to film by Martin Scorsese in 2016. *Silence* tells the story of Father Rodrigues, a priest trying to reach the Japanese, but finally caught and forced to step on a *fumi-e*. Yet, even after this, it is implied that he retains a weak, broken, hidden faith.

33 This is *not* peculiar to the entertainment industry. One finds such hiding in any arena where a secular mindset rules a *fumi-e* culture: higher education, news media, the art world and so on.

missionaries who arrived once Japan had opened up to the West after the Tokugawa era ended.[34]

- For these semi-hidden Christians, there is access to grace precisely through the darkness and brokenness they experience. Fujimura emphasizes the deep connection between beauty and brokenness. The Japanese word (in kanji) for 'beauty' (美, *bi*) combines the Chinese ideogram for a (sacrificial) sheep with the ideogram for 'great'.[35] As paradoxical as it may seem to Westerners, the Japanese concept of beauty is deeply intertwined with ideas of sacrifice, suffering, brokenness and death. Brokenness itself carries with it its own poignant, painful beauty: 'In Japan of old, cherry blossoms are considered most beautiful when they are falling.'[36] Japan also honours *kintsugi* artisans, who take broken pottery and mend it with a lacquer mixed with a precious metal – often gold but also silver or platinum. The idea is not to 'fix' the vessel in a way that hides where it has broken, but to beautifully illuminate the cracks, creating something more precious for its having been broken (see p. 2 in plate section).[37]
- Christianity, too, values brokenness. Christ for us was most precious and beautiful when broken. We recall and symbolically re-enact that brokenness repeatedly when we break bread and pour wine at the Lord's Supper.[38] His brokenness connects with ours, for in his brokenness we are made whole. Christians, then, are not the victoriously unbroken, but the broken-being-mended, on an ongoing journey towards wholeness. God is the ultimate *kintsugi* artist, and we are his walking, talking, loving, wounded-but-being-mended vessels, fragile 'jars of clay' – our cracks allowing Christ's beauty to shine through (2 Corinthians 4:7–11). This kind of brokenness, rather than clinging to an illusory perfection, should result in humility that mends divisions. It can make whole even a deeply fractured society.

34 This is *not* to endorse the religious relativism that denies the unique saving power of Jesus espoused by some of these hidden Christians. The real challenge is how to affirm the uniqueness of Christ from a posture of brokenness within a situation that necessitates a measure of hiddenness, and sometimes results in a 'failure' of faith.

35 Fujimura, *Silence and Beauty*, chapter 2, 'A culture of beauty', especially the section 'Beauty and sacrifice', pp. 65–66.

36 Fujimura, *Silence and Beauty*, p. 207.

37 For examples, see <www.instagram.com/academykintsugi>, accessed February 2023. Academy Kintsugi was founded by Makoto Fujimura and *kintsugi* artisan Kunio Nakamura.

38 Fujimura, *Silence and Beauty*, pp. 206–210.

Perhaps brokenness – the weakness and suffering that we share as human beings, both Christian and non-Christian – presents a way forwards for creatives in a *fumi-e* culture. It is not through presenting Christianity triumphant and conquering, the familiar game of the culture wars. Rather, the way forwards lies in presenting Christ – and ourselves – in humble brokenness. That path can connect Christian creatives to those born into a post-Christian culture.[39] Deep alienation can be bridged only through brokenness.

Only the broken plant oases

True oases are planted only by the broken. Just as Christ connects with our broken, helpless condition by being broken, so, too, art made by broken people finds a special resonance with the broken, and it gives the proud and self-assured new eyes to see brokenness. In this sense, art can be a means of grace, sacramental (though not a sacrament), breaking us open to grace. The actress told me of a powerful scene in which her character bridged different religions by unveiling her character's own brokenness, hurt and bitter disappointment. Art can heal a fragmented society when it humbly meets people in the low places of their lives.

This is slow work. Given the deep divisions in our current imaginary landscape, it will likely take generations for such efforts to bear substantial fruit. Part of the ongoing task of Christian creatives is to question a deeply entrenched cultural logic – 'What is true happiness?', 'What is true freedom?' – while simultaneously extending grace through brokenness. Are freedom and happiness to be found in the self-centred will? As occult philosopher Aleister Crowley put it, '"Do what thou wilt" shall be the whole of the Law'?[40] Or must true freedom and happiness be guided by love and care for others, as Augustine insisted, '*Love* and then do what you will'?[41]

---

39 We must be careful not to conflate Christ's brokenness with ours. His brokenness alone saves.

40 Aleister Crowley, *Liber AL vel Legis (The Book of the Law)*, III, The Law of Thelema, <https://lib.oto-usa.org/libri/liber0220.html>, accessed February 2023.

41 Augustine, Homily 7 on the First Epistle of John, paragraph 8, in H. Browne (tr.), Philip Schaff (ed.), *Nicene and Post-Nicene Fathers*, First Series, Volume 7 (Buffalo, NY: Christian Literature Publishing Co., 1888). Also revised and edited for New Advent by Kevin Knight, <www.newadvent.org/fathers/170207.htm>, accessed February 2023. Emphasis added.

Creatively addressing the collective imagination by questioning prevailing cultural narratives is delicate work. It must be done gently, in love, without pride, on the grounds of our common brokenness. Otherwise, our works will find no resonance among those who are not already of our tribe, and we will be barred from the larger cultural conversation. Without love, our cultural efforts are simply clanging cymbals (1 Corinthians 13:1), distracting noise not worth listening to. This is a call to love through cultural creativity, breaking up hard soil by revealing our own brokenness. In this way, oases can be planted.

The work of creative Christian cultural engagement in post-Christian culture requires a multipronged re-storying of our culture. Everyone has a part to play; it is a collective task for the whole church, not only creatives. To be effective, this questioning and telling and retelling of a different story must happen in secondary school and university lectures, law firms and financial institutions, church sanctuaries, politics, therapists' sessions and music, film, television and video game developer studios.

Christian creatives may need to rethink what they are trying to create and why. Those who aren't professional creatives may need to rethink how to support and pray for Christians who are. Both should frame their efforts within the larger call to reconciliation.

Do you remember the relationship that blossomed between Dan Cathy, CEO of Chik-Fil-A, and gay rights activist Shane Windemeyer described in chapter 2? I long to see other instances of creative cultural engagement that are aesthetic analogues of *that* relationship, overcoming the *fumi-e* cultures on both left and right. I long for cultural works made by Christians to do what Dan Cathy did, and to do it *as part of the mainstream.*

We have enough Christian popular culture that preaches to the choir, works that seek to win an unwinnable game of cultural tug of war. What we need now are stories, songs, films, television programmes and games that create spaces for conversation and connection, in which we discover one another's common humanity. Broken and needy, yes, but also full of depth and wonder, created for glory and made whole, ultimately, only in Christ. And we need Christians ready to show up and support Christian artistic excellence that dwells in and resonates with the cultural mainstream. We need audiences that have learnt to value works which resonate with beauty and brokenness rather than works that pander to the subcultural tribe. We need Christians who understand and value oases.

It will not be easy to find funding for works that dwell in that uncomfortable liminal space between faith and mainstream culture, but it will be worth it. Christians have a tremendous opportunity to create culture that, like an oasis in a thirsty land, invites the parched travellers of the post-Christian landscape into a cultural space that challenges and refreshes, rather than a culture that manipulates and repels by its strong-arm tactics or alienates because it only speaks using the insular language and images of Christian subculture. Such works would be 'aggressively gracious as we seek to be a counterculture for the common good'.[42] We want to be distinctive, yet draw those who disagree with us closer, not chase them away. In this way, we widen and deepen the imaginative horizons of those who may have started out alienated from us. *That* would be cultural engagement which is generative, prophetic and possibly landscape-changing. We need oases that breathe, refresh and challenge, not bubbles, not *fumi-e* cultures that guard tribal purity.

Oases aren't made by drawing battle lines; they are created by pouring out one's own life for the good of others, following our Lord in sacrificial love. By being vulnerable and honest, artists become transparent in their creativity, drawing the alienated in. Thus, oases tear down defensive walls and extend bridges. This path is filled with joy, but also pain. As we will see in part 4, the artists who plant oases in this way sometimes do so at great personal cost. This sort of loving creativity can open wounds as the creatives present their imaginative vision from a position of weakness. True oases are watered with blood, sweat and tears (of joy *and* sorrow). They mimic Gethsemane even as they partake of the Spirit of the empty tomb.

Through this costly love, Christians can help to shape the broader cultural conversation in ways that invite both Christians and non-Christians to join in, engaging the imaginary landscape – the shared hopes, dreams, fears and anxieties – of post-Christian culture so that they can begin to see the gospel *as* good news, *as* true and beautiful.

42 Vermon Pierre, interviewed by Collin Hansen, 'Faithful presence needs prophets', The Gospel Coalition (17 November 2015), <www.thegospelcoalition.org/podcasts/tgc-podcast/faithful-presence-needs-prophets>, accessed February 2023.

Conclusion: the potential impact of joining the cultural conversation – of sunflowers, escapist stories, and a Super Bowl half-time show

Imagine a future in which Christian communities grasp the unique role of the imagination and creative cultural engagement, building networks to support those who can do this sort of creative work well. This would be a decisive step away from culture wars and a strategy of sheltered distance from the world.[43] Instead, we could begin speaking life and peace into our common culture. In place of seeing culture as a battleground to be won or a monster to hide from, we could see it as a shared garden that needs care. Christian artist Makoto Fujimura proposes just this in his book *Culture Care*.

He tells a story of Koyu Abe, a Buddhist monk who lived near the Fukushima nuclear power plant after radioactive waste spilled into the soil when the reactor was hit by an earthquake and tsunami in 2011. The monk passed out millions of sunflower seeds to nearby residents. Sunflowers absorb radioactive contamination, storing it in the flowerheads and seeds. The people who live in the area have been planting sunflowers year after year in hopes that one day the soil will be safe enough to plant gardens in again. Likewise, Fujimura argues, Christian creativity can serve to renew the cultural landscape, removing toxic conflict and life-killing patterns that have poisoned our common culture for too long.[44] Well-planted oases can heal a broken culture.

These creative efforts may seem ethereal and insubstantial, unlike legislation or court decisions. But do not underestimate the power of stories told, performed, sung and played. Our very identities are patterned according to the story we imagine ourselves to be in, our 'narrative identities', as philosopher Paul Ricoeur called them.[45] Circulating stories shape our shared imaginary landscape, the background against which laws are made or unmade, courts decide one way or the other. Stories form

---

43 See chapters 2–3.

44 Makoto Fujimura, *Culture Care: Reconnecting with beauty for our common life* (Downers Grove, IL: InterVarsity Press, Kindle edn, 2017), loc. 1555.

45 See Paul Ricoeur, 'Narrative identity', tr. Mark S. Muldoon, *Philosophy Today*, vol. 35, no. 1 (Spring 1991), pp. 73–81, <www.scribd.com/doc/24868946/Paul-Ricoeur-Narrative-Identity>, accessed February 2023.

the imaginary backbone of culture. A Native American proverb says, 'Those who tell the stories rule the world.'[46] Those who tell stories that challenge the ruling narrative can change the world.

Fiction writer Neil Gaiman went so far as to suggest that humans are essentially hosts for the viral transmission of stories.[47] Stories shape how we believe and live in the world, and they seduce us into telling and retelling them, passing on their narrative DNA:

> A lot of stories do appear to begin as intrinsic to religions and belief systems – a lot of the ones we have, have gods or goddesses in them; they teach us how the world exists; they teach us the rules of living in the world. But they also have to come in an attractive enough package that we take pleasure from them and we want to help them propagate.[48]

Gaiman tells of his cousin Helen, a Polish survivor of the Holocaust. As a teenager, she and a group of other Jewish girls living in the Warsaw ghetto during the Second World War risked execution by reading a banned book, Margaret Mitchell's *Gone with the Wind*. For them, the imaginative escape from the ghetto was worth the risk. The escapes we find in entertainment are anything but ephemeral and inconsequential. They are powerful, reshaping our lives. Gaiman concludes:

> We [writers] decry too easily what we do, as being kind of trivial – the creation of stories as being a trivial thing. But the magic of escapist fiction . . . is that it can actually offer you a genuine escape from a bad place and, in the process of escaping, it can furnish you with armor, with knowledge, with weapons, with tools you can take back into your life to help make it better . . . It's a real escape – and when you come back, you come back better-armed than when you left.

46 This quote has also been attributed to Plato. On the power of stories, see Shane Snow's fascinating TEDx talk, 'Why commit?', TEDx Talks, YouTube (11 August 2014), 16:57, <www.youtube.com/watch?v=Asm2Ad49cyI>, accessed February 2023.
47 Maria Popova, 'Neil Gaiman on how stories last', *The Marginalian* (16 June 2015), <www.brainpickings.org/2015/06/16/neil-gaiman-how-stories-last>, accessed February 2023.
48 Popova, 'Neil Gaiman on how stories last'.

> Helen's story is a true story, and this is what we learn from it – that stories are worth risking your life for; they're worth dying for. Written stories and oral stories both offer escape – escape from somewhere, escape to somewhere.[49]

The content of the stories we encounter defines the kind of armour, weapons, tools and knowledge their audiences acquire. Shared culture is, in a sense, a living thing, a creature brought to life by the stories that have circulated within it, stories we *live* in. If *Gone with the Wind* is worth risking death for, for a fictional escape, what are we willing to risk to create stories that offer an escape *to* deepest reality? Want to see our culture change? Contribute compelling stories, performances, songs, images and games that themselves enter into the broader cultural conversation. Bring a cultural story to life and let it roam.

Can Christian storytellers, poets, artists, filmmakers and game developers make much difference when so much of our culture's storytelling is dominated by those with a very different vision of what the world should be? There have been times when recognizably Christian stories have shone in the wider culture, but today most Christian stories are told to other Christians. This can change if we, as a community, grasp the importance of the imagination and its benefits to post-Christian culture. We are not there yet.

The filmmaker I interviewed lamented that wealthy Christians do not see creative cultural engagement as something worth supporting unless it makes money. Unlike the LGBTQI+ community, their vision doesn't extend beyond a financial return. But Christian commitment in this area could result in the nurturing of generations of storytellers who could craft stories for *everyone*, and that could shift the cultural conversation. By itself, an isolated story rarely carries much cultural weight – like a lonely cloud. Given time and God's blessing, though, such stories could form 'weather systems' – each story contributing to an overall atmosphere that gradually gathers intensity, like darkening clouds bringing rain on the parched imaginary landscape, breaking up the dry desert soil so it can drink it in. They become another voice in the conversation, another motif

[49] Popova, 'Neil Gaiman on how stories last'.

in the cultural symphony. Now dissonant, now in harmony, but always voiced in love.

Even a single oasis can have a deep cultural resonance, given the right artist and the right circumstances. Consider U2's Super Bowl XXXVI performance in February 2002.[50] In the wake of the attack on the World Trade Center in New York on September 11, 2001, people in the USA were hurting, angry and grieving. Then, on the most widely watched annual television programme in America, four Irish musicians (one of whom makes his Christian faith no secret) stepped onstage and gave voice to that grief, while simultaneously offering hope in the power of a love that transcended and defeated death. The half-time performance started with lead singer Bono in the middle of a sea of fans, singing as he made his way through the crowd to a heart-shaped stage. He started in a place that erased the distance between performer and audience. He was one of them. It was a quiet rebuke to the way our culture exalts celebrities as gods, and simultaneously echoed the incarnation, how God became one of us.[51]

U2 opened with 'Beautiful day' – a song of energy and exuberance, even as it addresses how life can seem futile and grey. At the chorus, the stage was flooded with light from a huge triangle above the heart-shaped stage, visually suggesting a Purple Heart medal, a reference to the way America had been wounded. The song's lyrics affirm that there is indeed a wonder and beauty in everyday life that lies just under the surface, so be wary of letting yourself become bitter and hardened – you will end up missing the beauty. There is always hope.

The band then transitioned into 'MLK', a funeral song written for the slain civil rights leader, wishing him a gentle rest. And while the band was singing, a screen descended on which was projected the names of those slain on September 11, scrolling upwards, heavenwards. U2, on public television, were pronouncing peace on our dead, laying them to rest.

---

50 If you haven't seen it, it's worth a watch, at 'U2's POWERFUL tribute to 9/11 victims', FreshVideos, YouTube, <www.youtube.com/watch?v=iBzdittT3c4>, accessed February 2023.

51 When one reads Bono's interviews, it becomes clear that he has no illusions about his 'divinity'. He knows himself to be a sinner in need of grace, just like everyone else. See his interview with Michka Assayas where he affirmed that karma (we get what we deserve) is upended and defeated by the grace released by Christ's death. From *Bono on Bono: Conversations with Michka Assayas* (New York: Riverhead, 2005). An excerpt can be found on Greg Clarke's blog post, 'Grace, karma and Bono', Center for Public Christianity (18 March 2008), <www.publicchristianity.org/grace-karma-and-bono>, accessed February 2023.

I remember watching and feeling chills. Fans wept. With the seemingly endless list of names still scrolling, they began playing 'Where the streets have no name', a song about longing for a place where there is no hatred dividing people, no warring gang territories, as there were in Dublin during the 1970s and 1980s.[52] Without hitting the audience over the head with the message, the song affirmed a hope of life beyond death, a world made right, a new creation.

At the end of the performance, Bono opened his leather jacket to reveal an American flag sewn into the lining. The message was crystal clear: I might have been born in Ireland, but I am one of you. The whole performance communicated not simply solidarity but empathy and love as well. It was a moving reminder of what God's love accomplished in Christ, setting us on a trajectory that ends in peace and healing, even amid brokenness, pain and trauma.

Rolling Stone called it not only the best Super Bowl performance ever but also:

> one of the truly great live-TV rock & roll moments of all time . . . Only U2 could have made this so grandiose, yet so emotionally direct. Grown men wept buckets. Every daft ambition U2 ever had, every lofty claim they ever made, they earned tonight.[53]

Did everyone catch the Christian resonances of the performance? Probably not. But it's no secret that the lead singer of U2 is a Christian, and that the band's tireless campaigning on behalf of Africa's poor and other causes comes from a Christian perspective.[54] That night, they

52 The members of U2 come from Dublin where street names demarcated rival gang territories during the Troubles in Ireland. A place where the streets have no name is a reference to a place of peace and harmony, where a person can walk free of fear.

53 *Rolling Stone*, 'Every Super Bowl halftime show, ranked from worst to best to worst', RollingStone.com (14 February 2022), <www.rollingstone.com/culture/culture-lists/super-bowl-halftime-shows-ranked-from-worst-to-best-14201/beyonce-2013-3-228225>, accessed February 2023.

54 Though not all the band's members have been as willing to talk about faith matters as Bono, their music and charity work are permeated with biblical quotes, themes and implications. Even secular journalists notice. Bassist Adam Clayton, however, has publicly stated that he is not a Christian. See Richard Milner, 'The truth about the Christian background of U2', *Grunge* (26 April 2022), <www.grunge.com/844162/the-truth-about-the-christian-background-of-u2>, accessed February 2023. Concerning the slightly veiled biblical content of the band's lyrics, see Joshua Rothman, 'The church of U2', *New Yorker* (16 September 2014), <www.newyorker.com/culture/cultural-comment/church-u2>, accessed February 2023.

brought a country together, to a place of healing, and told its people that love conquered death, that it was safe to lay their dead to rest and they could place hope in a future in which they are not alone. That night, U2 planted an oasis.

Imagine what could happen if a sizeable number of Christians committed themselves and their churches to planting not simply an oasis here or there, but to building networks of them, a sustaining architecture of imaginative works not in opposition to mainstream culture but in a deep, compassionate conversation with it. *That* would be cultural engagement indeed. It could change the course of our cultural conversation, the shape of the imaginary landscape.

In some ways, creatives serve as the vanguard for the aesthetic witness of the church. But they are not the only ones with a calling to the imaginative life. As we are all made in the image of the imaginatively expressive and receptive triune God, the Creator, so we are all called to imagination and creation. The burden of this book, its purpose, is to encourage Christian communities to grow and nurture the imaginative life. From such communities come oases of the imagination large and small that can change the texture and direction of a whole culture.

Part 2

FRAMING A MYSTERY: WHAT IS THE IMAGINATION?

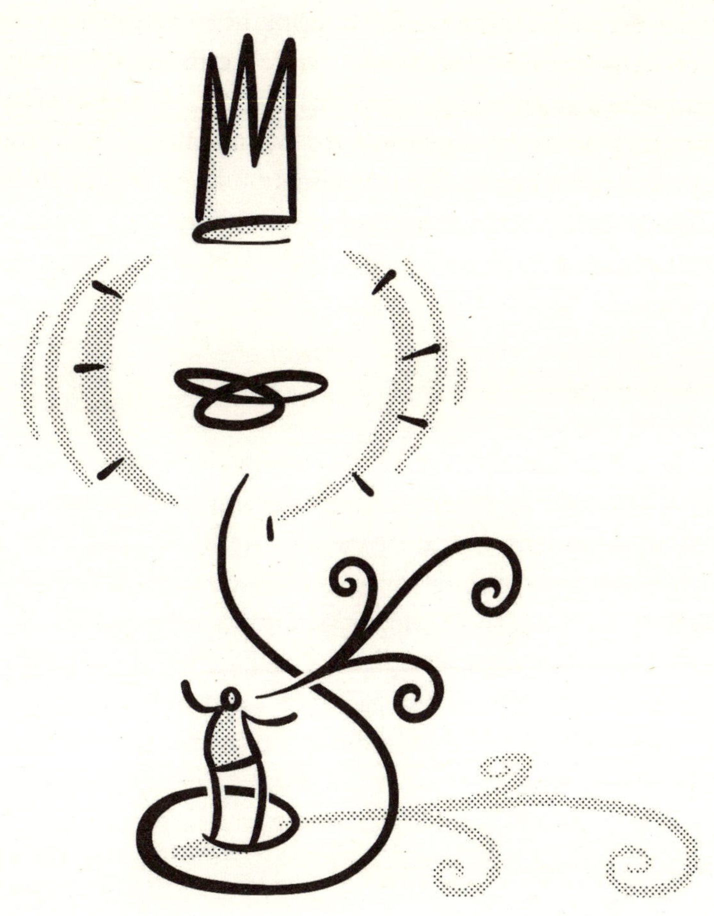

Part 1 laid out the case for creative cultural engagement. Engaging culture means (at least!) addressing imaginations, the 'imaginary landscape' that lies behind culture, the collective hopes and anxieties of a people. Engaging that landscape takes imagination.

A family picture

What is the imagination? Let me sketch you a scene that may help.

Several years ago, a few days before Christmas, my wife and I visited an old friend and his family. They live comfortably ensconced in an artsy town on a mountain. During our brief stay, their youngest – then a wavy-haired boy of seven – announced with delight that he could make paper dolls. I suppose he had learnt the skill during art lessons at school. He was eager to show that he could do it again and again. Not petite 'dress-me-up' paper dolls. No, these things towered, using whole large sheets of paper rolled into a cone so they would stand up. He started experimenting with the form, trying out variations, lamenting that the method didn't seem to work for male figures – they wear trousers, not dresses. I suggested samurai – they wear kimonos, not trousers.

His older sister – a wide-eyed precocious 11-year-old – entertained us one night by reading out loud chapter after chapter of her as yet unfinished fantasy novelette. The writing was precise, the imagery vivid, the dialogue clever but believable. She had then (and still does) all the makings of a good fiction writer. It didn't surprise me, as her father and mother are terrifically wise and intelligent people.

My wife and I spent the bulk of our visit just talking with our friend, the pastor. Although he doesn't draw or make music (though he's also a radio DJ), he paints with words. He sketches stories with sardonic wit, but always with a deeper point. Our conversations were peppered with extended metaphors drawn from sport, old songs, films, even jokes. This is a man who thinks in and through metaphors, searching for useful parallels that can open up new insights and applications. He is also always on the lookout for great music to share, constantly saying things like, 'Have you heard this new track from Dylan?' or 'You've got to hear this cut from the Shaggs tribute album.' He loves music and the places it can take him (and us) to.

His wife, busy making dangerously delicious muffins in the kitchen, chimed in from time to time, either to underline a point her husband had made or else to introduce a new angle that threw things into an altogether different light. Later, she excused herself to spend hours on the phone with her stepmother. It was the birthday of her recently deceased father, and her stepmother's first Christmas without him. She wanted to spend time grieving with and comforting her.

This is a family that walks the path of the imagination. There is joy, life, humour, wisdom and creativity everywhere. It is not a perfect family, but there is a colourfulness, a playfulness, a devil-may-care attitude mixed with compassion that I find profoundly attractive. It seems to me that their imagination-soaked lifestyle makes sense, given their faith in the Creator. Their way of life runs contrary to the stereotype of the Christian faith as a colourless, enslaving, antique religion inhabited by mindless sheeple. They were living Christianity as it should be lived.

Of course, there are different types of families and different ways of pursuing imagination, individually and collectively. Consider a single person who invites friends over for a film night where they watch, but also talk over what they watch. Consider a retired couple who finally have time to join a community choir and want to simply because they enjoy singing and getting to know their neighbours. Or parents who support their university-age daughter who wants to pursue a career in graphic design rather than take the 'safer' path of medicine or law. I know a retired man who uses his free time to serve the kids at his estate by creating an after-school homework club. A retired artist could as easily start an after-school art club that works on individual projects, but also a collective community project such as painting a mural on some blank wall (with permission, of course).

All these examples converge on one point: this faith of ours *should* foster actively creative people who embrace the way of imagination. Such people create a world that is welcoming and refreshing to body and soul.

Balking at DJ Jesus: Christian hesitations about the imagination

Contrary to the cosy pictures I've just described, many Christians have deep misgivings about the imagination. For some Christians, imagination and theological orthodoxy are very nearly antithetical terms. Imagination is seen as merely making up things that aren't real. Embracing the imagination for them means losing one's anchor in sound doctrine and godly living.

Where does this distrust and fear come from? Theologian Trevor Hart mentions four reasons the imagination has a bad reputation among many Christians.

1 Some English Bible translations use the word 'imagination' negatively, a term associated with sin, idolatry and rebellion in passages like Genesis 6:5 ('the imaginations of their hearts') and Romans 1:21 (the Gentiles became 'vain in their imaginations').
2 For English speakers, 'imagination' is associated with fantasy and illusion, whereas Christians want to be a people grounded in reality, a truthful people.
3 Christians fear that artistic creativity somehow undermines God's authority, challenging God by making competing creations.
4 Liberal theologians have claimed that God is beyond human knowing. All supposed revelation about him is the human imagination grasping after the divine.[1]

All these reasons, Hart argues, unfairly denigrate the imagination, by linking it not with creation but with fallenness.[2]

Let me add to Hart's list. Partly, Christian suspicion of the imagination stems from the lives and works of artists themselves. During the late eighteenth century into the nineteenth century, an artist-led intellectual movement known as Romanticism took root in Europe and North America. The Romantics believed the West faced a spiritual crisis that could be answered neither by the dry intellectual speculations of the Enlightenment philosophers, nor the outworn doctrines and moral conventions of the Christian church. What was left to feed empty souls? Art and the imagination. These alone could provide a doorway into the depths

[1] See Trevor Hart, 'A suspicion observed: Christian responses to the imagination', lecture delivered for the Billy Graham Center and Marion E. Wade Center Evangelism Roundtable V, 'Imagination and the gospel: Harnessing the imagination to engage contemporary culture and communicate the life-changing gospel', Wheaton College, Wheaton, IL (23–26 April 2008), pp. 6–11.

[2] In chapter 5 we will explore the depth of the connection between the imagination and our creation in God's image.

of the human heart. The imagination expressed through art would truly set us free.

The problem was, this new freedom often led to scandalous and self-destructive behaviour. The bohemian lifestyle of artists pushed boundaries past the breaking point, sometimes breaking the artists themselves. Church people mostly looked on aghast. Rather than reaching out to artists who were hurting and spiralling downwards, Christians distanced themselves from such notorious sinners. That chasm of mutual suspicion between artists and the church persists to this day.

During this same time, unbelieving intellectuals made ever more vigorous attacks on the integrity and veracity of the biblical faith. The Bible was simply a fairy story, an obsolete ancient legend. Adults have no need for childish tales of raised saviours and parted seas. Christian apologists felt obliged to respond. In so doing, they inadvertently adopted the rules laid down by their critics. They were so desperate to show that the Bible *was* grounded in fact, a book for grown-ups, that they ignored and suppressed the imaginative richness of the Bible and biblical faith. Imagination was, at best, overlooked as an irrelevance or, at worst, cast in the role of an enemy that undermined the Bible's truth claims.

Evangelical Christians have only relatively recently begun to question this automatic suspicion of the imagination. The works of J. R. R. Tolkien, C. S. Lewis and others have done much to allay Christian fears, but that chasm of distrust remains. Even today, artists can feel stifled by strict doctrines and conventional morality. They tend to innovate and experiment in their work, their thinking and their lives. They want to break free from rules that would restrain them, sometimes with dire consequences. For this reason, respectable Christians often draw away from such creative types. Anti-Christian apologists still denounce the Bible as legend and myth, and Christian apologists are still anxious to respond in ways that emphasize scientific and historical facts, ignoring or downplaying the Bible's imaginative richness.

Christian creatives see things differently. They view knowing and creating as intimately linked – creativity as a way to know God and his creation more deeply.[3] That makes less creative and rationalistic Christians

[3] Makoto Fujimura, *Art and Faith: A theology of making* (New Haven, CT, and London: Yale University Press, 2020), pp. 12–14.

suspicious – perhaps heresies are being smuggled in. These cultural currents, centuries old, have shaped Christian thinking, and alienation and suspicion between the Christian church and the imaginatively gifted have become entrenched.

Let us return to my example from chapter 1: the Christian DJ who received no support from people in his church. They thought that 'playing music for druggies' in a club was no place for a Christian. His question to me was, 'Should I be looking for some other line of work?' 'No, no, no,' I responded. 'You're *exactly* where you should be. That's where Christians *should* be. That's where Jesus would be.'

I believe this to be true. If Jesus were walking the earth bodily today, he would be hanging out with sinners (Matthew 11:16–19; Mark 2:13–17; Luke 19:1–10).[4] Today, that means being in the clubs, perhaps even at the turntables. After all, it was Jesus who provided wine for the wedding party. Why wouldn't he be the one to provide the 'sick beats', laying down banger after banger? As the Lord of creation, of *course* his set would be fire![5] Some might find such language shocking, but why? Because we *still* feel this tension, this mistrust of the imagination and artistic creativity.

It is understandable that Christians are sometimes hesitant and mistrustful of the imagination. But it is an unhealthy, unnecessary and, ultimately, unbiblical mistrust. Imagination is not the enemy. As we shall see, imagination and creativity are part of the fabric of the Christian faith itself.

---

[4] As Kevin DeYoung asserts, this does not mean that Jesus joined in sinning (see his blog post 'Jesus, friend of sinners: But how?', The Gospel Coalition (4 March 2014), <https://blogs.thegospelcoalition.org/kevindeyoung/2014/03/04/jesus-friend-of-sinners-but-how>, accessed February 2023. But it does mean that he made himself available to those whom religious people would find scandalous, and he did so as a reflection of God's wide mercy, even available to those we deem least likely to find God. And it meant that Jesus made himself accessible to those who weren't necessarily open to repentance (contra DeYoung). That is a reality that missionaries still face. In this sense, our DJ is a cultural missionary. Being in a club as a DJ to sinners is itself no sin, and may give access to those who would otherwise never consider entering a church. For a different and, I believe, more biblical understanding of Jesus as a friend to sinners, see Jonathan Parnell, 'Three tips on being a friend to sinners', Desiring God (22 March 2014) <www.desiringgod.org/articles/three-tips-on-being-a-friend-of-sinners>, accessed February 2023.

[5] Some Christians give art slight consideration because they believe that Jesus was not a performing artist. He wasn't a musician but he *was* a performing artist. He was a master storyteller.

To understand the imagination, we'll need *both* books

Part 2 of this book explores the imagination directly. The imagination is a mysterious, elusive beast, the Bigfoot of cultural theory: lots of blurry photos, not a lot of detailed definitions.

Part of the hesitation Christians have concerning the imagination can be traced back to a poor understanding of what it is and what it's good for. It remains a vague abstraction; a will-o'-the wisp that we fear will lead us into quicksand. As long as doubt remains about what the imagination is and what it does, we will be reluctant to embrace and utilize it fully and fearlessly. That reluctance then undermines a vivid, winsome, and absorbing cultural witness. Without an understanding of the imagination, we can't go on to plant vibrant and sustainable oases.

How to begin? Christians whose tradition stems from the Reformation look to the two great books: Scripture and nature.[6] In chapter 5, we will listen to the Bible, allowing it to lay out the fundamentals of human imagination according to the biblical pattern of creation–fall–redemption/ new creation. That is, the imagination was created by and filled with the glory of God, was twisted by sin, yearns for redemption and will be renewed in glory.

God also teaches us things not taught in the Bible through his second book, nature. Chapter 6 will explore the imagination using philosophy, literary theory and cognitive science. We shall find that the two books resonate in harmony.[7] Our goal is to arrive at a genuinely Christian understanding of the imagination.

---

[6] Article 2 of the Belgic Confession (or Confession of Faith), 'The means by which we know God'. If all truth is God's truth, then both books should be kept in mind when discussing the truth of the imagination. See Paul Arveson, 'Calvin's role in the history of science', a paper delivered on Calvin's 500th birthday, National Presbyterian Church, Washington, DC (May 2009), <www.arveson.com/chr//resources/articles/Calvins_role.pdf>, accessed February 2023.

[7] This understanding of the complementarity between natural science and biblical theology stems back to the influence of John Calvin. See E. L. Hebden Taylor, 'The Reformation and the development of modern science', *Churchman*, vol. 82, no. 2 (1968), pp. 87–103, <www.alloflieredeemed.co.uk/reformation%20of%20modern%20science.pdf>, accessed February 2023. See also Arveson, 'Calvin's role in the history of science', who shows that Calvin's understanding of how sin warps our thinking helps to clarify apparent conflicts between nature and Scripture. In reality the two are not at war, but there is often conflict between theology (Scripture interpreted by sinful and fallible humans) and science (nature interpreted by sinful and fallible humans).

That will prepare the way for narrowing our focus in part 3 on to what makes a Christian imagination distinctive.

A disclaimer for readers with short attention spans: the next two chapters lay out a Christian theory of imagination. It will be a deep and technical dive, the nuances of which might test your patience. If you want to understand the argument of the whole book, excellent! Do, though, feel free to cut to the chase by skipping part 2 entirely. You can always come back to it later.

5

A biblical theology of the imagination

Introduction: the freedom to make it new!

The very idea of the imagination makes some Christians uneasy because imagination innovates. Poet Ezra Pound commanded the poet and the artist to 'Make it new!'[1] That makes Christians nervous. We belong to an ancient tradition. We read the ancient Scriptures. We hear God say:

> Stand by the roads, and look,
>   and ask for the ancient paths,
> where the good way is; and walk in it,
>   and find rest for your souls.
> (Jeremiah 6:16)

Christians cling to the '*Old* rugged cross', which is the centre of our '*Old* time religion'. Christians revere the old and traditional.

You can understand why. In recent memory, new has not always meant better. Newness brings stresses, a more permissive, vulgar culture and more dismissive attitudes towards God and his gospel. Does that mean the imagination, with its pull towards innovation, undermines trust in the old and true? Not at all. Are there ways of expressing an ancient religion in new ways without compromising it? Absolutely. The imagination frees us to savour Christian insight, to mine deeply and richly, yet also discover new blessings, like polishing a gemstone to reveal new facets that refract and reflect the light in unexpected ways.

In fact, the very essence of the Christian faith beckons us towards the path of imaginative innovation. God repeatedly asks his people to 'sing a

[1] Ezra Pound, *Make It New: Essays by Ezra Pound* (London: Faber and Faber, 1934).

new song' (Psalms 33:3; 96:1; 98:1; 149:1), declaring to them, 'Behold, I am doing something new!' (Isaiah 43:19). In Christ, God brings to fruition something utterly new: the 'new creation' (2 Corinthians 5:17). In our daily lives, this means putting to death the 'old self' so that we might live a *new* life towards God in Christ by the power of the Spirit (Romans 6:6ff.; Galatians 2:20). In other words, God himself is in the business of innovation, taking the old and tired and twisted, breathing new life into it and transforming it into something utterly new, vibrant and alive. That takes imagination. God is the Master Imaginator, the Master Artist.

Our Creator and Saviour calls us to follow him, to imitate his ways. The Christian faith is a call to creativity. We tend to focus on Christianity as a set of dos and don'ts, but that is to completely miss what it is really about: Christ making all things new (Revelation 21:5), calling us to follow in his train. Christianity sets us free to explore, to discover, to innovate.

Of course, we need to respect tradition and God's law. There should be guidance and limits to the imagination. After all, the imagination can be turned to dark ends. The gulags and concentration camps of this world required imagination to plan and build them. Art can seduce people into foolishness and self-destruction. Being imaginative on its own doesn't guarantee goodness – that's the lie promulgated by the Romantics.

But for us, working and playing within the limits set by God's good and wise counsel, there are tremendous open fields, a whole countryside that we are free to explore. The imagination is like a kite. Untethered, it is blown aimlessly to its own destruction, tangled in telephone wires or impaled on a tree. But when it is connected to the ground, it can truly fly without wrecking itself. It is the *limits*, the *tether*, that give the kite the freedom to fly the way it was designed to. It is the same with God's law and our imaginations: that which limits us actually sets us free.[2]

Of Thwackums and dreamers: is the Bible anti-imagination?

Does a biblical perspective truly set the imagination free? A venerable tradition in the West holds that religious doctrine stifles the imagination. In Henry Fielding's famous novel, *The History of Tom Jones, a Foundling*

2 Thanks to my friend Chris Simmons for this brilliant analogy.

(1749), and the marvellous 1963 film adaptation, two characters especially stick out in my mind. The title character, Tom, illegitimate, with no social standing, is a free spirit – bawdy, all energetic imagination, cunning, generous of heart and guided by a keen inner sense of justice (played with a grin and a wink by the inimitable Albert Finney). One of the main villains is The Reverend Mr Roger Thwackum, who was Tom's tutor and is a clergyman. He is socially respectable, but a dour, self-important, judgmental and secretly greedy religious bigot (played with over-the-top odiousness and a permanent scowl by the redoubtable Peter Bull). By the end of the film, the viewer cannot help but conclude that religious belief acts as blinkers that narrow our vision and kill the imagination (and compassion). The biblically orthodox are locked in a long and bitter struggle with the free spirits of the world, and the free spirits must overcome. Go, Tom, go!

This motif is repeated again and again in arts and entertainment. The minister is the killjoy, the heresy hunter who is secretly a censorious hypocrite. Influential stand-up comic George Carlin was notorious for his contempt of the religious. *Doctor Who* and other sci-fi franchises repeatedly feature storylines of a privileged priest class that oppress and – through their ignorance – doom an entire civilization. Only the intervention of free-thinking atheist dissidents, such as the good Doctor, prevent disaster.[3] In a significant portion of the popular mind, religious orthodoxy and imagination (or reason, progress, freedom and so on) mix like oil and water. But is it true? Does the Bible disparage or hinder imagination or does it show us the true nature of the imagination?

If you look up 'imagination' (and related terms) in the Bible, you might get the impression that the Bible holds imagination in low regard. Imagination is linked to laziness and foolishness in Proverbs: 'He who works his land will have abundant food, but he who chases fantasies lacks judgment' (12:11) or 'A discerning man keeps wisdom in view, but a fool's eyes

[3] Tom Baker, the actor who played the classic fourth Doctor in *Doctor Who*, has been quite open about his own contempt for Christianity and how his Catholic upbringing scarred him psychologically. See Michael Idato, 'The true Doctor Who: Tom Baker', *Sydney Morning Herald* (15 November 2013), <www.smh.com.au/entertainment/tv-and-radio/the-true-doctor-who-tom-baker-20131115-2xks9.html>, accessed February 2023. Later seasons of *Doctor Who* took a more ambiguous view. See Stephen K., 'Is *Doctor Who* anti-religious?', *ArcadiaPod* (29 September 2011), <https://arcadiapod.com/2011/09/29/is-doctor-who-anti-religious>, accessed February 2023.

wander to the ends of the earth' (17:24), for example. The Teacher strikes a similar tone in Ecclesiastes: 'Whoever watches the wind will not plant; whoever looks at the clouds will not reap' (Ecclesiastes 11:4). The gist is clear: the imagination makes you a dreamy slacker. Be realistic, get busy and get something done. Today we might say, 'Sure, dear, your scribbles and drawings are fine. Just don't neglect getting your qualifications!' Imagination-driven people are of no practical use, little better than fools. They dream when they should plant and chase fantasies when they should harvest.

For other biblical writers, the imagination holds an even greater danger: seduction away from God. The second commandment forbids God's people from imagining a visual representation of him (Exodus 20:4).[4] You cannot imagine God any way you prefer and expect to please him; he must reveal himself to us. Imagination in this realm indicates a spiritual arrogance that leads to following *false* gods and alienating ourselves from the true God, who loves us. Imagination is thereby linked to self-destructive spiritual pride:

> All day long I have held out my hands
> to an obstinate people,
> who walk in ways not good,
> pursuing their own imaginations –
> a people who provoke me to my very face.
> (Isaiah 65:2–3)

Paul sees this type of imaginative stubbornness as part of the progressive numbing of the sin-warped heart: 'Although they claimed to be wise, they became fools and exchanged the glory of the immortal God for images' (Romans 1:22–23). Imagination, rather than freeing us can lead to idolatry, spiritual slavery and death.

Indulging the imagination can indeed lead to laziness or idolatry. Nevertheless, all the biblical writers *employ* imagination lavishly. The

[4] Some Christians take this prohibition to mean that *all* images are somehow inherently dangerous, that they distract from the word-based biblical faith. It's an unfortunate overreaction I call 'imagophobia'. See my book, *Popologetics: Popular culture in Christian perspective* (Phillipsburg, NJ: P&R, 2012), chapter 8.

narratives and poetry are full of literary inventiveness and creativity. Old Testament historians give us riveting accounts of events that stretch the imagination: a parting sea, a sun standing still, torches and smoking firepots. The prophets shared visions that still capture our imagination, with images of women in baskets, fiery horses and chariots, armies of locusts, stones with eyes, wheels within wheels, grotesque beasts and thrones surrounded by crystalline glory.

Being a biblical prophet takes imagination, not just eyes and a pen. The biblical poets used images, sounds and emotional textures to teach practical wisdom: joyful hearts that have a continual feast, an argument-prone wife like a constant dripping on a rainy day, beautiful hair like a flock of goats descending a hill, news from afar like cool rain, grasshoppers that drag themselves along, a pitcher shattered to pieces at a well. Jesus spun parables using the most ordinary objects and people – sowers and seeds, vineyards, housebuilders, wineskins, lost lambs, a father reunited with his son – to illuminate immense spiritual truths. The book of Acts and the letters to the early church abound with metaphors and other imaginative literary devices: creepy-crawly animals on a sheet, the different parts together forming one body, grafted branches, clanging cymbals, thorns in the flesh, fruits of the Spirit, the armour of God, tongues that set the world on fire, faith being refined like gold. Paul even draws on the pagan imagination, quoting pagan poets to get his point across to the Athenians in Acts 17 and elsewhere.[5] You certainly cannot read Revelation without knowing that its author had a particularly vivid imagination: dragons, flying scorpions, lions and lambs, healing leaves, a lake of fire and everlasting light.[6] The Bible is a book of imagination from beginning to end. Theologian Trevor Hart characterizes the Bible this way:

[5] He quotes Arastus in Acts 17:28. He also quotes the playwright Menander in 1 Corinthians 15:33 and Epimenides in Titus 1:12. And he draws liberally on pagan vocabulary and concepts in his letter to the Philippians, seeing Christians as Roman citizens in Philippians 3:20, listing Roman moral virtues that we should dwell on in 4:8 (see Moisés Silva, *Philippians*, Baker Exegetical Commentary on the New Testament (Grand Rapids, MI: Baker Academic, 2nd edn, 2005 [1992]), p. 197.

[6] I am not denying that John *received* a series of visions. As we shall explore below, imagination is vital for how we perceive and receive reality. It is clear to anyone who has studied the prophets in the Bible (including John) how expansive their literary imagination must have been.

> Scripture as a whole (while in fact it contains a wide variety of literary types) constitutes a single and singular trope – an appropriation by God of human realities to capture our imagination and so transfigure the world, granting us access to depths and dimensions of it which otherwise remain hidden and inaccessible to us.[7]

Furthermore, not only is the Bible imaginative but it also paints us a portrait of a God of immense creativity and imagination, presented in its first pages as *the* Creator. It is difficult to look closely at creation, with its hedgehogs, blue-ringed octopuses, paramecia, orchids, fly agaric mushrooms, strangler fig trees, lemurs, mountains, parrot fish, spiral galaxies and humans without discerning a vast imagination at work. How could such a Creator be anti-imagination or inspire a book that was anti-imagination?

Beyond being the Creator, God is the Redeemer, who initiated an epic drama of salvation in which he is both the author *and* main character, full of tragic falls, twists and comic delight (including a surprising and awesome eucatastrophe).[8] The Bible is steeped in imagination, because it comes, ultimately, from a master storyteller who weaves his tale with vividness and passion. The Bible gives no quarter to the Thwackums of this world who would quash the imagination in the name of religion.[9] The God of the Bible is not anti-imagination. As we shall see, imagination flows from the Spirit of God himself, and he maintains an ongoing relationship with our imaginations, sin-twisted though they may be.

When discussing the Bible's take on imagination, we should not expect the same breadth and level of detail that cognitive scientists, literary theorists, or philosophers bring to this subject. The Bible is not a science

---

7 See Hart, 'A suspicion observed', p. 15.

8 'Eucatastrophe' is Tolkien's term for a sudden reversal that results in unexpected joy, which we will explore further in chapter 13. See his essay 'On fairy-stories' in J. R. R. Tolkien, *Tree and Leaf* (London and New York: HarperCollins, 2001 [1964]), <https://archive.org/details/on-fairy-stories_202110>, accessed February 2023.

9 Clyde Kilby shares his perplexity at how a people of such an imaginative book as the Bible could have so little regard for the arts and imagination in his essay 'The aesthetic poverty of evangelicalism'. More than half a century later, we can still ask the same question. An edited version is reprinted in Leland Ryken (ed.), *The Christian Imagination: The practice of faith in literature and writing* (Colorado Springs, CO: Shaw Books, rev. exp. edn, 2002), pp. 277–278.

or philosophy textbook. It's a story, a moral and spiritual guidebook, a legal codex, a poetic reflection, a love letter and God thinking out loud, all rolled up into one. The Bible gives us a foundational vision of reality that we need to bring into dialogue with the testimony of creation (as revealed by cognitive scientists, literary scholars, philosophers and others). That is the task of chapter 6. For now, let us examine those foundations using the major categories of redemptive history: creation, fall, redemption/new creation.

Imagination through the lens of creation

The fact that God created the cosmos, us and all reality, shapes our understanding of the imagination in at least five ways.

Imagination and creativity are the overflow of a loving, dynamic relationship between members of the Trinity

It should surprise no-one that God's works in creation and redemption reveal a prodigious, dynamic imagination. Unless, of course, you picture God as a static, unitary, perfect being (an abstract first cause, a still pool of silent energy, a kindly grandfather, perhaps) who exists in stately detachment from the rest of the cosmos. But that's not the true God. The Christian God is a triune God.[10] The Trinity is anything but static and uninvolved. We believe and serve not the deist God but the triune, Christian God.

The early Greek church fathers described the Trinity as *perichoresis* (περιχώρησις), a mutual indwelling of the members of the Trinity as a community of three who are fully one.[11] The word itself strongly implies movement. It is derived from the Greek verb *chorein* (χώρειν), meaning 'to make room for', 'go to forwards' or 'contain', plus the prefix *peri-* (περί), which adds a note of mutuality and reciprocity.[12] Through a mistaken

[10] For centuries the early church fathers wrestled with what the Bible said of God: that there is one God called Yahweh, God is called 'Father', Christ is his Son incarnate and deeply identified with Yahweh, so much so that Christ is fully God (Mark 1:2–4, John 1:1–2, 8:19, 10:30), and the Holy Spirit is fully God as well (Acts 5:3–4). The full doctrine of the Trinity was established at the Council of Chalcedon (451). For an excellent short treatment of the doctrine of the Trinity, see Scott Swain, *The Trinity: An introduction*, Short Studies in Systematic Theology, ed. Graham A. Cole and Oren R. Martin (Wheaton, IL: Crossway, 2020).

[11] The term was first used to describe the relationship between the divine and human natures of Christ but was later applied to the Trinity.

[12] Dănuţ Mănăstireanu, 'Perichoresis and the early Christian doctrine of God', *Archæus*, vols XI–XII (2007–2008), p. 61, <www.academia.edu/4794642/Perichoresis_and_the_Early_Christian_Doctrine_of_God>, accessed February 2023.

etymology, several medieval theologians came to associate the Trinity with a divine dance (you can hear the similarity between *perichoresis* and the word 'choreography').[13]

Although the etymology was mistaken, the image of the dance resonates well with the hints we are given in Scripture about the relationship of delight, mutual indwelling and exchange between the persons of the Trinity.[14] The triune God is not static, but dynamic, like a conversation, an imaginative exchange between persons, a continual, creative giving and receiving between Father, Son and Holy Spirit. Think back to the rich and satisfying conversation with my pastor friend that I mentioned in the introduction to part 2. Now imagine a similar conversation between friends that is never less than entirely encouraging, challenging, loving, inspiring, trusting, intimate, fascinating, delightful, insightful, ever fresh, never boring . . . for all eternity.[15] That's but a dim picture of what the energetic, imaginative, creative, loving exchange between the members of the Trinity must be like.[16]

---

13 The mistaken etymology persists in contemporary theology as well. See, for example, Timothy Keller, 'The dance of God', in his book *The Reason for God: Belief in an age of skepticism* (New York: Dutton, 2008). But see Mănăstireanu, 'Perichoresis and the early Christian doctrine of God', pp. 62–63, and Larry Parkins, '182. The dance is not PERICHŌRĒSIS', *Internet Moments with God's Word* (2 December 2020), <https://moments.nbseminary.com/archives/182-the-dance-is-not-perichoresis>, accessed February 2023.

14 See, for example, Matthew 3:17; John 5:19–23; 8:29, 54; 13:32; 16:14–15; 1 Corinthians 2:10–11. Of late, systematic theologians have been debating the nature of the Trinity with some intensity. I do not intend to enter that debate here, except to say that historic Christian theology has always sought to understand God's threeness and oneness as equally ultimate. When I say that the Trinity is dynamic and has the nature of a conversation, I do not mean to undermine the perfect union of the persons of the Trinity. It is possible to honour passages that emphasize the perfect immutability of God, such as James 1:17, 'Every good gift and every perfect gift is from above, coming down from the Father of lights, with whom there is no variation or shadow due to change', *without* ignoring the relational aspects of the Trinity, as if God were somehow frozen and static. The Christian doctrine, as I understand it, embraces both the perfect plenitude and stillness of God's oneness *and* the relational dynamic (between persons as well as with us) of God's threeness. God is love, and love contains both ideas: unchanging steadfastness and dynamic responsiveness to the other.

15 God is never bored. We get bored because of our fallen existence within a single timeline in which time seems to coagulate and become a dull burden. God is neither fallen nor bound to linear time. He is sovereign over time, free from its burden. He is the 'Ancient of Days' (Daniel 7:9), faithful through generations (Deuteronomy 7:9; Psalms 100:5; 119:90), but never bored with time, with us or, especially, with himself. Each person in the godhead has an ever-renewing fierce love for the other two. From the overflow of that mutual passion and love, God passionately loves us with the kind of continual focus that we would find impossible to maintain.

16 The exchange between the persons of the Trinity is so much more than a conversation between friends. I am not advocating tri-theism (three Gods). It is an exchange so intense and interpenetrating that it can truly be said that they are *one* (*homoousios*, of one essence, as the Nicene Creed puts it) without obliterating the unique personality of each of the persons. The threeness is just as ultimate as the oneness.

Out of the overflow of that loving exchange, God created the world and, later, forged redemption for his people. In a sense, imagination and creativity are rooted in the very nature of the Trinity. Imagination, as we shall see, is all about creative reception and expression. In this way, human imagination dovetails with divine love: it is about the giving and receiving between persons. Both love and imagination may be twisted and distorted in a fallen world, but both are rooted in the nature of God.

Our creativity takes place against the backdrop of God's creativity, our imaginations derive meaning from his imagination

The most foundational truth about the creation is that the triune God created it. He *spoke* it into being – creation is a form of meaningful, personal communication, an intimate expression of his imagination. That is the ultimate context for our imaginations. We do not create against a blank slate of a random, purposeless universe. Rather, as Christian philosopher Herman Dooyeweerd put it, 'Creation *is* meaning.'[17] That is, because God made it, all creation's structures refer beyond themselves to a greater totality – namely, God. The meaning of creation lies precisely in that gesturing towards God's imagination, his speaking through creation that reveals his character and purposes (see Psalm 19; Isaiah 28:23–29; Romans 1:18–25).

The expressive, communicative nature of creation sets limits on our imagination *and* sets our imagination free (rather like a kite). Our imaginations are limited to remixing and reflecting what God has provided in creation. Strictly speaking, there is nothing new under the sun that God has not thought of (Ecclesiastes 1:9), no creativity (even rebellious creativity) that doesn't draw on God's prior creativity.[18] But those limits also provide a template – material, spiritual, narrative – out of which our own creativity emerges.

This is a touchstone of a Christian approach to the imagination: the God-given meanings woven into creation flow into and make possible the

---

17 Or, more precisely, '*Meaning* is the *being* of all that has been created', as he writes in his book, *A New Critique of Theoretical Thought*, Volume 1, tr. David H. Freeman and William S. Young (Jordan Station, Ontario: Paideia Press, 1984 [1953]), vol. 1, p. 4.

18 See Peter Leithart, 'Introduction: The devil has no stories', in his book *Heroes of the City of Man: A Christian guide to select ancient literature* (Moscow, ID: Canon Press, 1999).

meanings we create culturally. Even our stories draw on and reflect his story. In this way, human imagination and divine general revelation dovetail.

We have imaginations because we are created in the image of God, commanded by him to rule, subdue and 'recreate' the world wisely

Besides the meaningful backdrop of creation itself, why are humans imaginative and creative? Because we were made in the image of the Creator (Genesis 1:26–28). Note the connection between the image of God and God's command to 'fill and subdue' the earth.

> Then God said, 'Let us make man in our image, after our likeness. And let them have dominion over the fish of the sea and over the birds of the heavens and over the livestock and over all the earth and over every creeping thing that creeps on the earth.'
>
> So God created man in his own image,
> in the image of God he created him;
> male and female he created them.
>
> And God blessed them. And God said to them, 'Be fruitful and multiply and fill the earth and subdue it, and have dominion over the fish of the sea and over the birds of the heavens and over every living thing that moves on the earth.'

This passage employs a literary device that was common in Hebrew poetry called a 'chiasm', an 'x-shaped' mirrored and reversed symmetry to the wording. A simple example of a chiasm is:

> My name is Ted.
> I'm writing a book on the imagination.
> Imagination is my subject,
> and you can call me Ted.

A chiasm is a poetry sandwich: two slices of nearly identical poetry with a chewy, meaty filling between them. The purpose of a chiasm can vary.

It can highlight the meaty centre because it *is* positioned at the centre, so attention is drawn to it. Alternatively, it can indicate a connection between the centre and the periphery, the meat and bread, since it is all one poetic unit, a complete sandwich. Another way it can be used is to show progression by including slight differences between 'bread slice A' and 'bread slice B'. Once you've eaten through the sandwich, you end up in a slightly different place.

The chiasm in Genesis 1:26–28 serves all three purposes. It emphasizes the centre, the declaration that humans are the pinnacle of creation because no other creature has the privilege of bearing God's image. The chiasm also underlines the connection between our creation in God's image (the 'meat', v. 27) and the idea of dominion, ruling over the rest of creation as God's stewards (the 'slices of bread', vv. 26 and 28). It highlights the intimate connection between humans made in God's image and our call to imitate God's wise, life-giving lordship over creation.[19] Finally, the chiasm traces the subtle progression from 'bread slice A' (v. 26) to 'bread slice B' (v. 28). In both verses, God issues a command, but in v. 28 God adds his blessing.

For the first time in history, God addresses his new image-bearing creatures – the only creatures on earth who can intentionally answer him back – and what does he say? He blesses them and tells them to go and do what they were made in his image to do: fill and subdue creation. He commands them to use their imaginations to bring order and beauty out of his creation and adds his blessing as wind to their sails. He gives them the blessing/command that theologians call the 'Cultural Mandate': to go and create culture.

In the multivalent meaning of this chiasm, the author of Genesis makes his point poetically: human beings are uniquely made in God's image, and they image God (aided by his blessing) by using their imaginations to order the material universe just so, to fill it, develop its beauty and care for it, all for the glory of God. This poetic message is amplified when you place the chiasm within the larger context of Genesis chapters 1 and 2.

[19] Some Christians cringe at the thought of 'dominion' over creation, noting how our domination of the planet has brought disastrous results. The problem of dominion-as-domination can be avoided by remembering whose creation we are called to rule over. We rule/shepherd not as autonomous lords, but as stewards who have been entrusted with *God's* creation and are responsible for its flourishing as a whole, humans and non-humans alike.

Just as God filled the empty void and subdued it in Genesis chapter 1, bringing form and fullness to the formless and empty chaos-waters (תֹהוּ וָבֹהוּ, the *tōhū wā·bōhū* in Genesis 1:2),[20] so, too, he made us to subdue disorder, bring form to his creation and fill the empty spaces. Just as God used his imagination to bring something wonderful out of chaos, we also are to use our imaginations to bring something wonderful out of his creation. We are hard-wired, blessed and called to develop creation, not in the form of destructive exploitation but to draw out its hidden potential and beauty. Genesis 1:26–28's emphasis on forming, filling and subduing echoes God's own action throughout Genesis 1. Imaging God means imitating God's creativity, though in a creaturely mode and on a creaturely scale.

Genesis 1:26–28 also resonates with Genesis 2. Immediately after the blessing/command of 1:28, God rests, and the first creation account ends. A second, abbreviated creation account commences. We fast-forward to the point where there is empty land, a freeze-frame at a moment in creation before plants. There is an emptiness – God has not yet brought rain and 'there was no man to work the ground' (Genesis 2:5), as if the creation order is awaiting the arrival of Adam. He is needed to fill that empty space with growing things. God then brings a mist to prepare the land for plants (v. 6) and he gently, intimately forms man from the dirt, breathing into him his own Spirit (v. 7). God then fills his creation with plants and trees, rivers, gold and precious minerals (vv. 8–14), and he places Adam smack dab in the middle of it all to shape and care for it (vv. 8 and 15). This is our first picture of Adam in action – forming and filling what God had just created, imitating God's creativity. Genesis 2:15 gives us a concrete picture of Adam living out his nature and calling in conformity with the blessing/command given in Genesis 1:28. He starts by cultivating the garden, making a little world out of the whole world that God had entrusted to him.

20 The phrase תֹהוּ וָבֹהוּ (*tōhū wā·bōhū*) means formless and empty. Creation in Genesis 1 is framed in terms of giving shape to the formless and filling the empty chaos-waters of Genesis 1:2 (symbolized later in the Bible as a sea serpent hostile to God's creation and his people, a monster that God vanquishes to establish his rule (Psalm 89:9–10, for example). See Leland Ryken, James C. Wilhoit and Tremper Longman III (eds), entries 'Chaos', 'Creation' and 'Sea', in their *Dictionary of Biblical Imagery* (Downers Grover, IL: InterVarsity Press, 1998), and Bruce K. Waltke, 'The literary genre of Genesis, chapter one', *Crux*, vol. 27 (December 1991), pp. 2–10. For more on creation as God subduing the cosmic chaos, see Tremper Longman III and Daniel L. Reid, 'God wars against the forces of chaos' in *God Is a Warrior*, Studies in Old Testament Biblical Theology (Grand Rapids, MI: Zondervan, 1995).

The bottom line of Genesis 1:26–28: we humans image God precisely through expressing imagination by creating culture. We are hard-wired to be mini world-creators, following in the footsteps of God's creativity.[21] That involves, of course, the making and rearranging of stuff: wood into chairs or guitars, metal into ploughs or swords, flower petals into dyes and pigments for paintings and so on. But we creatively order not only stuff but also meanings, resonances and perspectives. In Genesis 2:19–20, Adam is told to give the animals names – in essence, to create categories of perception, avenues for understanding, a 'seeing-as', through which Adam and others can interpret animal life on earth.[22] The blessing/command of Genesis 1:28 applies not only to things but also to intangibles: imaginary art worlds, webs of narrative and metaphorical associations that colour our perception of the world around us. We create cultural works and performances – books, films, games, songs, paintings, poems – that reframe our experience of God's creation and cast it in a different light. We who bear the image of the Creator experience the world by recreating it through our imaginations.

Given how we were created, the relationship of image-bearers to reality *ought* to be fundamentally creative. Imagination is the nexus. In both perception and creation, imagination lies at the heart of what it means to be made in the image of the Creator.[23]

That said, each of us bears the image of God in a different way. God's image is refracted through a variety of individual imaginations, a dazzling array of colours and styles. Everyone has an imagination. Naturally there will be differences in cultural backgrounds, upbringing, training and calling that affect the shape, pace, pitch, flavour and intensity of each imagination – a near-infinite diversity. There are no cookie-cutter

[21] For more detail on culture as world-creation, see my book, *Popologetics*, pp. 57–58.

[22] As we shall see in the next chapter, metaphor, 'seeing-as', is the central operation of the imagination.

[23] Trevor Hart notes how more recent academic discussions of the imagination have moved away from viewing it as a discrete faculty and towards a more holistic approach in which the imagination is seen as fundamental to being human: 'Imagination is better thought of as *a way of thinking, responding and acting* across the whole spread of our experience, not some arcane "thing" with a carefully specified and limited remit . . . The imaginative is the psychical equivalent not of our appendix (which, when it becomes troublesome or painful, we can simply cut out and flush away without loss) but the blood supply which circulates things (both good and bad) around our entire body' ('A suspicion observed', pp. 4–5, italics in original).

imaginations, except where they are pressed or seduced into conformity (a very real danger in totalitarian or consumer-orientated societies).[24] That is a failure of what God intends our imaginations to be. When they are free, people's imaginations are expressed in amazing variety. Some orbit around words, others around colours and textures. Some focus on tones and harmonies, others on technological gadgetry. Some use maths as a lens on the world, others use lyric poetry or philosophical prose. Some visualize and craft using static space, such as architects; others use motion through space, as athletes or dancers do.[25] We all bear God's image uniquely. Our unique life experiences shape how we bear that imaginative God-image and what impact our imaginations will have on the world (some will have more impact than others). The human imagination mirrors God's, and that makes it powerful.

Human creativity, while a gift from God, is authentically human

The imagination – this power to re-envision reality and create according to that vision – is fundamentally human. This may sound blindingly obvious but consider the cultural context of Genesis. The Ancient Near East was full of myths about the origins of art and culture. Cultural creativity was considered as divine property – gifts from the gods who still held the title to the deed, as it were. Typically, the myths taught that a god was born and either became the patron of art and creativity or procured an artistic secret and passed it on to his or her worshippers. A Sumerian poem tells how the city Erech got its knowledge of the arts and music: its patron god Inanna stole them from the Lord of Wisdom, Enki, who dwelt in the sea.[26]

The early chapters of Genesis tell quite a different story. Yes, humans bear God's image, so are creators after his pattern. But the Bible also makes it clear that cultural creativity is something properly and authentically

24 The danger that the imagination will be overrun by commercial images and motifs is the driving concern of literary theorist Richard Kearney's magisterial *The Wake of the Imagination* (New York: Routledge, 1988).

25 My wife, educator Carolyn Turnau, noted that this insight lies at the foundation of the theory of multiple intelligences (that people are smart in different ways). See Thomas Armstrong, *Multiple Intelligences in the Classroom* (Alexandria, VA: ASCD, 4th edn, 2018).

26 See Edmund P. Clowney, 'Living art: Christian experience and the arts' in D. A. Carson and John D. Woodbridge (eds), *God and Culture* (Grand Rapids, MI: Eerdmans, 1993), <https://biblicalworldview21.org/living-art-christian-experience-and-the-arts>, accessed February 2023.

human. In Genesis 2:8–15, God creates a magnificent garden and then puts the man in it to care for and develop it. We are given no indication as to whether God gave him an extra gift or instructions or if he let Adam work it out on his own. Then, a few verses later (vv. 19–20), God brings all the animals to Adam, 'to see what he would call them'. This is a deeply significant act. In Ancient Near Eastern cultures, naming was more than simply assigning labels; it was an exercise of authority over the thing or person named, expressing and informing its meaning. Naming interprets and defines.[27] In Genesis 2, though, a question comes to mind: hasn't God already made the animals meaningful? Of course he has, but he stands back and allows Adam to exercise this very human form of cultural creativity, this imaginative/interpretive seeing-as, without micromanaging Adam. God made the animals, but naming them, working out what they mean, that was Adam's job, using his own imagination and wisdom. God doesn't interfere.[28] The passage culminates, beautifully, with Adam naming his wife in the first love poem ever composed (Genesis 2:23).

By the time we get to the end of Genesis 2, we have the origin stories of several types of cultural creativity: gardening/agriculture, biological taxonomy and poetry. They are not presented as discrete gifts from God but, rather, as the organic unfolding of human existence in God's world. One would think that the fall would derail human creativity and imagination but, as we shall see later in this chapter, it does not. The point is clear: arts and culture are human, a reflection of God's creativity, but properly and authentically human. God rejoices in the free development of his creation by his creatures.

Saying imagination is 'authentically human' is not to say that our imaginations are absolutely independent of God's. Rather, they are intimately linked to and dependent on God's creation and Spirit.[29] There is nothing we can imagine that God has not already thought of, no

27 For example, God renames Jacob 'Israel' in Genesis 32:27–28, changing his identity from 'deceiver' to 'he struggles (and prevails) with God'. It is significant that God does not reveal his own name to Jacob (Genesis 32:29). We also see this pattern of authority when Babylonian king Nebuchadnezzar changes the names of Daniel and his friends (Daniel 1:7) and when Jesus changes Simon's name to 'Peter', 'the rock' (Matthew 16:18).

28 That is not to say God was not sovereign over Adam at every moment. But in the story, God doesn't exercise that sovereignty in a way that restricts Adam's creativity. He *waits* to see what Adam will do. Adam is no puppet on a string. God allows him authentic, creative freedom here.

29 See under 'Even after the fall, God's Spirit is intimately involved in human imagination', later this chapter.

creative act that does not draw on God's original creativity.[30] Imagination in both perception (seeing the real anew) and creation (creating a new real) are rooted in God's creation and the image of God we bear. One gives us our world; the other gives us the world as it could be, as we wish it might be, perhaps as it should be. Both transform raw reality through desire and cultural work in a similar way to how God created the world, according to his desire and word.

The imagination, as presented in the early chapters of Genesis, is a God-given gift that is an integral part of being human, something that belongs to us, not to divine muses, not to the gods. Given by God, it unfolds naturally as we interact with his world. It is God-given, God-dependent, but also authentically human.

The imagination frees us from our cultural contexts and gives meaning to our moral lives

Moreover, having an imagination rooted in God himself (because we bear his image) allows us to make free and meaningful moral decisions. Just as God is not bound by cultural perspectives or biology, human imagination, likewise, is free. That freedom is limited, of course: we *are* creatures, bound to our time and place and biology, but we are not determined by them. We can – and sometimes do – choose to go against the grain of our culture. Consider William Wilberforce and his campaign against slavery in eighteenth-century England, when all in his culture insisted that it was a necessary evil. How did he arrive at the conclusion that his whole country and economic system were wrong? Or the man who faced down a tank in Tiananmen Square – where did he get his conviction that China needed to change direction? If our moral vision is simply constructed by our cultural location, it is difficult to explain moral innovation that goes against a culture's grain. But if the imagination is free, as God is free (though on a creaturely scale in our case), we can have a moral imagination that matters, that can defy current cultural categories.

30 See Leithart, 'Introduction'. Tolkien's term 'sub-creation' captures the same understanding of the human imagination as being derivative of divine imagination. But note Yannick Imbert's reservations in 'Covenantal faërie: A Reformed evaluation of Tolkien's theory of fantasy', *Westminster Theological Journal*, vol. 76 (2014), pp. 119–141. He faults Tolkien's theory for a lack of covenantal framework that renders our fantastical creations ethically autonomous.

The moral imagination enables us to reflect on and understand our place in the world from the vantage point of an 'other' reality of unrealized possibilities, a world of what could or should be real but isn't – philosophers call this the 'counterfactual imagination'.[31] We can and do question some cultural realities – we resist them as *wrong* – because we are able to see in ways that run counter to our cultures, to imagine the world as different from how it currently is. This ability to imagine counterfactually allows us to see evil as evil, and this is the foundation of all moral thought and action. It requires an imagination rooted in something (or Someone) that transcends cultures; a conscience ultimately rooted in God's law (see Romans 2:14–15). Imagination and cultural creativity should be understood as a *conversation* both between persons who are more than cultural constructs (because they are made in God's image), and between persons and an inherently meaningful (and morally orientated) universe, such as the Bible describes. These realities allow for imaginations that are free and truly countercultural.

Theories of the imagination that exclude the biblical God struggle at just this point. They propose alternative explanations for how a moral imagination that is able to defy cultural 'scripts' is possible. For some, contact with different cultures (through travel, education or the Internet) is the key, though the *motivation* for choosing other cultural perspectives as good remains unexplained.

Other theorists, such as Jacques Derrida, would say our imaginations are set free because language and cultural meanings are inherently unstable, always in flux.[32] Therefore cultures don't determine moral perspectives as every set of cultural symbols contains wiggle room. But, again, the moral motivation to choose this wiggle over that waggle, to

---

31 See Ruth M. J. Byrne, 'The counterfactual imagination: The impact of alternatives to reality on morality' in Anna Abraham (ed.), *The Cambridge Handbook of the Imagination* (Cambridge: Cambridge University Press, 2020). Monika Chylińska, drawing partly from Byrne, argues that the counterfactual imagination also lies at the base of creativity. See her 'Counterfactual imagination as a mental tool for innovation', *AVANT*, vol. VIII, Special Issue (21 November 2017), pp. 241–251, <www.researchgate.net/publication/321223287_Counterfactual_Imagination_as_a_Mental_Tool_for_Innovation/fulltext/5a157c920f7e9b925cd5525f/Counterfactual-Imagination-as-a-Mental-Tool-for-Innovation.pdf>, accessed February 2023.

32 Jacques Derrida asserts that linguistic meaning is in flux because of a structural instability that he calls 'différance'. See 'Différance' in Richard Kearney and Mara Rainwater (eds), *The Continental Philosophy Reader* (London and New York: Routledge, 1996).

choose a 'good' that runs athwart of our cultural scripts and group interests, remains a mystery.

Evolutionary theory supposes that the moral imagination developed from amoral tribal behaviours such as hunting and dancing.[33] Or perhaps the imagination started as a side effect of visual perception and language, which allowed early human children to pretend an absent loved one (a dead parent, for example) was present.[34]

Neuroscientists attempt to explain the moral imagination by locating it in the brain's neural networks.[35] But these networks are merely pathways, the wiring of moral reasoning, not the creative fire in the wire.

In each case, attempts to derive the moral imagination from amoral sources remain deeply problematic – moral motivation remains unexplained. Further, these explanations ignore the question of the *meaningful* freedom of the moral imagination. If we create our own meaning through culture, how can we transcend our cultural categories in a way that makes sense, in a way that leads to a moral vision that is meaningfully good or evil? If the imagination is an accident of another culture or language or early hominid behaviour or biology, then it can give us nothing more than the *illusion* of meaning. It can never supply us with meaningful moral discourse. Our imagination connects us to something *apparently* meaningful but, actually, it's a cosmic joke that we've taken a little too seriously.[36]

---

33 Steven Asma, *Evolution of the Imagination* (Chicago, IL: University of Chicago Press, 2017).

34 Peter Carruthers offers a helpful overview of the varied attempts to explain the evolution of the imagination in his 'Human creativity: Its cognitive basis, its evolution, and its connections with childhood pretence', *British Journal for the Philosophy of Science*, vol. 53, no. 2 (June 2002), pp. 225–249, <http://faculty.philosophy.umd.edu/pcarruthers/Creative-thinking.htm>, accessed February 2023.

35 For example, see Alexander Schlegel, Peter J. Kohler, Sergey V. Fogelson, Prescott Alexander, Dedeepya Konuthula and Peter Ulric Tse, 'Network structure and dynamics of the mental workspace', *Proceedings of the National Academy of Sciences*, vol. 110, no. 40 (16 September 2013), <www.pnas.org/content/110/40/16277.full>, summarized by Christian Nordqvist, 'Imagination: How and where does it occur in the brain?', *Medical News Today* (22 September 2013), <www.medicalnewstoday.com/articles/266426.php> (both accessed February 2023) and Evan D. Anderson and Aron K. Barbey, 'Moral reasoning: A network neuroscience perspective' in Anna Abraham (ed.), *The Cambridge Handbook of the Imagination* (Cambridge: Cambridge University Press, 2020).

36 There is an important distinction to be made here between that which resonates with us emotionally, subjectively – often quite powerfully – and something that exists beyond ourselves in which our subjective moral feelings are rooted (or rebel against). We should respect and respond to what people find subjectively meaningful, but it is a separate question as to whether or not there is anything beyond their subjective perceptions that is objectively part of some meaning structure larger than themselves and their feelings. That objective rooting is necessary

This is only a problem if you start by assuming that the world is a meaninglessness cosmos – random atoms colliding with others and interacting in interesting ways that, in the end, mean nothing more than a sneeze.[37] If, however, we begin by assuming that it is a *meaningful* cosmos, a connection with the Creator through his creation, we gain an imagination that gives us a meaningful moral vision because it is constantly in conversation with the woven-in created meaning within and without. Genesis 1 and 2 tell us where such an imagination comes from. It is not an accident of cultural contact or some quirk of linguistic instability or an evolutionary by-product, nor a side effect of neural networks. The imagination does not simply 'happen'. It emerges from who we are as beings made in the image of a Creator who lovingly breathed his very Spirit into us and surrounds us with his meaningful creation. From a biblical perspective, our imaginations play with and connect to meaning because we are virtually swimming in meaning.[38]

Because our imaginations are in constant conversation with God, his meaningful creation, and one another (as God's image-bearers), we can both meaningfully empathize (imaginatively transpose ourselves into others' shoes) *and* meaningfully distance ourselves from our own cultural assumptions, seeing them as sometimes wrong. We can critique our cultural categories meaningfully because the imagination flows from a Creator who *is* meaning himself. Our imagination responds to, or rebels against, the Creator's song and story embedded in creation itself, guiding us into countercultural visions of the good.[39]

for morally binding others who may or may not agree with what resonates emotionally with us personally. Otherwise, moral meanings can never be more than subjective emotional passion leveraged into (perhaps) an intersubjective social consensus surrounded by chaos – that is, nihilism, 'sound and fury, signifying nothing'. If there is no meaningful moral purpose to the universe other than the ones we temporarily ascribe to it (either individually or collectively), then our existence, objectively considered, renders us the butts of a cosmic joke: there is no ultimate meaning or morality. Atheists or agnostics may try to put a brave face on it, but finding meaning in ourselves or the universe is a quintessential example of trying to make an existential purse from a nihilistic pig's ear.

37 If that is the case, any *meaningful* investigation of the universe is something of a contradiction to begin with.

38 Theologians call this 'general revelation' about God's character and purposes in creation. See Psalm 19:1–4 and Romans 1:18–25.

39 Peter Leithart asserts that God tells his story through creation, history and redemption. Human storytellers draw on narrative themes that seem universal but are, in fact, God's story and perspective. The 'moral good' that we imagine, if it truly is good, is not an abstract, infinitely malleable concept but, rather, that which harmonizes with God's story for us. See Leithart, 'Introduction'.

The imagination through the lens of the fall and sin

The imagination has been corrupted by sin – creativity is bent towards destruction

Simply having an imagination – being set free to create – does not mean human creativity always leads to good. Quite the contrary. Since the fall of humans into rebellion against God, our imaginations have been marked by distortion and a fundamental antithesis.[40] This distortion is seen early in Genesis. The Hebrew word יֵצֶר (*yê-ṣer*) appears only twice in Genesis (6:5 and 8:2), immediately before and after the flood, expressing the twisted depravity that guided human action and culture-making. Modern translations render it 'intention' (ESV) or 'inclination' (NIV): 'The LORD saw that the wickedness of man was great in the earth, and that every intention [*yê-ṣer*] of the thoughts of his heart was only evil continually' (Genesis 6:5). I prefer the King James Version's translation here: 'imagination'. It clarifies *yê-ṣer*'s relationship to *wayyî-ṣer* (וַיִּיצֶר) in Genesis 2:7, which describes God 'forming' man out of earth. Both words share the same root: the creative, formative power we call the imagination.

Though Trevor Hart contends that it was the King James Version's use of the English word 'imagination' here and elsewhere that led to the Christian suspicion of it (see earlier in this chapter),[41] the translation of the Hebrew word as 'imagination' captures the breadth, depth and horror of human rebellion. We see God-given creativity betrayed. 'Intention' and 'inclination' lose the power of *yê-ṣer*. The hearts and minds of the prediluvian humans expressed not only bad intentions but also twisted imaginations, like a pack of war dogs straining at the leash, all tensed and ready to run amok to ruin and destroy. God judged them because their formative powers, their creative imaginations, were implacably bent

40 That is, two radically different paths were taken by the offspring of the woman and the offspring of the serpent (Genesis 3:15). The church father Augustine described this antithesis in terms of the City of God versus the City of Man. See Augustine, *City of God* in *St Augustine's* City of God *and On Christian Doctrine*, A Select Library of the Nicene and Post-Nicene Fathers of the Christian Church, tr. Marcus Dods, ed. Phillip Schaff (Edinburgh: T&T Clark and Grand Rapids, MI: Eerdmans, series I, vol. II, 1886), <https://ccel.org/ccel/s/schaff/npnf102/cache/npnf102.pdf>, accessed 2023.

41 See Hart, 'A suspicion observed'.

towards evil. Their imaginations, through which they formed and knew the world, had been warped and depraved beyond repair. The imaginative freedom given by God that makes moral vision and action possible had been weaponized and cruelly distorted.

Darren Aronofsky's film *Noah* (2014) did a brilliant job answering the question 'How bad must humanity have become if God decided that he had to send a flood to destroy the earth?' The film vividly expresses what Genesis 6:5 says in a single verse, showing how human creativity can be twisted, how proper dominion over creation can be bent into ruthless domination that turns the world into a desert, a living hell that God is justified in flooding and wiping clean.

Our imaginations bear the marks of our alienation from God, and they can be terminally corrupted by sin. The fall warps our moral imaginative freedom – how we distance ourselves from our culture, which allows us to make moral judgments 'outside the box'. Thinking outside the *cultural* box does not automatically result in virtue. Imagination and creativity do not equal goodness. They can, in fact, lead to hellish moral judgments and demonic innovations. Consider the engineering imagination that produced the ruthlessly efficient Nazi concentration camps, the glorious cinematography of Leni Reifenstahl that glorified Hitler's government, the administrative imaginations necessary to sustain the trans-Atlantic slave trade, the black face minstrel shows that denigrated black Americans during the Jim Crow era, the fine lighting, composition and technique of a *Playboy* photographer. The imagination is a properly human power that allows us to see a moral universe, but is not, in itself, redemptive. The fallen imagination can be twisted, and it can twist others.

Though warped by the fall, the imagination persists, accomplishing God's calling

The fall damaged so much. Humans were alienated from God. Death entered the world. The fall damaged but did not destroy human imagination or creative culture-making. As early as Genesis 3, we see Adam and Eve use their imaginations to hide from God, crafting leafy coverings for themselves, as well as verbal cover by shifting blame (Genesis 3:9–13). We see Cain use his imagination to devise and execute a murder (Genesis 4:8–9), but we also see him build a city (4:17). We see Cain's (Cain's!) descendants develop skills in tent-making, animal husbandry, music and metalwork (4:20–22). Though the imagination is bent by our rebellion, it is not broken. Imagination and cultural creativity persist, to accomplish God's call in Genesis 1:28, the Cultural Mandate.

The imagination through the lens of redemption and the new creation

Even after the fall, God's Spirit is intimately involved in human imagination

After Genesis we encounter another important Old Testament passage about human creativity and imagination. After instructing Moses in how to build the tabernacle (where he will dwell with his people), God concludes with a blessing (Exodus 31:1–6):

> The LORD said to Moses, 'See, I have called by name Bezalel the son of Uri, son of Hur, of the tribe of Judah, and I have filled him with the Spirit of God, with ability and intelligence, with knowledge and all craftsmanship, to devise artistic designs, to work in gold, silver, and bronze, in cutting stones for setting, and in carving wood, to work in every craft. And behold, I have appointed with him Oholiab, the son of Ahisamach, of the tribe of Dan. And I have given to all able men ability, that they may make all that I have commanded you.'

As he always does, God gives the necessary resources to fulfil his commands – in this case, materials plundered from the Egyptians. But God also provides the lead craftsman, Bezalel, *with himself*, his very Spirit. He likewise equips the rest of the artisans who are to work on the tabernacle. In short, God empowers human creativity by giving of himself, thereby bestowing a stunning dignity on human artistic imagination.

This fits well with the theological anthropology of Genesis 1 and 2: humans are beings of immense dignity because they are created in God's image to be in fellowship with God. Other Ancient Near Eastern creation myths, such as the Babylonian myths the *Enuma Elish* and the *Atra-Hasis*, see humans as degraded beings, created to carry out dirty work not fit for a god to do.[42] You get the distinct feeling that the gods keep their distance from 'the help'. By contrast, in Exodus 31, God dignifies human artistry with his presence, but without undermining the craftsmen's creative freedom (akin to Genesis 2:19–20).[43] God empowers his artists, filling Bezalel with himself, and the other artisans with knowledge and expertise, without running roughshod over their humanity.[44] God sees them not as pawns but as gifted artisans. The Spirit empowers Bezalel to 'devise artistic designs' (v. 4), illuminating and amplifying Bezalel's ability to see anew, to imagine new patterns and craft them, along with Oholiab and 'all able men' (v. 6). God doesn't micromanage his artists but leaves them to execute his plans as they will. He specifies materials and measurements but gives them freedom within those parameters. The style will be entirely Bezalel's and his team's.[45] God gives them more than artistic leeway; he gives them intimate access to his Spirit to get the job done. This is the delicate balance that a biblical understanding of the imagination must maintain: it is authentically human (and so free in expression) but also connected to and empowered by God's Spirit (and so derivative of God's imagination).

Was Exodus 31:1–6 a special gifting for a specific task – building the tabernacle, a 'one time only' offer? Or is it paradigmatic for all human creativity, available to everyone? Given the breadth of the Spirit's influence in Psalm 104:29–30, I am inclined towards the latter. In Psalm 104, God's Spirit is the foundation of the life and breath of all living creatures – animal and human, redeemed and unredeemed:

---

42 See the sixth tablet of the *Enuma Elish* and the *Atra-Hasis*, <www.sacred-texts.com/ane/stc/stc09.htm> and <www.livius.org/sources/content/anet/104-106-the-epic-of-atrahasis> respectively, accessed February 2023.

43 See under 'We have imaginations because we are created in the image of God, commanded by him to rule, subdue and "recreate" the world wisely', earlier this chapter.

44 This is the first instance in the whole Bible of a human who is referred to as 'Spirit-filled'. See E. Stephen Burnett, 'Imagination: For God's glory and others' good, part 3', *Speculative Faith: Exploring epic stories for God's glory* (9 June 2011), <http://speculativefaith.lorehaven.com/imagination-for-gods-glory-and-others-good-part-3>, accessed February 2023.

45 They surely worked within a then current artistic tradition – Western-style individualism was unknown to the Ancient Near East. The fact that the lead artists are even named, however, is significant. These are not faceless, nameless, traditional religious artists. Western individualism – the idea that individual humans and what they create matter – comes precisely from these stories, especially Genesis 1 and 2. We shouldn't be surprised to find elements of artistic individualism here.

When you hide your face, they are dismayed;
  when you take away their breath [רוּחָם, *rū-ḥām*], they die
  and return to their dust.
When you send forth your Spirit [רוּחֲךָ, *rū-ḥă-ḵā*],
    they are created,
  and you renew the face of the ground.

God turns away his face, and all creatures lose *rūaḥ*, their Spirit/breath. When God sends his *rūaḥ*, his Spirit/breath, life springs forth and the creatures come to life. This perspective on God's life-generating Spirit is found throughout Hebrew wisdom literature. Job speaks of his own life as 'the breath [*rūaḥ*] of God in my nostrils' (27:3). Elihu asserts that 'It is the spirit [*rūaḥ*] in a person, the breath [נִשְׁמַת, *niš-maṯ*] of the Almighty that gives understanding' (Job 32:8) and even life itself (33:4).[46] Proverbs 20:27 proclaims, 'The spirit [*niš-maṯ*] of man is the lamp of the Lord, searching all his innermost parts.' Taking their cue from Genesis 2:7, these writers assume an intimate, unbreakable bond between human life and the breath/Spirit of God.

If God's Spirit sustains the life of all human (and even animal) life, it stands to reason that his imagination-empowering Spirit in some sense courses through the creative life of all humanity as well. This resonates with passages such as Colossians 1:16–17 (through Christ all things were created, in him all things hold together) and Romans 11:36 ('For from him and through him and to him are all things'). God surely gives his Spirit to his covenant people in a more intense, intimate and redemptive way that is denied those who reject God as King and his Messiah as Lord. Nonetheless, the picture of God's Spirit presented in Psalm 104 and elsewhere is one of overabundant life, overflowing generosity that spills out into the existence of all living creatures. It makes sense, then, that God's Spirit would also overflow with creativity, an overabundance spilling into the imaginations of all people, not just isolated geniuses-under-contract like Bezalel. And just as one's Spirit-given life can be misused and bent for evil purposes, so too can the Spirit-given

[46] *Niš-maṯ*, though derived from a different root than *rūaḥ*, is virtually a synonym, used in poetic parallels. Like *rūaḥ*, *niš-maṯ* denotes both breath and spirit. In Genesis 2:7, God breathes the 'breath of life' into the man he formed from dust. That breath is *niš-maṯ*.

imaginative blessings. They can be used to create tabernacles or golden calves.[47]

This is heady stuff. God not only vaguely inspires human creativity from a distance; somehow, he *enters into* human artists.

Though the Bible doesn't present us with a detailed theory of art and the imagination, we can see this pattern – an authentically free human imagination empowered by God's presence – elsewhere in the Old Testament.[48] Consider David's artistic imagination. In 1 Samuel 16, Samuel anoints David with oil. At the same moment, God's Spirit settles on David (v. 13). We then discover that the Spirit has departed from Saul and has been replaced by 'a harmful spirit' from God that torments him. A search is made for a musician to give Saul relief (vv. 15–17) and David's name comes up (v. 18). David enters Saul's service, and his skilful (Spirit-empowered) musicianship gives Saul relief, as the harmful spirit is driven away (v. 23).

The narrative progression is rapid: from being anointed with oil to being anointed with the Spirit to using art to bring spiritual healing and refreshment. David wasn't only anointed as king but as a musician and singer as well. As David writes in 2 Samuel 23:1–3:

> Now these are the last words of David:
>
> The oracle of David, the son of Jesse,
> the oracle of the man who was raised on high,

[47] In fact, only one chapter later, in Exodus 32, we see imaginative craftsmanship gone horribly wrong, as gifted artisans create in *rebellion* against God's commands. In the total opposite of God calling attention to the skill of the artists in chapter 31, we see Aaron erasing his own role as creator, denying his responsibility for what he has made: 'I threw it into the fire, and out came this calf!' (v. 24). But this abuse of imagination does not sever the relationship between God and his people. After their failure, God reveals his name in a new way to Moses, his mediator (34:6–7). Then God, through Moses again, affirms the gifting of his Spirit to Bezalel and Oholiab, and their team begins to craft the tabernacle – the meeting place between God and his people (Exodus 35–40). God meets the people's rebellion with grace, restoring their sin-bent imaginations. Thanks to my wife Carolyn for these insights.

[48] Again, 'free' does not mean contrary to or independent of God's sovereign will. The human imagination remains derivative, drawing on God's creation and God's Spirit. He does not force our imaginations in one direction or the other (except in extreme cases, such as prophetic vision). Instead, our imaginations are organic expressions of the desires of our hearts, experiences, and the other stories, images and songs we've encountered along the way. Our imaginations are genuinely *ours*, but God remains our Sovereign. According to Proverbs 21:1, he can steer desire (our hearts) this way or that, like a stream in a channel.

the anointed of the God of Jacob,
the sweet psalmist of Israel:
The Spirit of the LORD speaks by me;
his word is on my tongue.
The God of Israel has spoken;
the Rock of Israel has said to me . . .

Obviously, David's role as 'oracle' refers to his role as prophet. But these oracles were also works of David's anointed imagination, highly esteemed works of art. Notably he doesn't refer to himself as an anointed prophet, but as the anointed 'sweet psalmist of Israel'.

All this highlights the intimate relationship between the Holy Spirit and the creative imagination. Again, we must ask, is this paradigmatic of all creative humans or is David a special case? After all, he was God's anointed king, 'a man after God's own heart' (1 Samuel 13:14). Nevertheless, the picture we get in both Exodus 31 and 1 Samuel 16 is striking: God neither overwhelms the artist (the artist is no puppet, art is a genuine expression of the artist's imagination), nor does God hold the artist at arm's length (art is not self-generated, but is fanned into flame by the breath of the Spirit).[49] God chooses not to stand aloof from the human imagination but, rather, his Spirit enlivens even imaginations that are used to rebel against him.[50] No doubt there are specially anointed, Spirit-empowered gifts that God uses in his service. We would not want to flatten a biblical distinction: some are specially called and gifted for extraordinary circumstances. But there is a sense in which every imagination, good or bad, is enabled by God's creative power.[51]

49 This is analogous to the writing of the Bible itself. God inspired the biblical writers, guided them, yet what they wrote bears the marks of their individuality and their human cultures. The verse 2 Peter 1:21 strikes just this balance. The Holy Spirit 'carried along' the human writers (φερόμενοι, *pheromenoi*, which primarily means 'to carry' but can also mean 'to bring along' or 'lead').

50 Christian apologist Cornelius Van Til was fond of the image of a little girl sitting on her father's lap, slapping him in the face. The little girl needed the father's support to even reach his face to slap it. So it is with us: our ability to reason, the air we use to breathe words that deny his existence, all come from God and are sustained by him at every moment. We depend on God and his gifts even to rebel against him. Isn't it the same in the case of the rebellious imagination? See Van Til's *Essays on Christian Education* (Phillipsburg, NJ: P&R, 1979), part III, section 5.D.3.

51 However, as Sinclair Ferguson warns us, we must be careful not to conflate the creative gift of the Holy Spirit distributed to all imaginations (particularly trained ones) with 'the marks of the covenant bond of salvation'. See his *The Holy Spirit*, Contours of Christian Theology, ed.

This is yet another perspective on common grace, the way God restrains evil and gives gifts even to his enemies: rain, sunshine, food, joy, justice and beauty (see Matthew 5:43–48; Acts 14:17). In this case, God's Spirit provides both the necessary condition for the imagination and restrains the sinful imagination from doing all the damage of which it is capable.

The imagination is an authentically human faculty, twisted by sin, yet intimately entwined with the Spirit's quickening power. Our ability to express ourselves creatively, out into the world, and so, in a sense, remake the world, is genuinely human. But it is also genuinely connected to the Spirit's creative and re-creative power and person, even after the fall.

Saving grace as a work of art

Creation was not God's only creative act. His redemptive work also displays an unparalleled creative imagination. Redemption is imaginative renovation, God writing a new song for us to sing (Psalm 40:3), making all creation new and us along with it (2 Corinthians 5:17; Revelation 21:5). The reconciliation that overcomes our alienation from God is a kind of artistic creation. Paul tells us that we are God's in-progress works of art: 'For we are his workmanship, created in Christ Jesus for good works, which God prepared beforehand, that we should walk in them' (Ephesians 2:10). We ourselves and the life-paths we tread are God's handiwork, his ποίημα (*poiēma*, from which we get the English word 'poem').[52]

This should not surprise us – God is an artist par excellence. You only have to look outside your window or watch the latest nature documentary to see evidence of his immense creativity. But his imaginative, creative work in salvation outshines even his work in nature, as glorious as it is. In creation ex nihilo,[53] newly formed nature cooperated with God. Other Ancient Near Eastern creation stories inevitably begin with battle, god slaying god and releasing creative energy. Not so in Genesis 1. God speaks, and light simply appears, and later sky and water and land and plants and

Gerald Bray (Downers Grove, IL: InterVarsity Press, 1996), p. 246. I will go on to argue in the conclusion of chapter 14 that the connections between the common grace operations of the Holy Spirit and the gospel can resonate very deeply.

52 Makoto Fujimura translates *poiēma* as 'masterpiece', to reflect the perfection and new creation we are already in Christ. See his book *Art and Faith: A theology of making* (New Haven, CT, and London: Yale University Press, 2020), p. 14. I believe Paul has in mind both the already (perfect in Christ) and the not-yet (we are new-creations-in-process).

53 Creation from nothingness.

dinosaurs and water buffaloes and armadillos and blue-tongued skinks and everything that moves. God says, 'Jump' and creation says, 'Yes, Sir! How high should we jump, Sir?'

God's saving work was different. He had the stubborn malice of his rebellious creatures to contend with – a gaping chasm of stinking sin that no-one but he alone could traverse and conquer. In so doing, he accomplished the most stunning and beautiful reversal that history has ever seen.

But we forget this. We get so hung up on the ways we fail and fall short, or the ways others fail, that we become blind to what has really happened: God, out of pure grace, has saved us in an astonishing act of creativity. Death produced life. Shame produced everlasting honour. A cruel miscarriage of justice resulted in unmerited mercy for the unjust. A twisted piece of torture produced peace and righteousness for the twisted. Ugliness produced everlasting beauty. A cosmic tragedy (God incarnate killed by his rebellious creatures) brings about deep comedy (rebels restored to fellowship with God for ever, the happiest of happy endings).[54] God graciously embraces his adopted children, welcoming them into a new family.

That is what the gospel is all about, not a list of dos and don'ts.[55] God is not a disapproving judge, storing up evidence that he can use to put us away.[56] Rather, he watches over us with love. He is working *with* us, *in* us, by his Spirit, to bring out of us his greatest artwork: our true humanity, which reflects our deeply good and magnificent Creator. That work remains unfinished until we are fully with him, when all things become new. Those dumb badges from the 1970s that said 'Please be patient, God's not finished with me yet' were right: we are works in progress. Or, better, we are *artworks* in progress.

God's creativity is so potent that when he creates his finest works of art, they so image him that they themselves become creators and shapers of

54 See Peter Leithart's *Deep Comedy: Trinity, tragedy, and hope in Western literature* (Moscow, IA: Canon Press, 2006).

55 I am not discounting God's law, but the Christian faith is not centred on the law. Rather, it is centred on an astounding act of grace that changes us into people who value his law and strive to keep it (though imperfectly).

56 Revelation 20:11–15 does indeed describe a book that records every individual's deeds for judgment. The decisive book, however, is the Book of Life, which lists those who have been saved by grace and follow the Lamb, Jesus. Grace triumphs over judgment before the great white throne (Revelation 20:11).

the world. We are called to follow the Creator in everything. We are called to unleash our imaginations in all our endeavours, even the most ordinary. Bringing up your kids should be a creative joy, not a dull duty. Preparing a meal should be a tasty work of art, not routine drudgery. Writing an essay for homework doesn't have to be boring (as a teacher, I deeply appreciate the students who put creative effort into their essays). Teaching should lead students into wonder, sparking their imaginations into flame. The imaginative life and the Christian faith fit together like hand and glove, because Christian salvation itself is the creative act of an immense imagination.[57]

Jesus and the artisanship of all believers

Because we are made in God's image, we are hard-wired to follow in his footsteps. We are made for love. We are made for imagination. As image-bearers, our very being calls us to creativity. As Christ-redeemed humans in the process of being remade by the Spirit, we are all called to a renewed imagination.

Consider Jesus, the picture-perfect image of restored humanity. He was an artist, his life full to bursting with imaginative innovation. He was forever spinning stories, metaphors, expertly moving into relationships, entering into human hurt, hunger and despair, and providing powerfully imaginative solutions. 'Here, put this mud on your eyes, then go wash. You'll find your vision clearing up, both physically and spiritually' (John 9). 'You temple officials want the taxes paid? Let's go fishing and see what we catch' (Matthew 17:24–27). 'You want to know how to love your neighbour? Let me tell you a story about someone you're used to hating – he's the *hero*' (Luke 10:25–37). He was constantly applying his imagination to the situation at hand, doing the unexpected, making it new. We have heard these stories so many times they seem cliché and trite. We overlook the ways in which he overturned expectations as well as moneychangers' tables.

Jesus was allergic to cliché. Being truly God, he could not act in any way that was less than imaginative. Being the quintessence of true humanity,

[57] Because we live in a fallen world with fallen hearts, we do not always experience imaginative wonder in life, but the Christian faith is a calling to an imagination-filled life.

he felt a calling to be creative rather than simply utilitarian.[58] Being less than creative would betray the image of God he bore. It would be to betray God, his Father, and the fecund nature of the Spirit. Following Jesus does not mean trudging a path of rote obedience. It means following along after him on the path of the imagination. Not only artists or writers. Everyone. One friend calls this the 'artisanship of all believers'.[59] Makoto Fujimura puts it even more boldly. The Christian faith is all about 'making' – producing something of beauty in the world. This is non-negotiable: '[W]e are all artists of the Kingdom, and the world needs to see such extravagant beauty in us, or else we are not the Bride of Christ, which is the church.'[60]

The imagination and faith: we need the eyes of the heart to see reality

If imagination and creativity are so central to the Christian faith, why aren't they mentioned more in the New Testament? Because, while the New Testament was being written, the people of God were scattered and in a position of relative cultural powerlessness. They did not have the resources to create large-scale art like the tabernacle. Yes, a church culture was *forming*, but that micro-culture was not to have a significant systemic impact on the larger society for another couple of centuries.

New Testament teaching on the imagination has a very different emphasis. There it is not so much a force for creation as a lens that shapes perception.[61] We get tastes of this in the Old Testament – singing a new song in Psalm 96, scales falling from a servant's eyes in 2 Kings 6 – but Christ's death, resurrection and giving of the Spirit unveils something new about the imagination.

58 Fujimura stresses that creativity is *gratuitous* rather than merely 'useful' (in *Art and Faith*, pp. 16–19). It reflects the overabundant generosity of God's creativity.

59 This is a riff on Martin Luther's famous 'priesthood of all believers', which means that every Christian stands in immediate relation to Christ. If Christ alone is our Mediator, we don't need priests – we *are* priests (though some are specially called to guide and teach the church community). Similarly, the inherent imaginative texture of the Christian faith frees all Christians to be artists of a sort (though some are specially called to pursue creative professions).

60 Fujimura, *Art and Faith*, p. 92.

61 The New Testament documents themselves are thoroughly infused with imagination: poetry, parables, colourful imagery and so on. All of that imaginative creativity was aimed at helping Christians see anew. Only later would there be a category 'Christian artist'. We will explore imagination-as-perception further in chapter 6.

Imagination is not only the driving force behind cultural creativity but also vital for a living faith. God must awaken our imaginations if we are to grasp him by faith. Paul implies this in his beautiful prayer in Ephesians 1:17–20:

> I keep asking that the God of our Lord Jesus Christ, the glorious Father, may give you the Spirit of wisdom and revelation, so that you may know him better. I pray that the eyes of your heart may be enlightened in order that you may know the hope to which he has called you, the riches of his glorious inheritance in his holy people, and his incomparably great power for us who believe. That power is the same as the mighty strength he exerted when he raised Christ from the dead.

What Paul calls the 'eyes of the heart' is the imagination. He explicitly links these 'eyes' to the creative (and re-creative/resurrection) power of the Spirit. The surface of the world and our lives can seem dead and godforsaken. Sons and daughters of God learn to see with the eyes of the heart into the deeper, truer context of their lives: God's love and power for those who believe, his glorious inheritance awaiting us, his awesome power that flows just under the surface of the dead, sin-twisted world. Christians are those who can see past the surface of *apparent* reality into *real* reality, the world and our whole lives seen as rooted and growing in God's love and power. Faith that sees past the apparent into the real takes imagination, the Spirit-awakened eyes of the heart.[62] As theologian Trevor Hart says:

> the way in which God makes himself known to us, and shares his redemptive purposes and promises for the world with us, is bound up with our capacity to imagine; to apprehend and hold in our

[62] 'Faith' and 'imagination' are not the same thing. 'Imagination' is an ability woven into the whole fabric of human existence that allows for creativity and seeing/feeling/experiencing the world anew – what we shall call later 'seeing-as'. 'Faith', by contrast, refers to the specific *orientation* of the imagination. True faith grounds the imagination in the redemptive love, power and purposes of God, expressed in Christ and applied by the Spirit. False faiths orientate the imagination towards other aims and purposes in service of an idol (that which is not God). Imagination is the compass; faith is the direction the needle points to. Our imaginations are drawn in faith, magnetically attracted to one faith orientation or another.

> 'mind's eye', as we would say, things which trespass far beyond the horizons of the things we can see and touch and hear.[63]

Both faith's genesis and continued growth lean heavily on the repeated renewal of our imaginations, on our capacity to see things anew.

Paul makes a similar point in another prayer in Philippians. We are to see everything through the lens of Christian love:

> And this is my prayer: that your love may abound more and more in knowledge and depth of insight, so that you may be able to discern what is best and may be pure and blameless until the day of Christ, filled with the fruit of righteousness that comes through Jesus Christ – to the glory and praise of God.
> (Philippians 1:9–11, NIV)

What the New International Version (NIV) translates as 'depth of insight' in verse 9 and the English Standard Version (ESV) as 'all discernment' is better translated as 'every sensation' (πάσῃ αἰσθήσει, *pásei aisthései*), the phrase's original use.[64] However, *aisthései* used in conjunction with ἐπιγνώσει (*epignōsei*, 'intellectual experience', translated by the ESV as 'knowledge') reveals the true scope of Paul's meaning. He is not saying that having love will give us a few new insights here and there. Rather, Paul's prayer is that the Philippians' love for God and for one another might colour their every intellectual, emotional and moral experience. That perception-shaping love is one of the key signs that God has begun his work in the Philippian Christians, a work that he will certainly bring to completion on the day of Christ Jesus (Philippians 1:6).

Paul's prayer is not only for the Philippians but also for all Christians. God longs to see this imaginative, loving texture of perception formed in all of us. Love is to shape the totality of what we experience moment by moment, regardless of what we are doing or with whom we are interacting. According to v. 10, the end result of that perception-shaping love is the development of a reliable discernment of what is most excellent. Verse 10

63 Hart, 'A suspicion observed', p. 13.

64 Calvin Seerveld interprets the Greek this way in his book *Rainbows for the Fallen World* (Toronto, Ontario: Toronto Tuppence Press, 2005 [1980]), p. 46. *Aisthései* later came to denote inner moral or emotional experiences as well.

shows what this love-seasoned judgment leads to: a life characterized by purity, integrity or 'blamelessness' (ἀπρόσκοποι, *aproskopoi*, literally, not stumbling around or causing others to stumble). Then we will be filled with 'the fruit of righteousness that comes through Christ' (v.11), which will shine (like a star in a dark place; see Philippians 2:15) to the glory and praise of God. Paul prayed that the Philippians might experience a love that would transform the creative ability to see the world, one another and ourselves differently, which we have been calling the imagination.

The message of these two passages is clear: Christians need imagination – the eyes of the heart – to see past the banal, sin-twisted surface of the world into real reality. We need a distinctive 'depth of insight' shaped by God's love, so that we may see everything in its true light, and live a life of love out of that reality.

Puritan pastor-theologian Richard Baxter urged his parishioners to something similar:

> You can open your Bibles, and read there of God and of glory; O learn to open the creatures, and to open the several passages of providence, to read of God and glory there. Certainly, by such a skillful, industrious improvement, we might have a fuller taste of Christ and heaven in every bit of bread that we eat, and in every draught of beer that we drink, than most men have in the use of the sacrament.[65]

What Baxter calls opening the creatures is what Paul called using the eyes of the heart: learning to read the world around us with the same Spirit-enlightened imaginative vision we have when we read the Bible. Imagination is central to living by faith in a fallen world. The health and shape of our imaginations makes all the difference.

Another illustration, this time drawn from C. S. Lewis' classic children's novel *Prince Caspian*. Lucy – the youngest and most open-hearted of the four Pevensie children – has a night-time adventure. All the children find

[65] Richard Baxter, *The Saint's Everlasting Rest* in *The Practical Works of Richard Baxter* (Ligonier, PA: Soli Deo Gloria, vol. 3, 1990), p. 293, cited in Eifion Evans, 'The Puritan use of the imagination', The Highway (n.d.), <www.the-highway.com/imagination_Evans.html>, accessed February 2023.

themselves transported to the land of Narnia, where they used to be kings and queens. Narnia has fallen on hard times and the children want to know why. Camping in the woods, Lucy finds that she can't sleep. 'Instead of getting drowsier she was getting more awake – with an odd, night-time dreamish kind of wakefulness.'[66] She walks into the woods and begins to talk to the trees, speaking to the spirits that she knows once lived in them. She knows how Narnia *should* be. She sees past the apparent deadness into the life beneath the bark. The next night, her 'dreamish wakefulness' helps her to see what the other children cannot: Aslan the lion, the creator and true king of that world. She wants to follow him, but the other children refuse to believe that what she saw was real, chalking it up to wishful thinking. They choose another, more obvious path, but it costs them precious time. They realize too late that Lucy's sight was clearer than their own.

Lucy's creativity/sensitivity is a good picture of what a faithful imagination looks like in practice. Imagination is not about making things up (or not *only* about making things up). The faithful imagination is also and primarily about being sensitive to the way things really are. The faithful imagination is a way of perceiving that is in line with God's own vision, despite the unbelief around us that sees only a dead, decaying world. What we *really* need to follow God, then, are faithful imaginations that can swim upstream, against the currents of unbelief that surround us. Imagination and spirituality are intimately related. We need imaginations that see and hear past the swirl of voices and images into the Truth itself. Nowadays, to catch a glimpse of truth, you *do* need imagination.

Conclusion: the Bible gives a rich understanding of the imagination

No doubt there are other fruitful areas of the Bible to explore. For example, what does prophetic or apocalyptic imagery say about the imagination?[67]

---

66 C. S. Lewis, *Prince Caspian*, The Chronicles of Narnia (New York: Scholastic, 1979), p. 116. Quote by C. S. Lewis © copyright 1951 CS Lewis Pte Ltd. Used with permission.

67 See Sharon Hodde Miller's insightful 'Evangelicals and the loss of prophetic imagination', *Mere Orthodoxy* (9 February 2017), <https://mereorthodoxy.com/evangelicals-loss-prophetic-imagination>, accessed February 2023. Drawing on the work of Old Testament scholar Walter Brueggemann, Miller asserts that the prophetic imagination's job is to disrupt and disturb the community, to make the community face up to unpleasant truths about itself. Many times, a faithful imagination is *not* encouraging and uplifting (we will examine this further in part 3).

What about wisdom literature and the poetic–ethical imagination? The historical imagination of the Gospel writers? At the very least, I wanted to establish that the biblical drama of creation, fall, redemption/new creation and the very nature of the Christian faith have something to say about the imagination.

This chapter has really been about giving you permission to explore and employ your imagination *because* it is rooted in the core realities of the Christian faith, in the nature of the triune Creator himself, in the nature of human existence, in the nature of our redemption, in the nature of the Spirit's dispensing of common grace, and in the nature of a living faith. Through the imagination, we reshape our experience. We reshape the world in faithful obedience to, or in rebellion against, our God. There's obviously more to the Christian faith than the imagination, but it is never less than that.

6

The testimony of (human) nature about the imagination

Introduction

In chapter 5 we laid out some basic biblical presuppositions regarding the imagination. But the Bible is not a science textbook, nor is it a philosophy treatise. It will not give us the depth of detail that is possible by exploring God's revelation in nature – in this case, *human* nature. We can, therefore, bring our understanding of the imagination into sharper focus by also listening to what science, philosophy and literary theory have to say.[1]

The idea that science and other forms of scholarship are inherently opposed to the Christian faith is a myth that has done great damage to both the church and academia. Christians have a long record of explorations in science and philosophy, and of thinking through their findings in light of the Bible (that is, general revelation in light of special revelation). While many of the thinkers I mention in this chapter are not believers, their insights resonate with what the Bible says. If all truth is God's truth, his revelation shines through the work of both Christians and non-Christians. This will help us to unpack the mystery of the human imagination.

However, there are a couple of caveats. The imagination has fascinated so many thinkers down the ages that I cannot hope to give a comprehensive account. I have had to be selective, focusing on the findings that make most sense to me as a Christian and are most salient for our discussion.[2]

---

[1] Art, poetry, architecture, music and so on are also explorations of natural structures of the world related to the imagination, but we cannot explore them all here. I have therefore chosen to focus on the subjects mentioned because they relate more directly than these others to a laying out of the nature of the imagination.

[2] For those wanting a more comprehensive historical account of the philosophy of the imagination, I recommend Mary Warnock's *Imagination* (Berkeley and Los Angeles, CA: University of California Press, 1976), Richard Kearney's *The Wake of the Imagination* (New York: Routledge, 1988) and Amy Kind (ed.), *The Routledge Handbook of Philosophy of Imagination* (New York: Routledge, 2016).

Further, I am not a cognitive scientist by training. Even if I were, scientists do not speak with a unified voice regarding the imagination.[3] Some refer to the imagination as the ability to visualize the world around us apart from what our eyes see; objects not present but tied to memory (the French toast I had for breakfast, for instance).[4] Others refer to it as the ability of the brain not simply to recall images but also to modify and combine them to create fictional, impossible objects and contexts (my French toast that now has eyes, ears and a mouth, speaking to me in a world where breakfasts converse with hungry breakfasters).[5] Still others refer to the imagination as creativity in general, something unable to be contained neatly in any single mental operation.[6]

What, then, *is* the imagination? In popular usage, the imagination is understood as that mystical, magical place where we make stuff up – songs, poems, films, pictures and so forth. Ironically, that's partly why the imagination has developed a bad reputation among Christians. Christians want to be level-headed truth-tellers, not fanciful weavers of fables. Why don't we trust medieval bestiaries for information about our natural world? Because they were often works of overactive imaginations filled with made-up monsters such as griffins and chimeras. Or consider the Hans Christian Andersen tale, *The Emperor's New Clothes*. Wasn't the real point of the story the inherent deceptiveness of the imagination, of seeing something where there was, in fact, nothing?

---

[3] For a fascinating overview of the current psychological, philosophical and neuroscientific theories of the imagination, see Jim Davies, *Imagination: The science of your mind's greatest power* (New York: Pegasus Books, 2019).

[4] See Association for Psychological Science, 'Imagination can influence perception', *ScienceDaily* (24 June 2011), <www.sciencedaily.com/releases/2011/06/110616193907.htm> or Brigham Young University, 'Neuroscientists watch imagination happening in the brain', *ScienceDaily* (28 August 2014), <www.sciencedaily.com/releases/2014/08/140828110935.htm>, both accessed February 2023.

[5] For example, Sandy Gautam, 'The faculty of imagination: Neural substrates and mechanisms', Science 2.0 (5 June 2007), <www.science20.com/sandygautam/the_faculty_of_imagination_neural_substrates_and_mechanisms>, Andrey Vyshedskiy, 'The science of imagination', TED-Ed, YouTube (12 December 2016), <www.youtube.com/watch?v=e7uXAlXdTe4> or Peter Zeidman and Eleanor A. Maguire, 'Anterior hippocampus: The anatomy of perception, imagination and episodic memory', *Nature Reviews Neuroscience*, vol. 17, no. 3 (March 2016), pp. 173–182, <www.openacademyofmedicine.org/sites/default/files/pdf/Bibliografia/Anterior%20hippocampus%20the%20anatomy%20of%20perception,%20imagination%20and%20episodic%20memory.pdf>, all accessed February 2023.

[6] John Kaag, 'The neurological dynamics of the imagination', *Phenomenology and the Cognitive Sciences*, vol. 8, no. 2 (2008), pp. 183–204, <https://citeseerx.ist.psu.edu/viewdoc/download?doi=10.1.1.471.2279&rep=rep1&type=pdf>, accessed February 2023.

In this post-Enlightenment age where we measure and quantify everything, imagining is often seen as simply making stuff up. Enlightenment philosopher David Hume famously called poets 'liars by profession'.[7] Understood this way, the imagination *undermines* the truth, whether the truth in question is empirical facts or God's revelation. This makes Christian truth-lovers nervous. But such a picture of the imagination only scratches the surface. Recall the preliminary definition I gave in the introduction:

> The imagination is a human power that orientates us – mind and body – in the world, through which we perceive and create. It orientates us both individually and collectively, so we can speak of a 'collective imagination' or an 'imaginary landscape'. The imagination inspires us to create, *and* it colours our experience of the world and our assumptions about reality. The imagination mediates: we shape our world through it, and through it our world shapes us.

There is more to the imagination than 'making stuff up'.

The imagination is a notoriously fuzzy concept; there is no consensus among the interested parties (philosophers, scientists, literary theorists and others). But just because the concept is fuzzy doesn't mean we can't spend some time defuzzing things, clearing up misconceptions. As things become clearer, they also become more interesting. It turns out that the imagination is more powerful and pervasive than you would . . . imagine. The testimony of science and philosophy is that the imagination not only creates made-up worlds but it also plays a more central role in our experience of the real world than we typically suppose.

The main takeaway from this chapter is that the imagination is a powerful mediator of reality – far more dynamic, complex and central than you might have supposed. Here are ten propositions that bring the imagination into sharper focus.

---

7 David Hume, *Treatise of Human Nature* (New York: Penguin Classics, 1986), book 1, part 3, section X, p. 170. For a fuller account of Hume's theory of the imagination, see Mary Warnock, *Imagination*, parts I and II.

Imagination is the arena of dialogue between body and mind

Generally, the word 'imagination' suggests conscious mental activity.[8] When someone says, 'I am imagining a giant lizard monster stomping Tokyo' (and who hasn't at one time or another?), what that person usually means is, 'I am intentionally forming a mental image of a giant lizard stomping Tokyo.' Such events are familiar, so we assume that the imagination is simply something that we guide effortlessly, consciously and intentionally with our minds.

But that is only part of the story. As odd as it may sound, the imagination situates us in the world *prior to* our conscious awareness of the world. According to art and literature scholar Janine Langan (drawing from perceptual psychologist Rudolf Arnheim), 'Any imaging of the world already orients our response to what it offers, and our perceptions already seduce, repel, and fascinate before the will and intellect kick in.'[9] Imagination rooted in the body – particularly the senses, emotions, desires, passions, attractions and repulsions – situates us in the world *before* imagining becomes a conscious mental activity. The imagination is as much a thing of the body as it is of the mind.

James K. A. Smith's book *Imagining the Kingdom*[10] seeks to correct a perceived overemphasis in conservative Christian circles on mind over body by insisting that the imagination is, first and foremost, embodied.[11]

---

8 Amy Kind, in the introduction to *The Routledge Handbook of Philosophy of Imagination*, asserts that the consensus among philosophers is that imagining is only intentional, when compared to perceiving, which is unintentional (p. 3). She then sets about 'carving up' the imagination, creating a taxonomy of ever more precise subsets of imaginative activity. Given the holistic nature of the imagination – not an 'appendix' but more akin to the circulatory system – that move seems to me to be unnecessary and unwise. See Trevor Hart, 'A suspicion observed: Christian responses to the imagination', lecture delivered for the Billy Graham Center and Marion E. Wade Center Evangelism Roundtable V, 'Imagination and the gospel: Harnessing the imagination to engage contemporary culture and communicate the life-changing gospel', Wheaton College, Wheaton, IL, 23–26 April 2008. As we shall see, the imagination seeps into both intentional and unintentional aspects of human existence.

9 Janine Langan, 'The Christian imagination' in Leland Ryken (ed.), *The Christian Imagination: The practice of faith in literature and writing* (Colorado Springs, CO: Shaw Books, rev. exp. edn, 2002), p. 64. See also Rudolf Arnheim, *Visual Thinking* (Berkeley, CA: University of California Press, 1969).

10 James K. A. Smith, *Imagining the Kingdom: How worship works* (Grand Rapids, MI: Baker Academic, 2013).

11 Smith draws especially on phenomenologist Maurice Merleau-Ponty and anthropologist-sociologist Pierre Bourdieu. See *Imagining the Kingdom*, chapters 1 and 2, especially pp. 43–44 and 70–72. Smith seems to swing the pendulum too far towards the body, leaving little room

He is right: we cannot simply think or consciously will our imaginations as though they were mental putty to be moulded any way we please. Rather, the composition of our imaginations is a product of a mixture of childhood formation, dispositions, passions, habits and desires that are thoroughly woven into who we are as embodied individuals within communities. Imaginative inclinations are stubborn and not easy to change.

Yet conscious reflection also plays a role. We can, and do, talk back to our imaginations. We fight dispositions and inclinations, trying to steer our imaginations towards certain objects or ideas. If we could not, it would make no sense for the psalmist to interrogate and chide his own imagination: 'Why are you so downcast, O my soul?' (Psalms 42:5, 11; 43:5). Likewise, if conscious reflection has no part to play in shaping imagination, we could make little sense of the experience of daydreaming – that free-floating imaginative journey nonetheless consciously guided by us. This conscious guiding differentiates daydreaming from night dreaming.[12]

Let us say, then, that the imagination is a *hybrid* of body and mind, a dialogue, rather like a game of tennis, a constant back-and-forth oscillation between our preconscious desires and dispositions (rooted in our bodies) and conscious reflections (rooted in our minds). Though our imaginations emerge from our embodied existence, our conscious minds can guide or resist, and that guidance or resistance can influence the shape of our imaginations in the long term.

We can see this dialogue in the creative work of an artist. Much of what an artist does flows out of muscle memory – actions trained over and over in what one artist friend calls 'a muscle liturgy in the body'.[13] Creative choices flow from the body – that brushstroke here rather than there,

(note 11 *cont.*) for conscious intellectual reflection. Smith has denied this charge. See, for example, Jesse Covington, Maurice Lee, Sarah Skripsky and Lesa Stern, 'Irreducibly embodied: 4 questions on *Imagining the Kingdom*, *Books and Culture*, January/February 2014, <www.booksandculture.com/articles/2014/janfeb/irreducibly-embodied.html?paging=off>, accessed February 2023. See also Smith's reply, 'Continuing a conversation with the Westmont 4', at *Fors Clavigera* (23 January 2014), <https://forsclavigera.blogspot.com/2014/01/continuing-conversation-with-westmont.html> and Jesse Covington's subsequent response to Smith, 'Cognition and embodiment: An ongoing conversation with Jamie Smith', *Civitas Peregrina* (1 February 2014), <http://civitasperegrina.wordpress.com/tag/james-k-a-smith>, both accessed February 2023.

12 I am intentionally ignoring the rare phenomenon of 'lucid dreaming'.

13 Alastair Gordon, email correspondence with me, 3 May 2021.

a film edit here, not there – often in ways that cannot be clearly articulated apart from 'it just felt right'. But it is not wholly a thing of the body. That training follows an idea of composition or sheet music or a script. The embodied imagination is guided into certain creative channels by the mind. It is a conversation that involves the whole person.

Another example is the heightened creativity that marks 'flow states'. Muscle memory formed by training in just about any field (music, painting, writing, sport, surgery) surfaces as mental attention on an activity that becomes laser focused, as the conscious awareness of self fades.[14] Conscious, focused attention and bodily memory merge into an optimal imaginative and creative whole.

The imagination, then, is neither primarily a thing of the body nor of the mind. It is a product of the exchange between the two.

We can speak about two aspects of the imagination: the *perceptive imagination* and the *creative imagination*

Typically we assume that the imagination is primarily about creativity, making stuff up (images or stories about giant lizards or naked emperors, for instance). But the imagination plays another important role: perception. It situates us in our world, allowing us to perceive the world and ourselves in the world.

Both body and mind are involved in these two aspects – creation and perception. We have seen how body and mind work together in creativity (such as flow states). Likewise, they both work together in the imagination to shape our perception. The imagination not only creates but also organizes how we perceive the world and ourselves in the world. Perception is rooted in our bodies as sense-data, dispositions, habits and desires. The mind is also involved, with conscious mental decisions being employed by perception to focus attention here rather than there, on this rather than that.

Just as the body and mind are in a constant conversation with each other – a conversation mediated by the imagination – so also are the two aspects of the imagination. Out of our imaginatively organized perception

[14] See Jeanne Nakamura and Mihaly Csikszentmihalyi, 'The concept of flow' in C. R. Snyder and Shane J. Lopez (eds), *Handbook of Positive Psychology* (Oxford: Oxford University Press, 2002), especially pp. 91–92.

flows our creative, imaginative productivity (the creativity we see in art, stories and mental images). And the creative products we enjoy, in turn, shape how we see the world. Here, too, imagination mediates, between bodily dispositions and mental reflection, shaping both perception and creation.[15] We could call these two aspects of the imagination the *perceptive imagination* and the *creative imagination*.[16]

The *perceptive imagination* gives us our world. In a sense, the real world is imaginary

While the imagination creates mental images of things that aren't there (a giant lizard or recalling a loved one who is away on a trip), there is also evidence that the imagination plays a decisive role in perceiving things and people who *are* present with us (the pet lizard in the cage, the beloved person sitting across the table from you).

Cognitive scientists have found that the brain is active in our perception of experience. It does not sit back and passively soak up information about the world like a sponge. Rather, our mind constantly filters information, highlights areas of interest, ignores or suppresses objects that are irrelevant (or, perhaps, painful) to us. Human perception is much more than stimulus–response.[17] The mind places a template of assumptions, desires and expectations on what we see, hear and feel. This is the ongoing work of the imagination: projecting patterns on to our experience that help us to interpret what is going on in the world.

15 I have oversimplified for the sake of convenience, focusing on two broad categories – creation and perception. These two categories, in fact, contain a complex variety of experience: remembering, trusting, solving, projecting, denying, deceiving, hypothesizing and so on. My main point: perception and creation interpenetrate far more than we suppose and, in each case, imagination serves as the mediator or conduit.

16 Other theorists (Spinoza, Kant, Coleridge, Wordsworth) have used different labels: dynamic and static, active and passive, primary and secondary, productive and reproductive. I prefer perceptive and creative for simplicity's sake (though the imagination is anything but simple). The use of these terms is not original to me. See Zong-qi Cai, 'Poetics of imagination: Wordsworth and Lui Xie on literary creation' in *Configurations of Comparative Poetics: Three perspectives on Western and Chinese literary criticism* (Honolulu, HI: University of Hawai'i Press, 2002), pp. 154–155.

17 This is not to say that stimulus–response plays no role. Light enters through the eye, hits the retina and is translated into information that forms images in the brain stem (specifically, an area called V1). But the *significance* of this imagery – even in terms of the recognition of objects or where they are located – happens further in the brain and is filtered through various processes that involve imagination. That is, imagination shapes the meanings that we attach to perception. See Davies, 'Perception and memory' in *Imagination*, chapter 2.

In the past two decades, much discussion in neuroscience and psychology has focused on 'mirror neurons' – a network of specialized brain cells that are activated when we see others perform an action, gesture or facial expression.[18] For example, when we see someone smile, an MRI will show the neurons associated with smiling light up, even when *we* are not smiling. This network may make social interaction and empathy possible.[19] For example, when we are in a conversation, we do not need to analyse a smile logically to perceive the intention behind it (pleasure, humour). Rather, a neurological system instantly recognizes the pattern and links it to our own experience. In this way we *project* meanings from our own experiences on to social situations, rendering them understandable.

More recent counter-evidence casts doubt on this, questioning whether mirror neurons play as wide and important a role as earlier researchers thought.[20] Even the sceptics, however, see them as the basis for how we learn motor skills through mimicking others. If mirror neurons do indeed lay the groundwork at least for social interaction (evidence is not yet conclusive), then we are hard-wired to interpret our social world through imaginatively projecting our own meanings on to what we see and hear.

Imaginative visualization even helps us to process basic visual information.[21] The imagination can 'prime' the parts of the brain used when receiving visual data, allowing for faster and smoother visual perception. Responding to different but related evidence, cognitive theorist Nigel J. T. Thomas argues for what he calls 'active perception theory'.[22] He postulates that our senses perceive the world around us,

---

18 See Susan Perry, 'Mirror neurons', BrainFacts.org (16 November 2008), <www.elegantbrain.com/edu4/classes/readings/depository/misc/mirror_neurons.pdf>, accessed February 2023.

19 Marco Iacaboni and Jonah Lehrer, 'The mirror neuron revolution: Explaining what makes humans social', *Scientific American* (1 July 2008), <www.scientificamerican.com/article/the-mirror-neuron-revolut>, accessed February 2023.

20 JohnMark Taylor, 'Mirror neurons after a quarter century: New light, new cracks', *Harvard University Science in the News Blog* (25 July 2016), <http://sitn.hms.harvard.edu/flash/2016/mirror-neurons-quarter-century-new-light-new-cracks>, accessed February 2023.

21 Association for Psychological Science, 'Imagination can influence perception', APS (16 June 2011), <www.psychologicalscience.org/news/releases/imagination-can-influence-perception.html>, accessed February 2023.

22 Theories of perception and imagination are still very much debated. Traditional theories of perception understand perception as passive – we receive sensory data and process that information. Imagination, dreaming, hallucination and other types of image-forming are clearly separated from perception. In active perception theory, perception and imagination are more closely linked. See Nigel J. T. Thomas, 'Are theories of imagery theories of imagination?

but the mind serves as an active filter during that process. According to Thomas' model, the mind continually projects queries and patterns to try to understand what it perceives. This question-and-answer activity happens so quickly that we don't notice it, but it is always happening in the background, testing to see if what we *imagine* to be there really is as we believe it to be. Thus, the imagination is continually bouncing queries off our surroundings. Is that a chair? Yes, it's a chair. A curtain? Yes, a curtain. I'm in a room? Yes, a room. Our perceptive imagination tosses patterns and possibilities out into the world repeatedly, like fishermen casting nets, seeing what it catches, what's confirmed, and what perceptions need to be adjusted in our understanding of our surroundings.

We notice this process only when there is confusion or doubt that momentarily derails our perception. For instance, I see a dark shape in the corner of the room, and my mind throws out a question, a possible pattern: 'Is that a cat? Is that Enkidu, *our* cat?'[23] Further questioning and testing will confirm that it is, after all, our small, grey-black cat Enkidu or it is not (and then my imagination will ask, 'How did a strange cat get into our house?' or 'Is it a pile of laundry?').

We perceive our world by seeing things *as* this or that, matching visual data with possible patterns of seeing-as (that shape *as* a cat, *as* Enkidu, our cat). Even more striking, just this morning I *saw* Enkidu sitting on a chair . . . until I turned my head and realized that it was a black plastic bag full of things that my daughter was taking to school for her book presentation.[24] But I would have sworn that Enkidu *was* there! I saw his

(note 22 *cont.*) An active perception approach to conscious mental content', *Cognitive Science*, vol. 23, issue 2 (11 February 1999), pp. 207–245, <www.academia.edu/3591301/Are_Theories_of_Imagery_Theories_of_Imagination_An_Active_Perception_Approach_to_Conscious_Mental_Content>, and his later 'The multidimensional spectrum of imagination: Images, dreams, hallucinations, and active, imaginative perception', *Humanities*, vol. 3 (15 April 2014), pp. 132–184, <www.mdpi.com/2076-0787/3/2/132/pdf>, accessed February 2023. Giovanni Pezzulo, Francesco Donnarumma, Pierpaolo Iodice, Domenico Maisto and Ivilin Stoianov attempt to reconcile the traditional and active theories by exploring how the brain uses internal models of the external world: 'Model-based approaches to active perception and control', *Entropy*, vol. 19 (9 June 2017), <www.mdpi.com/1099-4300/19/6/266/pdf-vor>, accessed February 2023.

23 Our beloved cat Enkidu died during the writing of this book. He is much missed, especially by my youngest daughter, Ruth. As homage to a very special cat, I refer to Enkidu in the present tense.

24 Please note that my imaginative visual reinterpretation of that object is still rooted in physical reality: I do not see a white cat, but a cat that matched the colour of the bag. Thanks to neuroscientist-artist George Shortess for this insight. I also did not see an unknown grey-black cat. Rather, that visual data – the fundamental materials of perception – was shaped by my imagination into a familiar and welcome pattern (I liked Enkidu; he was a good cat). It is this dialogue between visual input and the 'home making' imagination that I find so fascinating.

small, cat self . . . until I turned and saw that the pattern in my imagination did not fit and I needed to adjust what I *thought* I saw to what was *really* there. Perception, then, is not simply a passive reflection of things out there, like the image in a mirror. We do not soak up information neutrally like sponges. Rather, in perception, the imagination functions like a lamp, illuminating our world through its constant questioning and patterning activity.[25]

This patterning activity isn't only visual. We have a white-noise machine that we turn on at night. I hear patterns in the noise, audio hallucinations of a sort: short musical phrases, a choir singing, the ring of a distant bell, voices repeating words, cicadas whirring, a drum machine making a rhythm and so on. If these sound patterns aren't coming from the machine, where are they coming from? From my mind, my perception-shaping imagination. My wife hears them, too (though different patterns).

Hearing patterns in random noise such as fans or engine sounds is called audio pareidolia.[26] Carolyn and I both have normal hearing, and we are both also susceptible to 'earworms'.[27] These auditory hallucinations reveal something of the habitual function of our minds: the perception-patterning work of our imaginations. An auditory stimulus (white noise) has an impact on our ears, which our imaginations reshape into recognizable patterns.[28] Perception-shaping imaginative patterning is a characteristic shared by all humans. The world has various impacts on us, and we respond by creating patterns, compulsively, continually, reshaping the world in subtle and not-so-subtle ways. Perception is a conversation between the imagination and the world.

25 A similar dialogue involving visual perception happens in the famous Rorschach ink blot test. By presenting ambiguous visual information (a randomly produced ink blot), the patient reveals what's going on inside, what's driving his or her perceptive imagination. Thanks to my wife, Carolyn, for this example.

26 See Neil Bauman, 'Apophenia, audio pareidolia and musical ear syndrome', Center for Hearing Loss Help (9 July 2015), <http://hearinglosshelp.com/blog/apophenia-audio-pareidolia-and-musical-ear-syndrome>, accessed February 2023.

27 'Earworms' – songs, unbidden, playing continually in the mind – are typically experienced by people who have some degree of musical creativity, another instance of imagination shaping perception. Memories are 'heard' repeatedly, but in the mind, not the ears.

28 Though it is typically unconscious and reflexive, I can change the audio pattern if I concentrate on what I would *like* it to be. Sometimes the pattern reflects some idea or experience I have had that day. With white noise, I have found that this patterning activity is semiconscious, existing in the liminal area between reflex and intention.

This dialogue between our imaginations and our environment likely extends to our other senses as well, and to our overall sense of the world and ourselves within the world. Through this constant back-and-forth conversation with the world around us, we build up an imaginary landscape,[29] woven throughout with our expectations, presuppositions, biases, hopes, fears and, above all, desires.[30] The perceptive imagination is constantly interpreting our world, giving us the 'big picture', the overall sense of a story within which we are characters.[31]

In this sense, the real world *is* imaginary (though rooted, ultimately, in the physical reality around us). The perceptive imagination is the refracting lens through which our world is received and inflected. The imagination is 'our fundamental mode of insertion in the world',[32] situating us within the world we perceive around us.

This is not to endorse post-truth relativism – that each person *creates* his or her own truth about the world. In an age of 'fake news', conspiracy and science deniers, we must reassert: reality exists apart from our 'spin' on it. God's world is what it is, and our imagining activity can be in or out of line with *God's* original, authoritative imagining of his own creation. God's imagination has the final word. He is *God*, after all. But we shouldn't overlook the fact that this imagining activity is a fundamental part of our bearing God's image (Genesis 1:26–28). As we saw in chapter 5, we image our Creator by 'creating' a world in the act of perceiving it. Like God, we are fundamentally imaginative beings.

To experience God's world, we must imagine it. In continual conversation with the world around us, we project patterns, narratives and metaphors on it. The world, for every human, undergoes an involuntary

29 On the imaginary landscape, see the Introduction. It is the matrix that shapes perception, and out of which people in that society create, maintain or renew other imaginative works (art, institutions, entertainment, patterns of work and play and so on).

30 If this picture of the imagination is accurate, the implications for apologetics are enormous. Apologists often treat presuppositions and world views as though they were mere propositional information, mental data. Rather, world views are invariably embedded in a narrative, aesthetic, passional, imagistic and imaginative matrix. World views and presuppositions are creatures of this fundamental imaginative mode of human existence, this delicate interplay between human desire and the resistance of reality (general revelation) to our desires and assumptions. Christian apologetics needs to adapt to that imaginative context rather than expect non-Christians to adapt to their own linear, propositional methods.

31 See under 'The metaphors through which we see the world are shaped by the stories we inhabit (and vice versa)' later this chapter.

32 Langan, 'The Christian imagination', p. 64.

metaphorical transformation, so the world is seen *as* this or *as* that.[33] Naive empiricism assumes that our experience of the world is neutral, uninterpreted data. If this theory of perception is correct (there is still much debate), this much seems clear: our imaginations *are* active in our perception of the world. In fact, our world is infused with, experienced through and organized by our imagination. Imagination, far from being a distraction from rational thought, is necessary for any thinking, perceiving or interpretation whatsoever. The perceptive imagination – the lens of our 'eyes of the heart' – mediates our experience of the world. In this sense, the real world is imaginary.

The *creative imagination* creates *and* receives different worlds, alien imaginary landscapes

In addition to the perceptive imagination (the machine that's oscillating in the background, conversing with our surroundings to make sense of the world around us), there is also a more explicitly creative aspect to the imagination. The creative imagination is the tool storytellers employ when they say, 'Once upon a time, . . .' or when musicians compose and perform or film directors set up a shot or when children draw pictures or act out stories.

The creative imagination innovates and translates, allowing the mental images, sounds, colours, textures and words in the creator's mind to be realized in the external world as a cultural work. Such works create imaginary worlds. Thus, we image God, the original world-creator. J. R. R. Tolkien famously called it 'sub-creation', a derivative creating that draws on God's original creation.[34]

The creative imagination is required not only to create imaginary worlds but also to receive them. Enjoying cultural works – reading a story or a poem, listening to a song, watching a film or TV programme, or playing a video game – is never simply passive. To enjoy another's imaginative work, our imagination must *co-create* the world of the book,

[33] See under 'The perceptive and creative imaginations bleed into each other because they both operate by way of metaphor (seeing-as)' later this chapter.

[34] See J. R. R. Tolkien, 'On fairy-stories' in *Tree and Leaf* (London and New York: HarperCollins, 2001 [1964]), <https://archive.org/details/on-fairy-stories_202110>, accessed February 2023. An author or a child, by creating a world with internal coherence and consistency, becomes a mini-creator under God.

game, film or programme so that we can project ourselves into it and dwell there for a while. We must invest, 'buy into', that world using the currency of the energy of our creative imagination. The cultural work gives us a pattern according to which our imagination must build, and then we follow or resist that blueprint to co-create and inhabit the imaginary world.[35] Enjoying a cultural work is a collaborative imaginative project.

When I first saw *The Lord of the Rings: The Fellowship of the Ring* (2001), for example, it absolutely transported me. By the time the credits rolled, I had no idea what time it was. It took me a moment to reacclimatize, to return to the cinema. The experience of seeing it was like I had spent months travelling in and learning the ins and outs of this world, building it up in my imagination, thinking about where the story might go. Of course, it wasn't only the film having an impact on my imagination, as though I were being passively carried along by it. The film and I, *together*, shaped this imaginary world. My creative imagination inserted me into that world, creating space for me to travel with Frodo and company.

Perhaps you have had a similar experience, losing yourself in a book, film or computer game. Hours later, you look up at the clock and wonder where the time went. Time passes differently in these imaginary worlds. Your imagination becomes engrossed with learning detail after detail, getting a feel for the rules of the place, projecting outcomes and (in the case of games) planning strategies (a sort of flow state). This process is not merely an escape, diversion or distraction; it is a cooperative creation and inhabiting of an alternative reality. The 'work' part of a cultural work, then, is to provoke and guide our creative imaginations, and so goad us into world co-creation.[36]

35 Paul Ricoeur, considering the interaction between a novelist's and reader's imaginations, asserts that the novel lays down 'prescriptions for reading', a script that the author expects the reader to follow. But following that script requires imaginative work. See his *Time and Narrative*, Volume 3, tr. Kathleen Blamey and David Pellauer (Chicago, IL: University of Chicago Press, 1988), pp. 160–179. The role of the imagination in receiving a creative work can also be seen in imaginative failure or refusal. We put down the book or switch off the film saying, 'I don't get it' or 'It's just not my thing.' Without our permission and investment in the 'scripts' or patterns proposed by the creative work, the imaginative project cannot get off the ground.

36 For more on popular culture as projecting imaginary worlds for habitation, see my book *Popologetics: Popular culture in Christian perspective* (Phillipsburg, NJ: P&R, 2012), pp. 26–28. The idea of world habitation will become very important when we begin thinking through what Christian culture is for – the creation of oases, dwelling places for the imagination.

Dwelling in imaginary worlds projected by cultural works changes our consciousness, giving us a new perspective on the real world

Entertainment is never *mere* entertainment. Receiving culture, escaping into and dwelling in alternative imaginary worlds is anything but 'mere'.[37] Paul Ricoeur asserts that the experience of reading a novel 'refigures' the reader.[38] We come away profoundly changed.

How do creative works do this to us? Reading a novel or enjoying any creative work entangles the reader, viewer or player in a web of unfamiliar meanings and patterns.[39] In the case of a novel (Ricoeur's major focus), the reader's imagination is divided between the everyday experience of reality and the new reality that the novel is asking the reader to accept. As the reader plunges deeper into the work, the familiar patterns of life sink into the background and are replaced by the experience of a new, unfamiliar imaginary world. The reader learns to see things through other eyes. The imaginary world eventually loses its strangeness, but at a price: the reader changes. As the reader adapts to new, alien patterns of experience, his or her perspective alters, transforming the strange and new into the familiar and accepted, part of the reader. In this way, the imaginary world of the work shapes the reader, leaving its mark on his or her consciousness and perspective.

When reading a novel, we are inevitably drawn into a world of imaginative play, a place to experiment, to try on different perspectives and personas, seemingly without real-world consequences. We can slay a dragon without the danger of being burnt, feel what it is like to create a monster you cannot control without having the monster seek revenge on you. It seems risk- and consequence-free. But there are other

---

[37] Theologian and jazz musician William Edgar notes that, although entertainment can be degraded and trivial, the idea that it can have an effect on us runs deep. 'Entertainment' is derived from the French verb *entretenir*, to maintain a conversation. In its most profound form, entertainment 'is a conversation – with eternity'. See Glenda Mathes' interview with Edgar for *Ascribelog* (6 October 2010), <https://ascribelog.blogspot.com/2010/10/william-edgar-theologian-and-jazz.html>, accessed February 2023.

[38] See Paul Ricoeur, *Time and Narrative*, tr. Kathleen McLaughlin and David Pellauer (Chicago, IL: University of Chicago Press, 1984), vol. 1, pp. 70–82, and vol. 3, ch. 7.

[39] This paragraph draws heavily on Wolfgang Iser, *The Act of Reading: A theory of aesthetic response* (Baltimore, MD: Johns Hopkins University Press, 1978), pp. 155–159, and Ricoeur, *Time and Narrative*, Volume 3, chapter 7.

consequences. In being drawn into this fictional world with its new rules and assumptions, we are distanced from our old conceptions, biases and assumptions. The aesthetic pleasure of reading a book can transform our perspective on practical life and wisdom.[40]

Ricoeur and the literary theorists he draws on focused on novels, but we 'read' other cultural works as well. Though the effects differ from medium to medium, engaging and enjoying any imaginative cultural work leaves us subtly transformed. We acknowledge this implicitly when we say that a film or game 'took us on a journey'. We return from that journey not quite the same people we were when we departed.

Though we take it for granted, this facet of the creative imagination is the root of the moral imagination's freedom that we explored in chapter 5. It is part of being made in God's image – the ability to inhabit strange new worlds and see through strange new eyes.[41] As C. S. Lewis notes (about literature, but it applies to all creative works):

> We want to be more than ourselves . . . We want to see with other eyes, to imagine with other imaginations, to feel with other hearts, as well as with our own . . . We demand windows.[42]

Being able to enter other worlds allows us to gain a new perspective on our familiar world and assumptions. Fictional worlds set us free (or semi-free) from the world as we have known it. That limited freedom from our ordinary cultural perspectives mirrors God's absolute lordship over creation.[43] As we become disentangled and distanced from our status quo reality, we are freed to see the world afresh. That creative

40 Hans Robert Jauss, *Aesthetic Experience and Literary Hermeneutics*, tr. Michael Shaw (Minneapolis, MN: University of Minnesota Press, 1982), pp. 30–35. This dynamic – being drawn into an-other world, seeing through other eyes – may well drive the moral formation that Karen Swallow Prior notes in *On Reading Well: Finding the good life through great books* (Grand Rapids, MI: Brazos, 2018), especially pp. 19–22. Although her focus is on books, she recognizes that this happens in all art and entertainment (see p. 26).

41 God, being omniscient, sees and understands everything from every perspective immediately all the time, and can sift through these with perfect wisdom. For us, to learn even one other perspective, it has to be done over time. But the fact that we can do so at all testifies that we are made in his image.

42 C. S. Lewis, *An Experiment in Criticism* (Cambridge: Cambridge University Press, 1961), pp. 137–138. Quote by C. S. Lewis © copyright 1953 CS Lewis Pte Ltd. Used with permission.

43 Our freedom from cultural perspectives is not absolute. We do not attain a 'God's-eye view'. Our experience remains mediated through our cultural categories. But dwelling in imaginary worlds can reshape our cultural categories in ways that are real and significant.

insight is the beginning of resistance to evil in a world gone wrong because we can imagine the world *as different* from how it is. Though some may call entertainment 'escapism', this escape act has profound effects in the real world. We learn to escape from our usual assumptions into new ones. We gain, quite literally, a different 'world view', at least for a while.

One major consequence of this imaginative transformation is that it gives us empathy for those who are different from us. It moves us towards care. As Christian poet Wendell Berry puts it:

> Let [hope] be lighted also by the light that is within you,
> which is the light of imagination. By it you see
> the likeness of people in other places to yourself
> in your place. It lights invariably the need for care
> toward other people, other creatures, in other places
> as you would ask them for care toward your place and you.[44]

Within the imagination's ability to see other worlds, and so see this world differently, lie the sparks of resistance to evil. Langan asserts that we can 'distance ourselves from oppressive givens in order to re-interpret them' and 'empathize with situations different than our own'.[45] Writer and cultural critic Leon Wieseltier puts it even more vividly: the imagination, under the influence of art, helps us to transcend our own experience and pain to enter into the pain of others. This, he argues, is essential to moral goodness:

> Ethical principles are most commonly ascribed to the operations of reason, but we need to remind ourselves of the role of the imagination in moral action. Without the imagination, we would act only against wrongs that we ourselves have endured. We would be

44 Wendell Berry, excerpt from 'It is hard to have hope. It is harder as you grow old' in *This Day: Collected and new Sabbath poems* (New York: Counterpoint Press, 2013). Copyright © 2007 by Wendell Berry. Reprinted with the permission of The Permissions Company, LLC on behalf of Counterpoint Press, counterpointpress.com. Available online at <https://wordsfortheyear.com/2019/01/20/2007-vi-it-is-hard-to-have-hope-by-wendell-berry> and 'Wendell Berry reads a poem on hope', Moyers & Company, YouTube (3 October 2013), <www.youtube.com/watch?v=2j_r4jb9AYw&t=216s>, both accessed February 2023.

45 Langan, 'The Christian imagination', p. 65.

> prisoners of our experience – which is to say, the experience of people less lucky than ourselves would be incomprehensible to us . . . If this is so, then the old dichotomy between art and ethics, between the beautiful and the good, is not all we need to know about the place of art in life. Art, high and low, may play an indispensable role in the formation of virtue. One of the ways in which it does so is by picturing pain . . . Novels and poems and paintings and films and songs may bring the news of distant or hidden sufferings and abuses. By creating sympathy, art lays the ground, the internal condition, for moral behaviour.[46]

In the absence of such imaginative empathy, we care only for our own pain. Our politics becomes sub-ethical, selfish, abusive and deluded. By engaging the fictional, we relearn to see the real.

Through the imagination we can find hope in otherwise hopeless situations (as Neil Gaiman's account of his cousin Helen shows).[47] Hope gives us the leverage to resist evil. As Langan notes, 'Imagining is an act of hope, a challenge to fate, an effort to take matters to hand and to accept our unique role as human beings "in the world, but not of it".'[48] Thus, the creative imagination bleeds into the realm of the perceptive imagination. When we see something evil or ugly in the world, we can see it *as* evil or *as* ugly only because we can imagine the world in the light of hope, as better, as good, as beautiful. The human impulse to resist evil, decay, oppression and degradation, starts with the metaphorical imagination, with seeing-as. In this sense, every creative act of the imagination is at the same time potentially an act of resistance and subversion. The imagination gives humans dignity in the face of an oppressive or degrading reality.[49] For example, a well-publicized study of young readers of the

46 Leon Wieseltier, 'How voters' personal suffering overtook reason – and brought us Donald Trump', *Washington Post* (22 June 2016), <www.washingtonpost.com/posteverything/wp/2016/06/22/how-voters-personal-suffering-overtook-reason-and-brought-us-donald-trump/?utm_term=.dd65f67fef32>. A similar link between the imagination and moral compass/empathy is made by Sharon Hodde Miller, 'Evangelicals and the loss of prophetic imagination', *Mere Orthodoxy* (9 February 2017), <https://mereorthodoxy.com/evangelicals-loss-prophetic-imagination>, both accessed February 2023.

47 See Conclusion, chapter 4.

48 Langan, 'The Christian imagination', p. 65.

49 Langan, 'The Christian imagination', p. 65.

Harry Potter books found dwelling in that world reduced prejudice against migrants and minorities.[50]

There is no guarantee, however, that the transformation of perspective given by the creative imagination will lead inevitably in a direction that is good and right (the Romantic fallacy that 'art saves'). There have been periods of European and American history when politicians have captured the nation's imagination *not* to empathize but, instead, to demonize others, such as migrants fleeing persecution, deafening us to their pain. In the USA in the nineteenth century, the phrase 'manifest destiny' was wielded by presidents James Polk and William McKinley to agitate for the unjust and expansionist Mexican–American War, as well as anti-Mexican prejudice that persists to this day. A similar sort of imagination spurred Queen Victoria to expand the British Empire 'where the sun never sets', fuelling nationalist pride and racist sentiments that also can persist into the present.

Empathy does not, in itself, guarantee a better, more moral or biblical perspective on reality. It can leverage victimhood to generate a new intolerance of those it sees as past oppressors. Ironically, empathy can leverage hurt, bringing hurt to those who are now on the 'wrong side of history'. Empathy can be used to dispense with empathy, to humanize some and demonize others.[51] Imagination, apart from biblically guided compassion, is no guarantee of goodness.[52]

Good or bad, the creative imagination's overall influence on the real world around us is profound. Creating and inhabiting imaginary worlds leaves an enduring legacy of transformation.

---

[50] Loris Vezzali, Sofia Stathi, Dino Giovannini, Dora Capozza and Elena Trifiletti, 'The greatest magic of Harry Potter: Reducing prejudice', *Journal of Applied Psychology*, vol. 45, no. 2 (February 2015), pp. 105–121, <www.researchgate.net/publication/264162058_The_greatest_magic_of_Harry_Potter_Reducing_prejudice.>, accessed February 2023.

[51] See Wieseltier, 'How voters' personal suffering overtook reason – and brought us Donald Trump'.

[52] Christians, too, have been guilty of callous abuses (See Miller, 'Evangelicals and the loss of prophetic imagination'). Properly understood, the Bible gives us the foundation of true, complete compassion rather than a truncated, myopic focus on tolerance (a live-and-let-live perspective that is quite content to see people self-destruct spiritually). But compassion and empathy are essential. As Christian apologist Francis Schaeffer noted in *The God Who Is There* (Downers Grove, IL: InterVarsity Press, 1968), p. 36, 'There is nothing more ugly than a Christian orthodoxy without understanding or without compassion.'

The perceptive and creative imaginations bleed into each other because they both operate by way of metaphor (seeing-as)

Inhabiting the imaginary worlds of cultural works changes us and the way we perceive and act in the world. The creative and perceptive imaginations bleed into each other like watercolours on wet paper. The border between them is porous because the mental activity involved in perception and visual imagining mimic each other, employing similar brain pathways.[53] The patterns of eye movement are also similar, or even identical, when a person sees a scene or is asked to recreate a scene with eyes closed.[54]

What I have labelled the perceptive and creative imaginations are, in fact, two aspects of the same thing. They share a common modus operandi: metaphor, 'seeing-as'. A metaphor is a figure of speech commonly found in poetry but it also occurs far more widely. It means seeing one thing in terms of another: a sunset *as* a curtain of gold and crimson, a barbed-wire fence *as* death writ small. The imagination uses metaphor to connect our perceptions *and* creations to the meanings they elicit, the ways in which our experiences and creations resonate with us.

Thomas argues that seeing-as is the missing link between perception and creativity, between seeing what is there and inducing us 'to see things as we would not otherwise have seen them: to see fresh (or forgotten) aspects or meanings in an otherwise seemingly banal reality'.[55] The questioning, testing, patterning activity that enables perception and recognition[56] is a kissing cousin to the kind of creativity that illuminates unexpected connections between things, allowing the artist to dream up something that isn't really there. Normal perception is akin to creative metaphorical projection that opens up a whole new perspective,

---

53 See Zeidman and Maguire, 'Anterior hippocampus', particularly Figure 2.j. This mimicking activity happens particularly in the anterior medial hippocampus.

54 Bruno Laeng and Dinu-Stefan Teodorescu, 'Eye scanpaths during visual imagery reenact those of perception of the same visual scene', *Cognitive Science*, vol. 26, no. 2 (March–April 2002) pp. 207–231, cited in Colin Ware, *Visual Thinking for Design* (Burlington, MA: Morgan Kaufmann, 2008), p. 150. This mental mimicry may be related to mirror neurons.

55 Nigel J. T. Thomas, 'Are theories of imagery theories of imagination?' For an alternative but related philosophical account of creativity, see Margaret A. Boden, 'Creativity in a nutshell' in *The Creative Mind: Myths and mechanisms* (London: Routledge, 2004).

56 See under 'The *perceptive imagination* gives us our world' earlier this chapter.

a whole new imaginary world ('What if I try to play this song in a minor key or with a different set of chord changes?' 'What if I juxtaposed this image with this song, as in a music video or film score?' 'What if Abraham Lincoln slayed vampires in his time off?'). The activity of bringing unlike things into a close relationship to find something new – the business of metaphor – lies at the core of all cultural creativity.[57] Metaphor – this tensive vision that unites unlike things and projects strange models on to reality – links the two aspects of the imagination. The key to perception and recognition is also the key to creativity and innovation: seeing-as.[58]

Through metaphor, the imagination can transform our world in meaningful ways, enabling us to draw meaning from our experience. Consider a child playing with a beloved soft toy. For that moment, she imagines 'Mr Mittens' as a ferocious tiger, stalking prey in the jungle. She sees her toy cat *as* a terrifying predator by virtue of an imaginative projection of metaphorical meaning.

Imaginative seeing-as transforms the world in meaningful ways not only for children but also for us all. A director sees the boardroom as a battlefield. A student sees a ton of homework as a prison sentence. Jesus saw the crowds as sheep without a shepherd (Matthew 9:36). Each is doing what the girl is doing with her toy: seeing one thing in terms of another, finding meaning in the tension and space between the two. The girl is intentionally playing, whereas the director, student and Jesus were not, but the same imaginative transformative process informs the experience of each of them.

None of us simply perceives experience raw. Though our experience is rooted in physical reality, it is always more than that. We organize experience imaginatively, through one metaphorical lens or another. In this

---

57 Video essayist Kirby Ferguson has a fascinating study of cultural creativity in terms of three basic components: copying, transforming and combining. See his video essay, 'Everything is a remix remastered (2015 HD)', Kirby Ferguson, YouTube (17 May 2016), <www.youtube.com/watch?v=nJPERZDfyWc&t=4s>, accessed March 2023.

58 This applies as much to scientific creativity as it does to artistic creativity. Being able to create a metaphorical model so that it can help explain how the physical world works is the core component of scientific theorizing. Hence, physicists create metaphors to speak of light as a river (a 'flow' of energy) or a particle (photons 'bounce' off of different surfaces). See Paul Ricoeur, *The Rule of Metaphor: Multidisciplinary studies of the creation of meaning in language*, tr. Robert Czerny with Kathleen McLaughlin and John Costello (Toronto, Ontario: University of Toronto Press, 1977), pp. 239–246.

sense, the world we dwell in is *imaginary*, though not (wholly) fictional. Our worlds are inflected through the imaginative matrices of our anxieties, expectations, hopes and desires (our imaginary landscapes). The meaning of our world and everything in it is formed and informed by networks of interlocking metaphors.[59] Imagination informs perception through metaphor.

The creative imagination *also* works through metaphor; seeing-as is the creative engine that drives poetry. We can see time *as* a river; or my love *as* a red, red rose; or a hedgehog *as* a walking pincushion. We can even see poems *as* cars, complete with engines that drive them. Metaphor provides us with a way of seeing reality that goes beyond the obvious, penetrating into the meaning of things. Through the imagination we learn to see *and* create the world anew, bathed in a different light.

The practical implications of metaphor are immense. You can see an obstacle *as* an opportunity or an argument with your wife *as* a chance for you to understand her better (or, conversely, *as* another brick in the wall separating you). This ability to see things as different lies at the heart of all cultural creation, in songs, stories, games, images, dramas, architecture and so on. Each begins with a moment of seeing (or hearing or feeling) something known in terms of something other (scientific exploration in terms of self-destruction in *Frankenstein*, for example, or a symphony as an invocation of death in Beethoven's Fifth Symphony). Cultural creation and perception both begin in such metaphorizing.

Not that metaphor ever becomes wholly independent from the world around us – not if we remain sane, at any rate. Even the little girl playing with her toy responds when her mother calls her for dinner. She leaves the 'tiger' loose in her bedroom and goes to eat. In a similar way, the world (*God's* world) reserves the right to rein in, disrupt or confirm our assumed

---

59 The interface between metaphors and our social experience is explored in George Lakoff and Mark Johnson's classic *Metaphors We Live By* (Chicago, IL: University of Chicago Press, 2003). Different but complementary perspectives are offered by anthropologist Victor Turner's work, *The Ritual Process: Structure and anti-structure* (Hawthorne, NY: Aldine de Gruyter, 1969) and sociologist Erving Goffman's work that sees social interaction as drama in *The Presentation of Self in Everyday Life* (New York: Doubleday, 1959). Both ritual and the social drama are, at bottom, embodied metaphors that render our lives interpretable, ways of seeing oneself and one's community in terms of enacted symbols, a seeing-as (self as part of the whole, self as a member of a social stratum or as an advocate for a cause and so on). Aside from their functional uses, cultural performances and artefacts are embodied metaphors.

metaphorical associations.[60] The embattled director finds unexpected compromise. The homework-bound student finds herself enjoying her reading. Jesus found that the crowds were quite like wandering sheep and, worse, sheep with fangs. The real world has meanings of its own.[61] It intrudes and 'talks back' to our expectations and metaphorical associations. Meaning and truth emerge from that dialogue. The imagination is always in play throughout that conversation, through networks of metaphors woven into our perception of and creative responses to the world.

The metaphors through which we see the world are shaped by the stories we inhabit (and vice versa)

Where do these networks of metaphors come from? From parental wisdom, peer perspectives, communal assumptions that we absorb and, often, from the art and entertainment we connect with. These deliver stories, images, songs and gameplay that shape our experience of reality. The stories that capture our imaginations shape our sense of our *own* story, the narrative space from which we see, feel and live in the world. The story-worlds we inhabit grind the lenses (of the heart) and it is through these that we intuitively understand and respond to reality.

Smith asserts that:

> our action emerges from how we imagine the world. What we do is driven by who we are, by the kind of person we have become. And that shaping of our character is, to a great extent, the effect of stories that have captivated us, that have sunk into our bones – stories that 'picture' what we think life is about, what constitutes 'the good life'. We live into the stories we've absorbed; we become characters in the drama that has captivated us.[62]

---

60 For the Christian, God is both Creator and observing participant in his creation. His interpretation serves as an authoritative baseline of what reality truly is. Both general and special revelation ground our interpretations in the (mediated) real. For non-Christians (especially in postmodern/poststructuralist theory), nothing lies beyond our interpretations. There is no final authority for choosing between competing interpretations. There is no dialogue with the Real.

61 This is partly what I meant when I said meaningful creation is the ultimate context for our imaginations in chapter 5, under heading 'Our creativity takes place against the backdrop of God's creativity, our imaginations derive meaning from his imagination'.

62 Smith, *Imagining the Kingdom*, loc. 833 or p. 32 (and the whole of chapter 3). See also Paul Ricoeur, 'Life in quest of narrative' in David Wood (ed.), *On Paul Ricoeur: Narrative and Interpretation* (London: Routledge, 1991). See also Ricoeur, 'Narrative identity', tr. Mark S. Muldoon, *Philosophy Today*, vol. 35, no. 1 (Spring 1991), pp. 73–81, <www.scribd.com/doc/24868946/Paul-Ricoeur-Narrative-Identity>, accessed February 2023..

In other words, our imaginations render our lives meaningful by placing us in a story. The shape of that story is largely determined by the kinds of stories that 'have sunk into our bones'. Think of the director living out a story as the Boardroom Warrior, Captain of Industry, someone who *will* leave his mark (perhaps motivated by a father who repeatedly told him that he would never amount to anything or the film *The Wolf of Wall Street*). Our moral and spiritual character is formed by the characters we play in the narrative of our lives (a certain ruthlessness creeps in if one aspires to be the Boardroom Warrior). That story gives us a 'picture', Smith tells us – not a picture that we look at but a picture we see *through*, a lens. Given the story we inhabit, we learn to see the people and things in our lives *as* this or that, in light of certain meanings and perspectives. The imagination creatively, meaningfully shapes our raw experience[63] by positioning us in a story, a connected system of metaphors, ways of 'seeing-as'. That is how meaning emerges in our lives – through a creative and metaphorical perspective on things.[64]

Cultural creativity is important because creative works propose the way that the world is, or could and should be. That proposal can profoundly shape the life-story a person inhabits, the metaphorical lens through which he or she sees the world. Creation and perception are constantly engaged in intimate dialogue in the imagination. The creative imagination projects imaginary worlds that potentially can give us a new perspective on the real world, reshaping the perceptive imagination. Likewise, our perception equips us with experiences and metaphors through which we interpret the fictional worlds of the creative imagination. The creative and perceptive imagination are different in goal, but not in mode of operation. One reconstructs the *real* world in a way that is meaningful to us; the other

63 Remember that 'raw experience' is never simply empirical reality. It is empirical reality shot through with God's general revelation (empirical reality is general revelation). We formulate our stories in the ultimate context of God's story told through his creation (see Psalm 19:1–4; Romans 1:18–25).

64 See Calvin Seerveld, *Rainbows for the Fallen World* (Toronto, Ontario: Toronto Tuppence Press, 2005 [1980]), pp. 46–47, and Ricoeur's definitive work on metaphor, *The Rule of Metaphor*, especially chapters 6 and 7. See also his 'Metaphor and the central problem of hermeneutics' in *Hermeneutics and the Human Sciences*, tr. and ed. John B. Thompson (Cambridge: Cambridge University Press, 1982). For a Christian take on Ricoeur's analysis of metaphor and culture, see Theodore Turnau, 'Re-imagining Ricoeur: Popular culture as discursive text, metaphor, and narrative', PhD thesis, Westminster Theological Seminary, Glenside, PA (1999), especially chapters 3 to 5.

constructs *fictional* worlds in a way that is meaningful to us. Our overall sense of meaning, of 'at-homeness' in worlds (real and imaginary), emerges from the conversation between creativity and perceptivity. That conversation is possible because both speak dialects of the same language: narrative and metaphor, story-driven seeing-as.

Together, the perceptive and creative imagination shape, reflect and inform our emotional landscapes, drawing on desire in a subterranean way, making the world *our* world

This narrative and metaphorical shaping of creativity and perception changes not only how we think, but also how we feel and act. As noted under the heading 'Imagination is the arena of dialogue between body and mind', near the beginning of this chapter, the imagination isn't just rooted in the mind; it is also rooted in the body's habits and in our passional life. The imagination reconfigures desire.

For Smith, imagination-shaped desire lies at the foundation of human identity: 'human persons are not primarily or for the most part thinkers, or even believers. Instead, human persons are – fundamentally and primordially – lovers.'[65] By 'lovers', Smith means our deep affection for persons, things and (especially) visions of the world that express our take on flourishing and human happiness. Love is a disposition, a trained habit of the heart that lurks in the subterranean cellars of the psyche, below consciousness. Human identity centres not on what we think or believe, but on what we love and how we express that love.

Cultural stories draw us in because they connect with our loves at the level of our passions and emotions: 'such stories capture our imagination precisely because narrative trains our emotions, and those emotions actually condition our perception of the world.'[66] As I said, creative imagination (that which creates and inhabits fictional worlds) shapes our perceptive imagination (that which connects us to the real world). Through imaginative stories and metaphors, we receive and respond to a world interwoven with our loves and desires.

---

[65] Smith, *Desiring the Kingdom: Worship, worldview, and cultural formation*, Cultural Liturgies, Volume 1 (Grand Rapids, MI: Baker Academic, 2009), p. 41.
[66] Smith, *Imagining the Kingdom*, loc. 833 or p. 32.

In this way the world becomes *our* world, a 'home'. How? The imagination gives the world an expressive 'face', drawing on our loves and desires to give it a recognizable expression. In a fascinating account, philosopher Kathleen Lennon draws on Ludwig Wittgenstein's concept of 'physiognomy' to explain the 'imaginary texture of the real'.[67] What we perceive is not only data about the world but also a world interlaced with emotional value *for us*. 'Physiognomy' refers to the way a person's character or mood can be read immediately from the expression on his or her face. We don't analyse the physiological details of the face to read emotion (the eyebrows are raised X millimetres and so forth). Rather, we instantly see a whole pattern that tells us how this person feels inside. We 'read' faces and respond accordingly ('Better avoid him. He looks to be in a foul mood!').[68] We read the physiognomy, imaginatively and intuitively connecting what we see on the surface of the face and the emotional texture of the person's inner life.

The world around us has a physiognomy as well, an emotional weight that we can read and allows us to relate to it as our home. Lennon mentions an example from philosopher Martin Heidegger about visiting his old school:

> The high school building, for us who return to it, thirty years later, as for those who occupy it today, is not so much an object which it would be useful or possible to describe by its characteristics, as it is a certain odor, a certain affective texture which holds sway over a certain vicinity of space.[69]

In other words, the imagination is attuned to the emotional investments that make the world *our* world. We perceive our world according to its emotional texture – our attitudes, dispositions and desires regarding

67 The phrase was coined by French phenomenologist Maurice Merleau-Ponty, quoted in Kathleen Lennon, 'Re-enchanting the world: The role of imagination in perception', *Philosophy*, vol. 85, no. 33 (July 2010), pp. 375–389.

68 Lennon, 'Re-enchanting the world', pp. 376–377. Though Lennon does not mention mirror neurons, they might provide the biological mechanism that enables this intuitive pattern recognition. Individuals with autism spectrum disorder manifest damaged perceptive imaginations and are less able to make the instantaneous metaphorical connections needed to read emotional patterns. They compensate by focusing on details.

69 Martin Heidegger, *Introduction to Metaphysics*, tr. Ralph Mannheim (New Haven, CT: Yale University Press, 1974), pp. 27–28, cited in Lennon, 'Re-enchanting the world', p. 378.

it – or what Lennon calls 'affective logic'.[70] Our imaginative investments in the world are the precondition for valuing the world, for experiencing it as *our* world.

In this sense, our experience of the world is itself a creature of the imagination, creative and desire-laden.[71] We experience the world around us through the stories and metaphors that surround our lives, drawing on and configuring desire and our emotional responses. Our perception of the world creates an emotionally evocative terrain, an imaginary landscape. In perception, we involuntarily invest the world with emotional shape and weight. Desire courses through the narratives and metaphors that colour our world.

Desire emerges from the imagination by means of metaphor, seeing-as. For example, we *see* an apartment *as* our home (or *as* an intolerable dungeon); we *see* this school *as* our old stomping ground (or *as* our former prison); we *see* this child *as* a gift (or *as* a burden). A stranger might look at the same apartment and see only an apartment. It's our imagination that allows us to see the same bricks and mortar as something more – hopefully, home and all that means to us rather than a dungeon.

The imagination fills our world with stories and metaphorical associations that guide our emotional responses. Our imagination plants spreading networks of metaphor and narrative that fill our world with meanings rooted in our heart's desires. The real world is not neutral data – it is an imaginary landscape each of us carries within. It is not fictional; rather, it is the real imaginatively inflected.[72]

An analogous process occurs when we experience made-up worlds. We bring our everyday network of familiar narratives and metaphorical associations (seeing-as) into the realm of pure fiction – giving the fictional

70 Lennon, 'Re-enchanting the world', pp. 382–385.

71 Again, our experience is fundamentally rooted in physical reality. My point is that our experience is much more than unfiltered sensory data.

72 Lennon is quick to point out that 'to recognise the creative role of the imagination in perception is not to turn the shape the world takes for us into a mere fiction' ('Re-enchanting the world', p. 387). The world is as it is, and some imaginative patterns, some physiognomies, simply will not fit (such as conspiracy theories). See under 'The *perceptive imagination* gives us our world. In a sense, the real world is imaginary' earlier this chapter. From a Christian perspective, God's imaginative reading of his own creation rules, and we either conform or fail to conform our own imaginative perceptions of the world to his pattern. There are such things as obedient and disobedient imaginations.

world a physiognomy. We experience fictional worlds by extending our imaginative, desire-laden vision of the real world into conversations with unreal, fictional worlds (and vice versa).[73]

Over time, we become familiar with the physiognomies of those fictional worlds and so come to 'own' them. We call Oz or Tatooine or Middle-earth 'home' (especially when the real world becomes threatening or tiresome). Both real and fictional worlds are transformed into our worlds by imagination and desire.

This shift between receiving the real world and an imaginary one is a gear change for the imagination, but it is hardly a different vehicle. Not only do both the perceptive and creative imaginations employ metaphor and narrative; both draw on the very personal matrix of desire to invest in their respective worlds.

Imaginations are more like captured beasts than trained circus animals

Smith asserts that imaginations are trained by habit. Repeated social rituals carve familiar contours and furrows into the imagination over time, just as wind and rain erode riverbeds and canyons. Each set of social practices comes with its own implied imaginative vision of how the world is and should be.[74] These imaginative visions, in turn, shape our loves and desires, all without (much) conscious reflection. They habituate us to a certain imaginative perspective that inflames our hearts towards one ultimate aim or another.

Take shopping.[75] Shopping habituates us to a certain story in which we are inadequate (the ads tell us so), but not beyond redemption. Buying this or that product will make us better, sexier, more fulfilled versions of ourselves. Partake of the sacrament at the cash register and receive the promised salvation! Until, that is, the purchase becomes passé, boring and we hunger for a new salvific purchase.

73 That is, the conversation flows both ways. Not only do our perceptive imaginations shape our experience of imaginary, fictional worlds, but those fictional worlds shape our perceptive imaginations as well.

74 Smith, *Desiring the Kingdom*, pp. 46–71. Note the role of metaphor: reality is seen *as* this or that which is conducive to human flourishing.

75 The following account is a paraphrase of Smith, *Desiring the Kingdom*, pp. 93–103.

Thus, the consumer's imagination is formed; we are trained into consumer desire. Such social rituals become forms of worship that steer our imaginations away from the Christian faith. They erode our first love as we are sucked, imagination first, into desires that run counter to Christian compassion.

Culture, Smith says, is chock full of such anti-Christian sets of ritual and worship, practical regimes that shape our imaginations and desires *away* from the concerns of the kingdom of God. He advises Christians to abstain as much as possible from these non-Christian cultural practices. Instead, cultivate counter-practices, counter-rituals that radiate Christian compassion, not only on Sunday but every day through a 'new monasticism'.[76] He does not mean a 'strategic withdrawal' from culture (as Dreher does) but, rather, a set of spiritual disciplines (derived from Augustine) that help us to live for the City of God *within and with love for* those of the City of Man.[77] Left unchecked, worldly politics can warp our imaginations, leading to a culture-warring mentality, so he calls for a critical, ambivalent, cultural engagement in the Augustinian mode.[78]

For Smith, the pattern that forms imaginations is clear: habitual practice (ritual) shapes the imagination, and imagination shapes desire. Involving yourself in implicitly anti-Christian practices (such as consumerism) undermines the Christian imagination and desire. Recapture the correct practices and imagination is reformed, reorientating desire towards the right ends.

---

76 Smith, *Desiring the Kingdom*, pp. 209–213.

77 Dreher and Smith had been in dialogue, but parted ways in March 2017. Smith objected to Dreher's fear-stoking tactics, writing a trenchant and highly visible essay in the *Washington Post*, 'The new alarmism: How some Christians are stoking fear rather than hope' (10 March 2017), <www.washingtonpost.com/news/acts-of-faith/wp/2017/03/10/the-new-alarmism-how-some-christians-are-stoking-fear-rather-than-hope>, followed closely by his review of Dreher's *The Benedict Option: A strategy for Christians in a post-Christian nation* (New York: Sentinel, 2017), 'The Benedict option or the Augustinian call: Considering two ancient options for the contemporary church', *Comment* (16 March 2017), <www.cardus.ca/comment/article/the-benedict-option-or-the-augustinian-call>, both accessed February 2023. Smith's *Awaiting the King: Reforming public theology*, Cultural Liturgies, Volume 3 (Grand Rapids, MI: Baker Academic, Kindle edn, 2017) is essentially a guide for navigating the politics of the secular world without compromising the faith.

78 I am more optimistic than Smith that we can recognize and enjoy common grace in culture *and* maintain the antithesis between the City of God and City of Man. Smith prefers to replace common grace with what he calls 'craters of the gospel', cultural inheritances that have influenced liberal democracy which make sense only within the context of the Christian faith (what apologist Cornelius Van Til called 'borrowed capital'). See Smith, *Awaiting the King*, chapter 3, loc. 2763–3796. I believe common grace leads us to expect borrowed capital even in cultures that have not been influenced by a history of gospel proclamation and practice.

Surely habit shapes the imagination and desire – hence the long tradition of Christian disciplines. The pattern seems a bit too tidy, however, too linear: ritual X leads to imaginative vision Y, which in turn leads to desire Z. The imagination is not so predictable, not some tame animal that we can train to perform as we wish, like an elephant at the circus. The intertwining of the imagination and desire is messier and more surprising. At least, that has been the experience of fans of media franchises.

Media fans are, if nothing else, people in the grip of wild and powerful imaginations. If you ask fans for their 'origin stories' (how they became fans), you don't hear tales of training desire, shaping the imagination through repeated rituals. They didn't choose their fandom – it spontaneously 'chose' them. Listen to the fans and you hear stories about a gradual or rapid awakening of desire akin to falling in love or even religious conversion.[79] They weren't looking for it or working towards it through disciplined practice. Rather, they talk of imaginative cultural works sneaking up on them from behind and taking them down like a pack of wild dogs: 'A friend said I should watch this show, and I did, and it caught me, and I was hooked. I just fell in love with it.'

Phrases such as 'getting hooked' and 'falling in love' reveal the curious and unpredictable interweaving of the imagination and desire. It is not about repetition, practice and being in control – that comes later. It is about being magnetically drawn by something outside yourself that you find powerfully attractive. There is an unlooked for, surprising and addictive quality when dealing with the imagination. Addiction is a subtle mixture of active and passive, of being captured and wilfully pursuing, of control and losing control to something other than you (perhaps another reason why some Christians find the imagination so disturbing).

[79] Fans sometimes draw on the vocabulary of religious conversion. Becoming a fan is like 'getting saved' or 'finding God'. Such language reveals a sudden, unlooked-for transformation. The analogue runs deep – Christians say that they 'found God', but who found whom? Conversion depends not on our choice or effort but on God pursuing us and changing our desires and imaginations. Something like that takes place for fans when a particular show or piece of music reaches out and grabs them. For more of these parallels, see Daniel Cavicchi, *Tramps Like Us: Music and meaning among Springsteen fans* (Oxford: Oxford University Press, 1998), pp. 41–57, and Mark Duffet, *Understanding Fandom: An introduction to the study of media fan culture* (London and New York: Bloomsbury Academic, 2013), pp. 153 ff. See also Emily Mills, 'Ascent into madness: The story of my personal conversion to fandom', *Whoosh*, vol. 53 (February 2001), <http://whoosh.org/issue53/mills1.html#pussycat>, accessed February 2023.

Smith is right: habitual action (ritual) does play a big role in carving the canals through which imagination flows, paths that inform our worlds (both real and fictional). Imaginations are formed not only by how we think but also by what communities we are part of, what we do with our time and energy and the types of cultural experiences and entertainments we enjoy, the imaginary worlds we inhabit. We *should* be intentional and reflective about the culture we consume, and how we consume it. The Christian community also needs to think long and hard about the culture it creates. Cultural habits matter.

But Smith doesn't seem to leave much room for being blindsided by the imagination, a common experience among media fans. Can we do justice to both the habitual and unlooked-for/captivating aspects of the imagination? Is there a way to combine ritual and surprise?

I think there is. Repeated practice prepares us for imaginative revelation and transformation. Ritual sets the table for epiphany.[80] When Christians get a fresh grasp on God's grace and leave with their imaginations renewed, there is probably a history of struggle and persevering through dry times by repeated spiritual practices (prayer, reading Scripture, worship).[81] Likewise, media fans are generally involved in rituals involving the media (watching, listening, playing) that prime them for the 'revelation' of that new programme/musician/game a friend shared with them, the one that changed everything.

In both cases, usually there is an admixture of ritual and surprise. But not always. I would like to reserve a space for the imagination as a wildcard, for imaginative epiphanies that catch us with little preparation, that seem to come out of nowhere. Leave space for the imagination to be the wild beast that it is.

Though habits have an influence, no-one simply shapes their own imagination. It is always already in dialogue with desires and life experiences. It is notoriously hard to pin down, blowing this way and that,

80 This happens with negative experiences as well. Many of my 'Understanding media fandom' course students report being bullied and excluded at school because they were different. Repeated experiences of rejection and isolation prepared them for their 'fan conversion'.

81 Smith makes this point in *Imagining the Kingdom*, in chapter 4, but he never really explores the unpredictability of the imagination, emphasizing instead the habituated nature of desire and imagination.

like the wind, like the Holy Spirit (see John 3:8).[82] The Spirit can speak through the imagination in ways that rational argument cannot precisely because of this free, unpredictable, desire-pulling, addictive quality of the imagination. And that makes it slippery and resistant to the type of control that Smith envisages. Not that I'm against Christians undertaking repeated practices, being disciplined or undertaking rituals, but I remain sceptical that these can do all the heavy lifting Smith thinks they will. It can set the table for imaginative epiphany, but the beast can and often does come charging in unannounced and uninvited.

Still, there are ropes (or Poké Balls) that can lasso a wild imagination. The imagination *can* be enticed, fascinated, mesmerized and caught. That is why having Christian cultural works which are engrossing, inviting and awe-inspiring *to non-Christians* is so important for the church and our broader cultural witness to the reality of God.

As a people devoted to Christ, we need gifted members who are able to build enticing homes (oases) for the imagination, fictional worlds that delightfully ensnare wandering imaginations and so engage the addictive quality of the imagination, leading it towards what is most deeply good. If the imagination is as I say it is, we are called as a church to be about the business of creating works of the imagination that are compelling, don't turn people away and aren't easy to dismiss. I think much of the struggle that the church has had in post-Christian Europe and North America boils down to this: Christians don't understand the imagination, so they create kitsch and propaganda-led imaginative worlds that no-one but Christians are interested in visiting, much less living in.[83] Understanding the imagination better will help us become better imagination hunters.

Everyone has an imagination

Everyone has a beast dwelling within – that creative impulse through which we see the world and create and enjoy cultural works. Though every child intuitively knows this, we learn to suppress and silence the imagination. It lurks there nonetheless. The imagination is not the private reserve

[82] I did *not* say that imagination is the Holy Spirit, though I did say in chapter 6 that the Holy Spirit animates the imagination. He is the precondition for human imagination, breathing life into it and restraining it from being as wayward or evil as it could be (common grace).

[83] We will explore this in more detail in chapter 8.

of creative and artsy types, not an optional part of our personhood. It is a common possession that runs both wide and deep. When we talk about the imagination, we must remember that it is not a cast of the 'haves' (artists, musicians, writers) and 'have-nots' (accountants, janitors, shop assistants). *Everyone* has an imagination.

The real question is: what type of imagination does each person have? What sorts of narratives and metaphors guide the direction of their imaginative activity in their reshaping of the world? What glasses do the eyes of their heart wear? The imagination is the fundamental medium through which human experience is shaped. Desires, dreams, hopes, anxieties and terrors – not to mention more intellectual modelling and theorizing – all connect with reality through the imagination. And this is true of every human being.

All this is not to ignore the calling of those who are especially talented and have honed their creative imaginations to delight, challenge and encourage others. In chapter 16 we will examine the role of artists within the church. Their role, however, is not as specially anointed superhumans. It is pastoral, to encourage and strengthen the imaginations around them. Everyone has an imagination, and it has a huge role to play in the way we dwell in God's world and our aesthetic witness in post-Christian cultures.

Conclusion: gaining clarity on imagination

This is by no means a complete picture. It would take several books to cover the many thinkers who have weighed in on the topic. Nothing ignites the imagination of theoretical and scientific minds quite like the imagination. But the picture is clear enough: the witness of nature (general revelation) to the imagination dovetails with what we learn from the Bible. Together they form a Christian theory of imagination: a faculty not only of creation but also of perception of worlds both real and imaginary.

Now that we have a basic understanding of the imagination in general, we can ask the next question: is there such a thing as a distinctively *Christian* imagination? Is there a genuinely Christian focus of the eyes of the heart, a seeing-as, a pair of glasses that lays bare the reality of our faith? And more: is there a Christian way to imagine and create that is particularly effective in a post-Christian cultural context? That is our task in part 3.

Part 3

SHARPENING OUR FOCUS: CONSIDERING CHRISTIAN IMAGINATION AND ART

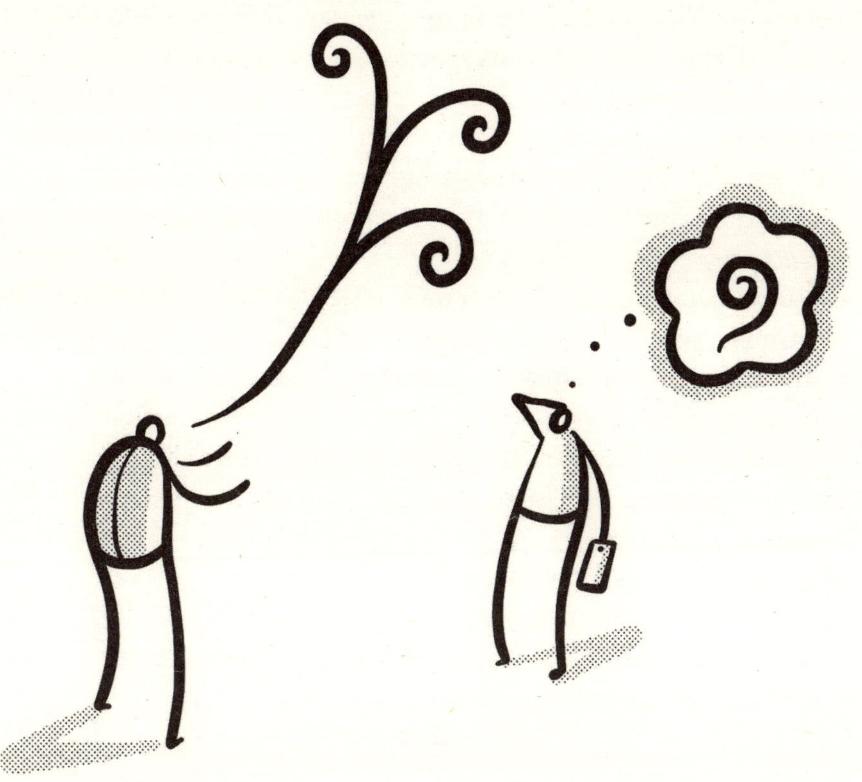

In part 2 we explored the imagination in general, the 'eyes of the heart' that shape both perception and creation. Surely the *Christian* imagination has a distinctive shape, right?

Not everyone agrees. Many artists of faith fear being pigeonholed. They would prefer to be known as 'an artist who is Christian' rather than 'a Christian artist'. Makoto Fujimura asserts, 'The Spirit does not read labels.'[1] He fears that labelling art undermines the generosity necessary for cultural healing and nurture, and that Christians will miss what the Spirit is doing in the arts *outside* the confines of the church. He's not wrong. In chapter 14 we will discuss a film by Krzysztof Kieślowski, a self-professed agnostic, that illuminates a Christian perspective on life better than most Christian films. And that's not an isolated case.

However, if the imagination shapes all life as a major conduit of faith, there *must* be something distinctive about the Christian imagination, a distinctively Christian prescription lens for the eye of the heart. There are certainly many examples of its opposite, sub-Christian imaginations – metaphorical networks that give us a life devoid of grace and mercy. A politics-shaped imagination sees life in terms of acquiring power, using alliances for leverage and so on. An economics-shaped imagination sees relationships as something to invest in so that you get some sort of return: affection, sex, friendship or networking contacts. An entertainment-shaped imagination sees life as an endless stream of potential amusement and distraction with an ultimate goal: collect as many entertaining moments as you can before you die. Each of these is sub-Christian. They quench the Spirit, undermine our motivation to live for God and make the gospel seem weird and superfluous rather than the pearl of great price it really is.

It is disturbingly easy to develop a sub-Christian imagination. Cultural voices and images surround us, pulling us towards the sub-Christian life. That is why culture and imagination are, above all, *spiritual* realities that cannot be ignored. We are constantly steered towards sub-Christian types of seeing-as that beckon us to envision:

- our jobs as simply a means to an end, a way to earn money;
- our marriages as convenient, comfortable relationships, if a bit boring;

1 Makoto Fujimura, *Art and Faith: A theology of making* (New Haven, CT, and London: Yale University Press, 2020), p. 35.

- our children as needy, annoying creatures we need a break from;
- the world as an address, a place to merely exist, perhaps finding a little joy while on holiday, and then we die.

The Christian imagination should open us up to so much more grace, mercy, beauty and *reality*. That is why creative cultural works that address and engage the imaginary landscape are vital not only for our aesthetic witness to non-Christians but also as a much-needed encouragement for Christians. Planting oases matters.

Part 3 asks the question, what makes an imagination Christian, and what sorts of imagination are best suited to planting oases? What's art for, and what sorts of Christian art help or hinder our witness to the watching world, and to one another?

7

Contours of the Christian imagination

Introduction: beyond the bubble into the oasis

These are challenging times for growing, forming, sustaining and creating from a Christian imagination. Close your eyes and envision the post-Christian world as a landscape. What do you see in your mind's eye? A desert? A wasteland? An overgrown, weedy swamp? A city-scape with a dazzling, chaotic array of lights and distractions? Each image emphasizes a different aspect of post-Christian culture (spiritual dryness, lack of direction, dangerous confusion, tempting glitter and energy).

But it's not all darkness. Culture is complex, never entirely good or bad. There are places that resonate with grace and beauty where Christians can find connections to the things God treasures: wisdom, mercy, forgiveness, integrity, humility, gentleness and justice. The imaginary landscape of any culture is going to be a mixed bag. It's into that messy mixture that we must learn to build bridges and speak our cultural peace with nuance.

Close your eyes again and picture a creative work that manifests a winsome and wise Christian imagination in a post-Christian imaginary landscape. What do you see? I see an oasis. You might see a shelter, a shady grove, a cool stream or a quiet park – all places that invite the weary, harried traveller in for rest, refreshment and reflection.

Too often, Christians see their culture not as an oasis but as a fortress, a walled city to keep undesirables out, a bubble that hermetically seals us off from the dangerous world around. Fortress culture is a sign of fear. We see the world as toxic and tainted, a holiness-corrupting contagion that might infect us or our children. That fear is understandable. No-one wants to expose children to cultural works that they are not ready for.[1] No-one who seeks to be faithful wants to be exposed to haunting temptations. Christians in post-Christian culture feel like salmon, tired of swimming against the current. It's tempting to erect a walled-off safe space, a subculture into which we can retreat, shielded from the currents of mainstream unbelief.

However, erecting barriers to protect ourselves from non-Christian culture (and non-Christians) is a luxury that we simply cannot afford. Such a cultural posture, in effect, means turning our backs on the rest of the world Jesus called us into. Refusing to engage and hunkering down in our bubble is not an option for biblically faithful Christians. Rather, we are called to engage the surrounding culture in a healing way, to share the shalom the Lord has blessed us with. Christian philosopher Calvin Seerveld puts it beautifully: 'The scriptural direction is singularly clear: give back to the Lord and to your neighbour the gifts the Lord has given you, in a ministry of reconciliation (2 Corinthians 5:17–19), joyously redeeming the time despite the tears (Colossians 4:5, 6).'[2]

Christian culture at its best is *shared* culture, a site of hospitality. It should invite the outsider to enter into a different imaginary world to be challenged, encouraged, enriched and renewed. Christian culture should strive to create breathable, open oases for the imagination, spaces both Christians and non-Christians can inhabit and explore. Such shared imaginary dwellings can lead to interesting and important spiritual conversations that lead both Christians and non-Christians to discover common human desires, questions and spiritual longings, challenging them to rethink and reimagine what they took for granted, encouraging them both to move deeper into the adventure and take the plunge. We don't need bubbles, we need oases.

What sorts of Christian cultural works plant oases for the imagination? What sorts of art and entertainment will open that space of invitation? And what sorts of Christian cultural works push away the jaded and uninitiated?

1 On guidance for encountering popular culture with kids, see a book I co-wrote with E. Stephen Burnett and Jared Moore, *The Pop Culture Parent: Helping kids engage their world for Christ* (Greensboro, NC: New Growth Press, 2020).

2 Calvin Seerveld, *Bearing Fresh Olive Leaves: Alternative steps in understanding art* (Carlisle and Toronto, Ontario: Toronto Tuppence Press/Piquant Press, 2000), p. 156.

Christian imagination that resonates most profoundly in a culture of unbelief has a characteristic tension and balance – what I call 'brightness control' and 'volume control'.

Brightness control: the tension between the darkness and the light

A Christian imagination sees all of life through the lens of the Christian world-story: creation, fall, redemption/new creation. It sees the world *as* God's (good because he created it), *as* twisted by sin (because we rebelled against him) and *as* heading for healing, redemption and cosmic renewal and reunion with God (because God mercifully intervened through Christ's death and resurrection, the inauguration of a new creation). But if we were to focus on one central aspect of the Christian story, the redemption accomplished through the cross and empty tomb surely

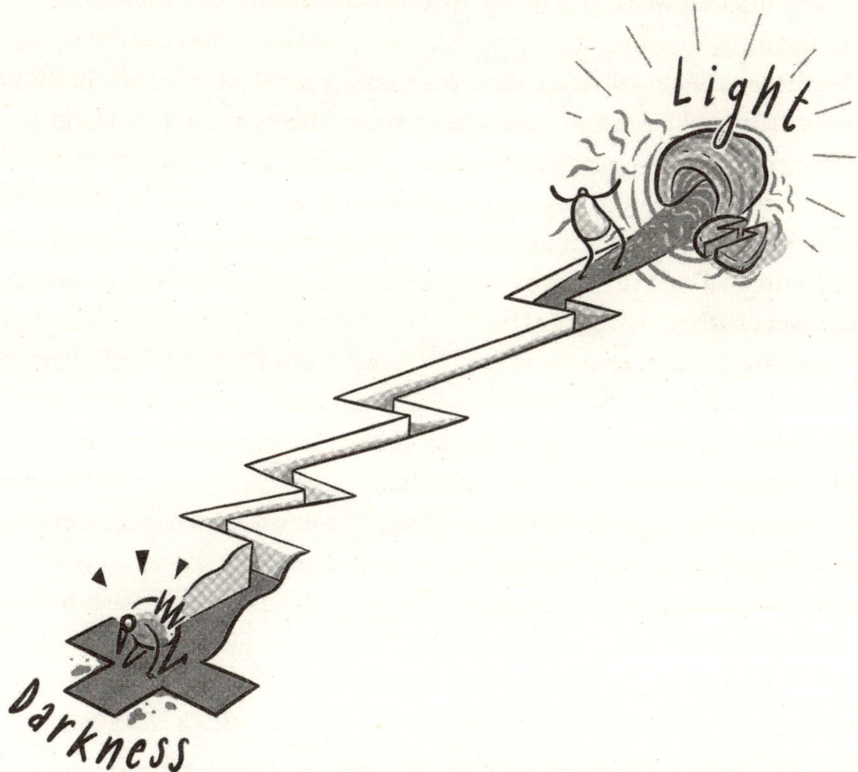

Figure 7.1 **Brightness control – holding both darkness and light in our vision as we look at the world**

qualifies. Crucifixion and resurrection are the hinge on which the whole story turns.

Brightness control (see Figure 7.1) means that the Christian imagination must keep *in tension* the dark, twistedness of the world (symbolized by the cross) and the light of our sure hope (symbolized by the empty tomb). A Christian imagination sees the world through the lens of the cross and the lens of the empty tomb simultaneously, seeing in tensive stereovision.

Seeing through the cross

What does it mean for the imagination to 'see through the cross'? The cross was a tool of execution, of death, an ugly thing that broke people's bodies and souls – an apt icon for human brutality and brokenness. But Christ resisted and defeated sin and death by embracing the cross, embracing that weakness and twisted brokenness as his own.

We Christians are called to do the same. We are to 'take up our cross' (Mark 8:34). Seeing through the cross means taking our eyes off ourselves to feel the brokenness of creation, to recognize how far this world has fallen from God's intention. We must learn to share Christ's heart and grieve for it enough to involve ourselves with it. Having a cross-shaped imagination means that we Christians do not turn away from what is ugly and dark. We have no right to sanitize reality by papering over the world's darkness with a sentimental lie.

Neither do we turn a blind eye to the darkness that still dwells within us, the inner struggles that we have with idolatry, for this is what drove Christ to the cross. We know that we are not yet as we shall be. We have a long way to go and we still desperately need God's mercy every day (1 John 1:8–10). A pastor I know used to sit on a committee that examines candidates seeking ordination to the pastorate. He asked each one the same question: 'What is the present value of the blood of Christ in your life today?' If the candidate could not answer the question – if he could not see that he was at that moment a sinner who still needed forgiveness every day – then this pastor would vote against his ordination. That pastoral intern needed more time to mature before he could serve others effectively in gospel ministry. All Christians need that humility and insight, especially those who seek to create oases of the imagination. We need to have a keen ear for the signs and symptoms of our own brokenness, as well as the brokenness of the world around us.

A cross-shaped imagination means paying attention to the tragic consequences of our rebellion in the world, and being moved to compassion the way Jesus was. It means paying attention to the tragic consequences of rebellion in our own hearts, and being moved to humility, sorrow, repentance and gratitude for God's mercy. Having a cross-shaped imagination means opening our eyes to the twisted wreckage that we humans leave in our wake. The world we live in *is* twisted, and our imagination ought not to suppress that core truth because we find it uncomfortable. Blind ourselves to the ugly reality we find ourselves in, and any art and culture we create will ring hollow. It will not express the way the world truly is.

Seeing through the empty tomb

The second seeing-as lens for the Christian imagination is the empty tomb. The story of Jesus does not end at the cross, in darkness and despair. Christ's death on the cross was a necessary first step towards light, life and beauty. In the Christian story, the cross *leads* to the empty tomb, to the death-breaking power of God displayed in the world.

Having an empty-tomb-shaped imagination means being able to see *past* the twisted brokenness to the potential for life and healing. It means seeing the glory hidden in what God has created, like seeing the life hidden beneath the shell of a bird's egg. If the Christian vision stops at the cross, we end at despair – an absurd world cloaked in impenetrable darkness, indistinguishable from the darkest of secular philosophies. The Christian imagination continues past the darkness to see the light of God's victory, which has already begun: death has been broken and a new creation is coming into being (2 Corinthians 5:14–17).[3] Seeing through the empty tomb means that everything in the Christian's world has a

[3] The verse 2 Corinthians 5:17 is often translated 'If anyone is in Christ, he is a new creation.' The 'he' was added for a smoother English translation, but it is better translated 'If anyone is in Christ, there is a new creation.' Reconciliation is not simply a matter of individual transformation – reconciliation in Christ is part of God's creation-wide grand project of 'making all things new' (Revelation 21:5). This includes personal spiritual renewal, but the Spirit's renewing scope is far wider and not primarily individual – it extends to the whole cosmos. See Herman Ridderbos, *Paul: An outline of his theology* (Grand Rapids, MI: Eerdmans, 1975), p. 45.

certain momentum towards renewal and redemption (or to judgment in the light of God's glory). The Christian imagination is inextricably interwoven with unbreakable threads of a sure *hope*.

In practice, having an empty-tomb-shaped imagination means revaluing everyone you meet and everything you touch. Paul, in 2 Corinthians 5:16, says, 'So from now on [in light of Christ's death and resurrection] we regard no one from a worldly point of view.' The light of the resurrection calls us to see the hidden glory of our neighbours, our wives, our husbands, our co-workers, our children, our friends, our jobs (even our bosses), our whole world! It means that, though the world is dark, it is not *only* dark. There is a light that pierces and shatters the darkness.

Eschatological desire: Christian imagination in the great in between

The faithful Christian imagination sees everything through both perspectives simultaneously, like seeing through the two lenses in a pair of glasses. Both perspectives must be held together, *in tension*: the world is *both* dark and sin-twisted, *and* full of redemptive hope and promise. It seems paradoxical, but that tension is vital. Put the cross and the empty tomb together, and you have a way of seeing the world that is mournful without despair, joyful without naivety, triumphant without triumphalism. You have a genuinely Christian seeing-as for *everything*.

Bear in mind that this tension applies to an artist's *collection* of work. Not every single piece must be suspended between darkness and light. There is a place for pure rejoicing (see Philippians, Paul's letter of joy) and pure lament (see Lamentations, Jeremiah's book of desolation). Looking over the collection of songs, stories or images produced by an artist, can we discern a *range* of emotional and spiritual colouration that acknowledges both the darkness and the light? Can we discern that distinctive tension?

That tension between darkness and light is vital for the Christian imagination because it is the reality, the world we live in. To speak with integrity to the post-Christian world, Christian culture must reflect life as it truly is, not as we wish it would be. The Christian imagination needs to tell the truth of the Great In-Between. Sin and rebellion against God have made the world a messed-up place, and we are messed up as well.

But because God is merciful, powerful, good and wise, and has intervened into our messed-up world, hope is real, more real than we could have possibly imagined. The job of Christian artists is to help the imagination grab hold of the real, both in its sin-twisted darkness and in the grandeur of its hope.

For life in the Great In-Between, hope has more of the texture of longing desire than fulfilment. We are not conquerors, Joshua's army marching boldly into the Promised Land. We are more like the Israelites wandering in the desert, living as pilgrims, finding a spring here, pastureland there, finding comfort in God's faithfulness. We are like the Israelites during the exile, learning to make a home in a foreign city. Their waiting and wandering did move them closer to their return home, but they had a long way to go. We, too, know that this world is not our home, that nothing in it can ultimately satisfy us . . . yet (Hebrews 11:13–16). But our wanderings on this earth are bringing us ever closer to our true home. There are, of course, great blessings and joys to be had, even here. We can (and should!) enjoy them gratefully (1 Timothy 4:4). But the twisted, destructive, hurtful things we see in the world and in our own hearts day after day remind us that this is *not* our home, that we ought not to settle in too much. We are pilgrims.

So we live by faith in the space between, patiently waiting for what God has in store for us. Our eyes search for signs of grace, both ordinary and extraordinary, because they are signs of hope that point to God's powerful, cosmic redemption, already on its way. We live in the tension, caught between sorrow and hope, simultaneously mourning over the world's (and our own) brokenness *and* longing for redemption, longing for creation released and restored (Romans 8:18–24). We know that redemption *is* coming because we have been given tastes and hints of it in the power of knowing Christ in our lives *now*.[4] We know God's grace in blessings both great (the forgiveness of sins, an increasing appreciation of God's faithful love for sinners like us, learning to turn from rebellion and step out in faith in a direction that's new, seeing justice expressed in society, watching a bitter relationship turn to friendship, seeing a child grow up into a

[4] Paul in Romans 8:23 calls this the 'firstfruits of the Spirit', the representative first portion that guarantees we will receive the balance in due time – the full redemption for which we hunger and thirst.

mature faith) and small (sharing a meal with a loved one, seeing a really good film, playing a fun game with your kids, bumping into an old friend or discovering a new friend, hearing a beautiful song, watching the autumn air weave through leaves making the trees' crowns shimmer in the light). This is life in the Great In-Between, caught betwixt the darkness and the approaching light (and we are assured that the light is *not* an oncoming train about to squash us). We live between sorrow and the sure hope of God's victory, between death and life eternal. For those in Christ, this is the truth of our situation.

Living in the Great In-Between provokes hunger and thirst, a complex and deeply conflicted sensitivity of the imagination I call 'eschatological desire' (see Figure 7.2). 'Eschatological' is a theological term that means 'having to do with the end of the world' (from the Greek word ἔσχατον, *eschaton*, meaning goal, purpose or end).

Eschatological desire is desire rooted in the future, the end of the world, but those roots stretch back to colour our understanding of the present. Makoto Fujimura refers to this reality, saying 'the wine of the feast will flow backwards from New Creation to our reality'.[5] Eschatological desire sees through the present darkness to the hope that is coming as surely as the dawn. It makes Christians feel sadness and gratitude, distress and peace, all at the same time. Looking at the world through Christian eyes, we see signs of decay and sin, but we also catch glimmers of redemption and grace, of God's future fulfilment of his shalom.

This is what I meant when I said that the Christian imagination, the eyes of the heart, is both cross-shaped and empty-tomb-shaped. We live in the reality of the ferocious power of sin and the suffering it causes, sin that led Christ to the cross, death woven into the fabric of the world. But we *also* see God's healing, death-reversing power in the victory of Christ when he strode out of the empty tomb. We know that Jesus' resurrection spells certain doom for Satan's armies, sure redemption and healing for this sin-sick world. The empty tomb and the reality of the resurrection Spirit mean that redemption and new creation have begun, coming for us with the unstoppable momentum of spring (see 1 Corinthians 15:20; 2 Corinthians 5:17; Ephesians 1:13–14, 18–21).

---

[5] Makoto Fujimura, *Art and Faith: A theology of making* (New Haven, CT, and London: Yale University Press, 2020), pp. 34–35.

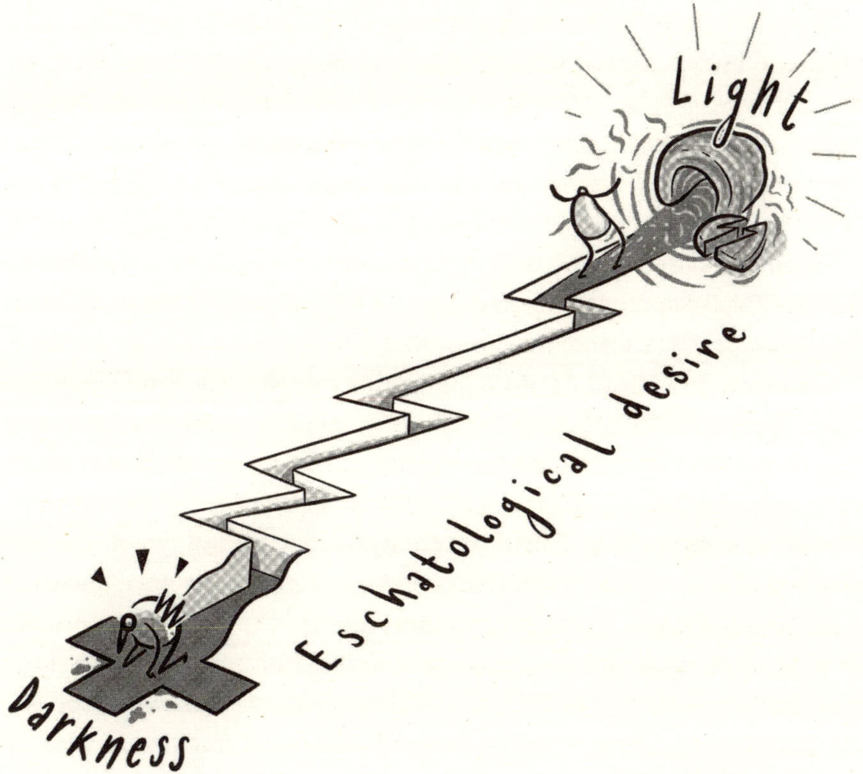

Figure 7.2 **Living in the Great In-Between of eschatological desire**

Eschatological desire is a *sensibility*, a sensitivity of imagination shaped by the experience of living in what theologians call the 'already/not yet' of Christian existence.[6] Already we have amazing riches in Christ, but we have not yet come to the kingdom. Already we have power over sin, but our struggle with sin is not yet over. Already we have victory in Christ, but we have not yet seen that victory definitively achieved. We see signs

[6] I say 'sensibility' and 'sensitivity' rather than 'emotion' because it is not a projection on to reality. Rather, it senses something objectively true, inherent in the structure of fallen creation, in reality itself. Because the Creator is also the Redeemer – the Author of the whole story – echoes of the end of the story resonate within the shapes and structures of the created order throughout the fabric of time. Think of time as a pond, and the end of the story (the redemption that all creation groans for, according to Romans 8) as a stone tossed into the middle of the pond. The ripples eventually spread across the whole pond. Eschatological desire taps into those ripples, those echoes in time. See my article 'Popular culture, apologetics, and the discourse of desire – Introduction', *Cultural Encounters*, vol. 8, no. 2 (November 2012), pp. 25–46, <www.turnau.cz/content/popular-culture-apologetics-and-discourse-desire-introduction>, accessed February 2023.

of hope, but not yet the healing of the world. We have the firstfruits of the promised eschatological redemption, but not yet the fullness.[7] That gap between what will be and what is now expresses itself as tension, as aching desire. The authentic Christian cultural imagination, inevitably, must wrestle with this tension-filled dual focus that comes from living in the Great In-Between.

The imaginative spaces that Christians create should be suffused with the scent of eschatological desire. Non-Christians are not averse to hope; they are averse to sentimental, Pollyanna, soft-focus, pie-in-the-sky hope. If Christian artists can produce cultural works that are simultaneously grounded in the brutal, tragic realities of a fallen world *and* in a hope that rings true, a hope that breaks the spine of darkness and despair, then they will provide a powerful challenge and enticement to the post-Christian imagination. Christian communities should encourage the creation of such spaces if we wish to build bridges to the non-Christian communities around us. Cultural creations that are familiar with real darkness, real brokenness, are also ones that can offer a real hope in love. Imaginative works of the Christian imagination should convey the tensive vision of aching hope and desire amid a fallen, hurting, messed-up world.

This tensive imagination is important for everyone, not only those called to creative professions. The everyday, practical impact of this Christian seeing-as varies widely.[8]

- You see your job not simply as a means to an end, to earn money, but as a calling from God. Despite its obstacles, petty politics and tedium, God calls you to be a source of healing and shalom for those around you who still dwell in darkness, longing for hope. The relationships you forge and the goods and services you provide ultimately mean something in the economy of God's coming kingdom.

[7] The classic theological expression of this dynamic can be found in Geerhardus Vos, *The Pauline Eschatology*, tr. John Richard De Witt (Phillipsburg, NJ: P&R, 1986 [1930]); John Murray, *Redemption Accomplished and Applied* (Grand Rapids, MI: Eerdmans, 1955); Ridderbos, *Paul*; and Richard B. Gaffin Jr, *Resurrection and Redemption: A study in Paul's soteriology* (Phillipsburg, NJ: P&R, 1987 [1978]).

[8] Compare the list here to the list at the end of the Introduction to part 3.

- You see your marriage not simply as a convenient, comfortable arrangement, but as a relationship with a fellow brother or sister in Christ who is destined for glory, but struggles deeply and desperately with sin, just as you do. God has called you into union with your spouse for the express purpose of healing, encouraging, pruning and beautifying, so that together you might become more and more like Jesus, a light to those around you. Marriage is a process that transforms you both away from your native selfishness into people who can love sacrificially, just as Jesus loved you.
- You see your children as delightful gifts who God has entrusted into your care, children who have rebellion wound round their hearts like twine and who often go astray. God has called you to love and teach them by word and example how to repent and forgive quickly, how to keep their hearts soft towards the Lord, how to have wisdom and grace in their dealings with the world and how to be agents of the new creation long after you are dead.
- You see this world as so much more than a place to do stuff and have experiences until you die. Rather, this world is a gift from a generous Creator, the arena in which his drama unfolds. It is a place that groans under its bondage to decay (Romans 8:20), longing for release. We have been called by God to take heart, have hope and to work towards its healing and restoration in light of the new creation.

This is what Paul prays for in Philippians 1:9 when he asks that our love extend to 'every sensation': a cross-shaped, empty-tomb-shaped imagination. It is what Paul calls us to in Romans 12:2: don't be conformed to the pattern of this world (which shrivels our imagination's ability to see the real), but be transformed by the renewing of our minds, so that we can discern the direction God wants our lives to take, and go out and love those around us. Imagination inflected through eschatological desire is central to a healthy Christian spiritual life.

Volume control: parabolic resonance – the balance between shouting and mumbling

We saw earlier that brightness control has to do with holding two perspectives in tension: the darkness of the fallen world and the light of the

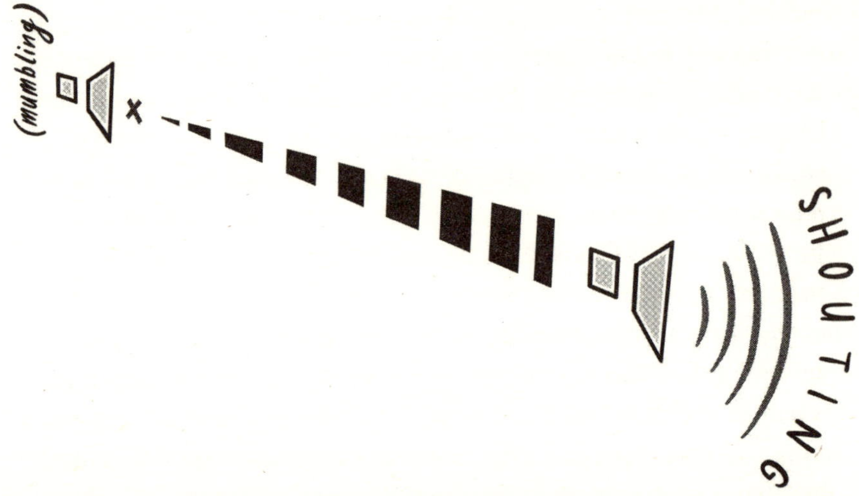

Figure 7.3 **Volume control – achieving balance between shouting and mumbling**

hope of redemption. Volume control (see Figure 7.3) isn't a tension as much as a balance: it's *how explicitly* the Christian imagination should express itself so that its works remain accessible to those in a post-Christian culture. It is a question of volume, a balance between shouting and mumbling.

The problem with megaphones

The question of volume is a delicate subject. Many Christians feel strongly that a cultural work isn't properly Christian unless it proclaims the gospel loud and clear.[9] That is, 'If it doesn't preach, it has no reach.' That is a mistake. Much of the most penetrating Christian culture often avoids

[9] For example, in 1998, following a controversy about the lack of Christian content in contemporary Christian music (CCM), the Gospel Music Association (GMA) defined 'gospel music' as music with lyrics 'substantially based upon historically orthodox Christian truth contained in and derived from the Holy Bible; and/or an expression of worship of God or praise for His works; and/or testimony of relationship with God through Christ; and/or obviously prompted by a Christian worldview.' Explicit, obvious Christian commitment was the necessary ingredient for Christian music. See Charlie Peacock, *At the Crossroads: An insider's look at the past, present, and future of contemporary Christian music* (Nashville, TN: Broadman & Holman, 1999), p. 17. After some popular artists were disqualified from the 1999 Dove Awards (CCM's Grammy Awards), the GMA rescinded the definition the next year. The controversy, however, reflects an opinion shared by many Christians, that Christian culture must explicitly evangelize, worship or testify.

preaching. Instead, it uses indirect ways to appeal to the imagination, subverting and challenging assumptions in ways that preaching cannot reach, in ways that *resonate* with the audience.

There is a time and place for strong, clear proclamation of the gospel. We are called to it and it is vital to the life of the church. But a Christian novel, film, video game, painting or song should not be mistaken for a sermon. In a post-Christian culture, producing cultural works that *trumpet* the good news can chase away non-Christians before they really hear anything of substance. Too often, preachy works fail to engage the imagination, not taking the time to factor in the obstacles and tensions inherent in post-Christian culture and unbelieving hearts.[10] Instead, its messages resonate with those already comfortable with Christianity rather than those alienated from the faith.

The direct, in-your-face approach reminds me of a family visit to a fan convention called Dragon Con some years ago.[11] The convention culminates with a parade. People of all shapes, colours and sizes dress up in costumes and walk through downtown Atlanta to the delight of cheering crowds. There are floats. There's music. It's a fun, festive event that displays the unifying spirit of the convention: we all may have different fandoms, but we come together and have an awesome time. Immediately after the parade passed, the street preachers descended. One megaphone-wielding preacher had a guy follow him with a huge placard that had a picture of the Incredible Hulk with the words, 'REPENT, OR SATAN SMASH YOU IN HELL!' The preacher probably thought that as he had included a picture of the Hulk, he was being culturally relevant. In fact, it was a display of stupefying cultural insensitivity. My eldest daughter overheard one fan mutter resentfully to another, 'We don't come into their church. Why do they invade ours?'

Was the street preacher telling the truth? Yeah, sort of.[12] He was shouting through a megaphone that Jesus forgives sinners, which is true. But the *way* he presented that truth was so loud and obnoxious, the

10 It should be said that good preaching *also* isn't preachy. That is, good sermons engage, even capture, our imaginations, reorientating our hearts. Art should preach, but good preaching should employ (and try to approach being) art.

11 I also recount this story (and my meeting with Cosplay Jesus) in a book I co-wrote, *The Pop Culture Parent*, pp. 44–45.

12 One obvious theological error: Satan in hell will be more smashee than smasher.

message of forgiveness never got through. No-one paid him any mind; he was just one more piece of evidence that Christians are rude, judgmental and profoundly out of touch. The street preacher had made no attempt to understand his audience, to walk in their shoes. His heart was in the right place, and he was making an effort in good faith to communicate with people to help them. He wanted their good, but he preached from a distance. He never entered their world.

Much (though thankfully, not all) Christian culture feels that way to non-Christians. We want to tell the truth so badly that we just blurt it out, megaphone-style. There is a place for praise songs, of course, but don't expect those songs to have much of an impact on people who have very different objects of worship, or for whom the very idea of worship provokes anxiety or disgust. If our cultural works simply repeat scriptural truths or Christianese phrases, how can they connect with people who don't know or trust the Bible? Such direct approaches betray a poor understanding of how the imagination works. Once upon a time perhaps, a direct approach worked, and we got good at it. But times have changed, cultural loyalties have shifted, and too many Christian creatives don't know what else to do except deliver sermons in our films, songs, TV programmes, novels and video games. Non-Christians ignore such cultural offerings in droves. As a result, we end up making Christian culture for Christians alone, then wonder why our creative efforts have no impact on the surrounding culture. We end up making bubbles, not oases.

The problem is not that our Christian beliefs are too strong, but that we convey those beliefs too directly, too bluntly and with too much Christian cliché. Perhaps we need to think outside the box about how we can communicate creatively and engage *less* directly. For example, at the same fan convention, I took Jesus out to lunch. To be more accurate, I took a guy out to lunch who went by the handle 'Cosplay Jesus'. He was olive-skinned, thin, medium height, with long hair and had the requisite beard and long white robes, complete with purple sash. He was there to participate in the convention, to talk to people. When other fans asked him why he dressed as he did, he answered, 'Jesus is my superhero.' He spoke their language in their space. And people responded, telling him what they thought of Jesus or of Christians. Cosplay Jesus would respond in character, as Jesus would, listening intently, loving them and having conversations about hurt, loss and other issues that matter. By subverting their expectations about blustering judgmental Christians, being surprising and indirect and in *their* space, he gained the right to be heard. Likewise, our cultural efforts can use disguise, misdirection, subversion, stepping into spaces where we are not expected and we may well find an unexpected welcome.

Much can be accomplished by not aiming directly at your target. We need less megaphone, more ninja.

Of turtles and chameleons

There is the ever-present danger of an imbalance in the other direction too. Christian creatives can become so subtle and clever that any hint of Christ is erased. Some Christian art goes so mainstream, it loses any Christian distinctiveness and merely repeats general moral platitudes.[13] Again, such artists have the best of intentions – to reach as many as possible – but they reach them with what? A 'gospel' of niceness, social morality, community or whatever? In such cases, our stories, songs and images lose their roots so the subversive power of the gospel doesn't come across. In a faith centred on the cross and resurrection of Jesus, there is no way we can remain faithful and avoid all offence. If we try to, we merely replace a shouted message with confusing mumbling. There is little left to distinguish a Christian imaginative work from any other.

Some Christian artists become so shy about their faith in the interest of reaching a wider audience that they become chameleons, blending into the post-Christian environment. Like turtles, they pull in anything that could cause non-Christians discomfort, hiding it from view. They mumble their message, hoping that they might fly under the radar and avoid alienating anyone. Turtling, mumbling, hiding in the shadows, becoming chameleons in non-Christian culture might help an artist to get an initial

[13] The actress from chapter 4 pointed this out. Studios are looking for stories that are the result of the Christian faith, but devoid of faith specifics, so non-Christian viewers will not feel uncomfortable. I called this 'bankable fruits safely detached from historical roots'. *Veggie Tales* creator Phil Vischer publicly repented of producing a gospel-free 'Christian' children's show: 'I had spent 10 years trying to convince kids to behave Christianly without actually teaching them Christianity. And that was a pretty serious conviction. You can say, "Hey kids, be more forgiving because the Bible says so," or "Hey kids, be more kind because the Bible says so!" But that isn't Christianity, it's morality.' Quoted in Megan Basham, 'It's not about the dream', *World* (24 September 2011), <https://wng.org/articles/its-not-about-the-dream-1617330209>, accessed February 2023.

hearing, but only at the cost of losing Christian distinctiveness. It is an attitude that borders on being ashamed of Christ (Mark 8:38), and that's *not* a good place for Christian artists to work from.

Neither megaphone nor turtle, but parabolic time bombs

There is a way that avoids trumpeting, megaphone-delivered messages *and* mumbling chameleon and turtle-like behaviour. Talented, Spirit-led creatives can indeed join a clear, strong Christian perspective with cultural sensitivity, creative indirection and nuance. We find a magnificent model in the imagination of Jesus himself. Of course, Jesus wasn't addressing a post-Christian culture, but his own context was as resistant to the gospel as ours is, ranging from the polytheistic Roman culture that wanted to fit God into its pantheon to the stubborn Pharisees and Jewish religious establishment addicted to their own traditions rather than God's Word. Jesus wasn't always indirect. He could be shockingly direct when he wanted to be (and use brutally vivid metaphors when he was, such as 'whitewashed tombs'). But, at other times, he avoided tackling issues head on, becoming ingeniously elliptical and indirect. He raised questions, challenged assumptions and told parables. Those parables resonated deeply within his audiences' hearts, setting up tremors in the imagination that might have gone unrecognized, until later. I call this 'parabolic resonance' (see Figure 7.4).[14]

In Matthew 21:33–46, Jesus tells a parable about workers who rent a vineyard but refuse to pay rent. Instead, they repeatedly abuse the messengers the owner sends to collect his due. Finally, in a desperate bid to displace the owner and claim the vineyard for themselves, they murder the owner's son. The crowd becomes so absorbed in the story that they respond by shouting for the death of those wicked tenants. It isn't until the parable is over that Jesus pulls back the curtain to give us the 'reveal'. He clarifies the meaning of his story with a Scripture passage so that the religious leaders understand that the resonance of the story had been directed against them. They finally feel the tremors, but too late. The damage had already been done. Using only metaphor and narrative, Jesus planted a time bomb and set it off.

[14] For you maths nerds, 'parabolic' here refers to parables, not to the symmetrical curve.

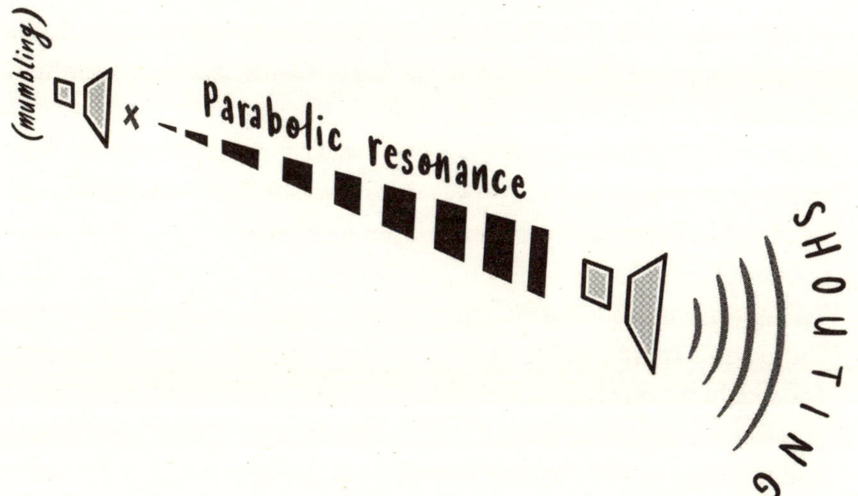

Figure 7.4 **The parabolic resonance between mumbling and shouting**

On another occasion, recorded in Mark 7, the Pharisees criticized Jesus' disciples for eating with 'defiled' hands (they didn't follow the Pharisees' hand-washing tradition). Jesus met their criticism head on, but then used odd, indirect, parabolic language to explain the nature of clean and unclean to the religious leaders (Mark 7:18–20): 'Nothing outside a person can defile them by going into them. Rather, it is what comes out of a person that defiles them.' He let that statement hang in the air, unexplained, and walked away. But some were curious and they pursued him. Only then did Jesus clarify this odd and seemingly offensive statement. 'Clean' and 'unclean' have little to do with food. They are, rather, matters of the heart, that pollution-spewing artesian well. For Jesus, that's *truly* unclean.

Notice what Jesus' odd, indirect words did. They opened a space for people to be brought up short, to have expectations challenged, to wonder and puzzle for a bit. Those who were curious had to pursue Jesus to ask for clarification. Their hunger was stirred so that they *wanted* to go deeper down the rabbit hole to illuminate the strange landscape that Jesus revealed to them.

That is what Christian cultural works ought to do: catch people's imagination in unexpected ways, plant time bombs, arouse curiosity, provoke a desire to go further and dig deeper. We Christians are often so anxious for our art to be on-message, and that the message will be received loud and clear, we deliver the whole package at once, leaving no room for exploration.

Poet Emily Dickinson also lived in a world that was becoming post-Christian, sceptical of the gospel. She sketched this resonant middle ground in her poem 'Tell all the truth but tell it slant':

> Tell all the truth but tell it slant –
> Success in Circuit lies
> Too bright for our infirm Delight
> The Truth's superb surprise
> As Lightning to the Children eased
> With explanation kind
> The Truth must dazzle gradually
> Or every man be blind –[15]

In the post-Christian West, telling the truth straight on, *unslanted*, will be dismissed as cliché or bombast – a kind of self-imposed blindness. Take into account what audiences can handle, deliver truth slant, always ready 'with explanation kind' to give as the truth gradually dazzles and dawns on them.

Christian art, then, can be overly direct or so muted that it's hard to tell it is Christian. Both approaches think of art as a vehicle for proclaiming a message: we must communicate X loud and clear or soft and fuzzy. Perhaps we ought to think less in terms of proclaiming a message and more in terms of clearing the ground for exploration. Construct imaginative works that don't preach the gospel but, instead, create spaces and worlds to explore *within which the gospel makes sense*. We don't have to say everything at once, and we don't always have to be direct. That is, we don't have to create Christian propaganda. Rather, we should conjure imaginary spaces that resonate at a deeper level, inviting – and rewarding – further exploration. Give glimpses, hints, rumours of gospel truth. Offer something to whet the appetite. Utter gentle whispers to

[15] From Thomas H. Johnson (ed.), *The Complete Poems of Emily Dickinson* (Boston, MA, and Toronto, Ontario: Little Brown & Company, 1960), pp. 506–507. Thanks to Dan Strange for suggesting the poem.

aching hearts that the Spirit could use to lead the alienated onwards, like echoes in a cavern. Gentleness and delicate resonances are ruined whenever we hit people over the head with the good news or mumble incoherently. Let the good news resonate rather than either blast out or blend into the woodwork.

How did Jesus' parables achieve such resonance in his hearers? He entered into *their* space. He started with their expectations, assumptions and narratives about the Messiah, God's kingdom, religious authority, fairness, mercy, death, judgment and so on. Jesus was incarnational in the way he communicated, stepping into the imaginary landscape of his audience to meet them where they lived. He delved into things that interested them intensely, places where they invested hope, felt frustrated, scared or hungry and thirsty. Most of the time, Christ's message resonated with those expectations, assumptions and narratives to overturn or subvert them. Christian cultural works ought to do the same thing, subverting expectations with the truth of the gospel. Subversive resonance is a difficult and subtle move to make, but it is essential if we are to build oases of and for the imagination.

Finding this balance and resonance is not simply a matter of cleverness or subtlety; it is a matter also of artistic passion, intensity and integrity. Our creative works must be willing to express what the world looks like through Christian eyes, and that vision will be messy and rough around the edges – darkness and shadow tinged with hopeful light, tragedy mixed with joy. It will not look or sound safe or prepackaged, as much Christian art and entertainment tends to do. And it will not behave. It may reach out and grab us by the shoulders and give us a good shake, yelling 'Wake up!' It may scream in anger, wail in sadness or frustration, or laugh at unexpected times. Christian art in these in between times may not be direct, but it will be wild.

Much Christian art and popular culture is too timid to strike a match to reach those in darkness. If Christian art is to ignite something in others, it must burn. Calvin Seerveld (my North Star when it comes to matters of art) captures this balance and passion well:

> You cannot bludgeon people with christian art into accepting Jesus Christ. But neither should you settle for just being as dispassionately

> good as the secular professional artist, adding: 'I do it for Jesus, you know.' It is the crux of your task as a communal body of fellow christian artists to fire your art until it emits sparks that warm, or burn, those it reaches. As Paul says in a different context (cf. Romans 11:11), in your artwork make the audience, believer or unbeliever, jealous of the power and richness and wholeness of life that is captured so convincingly and compellingly in the allusive forms you have fashioned. And then let God's Spirit spring your artistic trap.[16]

The Christian imagination must maintain a delicate balance between bludgeoning and dispassionately mimicking the secular artist's imagination. It must burn with a different, distinctive fire. Our oases must blaze with passion as they offer their challenges and consolations, grabbing the audience and giving them a good shake to wake them from their lethargy. Oases resonate best when they are neither a blaring megaphone nor confusing mumbling, but a fire that warms (and occasionally burns) those who draw near.

Of course, you might object that judging whether a piece of culture is too explicit about faith or not explicit enough is a dicey business. What one person calls trumpeting may sound like mumbling to another. A megaphone in one cultural context might sound like turtling in another. Agreed. It is a question of cultural discernment and sensitivity, and achieving balance will be different in different contexts. But it is a question worth wrestling with. Christian creatives should seek and strive to produce works the content, mode and tone of which resonate with the gospel. There is a space to be found that lives and breathes between blatant propaganda and chameleon-like turtle mumbling. Finding that subversive 'parabolic resonance' between those two extremes enables the creation of oases that invite and challenge Christian and non-Christian alike. It enables the creation of respectful, relevant and winsome cultural dialogue with the disenchanted, sceptical culture around us.

16 Seerveld, *Bearing Fresh Olive Leaves*, pp. 35–36. By 'allusive' Seerveld means to say that art communicates indirectly, gesturing beyond itself. We will explore this in more depth in chapter 8.

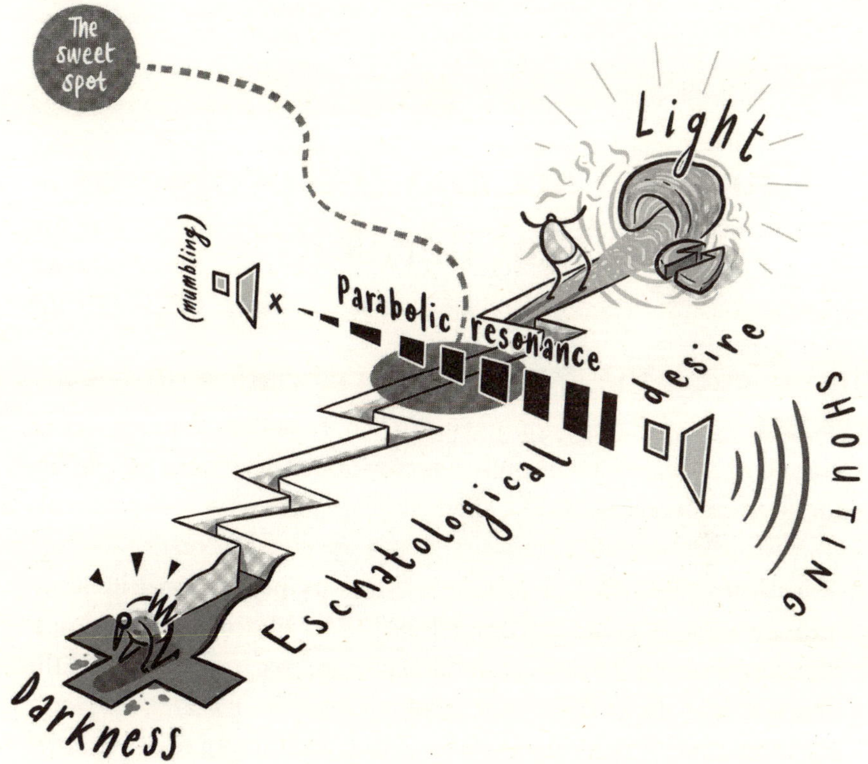

Figure 7.5 **Finding the sweet spot between eschatological desire and parabolic resonance**

Conclusion: finding the 'sweet spot'

These, I would argue, are the markers that distinguish an effective Christian imagination and its works. If Christian creatives can imagine and produce works that combine a distinctive tension between darkness and light (eschatological desire) *and* find a balance between shouting and mumbling (parabolic resonance), they can hit a 'sweet spot' that resonates and stirs desire in both Christians and non-Christians (see Figure 7.5). They will plant oases of power and depth in the post-Christian world. This kind of art is sorely needed now.

In chapter 8, we will spend some time reflecting on the nature and purpose of art. When Christians don't understand what art is and how it works, Christian art can sometimes go very wrong.

8

Christian art and the problems that derail it

Introduction: the importance of Christian aesthetic witness

A comment appeared in an online survey about what kept people from God, the church and the faith called 'The big objections':

> The Church has diluted Jesus' message. Its people are impotent and cowardly. Its music and Art reflects [sic] its nature – mediocre and blandly revolting. The media condescend and pacify its people with anoemic [sic] shows like S of P [*Songs of Praise*] – it's a horror story on prime time. If Jesus was dead he'd be at 12 000 rpm in His grave.[1]

These are bracing words. Other commenters mentioned contradictions in the Bible, the problem of suffering, the church's stance on gay marriage and many other issues. Below the many intellectual objections non-Christians have, there are often unspoken emotional and aesthetic objections as well. Christian culture makes it seem as though we are afraid of reality's hard edges, preferring to surround ourselves with vapid niceness. It is hard to take the Christian faith seriously when so much of its culture seems aesthetically trivial (or 'blandly revolting'). Our culture disqualifies us before any serious conversation begins.

I teach a world religions class. A perennial favourite is Zen Buddhism. Students take its paradoxical, non-logical claims in their stride because of its aesthetic appeal. White empty spaces, clean lines, uncluttered, focused: reason enough to give Zen a hearing. It's amazingly attractive for

1 From an unnamed commenter, 'The big objections', Kings Church Eastbourne (n.d.), <www.kings.church/bigobjections.php>, accessed February 2023.

anyone seeking peace, quiet and simplicity. By contrast, what sort of aesthetic witness is associated with contemporary evangelical Christianity? Nineteenth-century 'white Jesus knocking at the door of your heart' paintings? A decorative cushion with a Bible verse, rainbow and fluffy rabbit? Country cute? Soft-focus floral photographs? Aggressively 'cool' slogans on T-shirts? Contrived, triumphalist cinematic stories? Music that tends towards easy listening, afraid to take risks? It's an aesthetic that turns the curious away. If they come to faith, they come *despite* such cultural works.

Obviously, the barriers between Christian faith and the unbeliever run deeper than aesthetics. Christianity's values and vision threaten the moral autonomy so precious to secular folk ('No-one tells *me* how to live!'). But presenting those values and vision without real imaginative insight or consideration for the aesthetic impact doesn't help. Unimaginative, kitschy, saccharine, sentimental, out-of-touch culture effectively hamstrings Christian witness. Knowing the truth matters little if our aesthetic witness renders the truth ugly and ineffectual to those who need it most (including Christians themselves). For this reason alone, the Christian artistic imagination is worth considering. All of us need to know something about art.

Some readers might object, 'I'm no artist! What practical value does this information have for people like me?' Because artists need you. The church needs professional creatives, but it also needs aesthetically discerning members of the Christian community. Artists[2] do not simply happen; they are grown. They grow best in supportive, involved communities.

Remember the Christian DJ from the beginning of this book? He needs that kind of community, as do others I know. Artists want to be understood. They want friends who can speak into their working lives with wisdom and compassion. They want to be valued for what they do – knowingly praised when they do it well, constructively critiqued when they do it badly. And, obviously, it is your money that helps to support them and allows them to make a living.

2 In chapter 5, I said that all God's people are artists. Here I am using 'artist' as shorthand for professional creatives.

We must support art that is worth supporting. The wider Christian community has a crucial role as the matrix within which good (or bad) art happens, a greenhouse for the Christian imagination and for artists. We should be intentional, to know what we're about vis-à-vis art and the Christian imagination. We will look at the role of the wider Christian community in the life of the artist further in part 5. For now, let us focus on what art is and what it's for.

What is art, and what's it for?

Before we explore Christian art and what typically derails it, let us explore what art is and its purposes. Calvin Seerveld gives a helpful, concise definition:

> Art is an object or event conceived and structured by human design to be perceived by our senses, and characterized by an imaginative and allusive finish that affords the piece its own independent identity.[3]

Let's break that down point by point.

First, art is 'an object or event conceived and structured by human design'. Art is the result of a planned project on the part of humans. As I said in chapter 5, art is authentically, uniquely human. No other creature practises art. The spider weaves her delicate web by instinct, not design. The weaver bird is a craftsman (or a craftsbird), but no artist. Only humans mimic the Creator by employing the imagination in a concrete project.

Second, art is designed 'to be perceived by our senses'. Art is for people dwelling in bodies, not disembodied minds. Good art is primarily sensual, not primarily intellectual, even if it makes you think (as good art should). Even a complicated novel derives its power from how it evokes a sensual, imaginary world, and how what goes on in that world hits you in the gut. Seerveld eschews a disembodied spirituality and affirms the goodness of physical creation, including our bodies. Art is made for the senses, made to be felt and not simply thought.

---

3 Calvin Seerveld, *Bearing Fresh Olive Leaves: Alternative steps in understanding art* (Carlisle and Toronto, Ontario: Toronto Tuppence Press/Piquant Press, 2000), p. 8.

Third, art has an 'imaginative and allusive finish'. A piece of art is different from a neon sign on a restaurant, blinking on and off: 'Eat at Joe's'. Such a sign communicates its message in a standard, straightforward manner. Not so a work of art. Art is imaginative, creating worlds of meaning for exploration. Art is allusive, gesturing beyond itself to larger, deeper realities. Art always means more than it says outright, and what it says cannot be reduced to a soundbite. It is more than utilitarian and functional.[4] Art leads us beyond itself to a wider and deeper context of meaning.

When Christian fiction writer Flannery O'Connor was asked to summarize the meaning of one of her stories, she is supposed to have replied, 'If I could tell you the meaning, I wouldn't need to write the story.'[5] Stories are organic, imaginative meaning structures:

> The meaning of a story has to be embodied in it, has to be made concrete in it. A story is a way to say something that can't be said any other way, and it takes every word in the story to say what the meaning is. You tell a story because a statement would be inadequate. When anybody asks what a story is about, the only proper thing is to tell him to read the story. The meaning of fiction is not abstract meaning but experienced meaning, and the purpose of making statements about the meaning of a story is only to help you to experience that meaning more fully.[6]

This organic, complex meaning structure that resists paraphrase is what Seerveld means by 'imaginative finish', which gives a piece of art its

---

[4] Makoto Fujimura insists that art cuts against the grain of our utilitarian, commodified society. Rather, it is *gratuitous*, mirroring God's generosity on display in his creation and redemption, partaking more of the nature of a gift than a commodity. See Fujimura, *Art and Faith: A theology of making* (New Haven, CT, and London: Yale University Press, 2020), pp. 17–18 and 66–72.

[5] This quote, popularly attributed to O'Connor, seems to be a conflation of two separate quotes. First, when asked in an interview what happened in her short story, 'The life you save may be your own', she replied, 'I don't think you can paraphrase a story like that. I think there's only one way to tell it and that's the way it is told in the story.' From *Conversations with Flannery O'Connor*, ed. Rosemary M. Magee (Jackson, MI, and London: University of Mississippi Press, 1987), p. 8. Second, in a letter to 'A', 'If I had the abstraction first I don't suppose I would write the story.' From T*he Habit of Being: Letters of Flannery O'Connor*, selected and edited by Sally Fitzgerald (New York: Vintage, 1980), p. 178. It's similar to another unsourced quote by the pioneer of modern dance, Isadora Duncan, 'If I knew what it meant, I wouldn't have to dance it.'

[6] Flannery O'Connor, 'Writing short stories' in Sally and Robert Fitzgerald (eds), *Mystery and Manners: Occasional Prose* (New York: Noonday Press, 1969), p. 96.

unique identity. An artwork communicates and opens a world for exploration using the specific imaginative 'language' of its particular medium and form. Only in this way does the audience gain an entrée into its 'experienced meaning', its particular imaginary world.

This imaginary world, however, is not sealed off from the real. Seerveld does not promote 'art for art's sake'. Art is 'allusive', that is, it gestures beyond itself. It resonates in its own peculiar way with the depths of human reality, like a low bass note vibrates your skull and stomach. It has an impact beyond its own meaning structure. In this way, art mimics creation, which also resonates beyond itself with the larger reality of the God who made it (or what theologians call 'general revelation').[7] Christian art intentionally amplifies and focuses general revelation. Christian or not, art crystallizes, resonates and gestures. That's its nature.

Fourth, this imaginative and allusive texture of art 'affords the piece its own independent identity'. Seerveld is careful to guard art's autonomy, its self-identity. He insists that we distinguish between art's validity and the uses we might have for it. A work of art is valid on its own terms, as an artistic contribution to God's world. Its value is not determined by how 'useful' we find it. To say, for example, that a piece of art is only good if it evangelizes is akin to saying that art is only good if it sells its message. Is that so different from saying art is only good if it sells a product, like tights or hotdogs or propaganda? It may be a great message, but pinning art's worth on how well it sells its message effectively prostitutes art, undermining its integrity and authenticity. A piece of art stands or falls on its own artistic merits, not on how well it performs other functions. That is not to say that it can't have other functions or that it cannot have a message, but that isn't its primary job. Art's task is to open imaginary worlds, gesturing in an imaginative way beyond itself.

Finally, notice what Seerveld does *not* say. He does not say that art can't be commercial, that only art made for museums and concert halls is real art. The purist, high-culture snobbery that runs through so much

7 Musician and theologian David Covington calls this aspect of aesthetics 'translucency', that we see light *through* the beauty and emotional impact of creation and art, as opposed to secular art's insistence on 'opacity', art being an end in itself. See his book *A Redemptive Theology of Art: Restoring godly aesthetics to doctrine and culture* (Grand Rapids, MI: Zondervan, 2018), pp. 92–93, 185 and 214–215.

talk about art is absent from Seerveld. Instead, he makes the case for what he calls 'encapsulated art' – art that finds a home in institutions other than those dedicated to art itself.[8] You can find art that is both artistically valid *and* serves a church, an entertainment media company or an ad agency. Art can legitimately be imaginative and allusive *and* guide worship, entertain or even sell something (if it does so honestly and in a way that honours the consumers' real needs). From his perspective, popular music, Hollywood films, video games, worship songs, adverts on TV, all can be art, *if* they maintain their own independent identities as art while they serve their other functions.[9] There is, of course, the danger of a work failing to maintain its identity as encapsulated *art*, debasing itself in servile obeisance to the whims of the market. Still, it *is* possible (and necessary) to call good, popular culture art.[10] Indeed, such works are important precisely because their impact is *not* confined to a museum or concert hall. Good art, as Seerveld defines it, creates oases.

So a work of art is designed by a human and is a sensual, imaginative and allusive thing or event that has its own creative identity. What's it for? Why is there art in God's world? Where does it fit in God's plans for us? Isn't it simply a luxury? After all, people don't starve from lack of art like they do from lack of food. Answer: art is an important part of what it means to be fully human in God's world. There has never been a culture without some artistic activity going on in it. Art of all sorts (popular, fine, commercial, museum) are things that feed, refine and reform the imagination in different directions. Art brings encouragement, escape, entertainment, questions, challenges, wonder and glory to those who partake of it. Art crystallizes and focuses our shared human existence. It helps us to live beyond our own little worlds, helping us to understand and empathize with one another. It helps us to live in a bigger world or, conversely, it can shrink the borders of our world to something quite small and constricting. Art, in its own way, tells the truth about God and his world, or else it deceives and helps us to believe the lie that God is distant,

8 Seerveld, *Bearing Fresh Olive Leaves*, pp. 37–38.

9 To put this in Fujimura's terms, they all can be art if they are truly gifts first, generous and generative in nature.

10 Media scholar William D. Romanowski uses the term 'popular art' for just this reason. See his *Eyes Wide Open: Looking for God in popular culture* (rev. exp. edn 2007 [2001]) (Grand Rapids, MI: Brazos Press, 2001), chapter 7.

uncaring or dead. Art does this in a way that gets under our skin, skirts around our defences and enters through the back door of our minds, seeping into our very dreams and desires. Art is powerful, and it ought not to be ignored by the church – not if we wish to develop a faithful imagination and a faithful aesthetic witness.

What, then, is *Christian* art? Christian art is this allusive and imaginative world-building done with 'a spirit of compassionate judgment honouring Christ's rule'.[11] Given what we have learnt about the Christian imagination, 'honouring Christ's rule' with our art means creating works of allusive power that create oases for the imagination through:

- a tensive vision that includes both the twisted darkness of the fallen world and the piercing light of our hope;
- a balanced voice that neither shouts nor mumbles.

Christian art doesn't differ from non-Christian art in its subject matter, but in *how* that subject matter is expressed. It's a matter of ensuring that its perspective, vision, voice and inflection maintain that tension and balance.

Problems that derail Christian art

What happens when the balance and tension are *not* maintained, when the Christian imagination derails its aesthetic witness before the watching world? Let's explore some of the fundamental problems that derail Christian creativity in a post-Christian world: kitsch, propaganda, triumphalism and a hopeless vision.

Death by cute niceness: kitsch

'Kitsch' is a German word that is often invoked but seldom defined. We know it when we see it: the bouncy hula doll on a trucker's dashboard, the trashy paperback novel, the all-too-typical romantic sunset picture, the Christmas card adorned with chubby cherubs. We all recognize it. And we all know Christians who own, enjoy, share, and even possibly produce, kitsch. It seems harmless enough, so what's the problem?

[11] Seerveld, *Bearing Fresh Olive Leaves*, p. 17.

Secular art theorist Tomas Kulka identifies kitsch using three markers:

- **sentimentality** it manipulates its audiences' emotions;
- **instant accessibility** it is obvious, no need for reflection or investigation;
- **cliché** it employs overused images and tropes, conjures no surprises, gives no new imaginative insight.[12]

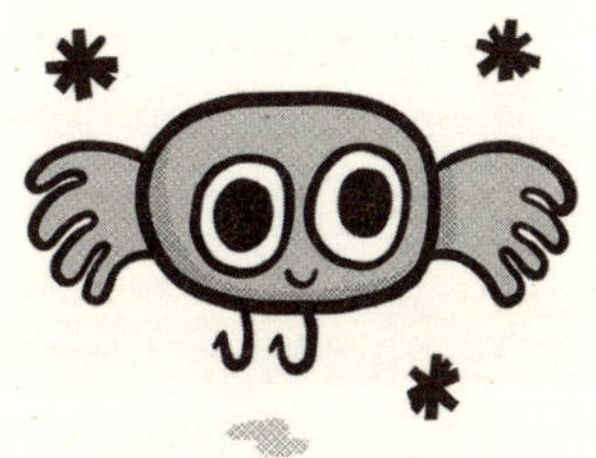

Kitsch manipulates us emotionally, dumbs things down and leads us to where we've all been before. It breaks no new emotional, intellectual or imaginative ground. Kitsch is lazy art.

For Seerveld, the stakes are even higher. He categorizes kitsch as aesthetic sin:

> Kitsch is anything impressive, sentimentally endearing, but fake. Kitsch is a luxurious trifle correlated with immature sincerity . . . Kitsch reduces the rich troubles of life to a single, all-absorbing, temporary pleasure that is essentially unsatisfying. According to Milan Kundera, kitsch presents a world in which there is the absolute denial of shit. So, to my mind kitsch superficializes the quality of human life because it makes you feel good by insulating you from the real world we inhabit.[13]

Isn't Seerveld being too severe? I don't think so. Kitsch takes something with amazing potential – art – and diverts its power in destructive, mendacious ways.

- Kitsch is a sin against the Creator and creation. It's replacing the amazing complexity of created reality with a simplified surrogate.

---

[12] Tomas Kulka, *Kitsch and Art* (University Park, PA: Pennsylvania State University Press, 1996), pp. 25–42.

[13] Seerveld, *Bearing Fresh Olive Leaves*, pp. 181–182. The quote from Kundera comes from 'The Grand March', part 6 of *The Unbearable Lightness of Being*, tr. Michael Henry Heim (Cambridge, MA: Harper & Row, 1984). By his memorable phrase Kundera means that kitsch is a way of protecting the viewer/reader/listener from the hard, messy realities of life.

- Kitsch is a sin against our neighbours. It turns us away from the darkness of this twisted world (the cross-shaped imagination), insulating us from our neighbour's troubles by transporting us to a happy place full of sunshine, unicorns and rainbows. Kitsch deafens us to the brokenness of the world.
- Finally, kitsch is a sin against the imagination itself. It stifles the imagination, making it weak through lack of exercise. It takes no risks and asks us to risk nothing.

The fundamental problem with kitsch is that it tells a sentimental lie. Sentimentality is, according to philosopher Mark Jefferson, a 'misrepresentation of the world in order to indulge certain emotional states'.[14] Sentimentality (the major emotional ingredient in kitsch) ascribes 'qualities of innocence' to its objects (whether kittens, sunsets or nations), 'sweetness, dearness, littleness, blamelessness, and vulnerability'.[15] It is a denial of darkness, complexity, fallenness and suffering.

Christian kitsch becomes a signal to the watching world that the Christian faith denies the truth about hard reality and is too cliché to be relevant to real lives – lives filled with pain, confusion and trouble. In the minds of non-Christians, our love of kitsch disqualifies us from speaking with authority about the struggles of real people. It seems that we prefer to dwell, instead, in our snug, comfortable fantasy world, isolated from the evil and mess of reality. Kitsch hamstrings our cultural witness. Aesthetically committed to unreality, our proclamation rings hollow. Kitsch is the kiss of death for Christian apologetics and evangelism *before any arguments have even been spoken.*

In other words, kitsch places us in a Thomas Kinkade painting, a fantasy world of self-satisfaction and candy-coated scenes with cosy fireplaces, isolated from the twisted, evil world that we struggle in every

14 Mark Jefferson, 'What's wrong with sentimentality?' *Mind*, vol. XCII, no. 368 (October 1983), pp. 519–529, cited in Gregory Wolfe, *Intruding upon the Timeless: Meditations on art, faith, and mystery* (Baltimore, MD: Square Halo Books, Kindle edn, 2003), loc. 1612. The main failing of sentimentality is that it morally oversimplifies its object, ascribing to it an absolute innocence, which deserves unreserved sympathy. But holding something or someone absolutely innocent has a dark side. It can lead to a brutal repression of anything or anyone seen as threatening the sentimentally beloved thing or person. See Jefferson, 'What's wrong with sentimentality?' pp. 526–528.

15 Jefferson, 'What's wrong with sentimentality?' quoted in Wolfe, loc. 1579.

day. The self-proclaimed 'Painter of Light'™ wanted to 'portray a world without the fall'.[16] Kitsch seeks to place us beyond trouble, darkness and evil.

Not only does kitsch distance us from the pain of a fallen world but it also oversimplifies and defangs the beauty and majesty of God's work in his creation and redemption. Christian literary scholar Clyde Kilby is worth quoting at length on this point here:

> There is a simplicity which diminishes and a simplicity which enlarges, and evangelicals have too often chosen the wrong one. The first is that of the cliché – simplicity with mind and heart removed. The other is that of art. The first falsifies by its exclusions; the second encompasses. The first silently denies the multiplicity and grandeur of creation, salvation, and indeed all things. The second symbolizes and celebrates them. The first tries to take the danger out of Christianity and with the danger often removes the actuality. The second suggests the creative and sovereign God of the universe with whom there are no impossibilities. The contrast suggests that *not* to imagine is what is sinful. The symbol, the figure, the image, the parable – in short, the artistic method – so pungent in the Lord's teaching and acting, are often noteworthy for their absence in ours.[17]

We wrong the Author of creation and redemption when we produce such failures of imagination and take the shortcuts offered by kitsch and cliché.[18]

---

16 Quoted in Randall Balmer, 'The Kinkade crusade', *Christianity Today* (4 December 2000), <www.christianitytoday.com/ct/2000/december4/6.48.html?start=2>, accessed February 2023. Incidentally, an artist named Jeff Bennett did a series of illustrations altering Kinkade paintings by adding a military presence of the Empire called 'Wars [short for *Star Wars*] on Kinkade' (digital art), *Deviant Art* (24 October 2013), <http://alienartisan.deviantart.com/gallery/46432162/Wars-on-Kinkade>, accessed February 2023. By adding a sense of impending doom (a hovering Imperial Star Destroyer, approaching AT-AT walkers), Bennett inserts a note of menace that completely subverts the serene nostalgia of Kinkade's paintings. I confess, I would gladly hang a Bennett-altered Kinkade painting in my home.

17 Kilby, 'The aesthetic poverty of evangelicalism' in Leland Ryken (ed.), *The Christian Imagination: The practice of faith in literature and writing* (Colorado Springs, CO: Shaw Books, rev. exp. edn, 2002), p. 278.

18 See also Daniel Strange's critique of sentimentality in 'I'm (not) getting sentimental over you', *Themelios*, vol. 42, no. 3 (December 2017), pp. 440–445. He argues that sentimentality massages feelings, allowing modern people to swap feelings for truth and meaning. This can then be leveraged against those who feel differently. Feeling itself becomes sacred and, therefore, a potential weapon.

Kitsch does have its defenders. Art scholar Betty Spackman sympathizes with many of those who produce kitsch because it so often represents the voices of the powerless.[19] Kitsch offers the poor and marginalized a way to deal with a dark and disconcerting world. She recognizes something deeply human in these plastic pieces that seek to tug on the old heartstrings. Perhaps despising kitsch is a form of middle- and upper-class privilege and snobbery – people in those strata have not experienced the depth of brokenness to which kitsch offers its consolations.

While I am sympathetic to Spackman's arguments, kitsch remains kitsch. Just as we expect Christians to mature in their understanding of the truth, so we should expect Christians to mature in their understanding of art and imagination. The church should help Christians to grow out of their yearning for the comforts of kitsch. Our ultimate comfort resides in the gospel itself, and the gospel is full of blood, sweat and agony – it is anything *but* kitsch. Further, kitsch undermines our aesthetic witness to the truth of the gospel. In a culture that has been inoculated against the gospel, averse to any solution the church might offer, Christians' love for kitsch only confirms their suspicion that we (and the gospel) are out of touch with reality. If there's going to be a stumbling block, let it be the gospel itself, not sentimentality.

One final thought on kitsch. Some non-Christian scholars believe that any hint of hope, light or salvation is, *by definition*, kitsch. In 1990, the editors of academic journal *Salmagundi* organized a symposium on literary kitsch. There was much debate and disagreement over which pieces of literature might qualify as kitsch. They all agreed that Fyodor Dostoyevsky's character Sonya, the original 'hooker with a heart of gold', qualified. She redeems (and is redeemed) by her love of God and Raskolnikov in *Crime and Punishment.* Barry Goldensohn explains Sonya's kitschness this way:

> she represents a mass middle-class fantasy of the prostitute: a Christianized vision of the soul that can be saved through orthodox

[19] Betty Spackman, *A Profound Weakness: Christians and kitsch* (Carlisle: Piquant Editions, 2005). Frank Burch Brown makes a similar point in *Good Taste, Bad Taste, and Christian Taste: Aesthetics in religious life* (Oxford: Oxford University Press, 2000). If we are to avoid elitism, we must also keep the social context of both artist and audience in view.

means ... Why we call the conventions of sentimental romance kitsch is that they have lent themselves so well to mass fantasies, mass wish-fulfilment. They have been used again and again in bad art; they gratify the assumptions that we can very clearly identify with a mass audience.[20]

In other words, the problem was not *how* Sonya was portrayed by Dostoyevsky but that she was portrayed *at all*, as a pointer towards the possibility of Christian redemption. Goldensohn's reasoning seems to be, 'Since the intellectual elites know that Christian redemption is simply mass wish-fulfilment, any art that depicts that redemption is, by definition, kitsch.' In a world where reality is seen as ultimately dark and futile, such critics believe that salvation for sinners is our cute, bobble-head puppy figurine, our stereotypical sunset picture. For those critics, only a nihilistic embrace of the *ultimacy* of shit (to adapt Kundera's phrase) avoids being labelled kitsch.[21] That is sheer prejudice and it is bad for art and bad for the human spirit.

Attitudes like this remind us that Christian artists are not competing on a level playing field. Christian artists will have to put in extra effort to make sure that their stories, songs, images and games are as unsentimental as possible, but without slipping into brutality and despair. We need artists who can conjure compassion without cliché, hope devoid of saccharine sweetness, a *subversive* hope that overturns expectations. *That* is the agenda for the Christian imagination in a cultural context disillusioned with the gospel.

We need artists like (atheist) Joss Whedon of *Avengers, Firefly* and *Buffy the Vampire Slayer* fame. Though in recent years he has blown up his personal and professional life,[22] he was an amazing writer with an *absolute* allergy to cliché and sentimentality. He sought to undermine them

---

20 Barry Goldensohn, 'On kitsch', *Salmagundi: A quarterly of the humanities and social sciences*, vol. 85–86 (Winter–Spring, 1990), p. 248, cited in Kulka, *Kitsch and Art*, pp. 94–95.

21 Nihilism is the belief that, ultimately, existence is a meaningless riddle. Human life has no intrinsic purpose or worth.

22 Whedon has been embroiled in a number of scandals involving affairs with actresses in his shows (leading to a bitter divorce) and on-set verbal abuse (which led to his removal from several projects). See Aishwarya Sinha, 'Is Joss Whedon heading towards retirement? Drink all the tea with us', *Film Daily* (7 December 2020), <https://filmdaily.co/news/joss-whedon-retirement/>, accessed February 2023.

whenever he could in his writing and directing, leaving the audience flanked, surprised and delighted. Or Charlie Kaufman, the screenwriter behind *Adaptation*, *Eternal Sunshine of the Spotless Mind* and *I'm Thinking of Ending Things*. His scripts burst with imaginative weirdness, often traversing disturbing territory, raising difficult questions, but always with deep compassion for his characters. Or Greta Gerwig, the writer and director of *Lady Bird* and *Little Women*, one of the few screenwriting talents I know of who can portray deep human goodness without making it feel static and boring. Instead, goodness feels dynamic, full of life and risk. None of these filmmakers is Christian, but they all share a deep aversion to kitsch, so their films have a profound impact on audiences. We need Christians who can do that, and more.

The message must go through: propaganda

Another pitfall for the Christian imagination is propaganda. Despite its bad reputation, propaganda need not be manipulative; it simply needs to be passionately direct.[23] But propaganda is not art. Art should be allusive, subtle, indirect, playful. Propaganda has but one passion: it must, must, *must* get its message across so that its audience will get on board and believe the Right Things. Art, too, burns with passion, but it doesn't shout. It whispers seductively to the imagination, opens doors in unexpected places and allows room for exploring strange new worlds.

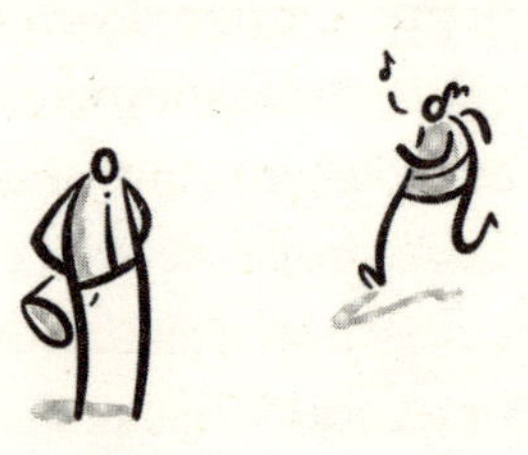

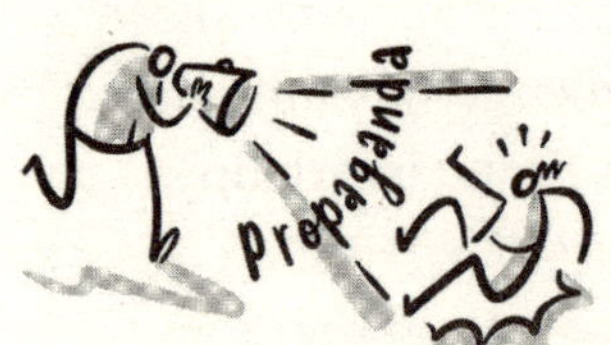

Propaganda is a problem for earnest conservative Christians precisely because we care so much about our message. The gospel brings life and health and peace, and people should know about it. But those in the current generation have grown up in a media-saturated culture; they know how propaganda works. They can spot, deconstruct and dismiss an overly earnest plea from a mile away. Too often, such directness meets with exactly the same level of success as a pigeon flying directly into a plate glass window. There is an impressive smack, to be

23 Seerveld, *Bearing Fresh Olive Leaves*, pp. 126–127.

sure, but nothing of the message gets in. It just slides down and lies there, inert . . . like a dead pigeon.

There are contexts in which directness is called for, situations where subtlety and misdirection are absolutely out of place. In the life of the church, preaching is clearly of central importance. But art offers jaded, unchurched people freedom to explore, to find hidden passageways, to wrestle with the monsters that lurk within this imaginary world and within their own souls. Christian artists therefore need to think incrementally, in terms of a process rather than an immediate result. In a post-Christian culture, the journey from hard-hearted unbelief (or stubborn agnosticism) to joyful surrender to Christ takes years, maybe decades. Creating relationships and an ongoing dialogue are part of that process.

One overlooked aspect is a progressive openness to, and acceptance of, the aesthetic of the Christian community. We need narratives, songs, games and images that give people the freedom to discover truths for themselves within these imaginative oases. Our art should allow people to become *participants* in the imaginary worlds portrayed. An emphasis on process and participation encourages repeat traffic and ongoing engagement with the Christian imagination. Our anxiety that they won't 'get it' without overly simplistic, neon guideposts is a recipe for continued alienation, for shutting down that crucial, participatory process.

Good Christian art treats its audience as people with intelligence and imagination. It raises questions more than it gives answers. That sort of art leads to prolonged audience engagement rather than a one-and-done mindset. Look for and support Christian art that opens up spaces for exploration rather than settling for propaganda that closes doors.

We are the CHAMPIONS: triumphalism

Kitsch and propaganda are pitfalls of technique or strategy in relation to expressing the Christian imagination. Triumphalism is more of a pitfall of the heart, a product of poor theology and attitude rather than aesthetic carelessness. Triumphalism elevates the culture war and proclaims victory (prematurely) because God is on our side. In chapter 7, I said that our position is not one of the victorious army of Joshua marching in to conquer the land. Rather, we are more like the exiled people of God, waiting for him to bring us home. In the meantime, we work for the common good of our adopted land (Jeremiah 29:4–7). Christian art that projects us as victors over the land misapprehends our real situation.[24] Triumphalism is deeply alienating to the very people we are trying to reach with the love of Christ.

Given the historical legacy (not to mention the more recent conquests) of a politically muscular Christianity, post-Christian cultures are hypersensitive to any hint of coercion or attempted political takeover that pushes us towards what they perceive as theocracy.

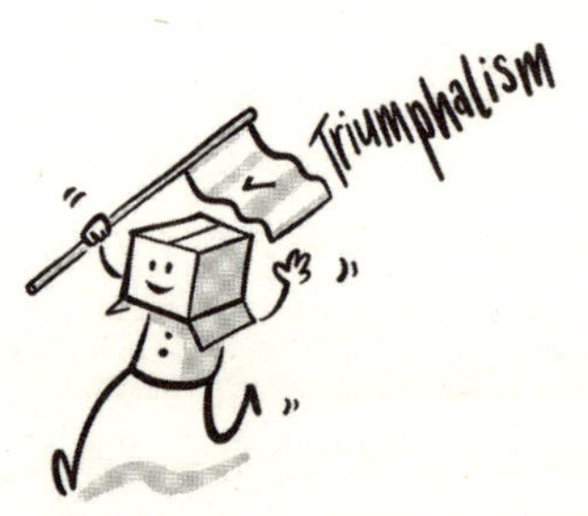

The other-enchanted[25] and post-Christians are firmly in the majority.[26] If the faithful want to push a religious agenda down their throats, they are all too ready to push back. And they are repulsed by a hasty confession that we are only doing this because we love them. What too many Christians dish out doesn't look or feel like love. They are right. All too often, we mouth our love for non-Christians, but in our imaginations the non-Christian 'other' (gay people, liberal political activists, secular media and others) are cast as 'Enemies of the Kingdom of Righteousness'. They can feel that hypocrisy. We act out of tribal self-interest and try to convince ourselves that it's love.

---

24 Triumphalism often goes hand-in-hand with Christian nationalism, a theological perspective that insists God's favour shines especially on one's own country, obscuring the international and multi-ethnic nature of the church. Conflating God and country blinds us to what God is doing among people different from us and deafens us to calls for justice from the oppressed – oppression in which, too often, we are implicated. Jesus' command to 'go and make disciples of all nations' (Matthew 28:19) and John's vision of a multitude 'from every tribe and nation' (Revelation 7:9) both mean that loyalty to Christ supersedes loyalty to nation. Our true citizenship is in heaven (Philippians 3:20). Christ stands in judgment over every nation, including our own. We must keep our dual citizenship in view, ready to critique our own nation in light of Christ's lordship. James K. A. Smith, *Awaiting the King: Reforming public theology*, Cultural Liturgies, Volume 3 (Grand Rapids, MI: Baker Academic, Kindle edn, 2017), argues that Christian attachment to nation must be marked by learned (liturgical) ambivalence: affection, but also critical rebuke when that nation violates the life of mercy Christ has commanded us to follow (see especially chapter 6 and loc. 6004–6173 or pp. 213–221). Timothy Keller highlights the varieties of Christian nationalism in his review of Samuel L. Perry and Andrew Whitehead's book, *Taking America Back for God: Christian nationalism in the United States* (Oxford: Oxford University Press, 2020), 'A book review on the topic of Christian nationalism', Life in the Gospel (Spring 2021), <https://quarterly.gospelinlife.com/book-review-on-the-topic-of-christian-nationalism>, accessed February 2023.

25 See the Introduction to chapter 2.

26 See the statistics in the Introduction to chapter 2. Evangelical/conservative Protestant Christians constitute a distinct minority in both the USA and the UK.

Further, triumphalist Christians are often blind to their own weaknesses and failings. If they do catch a glimpse of them, they dare not speak of them because 'We are the Good Guys. We are *not* like them.' By hiding behind masks, triumphalism cheapens our common humanity to posture on the moral high ground.[27] Nothing good comes from art born of such an ugly spirit.

One example of triumphalism I mentioned earlier is *God's Not Dead* (2014). More propaganda than art, this film presents Christians as unerringly sweet (and victimized), while the atheists are unbearably smug, hate-filled and devoid of compassion. That's not just bad writing; it's a form of self-comfort that sings to the choir while pretending to convey an important message to a secular audience. That is why it has been panned universally on important film review sites such as Metacritic and Rotten Tomatoes.[28]

YouTube film critic Josh Keefe analyses the film in his video essay, 'Why Christian movies are BAD'.[29] In the most disturbing part of his video, he shows footage of moments at a Newsboys concert.[30] They performed their song 'God's not dead' while clips from the film played behind them. Whenever the clip showed the atheist Professor Radisson, the audience booed loudly. Whenever the clip showed one of the Christian characters, they cheered. Keefe comments, 'It felt like the Two Minutes Hate from George Orwell's *1984*.' He then asks how he would feel if he were an atheist teenager who had been invited to that Newsboys concert. 'Would he feel that Christians are loving and not judgmental?' Sometimes Christian entertainment reveals a dark, ugly side that completely undermines who we are called to be: honest about our own failings and compassionate towards the failings of others. Triumphalism betrays the love Christ calls us to.

27 As I write this, a series of media stories about sexual abuse scandals involving churches (and, in one case, a seminary) are making their way through social media. Most often the abusers were protected and the victims were discredited and driven away. These are only the most extreme examples of the way in which abuse and dysfunction hide themselves within the conservative Christian community, a symptom of a triumphalistic culture that insists on masks.

28 In October 2021, *God's Not Dead* was scoring 16/100 on Metacritic, and 12/100 on Rotten Tomatoes. Both sites survey a wide number of critics and users to determine the consensus about a film. For reference, Rotten Tomatoes scored *Birdemic: Shock and Terror* (a truly inept piece of filmmaking) at 18/100.

29 Josh Keefe, 'Why Christian movies are BAD', Josh Keefe, YouTube (14 August 2017), <www.youtube.com/watch?v=50_3J6Go5Ng>, accessed May 2023. The analysis of *God's Not Dead* begins at 8:50.

30 The Newsboys are a popular Christian musical group. Keefe relates this story beginning at 12:30.

In fact, triumphalism betrays the gospel itself. There is no gospel – no good news – without a reckoning with the bad news. We must acknowledge our helplessness (not power) and sinful brokenness (not righteousness) if we are to be saved. As Christian author Philip Yancey says:

> The truth, about ourselves and about our need for outside help, sets us free. We don't need to pretend that things are fine or that goodness comes easily. We admit we are needy and look to God for both vision and strength to subvert the world.[31]

Triumphalism, by pretending that we are better than we are (or better than our cultural opponents, at any rate), hamstrings the subversive power of the Christian imagination.

Of course, there are still areas of deep disagreement between Christians and non-Christians. There are times when Christians (and Christian art) must speak up for the voiceless, who are endangered by a callous society. But when we disagree with the non-Christian majority, *how* we do so makes all the difference.[32] We should grieve over the alienation between us and those who see things differently. We should strive to love. Love seeks common ground to heal rifts where it can[33] but, too often, we seem to revel in those rifts. We end up mimicking the Pharisee who thanked God that he was not like the tax collector (Luke 18:9–14). That is not the ministry of reconciliation Paul wrote about in 2 Corinthians 5:16–21. The Christian posture before the watching world must be one of humility and compassion rather than that of exhibiting an angry, judgmental, triumphalistic spirit. We need art that reflects gentleness, mourns the alienation between us and our neighbours, seeks to heal, restore and speak wisdom into our culture for the common good. Only that can be called Christian triumph, for only then do we reflect God's mercy to messed-up humans like us.

---

31 Philip Yancey, *Vanishing Grace: What ever happened to the good news?* (Grand Rapids, MI: Zondervan, 2014), pp. 262–263.

32 See the end of chapter 2.

33 'Common ground' here refers to areas of common cause (common grace) where Christians and non-Christians can work together and build relationships, not *presuppositional* common ground.

Turning to the dark side: hopeless vision

Sometimes, Christian artists who want to avoid kitsch and triumphalism in the name of artistic (and personal) integrity will wander into very dark territory – a place without light or hope. Such artists will push the envelope, becoming edgier in their language or visuals than most conservative Christians will accept. They don't venture into darkness because they lack empathy, but precisely because they *do* have empathy, particularly for those who suffer.

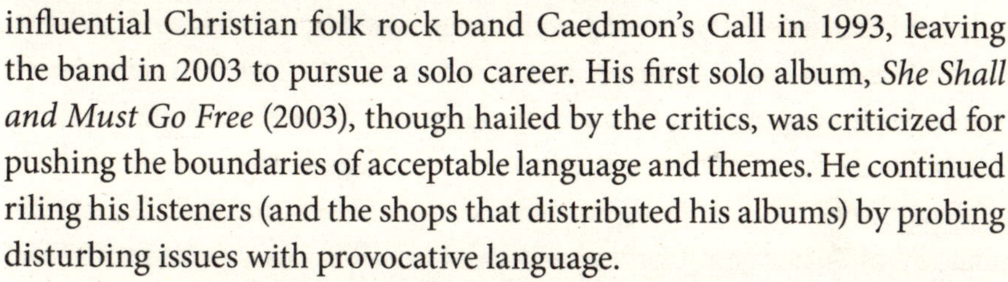

Dwelling in dark places leaves them feeling angry at the injustice and pain they see. Sometimes, it leads them away from the Christian faith entirely, as witnessed by the spate of high-profile Christian artists who have become 'exvangelicals'.[34]

Derek Webb is perhaps the most famous Christian artist to 'deconvert'. He founded the influential Christian folk rock band Caedmon's Call in 1993, leaving the band in 2003 to pursue a solo career. His first solo album, *She Shall and Must Go Free* (2003), though hailed by the critics, was criticized for pushing the boundaries of acceptable language and themes. He continued riling his listeners (and the shops that distributed his albums) by probing disturbing issues with provocative language.

In 2014, Webb divorced his wife, Christian singer-songwriter Sandra McCraken, after he acknowledged having an affair. He described his first album after the divorce, *Fingers Crossed* (2017), as 'a deeply personal tale of two divorces' – from his wife *and* God.[35] In a podcast in 2018, Webb decisively rejected the Christian faith. One ex-fan recalled that

---

[34] The term exvangelical refers to a category of religious nones – namely, those who have left the evangelical Christian faith, typically over their church's politics or teaching on sexuality. For a profile of exvangelicals, see Bradley Onishi, 'The rise of the #exvangelical', *Religion and Politics* (9 April 2019), <https://religionandpolitics.org/2019/04/09/the-rise-of-exvangelical>, accessed February 2023.

[35] From a tweet dated 10 October 2017, 5.34 p.m. Quoted in Matthew Loftus, 'Curse your listeners: Making sense of Derek Webb's *Fingers Crossed*', *Christ and Pop Culture* (7 November 2017), <https://christandpopculture.com/curse-your-listeners-making-sense-derek-webb-fingers-crossed>, accessed January 2023. See also Phillip Luke Sinitiere, 'Derek Webb beyond belief', *Sacred Matters* (20 February 2020), <https://sacredmattersmagazine.com/derek-webb-beyond-belief>, accessed February 2023.

Webb 'explained how he found more comfort in alcohol than he did in the truths of the gospel. At one point, he expresses that, in light of the suffering in the world, either there is no God or the one that exists is a 'f***ing ***hole.'[36] Since then, Webb's albums have continued to explore life after faith, finding freedom away from the 'needless yoke' of the Christian faith.[37]

What happened to this talented and influential artist? We cannot know his heart, but his public statements indicate at least two causes: pain and desire for freedom. He felt pain as a result of his own sinful failures, the damage he caused, as well as the injustice and suffering he saw in the world. Unwilling to wear a mask and hide his pain, Webb decided to walk away from what he perceived to be the source of his pain: his faith. He also craved freedom, seeing the Christian faith as a straitjacket. Throughout his association with his Christian record label, Webb chafed against the narrow confines of evangelical politics and sensitivities, often using deliberately provocative language to push back.[38] Together, his pain and yearning for freedom cast a shadow that, for him, extinguished the light of hope the gospel provides. God's arm seemed too short to save (Isaiah 59:1), and did he really want to be saved by *this* kind of faith?

Webb's journey is unique, but instructive. Artists have raw souls, emotionally exposed to the world. They are empathetic, often taking others' pain on themselves. When they see Christians *cause* people pain (through, say, triumphalistic attitudes), they feel shame and resentment that can alienate them from other Christians. They can feel unheard and unloved, lonely within their own spiritual communities.

Artists are also innovators and free spirits. They hate conventional confines. When a boundary presents itself, many instinctively – and creatively – push against it. They are explorers by nature and often delve

36 Dustin J. Coleman, 'Derek Webb, wrestling with the category of "ex-Christian", and the nature of true saving faith', *Theology Along the Way* (10 April 2018), <https://theologyalongtheway.org/2018/04/10/derek-webb-wrestling-with-the-category-of-ex-christian-and-the-nature-of-true-saving-faith>, accessed February 2023. The specific podcast was not named.

37 From a tweet dated 27 July 2019, 6.49 a.m.: 'thanks, brandon. i receive that as an expression of care. respectfully, i feel the same way. i hope you can one day feel free of the need for a needless yoke, regardless of how light.' Quoted in Ryan Hawkins, 'Exchanging Christ's yoke: A response to Derek Webb, Josh Harris, and others leaving Christianity in search of freedom', *Looking at Christ* (2 September 2019), <www.lookingatchrist.com/exchanging-christs-yoke>, accessed February 2023.

38 The song 'What matters more' uses profanity to make the point that Christians care more about obscene language than they do about human suffering (track 6 on *Stockholm Syndrome*, 2009), Fair Trade Services, <www.youtube.com/watch?v=s5pBXY2AkeY>, accessed February 2023.

into dark, uncomfortable issues such as sexuality, violence, abuse. Such explorations take an emotional and spiritual toll, opening doorways into a world of shadows.

This is not to pretend that artists who drink too deeply of darkness bear no responsibility. But if churches want creatives to be part of their communities, they will need a heightened sensitivity to creatives' pain, and ways to nurture them to keep them from falling into the darkness. Artists need and crave pastors and friends along the way to help keep them in touch with the light, to help them drink deep of the hope Christ provides, so they will have light to share.

The big picture

Now that we have sketched the major pitfalls for Christian imaginative, artistic work – kitsch, propaganda, triumphalism and a hopeless vision – we can combine them with the positive tension and balance we discussed in chapter 7, which Christian artists should strive for:

- to explore the tension of an existence coloured by both the darkness (a cross-shaped imagination) and the light (an empty-tomb-shaped imagination) that finds its centre in 'eschatological desire' (a thirst for the light that pierces the darkness);
- to find a balance between shouting and chameleon-like mumbling, finding a 'sweet spot' in a whispered 'parabolic resonance' (setting up vibrations in our audience the way Jesus did in his parables).

When Christian creatives lose that balance and tension, they end up in one or more of the 'four kingdoms' – false paths that derail aesthetic witness. When they are combined correctly, however, the pitfalls and centres we aim for (the 'sweet spot') form an overall landscape (see illustration on page 3 in plate section).

Each pitfall, or 'kingdom', has its own distinctive hue and texture.[39]

[39] This list of pitfalls is by no means exhaustive. Rather it focuses on what contributes to the failure of Christian art within a post-Christian audience – the failure to plant oases. For another perspective, see Eleanor Nickel, *Christian Popular Culture: From* The Chronicles of Narnia *to* Duck Dynasty (Eugene, OR: Wipf & Stock, 2021). She explores how Christian popular art represents people of colour and women, either seeing them as fully human or stripping them of dignity by using sexist and racist stereotypes.

The kingdom of fluff

Also known as the 'realm of the vaguely uplifting', it's full of blue skies, flowers, sunsets, fluffy kittens and unicorns – that is, cultural works long on feel-good sentiment, short on substance. Any Bible verses mentioned will be comforting and blandly encouraging.

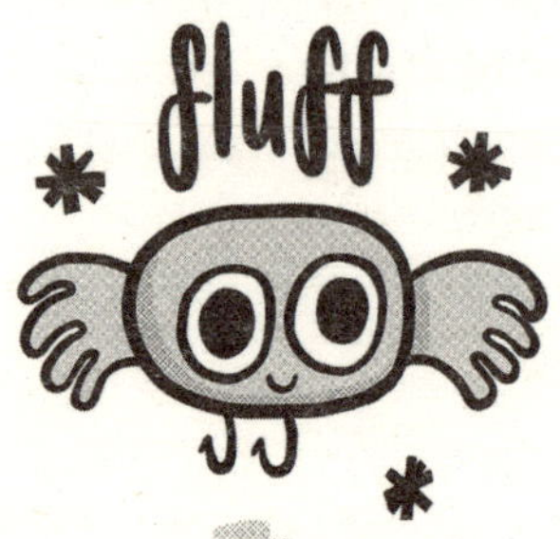

The result? A vague, spiritually inspiring feeling. Sentimental and overly cute figurines and Kinkade paintings fit into this category. So do email slide shows with synthesized classical music and animated fluttering butterflies that wish you a 'Blessed day'. So, too, does most kitsch.

Nothing too disturbing or challenging will be found here, certainly not bumping into the real God and facing psychological devastation, as Isaiah did in Isaiah 6: 'Woe to me, I am undone, for I am a man of unclean lips and I live among a people of unclean lips!' Nothing is risked. All is niceness and positive energy, hazy comfort and reassurance, with a slick Hallmark-type sheen. Gone is the tension that recognizes the darkness and brokenness of a fallen world (the cross-shaped imagination). All is mumbling niceness.

The kingdom of forced smiles

Also known as the 'kingdom of Christian swagger'. This kind of Christian culture sometimes manifests itself in sentimentality that boils down to emotional manipulation. These works avoid emotional honesty, the raw wounds that Christians sometimes bear in their hearts but dare not acknowledge openly.

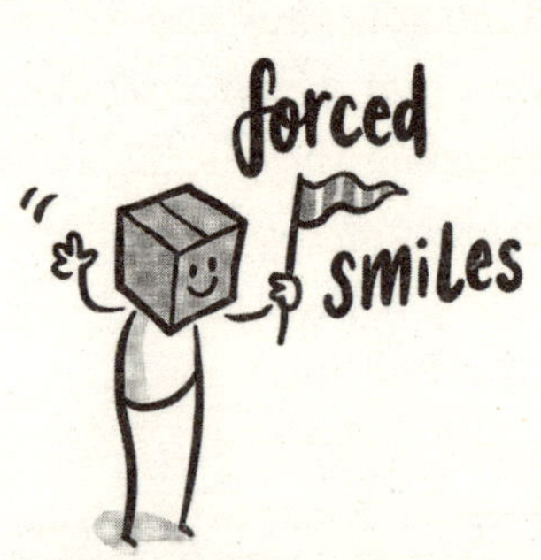

This kingdom can also manifest as an aggressive, trumpeting triumphalism that treats the Christian church as a conquering army that routinely puts the pagans to flight (if only we had enough faith!). But this cultural posture forgets that we are to be servant-lovers of those who have set themselves against God. In either case, what is opened by such art is not an expanse for exploration, but a narrow passageway that leads in one direction: the gospel message simply

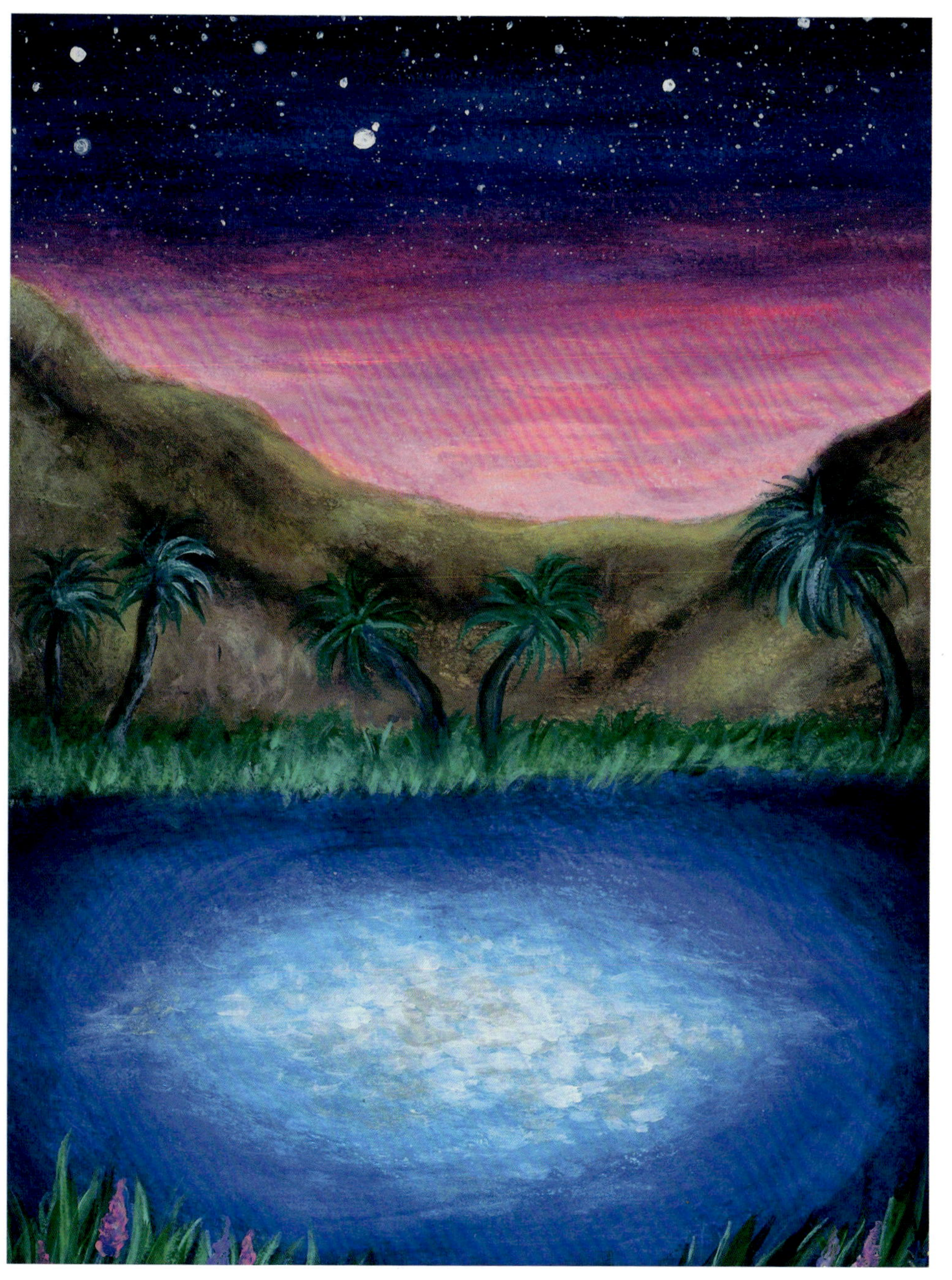

The portal
(Claire Elise Turnau Ward, 2019)

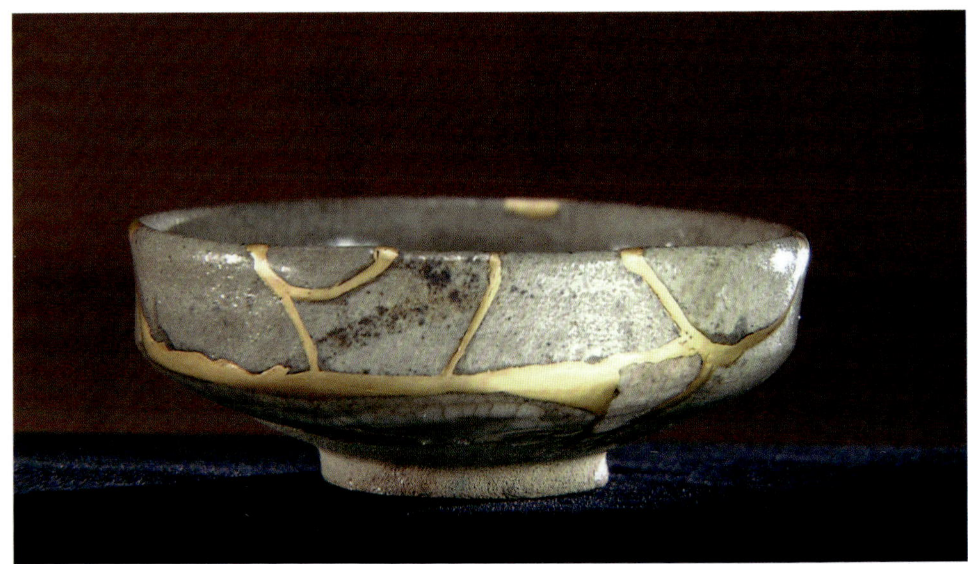

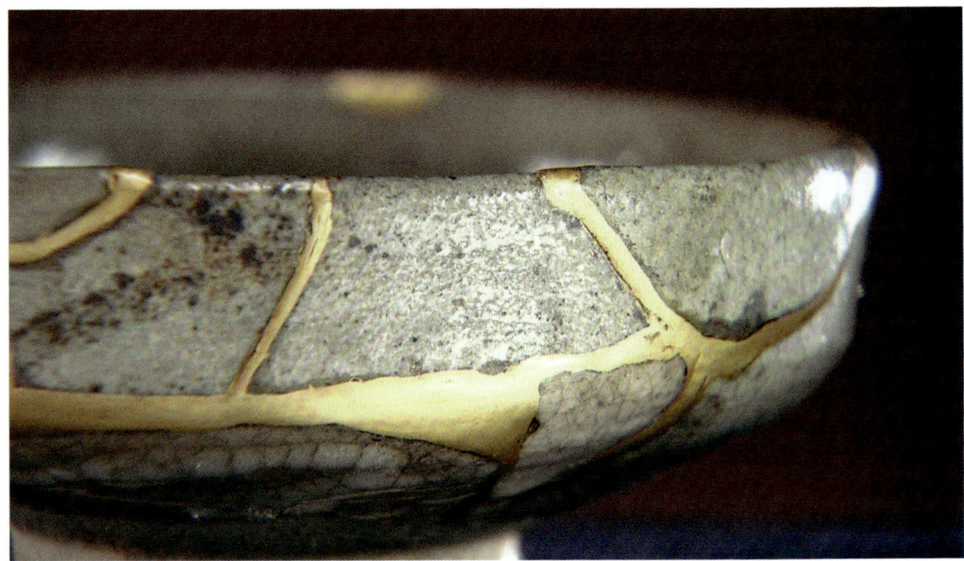

Photos of *kintsugi* (Dave Pike, 2015)

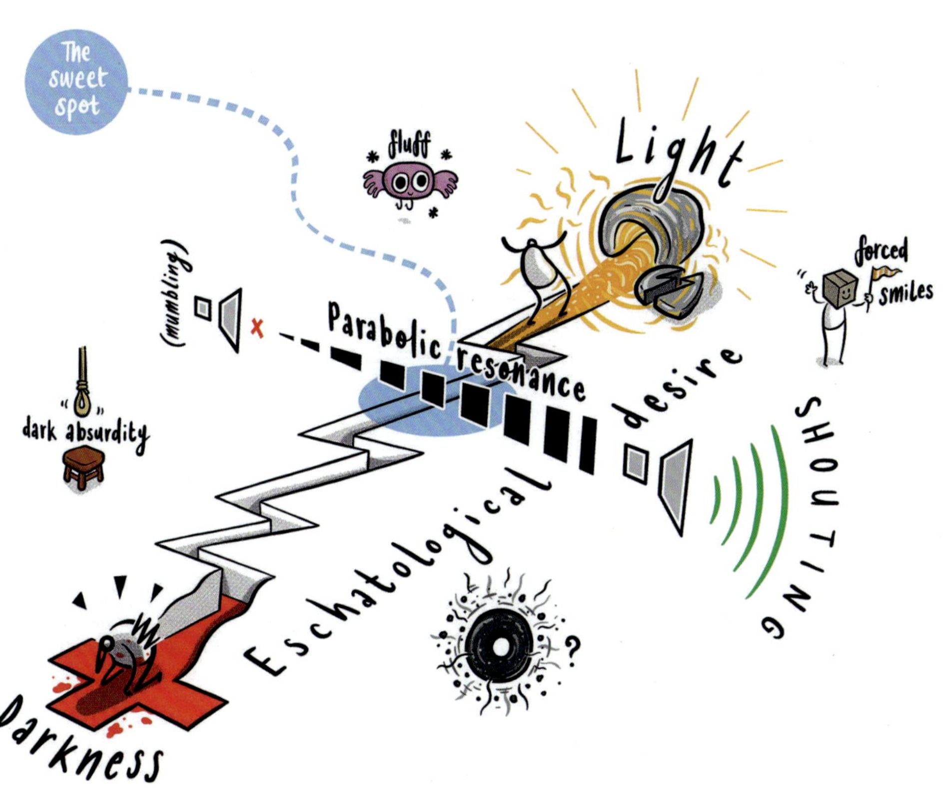

The big picture: 4 kingdoms and a sweet spot
(Jason Ramasami, 2023)

Light, apples, and shadows (Ruth Naomi Floyd, 2015)

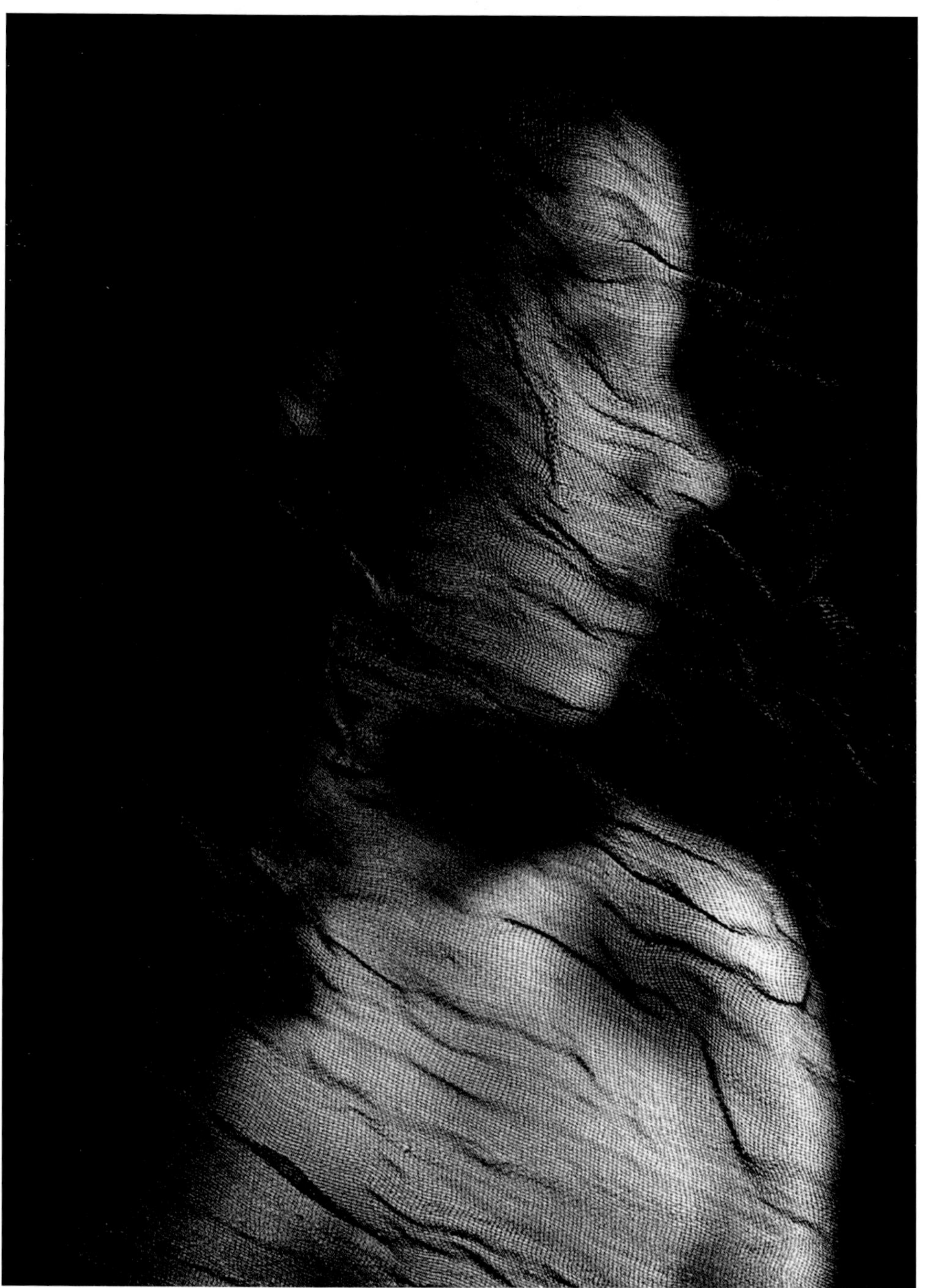

Woman and the veil (Ruth Naomi Floyd, 2007)

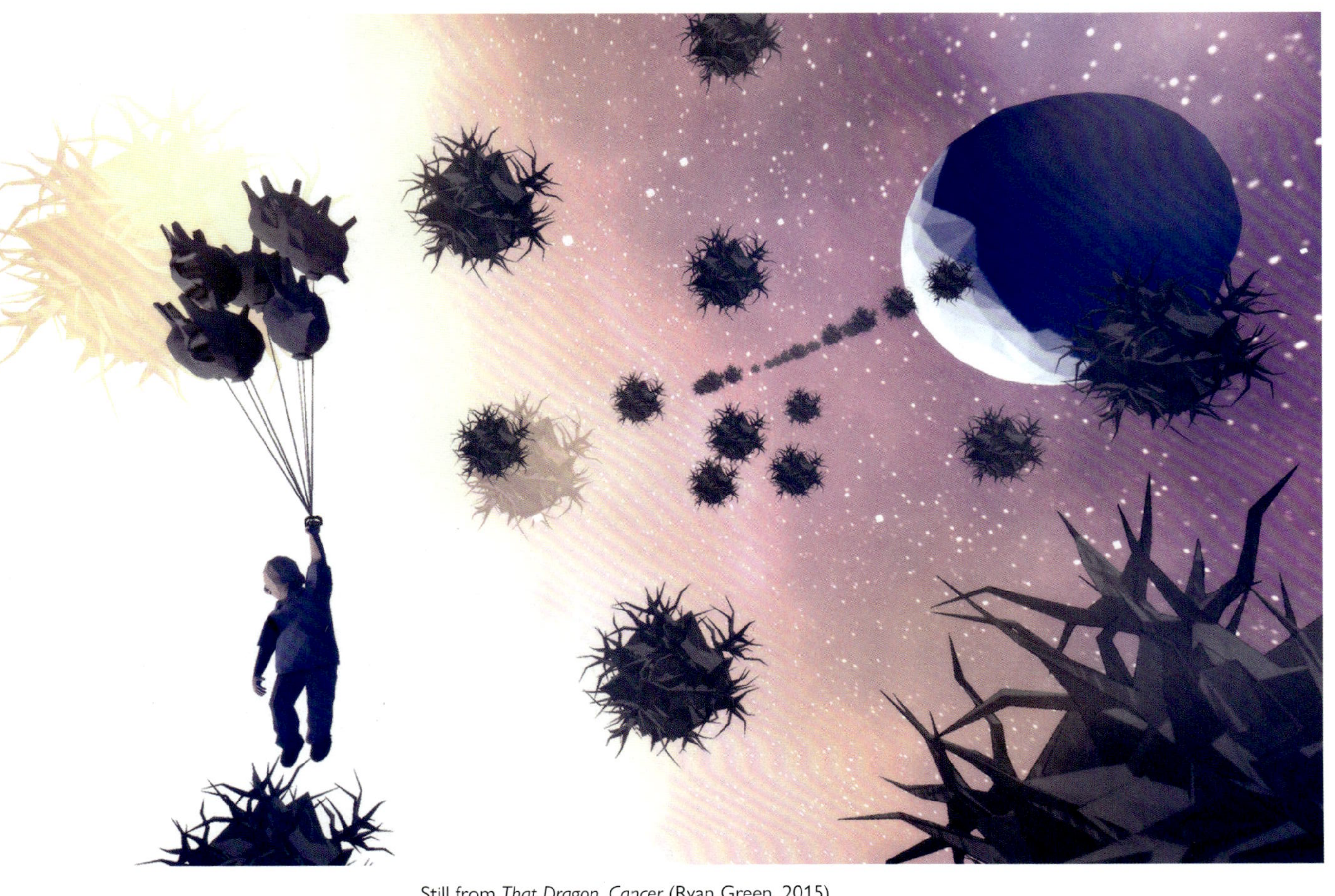

Still from *That Dragon, Cancer* (Ryan Green, 2015)

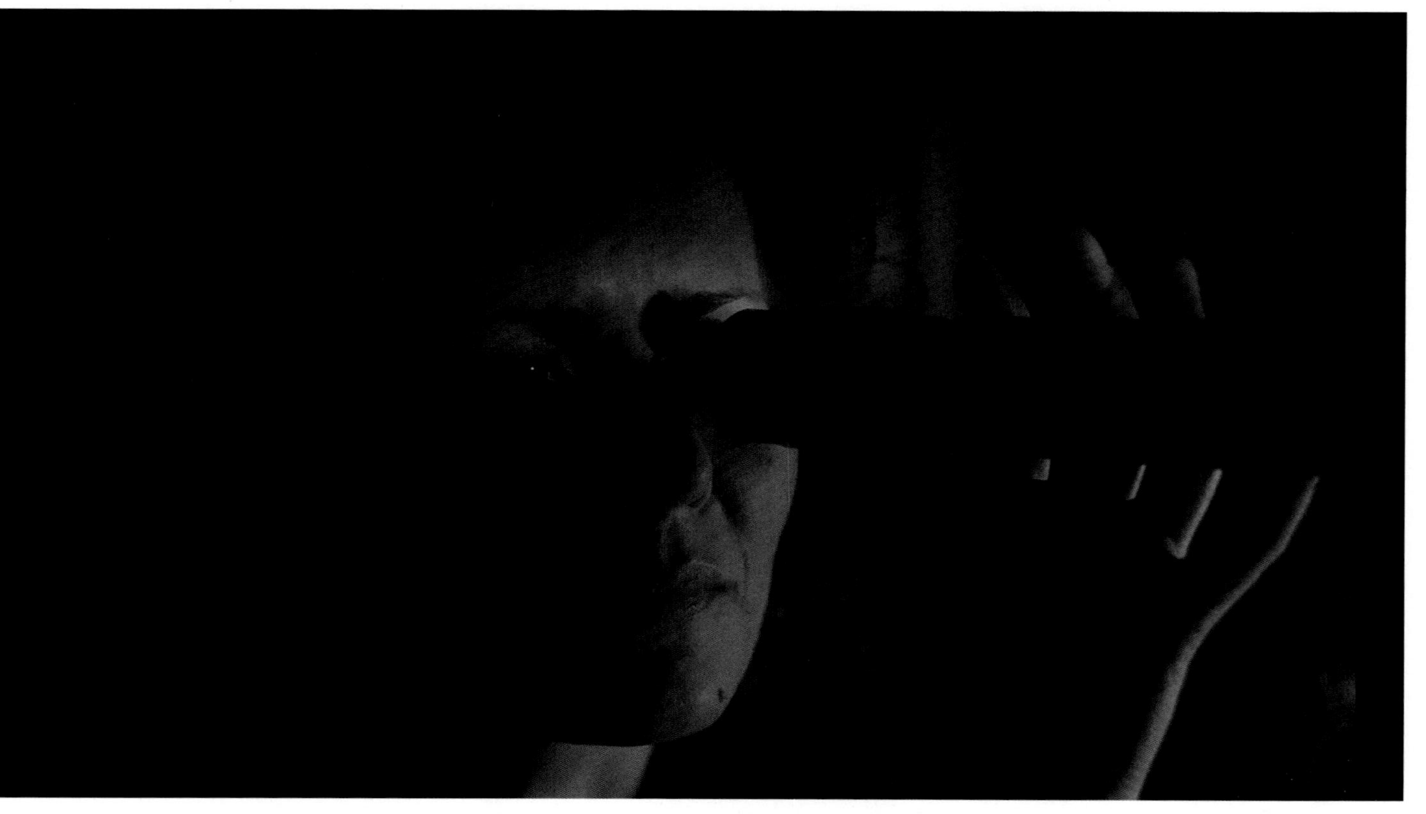

Still from *A Short Film about Love* (Krzysztof Kieślowski, 1988)

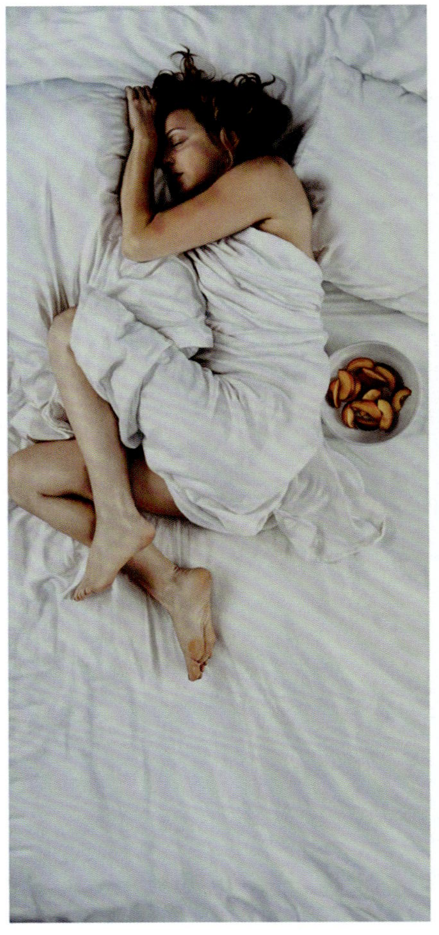
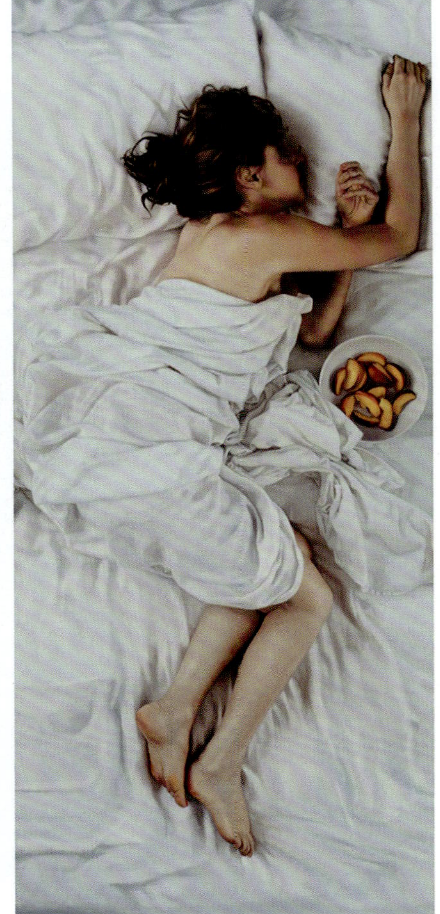
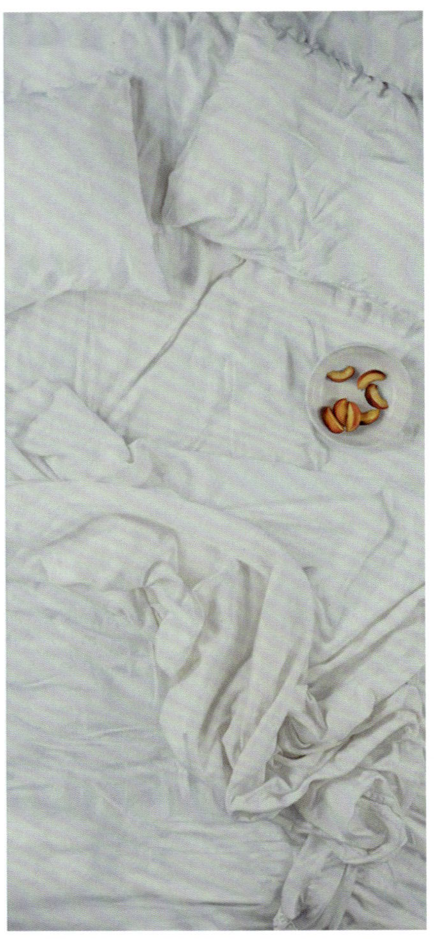

Sleeping with peaches (Lee Price, 2011)

must get through loud and clear. There is no room for reflection or questions, no room for ambiguity, no room for lament. Everything must be spelt out in **BOLD CAPS**. Chick comic tracts live here.[40] Those dwelling in this kingdom seem to take perverse delight in the hellish destination of sinners, while simultaneously hitting the lost over the head with the gospel.

Many Christian films and some contemporary Christian music fall into this category. Such works will be anathema to non-Christians, who don't care for gospel megaphones. They will treat such Christian culture with ridicule. But the works of this kingdom damage Christians as well. They express a vision of an unrealistically tidy life where all struggles are resolved within two hours of film time and everyone with faith is happy and content (or soon will be). This forgets that we still dwell in a dark and twisted land (with dark and twisted hearts), that walking by faith costs us something, that sometimes God doesn't answer our prayers as we would want, that life itself makes us feel weak and hurts like hell, that we look *forward* to our full adoption and redemption in faith with aching desire.

The kingdom of dark absurdity/a distant God

Some Christian artists, overreacting to the kingdom of forced smiles, shed most or all of their Christian distinctiveness and take refuge in a grim acknowledgment of the twisted darkness of the world. In their pain, any real sense of hope and light is lost.

This type of Christian culture is rare since the Christian culture-buying public doesn't like wallowing in darkness. But such works do exist on the margins of the Christian imagination (the novels of John Updike, perhaps Graham Greene and many exvangelicals, for example).

40 For the uninitiated, Chick tracts are mini comic books written to be evangelistic tools by fundamentalist comic artist Jack T. Chick. They often featured violence (a sinner falling to his death after rejecting Christ and so forth) and over-the-top, buffoonish portrayals of non-Christians and demons. Subtle they are not. They are available for free on the Internet at <www.chick.com>.

The kingdom of ?

There is not much to say about this category – I don't think it exists. There aren't many self-consciously Christian artists who both trumpet their theological commitments *and* forget about the light of hope in the gospel. Perhaps the music of quasi-Christian musician Nick Cave counts (great stuff, but he countenances no redemption). The strident atheism of several exvangelicals (including Derek Webb) fits into this category, but they would not want to be called Christian creatives any more. Given the character of the gospel, it is almost impossible to be very explicit about it without also inevitably sharing hope.

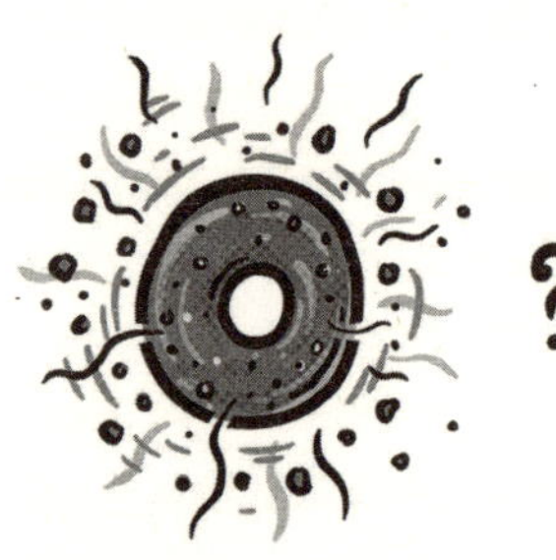

Conclusion: on maintaining subversive power

Art's purpose is to open imaginary worlds for exploration, not to deliver our messages, nor insulate us from the world. Christian art must enter into conversation with the world as it truly is, as well as with our hope for what the world shall become.

The 'four kingdoms' serve to illustrate vividly what happens when Christian creatives (and their audiences) lose sight of Christian art's characteristic tension (between the cross and empty tomb) and balance (between shouting and mumbling): it loses all subversive power in a post-Christian culture. But if it manages to maintain balance and tension, works of the Christian imagination have a deeply subversive power to create oases in the desert. What does that look like in practice? We shall explore this in part 4.

Postscript: on artists and systems

All this talk of kingdoms, balance, tension and 'sweet spots' could lead to the mistaken impression that it all comes down to the intention and talent of the artists. But it is not only about them. We often have romantic notions of artists as free spirits, unhindered by the limits that the rest of us struggle with. In fact, artists have never been completely free. Not if they want to eat. The system they must work within can have a profound impact on them.

I sat down with a friend from church named Zach Zegan. From 1998 to 2013 he fronted a Christian rock band called Dizmas.[41] Full disclosure: I am not a fan of contemporary Christian music (CCM). It's too slick, too overproduced, too conformist, too safe to be interesting. I had been under the impression that it sounded that way because the musicians were risk-averse, that they liked playing it safe. But Zach showed me a more complicated picture.

Zach and some friends started playing local gigs in their home town before they left secondary school. The music they played was hardcore, what would later be called 'screamo' – heavy guitar and drums, aggressive vocals – which was cutting-edge stuff at the time. It was the antithesis of stereotypical CCM. As they played festivals and found success, they signed to a small, independent Christian record label, then to a larger one (Sparrow).

They started maturing as a band, with the help of a professional record producer, at an interesting time in the music business. In the late 1990s and early 2000s, two things were happening simultaneously. The first was that major record labels (Sony/BMG, EMI-CMG, Warner and Universal)[42] started aggressively buying up smaller independent labels. Their control of distribution channels made it difficult for independent labels to survive.

The second thing that happened was the rise of Internet sites such as YouTube and Spotify. They offered music for free,[43] putting pressure on all the labels, major and independent. Most of the independent record labels were bought by larger, multinational corporate giants, which themselves were being squeezed financially. While the major labels claimed that they would maintain the character of the smaller Christian labels they bought (now subdivisions of much larger companies), they were actually interested in only one thing: whether or not they would generate revenue. All other objectives were purely secondary.

Dizmas was on the roster of Credential Recordings, one of the labels owned by EMI-CMG. It was supposed to appeal to Christians who liked a heavier, more raw sound than mainstream CCM. But Credential wasn't

---

41 According to church tradition, Dismas was the name of the thief crucified next to Jesus who asked to be remembered when Christ came into his Kingdom (Luke 23:39–43).

42 Universal bought EMI in 2012, so the Big Four is now the Big Three.

43 Spotify was later forced to offer its service as a paid subscription. Musicians still complain about the minuscule compensation they receive.

earning as much money as EMI wanted. Zach told me that affected his mentality as a musician.

> We realized: we're not really impacting anybody on this unknown subsidiary record label. We're going on all these small tours, we're *headlining* tours, and nobody knows who we are, and it's getting hard to get people to come to our shows. To, 'OK, well, I guess next album we'll have to try to figure out some way for more people to like our music, or something.' So maybe we tone down the radicalness of our music a little bit.
>
> . . . as we looked at things and talked to our record label, there was definitely logic and reason behind [it], like, 'Hey, if you want your career to keep going, and be successful, we just have to advise you that it would be best if you guys were writing some songs that are more accessible for multiple audiences, instead of just the underground scene . . .'
>
> I think the record label let us record our first album the way we wanted, and when it didn't hit as well as everybody thought it would, I think that's when people's opinion started to come like, 'Hey, we were thinking . . . ' We never felt forced, like, 'You *have* to do this', but there definitely were opinions coming from our record label's direction. It could make the record label sound like 'bad guys', but I would say our parents were always saying the same things too . . . [44]
>
> The thing I have to look back on is that we were young and impressionable, and we respected the people that worked for our record label, we respected our management, we respected the music scene and different things. But we were just trying to figure out how to balance all those things. Certainly, we wanted our own sound. We wanted to be artistic. We wanted to have that 'This is *us* [sound].' And yet, in that element, we are maturing, growing young adults. Our writing style, our understanding of music, the music that influences, it was changing from year to year as we were growing . . . there are things you're learning to appreciate more that maybe you

[44] The members of Dizmas were secondary (high) school students at this point.

> didn't before. And as an artist, artists are very existential in many ways, so it's kind of being *whoop* into anything and everything. So you're trying to keep an open mind to whatever it is as an artist that you can do, but at the same time be yourself: This is who I am. And in those cracks of uncertainty and being in between 'I know who I am, but I want to be open', that's where I think some of the influences of the record label's management begin to creep in. 'Creep in' makes it sound negative. But they kind of infiltrate and get in.
>
> . . . it's not my intention to paint the Christian record labels or the Christian ministry as these people who are intentionally trying to cause you to be unfaithful to who you think Christ has called you to be. Never once did I feel that our record label or anybody in our label was trying to draw us away from a Christ-centred ethic into a business-centred ethic. But there certainly *was* an element of 'We are Christians, but we are a business.'[45]

In the subtle but constant pressure of a business under financial strain, Dizmas was nudged towards middle-of-the-road music so that they could make a profit. This meant they were no longer making music that would necessarily appeal to the non-Christian hardcore music fans that they used to have. From the label's perspective, you go where you can make the most money. It's simple demographics: the audience spending the most on Christian music is (surprise!) Christians. At the moment, Christians want their music to be inspiring, nice, uplifting, not rocking the boat or screaming at the darkness. The dynamics of the industry itself produce conformity.

But Zach also pointed out that the very thing putting so much pressure on the music industry (the Internet) also provided opportunities for musicians to create and distribute their own music, free from the pressures of the big labels. The very technology that helped to create the pressure to conform was now also creating momentum for artistic diversity.

My point: artists do not work in a vacuum. They are humans who want to connect with their audiences. They need to earn a living. And they want

[45] Personal interview with Zach Zegan (7 June 2016). Zach is now a missionary who assists churches in discipleship and evangelism. He and I both go to the same church in Prague, Czech Republic. It is strange seeing a younger Zach screaming his lungs out on YouTube videos, but there they are.

to feel that they are not playing or writing or directing to an empty space. Staying true to an original artistic vision is not easy and, in some instances, it is unworkable. In a consumer economy, artists are part of a heavily integrated economic system, and systems are notoriously hard to change.

In a *consumer* system, the fastest and most decisive way to change the system is to change consumer desire. If your audience wants something different, challenging, original and creative, rather than conformist, staid and safe, then that is what it will get . . . *if* the audience is willing to support that kind of art financially.

There is another alternative: we could rethink the relationship between art and the economy. A consumer economy demands that the arts conform to consumer desires: the customer is always right. But that dynamic produces tame conformity rather than the imaginative freedom that both artists and audience need. Makoto Fujimura asserts that if the arts are to flourish, we must develop an alternative economy that operates alongside consumer capitalism, a 'gift economy'.[46] Art, like the gospel itself, must be seen as a gift rather than a commodity, a grace freely given rather than an item of consumer exchange. Art within a gift economy – shared and received in a spirit of generosity and self-giving – has the potential to transform cultures. Art-as-gift can alter the increasingly commodified culture of the American church (church-as-spiritual-customer-service-centre), setting it free to participate in the coming new creation.

Let us apply Fujimura's idea of a parallel gift economy that allows the arts to flourish and transform our culture to Zach's band. How differently would Dizmas have developed as a band had churches or other Christian organizations provided a space within which their music could have been offered as a gift rather than a commodity (perhaps by churches providing financial support, giving a gift to allow another gift to develop away from financial pressure)? What if they were spared the conforming pressure of profit in a consumer economy? What if their songs were treated not as commodities but as gifts? Had they been given the freedom to follow their own path, their music might have had the chance to resonate more deeply

[46] The following draws from Fujimura's *Art and Faith*, pp. 66–70. Fujimura himself draws deeply from poet Lewis Hyde's book, *The Gift: Creativity and the artist in the modern world* (New York: Vintage, 2007 [1983]).

with both Christian and non-Christian listeners, transforming their imaginations. It might have developed the roots of an oasis.

Perhaps there's a better way for Christians to relate to art than just leaning into the consumer economy. We need to consider developing a gift economy to fully realize the transformational potential of the gift of art.

In part 4, we will begin to put meat on the skeleton of the framework presented in part 3, exploring concrete examples of the Christian imagination done well. We shall find that it can take a dazzling variety of forms and styles.

Part 4

THE CHRISTIAN IMAGINATION DONE RIGHT: EXPLORING SUBVERSIVE CULTURAL RESONANCE

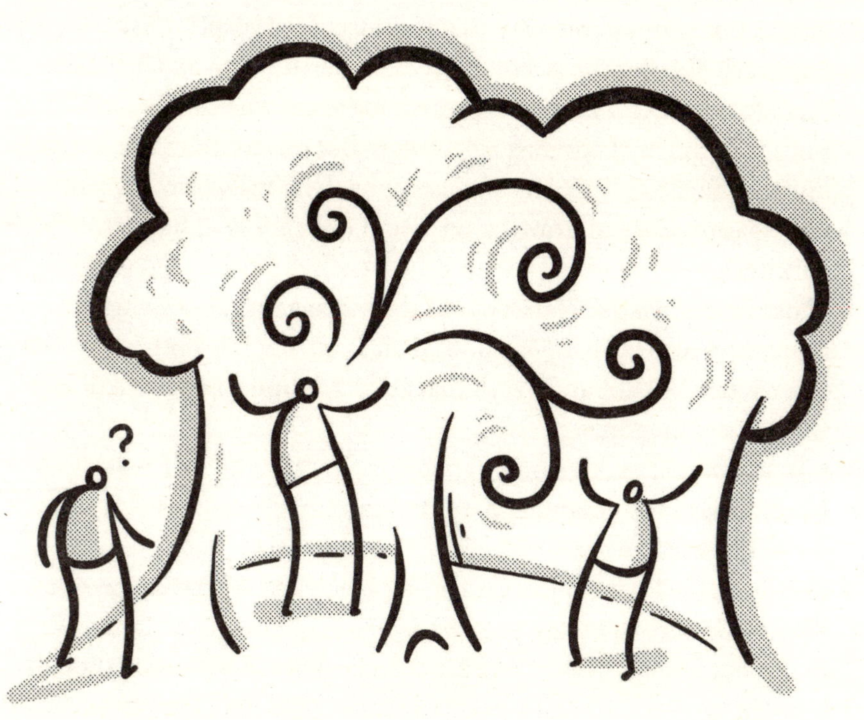

Part 1 explored the issue of cultural engagement, and proposed the Christian imagination as an alternative, positive path for engaging a post-Christian world by planting oases. Part 2 presented a theory of imagination informed by Scripture, science and philosophy. Part 3 narrowed our focus to the Christian imagination and what makes it resonate well in a post-Christian world. In part 4, we will flesh out the theory with concrete examples of works by Christian artists who plant oases well, revealing the subversive, expectation-overturning nature of the Christian imagination in art and entertainment.

The creative works we explore in this part capture that characteristic tension between the darkness and the light in different ways. Each artist's voice finds a different balance between being overly explicit about faith convictions (trumpeting) and hiding them entirely (mumbling) to find resonance in post-Christian culture. We shall explore a *spectrum* of approaches, from the fairly direct to the extremely indirect.

- At one end of the spectrum we find Blind Willie Johnson. He pulls no punches – his music is direct and explicit (he could be in 1930s Texas), but with an intensity that is unusual for gospel music.
- Rap artist Sho Baraka is a bit more oblique, drawing on Christian themes and imagery. Faith is present for those who dig deeper.
- Ruth Naomi Floyd covers gospel songs, but makes more suggestive, indirect music as well. Her photographs don't make any explicit faith claims, instead drawing on visual metaphors of hope in darkness.
- Those in the creative team behind the video game *That Dragon, Cancer* are also fairly open about their faith, but it is faith expressed in a context of pain and death that seeks to connect empathetically with others in pain.
- J. R. R. Tolkien's faith is more muted in *The Lord of the Rings.* Nevertheless, the contours of a Christian imagination undergird the entire work.
- Finally, at the least explicit end of the spectrum, we have Krzysztof Kieślowski's master work *A Short Film about Love.* Here faith dwells in the shadows, heard only in hints and echoes. Kieślowski, though brought up in a Catholic Christian culture, did not claim to be

Christian. Yet his work resonates powerfully with that tension, the hope-in-darkness that characterizes a Christian imagination.

Each of these works transcends the categories typical of contemporary Christian art and entertainment. Apart from Tolkien, they appeal mostly to niche audiences because these types of cultural creativity don't fit the marketing structures of the Christian culture and entertainment industry. Nevertheless, they are important because they offer a creative subversion of post-Christian culture.

Subversive, hopeful protest against the twisted realities of the fallen world lies at the heart of what makes Christian creativity resonate with integrity, compassion and intensity. Not all culture that labels itself as 'Christian' has that subversive power. Plenty of works fall short. But when they have it, such works can serve as a powerful challenge to the post-Christian status quo.

What do we mean by 'subversive'? Must Christian artists be involved in radical politics or revolutionary movements? Yes and no.

Yes, to the extent that Christian artists share God's passion for justice and his sorrow at the way the world has been warped, they may be involved with causes that don't fit neatly with standard political party platforms. Such artists may look for solutions that depart markedly from 'business as usual'.

Also no, as, when I mention imaginative subversion, politics is *not* primarily what I have in mind. Rather, Christian art takes on a subversive resonance when it draws energy from a first love that is rooted in something radically[1] different from the loves of mainstream popular culture. It is subversive when it channels that energy in a way that refreshes, challenges and awakens a deep hunger in those who come into contact with it. The Christian imagination subverts by building shared oases: the cool shade invites but with a different texture and aroma from that of the world.

I am particularly interested in *popular* culture. Not all the case studies in the following chapters are drawn from popular culture – important work is being done in arthouse cinemas and galleries. But imaginative

[1] 'Radical' comes from the Latin *radix*, meaning 'root'.

waves within popular culture spread further and invite more people into its shade. Joss Whedon, once one of Hollywood's most sought-after writers (before his troubles in more recent years), was asked why he incorporated fantastic/sci-fi elements into his work rather than writing 'grown-up' TV programmes. He responded, 'I don't want to create responsible shows with lawyers in them. I want to invade people's dreams.'[2] He did that for the millions of viewers of *Buffy the Vampire Slayer, Firefly* and *Marvel's Avengers. That* is effective cultural subversion. Whedon is an atheist. What I long for are creatives who can invade the dreams and desires of the many, but with a distinctively Christian imagination. When that happens, oases are created that are big enough for everyone.

2 Quoted in Emily Nussbaum, 'Must-see metaphysics', *New York Times Magazine* (22 September 2002), <www.nytimes.com/2002/09/22/magazine/must-see-metaphysics.html.>, accessed February 2023.

9

Towards a subversive Christian popular culture: learning from the blues

What can the blues teach us about creating authentic, resonating Christian popular culture? The blues helped give birth to jazz, rhythm and blues, rock, funk and (at a further remove) pop and various other types of dance music. The blues taps into a spirit that is at once poignant and terrifically powerful, a spirit that has a deep affinity with the Christian ethos. We will focus here on how the blues imagination expresses the tensive vision between the darkness and the light that gives authentic Christian culture its subversive power.[1]

The roots of the blues

The blues originated in a complex mix of different African and European cultural influences. It could hardly have been otherwise, given the social context that gave birth to the blues: forced deportation, slavery, a people inserted into another culture against their will. The blues' rich cultural resonance stems from that painful, bloody, tragic history. Musically, the blues grew from two main roots: the work song and the Negro or African-American spiritual.[2]

The work song (or field holler) was a call-and-response vocal music that black slaves, prison work gangs and sharecroppers used to pass the time.

---

1 For the moment we will ignore the balance between shouting and mumbling.

2 One important source of the blues that I will not be discussing here is griots – West African troubadours who served as models for the lone, wandering blues musician. See Debra Devi, 'The language of the blues: Griot', *American Blues Scene* (10 July 2014), <www.americanbluesscene.com/language-blues-griot>, accessed February 2023. See also William Ferris, 'Blues roots and development', *The Black Perspective in Music*, vol. 2, no. 2 (Autumn 1974), pp. 122–127; and Ed Kopp, 'A brief history of the blues', *All about Jazz* (16 August 2005).

It took their mind off the back-breaking, repetitive work they did, such as chopping wood, picking cotton or breaking up stones. The spiritual was also sometimes sung during work, but was more at home in the black church, a distinctively African-American adaptation of white Christian hymns. The spiritual was the worship music of the black church, expressing the hopes and laments of that community.

Both the work song and the spiritual came out of an experience of suffering and oppression. Black slaves sang them to articulate their misery and trouble. But the songs could also communicate hope, even joy, particularly the spiritual, which stared twisted injustice and sorrow in the face and proclaimed an unshakeable hope, anchored in the realities of God's power and hunger for justice for the oppressed. These were songs rooted in the confidence of an eventual, inevitable liberation.[3]

This commitment to liberation made the spiritual implicitly subversive to the white-dominated culture of the American South. These songs were sung not simply for emotional and spiritual support – sometimes they contained messages used to subvert the practices of oppressive institutions, such as slavery, through hidden double meanings. 'Go down Moses', for example, was both a retelling of the biblical story of the exodus *and* a proclamation that God was going to judge the *contemporary* pharaohs, the slaveholders, and demand that they must 'Let my people go'.[4] 'Wade in the water' served as both an invocation of God's redemptive act of parting the Red Sea *and* advice to runaway slaves on how best to shake bloodhounds off their trail.[5] 'Steal away to Jesus' invited slaves both to find spiritual solace in Christ *and* to steal their master's property – their very selves – away to the North and to freedom.[6]

The spiritual was born of a tension rooted in a life-perspective profoundly shaped by the story arc of the Bible. The creators of the spiritual understood that the world is twisted and wrong *and* that there is hope, because God rescues his people. Through these songs, slaves not

3 Wyatt Tee Walker, *Somebody's Calling My Name: Black sacred music and social change* (Valley Forge, PA: Judson Press, 1979), p. 46.

4 Walker, *Somebody's Calling My Name*, pp. 56–57.

5 William Edgar, 'The deep joy of jazz', *byFaith Online* (1 October 2006), <https://byfaithonline.com/the-deep-joy-of-jazz>, accessed February 2023.

6 Tim Alexander, 'Double entendre: A glimpse into the meanings of slave songs', *UC Merced Undergraduate Research Journal*, vol. 7, no. 1 (2014), pp. 114–120, especially pp. 116–117, <https://escholarship.org/content/qt4h3778q2/qt4h3778q2.pdf>, accessed February 2023.

only took heart but also actively confronted and subverted the evil that they found in the world. Through the spiritual, the people not only sang about hope and liberation, they worked for it.

The spiritual later passed on to the blues a powerful tensive imaginative vision that grew out of the Christian world view, the eyes of the heart focused simultaneously on the evil and twisted wrongness of the world *and* the hope that lives because God is the powerful Redeemer who brings life out of death, freedom out of bondage. Out of that tensive vision came a powerful music of both lament and liberation.

The blues as scandalous truth-telling

How did the spiritual pass on its 'cultural DNA' – the dual focus on the sinful distortion of the world and the reality of hope – to blues musicians? The early blues musicians were all brought up in the black church, and they absorbed the imaginative vision of the church through its music and preaching. Though not typically model members of the church, when they were children they spent time in the pews, participating in worship. That left its mark on the blues musicians and their music.

There were, of course, differences between the church communities and blues musicians, and most ended up leaving the church behind. Some of them were fed up with the deadly mixture of self-righteousness and hypocrisy they found there.[7] Some felt that they could not live up to the moral standards expected of church people. As preacher-turned-blues musician Son House sang in his song, 'Preachin' the blues':

> Oh, I'd'a had religion, Lord, this very day
> But the womens and whiskey, well, they would not let me pray.[8]

Perhaps the decisive reason for their departure from the church was the music itself. Both church people and blues musicians believed that the blues possesses a spirit absolutely antithetical to church music. At a

[7] See Jon Michael Spencer, *Protest and Praise: Sacred music of black religion* (Minneapolis, MN: Fortress Press, 1990), p. 115.

[8] Son House (Eddie James Jr), 'Preachin' the blues, Part 1', *The Roots of Robert Johnson* (Shenachie Entertainment, 1989 [1930]), track 12. Reasonable attempts have been made to discover and contact the copyright owner of these lyrics. The copyright owner is invited to contact the publisher so that acknowledgment may be given in future editions.

concert in 1964, before performing, Son House said, 'I can't hold God in one hand and the Devil in the other. Them two guys don't get along together too well. I got to turn one of 'em loose. So I got out of the pulpit.'[9] And then he sang in 'Preachin' the blues':

Oh, in my room I bowed down to pray
Oh, up in my room, I bowed down to pray
Then the blues come along, and they blowed my spirit away.[10]

He was not alone: at that time, people had to choose – the blues was simply not considered respectable music by anyone on either side. Sung not in churches but in bars, brothels or out on the street, the blues dealt with sensual, rowdy subject matter. Furthermore, the blues saw things with a scandalously exacting eye. Like the spiritual, its lyrics are about the troubles of the world. But a blues song by Otis Spann that has a deliberate dig at the spiritual 'Nobody knows the trouble I've seen', got uncomfortably specific:

Nobody knows, nobody knows, people, the trouble that I've seen.
Now you know I done lost all my money, and my woman she
treated me so mean.[11]

Whereas church people might be tempted to gloss over ugly details with an 'Hallelujah!' or a 'Have mercy!', blues singers told the low-down dirty truth. They simply didn't care if they offended anyone; the blues was going to speak the truth, no matter what.

Truth-telling is the cardinal virtue of the blues, its first commandment. Blues musicians are duty-bound to tell the truth. In this sense, for all its sensuality and revelling in sin, the blues often *is* redemptive. Its artists walk in the footsteps of those earlier truth-tellers, the prophets (who themselves

9 Son House, before a concert audience in Wabash, Indiana, in 1964. Quoted in Spencer, *Protest and Praise*, p. 119.

10 Son House, 'Preachin' the blues, Part 1'.

11 Otis Spann, quoted in Paul Oliver, *Conversations with the Blues* (New York: Horizon Press, 1965), p. 52, quoted in Spencer, *Protest and Praise*, p. 114. Reasonable attempts have been made to discover and contact the copyright owner of these lyrics. The copyright owner is invited to contact the publisher so that acknowledgment may be given in future editions.

knew how to turn a scandalous phrase or two).[12] Blues singer Henry Townsend protested regarding the rejection of the blues by the black church:

> Some people think that the blues is something that is evil – I don't. If the blues is delivered in the truth, which most of them are . . . if I sing the blues and tell the truth, what have I done? What have I committed? I haven't lied.[13]

On the one hand, it is true that the blues often presents a 'salvation' that's at odds with what the church offers. 'Finding my baby', getting drunk or getting rich were the standard pathways to blues heaven. That is, the blues presents a secularized, earthly (and earthy) version of salvation. Not heaven, but the love of a good woman, physical pleasure and material success. That secularized version of salvation would be passed down to rock 'n' roll.

On the other hand, for all their hedonism, blues musicians were still committed to telling the truth through a lens that bears the unmistakable marks of the spiritual. Blues veteran John Lee Hooker once said, 'when the spirituals was born, it was born on the blues side', and that was why he stopped singing spirituals and moved over to the blues.[14] It is an oversimplification to say that the blues is a secularized form of the spiritual, but 'preachin' the blues', despite its earthiness and sensuality, *is* prophetic and points towards redemption in its own scandalous way. The blues offers 'a way of rendering meaning to the cosmos by being brazenly truthful about it'.[15] And, like its progenitor, the spiritual, the blues path for finding meaning through truth-telling is deeply shaped by a Christian imaginative vision of the world. Like father, like son.

The tensive vision of the blues: 'it's a sad thing and it's a rejoicing thing'

How does the blues communicate this tension between lament and expectation, between a sorrowful recognition of human brokenness and the

12 See, for example, Isaiah 47:1–3; Jeremiah 5:7–9; Ezekiel 23; Nahum 3:5–7; Habakkuk 2:15–17.

13 Henry Townsend, quoted in Oliver, *Conversations with the Blues*, pp. 169–170, quoted in Spencer, *Protest and Praise*, p. 122.

14 Oliver, *Conversations with the Blues*, pp. 160 and 168, quoted in Spencer, *Protest and Praise*, p. 125.

15 Spencer, *Protest and Praise*, p. 113.

awareness of hope? The stereotype is that blues songs are songs of despair. Things aren't that simple.

The dark vision of the blues

Certainly, blues songs present sorrow, even despair, in a powerful way, showing a remarkable sensitivity to the brokenness of the world. The lyrics focus on betrayal, bad luck, racism, social oppression and humiliation, suffering, and other realities that degrade and drag people down.

The blues can also express lament that transcends words – a moaned, wordless complaint reflecting profound suffering. The blues moan is an echo of the earlier African-American field holler, the work song of the slaves in the fields. The work song existed somewhere between a shout and a melody.[16] It gave slaves (and, later, prison work gangs and sharecroppers) a way to alleviate the soul-crushing tedium of repetitive and physically demanding work, breaking up the monotony and oppression they found themselves in by expressing their frustration and sorrow creatively. They vocalized their pain, which made it a little more bearable. That cry of the heart is preserved in the blues singer's (or guitar's) moan. The blues looks at the brokenness and twistedness of human existence and responds with a mournful wail.

The twenty-first century West prizes happiness above all. We try to avoid sadness – it's a downer. But sorrow can be deeply good and cleansing. In fact, the blues' moan may be the voice of wisdom. The Teacher says, 'The heart of the wise is in the house of mourning, but the heart of fools is in the house of pleasure' (Ecclesiastes 7:4). Of all the different styles of music that the West has known, the blues moan comes closest to what Paul describes as 'interceding with groans that words cannot express' (Romans 8:26). Of course, Paul was referring to the intercession of the Holy Spirit, but that only shows the rightness of this kind of lament. Blues moans harmonize with the Spirit's groans. Faced with a world so broken and hearts so sinful, even the Holy Spirit gets the blues.

This awareness of the world's brokenness penetrates into the very structure of its unique musical language and style – the blues scale. When

---

16 See William Edgar, 'Ain't it hard: Suffering and hope in the blues', *Modern Reformation*, vol. 14, no. 1 (January–February 2005), p. 31, <https://issuu.com/modernreformation/docs/the-blue-note-january-february-2005>, pp. 3 –39, accessed February 2023.

W. C. Handy standardized the blues scale by writing the blues down on sheet music around 1909, he invented a notation for the way black folk singers slid between notes and 'broke' the third and seventh tones of the major scale.[17] The blues scale gives the music a particular feel, a weight all its own, a 'brokenness'. Sometimes, blues music can feel happy (as in the up-tempo 'Jump Blues' style) but, more often than not, its classic melodies and harmonies communicate loss and longing, desire and disappointment. The music's brokenness is not simply about structure or style; it is an imaginative vision refracted *through* the musical style, a musical language deeply rooted in an awareness of human brokenness, of the screwed-upness of the world.

These facets of the blues – lyrical content, the moan, broken blues scale – all communicate an awareness of life being wrong, of suffering, of plaintive lament. Despite its alienation from the black church, the blues communicated the reality of brokenness in explicitly Christian terms. Whether blues singers are talking about a two-timing lover or their own evil behaviour, they're likely to proclaim, 'It's a sin',[18] telling it like it is using Christian categories. Further, when the blues offers its lament about injustice, it calls on God to witness the suffering of ordinary people.

African-American studies scholar Jon Michael Spencer points out the frequent references to God in blues songs – 'Lordy, Lord', 'God have mercy', 'for God's sake', 'great God above' and so on. These are not meaningless utterances at all, not simply black cultural baggage. Rather, they are invocations of and petitions to God, just as surely as they are in spirituals, but not done in a churchy style. The classic blues musicians, brought up in the church, always felt God surveying the scene, and that affected the way they saw themselves, as truth-tellers. The blues singers 'told the truth in the presence of God'.[19]

For all of its sensuality and decidedly un-churchy, raucous behaviour, the blues still communicates a deeply Christian vision of the world by telling the dark truth about human depravity, brokenness and suffering.

---

[17] James Haskins, *Black Music in America: A history through its people* (New York: HarperCollins, 1987), p. 45.
[18] Spencer, *Protest and Praise*, p. 120.
[19] Spencer, *Protest and Praise*, p. 112.

Where the light leaks in

But the blues isn't only about darkness and despair. It sees *past* the darkness. The blues carries deep within its belly both an awareness of the brokenness of the world *and* an unquenchable desire for something better.

The blues expresses an ache so bad, you feel your heart is going to break, whether it's longing for 'my woman', money, a drink or simply some peace of mind. This desire, though, sets the blues apart from despair. Despair is content to name the darkness as it succumbs to it.[20] The blues, by contrast, contains both an awareness of darkness and an implicit protest *against* the darkness through its heartbreak and longing for something better. The blues implies that things could and *should* be better. As musicologist and theologian William Edgar argues, 'the blues is about lament and defiance, all at once'.[21] In that mixture of lament and defiance, the light leaks in. The blues cries out *because* it hopes. And, often, it calls out to the Lord above as our witness and Redeemer.

Just as its dark vision of human brokenness penetrates into the musical structure of the blues (the 'broken' blues scale), its desire for redemption leaves a structural imprint. William Edgar also notes that the particular arrangement of the blues verses means optimism emanates from them despite the darkness.[22] Using an arrangement reminiscent of the call-and-response pattern characteristic of both West African music and Protestant hymns, blues singers typically employ an A–A–B structure. Repeating the A line twice, they then answer the call using the B line. Take this famous example by the legendary blues musician and songwriter Robert Johnson:

> A: I went to the crossroads, fell down on my knees
> A: I went to the crossroads, fell down on my knees
> B: Asked the Lord above, have mercy now, save poor Bob if you please.[23]

---

20 Despair characterizes various types of popular music such as 'emo' and 'suicidal depressive black metal' (yes, it's a real genre). See Christan Grant, 'Top ten most depressing music genres', The Top Tens (n.d.), <www.thetoptens.com/depressing-music-genres>, accessed February 2023.

21 See Edgar, 'Ain't it hard?' Edgar notes that this spirit of defiance was passed on from the black church as they learnt about the freedom and forgiveness that God gives sinners through Christ.

22 See William Edgar, 'How does music mean?' in *Taking Note of Music* (London: SPCK, 1986), pp. 57–58.

23 Robert Johnson, 'Crossroad blues', *Robert Johnson: King of the Delta blues* (Columbia Records, 1997 [27 November 1936]), track 1.

Even the chord pattern of the 12-bar blues is designed to fit this call-and-response pattern. The A-section chord changes are resolved by the B-section.

The meaning of this A–A–B structure varies depending on the specific lyrics involved. Sometimes A asks a question that B answers. Sometimes B reveals a new detail that casts new light on the situation presented in A. Whatever the specifics, B always moves the story on to another plane. In so doing, Edgar argues, the A–A–B pattern implies not only musical resolution but also hope in a promised resolution of the singer's problem (in this case, that the Lord will have mercy on poor Bob and get him out of his fix). It gives a subtly hopeful tint to the whole song, that perhaps things *can* change. In this way, even sad, depressing blues songs gain a resonance of an anticipated resolution (whether the problem ends up being resolved by the final line or not). This is not to say that all blues songs are happy or optimistic, but within the musical and lyrical structure of the blues, there *is* a reflection of the desire for redemption, a buried hope, even when redemption seems impossibly far away.

The blues as a messy and powerful tension

This is what gives the blues its arresting, gritty character that resists cliché and sentimentality: a powerful, messy combination of clear-eyed, sorrowful truth-telling about a twisted, messed-up world, and a growling protest against that messed-upness that lets the light leak in. Tennessee blues musician Zula Van Hunt said of the blues, 'It's a sad thing and it's a rejoicing thing.'[24] It's *both*, in tension, that give the blues its peculiarly cathartic, cleansing power (what Spencer calls 'a crooning, crying and moaning confession that left the blues soul washed clean at the blues altar').[25] Van Hunt explains in more detail:

> The blues is something . . . Oh, Lord, you don't care, you get to the point, you give up and don't care for nothing. Right alone in there, you got the blues . . . The blues is a feeling that can't nobody do

---

[24] Mrs Zula Van Hunt (b. 1902), oral history interview, by George McDaniel, Center for Southern Folklore, Memphis, Tennessee (5 January 1983), tape 3, p. 13, quoted in Spencer, *Protest and Praise*, p. 111.

[25] Spencer, *Protest and Praise*, p. 112.

> nothing with, it's a thing that will get on you . . . It's a good feeling and it's a sad feeling and it's a sort of low-down feeling. Now that's deep, deep inward, see, and it's got to – you can't push it or you can't shove it – it's got to die down itself for you just to feel like normal again. And it's a striking thing, it will strike you when you are not thinking of it or nothing of the kind.[26]

What makes the blues so striking, and such a powerful truth-teller, is this tension that sees the world as broken, reality as out of joint and, beyond that brokenness, a deep desire for things to be put right, a fundamental orientation towards hope.[27] The blues feels grounded and real in a deeply Christian way.

Earlier, I called this the tension between a cross-shaped and an empty-tomb-shaped imagination – a recognition that life is broken, but that brokenness is not the last word. What makes the blues unique, most itself, is this perspective that was formed out of the Christian imaginative vision as those church-moulded imaginations interacted with a history of suffering and oppression. That is what an authentic communication of the Christian imaginative vision of the world is all about.

The blues has taken the hope and longing of the spiritual and secularized it, but it *also* intensified its dark, hopeful, longing vision precisely because it wasn't obliged to behave and sound nice and respectable, as church music was. Nothing kills the authentic communication of the Christian imagination better than 'niceness', sugar-coated sentimentality that undermines directness and avoids saying what really needs to be said. The Christian imagination isn't about niceness. Rather, it is anchored in the reality of the screwed-upness of the world, and the hope that stems from a powerful, merciful God. This prophetic truth-telling about the ugliness of evil and the reality of hope makes authentic Christian culture subversive in a world where redemption is dismissed and scoffed at. No-one scoffs at the blues.

---

[26] Mrs Zula Van Hunt (b. 1902), oral history interview, by George McDaniel, quoted in Spencer, *Protest and Praise*, p. 125, n. 64.

[27] In chapter 7, I called this 'eschatological desire' – an aching hope that stems from the sure promise of future redemption, the new creation.

Blind Willie Johnson sees blue

Let us look at a concrete example of the tensive vision of the blues: the songs of Texas blues musician Blind Willie Johnson (see Figure 9.1). There is a profound irony in exploring the vision of a blind man who saw light and darkness more clearly than most sighted people. Another irony: Blind Willie Johnson, one of the most respected blues musicians in history, would not have called himself one. He was deeply committed to the church and played his music for church people, but they didn't much care for the blues. I believe that Blind Willie's reluctance to name his music 'blues' was due to another kind of blindness – cultural blindness. The church people themselves were blind to the redemptive possibilities of the blues, so there simply wasn't a category for people like Johnson – that is, people of deep faith who also play the blues. They are rare, but they exist.[28] Such musicians understand the meaning of the blues best. And, without a doubt, Blind Willie Johnson was one of the most gifted and influential blues musician in his or any other generation.

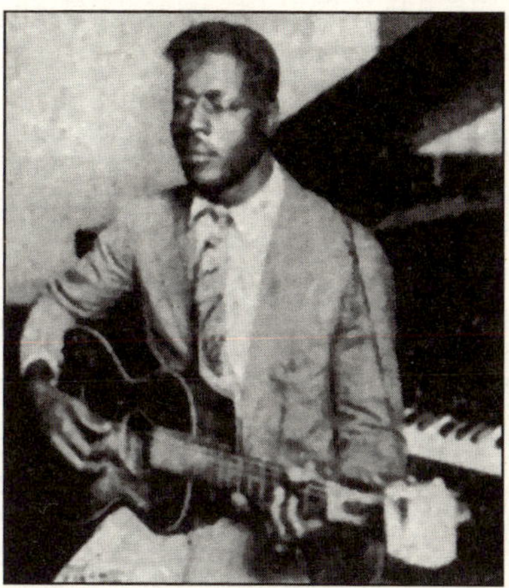

Figure 9.1 **The only known photograph of Blind Willie Johnson (public domain, 1927)**

[28] The Reverend Gary Davis, Joseph Spence, Skip James and Sister Rosetta Tharp are among those who also bridged the cultural and musical divide between the blues and the black church.

'Motherless children have a hard time': the life and influence of Blind Willie Johnson

One look at Blind Willie Johnson's biography reveals a man well acquainted with suffering.[29] To quote Billie Holiday, if anyone had a 'right to sing the blues', Johnson did.

Born around 1902 in Temple, Texas, he was brought up in Marlin, a small town south of Dallas. His church encouraged its members to make music, so Willie started playing a cigar-box guitar at the age of five, and declared that he intended to be a preacher. His mother died when he was very young, and his father married again, but his new wife proved unfaithful. After his father found out about an affair, he beat her severely. To get revenge, she threw lye – an alkaline substance similar to oven cleaner used in making soap – in her stepson's face, blinding him. One version of the story is that she was aiming for Willie's father and hit the boy by mistake. Another is that she deliberately blinded her stepson to get at his father. Whatever the case, Willie Johnson was blinded for life at the age of seven. As he couldn't work, his parents put him on the street to play for money. He would play at church functions and became well known both in Dallas and Houston for his incomparable slide guitar playing. Popular legend has it that he used a penknife as a slide, though it was likely the sawn-off neck of a wine bottle.[30] Willie Johnson also gained fame for how his singing voice changed to an unearthly growl whenever the Spirit moved him. His popularity earned him a deal with Columbia Records from 1927 to 1930. Sometimes his wife, Willie Harris, would back him up on vocals. He later divorced her and married Angeline (we don't know her maiden name). They sang together regularly at a Baptist church in Beaumont, Texas, travelling to Houston occasionally to perform at revivals. In 1947, their house burnt down. He and Angeline had to sleep on a bed of damp newspapers in the cold. Two weeks later, Johnson contracted pneumonia. According to Angeline, the hospital

[29] Biographical details drawn from Jas Obrecht, liner notes for *Dark Was the Night* (Columbia/Legacy, CK 65516, 1998); and Joslyn Layne, 'Blind Willie Johnson', *All Music*, <www.allmusic.com/artist/blind-willie-johnson-mn0000040137/biography>, accessed February 2023.

[30] Guitarist-blogger Y2Karl finds evidence for the wine bottle neck on the pinkie of his left hand in the one surviving photograph of Blind Willie Johnson. See 'Dark was the night – cold was the ground', *Metafilter* (15 September 2005), <www.metafilter.com/45137/Dark-Was-The-NightCold-Was-The-Ground-by-Blind-Willie-Johnson>, accessed February 2023. Regardless, his slide playing is universally recognized as transcendent.

refused to treat him because he was blind. He later died of pneumonia at the age of 45.

Though he died in poverty and obscurity, his legacy endures, proving a seminal influence for later musicians. Christian blues musician Reverend Gary Davis learnt his songs and passed them on to a new generation of blues musicians. Those who have covered Blind Willie Johnson's songs are diverse, including black gospel groups such as the Staples Singers, folk singers Peter, Paul and Mary, contemporary blues musicians Chris Thomas King and Taj Mahal, and even rock bands such as Hot Tuna, the Grateful Dead and Led Zeppelin. American roots guitarist Ry Cooder said of Willie Johnson:

> Beyond being a great guitar player, I think this guy is one of these interplanetary world musicians – and there are only a few. Blind Willie Johnson is in the ether somewhere. He's up there in the zone.[31]

It makes sense, then, that when NASA had a gold disc made to send up with the spacecraft *Voyager*, they chose his song 'Dark was the night', along with pieces by Beethoven and Bach, a song by Chuck Berry and folk songs from Peru and Africa. They felt that Johnson's wordless, moaning lament was one of the best representations of the music of the planet.

Blind Willie Johnson sings of light in darkness

Johnson's music perfectly expresses this tensive vision: a deep awareness of suffering and sin, yet an indefatigable hope amid suffering. Some songs stress the suffering, some a defiance born of hope, and some express both at the same time. If you have never heard his music, do listen to the tracks we discuss here (available free on YouTube and elsewhere). It is one thing to describe the music and lyrics, quite another to hear his vocal textures, his timing and the ferocity with which he attacks his slide guitar solos. Be warned: his voice is an acquired taste and takes some getting used to.

That said, let us consider how his songs explore the tension between darkness and light inherent in the Christian imagination. First, many of his songs poignantly express darkness, evil and the sorrows he endured.

[31] Quoted in Obrecht, liner notes for *Dark Was the Night*.

His 1927 recording of 'Dark was the night' is a wordless meditation on the crucifixion of Jesus.[32] A slow, reflective slide guitar serves as the backdrop for Johnson's quiet moans and humming of the melody, sometimes in unison with the guitar. He penetrates the emotional core of the abandonment and darkness that Jesus must have felt, and that Johnson felt as well. It is deeply moving to hear someone who was maliciously blinded as a child singing a song entitled 'Dark was the night'. He knows better than any of us the darkness and cruelty of the world. But the fact that he is singing and playing about the suffering *of Jesus* means something as well. In that darkness, Christ was gaining for us forgiveness, liberation, restoration and healing. There is in Johnson's moans a plaintive searching, perhaps searching for the meaning of his own darkness as he connects it with the darkness his Lord felt. Here is a song that mourns deeply over the evil the world can throw at a person, but also is deeply in touch with reality – that such suffering *means* something and suffering will not have the last word.

Another song that explores his own sorrow, but with a profoundly different emotional texture, is his classic 'Motherless children'.[33] Instead of meditative sorrow, the mood here is one of protest, even barely restrained anger. He begins the song with an up-tempo, aggressive slide guitar solo, interrupted by a growling, knowing, 'Well, well, well.' He then begins the refrain:

> Motherless children have a hard time.
> Motherless children have a hard time, mother's dead.
> They'll not have anywhere to go,
> Wanderin' around from door to door.
> [Motherless children] have a hard time.

---

32 'Dark was the night' is on *Dark Was the Night* (Columbia/Legacy, CK 65516, 1998 [this track originally recorded in 1927]), track 2; 'Dark was the night, cold was the ground', Blind Willie Johnson – Topic, YouTube, <https://www.youtube.com/watch?v=71Ti_TdpJHE>, accessed February 2023.

33 The title has been widely mistakenly given as 'Mother's children'. The combination of bad tape quality and Johnson's hard-to-decipher diction may have led early transcribers to drop a syllable. Given the lyrics, 'Mother's children' makes absolutely no sense, however. You can hear it here, though it has been given the incorrect title here too: Blind Willie Johnson, 'Mother's children have a hard time', Traveler Into The Blue, YouTube, <www.youtube.com/watch?v=ywTC7yt7XZw>, accessed March 2023.

Then, verse by verse, Johnson explains that no other family relationship can ever replace the care and nurturing a mother can give. Wives can prove unfaithful. A sister will eventually marry and 'turn her back on you'. Fathers do the best they can, but there are 'so many things a father can't understand'. Johnson then launches into two more aggressive slide guitar solos, restating the melody line of the refrain in the middle of the song and at the end, all while interjecting, 'Lord, Lord . . .'. There's even meaning in the *way* he sings (or, rather, growls) the words. Each verse contains five lines with short pauses between each line so that his guitar can state and restate a short musical phrase. It took me a while to realize, but that short phrase he plays over and over is the same melody that Johnson sings in the refrain to the words, 'When mother is dead.' The idea that 'mother is dead' is relentlessly repeated by the guitar throughout the song. The song is literally haunted by his mother's absence, and by Johnson's barely suppressed rage about that.

The theme is similar to that in 'Dark was the night' – the feeling of being abandoned – but, in place of a gentle lament, he lashes out with his voice and his guitar in anger and grief at the way he has been abandoned. His anger is understandable, given his own mother's death and his treatment at the hands of an unloving stepmother.

When I listen to 'Motherless children', I get the same feeling of rage at the outrageous injustices of life as when I read Job's laments. But in both cases, there is also a feeling that, as they struggle with their abandonment, ultimately, they are wrestling with God himself, though he is hidden and distant. And through that wrestling, God is listening, present – and his presence changes things. Wrestling with one's rough treatment at God's hands is not at all the same thing as wrestling with despair in an empty, absurd universe. It is complaining *to* someone, wrestling *with* someone, as Johnson acknowledges by calling out 'Lord, Lord' during his guitar solos. Even in the wrestling, in the attitude of defiance in suffering, hope remains in seed form, because the one with whom you wrestle is there, shadowy, perhaps about to make his entrance.

Johnson's music deals not only with the darkness and suffering, whether in meditative sorrow or angry grief, but also holds out hope in explicit and startling ways. My favourite Blind Willie Johnson song is 'Let your light shine on me'.[34] Even though the guitar work is simpler than in the other two songs, lacking his brilliant slide technique, this song contains something just as wonderful. He begins with slow strumming and, in a quiet, plaintive voice, sliding and bending notes, he sings a simple introduction:

Let it shine on me.
Let it shine on me.
Let your light from the lighthouse shine on me.
Let it shine on me.
Let it shine on me.
Let your light from the lighthouse shine on.

Then the music picks up to a walking tempo as he plucks out a catchy bassline, and he sings the first verse:

My Lord, he done just what he said.
Let your light from the lighthouse shine on me.
Heal the sick and raise the dead.
Let your light from the lighthouse shine on.

Johnson declares his trust in the faithfulness of his Saviour, one who keeps his word. He proves it by healing the sick (including the blind) and raising the dead. Johnson then launches into the chorus, and his voice soars:

Oh, let it shine on, oh, let it shine on.
Let your light from the lighthouse shine on me.
Shine on, oh, let it shine on.
Let your light from the lighthouse shine on.

Stop and think about that image for a moment. What does a lighthouse mean to a blind black man living in the American South in the 1930s,

---

34 Blind Willie Johnson/traditional, 'Let your light shine on me', *Dark Was the Night* (Columbia/Legacy, CK 65516, 1998 [this track originally recorded in 1929]), track 7; Blind Willie Johnson – 'Let your light shine on me', Traveler Into The Blue, YouTube, <www.youtube.com/watch?v=IcYKEGNQGJc>, accessed February 2023.

surrounded by the darkness of poverty and racial oppression, as well as literal, unseeing darkness?

A lighthouse's job is to pierce the darkness, making itself visible even from far, far away. The kind of redemption that God gives his people is like that: a light in the darkness seen from far away. It doesn't have to be close for us to know that it is real. You can put your hope and trust in it, even when you find yourself engulfed by present darkness.[35]

As he begins the second verse, Johnson's voice changes. Gone is the plaintive, gentle tone. He now growls with that unearthly growl for which he was famous, galvanized, all resistance and defiance against the dark:

> I know I've got religion, and I ain't ashamed.
> Let your light from the lighthouse shine on me.
> Angels in the heaven done wrote my name.
> Let your light from the lighthouse shine on.

While he growls out the lyrics, you can hear a thumping in time with the music, whether it is from a hand against the guitar or a foot stomping, I can't tell. But it gives the music a feeling of rock-solid steadiness. After every line, he keeps repeating, 'Let your light from the lighthouse shine on me.' It is even more relentless than the statement of his mother's death in 'Motherless children'. He acknowledges the darkness and simultaneously issues a powerful challenge against it: 'Go on, you damned darkness, do your worst! I'll outlast you yet, because this light is real, and it will snap your spine and break you to pieces.' Even though I've listened to this song countless times, I still sometimes get chills when his voice goes into growling high gear – the way he shakes his fist at the darkness and proclaims an unshakeable confidence in the Lord of Light. And this, coming from a blind man! As I said, he knows the light a lot better than most of us who can see.

The song closes with him repeating the chorus a couple more times, slowing down, his voice reverting mid-line to the gentleness with which

[35] The contrast between the distant light and the present is to be taken eschatologically, not solely spatially. We see the victory of Christ and the new creation from afar, in a future we know not how distant it is. Even so, the light cuts through the darkness that we see around us now, a beam of hope that disperses darkness.

he started the song, asking the light to shine on him. It leaves me with a deeply peaceful feeling. The redemption light from the lighthouse remains so far away, but we can still see it shining. And that's enough for now. Just keep shining on us, Lord, and we'll make it, by your mercy.

There are plenty of other Blind Willie Johnson songs that we could talk about in which he voices a keen awareness of pain and suffering, even amid Christian hope ('Lord I just can't keep from cryin' sometimes'), and of the reality of a Saviour who inspires us to defy the darkness ('Trouble will soon be over', 'If I had my way I'd tear the building down', 'I know his blood can make me whole'), but then I'd spoil the surprise and wonder of his other songs. My point is clear enough using only these three.

In Blind Willie Johnson's music, the blues shows its finest colours: a tensive vision that encompasses the sin, fallenness and darkness of the world, *and* the light of hope grounded in the reality of God's saving power for his people. We find a powerful and winsome communication of the Christian imagination in a popular cultural medium, a potent apologetic against the darkness and for the light. In its tensive blues vision of the world, Blind Willie Johnson sings, plays, and sees the truth.

But we don't live in Willie's world

One issue that I have ignored is the balance between shouting and mumbling. Blind Willie Johnson is many things – subtle and nuanced he is not. He's a blues preacher, an evangelist with a guitar. Imaginative? Yes. Passionate? Very. Oblique and indirect? Not so much. But I wouldn't think of holding that against his music for two reasons.

First, his world (1930s Texas) was very different from ours, his audiences miles away in terms of the shape of their imaginations and world view (their imaginary landscape). While the intelligentsia might have been post-Christian (though, in 1930s Texas, I doubt that they would have been open about it), the ordinary people would have lived in the thickest, leatheriest part of the Bible Belt. Willie Johnson sang his songs into a solidly Christian culture. We don't have that luxury any more. Not even in Texas. Christian artists today have to contend with additional obstacles.

Second, Johnson's songs are so flawlessly unsentimental, so powerful, brutal even, in their execution that their influence has travelled far beyond the cultural boundaries of the faithful. His voice and guitar ring with authenticity, with suffering, with joy. Nobody's going to mistake this for nice, syrupy CCM. You can't. This music is real. It growls. It touches the face of the deep, even if you don't agree with his theology. That depth and ferocity is something that Christian oasis-makers need to consider and generate in their own works.

In short, Johnson illustrates the tension between darkness and light beautifully, but not with the indirectness and subtlety needed for the balance between shouting and mumbling. But I'll plead extenuating circumstances in terms of context and his peculiar genius. He's still my pop culture hero.

In the next few chapters, I want to meditate and expand on what we've learnt from the blues about the tension between the dark and light that gives good Christian cultural works their peculiar gravity and subversive power. We shall expand our exploration to include an indirectness and subtlety that comes from a creative voice which neither shouts nor mumbles.

10

Sho Baraka: speaking truth and hopeful protest to the church family and beyond

Introduction: engaging the church along with the world

One chilly February evening, my wife and I went with a group from our church to see *Union: The musical*. It retells the story of the 1968 refuse workers' strike that paralysed Memphis, Tennessee. After two workers were crushed in the compactor of a refuse truck, black workers went on strike, demanding humane working conditions. Black women joined in, with an economic boycott of white-owned businesses, challenging the racism woven into the economic structures of the city. As tensions rose, the strikers kept Dr Martin Luther King, Jr, informed about developments and he went to Memphis. It was the last civil rights action he took part in. King spoke to a group of the workers when he arrived in Memphis, and was assassinated the following evening. The musical focused not on the assassination, but on the lives and stories of the black protesters.

Tickets for the main venue were sold out, so we watched a livestream at a church a few blocks away from the performance. Beset by technical issues, the power of the music still came through. Afterwards, the writers and performers came to the church for a debriefing session. Many talented and creative people were there, each with a story to tell. But one stood out to me: Sho Baraka, co-writer of the show, and a rapper much respected among black Christians.

During the Q&A, he said something about artistic creativity and the gospel that struck a chord: a full understanding of the gospel leads to cultural engagement because Christ is Lord of everything.

> What is your 'Christ crucified'? One of the things I had to wrestle with is this mistruth that Christianity was just about a relationship with God. What is true religion? True religion is Jesus reconciling *all* things. So, he's not just cool with us having our personal pious relationship with God; Christianity is about *relationships.* It's not just about relationship with God; it's relationships with other people, and a relationship with the land, the Cultural Mandate, and how we create, and how we cultivate. And we've cultivated some terrible systems within the faith, and the church is responsible. If Jesus is calling us to redeem and reconcile all things, then it's the church's job to not only have relationships with the Lord, relationships with other people, but [to ask] how do we redeem and restore the inverted systems that were created in the fall? God has called us to redeem and reconcile all things. This is the gospel I now believe in. 'Cause before it was just about our personal piety. But now I see that God has called me to not only love him and love others but also love him in how I create . . . Am I contributing to the *imago Dei* of people in my creation? I would hope that this play is doing just that - in our storytelling, we're encouraging people to see and create in the image of God.[1]

Sho Baraka is an artist who has thought through the implications of the gospel for engaging our shared culture and culture-making. As I explored his music, it became clear that his was an imagination I needed to know better.

The next day, a local black church hosted a panel discussion and worship service regarding racial justice in Winston-Salem, North Carolina. It was painful to hear how a city that seems so prosperous excludes so many of its citizens from that prosperity. The county surrounding the city is one of the worst in the USA for keeping people trapped in poverty,[2] and we heard how the school system had become resegregated, ensuring that white kids got the best education, leaving black and Hispanic kids behind.

---

1 Recorded at First Presbyterian Church, Winston-Salem, North Carolina, 8 February 2019 (lightly edited).

2 Piedmont Renewal Network, 'Our city: the present', <https://renewalnetwork.org/the-present>, accessed February 2023.

And, most painful of all, we heard how the white church had often actively supported an unjust status quo.

The white church has often been resistant to calls for racial justice.[3] Pastor Greg Thompson – grandson of a Klansman – became so frustrated at that resistance in his own church that he called Sho Baraka. Together, they created *Union: The musical.* As Thompson put it, after beating his head against a wall with church leaders, he sought a creative 'end run' as a way round the defences white Christians often erect. He wanted to put the issue in a different light, to tell stories that would engender empathy. He believed that the music he and Sho wrote could help to change the church and the wider communities beyond its walls.

The experience of watching the musical and the dialogue that followed challenged a major premise of this book. I had assumed that what the church *really* needs is creatives who will engage the world – artists who can serve the church as a creative interface with post-Christian culture. I began to understand that if we are to reach the world with any integrity, creatives might have to focus on reaching the church first. If we, as the body of Christ, haven't got our act together on something as basic (and difficult!) as ensuring justice for all those who bear God's image, then we have serious work to do. We need artists who can serve the church as a creative interface with *itself.* Perhaps a major calling of Christian artists is to reach their communities *before* taking their work to the world. In other words, we need oases – prickly, provoking oases[4] – to challenge not only the 'pagans' but also, just as important, Christians when they start thinking and acting and feeling 'pagany'. That is, artists help the church not only with outreach and building bridges but also in our discipleship.

Perhaps rap can be a vehicle for changing both church *and* world through planting oases.

Rap as an artistic genre

Some Christians might be genuinely shocked when I say that rap could build oases that are useful to God in challenging, confronting, encour-

3 For details on the white church's complicity with racism in the USA, see Jemar Tisby's 'The color of compromise' in *The Color of Compromise: The truth about the American church's complicity in racism* (Grand Rapids, MI: Zondervan, 2019)

4 See part 4, chapter 12, under heading '"Art judges us": Christian creativity provokes reflection and critique'.

aging and refreshing both church and world. In fact, rap – like the blues and so much black music – has roots in the black church, in the cadence of the preacher's delivery, and in the prayers and vocal responses of the congregation.[5] Some black gospel groups 'rapped' over music decades before L. L. Cool J or the Sugar Hill Gang. Consider the spoken-word stylings of J. C. Ginyard of the Jubalaires in 'Preacher and the bear' (1945).[6] Granted, Ginyard sounds more like Cab Calloway than Notorious B.I.G., but the lineage is there, though too often ignored by secular music historians.[7]

Like the blues, rap has had a troubled history with the black church. Many black Christian mothers wanted their children to steer well clear of gangsta culture, and rap was the soundtrack of that culture in the 1980s and beyond. In more recent decades, there has been a rapprochement between the black church and rap, and for good reason: they both speak the language of resistance, protest, celebration and proclamation. Rap, like the blues, seeks to tell the scandalous truth. Rappers call this commitment to truth-telling 'keepin' it real'. It gives rap an uncomfortable edginess that comes from integrity. It can say things that we would rather not hear but need to.

Most white conservative Christians will recall DC Talk, an evangelistic rap group that has been around since the 1980s. More recently, young black men, fresh from Reformed seminaries, have started using rap to explain the gospel, often in explicitly Calvinistic terms.[8] Lecrae emerged

5 See Janice D. Hamlet, 'Word! The African-American oral tradition and its rhetorical impact on American popular culture', *Black History Bulletin*, vol. 74, no. 1 (Spring 2011), pp. 27–29, <https://docplayer.net/29619780-Word-the-african-american-oral-tradition-and-its-rhetorical-impact-on-american-popular-culture-by-janice-d-hamlet.html>, accessed February 2023.

6 The Jubalaires, 'Preacher and the bear', Soundie; The Jubalaires 'Preacher and the bear' (1941), vintage video clips, YouTube (1945), <www.youtube.com/watch?v=1mNP9f84Zk8&ab>, accessed February 2023. (Note that the YouTube recording mistakenly gives the date as 1941.) For more information on Ginyard and the Jubalaires, see 'Spotlight on J. C. Ginyard – Part One (The Jubalaires)', *Vocal Group Harmony*, no. 924 (25 May 2019), <www.vocalgroupharmony.com/6ROWNEW/BeforeThisTime.htm>, accessed February 2023

7 See Justin Sarachik, 'The Jubalaires were doing gospel rap back in the 1940s', *Rapzilla* (11 July 2016), <https://rapzilla.com/2016-07-the-jubalaires-were-doing-gospel-rap-back-in-the-1940s>, accessed February 2023.

8 See Matthew Barrett, 'Reformed rap: Shai Linne', *Credo* (24 September 2011), <https://credomag.com/2011/09/reformed-rap-shai-linne>, accessed February 2023. Reformed rap, also known as 'holy hip hop', caused much (needless) debate and handwringing among white conservative Protestants, including an infamous panel of the National Council of Families in Churches (NCFIC) in 2013. The NCFIC has removed the video of the panel, but you can find a transcript (and push back) here: Brent Hobbs, 'Critiquing NCFIC arguments against Christian rap', *Deeper into Grace* (27 November 2013). The best response I've seen is Mike Cosper's

from this group. Faith perspectives have penetrated mainstream rap as well, both in the upbeat, positive, gospel choir-infused music of Chance the Rapper (from Chicago's Southside) and in the dark, disturbing soliloquies of Kendrick Lamar (from Compton). In the past decade, rap has become a rare venue for conversation about the Christian faith.

It is in this cultural context that we should consider Amisho Baraka Lewis, better known as Sho Baraka.

The narrative of Sho Baraka: a short biography

As with many creatives, his art flows from his life, particularly the tension between two often conflicting perspectives: the gospel as preached in white, theologically conservative Protestant churches, and his own God-given racial identity. Brought up in California, his mother passed on to him a strong sense of the black community, encouraging him to read black history and to 'do reports of Black people who didn't fit into the master narrative of Black History that was taught in grade school'.[9] Later, when he became a Christian, he felt profound tension between being proud of his heritage and 'a faith that seemed to "whitewash" everything about me'.[10] That crisis of faith led him to Christian thinkers and church fathers outside white conservative Protestantism: 'Once I had the confidence to embrace these non-white luminaries in history, while knowing that Christ loved the whole me, is when I became comfortable in my skin.'[11]

Perhaps it was the struggle to reconcile his racial identity and his identity in Christ that led him to an understanding of the gospel that resists the dualism between the spiritual and the secular, between the personal and the social. The gospel must address the whole of life or it isn't really the gospel. 'ALL WRONGS AND EVILS are being redeemed and reconciled unto GOD. If you don't believe that the gospel is a tool to

(note 8 *cont.*) 'Creation, culture, redemption, and hip hop: A response to the NCFIC panel', *Mike Cosper* (29 November 2013), <https://web.archive.org/web/20140203075613/http://www.mikedcosper.com/home/creation-culture-redemption-and-hip-hop-a-response-the-ncfic-panel>, accessed February 2023.

9 From my email interview with Sho Baraka, 16 June 2019.

10 From my email interview with Sho Baraka.

11 From my email interview with Sho Baraka. White conservative Protestants may find these musings difficult to hear but, in American history, much of white evangelical faith and theology have been intertwined with white identity and racial oppression (see Tisby, *The Color of Compromise*). That distortion has left its imprint on black believers.

redeem the broken systems that created racism then you don't have the same gospel as me.'[12] Or, as he put it on that night in February, the church is to be about relationships and righting the 'inverted systems' that cause injustice. We are to be part of God's project to reconcile and heal *all* things.

At Tuskegee University and the University of North Texas,[13] he studied television, film, anthropology and public administration.[14] He came to rap gradually. A turning point occurred when friends started a record label and asked him to join. Though he's best known for his rap albums, rap is only 'one of many things I felt gifted in'.[15] He also pursues faith-informed political and social advocacy,[16] international activism and relief work, and he is an in-demand speaker.

He is married and has a daughter and two sons, one of whom is autistic.[17] He takes fatherhood seriously. He is present for his family despite his busy schedule. I asked him about the sacrifices he has had to make for his art. He responded:

> I don't know if I would say that I've had to sacrifice much. If anything, I'm scared to give too much attention to my career while missing the important moments with my family. The moment my family says [I'm] sacrificing them is the moment I press pause. Which hasn't happened often. I want to be a star in my family's eye. That's success to me.[18]

---

[12] From my email interview with Sho Baraka. Capital letters as in the original.

[13] The University of North Texas is famous for its jazz music programme. Although Baraka did not get a music degree there, his rap shows a deep affection for jazz.

[14] 'Sho Baraka: About', Humble Beast, <https://humblebeast.com/books/sho-baraka>, accessed February 2023.

[15] From my email interview with Sho Baraka.

[16] He is one of the founding members of the AND Campaign, an organization that seeks to address systemic injustice from a perspective that honours Christian values. Its motto: 'Biblical values AND social justice'. See <https://andcampaign.org>, accessed February 2023.

[17] He revealed the frustrations, insecurities, learning curve and contentment that comes from being the parent of an autistic child in an address he gave in Atlanta for Kulture City, an autism advocacy group; KULTURECITY, YouTube (3 March 2016), <www.youtube.com/watch?time_continue=988&v=iqiQR7qJoac>, accessed February 2023. His experience with his son shines through in the empathy, humility and deep appreciation for grace in 'Words, 2006', *The Narrative* (Humble Beast, 2016), track 12; see 'Words, 2006', Sho Baraka, YouTube <www.youtube.com/watch?v=C_6ieBZkVlU>, accessed February 2023. In the song, he reflects explicitly on his relationship with his son and what he has learnt, as a wordsmith, being confronted by a situation that he cannot fix with words

[18] From my email interview with Sho Baraka.

Through his dedication to finding a healthy balance between work and family, Sho Baraka presents a strong model of what successful manhood looks like, and a counter-narrative to our culture's perspective on black men and fatherhood.[19] Celebrations of marriage and family are rare in rap, but that is where Sho's heart is.

Since we are focusing on creative cultural engagement, let us explore his music.

A controversial artist

Sho Baraka has been putting out albums since 2007. They are generally well received by the rap community but tend to generate controversy in Christian circles because he calls out systemic social sin ('inverted systems') as well as individual sin.[20] His 2013 release, *Talented 10th*, stirred controversy because Baraka confronted racist language by using those very same offensive words in his songs. Nevertheless, the album charted exceptionally well on *Billboard,* placing first in gospel, fifth in Christian music overall and twelfth in US rap albums.[21]

His next album, *The Narrative* (2016),[22] charted somewhat lower (ninth in rap albums, fourteenth in Christian albums),[23] possibly because (the now defunct) LifeWay Christian bookshops pulled the album from its shelves. They objected to one word in the lyrics of the final song: 'penis'.[24]

---

19 A study done by the US Centers for Disease Control in 2013 found that black men, even when they lived away from their children, actually spent more time with their children than white or Hispanic men. See Jo Jones and William D. Mosher, 'Fathers' involvement with their children: United States, 2006–2010', *National Health Statistics Reports*, no. 71 (20 December 2013), <www.cdc.gov/nchs/data/nhsr/nhsr071.pdf>, accessed February 2023. See also Kenrya Rankin Naasel, 'It's a myth that black fathers are absent', *New York Times* (12 March 2014), <www.nytimes.com/roomfordebate/2014/03/12/the-assumptions-behind-obamas-initiative/its-a-myth-that-black-fathers-are-absent>, accessed February 2023.

20 Racism is both individual and systemic. See Tisby, *Color of Compromise*, chapter 1, especially pp. 16–17; Timothy Keller, 'Racism and corporate evil: A white guy's perspective', Desiring God, YouTube (26 August 2017), 26:05, <www.youtube.com/watch?v=EhJJcTKTVGo>, accessed February 2023.

21 Steven, 'Sho Baraka "Talented 10th" debuts #1 gospel, #5 Christian and #12 rap on Billboard', *Rapzilla* (25 January 2013), <https://rapzilla.com/2013-01-sho-baraka-talented-10th-debuts-1-gospel-5-christian-a-12-rap-on-billboard>, accessed February 2023.

22 Sho Baraka, *The Narrative* (Humble Beast, 2016).

23 David Daniels, 'Sho Baraka's "The Narrative" and Bizzle's "Crowns & Crosses" share several Billboard charts', *Rapizilla* (1 November 2016), <https://rapzilla.com/2016-11-sho-baraka-s-the-narrative-and-bizzle-s-crowns-crosses-share-several-billboard-charts>, accessed February 2023.

24 See Justin Sarachik, 'Sho Baraka's "The Narrative" pulled from LifeWay bookstores for offensive language', *Rapzilla* (8 February 2017), <https://rapzilla.com/2017-02-sho-baraka-s-the-narrative-pulled-from-lifeway-bookstores-for-offensive-language>, accessed February 2023.

The offending lyric was actually a gesture of repentance from the song 'Piano break, 33 A.D.': 'I was an insecure boy who just thought he was a genius/But always pissed off, that's because I thought with my penis.' Regardless, *The Narrative* has gained substantial critical success and is considered a latter-day Christian rap classic.[25]

Sho responded to LifeWay's decision with a video statement that was gracious, but also highlighted the problem that many Christian artists face: either abandon the Christian market or conform to a culturally homogenized identity to make their art palatable for the 'soccer mom' (the average middle-class suburban mother) demographic. Baraka called for a redefinition of the role of the Christian artist by building alternative institutions and distribution networks.[26]

More recently, Sho Baraka teamed up with Vanessa Hill to make *So Many Feelings*, an album about marriage. It started out as a joke. He and his wife posted some photos of the two of them in hip-hop poses on social media, complete with a made-up track list. It caught on, and he ended up calling on vocalist Vanessa Hill as co-writer and singer to perform as his wife. The album was released on Sho and his wife's fifteenth wedding anniversary. It has been labelled 'controversial' because it addresses mature subjects that married couples face (without being explicit), such as problems with money and sex. Sho Baraka responded to such reactions in an interview:

> The problem is we sanitize everything, and when people come into real-life issues, we don't know how to deal with it. People have real-life issues around sex. When we don't talk about it openly and explicitly, that's when you have issues with sexuality and people being confused. That's when you have children getting information from popular culture rather than from their pastors, parents and spiritual leaders. Most marriages have problems because of money and sex. When you don't talk about these things in an adult way, marriages fall apart.[27]

[25] See Sarachik, 'Sho Baraka's "The Narrative" pulled from LifeWay bookstores for offensive language'.

[26] 'Sho Baraka responds to the LifeWay decision', Forth District, YouTube (10 February 2017), 5:00, <www.youtube.com/watch?v=IlKxmkxZLoI>, accessed February 2023. This is precisely the issue we explored at the end of chapter 8.

[27] See Seth Tower Hurd, 'Sho Baraka and Vanessa Hill speak out about their controversial new album', *Relevant* (20 March 2018), <https://relevantmagazine.com/culture/music/sho-baraka-vanessa-hill-speak-controversial-new-album>, accessed February 2023.

He's not wrong. One YouTube commenter described *So Many Feelings* as a 'Marriage seminar on an album'. Real marriages are messy, unsanitized lifelong projects. Sho Baraka and Vanessa Hill are keeping it real. Perhaps adult Christian music consumers need to mature to a place where they are OK with uncomfortable explorations of real marriage. Song of Songs, though sanitized in English translations, is a little uncomfortable as well.

Sho Baraka does not court controversy but, rather, strives for reconciliation. Here is what he said in his video about the LifeWay lyrics controversy:

> I know some people may think that my music is provocative and that I'm provocative. But I don't run around looking for confrontation. Like, I don't think there's joy in conflict alone. That's psychotic. I find joy in conflict *resolution*. I make my music to conflict with ideologies that I think need to be challenged and tested to hope that that brings reconciliation, and joy in that reconciliation.[28]

Rather than a provocateur, Sho Baraka sees himself in a prophetic role, speaking difficult truths to people he loves so that they might turn from foolishness to the path of life. He's doing what Jesus did. Those who practise creative Christian cultural engagement are called to walk the hard path of the prophet, facing resistance even from those who call themselves brothers and sisters. Prophecy starts in-house, with the family of faith (see 1 Peter 4:17).[29]

Sho me the music

Sho Baraka's music is diverse and lyrically complex, as rap tends to be. We only have space to explore one song here, but it contains many themes that recur in Baraka's albums. It is the last track from *Talented 10th*, 'Epilogue 2: KJPJ'.[30]

---

28 Sho Baraka in 'Sho Baraka responds to the LifeWay decision'.

29 'For it is time for judgment to begin with God's household; and if it begins with us, what will the outcome be for those who do not obey the gospel of God?' (1 Peter 4:17).

30 Sho Baraka, 'Epilogue 2: KJPJ', *Talented 10th* (Lions and Liars Music, 2013), track 16. The album's title refers to a phrase coined by W. E. B. DuBois regarding the need for the US government to provide intellectual training for the top 10 per cent of the black population. See 'Talented Tenth', *DuBoisopedia*, <https://web.archive.org/web/20160329212603/http://scua.library.umass.edu/duboisopedia/doku.php?id=about:talented_tenth>, accessed March 2023.

Resistance to injustice and idolatry

The title alone is shocking: 'KJPJ' stands for 'Kill Jesus, praise Judas'. In the description of the live version, Baraka explains:

> When the hearts of men are bent towards greed, selfishness and hate, there was an example of Love, Sacrifice and Service. But we would rather remove purity to make room for perversion. I can hear my Grandmother say, 'Baby, we kill Jesus to praise Judas!'[31]

The song laments and protests against how greed turns things upside down. Just as Judas betrayed the One more precious than all the gold in the world for thirty pieces of silver, we too often do the same. When greed blinds us, we turn the world upside down, taking wrong for right, selling out biblical principles such as the call to love those around us. In service to money and power, we kill that which is precious. In reality, we're not so different from the crowds that bellowed for Jesus' blood; we're no different from the betrayer. Sho does not mince words:

> Corrupt kings, corrupt queens
> Do ugly things with a pretty please
> I seen abuse of a King's dream[32]
> Slave for the money – it's whipped cream
> Serve people or serve dollar signs
> *Grand Theft Auto* or Columbine
> Israel and Palestine
> The world been crooked
> How am I out of line?
> And I don't know why we do this
> Only the foolish kill Jesus to praise Judas

His indictment is simple: as a society, we have become foolish, praising and practising what we should condemn, killing off Jesus to exalt Judas,

[31] From the notes on 'Sho Baraka presents: Hello Rev – Kill Jesus, Praise Judas – Live Music Video (@hisocieties)', *Rapzilla*, YouTube (12 March 2012), 5:19, <www.youtube.com/watch?v=-NPemiiEVwA>, accessed February 2023. In my opinion, the live version is better than the version on the album, more jazz-infused energy.

[32] The reference here is likely to Martin Luther King's 'I have a dream' speech.

bowing to a system that lionizes greed. As we rush for money, corruption festers. The result is a crooked world that causes real suffering.

Joy amid a dark world because we are not abandoned

In the middle of this dire message, there is an unexpected positive element: the music. It's neither angry nor mournful but, rather, joy-filled. Watch the video of this song performed live on YouTube. Backed by a solid jazz rhythm section, with Jamm (rapper-singer-pianist Jamie Porter) leading on piano and adding vocals on the refrain, this group swings *hard*. Lara Polangco sings wordlessly, playfully weaving around the melody. Sho raps with conviction, pouncing on the rhythm to make his point. It's difficult not to feel the exuberance, the flow, the energy.

Sho's music often features jazz. He aims to honour the history of African-American music, and it adds depth to his songs. As he told me, 'Jazz has challenged my cadence and tone. It's a different mood and feel. I truly love the organic atmosphere that Jazz gives my music.'[33] Jazz gives a joy born out of a history of suffering and endurance, a celebration that doesn't ignore oppression but, rather, resists and transcends it.[34]

The lyrics contain an irrepressible joy and optimism as well.

> Am I alone in this nightmare?
> Well I guess I'll be a light then
> I'll walk with wolves and baboons
> There'll be a church up in the wild soon.

Underneath the sharp critique and denunciation, he is confident because he knows that he is not alone. God is at work in history, still in charge, and God's people will come round: a church will emerge from the wilderness. It's a paradoxical but, ultimately, hopeful situation. As Jamm sings in the refrain:

> And he walked down through the valley
> Full of mercy, full of grace

---

33 From my email interview with Sho Baraka. 'Jazz' was capitalized in his response.

34 See William Edgar, 'The deep joy of jazz', *byFaith Online* (1 October 2006), <https://byfaithonline.com/the-deep-joy-of-jazz>, accessed February 2023. See also William Edgar, *A Supreme Love: The music of jazz and the hope of the gospel* (Downers Grove, IL: InterVarsity Press, 2022).

Kill Jesus, praise Judas
Lord, forgive them for their evil
And all their wicked ways
Kill Jesus, praise Judas.

The 'valley' refers to Psalm 23's 'valley of the shadow of death' (v. 4). Sho characterizes that valley as the home of the warped system that kills Jesus to praise Judas. And Jesus walked straight into it, 'full of mercy, full of grace', and on to resurrection on the other side.

We have hope because Jesus has gone before us, purchasing forgiveness and life for us in the midst of death, asking his Father to forgive them (us!) for their wicked ways, showing that resurrection is possible. Society is messed up, but God is still good, and he still has the last word. This has been the refrain of the black church for centuries, and it is a theme that pulses throughout Sho Baraka's music. Sho nails the tension between the darkness and the light that lies at the core of the Christian imagination.

Recognition of the darkness within

Sho Baraka is too self-reflective to pretend that the problem is only 'out there', in the world, in society. Society is made up of people: us. His songs contain a humbling dose of self-criticism, the very antithesis of triumphalism (and the self-aggrandizing posturing found in much rap music). Right after he accuses our society of injustice and betrayal, he adds, 'Hold up, I take the blame too/We love ourselves, we'd rather change you.' He becomes uncomfortably specific about the inner demons he faces – the siren call of sins that tempt him to betray his Saviour:

There'll be a church up in the wild soon
In the valley of death
'Cause ain't much changed since the last I left
Envy asking me to come back
Jealousy wants me to unpack
Lust been talking about she miss me
Death's been dying to kiss me
Greed whispers with a coolness
'I love it when you act like Judas.'

Even where he feels most gifted and righteous – his outspoken prophetic critique – he recognizes the need for grace:

Yeah, the many mistakes, the multiple apologies
The pride in my heart when the rest didn't acknowledge me
The many times I've opened my mouth
When silence could've been the best route (yeah)
We all gotta learn, one day.

For all their 'throwing down the gauntlet' edge and challenge, his songs incarnate something not commonly found in rap: humility. This is not Christian propaganda. Rather, it's an invitation to struggle with and draw alongside strugglers, because he knows his own inner darkness. This is something sorely needed in Christian art and popular culture.

Hope that change will come, that beauty grows in the dark world because God's light still shines

Though society is a tortured mess of our own making, and that mess seeps down into our own souls, hope remains because God *still* works in our world. More astonishing, he works through *us*, through our fumbling attempts, our broken protest and poetry. Baraka reveals his de facto mission statement in the second verse:

Protest music I might say stuff
Crazy enough to make change come
The freedom writers [or riders] may like this
Pick in an Afro with a black fist
Words that decorate a real father[35]
Who love on the queen's daughters
Who blossom the king's flowers
Cause ain't no hoes up in God's garden.

Sho sees himself in the tradition of the 'freedom riders' who struggled for liberation in the early 1960s. He is a writer who embraces his own ethnic

35 The 'father' here may be God the Father, but more likely Baraka is highlighting the role 'freedom writers' play in encouraging human fathers, as the next lines explain. Being a father – especially of daughters nowadays – is a tough gig. We need all the encouragement we can get.

identity *and* his calling to write words that bestow dignity and beauty on others: the faithful fathers too often forgotten, the daughters too often denigrated as 'hoes', making all 'God's flowers' blossom by bringing out people's hidden inner beauty. Hope for a warped society and warped souls lies precisely in walking this path, writing and performing words that affirm God's power, grace and the beauty of his creation. Hope lies in protesting against the darkness to protect and preserve what was meant to be God's garden.

Sho places hope especially in the legacy of strong families: husbands who love their 'queens', 'real fathers' who love their kids and teach them God's wisdom rather than passively sit back and watch them degrade and destroy themselves through foolishness. The line, 'Ain't no hoes up in God's garden' functions on several levels at once: a clever wordplay (hoe as garden implement v. ho as a sexually loose woman), *and* a call to men to treat women with respect (they are queens and flowers, not sexual objects), *and* a call for fathers to bring their daughters up to become women of virtue, to live lives worthy of a true queen and beautiful flower. There is hope, real hope, for those who seek shelter in God's garden.

There is a lot going on in this one song. Sho Baraka protests against a messed-up world with an imagination that is at once full of lamenting protest *and* confident hope, because God is with his people, a people who know that they too need God's mercy. Baraka gets the tension exactly right: an utterly realistic recognition of the dark, twisted nature of this world, but a firm grasp on the light of hope that comes from God's covenant grace and power, active in the world, even active through his people.

In terms of volume control (see chapter 7), Baraka's songs are unmistakably Christian, but are in no way triumphalistic propaganda.[36] His use of metaphor, double entendre, references both cultural and biblical, all create a thick text that invites Christians and non-Christians in to explore. His songs often share his own brokenness in painfully honest, transparent and vulnerable words. This is not hip-hop posturing; this is wisdom born of pain. It resonates in a way that commands tension because of its empathy. Baraka creates a peculiarly Christian space that breathes – an oasis for both the wayward church and wayward world.

[36] Not to be confused with Propaganda, another fascinating Christian rapper/spoken-word artist.

Conclusion: speaking truth to family is hard, but necessary

One song doesn't really show the diversity of styles and tones Sho Baraka employs. He can be hard-hitting, as in 'Kill Jesus, praise Judas'. He can be gentle, reflective and exuberant, as in 'Piano break, A.D. 33' (the one that got him in trouble with LifeWay). Or he can be playful, as in 'Kanye, 2009'. He has a deep passion to see God's justice worked out in contemporary society, and a remarkable capacity to hold on to lament and hope simultaneously. He has the courage to expose his own limits and weaknesses. He has an eye for grace and beauty in the ordinary, such as the way a husband revels in the beauty of his wife when she's at her least glamorous, as in 'Headwraps and sweats', from *So many feelings*.

All in all, this is what a healthy Christian imagination (and spirituality) looks like: grounded in the beauty of God's generous creation, it has wisdom to see how sin warps and ruins that creation (including us), and a sure hope that catches sight of our redemption in Christ, looking forwards, to the grace and power that, ultimately, will triumph in a new creation.

His music has no patience for tidy spiritual dualisms that sideline this-worldly questions of justice, race, marriage and sex, fatherhood, money and power. Either Jesus is the rightful King of it all or he is not King at all. Faithfulness demands attention to everything under his rule. Sho Baraka believes in the power and grace of King Jesus over the whole world, and he raps accordingly.

The world needs this perspective, but perhaps the church needs it more – that is, if we are to incarnate God's love for the world. Baraka tries to reach both church and world, though he gives a certain (if not exclusive) priority to his church family:

> my primary audience is the church . . . It's like your family. I know the core values for which we operate. However, I attempt to reach people who are willing to wrestle with the general themes I address in my music. Fatherhood, marriage, justice and much more. These are not issues isolated to the church. I find that people outside the church connect more deeply to some principles I communicate

> than folks inside the church. We bring our experiences to the party. Sometimes people experience [the same] things you do [about] fatherhood but don't share much else. I hope they are encouraged by my music. It's a truth that Jehovah has given me about life that's not exclusive to Christians.[37]

This is oasis music that breathes and invites in both Christian and non-Christian.

Baraka focuses mainly on the church because, too often, Christians are part of the problem. Church is family, and he's honest about family issues:

> I have an intrinsic common ground with those who identify as the church. We should know where to start and where the finish line is. My greater challenge is to wake us to the ways we use the tools of our faith for detriment. Just as much as we can be the solution we can also be the problem. The title of Christian doesn't keep us from using the principles as tools of oppression.[38]

Sho Baraka is an artist who serves as prophet first to the church, then to the world. I asked him what he wants his music to accomplish. He gave me a quote from Christian recording artist and producer T. Bone Burnett (borrowing from C. S. Lewis):

> T. Bone Burnett said, 'I can either write songs about the sun or I can write songs about what the sun helps me see.' If Jesus is the sun, then my goal is to create stories and opportunities for people to see the 'sun' and what the 'sun' helps me to see.[39]

Sometimes sunlight reveals distortions that need to be corrected, like systemic racism. Social justice is not the gospel, but it is intrinsic to our

---

[37] From my email interview with Sho Baraka.

[38] From my email interview with Sho Baraka.

[39] From my email interview with Sho Baraka. I am not sure where the T. Bone Burnett quote came from (possibly a private conversation with Sho Baraka), but the full wording from C. S. Lewis is, 'I believe in Christianity as I believe that the Sun has risen, not only because I see it but because by it, I see everything else.' It comes from Lewis's famous sermon, 'The weight of glory', delivered at the Church of St Mary the Virgin, Oxford (8 June 1942), <www.wheelersburg.net/Downloads/Lewis%20Glory.pdf>, accessed February 2023. Quote by C. S. Lewis © copyright 1961 CS Lewis Pte Ltd. Used with permission.

calling as gospel-formed people. Jesus saves, but he saves us not only *from* sin but *to* a mission: to be lights in darkness, to be agents of healing in a sin-warped world. Baraka believes that his specific mission as an artist is to draw alongside those actively engaged in the fight and encourage them.

He knows some will oppose him, but that's par for the course: 'anyone submitted unto Jesus will face resistance of some kind so I'm not special or an outlier in any sense. The supporters and the narrative of Jesus keep me hopeful.'[40]

I asked him what 'success' looks like for him, what sort of change he hopes his music brings.

> For me, success is being true to my mission and vision while hearing that those who engage my work have found an entrance into a more complete truth of who Jesus is while entering into a great connection to their neighbor.[41]

That would be more than enough for any Christian artist. *That* is an oasis.

40 From my email interview with Sho Baraka.
41 From my email interview with Sho Baraka.

11

Being present in the broken dance: the improvisational, pointed art of Ruth Naomi Floyd

Introduction and confession

You may have noticed that I'm not exactly neutral about the artists featured in these chapters. I'm excited about their work, invested, a fan. Jazz vocalist, composer, photographer, educator and poet-lyricist Ruth Naomi Floyd is no exception. But I need to come clean: I have a deep affection and admiration for Ruth's person as well as her art. She is a dear friend.

My family originally connected with Ruth through my friend and mentor Bill Edgar (himself a formidable jazz pianist), and I've seen her perform several times over the years. Each time, I have been blown away by the depth, dignity and resonance of her presence and voice. I love the textural quality, the sadness, the twilight sensibility that infuses her photography. But that's just her art. In person, she has a wonderfully generous spirit. Her words hit you with both beauty and blunt power, speaking truth with the empathy and urgency of the prophets of old. In short, in her music, images and conversation, she tells it like it is. Plus, she's one of the very few of my artist friends who loves sport as well. That alone puts her in a class by herself. So, no disinterested analysis here. I am a fan and a friend.

I almost didn't include her because of that, but my wife was adamant that this book needed Ruth's perspective as an African-American woman. Turns out she was right. I interviewed Ruth in August 2015,[1] a summer that saw a lot of turmoil and soul-searching concerning racial tensions in

[1] Ruth requested several changes to the transcript to reflect her present position.

America – turmoil that has only increased over the years. For Ruth Naomi Floyd, race, faith, imagination, artistic integrity and vulnerability all interweave in ways that are important for Christians to hear, especially in a post-Christian cultural context. I will draw out themes from her music, photography and our conversation, to see how they illuminate one another to shed new light on Christian creativity.

Imagination, improvisation and presence

I listened to the whole of Ruth's album *Root to the Fruit*.[2] What struck me most wasn't the high level of musicianship, the solid and satisfying compositions and arrangements – or even how hard the band swung – but, rather, the texture of emotional vulnerability, which was arresting and sometimes disconcerting. No-one is going to mistake this for your typical contemporary Christian music album. Her heart lay exposed, as a raw wound, a pain brought closer than most Christians find comfortable.

Though her photography is gentler, that sense of emotional transparency is just as clear. According to Ruth, her images expose her more than her music. When I talked to her, her mother was dying (she has since passed away). She was also looking after her father, who was ailing and needed round-the-clock care (he passed away as well, though years after our interview). Amid all this, her images laid her soul bare:

> With photography, I can't hide . . . I feel completely naked when I create an image. I feel like everyone can see into my soul. I had a war and a battle about putting up [on Facebook] this series called 'Morning light series' that just shows light and shadows at morning and dusk. Because of what's going on with my parents and everything, I just felt, 'You are exposing yourself to the world!' And then, as any artist, you hope that your images touch people. And probably the image that was the hardest for me is in some ways the most beautiful. It was in colour, which is rare; just apples on the table by a wall with light and darkness. And for me, there was so much in there: fruit, 'Is the fruit good from the root?' There were just so

2 Ruth Naomi Floyd, *Root to the Fruit* (Contour, 2007). At the time of writing, Ruth is working on an album based on the works of Frederick Douglas. See <https://fredrickdouglassjazzworks.com>, accessed February 2023.

> many metaphors in that that it was just very, very hard for me to put up. So I am most transparent in my photography. If you want to know who I am, my images will tell you. And each exhibit is hard because I feel like I come to the exhibit with no clothes on, just nude and vulnerable. I'm a very different person at the premiere of an exhibit than I am on stage . . . because I just cannot hide. I wish I could (which is sad, too), I wish I could not be so transparent, so vulnerable.

I had no idea what she meant until later when I looked at her image 'Light, apples, and shadows' (see p. 4 in plate section). It is a deceptively simple still life: green apples in a rush basket on a table in front of a richly detailed wall with morning light slanting in from an unseen window. With the exception of the green apples, the colour palette is muted: brown table, brown basket, greyish-brown wall. The texture is grainy, perhaps from using a fast shutter speed for low-light photography. But that grain gives the image a tangible roughness, an unvarnished quality.

Ruth's commentary on the image says, 'The vivid rays of morning light cast upon shadows of the vanishing night.'[3] So you'd think it's an image of hope. But the way the shadow from the table falls away and down, how the whole image descends into darkness as the eye scans from left to right, suggests the inevitability of death, of fading light, while still pointing to the hope contained in the passing of the night, of resurrection after death. At least, that was my interpretation. Through it I could see the muted grief of my friend. I felt her presence in the image.

'Being present' is the undertone that unites all her work. It means not hiding, being transparent, vulnerable, showing need, grief, joy, desire and brokenness. For her, this is what the imagination is for, a gift through which we become present to one another. When I asked her to define the imagination, instead of giving a technical definition (such as you can find in chapters 5 and 6), she described it as a vital aspect of God himself that he bequeaths to us:

[3] The image plus Ruth's commentary can be found on her Facebook profile, <www.facebook.com/129687350403451/photos/pb.129687350403451.-2207520000.1446453042./999135776791933/?type=3&theater>, accessed February 2023.

> I absolutely love that our first introduction, that our first image, glimpse, understanding of God, is not as Lord and Saviour, not as Redeemer, not as a babe wrapped in swaddling clothes, not even the great sacrificial Lamb on Calvary's tree. We are first introduced and shown who God is as an artist. 'In the beginning, God created.' And so the first and greatest Artist, the one who created out of nothing, paints himself, reveals himself as an artist. I'm reminded of that Schaeffer quote, that the imagination of the Christian should just enable us to fly, that it just zooms, that we should have the greatest gift of imagination.[4] So it's our heritage. It's our birthright. It's a tool that God uses throughout his world in conjunction with his word, and that it is woven through with who he is. So, in the struggles of my life as an artist, that's where I go back to.

For Ruth, the imagination is invariably improvisational. Obviously, jazz is an improvisational musical genre, even for a vocalist. You will never hear a jazz singer sing something 'straight'. Rather, the singer will vary the phrasing and intonation, making the song her own. Ruth does that in her singing, but improvisation is involved in her photography as well:

> The gift of imagination for me is very improvisational. As a photographer, I'm a pre-visualist, which lends itself, I think, for people to think that it's not improvisational. But I pre-visualize an image, and when I go to execute it, I let that go; I let it take its own form.

Creating through improvisation opens the artist to risk. In this, it resembles the life of faith, being available in the flow rather than planning out a regimented performance. One cannot call on the imagination without risk:

> [The gift of imagination is] absolutely about taking risks. And being willing to fall. I think this Christian life is much the way that I teach jazz vocalists. You're jumping off a mountain without a parachute.

[4] The reference here is to the famous Christian apologist and philosopher Francis Schaeffer, likely from *Art and the Bible* (Downers Grove, IL: InterVarsity Press, 2006 [1973]).

> Sometimes you'll fly, sometimes you'll fly for a long time. Sometimes you'll crash right to the bottom. But in taking those risks, you learn a lot about yourself, you learn a lot about the craft, and you learn a lot about the One – directly or indirectly – who created that gift. And you don't make the same mistake again. It's a tough learning tool, but I think we as Christians, in conjunction with the imagination, need to have that kind of posture.

Ruth calls that posture of creative risk 'being present', whether it applies to improvisational art or emotional honesty. In life or art, one has a choice: to be real, vulnerable, transparent, or to hide and manipulate. In this, her perspective challenges the culture-war mentality. The Christian life is not (or, rather, should not be) about the conquest to reclaim culture. It's about being present. Her model of artistic and Christian integrity is Christ in the Garden of Gethsemane, Jesus at the end of his rope, struggling:

> Vulnerability, transparency and truth: that's really what the Garden of Gethsemane is, a gift of all those things. This is Jesus' Rambo moment. He's going to come and destroy the Evil Empire. He's going to bring it down. And we find him on his knees crying, sweat, blood, asking if this bitter cup can pass, is there another way. Not really the way we want to see our heroes. And so he paints a picture for us of that cup of suffering. He's transparent, like the great African-American spiritual, 'Prepare a body for me and I'll go down and die'. It's game day. This is what you've worked for since you're eight years old. It's the Super Bowl. Can you imagine the quarterback saying, 'Is there any way another team could do it? Is there any way another quarterback could play?' He shows us his transparency. He gives us the gift of transparency. He shows us his vulnerability. He asks for comfort. He needs something, the Saviour of the world *needs* something from the Father, his Father, who *will* turn away from him in a matter of hours. And then, like all of us, he says, 'Not my will but thine be done' and marches to the cross.
>
> So I love that gift. I think that we need to be truthful about all the layers of imagination, which comes down to that small line between deep lament and unspeakable joy, and teetering on both sides. And

> being real in it: that in deep lament you're waiting for unspeakable joy. You need it. You're waiting for it. When will it turn a corner? And in the midst of unspeakable joy, a deep lament around the corner. But it's about being *actively present* and to *do that dance*, whether it's deep lament or unspeakable joy; a *real* dance, and a deep lament, that dance, that burden that's heavy-laden that's asking, 'Do I have to drink this cup?' to that unspeakable joy where there's dancing and light, you know, just jumping around and pure joy. But we must address that cup and be honest about that cup. And so, for me, that's just a beautiful picture of what I feel imagination is. And struggle.

Imagination, then, is all bound up in improvisation, a being present in the moment, being vulnerable, transparent to one another. Imagination is intertwined with allowing ourselves to love and be loved, being the church for strugglers. It's about refusing to put on an act as though things are OK. It's about being real.

Broken and dancing between deep lament and inexpressible joy: what white Christians can learn from the African-American experience

What reality are we to be present in? For Ruth, it is about living in the tension, being present as we walk a sometimes depressing and sometimes elating path. It's about not narrowing the emotional spectrum the way that the kingdom of forced smiles does in its triumphalism or the kingdom of fluff does in its kitschy comfort zones. Rather, we must allow ourselves to feel and be transparent in the tension between the cross and the empty tomb. It's about dancing between the darkness and the light, and in all the shades of grey in between.

Take Ruth's music – her 2007 album *Root to the Fruit*, for example. In this album alone, she explores a vast emotional spectrum.[5]

- 'Mere breath' is a sombre meditation on the delicate beauty and brevity of life.

[5] There are other tracks – we will explore them later this chapter.

- Her cover of Randy Weston's 'Where? (Can a soul find release)' expresses a prayerful, exhausted longing and searching, at times her voice loping lazily just behind the beat. She's backed by a gently understated piano trio and that gives the song a gentle intimacy.
- The band's cover of the spiritual 'O, freedom' is sung with a sharp defiance as the band descends into a free jazz chaos that feels like death and isolation (the line 'Before I'd be a slave, I'll be buried in my grave' stands out). At one point, Ruth and James Newton's flute are nearly screaming in unison as she proclaims, 'There'll be shouting over me'. (Over her dead body, death being the only passageway into absolute freedom?) But the song isn't only about disorder and pain. It breaks *through* the chaos into an up-tempo flute solo that suggests hope taking flight, gradually resolving into a rock-steady groove, as if to affirm that we've got to keep moving through life in this too often dark world.
- The mood on Mary Lou Williams' 'Act of contrition' moves from a slow, sorrowful repentance to a hope-filled determination to press on because God has shown mercy in Christ. The Hammond B-3 organ, bass guitar and ride cymbal propel her vocals gently but irresistibly forwards in a sleek groove.
- Her cover of another spiritual, 'Sometimes I feel like a motherless child', moves gradually from keening and mourning to a deep rage (though different from Blind Willie Johnson's). At one point, after the line, 'Sometimes I feel like a motherless child a long, long way from home', Ruth ad-libs about the homes she's been snatched from (Africa, and heaven). You get a sense of the deep hurt and alienation that have resulted from the injustices inflicted on her people collectively and on her individually.
- The album ends on a note of wistful hope, expressed in 'Goodbye for now' (a song Ruth wrote on the passing of her grandmother).

Overall, it's a powerfully transparent musical testament of her experience, grounded in a deep history of suffering and hope. Ruth's music embraces the tension between the darkness and the light. Listening to the entire album straight through, I felt as though I'd travelled a good distance with her, that I knew something of what she's been through because she had allowed me into her heart to hear the ups and downs of clinging to hope in a fallen, broken world.

Her photography does the same thing, though in a quieter way. 'The veil series' consists of mostly black-and-white images of individuals (predominantly their faces but also their hands or feet), each draped in a translucent black veil. The people behind the veil are still visible, though partly obscured, as through a glass darkly (1 Corinthians 13:12). The subjects' eyes are often averted, looking to the side or downcast, or closed in pain (see page 5 in plate section).

These are images of grief, mourning, loss, death. But even here, we catch glimpses of hope. In one image, the veil covers only part of the subject's face. Her eyes can be seen, unobscured by the dark fabric, looking at the world beyond the veil. In another, tensed hands beneath the veil are grasped by a hand from above, offering help and comfort – this person need not struggle under the veil alone. These images acknowledge the weight of the shadow we labour under, but the shadow does not get the final word.[6]

It is exactly here that white Christians can learn from artists such as Ruth Naomi Floyd. She is not afraid of addressing the issue of race, even though it makes many of her fellow Christians uncomfortable. White Christians often assume that when race is broached, it is simply about lobbying for black self-interest in the name of political correctness and identity politics. I have come to learn that, too often, we white folk simply don't understand the countless indignities, injustices and exclusions that black people still endure in a majority white society, even in church. Floyd calls it 'being invisible', and it is degrading.

Brought up the daughter of a black Baptist minister, Ruth later became interested in Reformed theology and attended a long-established church in a biblically conservative Reformed denomination. But she was a tiny minority within it, ignored, overlooked, dismissed and pigeonholed. Instead of being treated as a complex and fully human being in her own right, she was put into a box.

> When I was seen, I was viewed as a house Negro, acceptable Negro, 'Ruth you're a credit to your race. You're not like those welfare mamas

6 To view these images online, go to <https://rnfimages.com/#!/veil-images/>, accessed May 2023.

out there. You're amazing. Wow! And you're articulate. And you're smart. And you're my friend.' Or 'Sing for us, Ruth. We need a spiritual. We need to mourn. Sing and make us cry. Be Mammy. Cradle us in the arms of your voice.'

Sometimes the racism was more explicit, such as the time she was called a racial epithet by an elder in the sanctuary of the church she had begun to call home. On top of that, there was no recognition of the damage that this part of the white church had done to black people throughout American history. It made her want to leave her newly adopted church home.

When we talk about ISIS, when we talk about all that, there's no misunderstanding about that. But then when we see the Ku Klux Klan meeting with a white Southern pastor, meeting in a church with a cross behind him with 'Jesus saves', there is not a clear understanding of the religious terrorism that went on in the name of Jesus, and my theological tribe's deliberate silence during slavery, and my tribe's deliberate non-action during the civil rights movement. It points to the fact that there's a *huge* disconnect between the theology that is preached and the theology that is practised. So I decided to walk away. I just thought, 'I love this theology, but I can't take this anymore.'

She would have left, were it not for the words of another elder in that church – a black man who had been attending for decades. As he lay dying of cancer, he asked her to visit. It was the beginning of a painful, but ultimately liberating, journey towards brokenness.

He looked me in the eye and said, 'If I could stay, you could stay. I too, like you, heard this theology on the radio. And something, I believe the Holy Spirit, pulled me towards it. And when I walked into that church, daughter, the only place I could sit was in the balcony. I endured to become the first African-American elder in the church and *still* be invisible. If I can do it, you can do it.' Sometimes continuing to show up is resistance. And so, I stayed. But I thought, 'If I'm going to stay, I am going to tell the truth.' The way I told the truth, in the beginning, was with a lot of justified rage.

> Justified rage can be a necessary tool towards transformation and justice. But one can only sustain rage (justified or not) for so long. God broke me, and He chose to break me in a place where my full humanity was invisible and where deep hurt resided. I was saddened when God chose to break me in this place of pain. During the process of brokenness, I learned how to actively listen in a deeper way, not to come back with a witty response, but to actively listen and learn. And how to be present when presented with teachable moments and opportunities for that, to have teachable moments. I learned to recognize and utilize teachable moments for the possible opportunity of repentance, healing and restoration. I am grateful for the process of brokenness as it was also a place of preparation. This long season of brokenness prepared me for something I could not fully navigate then but, by the grace of God, I am able to navigate in a better way with existing and new communities where racism exists and is reinforced. Brokenness helped me understand *imago Dei* in deeper ways and it pushed me to boldly speak the truth in and with love.

In short, that painful experience of being broken has given Ruth strength, patience, sensitivity and compassion for those she speaks and sings to.

Because her experience is informed by generations of suffering and exclusion by a majority American culture that instinctively protects its position of privilege, white conservative Christians can learn something, both in the USA and in the wider Western world. The majority culture around us has become more solidly post-Christian and, in some cases, even hostile to Christians. I need to choose my words carefully: I do not mean for a second to equate what white conservative Christians now suffer with hundreds of years of brutal slavery, Jim Crow laws[7] and racism that has continued ever since. But a time is coming, and has now come, when the sorts of indignities and injustices that are routinely suffered by African Americans will be felt by white Christians also. The question that

[7] Jim Crow laws were a system of local laws that were established, beginning in 1865, immediately after the US Constitution's 13th Amendment outlawing slavery. They were intended to solidify segregation and ensure that black people could not gain financial independence or seek redress for crimes against them. In effect, these laws continued the subjugation of black people that they had endured under slavery in a country that had outlawed slavery.

ought to capture the church's attention is not 'How do we win back the culture?' but, rather, 'How do we speak truth to power in ways that are both passionate and winsome?' This is territory that black church communities know with grim familiarity. The white church, not so much. We have no frame of reference for the kind of slow-burn, everyday suffering that African Americans know so well. But we will have to learn, and soon.

For historical reasons, until relatively recently, those of us in the West, especially the UK and USA, have lived in a Christian majority culture (even a Protestant majority culture). Sociologist James Davison Hunter has called it a 'pan-Protestant hegemony', but one that is increasingly being replaced by a secular hegemony.[8] For a while, we laboured under the illusion that we lived in a Christian part of the world. We lived enjoying the comforts of an illusory empire. Hence the attitudes of triumphalism that haunt much of Christian culture. But that illusion is fast evaporating. So now what?

Perhaps, like Ruth, we need to learn how to listen actively to those who differ with us, knowing when to speak, when to hold our peace and how to love those who make life difficult for us (Matthew 5:43–48). In learning how to be humble, broken yet unbowed, speaking truth to power with passion and patience, the black church has much to teach us. Not that black churches are perfect, but they have occupied a cultural space that is similar to the one we are entering now. We must learn to dance, broken, in the tension between deep lament (for the world and our own hearts) and inexpressible joy.

'Art judges us': Christian creativity provokes reflection and critique

One aspect of Ruth's music that differs from the 'balanced' ideal I presented in chapter 7 is that she is an evangelist, and the daughter of an evangelist. Her music doesn't beat around the bush; it often proclaims its message directly and in no uncertain terms. In *Root to the Fruit* she opens with the spiritual 'No hiding place'. The arrangement is spare: just her voice and Ron Howerton's conga drumming. It's the perfect vehicle to convey a message of exposure – her voice has no hiding place.

---

[8] James Davison Hunter, *Culture Wars: The struggle to define America* (New York: Basic Books, 1991).

In the song, a sinner tries to hide under a rock, but the rock answers, 'there's no hiding place down here'. The lyrics then proclaim the end of Pharaoh's reign (a reference to the slave master's oppression and, by extension, the twisted oppression that pollutes this world) and that sinners better run (because they can't hide), that evil will be exposed and judged. But the song also affirms that God is our 'shelter in the storm'. There's 'no hiding place down here', but God provides shelter for his own. Pretty direct stuff, and a good preamble to an album that leaves not only the artist's heart exposed but the listeners' hearts as well.

On the fourth track, Ruth borrows from Czech composer Antonín Dvořák (who borrowed from the Bible) to proclaim that 'God is my Shepherd'. And the seventh track, 'Open the door to him', is as close to an altar call as you'll find in jazz. Though sometimes she uses oblique or metaphorical references, much of the time it's gospel straight up.

Nevertheless, Ruth's music succeeds and gains respect (at least with reviewers)[9] where so much evangelistic contemporary Christian music fails. There are three reasons for this. First, the music is *so* good. She chose her musicians not because they are Christian but because they are excellent and proven. It's got her into trouble with some Christians, but their contributions give her music a depth and power it would not have otherwise.

Second, Ruth draws masterfully on the history of suffering and hope that characterizes so many African-American spirituals. She told me:

> It's been my goal to take from past generations, to honour those who've come before me who've sacrificed and laid down their lives to create, to explore, to develop their art forms, to share that music. Hopefully, my goal has always been, besides the spiritual (and obviously this is tied to the spiritual), to take what generations have done before, to honour that, to talk about where we are, honestly, as a human race, but then also social-politically, and certainly the racism. And to point to where we can go, and hopefully will go.

9 For example, see Bill Milkowski's review, 'Ruth Naomi Floyd: Jazz mass', *JazzTimes* (1 April 2007 [updated 25 April 2019]), <https://jazztimes.com/archives/ruth-naomi-floyd-jazz-mass>, accessed February 2023.

This is a musically expressed spirituality that is not to be dismissed lightly, for it draws on a well of experience that stretches back through the generations, ancient and proud. Her sensitivity to that history gives her music gravitas.

Third, Ruth's music succeeds because she is doing something unusual and arresting: setting gospel content to straight-ahead (even edgy, 'outside') jazz music. Bridging the gap between jazz and Christian spirituality is not something that many have done well. Her music leaves no room for cliché or cheesiness because her performances are both excellent and emotionally honest, transparent and vulnerable. And they never come across as preachy. Rather, she conveys hope, sadness, anger, conviction and joy. The resonance of her voice and music is her argument, and even non-Christians respond (not necessarily in faith but with deep respect). In so doing, she creates an oasis, a space that draws in Christians and non-Christians in a way that encourages reflection and conversation.

Ruth's photography does the same thing, though in a different way. She told me about one of her first exhibitions of 'The veil series'. An art critic showed up to review her work. After studying perhaps three images, he became visibly agitated and left. Ruth followed him, not to try to salvage a good review but to see what was going on inside the man.

> I went out and said hello. He knew who I was, and he goes, 'I don't want to talk about it. I don't want to talk about it.' The art from 'The veil series' images confronted him. And what it did was confronted him with his own veils in his life. And he didn't like seeing those veils. He didn't want to answer 'Which veils are in my life?': a woman embracing a veil, a woman pushing against a veil. Which veil is this? And I just said, 'Look, you're going to write what you're going to write. The good thing is, I'm an emerging artist. Half the people won't pay attention. I have nothing to lose. At this point, you can help me a lot, but you can't hurt me a lot. So I'm just going to gamble. I'm more interested in you.' And I told him, 'My job as an artist is to provoke a response, and you gave me a huge response, and it's negative. I want to know – as human being to human being, not artist to critic – talk to me about that response.' And he did.

They met for coffee later. She learnt that the critic was going through a messy divorce. His wife had cheated on him and he had taken comfort in being the innocent victim. But those images of loneliness and loss haunted him. After reflecting for a time, he realized that he, too, was to blame. His own distance and cold hostility had isolated his wife, leaving her no option, she felt, but to seek solace in the arms of another or commit suicide. Those images helped him to own his responsibility in the dissolution of his marriage and he asked his wife for forgiveness. It was too late to save the marriage, but they parted in peace, as friends.

That is what Ruth meant when she told me, 'I really, truly believe that we don't judge art; art judges us.' Art has the ability to communicate emotionally and spiritually in a way that flies under our conscious intellectual radar and provokes reflection and self-criticism. Art can take us off our high horses and help us to see our own brokenness. Great art humbles and humanizes us.

Hearing the story about that critic made me rethink the central metaphor of this book: the oasis. I still like the metaphor of works of art as oases, Christians using cultural creativity to open spaces for reflection and conversation. At the same time, perhaps the metaphor is too passive. In Ruth's way of thinking, art has sharp, pointy edges that poke the audience or viewer. That means it not only allows for reflection and discussion but, further, provokes and prods us into doing so. Art judges us, backs us into a corner, and we must respond. It's true. So if you can hold that thought in your imagination of an oasis that is at once inviting and pointed, refreshing and provoking, attractive and gets under your skin in ways that are painful and impossible to dismiss, *that's* what I mean. That is what Christian art should aspire to.

Don't play the Holy Spirit: leave room for the art to speak

That is why Ruth believes artists should resist playing the Holy Spirit by trying to control how the art is received. If it's worthy art, it will stand on its own. Part of being an artist is relinquishing control, letting the art find its audience and speak for itself. She told me a story from early in her career, a performance she gave at one of the most revered jazz clubs in Philadelphia, Zanzibar Blue. A pastor-theologian she deeply respects came to the performance. Before each song, she'd read a Bible verse or say a few words to help the audience to interpret the lyrics.

> After the first set he came up, he goes, 'Can we talk?' And he said, 'What are you doing?' I said, 'I'm singing my music and I'm sharing the gospel of Jesus Christ.' And he said, 'Look, you have poured over your lyrics. You have thought through them. You have reflected on them. You have checked with other theologians on them. You thought. Seriously, let the music speak for itself. You don't need to introduce the tune. You don't need to say, "Lamentations 3:22 and 23" for "Mercy". All that's needed is in there. Allow room for the Holy Spirit to work.'
>
> It was really important. What it does is that, although I don't evangelize, I let the Holy Spirit do his work. It also holds me to, in a deeper way, integrity and accountability, of making sure that the lyrics I do put out there present the gospel, either in sometimes a direct way or maybe in a more artistic, veiled way, that they're pointed to the gospel in the foundation of what I'm trying to communicate. In other words, there is the presence of the gospel for the Holy Spirit to do his work. So instead of wondering and trying to do the Holy Spirit's work of 'Will it touch lives?' 'Will it change people?' (I can pray for that), I'm more saying, 'Make sure the vehicle that carries the gospel is on point.'

Even so, Ruth doesn't believe that art must always evangelize. Rather, she told me, 'I think the theology of beauty shows that they don't need to have the Four Spiritual Laws or a Scripture verse in every song. A flower in and of itself is just the gospel, is the Word, it reflects the beauty of Jesus.' In other words, the doctrine of creation is inseparably tied to the doctrine of redemption. All truth is God's truth. All beauty is God's beauty. The creation of God vibrates with the resonance of the redemption of God.[10]

---

10 For my thoughts on how creation (general revelation) interweaves with redemption (special revelation), see my article 'Reflecting theologically on popular culture as meaningful: The role of sin, grace, and general revelation', *Calvin Theological Journal*, vol. 37, no. 2 (November 2002), pp. 270–296, <www.calvin.edu/library/database/crcpi/fulltext/ctj/88090.pdf>, and thoughts on popular culture, apologetics and the discourse of desire summarized in chapters 3 and 4 of *Popologetics: Popular culture in Christian perspective* (Phillipsburg, NJ: P&R, 2012). For a different but complementary perspective, see Craig Detweiler, *Into the Dark: Seeing the sacred in the top films of the 21st century* (Grand Rapids, MI: Baker Academic, 2008), pp. 29–37.

For the artist, the entire cosmos, the whole spectrum of human experience, is fair game. Sing, write, dance, photograph, make films or TV programmes, video games about *everything*, because it all belongs to God's creation, marred by the fall, and involved with his redemption. Don't play Holy Spirit. Allow your art to speak. But, remember: it can (and should) speak about *anything*.

'If we could just tell the truth about the blues': embracing the mess

The last theme we will touch on in this chapter flows from the gospel itself: tolerance for human hurt and mess. Not simply telling the truth, being present and vulnerable, but also creating spaces and communities in which that kind of truth-telling and transparency is safe, met with compassion and empathy. Not simply 'art judges us' but also art leads to *self*-judgment, not judgmental Christians making (other) sinners feel small and excluded.

Ruth's music and images do this. They can hit hard, but she's not lashing out at anyone. Her directness is always guided by compassion. Even when she proclaims that 'sinners better run', she is always quick to present a destination they can run *to*. This art flows from a theology of sovereign grace that is available to the messiest of people. We can be honest about the struggle, about our broken dance between lament and joy, precisely because gospel grace surrounds us in the struggle and joins us together as communities of strugglers.

Understanding grace deeply enough to allow the truth of our messy lives to surface in our art and communities will draw people to the faith, Ruth asserts. Having relationships strong and mercy-filled enough to encourage and embrace the messed-up will attract sinners to Jesus.

Several times during the interview, Ruth touched on what she called telling the truth about the blues.

> If we had good relationships, good marriages . . . [and] if Christians *told the truth about the blues*, our churches would be filled . . . I'm talking about loss, abandonment, grief, everything that is a language that all of us have spoken. You live in this world long enough, you *will* have the blues. That is a promise. That is a guarantee.

As examples of those who told the truth about the blues, she mentioned the prophet Jeremiah. He wept and yelled at God for giving him the thankless, seemingly futile task of delivering a message that the people didn't want to hear . . . again and again and again. Ruth likened him to Billie Holiday, who sang 'Strange fruit' (Abel Meeropol's poem about lynchings in the southern states in the USA, set to sombre music) repeatedly to audiences who simply didn't want to hear it.

These are stories that don't have neat, tidy solutions. Rather, they resonate with the pain and corruption of fallen existence. Jesus in the Garden of Gethsemane understood that, as did the slaves who wrote the spirituals. *They* told the truth about the blues. Christians should as well. Tell the truth about the mess and pain, and so welcome the messy and afflicted.

Ruth held up a church that she formerly attended (the same one she criticized earlier for displaying subtle racist attitudes) as an exemplar of what it means to welcome the messy. She told the story of a prodigiously talented painter who lived on the street and struggled with mental illness. The church community embraced him, exhibited his work in the church, and some bought his paintings. They cared for him amid his struggle when he went off his meds, when he hadn't showered in a week. That church community acted as all churches should.

Ruth mused on how Vincent van Gogh's story might have turned out differently if Christians around him had, similarly, been willing to love him, even through his messiness and scandalous lifestyle.

If we were to do this, consistently show the mercy that we preach about to those who are difficult to love, to the artists we don't understand and whose art makes us feel uncomfortable, how would our post-Christian culture view us then? To do this, churches must be committed to transparency, vulnerability and risk. They must be places where the messy can find shelter without being judged and discarded, refusing to put a shiny patina on life. Instead, they must tell the truth about the blues.

Something about Ruth's music and art clues in the listener or viewer that this woman is honest about the struggle, and she harbours no bitterness, nor a judgmental spirit. Rather, she is one who is ready to draw alongside and embrace the pain and the mess. There is a warmth in the tone of her vocals that embraces. There is a stillness in the light of her images that draws us in. And she lives this out day by day. She poured herself out for her ailing father. She goes into bars and sits and talks with people hurt and confused about their own gender and befriends them. In this respect, her art and life organically imply one another. Out of the overflow of her heart and life, her art speaks. It points through the artist to a God who is ready and eager to embrace the messy and the broken.

Conclusion: practical advice on not abusing Christian artists

What I appreciated most during our time together was her unflagging practicality. I tend to intellectualize, see life as a set of mental problems in search of solutions: we need to contextualize better here, we need a more creational emphasis in our theology there. What Ruth made clear to me is that, for both Christian art and Christian life, it's not about theory, it's about love. Not about the talk, but about the walk.

We also discussed the relationship between the church and artists, how Christians can elevate artists to rock star status within the small pond of Christendom (and so paralyse their artistic development), rather than encourage them to make it in the large pond of the wider culture. Or Christians can denigrate artists and expect them to work for free in the church because it glorifies the Lord (as if hanging work in a secular gallery or singing in a jazz club does not).

We discussed how some Christians don't see artists as creators, but simply as vessels of the message (and so artists shouldn't get copyright protection for their work because the images or songs don't *truly* belong to them).

We will have a chance to talk about these attitudes in more depth in chapter 17, but for now, the most important themes I take from Ruth's art and our conversation are the ideas of being present, brokenness, transparency (being unafraid to explore the entire emotional landscape), creating art that provokes a response (negative or positive), letting the art speak, and telling the truth about the blues. There is much here to learn, not only for Christian creatives but also for the wider Christian community, about how to live out the gospel in relationship and creativity.

12

'Becoming transparent': sharing pain and hope in *That Dragon, Cancer*

The power of art – especially narrative – is its ability to make the abstract concrete, the universal personal, to bring the distant close, to put you in someone else's shoes. No other kind of storytelling does this with quite the combination punch of video games. They combine the visual impact of cinema and television, the interiority of novels, the subtle persuasion of music and, if done well, the lyrical depth of poetry. *That Dragon, Cancer* is one such game.[1] It is quite unlike anything that I've ever played before or since. It invites you to tread the terrible and exhausting path of losing a child to terminal cancer. But it treats this awful subject with such a vivid, imaginative approach, amazingly, I found that I *wanted* to walk this path.

The story behind the game

In 2016, Numinous Games, a small independent video game studio, released *That Dragon, Cancer.* It made waves, not least because the creative team at Numinous – Ryan and Amy Green, and Josh Larson – were open about their Christian faith. They defied expectations of what a Christian video game is supposed to be.

The story, or better, the space in which the player is placed, reflects the real-life story of the Green family. In 2010, one-year-old Joel, Ryan and Amy's third child, was diagnosed with a rare brain cancer.[2] Doctors treated it aggressively, and there seemed to be hope of survival. A year

[1] Ryan and Amy Green, and Josh Larson, *That Dragon, Cancer* (Numinous Games, 2016).
[2] Background information taken from Jason Tanz, 'Playing for time: A father, a dying son, and the quest to build the most profound videogame ever', *Wired* (January 2016), <www.wired.com/2016/01/that-dragon-cancer>, accessed February 2023.

into the treatment, the cancer returned, and the doctors stopped aggressive treatment and started palliative, end-of-life treatments instead. They estimated he had four months to live. Joel spent a lot of time in the intensive care unit (ICU). There were partial victories, many relapses. Joel survived, but suffered a severe developmental delay and lost the ability to speak.

Ryan cut back his hours as a programmer for a dialysis company, then quit altogether so he could help to shuttle Joel to and from the hospital for tests and treatment. To make ends meet, Ryan began doing contract work for video game companies. At a conference, he met Josh Larson, another programmer who had an intense interest in creating games that would break new imaginative ground (a genre called 'not games').

In 2012, they discussed creating a game that would communicate what Ryan, Amy and Joel were going through. Ryan suggested quitting contract work to focus on the project full time. Amy felt led by the Spirit and agreed. They would live off their savings.

They produced a sample scene of the game between Ryan and Joel set in the ICU. Joel is feverish and miserable, and everything the player (as Ryan) does to soothe Joel only makes him scream louder. They took the scene to game expos and many who tried it found it powerful, even devastating. It captured the imaginations of the indie game-development community,[3] and the project gained momentum. They got funding from a Kickstarter campaign.

As Joel survived into his third year, Amy was convinced that God was preparing to do something miraculous for Joel. She wanted the game to document events leading to the impending miracle. The Greens even allowed a film crew to record their lives and the making of the video game. Their initial hesitation was overcome by the idea that this independent documentary would be ready to record the miracle that *was* going to happen.[4] Amy was sure that God was going to achieve victory in the

[3] 'Indie games' are made by small, independent studios such as Numinous, as opposed to 'AAA games' that have the financial backing of huge companies of the likes of Nintendo, Microsoft, Electronic Arts, Ubisoft. AAA games have higher-quality graphics and overall production values. Indie gaming studios, unable to afford that level of production quality, focus on innovative stories and gameplay.

[4] The film is entitled, *Thank You for Playing*, written and directed by David Osit and Malika Zouhali-Worrall, who won an Emmy for it for 'Outstanding arts and culture documentary' in 2015. The film can be streamed via AppleTV, Amazon Prime and other streaming sites.

shadow of death. Ryan called it Amy's 'Elijah moment'.[5] They just had to wait for God to show up and heal.

And then . . . God *didn't* show up. Or, at least, he didn't show up in the way they had hoped. The tumours multiplied. They moved from Colorado to San Francisco, seeking cutting-edge experimental treatment. Nothing worked. Joel died at the age of five, on 13 March 2014.[6]

At that point, the game morphed into something else – a memorial to Joel. It became the Greens' way of expressing their grief and disappointment with God, who did not intervene as expected. Through the game, they shared their pain and hope in the middle of a tragedy. By being brutally honest, they found that the game unexpectedly opened all sorts of doors.

The creatives behind *That Dragon, Cancer* generously gave me a beta-key so I could play it a couple of months before its release. Even more generously, they spent hours of their time letting me interview them. What I learnt was fascinating and moving.

Video games are for being

Before we explore this particular game, let's talk about video games in general. Many people don't take video games seriously. They are escapist fantasies for kids, not a venue for serious culture. And they are never, ever art.[7]

Wrong. Video games done well (and *That Dragon, Cancer* is done well) can be works of great beauty and depth. They express creativity in a different way from books or films, but no less profoundly. And they have one element other art forms lack: agency. In a video game, you do not simply *vicariously* identify with a character, you *are* that character, insofar as *you* are the one acting (lifting this rock, running over that hill).

[5] From interview with me, 10 December 2015. Ryan was referring to Elijah on Mount Carmel demonstrating to the wavering Israelites that the Lord was the true God by calling down fire on the sacrifice, revealing the impotence of the prophets of Baal. See 1 Kings 18:16–45.

[6] Mike Futter, 'Joel Green, inspiration for That Dragon, Cancer, passes away at age 5', *GameInformer* (13 March 2014), <www.gameinformer.com/b/news/archive/2014/03/13/joel-green-inspiration-for-that-dragon-cancer-passes-away-at-age-5.aspx>, accessed February 2023.

[7] Even revered film critic Roger Ebert denied that video games could ever be art. See his article 'Video games can never be art', *Roger Ebert.com* (16 April 2010), <www.rogerebert.com/rogers-journal/video-games-can-never-be-art>, accessed February 2023. The historical irony, of course, is that culture critics had the same attitude towards film a few generations previously. See F. R. Leavis, 'Mass civilization and minority culture' in John Storey (ed.), *Cultural Theory and Popular Culture: A reader* (New York: Routledge, 4th edn, 2009 [1930]), p. 14.

Player agency puts you *inside* an imaginary space in a way that books or films cannot. In the words of Ryan Green, 'if books are to tell, and films are to show then, to me, video games are to be'.[8] A video game immerses the player in a specific moment at a specific location. It's about presence, being. Not all video games explore fully what it means to be in an imaginary space and time, but many do. One genre that exceeds in this is called 'empathy games'. They help the players to understand another's experience intimately.

That Dragon, Cancer also enables empathy in powerful ways. Gameplay mechanics compel the player to slow down and just be, to exist in that time and place with the Greens, *as* the Greens (Ryan, Amy and Joel). Through story and gameplay elements, the game bears witness by 'exploring an emotional landscape' and 'analysing interactive poetry'.[9]

Playing the game

Note: You will get more from this chapter if you stop reading and become acquainted with the game. Watch a playthrough on YouTube or buy and play the game yourself. Spoilers lie ahead.

When you enter into the world of the game, you find yourself walking on a sunlit path through a wooded park to a duck pond. The first thing that jumps out at you is that are no AAA graphics here, no photorealistic, high-definition renderings of Lara Croft's face.[10] Instead, you are immersed in a world of polygons and colour. The graphics are more visual gestures than fully realized renderings.

Oddly enough, the low-resolution graphics don't get in the way of connecting and bonding with the characters. Connection is achieved by voice (the game uses recordings of the real-life protagonists, Ryan, Amy, Joel and their doctor), music and walking in their shoes, seeing through their eyes, sometimes even into their dreams and imaginative visions.

The second thing that jumps out at you on arriving at the duck pond is that you *are* the duck. Then, with a graceful sweep of the camera, you are

8 From interview with me.

9 Amy Green, 'A video game to cope with grief', TEDNYC (February 2017), <www.ted.com/talks/amy_green_a_video_game_to_cope_with_grief>, accessed February 2023.

10 Lara Croft is the heroine of the AAA game (and later, film) franchise *Tomb Raider*.

Joel, throwing bread to the duck. This is one hallmark of the game: shifting viewpoints that lead to a multifaceted appreciation of situations. In one pivotal scene, when the doctor delivers devastating news to the anxious parents, you actually play out parts of the scene, moving from being in the father's head, to the mother's, the doctor's and the nurse's, as the room fills surrealistically with water.

It doesn't have the sort of freighted narrative complexity of Akira Kurosawa's *Rashomon* (1950) or even Alan Moore's *Watchmen*.[11] The idea is not to add contradictory layers or even backstory. Rather, the effect is to introduce, reinforce and reiterate a sense of helplessness in the face of blank tragedy by showing that helplessness from a variety of differing but complementary points of view. The game doesn't shift perspectives to spice up the story or be flashy. Instead, it humanizes the situation, reminding us that this happened to real human beings, who each responded in his or her own way.

A third aspect of the game that stayed with me is its use of visual metaphor. Cancer was shown as the shadow of a dragon flying overhead or as black, prickly, menacing balls of tumbleweed, growing ever larger. The feeling of impotence, panic and grief is visualized as rising water that submerges the parents – you drown in their grief.

Several mini-games are also included to help you understand where this Christian family is coming from and what they have gone through. Joel becomes a gallant knight in a platformer, ducking fireballs from the dragon, cancer.[12] In the hospital, receiving treatment, mother and child are transported to a Mario Kart-type racing game, picking up oddly shaped balloons that the player assumes are bonus points. At the finish line, the scoreboard reveals that the 'bonuses' earned were invasive and painful medical tests that Joel had to undergo. The sudden change in mood hits you like a kick in the gut.

---

[11] Akira Kurosawa (director), *Rashomon* (Kadokawa Pictures, 1950; DVD, Criterion, 2012); Alan Moore (writer), Dave Gibbons (illustrator) and John Higgins (colourist), *Watchmen* (New York: DC Comics, 1986–1987). Both *Rashomon* and *Watchmen* build an overall story using layer on layer of often conflicting character perspectives. *Watchmen* in particular takes the reader into the in-depth backstory of the various characters, enabling the viewer to empathize with the profusion of conflicting viewpoints.

[12] A platformer is a type of video game in which the player must advance up levels (platforms), avoiding obstacles and dangers, to reach the goal at the top of the screen or end of the course. *Donkey Kong* and *Super Mario Brothers* are the most famous platformers.

Another mini-game shows the game's penchant for visual poetry. Joel is given a bouquet of helium-filled rubber medical gloves. He gently floats out of the hospital window to freedom (we hope). But barring his way are horrible, black, spiky balls of tumbleweed that threaten to pop Joel's balloons (see page 6 in plate section). You must guide Joel up, under and around the moving maze of tumbleweeds. But the tumbleweeds grow and the pathway shrinks. One by one, Joel's balloons pop and it suddenly dawns on you, 'I can't win. There's no way out of this. I cannot protect Joel from these things . . . from death.' The game forces you into that space of horrible futility, unable to shepherd this child to safety.

A fourth characteristic of the game that stood out to me was the messages and user-donated artwork displayed everywhere. This is, of course, due to the way the game was funded. Often, as a perk for supporting a video game on Kickstarter, messages or art from donors are included in them. In this case they took this idea further.

As I read a card on a table in Joel's hospital room in memory of a child who had passed away years earlier, and another, and another saying, 'We miss you', it made me realize that, though this is an intensely personal story, it is not unique to Ryan, Amy and Joel Green. It is a story that has played out many, many times, with different variations – different people of all ages suffering from different deadly diseases, again and again and again. The game expresses a solidarity in suffering. The Greens are not alone. We are not alone. I thought of when I lost my dad to cancer in 1996, the helplessness, the feeling of being disconnected from the world, the terrible solitude. In the face of bereavement, we need to know that human solidarity. We are in this together.

The last characteristic of the game that I want to mention is the rails. One way to characterize adventure or story games is as 'rail-y' (like a roller coaster – the player must stick to a certain path, do certain missions to advance the game) or as a 'sandpit/open world' (the player explores more or less freely).

This game is on rails, with occasional sandpit/open world spaces. Much of the time, the player is hunting for a prompt to click on, some clue that will move the game on to the next activity, the next message, the next setting, the next whatever. Sometimes it got oppressive. 'Adrift' (the chapter where the Greens process their worry and grief in different ways) seemed to last for ever. At one point, you are forced to be with Ryan, to *be* Ryan, as he tries to quiet the crying Joel, who is miserable and in pain. Later, you are obliged to listen to each and every prayer at Joel's funeral, prayers filled with expectation and doomed to go unanswered (he was not raised from the dead). It gets heavy at times, but that narrow corridor of limited choices mirrors the reality – the constraints of the experience of watching a loved one die of cancer. Not a lot of choices, no way out, on restrictive rails. The gameplay imitates life.

In fact, the game deliberately subverts the normal dynamic of video games. Typically, even games on rails let the player choose new pathways, getting stronger along the way, allowing the player to win. In *That Dragon, Cancer*, the player is trapped in a series of dead ends, closing pathways, feeling weaker and more emotionally vulnerable along the way. Amy Green explains it this way:

> We took that vulnerability that Joel taught us, and we encoded the game with it. Players expect their video games to offer them branching narrative so that every decision that they make feels important and can change the outcome of the game. We subverted that principle of game design, collapsing the choices in on the player so that they discover for themselves that there is nothing that they can do that will change the outcome for Joel. And they feel that discovery as deeply and desperately as we felt it on nights when we held Joel in our arms praying for hours, stubbornly holding out hope for a grace that we could not create for ourselves.[13]

This game is a deterministic system: you know from the outset that Joel dies in the end. But there is still room to breathe, room to explore. In this way, the game coaxes you into lingering, reflecting, feeling with, being with the Greens.

All told, its brilliant (and brutal) game design mirrors the emotional rawness of the experience the Greens had to endure. But because it is so visually imaginative (and, dare I say, fun?), it also feels inviting. The title itself comes from a visual metaphor – cancer as a horrible dragon – that

13 Green, 'A video game to cope with grief'.

Amy used in an ongoing bedtime story she told Joel's two older siblings, so they could wrap their minds around what was happening to their younger brother, visualized in the mini-game of Joel as a knight v. the dragon. It's a playful way of dealing with an utterly terrifying reality, and the game is full of such moments.

The space you're invited into is extremely intimate; you hear voices recorded from the Greens' day-to-day lives. It makes the loss that much more real and devastating. But, through it all, the game never loses sight of hope, even when all seems lost in the dark. God's presence is there, just beyond sight – not felt exactly, but sensed somehow, most powerfully in the ending: Joel is still alive, and thrives, in a beautiful new space we can only imagine.[14] In this way, the game allows players of different faiths, or no faith, to dwell in a space that mirrors the Greens' faith. It is strange, but profoundly moving.

The one thing that I wish the game had included was some scenes of Amy and Ryan's post-funeral processing, sort of a video game equivalent to Sufjan Stevens' 'Casimir Pulaski Day'.[15] I wanted to see how they came through it, what their faith looks like now.

Then again, that story is still being written and no game can continue indefinitely. On reflection, it ended at the perfect spot: the picnic at the edge of the universe. I loved how the game made heaven as concrete as pancakes and pug dogs. I don't cry at media . . . ever. But that picnic nearly broke me, when Joel welcomed me into his party, where he was perfectly healthy, content and just happy to be alive. The game ends on a note of hope that transcends this too often dark world.

Overall, the game made me feel as though I had really known Joel, not just as a victim, developmentally delayed, doomed. I got to know Joel as he could and should have been: playful, confident, full of imagination, a lover of dogs, lions, stars and bubbles. I'm grateful for being given that chance.

I also felt that I understood the Greens better, their faith, their pain, their loss and their hope. By being so emotionally honest, brutally transparent

---

14 For more on the impact of this moment, see Jenn Frank's beautiful think piece on the game, 'He's still alive', *Unwinnable* (5 April 2013), <www.unwinnable.com/2013/04/05/that-dragon-cancer>, accessed February 2023. She relates the Greens' experience to her own experience of losing her adoptive mother to cancer.

15 'Casimir Pulaski Day' is track 10 on Stevens' album *Come On, Feel the Illinoise* (Asthmatic Kitty, 2005), in which he reflects on the death of a beloved friend from bone cancer.

and allowing us to walk through this crisis with all its hard edges (including relational tension between Ryan and Amy), their faith and humanity become real. Putting flesh on faith, seeing through eyes filled with tears and hope, this probably accomplishes more than any apologetical argument ever could. It brings God close (as he was when Ryan prayed in the ICU for peace, for Joel to sleep), even when God seems so distant.

Making 'questioning art'

This is uncomfortable territory for Christians. We want to affirm that God is good, powerful, with us and for us. Going through prolonged suffering casts doubt on that. When their expected miracle turned into devastating loss, the Greens were left with more questions than answers, and that haunted them. Should we keep making the video game? Would it bring disgrace on God's name, showing that he sometimes *doesn't* intervene when we need it most?

In our interview, both Ryan and Amy voiced these concerns. Both admitted that before they started this project, they disliked 'questioning art'. Art should have an opinion, it should take a stand. But in that situation, they felt answers slip away along with any hope of Joel's recovery.

But what could they do? Stop making the game? It was the only piece of Joel they had left. They decided they would keep at it as a memorial to Joel, to show that even with his disabilities, his life mattered to them, to God, to us all. It still felt weird and uncomfortable, but it led to a good place. Amy told me:

> It almost felt anti-Christian, creating this questioning art, and we didn't like it. And we've had to come to terms with the fact that we're creating art with a lot of questions that doesn't offer a lot of answers. But now I see the value in that and how the Holy Spirit can move through that. Instead of assuming that I can create an answer and give it to someone, instead I can just say, 'I can ask the questions and hope that God answers it for you in a personal way however he chooses to do that; it probably won't be through what I create.'[16]

16 From interview with me.

By forcing the game out of 'sermon illustration mode' ('See how great God is?!'), it brought the game into a space where it could converse more intimately with each player, coaxing them to wrestle through the issues for themselves. 'Where is God? Where is hope? How do I get through this?' This was a theme I heard from all three developers again and again: we need to abandon teaching and preaching and just be, let the questions stand, let players struggle in our space for a while. Because the game allows for exploration and struggle, the players *own* the struggle and the answers they find. It becomes a part of them in a way that simple storytelling or teaching never could.

The moral for Christian creatives and communicators, a lesson the Greens learnt through painful experience: give your audience room to struggle. Don't be too quick with the answers, even if you think you know what they are. Life often throws us into situations where easy answers melt away and we are left either to despair or to find hope and assurance beyond the easy answers. It's a hard place to create from, a hard place to be. But it is also deeply good, and can be life-changing.

Where does this kind of creativity come from?

That Dragon, Cancer is striking, unusual. Where does such questioning, difficult, devastating, beautiful art about brokenness and hope come from? Obviously, it's drawn from the real-life pain the Green family went through day by day, but plenty of Christians go through heart-wrenching tragedies and never create anything like this game. What makes this different? What sort of mindset did these creators have for this project?

The interview with Ryan, Amy and Josh revealed a few important creative characteristics.

The posture of cultural missionary v. culture warrior

The developers intentionally adopted the posture of missionaries, trying to serve and reach their culture rather than culture warriors trying to conquer their culture. The founders of Numinous Games also see themselves as missionaries to other indie game developers, indie gamers and wider geek culture. They're not interested in reaching church people – they're trying to reach people who'd never darken the door of a church.

To do that, they rejected the idea of 'us v. them', our culture v. their culture. For Josh, Ryan and Amy, it's *all* our culture, and they want to be present in that shared culture as participants. As Ryan put it (with a nod to Andy Crouch), 'there's a lot to be gained by consuming, criticizing and contributing to that culture'.[17] Only by valuing and fully participating in our common culture can we hope to reach those alienated from Christ in that culture.

That meant, however, surrendering something that is precious to many conservative Christians: the 'persecution complex'. This is the idea that Christians in the West (particularly in the USA) are an oppressed minority.[18] A Christian persecution complex is problematic.

First, it isn't exactly true. Christians may get pushback, even harassment, from secular culture, but they don't tend to be marginalized and silenced as much as others (at least in the West). Further, for those who truly *are* oppressed, watching a culturally dominant group (such as white Christians) claim victim status is extremely upsetting. As Ryan put it:

> As a Christian white guy, I'm the majority. I have the power. I have the influence. I have the ear of the media, and of people, and everything else. And anybody who's a minority in that space is feeling threatened. I think what's weird is that, as Christians in America, we think of ourselves as always in danger of losing everything ... What we don't realize is that *we're* the majority, even when we don't feel like it. So when we act like the minority, when we're the majority, that's so false to them. And so insulting to them. That causes so much antipathy.[19]

Second, posing as a victim is unnecessary. As Josh explained, they aren't out to get Christians:

17 From interview with me. Andy Crouch is the author of *Culture Making: Recovering our creative calling* (Downers Grove, IL: InterVarsity Press, 2008).

18 The term 'persecution complex' was suggested by both Josh Larson and Ryan Green during their interview with me.

19 From interview with me. I argued earlier in this book that the USA and UK are post-Christian cultures – the culture's momentum for the past 50 years has been away from the Christian faith. That doesn't mean that Ryan is wrong. Even with the more recent decline, the USA is still a majority Christian nation (7 in 10 according to the latest polls). White evangelicals *alone*, however, comprise 14.5 per cent of the population in 2020. See Public Religion Research Institute (PRRI), 'The 2020 Census of American Religion, PRRI (8 July 2021)', <www.prri.org/research/2020-census-of-american-religion>, accessed February 2023.

> When you actually engage the culture and create a cultural artifact that people find valuable, or not necessarily valuable in the sense of getting tons of praise and acclaim, but even just something people find worth talking about and engaging with you about, that persecution doesn't exist. It's just something I built up in my own mind.[20]

When you create oases – cultural works that people want to talk about – persecution becomes a non-issue because you are contributing to the common good in good faith. People around will respond in kind.

Third, and most important, a victim posture reflects poorly on our calling. We are not called to nurse perceived wounds or lament our loss of cultural power. We are called by Jesus to go and love those who are alienated from him, to be for them, *especially* if they belong to a hated or socially disadvantaged group. As Ryan put it, 'my mandate from Christ is to go to people who feel oppressed and to lift them up, and to defend them, and to have dinner with them and hang out. That's our job.'

Taking the posture of cultural missionary/servant, loving those in the culture as our own, requires a deep humility and willingness to listen. In a cultural context where different groups are all jockeying for position, trying to shout one another down, Christians can choose *not* to play that power game. Instead, we can listen humbly and create space for those who feel oppressed and silenced. In this way we gain the right to speak into culture. We will have something worth sharing with the culture around us. As Ryan put it:

> It's our job to make space for them rather than for other people to make space for themselves. And I think a lot of the culture war right now is those people who feel marginalized making space for themselves. And then we're yelling at them . . . 'Stop making space. You're going to threaten us.' And they're like, 'What on earth? We can't possibly threaten you.' So, to me, that's changed my thinking in the past few years more and more, when I'm like, 'Oh. I'm a guest, and I'm an aggressor to them.' So I have to come in meekness and

20 From interview with me. Note the use of the first person. Both Josh and Ryan recognize this to be a mindset that they personally struggle against. (Amy wasn't there for this part of the interview.)

> gentleness and love. I can't possibly share the pain they've had, but I can share my pain. And I can share my comfort.[21]

Contributing meaningfully to culture means, in part, giving up on seeking to control culture like a culture warrior.[22] It means refusing to withdraw into subcultural bubbles to ensure our own purity.[23] And it means doing more than just accepting the status quo. Rather, it means loving those around us actively, creating spaces (oases) in which we can enter into conversation and relationship with them. It sounds simple, but for those who are accustomed to postures of culture warring or cultural withdrawal, it feels like capitulation. But we reach those alienated from Jesus only by taking on a servant role, like Jesus did.

Interestingly, a relativistic culture gives Christian creatives a space to tell their stories and find an audience. As Ryan put it:

> We're really upfront about that we're Christians and that this [game] will have spiritual content in it. And yet we had support across the board, from the theistic to the atheistic, gender identities, political leanings, all of it. They all support what we're doing. And I think the main thing is that we're not coming with a prophecy, we're not coming with a . . . 'thou shalt not'. We're just coming with our testimony. And for us, I feel like we've kind of stumbled into this space where it's OK for us to talk about the things that have made us who we are. Because we're saying, 'It's our testimony.' And who are they to argue with that? It's very disarming. And I think they've been conditioned in this culture to be like, 'Yeah. Mutual respect, and listen to each other. And you all can believe what you want to believe.' So, in that sense, I feel that there's a seat at the table that, I feel, maybe Christian culture doesn't sit at the table, even though there's a seat open.[24]

The Christian community simply has to be willing to serve by participating in a common culture with humility and gentleness. Out of this

21 From interview with me.
22 See chapter 2.
23 See chapter 3.
24 From interview with me.

posture of humility, oases – cultural creativity that opens spaces for hospitality – are created.

Being vulnerable and honest about your testimony and struggle with God

Humility doesn't come out of thin air. It is hard won, typically through gut-wrenching struggle. If the struggle doesn't leave you embittered, it will leave you humbled. That was my sense talking to Amy, Ryan and Josh. The loss the Greens suffered left them with pain and hard questions. It also left them humble and open to others in ways that perhaps prosperous, comfortable Christians wouldn't be.

Their humility is expressed principally in their willingness to be vulnerable and brutally honest about their struggles with God. In-game, Amy was often the voice of unshakeable faith: God *will* come through with a miracle. Ryan was often the voice of anger and despair: why isn't God showing up when my son is dying? They each processed their grief and helplessness differently, and sometimes they clashed. As a player, you get to hear it all. It is uncomfortable, but very real. In Ryan's words, the game was, for them, a process of 'making ourselves transparent'. No hiding, no stiff upper lips, no soothing platitudes. Just hurt and grasping for hope beyond the hurt.

I was particularly struck by Ryan's honesty in being unable to see God as 'Father' and 'healer' in light of his son's death:

> I think it's our abiding hope – that God is 'working all things together for our good'[25] – that we have to wrestle with. And I don't understand him as a father . . . as much as I understand him as God of the universe right now. I don't understand him as healer right now. I think I'm OK with that because he still calls himself healer, and he calls himself Father. These aren't names I gave him. I didn't come up with these names. He gave us his names. And so when I don't see it, I just have to sit in the 'Wow, I don't see it.' And I have to be honest about it. And I'm not going to trick him by saying I see

25 Romans 8:28 is a go-to passage of comfort for hurting Christians seeking assurance that God is always in control for our good.

> it. But at the same time, I listen to that song that's so popular right now, 'You're a good, good Father' [by Chris Tomlin], I just listen to that on repeat because I don't see it, but I believe it's true.[26]

Amy's struggle was more a fear that they would somehow bring disgrace on the name of God by sharing their pain when God didn't deliver the miracle that they had desperately hoped and prayed for. What effect was their art going to have on non-Christians? Would it discourage anyone from seeking God?

> There are scenes in the game where we share the prayers people prayed for Joel, and we make it obvious in the game that we were expecting a miracle. So, in a way, it feels like we're creating a testimony to God *not* answering our prayers. And I think we've both questioned whether or not that's evangelistically responsible. Because our heart is that we hope people would play this game and learn about God's great love for them. And I think there's a fear that perhaps they'd play this game and not feel that. But we've been able to continue, I guess, because we have such a strong knowledge that God is good, and that he's not depending on our ability to tell a good story. He can use whatever we create. I think now my prayer is that he'd anoint the project for whatever he wants to do with it. Because I can't tell the story: A + B = Jesus loves you and you should be saved. I have to just tell the story: A + B = this is how I relate to God, and how God seems to relate to me in the midst of tragedy.[27]

They both feel that they can't really do otherwise. They dare not sugarcoat things to make God look good. For Amy, this was the testimony that God gave them and, therefore, they must tell it. Like the blues, they are called to be truth-tellers first and foremost. She said:

> I think the main reason we continued was we were so committed to sharing our experience exactly as it happened, like, in the process.

26 From interview with me.
27 From interview with me.

> I think it would've felt very disingenuous to say, 'We only want to share our story where God does what we want him to do.' And I think we had to trust that, even though God had done something we didn't want him to do, he was still good, and therefore our testimony was still good, even though it wasn't the testimony we wanted to share. And, honestly, it's a struggle we continue to have . . .
>
> I had to wrestle with the fact that I could only share the testimony God gave me. So if I'm called to share our testimony, and this is the testimony he gave us, then it must be OK to share it. [28]

For Ryan, continuing to make the game and tell the truth is just part of who he is. His creativity entails transparency:

> You asked us why we kept going [after Joel died]. I don't know what else I'd do. As soon as Joel got sick, Amy was writing blogs and I was making art. That's just what we did. That's the natural expression of the thing that we could do. We can't fix our house or keep it clean or teach our kids how to wire a house. But we can create art, and we can talk about what we're going through. We can share that with people, and so it gives me a purpose in the midst of this. This act of making ourselves transparent is the only thing I'm good at. I think there's that compulsion as a creative person; that's how I was wired to do things.[29]

Josh Larson found that sharing the Greens' pain and telling their story transformed him:

> JOSH: Sharing the Greens' testimony over and over again with people, it teaches you, it changes you. It changes how you relate to people, how you look at them and how you treat them as people made in God's image. Sharing that testimony of faith and hope and

[28] From interview with me.

[29] From interview with me. Ryan also wondered aloud if 'creative people go through certain types of trials so that they can be comfort to other people'. We will discuss the costs of honest creativity below. It's a point worth pondering: perhaps one of the costs of being a Christian creative is that God might call you to endure certain types of suffering *precisely because* you're 'wired to do things'.

pain, all wrapped together around each other, you relate to people differently than before.

RYAN: 'Cause people aren't coming to you in anger; they're coming to you in brokenness over the same things, you know? You just hug people.

All three of these creators had a sort of 'Here I stand' moment.[30] They all felt highly committed to tell the truth, the whole truth and nothing but the truth. They told it creatively, in the form of a video game. They shared their pain and hope without fudging or sprucing it up to make it nice. That process of unrelenting artistic transparency changed them and opened doors in unexpected ways. It created an oasis.

The costs and benefits of honest creativity

What, finally, is the impact – on creators and players alike – of a game that raises more questions than answers, a game in which players dwell in a space where they must share the pain and hope of the creators? What did the creators want the game to do, and did it succeed? Was it worth it?

All creation costs. To create something in which you share your personal pain, the cost is especially dear. For Amy, the death of her son and documenting his final year in a game was, essentially, surrendering any hope that God would show up and make things OK. Or, as she put it, it was a 'gradual loss of faith and hope'. When Joel died, something inside of her died as well. That inner death made her hesitate and reconsider whether or not the project was worth doing.

Paradoxically, out of that double death came a potential doorway for new life. She came to realize that, by being willing to share her disappointment and hurt, the game could connect more intimately with those who had been disappointed and hurt. By suffering death, the game could connect with those who felt dead inside. By sharing brokenness, bridges were formed with the broken:[31]

---

30 'Here I stand' ('Hier stehe ich') is the famous phrase that Martin Luther used to conclude his defence at his trial for heresy at the Diet of Worms, 1521. He had refused to recant his writings.

31 See chapter 4, under heading 'Christian cultural witness in Hollywood: building bridges through brokenness'.

> I thought, 'Wow, the people we could speak to with a miracle testimony are the people who are sort of looking for miracles already, and those people are probably doing OK. And the people we can speak to with a tragic testimony are the people who have been hurt, disappointed and frustrated, and perhaps have rejected God because of those things. And having now experienced some of that, I'm more convinced that those are the people who really need to think of God in a new way.[32]

For Ryan, the emotional cost of the game came in the form of emotional distance from God, being unable to call him 'Father' because of his overwhelming pain *as* a father who had lost his son. But even that pain gave opportunities to draw alongside those who had issues with their fathers to share the Father's love. I asked him if the game had provoked any significant conversations:

> We share stories, and we share our hearts, and I talk about things in a much different way . . . I remember one kid in Denmark. I shared clips from the game, and I talked about the game. And he stayed afterwards and said, 'You know, what you said about doing things out of love really struck me, because I don't feel I've been creating out of love, but out of anger at my father.' And that just really stuck with him because he wanted to prove his worth to his father. And so I just got to share a father's love with him, you know? I just got to tell him about his value to God. And this was the moment I could share with this stranger in the middle of Denmark, out of sharing this story . . .
>
> In this space [of indie game culture] there's a lot of people with wounds from their fathers, from their parents. And I feel like I can hopefully show what a loving father [is] like, how he behaves, what he cares about, and that's a testimony through what we've created, which is, hopefully, characterized by love, and of what's documented of us in the film and stuff. Hopefully, they see a reflection of love. I'm more just like, 'I want to show you that brokenness does not cause a father to love you less. It should cause a father to love you

32 From interview with me.

> more.' I want to exemplify that through my love of Joel, and I want to exemplify that through my love of this community, because it's made up of people who have value just because they're God's children, you know? And in this subculture, they're in a space, and they value things that their parents might not necessarily have valued. And I value it. I think it's meaningful, and I think it's worth investing a career in. And it's worth cultural artifacts, even if it's video games. I want to impart a picture of how I believe God sees us to this culture, and that act alone speaks volumes to how people see themselves. And if I can do that in some small, representative way of how I'm a father, and so I can impart that love that I have, then that's the one way I can do it.

The impact of the game is to create space in which to be present with others, to share love through one-on-one conversations. This is one important reason for planting oases. I asked Ryan what he wanted players to take away from the game. He responded:

> I want you to play the game, and I want to ask you what you took from it. Because I had a pat answer for a long time, and I'm just like, 'I don't know if it succeeds. I don't know.' Early on we said we wanted people to face death and not be afraid of it. Other times I've said I want people to fear, and I wanted people to love Joel . . . I just want to give people space to shake their fists a little bit, and acknowledge them, and acknowledge their pain, and not really give them answers, but just sit with them in it, you know? I think my motivations, personally, have changed over time, where I'm less concerned about communicating something to you, and more concerned about, just [pauses, reflecting] . . . I think the one thing that's stayed true is that I hope the cultural benefit of the game happens *outside* the game. To me, it's the conversations afterwards. It's the people sharing their stories as a result of it. That to me has the lasting impact, because, other than that, it's just a video game.

For the team, creating out of pain cost a lot, but it was worth it. Creatively, vulnerably expressing pain (and hope born of pain) created connections and opened doors to those in pain. And who knows how God can use those open doors?

The audience also has to count the cost of honest creativity. *That Dragon, Cancer* is the very opposite of mindless fun. For each player, there is an emotional weight to be borne, a price to be paid. Christian creators need to take this into account. Ryan addressed this explicitly:

> In some cases, I just did a play-through with somebody, and he said, 'Oh, I'm surprised by how hopeful and joyful it was.' And I'm like, 'Oh, really?! You saw that? That's great! That's what we were going for!' But I think a lot of people, they evaluate the emotional cost of it, and then just say, 'I don't think I can play that.' Our hope is that we can return something, you know? Part of our struggle is convincing people that it's worth going through.

For me, as a player, it was definitely worth it. It presented a picture of hope that transcends suffering even in the midst of real, lasting pain. In that sense, *That Dragon, Cancer* captured the elusive balance between darkness and light, the cross and the empty tomb, as it whispered a hope that resonates across eternity.

Conclusion: sacrificial love in post-Christian culture

That Dragon, Cancer is emotionally draining and may not be everyone's cup of tea, but I believe that Numinous Games presents us with a model of how the Christian imagination can speak winsomely and meaningfully into a post-Christian culture. It is costly oasis planting, but God honours this kind of sacrificial love in art, using it to open doors and heal wounds. Of course, there are no guarantees that doors will open or wounds will be healed, but that is life in a fallen, post-Christian world. What *is* certain is that this kind of art – in any and every medium – is desperately needed.

13

Contagious evil and hope against hope: Tolkien's Middle-earth

Introduction: the influence of Tolkien's *The Lord of the Rings*

The Lord of the Rings is an obvious choice for studying a Christian imaginative work in a post-Christian context. Though written at a time when Western culture was friendlier to the Christian faith than it is now, it has endured into the present as a monumental force in popular culture, even before Peter Jackson's films. Since its publication in 1954 and 1955, *The Lord of the Rings* has had a long-lasting impact on the English language-reading public, one that is unparalleled in the late twentieth/ early twenty-first century.[1] In the late 1990s, Waterstones, the BBC, Nestlé and several newspapers surveyed the reading public in the UK about who they thought should be named 'author of the century'. To the consternation of many 'proper' literary critics, Tolkien placed first in all the polls but one (in the Nestlé poll he came in second to the Bible).[2]

Tolkien's influence is not limited to the UK. *The Lord of the Rings* became a countercultural force in the USA during the late 1960s and 1970s. Hippies, attracted to the depth and beauty of Tolkien's world, wore badges and sprayed graffiti that proclaimed 'Frodo lives!'[3] Another US contribution to Tolkienmania: Dungeons & Dragons (D&D), the tabletop role-playing game created in 1974, which, in turn, spawned the whole

[1] The exception being, of course, another product of the Christian imagination: J. K. Rowling's Harry Potter books. Both Tolkien's trilogy and her Harry Potter books get an excellent treatment in Jerram Barr's *Echoes of Eden: Reflections on Christianity, literature, and the arts* (Wheaton, IL: Crossway, 2013).

[2] Tom Shippey, *J. R. R. Tolkien: Author of the century* (London: HarperCollins, 2000), pp. xx–xxi. In the Waterstones poll in Wales, Tolkien placed second after James Joyce.

[3] See *Fanlore*, 'Frodo lives!', *Fanlore* (14 January 2022), <https://fanlore.org/wiki/Frodo_Lives!>, accessed February 2023. The slogan is called a 'pre-Internet meme'. See also documentary film by Carlene Cordova (writer, director) and Cliff Broadway (writer), *Ringers: Lord of the fans* (Sony Pictures Home Entertainment, 2005; DVD, Planet BB, 2005).

genre of fantasy role-playing games.[4] There is no doubt, however, that Peter Jackson's films (2001–2003) catapulted Tolkien's trilogy into the spotlight, making them a global pop phenomenon. The films have since gone on to become one of the highest-grossing film franchises of all time, earning more than $8 billion worldwide.[5] Taken together – the books, films, computer games and other merchandise – Middle-earth has earned somewhere between $10 and $15 billion worldwide.[6] Those films led to a television series, but it hasn't been quite as successful, at least in its first season (though I quite enjoyed it).[7]

Even in non-English-speaking countries, such as my adopted home, the Czech Republic, Tolkien has had a seminal and enduring impact. The books were banned under communism by the pro-Soviet authorities. They disliked the location of Tolkien's 'evil empire', Mordor, to the east, same as Russia. The books had to be circulated underground in the form of mimeographed copies. According to the documentary film *Ringers: Lord of the fans* (2005), Tolkien's imaginative universe has inspired a deep loyalty among an international fan base that has spanned generations.

What is it about Tolkien's works that has made them so compelling for so long? Certainly, his vivid writing that brings an ancient and mysterious world to life, relatable and fleshed-out characters and the novels' elegiac tone all play a part in their enduring popularity. Tolkien is a master storyteller, building suspense through cliffhangers and hair's-breadth escapes. But *The Lord of the Rings* also owes its magnetic attraction to

---

4 The creator of Dungeons & Dragons (D&D) Gary Gygax maintains that he was influenced very little by Tolkien. The fact that his game contains vital elements of Tolkien's universe – elves, dwarves, orcs, hobbits, ents and even a Balrog – says otherwise. He was later forced to change the names of hobbits and Balrogs to avoid copyright infringement. See Jeff McLeod, 'Tolkien and Dungeons & Dragons', *The Artifice* (20 September 2019), <https://the-artifice.com/tolkien-dungeons-dragons>, accessed February 2023. See also my article 'Inflecting the world: Popular culture and the perception of evil', *Journal of Popular Culture*, vol. 38, no. 2 (November 2004), pp. 391–392.

5 As of August 2021, Peter Jackson's *Lord of the Rings* film franchise ranked tenth in a list of all time with international and domestic box office earnings of $8.38 billion (domestic box office adjusted for inflation). See The Numbers, 'Movie franchises', The Numbers <www.the-numbers.com/movies/franchises#franchise_overview=od4>, accessed February 2023.

6 See Garrett Parker, 'How much is the Lord of the Rings franchise worth?', *Moneyinc.* (14 June 2016 [updated 8 April 2020]), <https://moneyinc.com/lord-of-the-rings-franchise>, accessed February 2023.

7 John F. Trent, '"The Lord of the Rings: The Rings of Power" completely falls off Nielsen charts just two weeks after season finale', *Bounding into Comics* (30 November 2022), <https://boundingintocomics.com/2022/11/30/the-lord-of-the-rings-the-rings-of-power-completely-falls-off-nielsen-charts-just-two-weeks-after-season-finale>, accessed February 2023.

Tolkien's use of a tensive vision that expresses the heart of the Christian imagination. That vision doesn't trumpet its Christian perspective. Rather, it subtly permeates his imaginary world, flying under the radar of post-Christian cultures. Though the story contains fantasy elements, such as elves, dwarves, orcs, hobbits and wizards, it nonetheless taps into something real and everyday in myriad ways. I will focus here on only two of its themes: the complex and realistic portrayal of evil, and how grace is woven into the story, giving its heroes hope.

Evil and sorrow: reality in the twilit world

Tolkien's works stand out from other fantasy and adventure novels because of his subtly nuanced – even ambiguous – understanding of evil. That ambiguity and nuance arises in both *who* is evil and *what* evil is.

The locus of evil in the books is, of course, the One Ring: a weapon of enormous power sought by the armies of both major villains, Sauron and Saruman. The 'good guys' of the story, who possess the Ring, set out on a quest (or, better, an 'anti-quest')[8] to destroy it in the fires of Mount Doom. It is simply too dangerous for it to be allowed to exist. But the danger posed by the Ring is not physical, such as the various 'doomsday devices' that appear in James Bond films. The power of the One Ring is not destruction but domination. It promises the ability to command wills, to rule.[9] The danger of the Ring is fundamentally spiritual: playing God by enslaving others, making them less than human.[10] Grasping for power over others and laying waste to human lives and wills has become all too familiar in the twentieth and twenty-first centuries.[11]

The Ring contains another danger that forces the wise of Middle-earth to undertake their drastic and risky plan to destroy it: the temptation to wield the Ring's power. The Ring corrupts the wills of those who attempt to use it, even for good. So argue Gandalf the wizard and Elrond, the wise

[8] The adventurers in the story are not on 'a quest, but an anti-quest, whose goal is not to find or regain something but to reject and destroy something', Shippey, *J. R. R. Tolkien*, p. 114.

[9] So argues Matthew Dickerson in *Following Gandalf: Epic battles and moral victory in* The Lord of the Rings (Grand Rapids, MI: Brazos Press, 2003), pp. 96–100.

[10] I do *not* mean to imply that God himself reduces us to slaves, subhuman beings. But when sinful humans try to exercise divine authority (without God's perfect love and wisdom), the result is always dehumanizing.

[11] Shippey (*J. R. R. Tolkien*, pp. 112–119) points out that, for all its grounding in ancient folklore, *The Lord of the Rings* displays a remarkably contemporary concern with and understanding of evil.

half-elf and head of the Council of free peoples.[12] Ironically, the Ring promises power to command wills while it enslaves the wielder. The One Ring is not simply a danger if it falls into the wrong hands; it is a danger if it falls into *any* hands. The Council assigns Frodo the hobbit to carry the Ring, not because it poses no danger for him but because hobbits, typically, are uninterested in power, having been sheltered from the politics of Middle-earth. It is safer with him than it is with any of the heroes who attend the Council.

Tolkien's take on evil is not simply Lord Acton's adage that 'power tends to corrupt and absolute power corrupts absolutely'. Linguist and Tolkien scholar Tom Shippey argues that evil's power in the One Ring takes the form of *addiction*.[13] Gandalf's and Elrond's warnings that the Ring cannot be used, even for good, are proven true several times as the story unfolds. Bilbo, the affable old hobbit, shows signs of addiction in his reluctance to part with the Ring at the beginning of *The Fellowship of the Ring*. He lashes out at Gandalf, accusing him of trying to steal it, and when that doesn't work, almost leaves, 'forgetting' that the Ring is still in his pocket.[14] The withered, slinking creature Gollum, who kept the Ring as 'his precious' for 478 years,[15] spends most of the story obsessing about the Ring and trying to recapture it for himself. A gnawing addiction to the Ring has clearly eaten him up inside. Even the honourable and valiant warrior Boromir breaks the fellowship of the nine heroes by attempting to take the ring from Frodo, first by persuasion, then by force.[16]

Shippey suggests that this addictive corruption of the will can be seen in fullest flower in the Nazgûl, or Ringwraiths, powerful beings who hover somewhere between the dead and the living. They were once human kings, but because they accepted rings of power from Sauron – rings that

12 'The Council of Elrond' in *The Lord of the Rings* (London: HarperCollins, 1995 [1954–55]), pp. 260–262. Throughout, all references given are to this unabridged, one-volume edition of *The Lord of the Rings*, but I will use abbreviations to refer to the specific books it includes to better orientate you: FOTR = *The Fellowship of the Ring*; TT = *The Two Towers*; ROTK = *The Return of the King*. Note: All extracts from *The Lord of the Rings* (London: HarperCollins, 1995 [1954–55]) that appear in this chapter are reprinted by permission of HarperCollins Publishers Ltd © 1954–55, J.R.R. Tolkien.

13 Shippey, *J. R. R. Tolkien*, p. 119.

14 FOTR, I/1, 'A long-expected party', pp. 32–34.

15 See *The One Wiki to Rule Them All*, 'One ring: Ring bearers', *The One Wiki to Rule Them All*, <https://lotr.fandom.com/wiki/One_Ring#Ring-bearers>, accessed February 2023.

16 FOTR, II/10, 'The breaking of the fellowship', pp. 387–390.

answer, ultimately, to the power of Sauron's One Ring – the kings withered and became enslaved to his will.[17] They are now fear-inspiring foes, but also subhuman, insubstantial things.[18]

Tolkien implies that one who gives in to the temptation and addiction of the Ring lessens, begins 'wraithing' away to a corrupt, enslaved, faded existence. Saruman, consumed by a hunger for power and for the Ring, dies in a wraith-like fashion: a mist leaves his body and blows away in the wind.[19] The emaciated, shrivelled Gollum seems well on his way to wraithhood. One can assume that had Boromir obtained the Ring, he would also have become enslaved after a few moments or years of glory. Frodo, too, is slowly being 'wraithed', corrupted by the power of the Ring throughout the story after being stabbed by one of the Ringwraiths on Weathertop. And at the end of the epic journey, he even takes a decisive step down the path of corruption when he succumbs to the temptation to claim rather than destroy the Ring. Indeed, we feel that Gollum has done him a profound mercy by biting off his finger, sparing him from a fate worse than death: a living death, a slow decline into an obsessive, addictive existence like Gollum's and, thence, into the half-life/half-death state of a wraith.[20]

Because of the Ring's addictive power, Tolkien avoids giving us a conventional 'good guys versus bad guys' scenario. *Everyone*, potentially, is a bad guy, and especially prone are those who crave power (as Saruman and Boromir did) or those who come into contact with the Ring (as Gollum and Frodo did). The wise and good are those who fear even to touch it. By complicating evil, making it a dangerous, addictive force – like sticky sap that traps insects in amber – Tolkien undercuts the naive conceptions of evil found in most adventure tales.

From a biblical perspective, such a move is altogether realistic and healthy. Our fallenness means that everyone is susceptible to temptation;

17 See J. R. R. Tolkien, 'Of the Rings of Power and the Third Age', *The Silmarillion*, ed. Christopher Tolkien (London: HarperCollins, 1999 [1977]), p. 346. See also Shippey, *J. R. R. Tolkien*, p. 123.

18 Shippey, *J. R. R. Tolkien*, pp. 123–124.

19 ROTK, VI/8, 'The scouring of the Shire', p. 996. See also Shippey, *J. R. R. Tolkien*, p. 127. Jackson's more gruesome falling/impaling death of Saruman in *The Return of the King* film rather misses the subtlety of Tolkien's vision here.

20 Might Tolkien have had Matthew 5:30 in mind when he wrote this scene? 'And if your right hand causes you to sin, cut it off and throw it away. For it is better that you lose one of your members than that your whole body go into hell.'

everyone is capable of evil. There *are* good guys and bad guys in *The Lord of the Rings*, obviously, but evil is not primarily something 'out *there*'. The more terrifying power of evil lies within – an ever-present potential to be drawn down the path of corruption. Even heroes like Saruman (leader of the White Council or Council of the Wise) and Boromir can be perverted in this way. Because evil is an addiction to self-will, *anyone* can be evil. Evil is a threat and pull within one's own heart.

Certainly, evil in *The Lord of the Rings* has an external component as well. Evil is not simply internal corruption and weakness. It emerges also in the malice of the Enemy. Tolkien not only complicates evil with respect to *who* can be evil (anyone can be corrupted) but he also complicates evil in terms of *what* evil is. In evil studies,[21] evil is defined in one of two ways: as essentially negative (an absence of good) or positive (a force for malevolence). Shippey asserts that both views are expressed in *The Lord of the Rings.*[22]

The negative view can be traced back to the church father Augustine and was given its classic expression by Boethius, a Roman senator and moral philosopher of the sixth century AD: evil is not a thing in itself, but simply a *privatio boni*, a privation of the good. Darkness in itself is nothing but a lack of light. Likewise, evil is nothing but an absence or distortion of the good. Tolkien seems to reflect this understanding of evil in his representation of the wraiths and Gollum. In their characters you can see the corrupting, warped, withering influence of evil. Evil saps away reality, leaving nothing but shadow.

The positive view sees evil not simply as an absence but also as a presence, a force to be reckoned with. This view traces its roots to Manichaeism, a religious cult stemming from the writings of the self-proclaimed 'Apostle of Light', Mani, in the third century AD. The cult spread throughout Europe and Asia up to the Middle Ages. Manicheans saw reality as a dualism, a never-ending struggle between two ultimate principles: good

21 Yes, there is such a discipline or, rather, an interdisciplinary field. Evil studies involves a number of fields, including theology, philosophy, cultural studies, literature, literary theory, sociology, law, history, psychology, holocaust studies, gender studies and others. See 'Research on evil: An annotated bibliography', *Hedgehog Review*, vol. 2, no. 2 (Summer 2000), pp. 100–111, <https://hedgehogreview.com/issues/evil/articles/research-on-evil-an-annotated-bibliography>, accessed February 2023.

22 Shippey, *J. R. R. Tolkien*, pp. 128–143.

and evil. The world is a battlefield where neither finally conquers the other, for both are ultimate. We must commit to fighting evil in the universe even though we know that no victory is final.

This positive understanding of evil as a 'hideous strength'[23] surfaces in Tolkien's narrative in a variety of ways. The Ringwraiths are not simply subhuman shadows; they emanate a power that inspires irresistible terror and despair.[24] The Ring, too, proves to have a menacing will and power of its own. It tempts not only through internal corruption but it also calls and beckons. The Ring possesses an intelligence, a magnetic power that actively tries to seduce Gollum, Boromir, Frodo and even Sam.[25] The Ring's power grows as Frodo approaches Mordor, the place where it was forged by the evil and powerful Sauron. It becomes all but overpowering. Evil in Tolkien's universe is not simply an absence or distortion of the good: it is a terrible, malicious presence.

Is evil negation and privation or malice and power? Tolkien affirms both. Further, Shippey argues that this ambivalence concerning the nature of evil is 'at the absolute heart of the Christian religion itself', reflected in the sixth and seventh petitions of the Lord's Prayer (Matthew 6:13): 'Lead us not into temptation [that is, spare us from our own weakness and corruption], and deliver us from evil [save us from evil's magnetic and abusive power]'.[26] Evil in the Christian world view is both an internal and an external threat, both distorting privation and malicious power.

Tolkien's imaginary world is one that dwells, even broods, on the fallenness of the world and our own hearts. The dark part of the tensive vision is found in Tolkien in spades. There is no mistaking the texture of Tolkien's imaginary world for the triumphalist or sentimental works of much of popular Christian fiction. The heroes do win in the end, but only at a terrible cost. Much that was precious and beautiful in Middle-earth is doomed to pass away for ever.

One feels, in the overall tone of *The Lord of the Rings*, a melancholy sensibility that recalls Ragnarök, the twilight of the gods of Norse mythology. The gods bravely battle the forces of chaos knowing that they are

---

23 The reference is to the title of a novel by Tolkien's long-time friend C. S. Lewis.

24 Shippey, *J. R. R. Tolkien*, pp. 124–125; ROTK, 'The siege of Gondor', V/4, pp. 790–791. J. K. Rowling may well have modelled her despair-inducing dementors on Ringwraiths.

25 Shippey, *J. R. R. Tolkien*, pp. 137–140.

26 Shippey, *J. R. R. Tolkien*, p. 141.

fated to die. As a linguist, Tolkien was fascinated by Scandinavian and Germanic folklore and their sense of tragic, inescapable fate.

Tolkien does not present to us a world that is easily healed of its scars and moves merrily on its way. Even the finding of the One Ring inevitably means that things cannot stay as they are. As Elrond says, 'many fair things will fade and be forgotten'.[27] The Elf-queen Galadriel echoes this sentiment, explaining her and her husband's mission to Frodo: 'together through the ages of the world we have fought the long defeat'.[28] One of the wisest and most powerful beings in Middle-earth sees her task as essentially hopeless: the world will fade regardless. Tolkien paints for us a twilit world, its beauty fading irretrievably until, perhaps, it is remade again. In biblical terms, this is a fallen world, bound to decay (Romans 8:21).

Grace woven into the order of things or reasons not to abandon hope in Middle-earth

And yet, such a dimming of the glory of the world is not a cause for despair. In fact, Galadriel is happy to fight the long defeat, because the alternative – not fighting – is intolerable. Repeatedly, despair is linked in *The Lord of the Rings* with evil, a device of the Enemy. The deadliest weapon of the Nazgûl, the Ringwraiths, captains of Sauron's armies, is the power to inspire despair, to tempt enemies to give up and cave in. Gandalf, the wisest of the story's heroes, has but one main task: to *encourage* the peoples of Middle-earth to resist evil, to draw them out of despair into hope.[29] He does this quite literally with Théoden, King of Rohan, curing him of the spells of despair and passivity woven about him by his traitorous chief counsellor Wormtongue.[30] He does it again for the soldiers of Gondor during the siege of Minas Tirith when the army is in danger of despairing when confronted by the Nazgûl and an uncountable enemy.[31]

One could say that the only unforgivable sin is despair, giving up hope. The power of evil to inspire despair causes even Denethor II, the wise

27 FOTR, 'The Council of Elrond', II/2, p. 262.
28 FOTR, 'The mirror of Galadriel', II/7, p. 348.
29 See Dickerson, *Following Gandalf*, chapter 7.
30 See TT, 'The King of the Golden Hall', III/6, pp. 503–504.
31 ROTK, 'The siege of Gondor', V/4, 'Wherever [Gandalf] came men's hearts would lift again, and the winged shadows pass from memory', p. 806. See also Dickerson, *Following Gandalf*, pp. 138–143.

steward of Gondor, to turn traitor and give up hope when his city is attacked, choosing pagan suicide rather than resistance for himself and his son (had Faramir not been rescued from the flames).[32]

Why is despair evil? Because, in despair, one turns away from hope and cedes the field to the Enemy uncontested.[33] Again and again, the path of integrity and heroism is strewn with suffering and obstacles, a call to fight the battle against all odds, despite the likely outcome. Galadriel knows that she and all good folk are engaged in a hopeless struggle, but still she fights, and wants to fight.

What's the point? Isn't despair the only logical course? Isn't hope sometimes pointless? There are two answers to this question. In exploring them, we shall see how Tolkien's imaginative vision encompasses not only the fallen brokenness of the world but also hope and grace, and does so with a subtlety that resonates in a post-Christian world.

The everyday texture of grace

Middle-earth, though fading, deserves protection – grace is woven into its tapestry. One of Tolkien's recurring themes is the goodness of creation. In his books, grace can be ethereal, as it is with the elves. But it can also be commonplace and down to earth, as it is with the men and hobbits. The good and the wholesome (a word Tolkien is fond of) are found in everyday, natural things: the outdoors, trees, a good meal and ale, smoking one's pipe with a friend. These ordinary blessings often serve to encourage the characters in their fight against despair.

For instance, Pippin, a young hobbit, overcome by curiosity, steals a palantír (a seeing-stone) from Gandalf. Gazing into it brings him face to face with the Dark Lord Sauron himself. The experience leaves him shaken, his spirit broken. But he soon recovers under the influence of such unremarkable things as the feel of wind on his face, the light of the moon and the warmth of Gandalf's words and presence as they ride together to Minas Tirith.[34]

---

[32] See ROTK, 'The pyre of Denethor', V/7, pp. 832–839.

[33] The enemy of Middle-earth is Sauron. The imagery associated with Sauron and his land is stereotypically hellish: shadow, sulphur and fire. Sauron is a stand-in for Satan, though, according to Tolkien's wider lore, he is only a minion of Melkor, the Satan of Tolkien's mythology. See Tolkien, *The Silmarillion*, pp. 4, 7–8 and 23.

[34] TT, 'The palantír', III/11, p. 582.

Earlier, Gandalf heals Théoden of despair by coaxing him to stand and walk out of his dark hall and into the wind, rain and sunshine.

> 'Now, lord,' said Gandalf, 'look out upon your land! Breathe the free air again!'
>
> From the porch upon the top of the high terrace they could see beyond the stream the green fields of Rohan fading into distant grey. Curtains of wind-blown rain were slanting down. The sky above and to the west was still dark with thunder, and lightning far away flickered among the tops of hidden hills. But the wind had shifted to the north, and already the storm that had come out of the East was receding, rolling away southward to the sea. Suddenly through a rent in the clouds behind them a shaft of sun stabbed down. The falling showers gleamed like silver, and far away the river glittered like a shimmering glass.
>
> 'It is not so dark here,' said Théoden.[35]

Why does Tolkien go into such meteorological detail? Certainly, it is dramatic and foreshadows elements of the story. The storm that has come from the East (from the direction of Mordor, the enemy's land) is beginning to break up towards the sea (a symbol of transcendence and heaven in the book – the place where elves go when they depart Middle-earth). But beyond stylistic or thematic considerations, Tolkien is making a point: it is through the details of wind and weather that healing comes to Théoden. Connecting with the natural world allows him to feel more himself, more like a king of men and less like a withered, senile dotard. Gandalf's *words* surely bring hope and healing, but even more healing grace comes through everyday blessings such as rain, green grass and a shaft of sunlight breaking through the clouds. This is the world God has made, and through it comes healing. It *is* worth fighting for.

That 'fighting hope' also informs a much remarked on theme in the book: care for the environment. It is no accident that the enemies of Middle-earth ruin the lands they occupy. Sauron makes Mordor into a wasteland of pits and noxious fumes. Saruman, the wizard turned

---

35 TT, 'The King of the Golden Hall', III/6, p. 504.

traitor, destroys much of the forest surrounding his home, Isengard, pursuing technologies of war. And when Saruman flees to the hobbits' homeland, the Shire, he builds factories and fells trees simply out of spite.

But it is also no accident that the faithful servant of Frodo, Samwise, is a gardener. Galadriel's gift to him on their departure from her land is a box containing blessed earth with the power to renew a ruined land: 'Though you should find all barren and laid waste, there will be few gardens in Middle-earth that will bloom like your garden, if you sprinkle this earth there.'[36] Faramir, one of the noblest characters in the book, holds gardeners in high esteem, and aspires to be one himself when the War of the Ring is over.[37]

In Tolkien's universe, the bright line that separates the armies of evil from the armies of good is that the former seek to dominate while the latter seek to preserve, nurture and bring to full flower. Despair cannot be an option; hope must be embraced tenaciously. Otherwise, the dominators will destroy all that is good on earth.[38]

Even when all seems lost, there is a grace written on the very face of Nature herself that brings hope to the heart. The best illustration of this appears towards the end of the tale. Frodo and Sam have journeyed through the dry and weary land of Mordor. They are parched, and clean water is nowhere to be found. Exhausted, close to collapse, depressed almost to the point of despair, they crawl under some brambles to rest, trying to find the courage and strength to cross the barren plateau of Gorgoroth, and thence go to Mount Doom and the end of their quest. Suddenly, Sam sees a star:

> There, peeping among the cloud-wrack above a dark tor high up in the mountains, Sam saw a white star twinkle for a while. The beauty of it smote his heart, as he looked up out of the forsaken land, and hope returned to him. For like a shaft, clear and cold, the thought

---

36 FOTR, 'Farewell to Lórien', II/8, p. 366.

37 TT, 'The window on the west', IV/5, p. 666; and ROTK, 'The Steward and the King', VI/5, p. 943.

38 God, too, holds the earth in high esteem and as accountable those who corrupt and destroy its beauty (Revelation 11:18). See chapter 1, under heading 'Does it matter in the long run?'

> pierced him that in the end the Shadow was only a small and passing thing: there was light and high beauty for ever beyond its reach.[39]

Here we catch a glimpse of *why* the everyday grace derived from nature has this peculiar encouraging, even healing, power: it points *beyond* itself to something (or Someone) that transcends it, untouched by the evil and destruction wreaking havoc in the world. Everyday grace reminds us that hope is real because other powers are at work in the world besides dominating evil.

An invisible guiding hand

Another reason the characters do not to give up hope is that they understand themselves to be part of a grand drama written by a greater Author. Tolkien never says so outright, but there are more than enough hints of an all-encompassing plan at work. Early in the story, Gandalf tells Frodo about the Ring left to him by his uncle Bilbo, who just happened to be in the right place at the right time because 'there was more than one power at work' thwarting evil.[40] He concludes:

> Behind that [Bilbo's finding the Ring apparently by chance] there was something else at work, beyond any design of the Ring-maker. I can put it no plainer than by saying that Bilbo was *meant* to find the Ring, and *not* by its maker. In which case you also were *meant* to have it. And that may be an encouraging thought.[41]

Later in the tale, Aragorn, the leader of the company, finds himself at a crossroads, waiting for Frodo to choose their next step. Aragorn decides against trying to force a choice on Frodo: 'I do not think that it is our part to drive him one way or the other. Nor do I think we should succeed, if we tried. There are other powers at work far stronger.'[42] It is unthinkable that the 'powers' he mentions belong to the Dark Lord. Rather, Aragorn is making a veiled reference to some Providence that guides events quite

39 ROTK, 'The land of shadow', VI/2, p. 901.
40 FOTR, 'The shadow of the past', I/2, p. 54.
41 FOTR, 'The shadow of the past', I/2, pp. 54–55 (the emphases are Tolkien's).
42 FOTR, 'The breaking of the Fellowship', II/10, p. 394.

apart from the will of men (or elves, hobbits, dwarves, orcs, wizards or Dark Lords). Our heroes struggle against evil, but not alone. Even in supposedly chance events, there is an invisible hand guiding the story.

In fact, 'chance' plays a key role in Tolkien's writings. More than once, Tolkien's characters mention chance, but they often qualify it. The ageless, jolly, inscrutable Tom Bombadil *happens* to be passing by just when Frodo and his companions need to be rescued from a murderous tree-creature. When Frodo asks Bombadil if he had heard their screams, he answers, 'Nay, I did not hear you. I was busy singing. Just chance brought me then, if chance you call it. It was no plan of mine, though I was waiting for you.'[43] Earlier, Aragorn *happens* to be in Bree as the Black Riders attack, and elves *happen* to be in the area to help them to escape.[44] Much later in the story, the hobbits Merry and Pippin are about to be slain by the evil orc captain Grishnákh, but are saved by a 'lucky' shot from a Rider of Rohan: 'An arrow came whistling out of the gloom: it was aimed with skill, or guided by fate, and it pierced his right hand.'[45] There are so many such 'chance' events that literature scholar Kathleen Dubs calls this a 'providential pattern'.[46] Standing behind the apparent random events in Middle-earth are an order and purpose. And that may be an encouraging thought.

The owner of the invisible hand guiding events is never named. We know from Tolkien's other writings, however, that it is the hand of Eru Ilúvatar, the creator of Middle-earth.[47] Every event is guided by his music. Even creatures who rebel find their discord playing a part in the greater harmony of Eru.[48] But though Ilúvatar guides, the characters of his story are no mere marionettes. Their choices matter. The invisible hand of guiding providence is woven *into* the choices the characters make, using them to steer events to his preordained destination. The result: virtuous choices are rewarded in ways that are often impossible to foresee.

The most dramatic example of this subtle pattern is the saga of the wretched, treacherous Gollum, which begins in *The Hobbit*. Bilbo Baggins,

---

43 FOTR, 'In the house of Tom Bombadil', I/7, pp. 123–124.

44 FOTR, 'A knife in the dark' and 'Flight to the ford', I/11, p. 12.

45 TT, 'The Uruk-Hai', III/3, p. 446.

46 Kathleen E. Dubs, 'Providence, fate and chance: Boethian philosophy in *The Lord of the Rings*' in *Tolkien and the Invention of Myth: A reader*, ed. Jane Chance (Lexington, KY: University of Kentucky Press, 2004). See also Shippey, *J. R. R. Tolkien*, pp. 143–146.

47 Tolkien, *The Silmarillion*, p. 3.

48 Tolkien, 'The music of Ainur', *The Silmarillion*, pp. 3–12.

the hero of *The Hobbit*, finds himself separated from his friends and lost in a cave where Gollum has long lived and brooded in the dark. He decides to play a riddle game with Bilbo, then kill and devour him. What Gollum doesn't know, however, is that Bilbo has found Gollum's magic ring, which gives him the power of invisibility. After Gollum finds that his ring is missing, he is enraged. Bilbo is frightened and accidentally slips on the ring. He then ponders how to escape the murderous, disgusting Gollum, who has blocked the only exit. The easy option would have been for Bilbo to slay him, but he has a sudden insight out of empathy, of what life must be like from Gollum's perspective: alone in a cold, dark cave for endless days. He pities him and decides instead to jump over Gollum, sparing the miserable creature.[49]

Later, Frodo learns that the ring he inherited from Bilbo is the One Ring. Hearing of the evil that Gollum has done since trying to find it, he asks Gandalf why he hasn't killed him yet as he deserves death. Gandalf replies:

> Deserves it! I dare say he does. Many that live deserve death. And some that die deserve life. Can you give it to them? Then do not be too eager to deal out death in judgement. For even the very wise cannot see all ends. I have not much hope that Gollum can be cured before he dies, but there is a chance of it. And he is bound up with the fate of the Ring. My heart tells me that he has some part to play yet, for good or ill, before the end; and when that comes, the pity of Bilbo may rule the fate of many – yours not least. In any case, we did not kill him: he is very old and very wretched. The Wood-elves have him in prison, but they treat him with such kindness as they can find in their wise hearts.[50]

Here we gain two important insights into Tolkien's perspective on things (Gandalf is always worth listening to as he often serves as Tolkien's mouthpiece). First, the path of mercy and kindness is wise, always to be preferred to the path of vengeance and death. Second, choosing mercy can set in motion a pattern of events that may prove decisive in the end.

49 J. R. R. Tolkien, *The Hobbit, or There and Back Again* (New York: Ballantine Books, rev. edn 1973), pp. 92–93.

50 FOTR, 'The shadow of the past', I/2, p. 58.

Later in the story, Frodo and Sam are tracked and attacked by Gollum as they try to find their way into Mordor. In the fray, Frodo has the chance to kill Gollum, but finds that now he has seen Gollum, he *does* pity him, and he spares him, just as Bilbo did.[51] Instead, Gollum becomes their guide, and it is likely they would have become hopelessly lost if not for Gollum, despite his treachery.

Much later, as the quest nears its end, Sam also has the chance to kill Gollum. It would have been just and, as Sam reasons, the only safe thing to do, but, again, mercy prevails.[52] That last act of mercy does indeed prove decisive. When put to it, Frodo is finally overcome by temptation and decides not to part with the Ring. It takes Gollum biting off Frodo's ring finger and falling into the fires of Mount Doom to complete the quest.[53]

The whole Gollum saga, then, exists in *The Lord of the Rings* not simply to add colour to the story but also to make a point: that there is always a reason to hope, a reason to choose rightly, a reason to show mercy, a reason to press on, because grace is woven in and around those choices.

These two sources of hope in Tolkien's mythical universe – the grace woven into the goodness of all natural things, and the invisible hand guiding events – spring from the same source. The One who made the star that Sam sees – untouched and untouchable by the Shadow – is also the One who is actively working in and around character choices, leading the story to a new dawn, and the Shadow's demise.

Eucatastrophe

Perhaps the most discussed aspect of Tolkien's hopeful vision is 'eucatastrophe' – that is, the sudden, surprisingly happy ending that defies belief. Tolkien's famous definition:

> The consolation of fairy-stories, the joy of the happy ending: or more correctly of the good catastrophe, the sudden joyous 'turn' (for there is no true end to any fairy-tale): this joy, which is one of the things which fairy-stories can produce supremely well, is not essentially

51 TT, 'The taming of Sméagol', IV/1, pp. 600–601.
52 ROTK, 'Mount Doom', VI/3, p. 923.
53 ROTK, 'Mount Doom', VI/3, p. 924–925.

> 'escapist', nor 'fugitive'. In its fairy-tale – or otherworld – setting, it is a sudden and miraculous grace: never to be counted on to recur. It does not deny the existence of dyscatastrophe, of sorrow and failure: the possibility of these is necessary to the joy of deliverance; it denies (in the face of much evidence, if you will) universal final defeat and in so far is evangelium, giving a fleeting glimpse of Joy, Joy beyond the walls of the world, poignant as grief.[54]

Eucatastrophe brings hope unlooked for, as when Sam and Frodo collapse after completing their quest, the landscape itself crumbling around them, certain that they will not survive. But they do, rescued by giant eagles sent by Gandalf. Sam awakens to find Gandalf by his bedside. He blurts out, 'Gandalf! I thought you were dead! But then I thought I was dead myself. Is everything sad going to come untrue?'[55]

The answer, as Shippey rightly points out, is 'No.' There is still sadness left in the world. A great battle has been won, but evil is not completely banished.[56] But you can hardly blame Sam for his mistake. He has had a foretaste, a glimpse, of the final victory to come, a dose of concentrated hope, a divine twist of fate that points to the 'Joy beyond the walls of the world'.

So, if tragic events *can* turn to victory and joy so suddenly, is there *ever* reason to give up hope? As Gandalf says during the Council of Elrond, 'despair is only for those who see the end beyond all doubt'.[57] Contrast his wisdom with Denethor's, the Steward of Gondor. Faced with insurmountable odds, he despaired and, thenceforth, sank into madness and suicide because he *thought* he saw the end beyond all doubt. By being 'realistic' he lost touch with real reality, which contains the ever-present possibility of eucatastrophe.

Eucatastrophe's reminder never to despair because we cannot see the end beyond all doubt is a deeply Christian insight. Resurrection, life renewed after the apparent victory of death, lies at the core of the

---

54 J. R. R. Tolkien, 'On fairy-stories' in *Tree and Leaf* (London and New York: HarperCollins, 2001 [1964]), p. 31, <https://archive.org/details/on-fairy-stories_202110>, accessed February 2023. Reprinted by permission of HarperCollins Publishers Ltd © 1964, J.R.R. Tolkien.

55 ROTK, 'The Field of Cormallen', IV/4, p. 930.

56 Shippey, *J. R. R. Tolkien*, pp. 207–208.

57 FOTR, 'The Council of Elrond', II/2, p. 262.

Christian faith. The Christian universe, like Tolkien's Middle-earth, essentially is eucatastrophic, always haunted by something beyond the temporary victory of evil and death. The God of grace will have the last (eucatastrophic) word.

Conclusion: but is it 'Christian'? Tolkien's impact beyond the faithful

The putative Christian character of *The Lord of the Rings* has been much debated by scholars and fans, and for good reason. The relationship between Tolkien's mythical world and the Christian world view is complex and subtle.

Tolkien did not want to write a story that wore its convictions on its sleeve, so to speak. He famously disliked allegory, so he could honestly say, 'As for any inner meaning or "message", it has in the intention of the author none.'[58] There is little talk of religion or religious rituals. The closest we get is Faramir's explanation of the Gondorian custom of a moment of silence looking towards 'Númenor that was, and beyond to Elvenhome that is, and to that which is beyond Elvenhome and will ever be'.[59]

Yet there are hints and Christian motifs, even Christ figures. Frodo and Gandalf both sacrifice themselves for their friends and are resurrected (Frodo figuratively, Gandalf physically). Aragorn, the returning king with the 'hands of a healer', literally passes through the realm of the dead to save his people, much as Christ passed through hell to save his. Even Boromir, who tried to take the Ring, repents and dies trying to protect Merry and Pippin. At the very least, in his repentance and self-sacrifice, we can see a reflection of Christian salvation and the dying to self that Jesus speaks of in Mark 8:34–36. But there are Christ figures aplenty in non-Christian stories as well. And, as literature scholar Matthew Dickerson points out, Tolkien also draws on pagan sources, such as the Germanic and Scandinavian heroic tales of which he was so fond.[60] Tolkien was not out to write a piece of Christian propaganda.

---

58 FOTR, 'Foreword to the Second Edition', p. xvi.
59 TT, 'The window on the west', IV/5, p. 661.
60 Dickerson, *Following Gandalf*, pp. 204–206.

No, what makes his tale Christian is harder to pinpoint. It has to do with his assumptions about reality, the values of the heroes, the imaginative *texture* of the story, the *mood*.[61] Above all, his tale is characterized by that distinctively Christian tension, the dual imaginative vision – here, a fading, dying world plagued with evil, yet filled with undying hope rooted in a power that transcends that world. This is the imaginary world within which the characters act, persevere and hope. This is the territory out of which an authentically Christian imagination produces imaginary worlds that can resonate in a post-Christian culture. As Tolkien confessed to a priest friend:

> *The Lord of the Rings* is of course a fundamentally religious and Catholic work; unconsciously so at first, but consciously in the revision. That is why I have not put in, or have cut out, practically all references to anything like 'religion', to cults or practices, in the imaginary world. For the religious element is absorbed into the story and the symbolism.[62]

Because its Christian commitments are so thoroughly kneaded into the imaginary world, and Tolkien presents this world and all its textures with such a natural touch, no-one walks away feeling preached at. Rather, they depart that world feeling moved. This meaningful texture flies under the radar and creates a space that is uniquely Christian, but does not register as such.[63] Hence the debate about whether his books are or are not truly Christian. That debate is a marker of its success – so many non-Christians care so deeply, they fight for it to belong to them and not be a solely

---

61 By 'mood', I mean the emotional texture that informs a poem (or, in this case, a tale), evoking a distinctive imaginary world.

62 Letter to Robert Murray, S.J., dated 2 December 1953, in Humphrey Carpenter (ed.), *The Letters of J. R. R. Tolkien* (New York: Houghton Mifflin, 2000), p. 172. Extract reprinted by permission of HarperCollins Publishers Ltd © 1981, J.R.R. Tolkien. See also Joseph Pearce, 'Is *The Lord of the Rings* an allegory?', *Faith and Culture: A Journal of the Augustine Institute* (4 May 2018), <www.faithandculture.com/home/2018/5/4/is-the-lord-of-the-rings-an-allegory>, accessed February 2023.

63 Some clearly have been brought to (mostly Catholic) faith through his works. See, for instance, Kaitlyn Facista, 'How Tolkien's Middle-earth introduced me to Catholicism', *Tea with Tolkien* (n.d.), <www.teawithtolkien.com/blog/2017/2/10/tolkien-my-conversion-to-catholicism>, accessed February 2023. See also a thread posted by Reformed-ish-Homeboy in the Tolkienfans subreddit, 'Does reading Tolkien make you more interested in Christianity or Catholicism?', <www.reddit.com/r/tolkienfans/comments/9t03wl/does_reading_tolkien_make_you_more_interested_in>, accessed February 2023. The responses vary widely.

Christian property.[64] Shared imaginative spaces often generate debate. Oases, while refreshing and potentially transformative, are not always the most tranquil places. That is to be expected, and welcomed. Tolkien has done the Christian imagination a great service. He used it the way it should be used.

Though I have focused on theological themes running throughout *The Lord of the Rings* that may serve as a Christian witness in a post-Christian society, its witness has been broader than simply evangelistic. Tolkien's own affection for the natural world in his stories – illustrated by the elves, ents and the disdain for Saruman's and Sauron's destruction of trees – served to clear an imaginary space for a generation to think about nature in a new way.

Though culturally they were oceans apart, Tolkien's work inspired the hippies, becoming a touchstone of modern environmental activism.[65] Robert Hunter relates how, for Greenpeace's first environmental protest, their action was framed explicitly in terms of Middle-earth: 'We are on our way to the dread dark land of Mordor, and Amchitka is Mount Doom . . . somehow we have to hurl the Ring of Power into the fire and bring down the whole kingdom of the Dark Lord.'[66] From very early on, *The Lord of the Rings* fandom and other examples of environmental activism were tangled up with one another: to love Middle-earth meant protecting *this* earth.

Though Tolkien himself was not an environmental activist, his tales inspired others to activism, or what Christians now call 'creation care'. *The Lord of the Rings* is, among other things, a call to nurture the world we have been entrusted with. His creative vision honoured creation and worked for the common good. It even led some to the Creator.

64 Though we will not explore the works of C. S. Lewis, his stories have often provoked a similar response in non-Christians. When my eldest daughter was in primary school, she would not tell her Czech classmates (who came from atheist families) that Lewis was a Christian for fear that they would stop reading him.

65 William E. Ratliff and Charles G. Flinn, 'The hobbit and the hippie', *Modern Age*, vol. 12, no. 2 (Spring 1968), pp. 142–146, <https://isiorg.b-cdn.net/wp-content/uploads/2014/10/ratliff.pdf?x65817>, accessed February 2023. Ratliff and Flinn mention two points of convergence between Tolkien's stories and hippy counterculture: the rejection of materialism (that the world is only physical) and the 'rationalist progressive' view of history (that 'progress' is always a good thing); p. 144.

66 Robert Hunter, *The Greenpeace to Amchitka: An environmental odyssey* (Vancouver, British Columbia: Arsenal Pulp Press, 2004), p. 31, quoted in Doyle Irvin, 'The ent activist: Why "The Lord of the Rings" became a counterculture icon', American Forests (23 May 2017), <www.americanforests.org/blog/tolkien-lord-of-the-rings-became-counterculture-icon>, accessed February 2023.

Postscript: the Christian imagination in non-Christian hands

D&D, Peter Jackson, EA Games and, more recently, Amazon have got hold of *The Lord of the Rings*, but how 'Christian' are these later, post-Tolkien iterations of Middle-earth?

No doubt some of the themes and textures we explored earlier in this chapter have been attenuated and replaced, somewhat distorting Tolkien's vision. For example, in Jackson's *Lord of the Rings: The Two Towers* (2002), the screenwriters rewrote the important character Faramir. In the books, Faramir is the quintessence of faithfulness and nobility, treating Frodo and Sam as honoured guests. Importantly, he is wise enough to keep his distance from the Ring. In the film version, Faramir imprisons Frodo and Sam, beats and threatens Gollum like an overzealous 'bad cop' and decides to take the Ring to Gondor (something his brother, Boromir the traitor, couldn't manage) . . . until he resists temptation at the eleventh hour. It's as though the writers found simple goodness and faithfulness too boring a character arc for a film. Not enough conflict. But such a subplot is wholly out of tune with Tolkien's reverence for moral integrity; he doesn't find goodness boring at all. And don't get me started on characters that Jackson decided to create and shoehorn into Middle-earth, such as Tauriel. In *The Hobbit: The desolation of Smaug* (2013) and *The Battle of the Five Armies* (2014), she seems to exist solely for the purpose of a romance subplot, and to make sure Middle-earth has its quota of hot women warriors.

The fantasy role-playing tabletop and computer games inspired by Tolkien changed his vision as well. For Tolkien, battle is part of the drama of Middle-earth, but always as a necessary evil to preserve the good and to establish the rightful King. In the games, the battles *are* the point.[67] For Tolkien, who served in and was traumatized by the Battle of the Somme

67 Tolkien scholar and artist Jeff McLeod notes obvious connections between Tolkien's works and the first fantasy role-playing game, Dungeons & Dragons (D&D). But he also notes a fundamental disconnect. D&D (and the vast majority of fantasy role-playing games since) follow what he calls a crush your enemies (CYE) narrative pattern centred on violence and accumulating power. Tolkien, he argues, follows an 'enchantment narrative', in which the free peoples of Middle-earth eschew power and violence unless absolutely necessary. Violence violates the delicate balance of nature, the beauty of the earth. See his 'Tolkien and Dungeons & Dragons'.

in the First World War and experienced two of his sons serving in the Second World War, war is an ugly scar on existence, never to be taken lightly. It was not something to be played at for amusement.

As for the latest instalment in *The Lord of the Rings* universe, *The Rings of Power*, there are both joys and disappointments. Amazon spent a *lot* on this production, and it shows – frankly, it's gorgeous.[68] The dialogue, sometimes stilted, sometimes anachronistic, seems to have been a problem for writers.[69] The accents were odd and fluctuate at times. The story is sprawling – understandable, given the source material. But one of the things that attracted me to this world (and world-building is this series' forte) was an atmosphere of moral health, for lack of a better term, a commitment to what was clearly good on the part of key characters, as opposed to, for example, the studied moral ambiguity of HBO's *Game of Thrones: House of the Dragon* series.[70] In *The Silmarillion*, the source of that commitment among the elves is fairly clear: Eru Ilúvatar, the creator of Middle-earth. But that commitment, and the blessedness of the Valar, are curiously obscured in the series – perhaps so as not to upset anyone's secularist sentiments.[71] As a result, it's a goodness without much reason behind it. Perhaps that's a good thing, in terms of aiming for a balance between shouting and mumbling (Tolkien hints at more than he discloses). But the series falls short of what Tolkien wrote. It mumbles a bit too much for my taste.

What are we to make of these distortions of Tolkien's oasis? Simply this: once they are committed to paper, video, disk, MP3 or computer code, oases cease to be private reserves. They become public and, once public, then they can be enhanced or abused, deepened or subverted. If they succeed at attracting inhabitants, the one thing that they will never

---

[68] *The Lord of the Rings: The Rings of Power* is officially the most expensive television production in history. Amazon spent more than $1 billion to bring it to life, $452 million on the first season alone. See Matthew Biggin, '*LOTR: The Rings of Power* show budget: Will cost more than $1 billion', *ScreenRant* (11 February 2022), <https://screenrant.com/lotr-rings-power-show-budget-billion-amazon-details>, accessed February 2023.

[69] On this particular problem, and finding the correct tone for characters in a fantasy novel or film, see Ostadan's excellent essay, 'From The Rings of Power to Poughkeepsie', *The OneRing.net* (26 September 2022), <www.theonering.net/torwp/2022/09/26/115304-from-the-rings-of-power-to-poughkeepsie/>, accessed February 2023.

[70] *House of the Dragon*, in fact, fared better in terms of viewership than *The Rings of Power* – perhaps a testament to a post-Christian cultural affinity with moral relativism.

[71] See Hannah Matis' review, 'The Rings of Power', *Covenant* (10 November 2022), <https://covenant.livingchurch.org/2022/11/10/the-rings-of-power>, accessed February 2023.

remain is static. And yet, one still catches an aroma of the original. That alone may entice some to dig deeper into the source material. Oases suffering change is no excuse to stop creating or supporting creatives. Rather, let us take it as a challenge to create better, deeper and with more care.

14

Rumours of grace in the Christ-haunted world of Krzysztof Kieślowski's *A Short Film about Love*

Introduction: Kieślowski's portrayal of hope in a dark world

Our final example of the Christian imagination done right is the work of Polish filmmaker Krzysztof Kieślowski (1941–1996) and his screenwriting collaborator Krzysztof Piesiewicz (b. 1945). Together they produced some of the most brilliant expressions of hope and meaning in a dark world that I have ever seen. We will explore just one of these here – their 1988 masterpiece *A Short Film about Love* (*Krótki film o milosci*).[1]

Lauded by both viewers and critics, it is one of my favourite films by any director. Be warned: this film is not for children and not easy to watch, even for adults. Some will find this film profoundly distressing due to its sexual content (though there is no nudity) and disturbing themes and imagery (including a seduction scene and a suicide attempt). If you think it will be too much, feel free to skip it. For the rest of you, *go watch the film*, as my comments and plot summary will contain spoilers.

A Short Film about Love

Originally part of Kieślowski's *Dekalog* series made for Polish television in the late 1980s, *A Short Film about Love* was extended to make it into a feature-length film.[2] Each film in the series is a meditation on the ethical and existential meaning of one of the Ten Commandments – how we

[1] Krzysztof Kieślowski (screenplay, director) and Krzysztof Piesiewicz (screenplay), *A Short Film about Love* (*Krótki film o milosci*) (Zespol Filmowy 'Tor', 1988; DVD, Artificial Eye, 2002).

[2] Kieślowski also lengthened one other *Dekalog* film, the harrowing *A Short Film about Killing* (1988).

violate them, how we understand life better through them. *A Short Film about Love* explores the meaning of the sixth commandment: 'You shall not commit adultery.'[3] Kieślowski changed very little when he extended it, except at the end, to give the film more closure or what actress Grażyna Szapołowska called a 'fairy-tale ending'.[4] It isn't really (no Tolkienesque eucatastrophe), but it does provide more visual consolation than the original abrupt, austere ending. By all accounts, the added material completes the film, making it a much richer cinematic experience.

A Short Film about Love is not popular cinema. The pace is much more deliberate than, say, an instalment of the Marvel Cinematic Universe. No gunfights, car chases or superpowers. For those accustomed to Hollywood films, it will require patience. Also, the film raises more questions than it answers.[5] It is worth it, though, as Kieślowski was a master of his craft, known and revered by more popular filmmakers. Through them his influence has been felt widely.[6]

I turn to Kieślowski because, truth be told, Christian filmmaking is in pretty bad shape. Cinema is a difficult art form to master. It forces artists to deal with multiple stylistic vocabularies at once: the script, lighting, visual composition, music, dramatic performance, set design, editing and on and on. It is so easy to get it wrong.

It doesn't take much to turn an OK film into manipulative kitsch or propaganda. In addition, many Christian filmmakers are so anxious to give faith-filled answers that they ignore how adept film is at raising questions, then leaving the viewer room to wonder and reflect. That is what sets Kieślowski apart, as a writer and director: his trust in the audience, his willingness to let viewers explore the length and breadth of his imaginative vision. He hints at possible answers but subtly, without hitting the viewer over the head with them (rather like Jesus did in his parables). He respects the medium and knows how to invite us into his stories, into

---

3 Sixth in the Catholic tradition; for Protestants, it is the seventh commandment.

4 Grażyna Szapołowska, interview on the American and Artificial Eye Region 2 DVD releases of *A Short Film about Love*, Tom Patson & Partners, YouTube (2003), <www.youtube.com/watch?v=5I5va4HmNAU>, February 2023.

5 Recall Ryan Green's comments about 'questioning art' in chapter 12.

6 Just two examples of Kieślowski's fingerprints on popular film: the montage at the end of Richard Kelly's cult classic *Donnie Darko* (2001). The camera pans left, slowly and deliberately, from character to character, implying a deep, mysterious connection between them, mimicking the final montage of Kieślowski's film *Three Colours: Blue* (1993). A similar montage occurs near the end of John Michael McDonagh's film *Calvary* (2014) too.

the lives of his characters.[7] This is something that Christian filmmakers are still learning: storytelling without emotional manipulation, without spoon-feeding the audience, without putting Christian values on parade. Kieślowski's films ought to be required viewing for any aspiring Christian filmmaker.

The story

Tomek is a 19-year-old orphan who lives with his landlady (his best friend's mother) in an apartment complex in Warsaw. His friend is away in foreign lands for the Polish military, so Tomek has become a substitute son for his landlady. But Tomek has a secret: he enjoys spying on a neighbour through a stolen telescope. The neighbour, Magda, a beautiful and promiscuous thirty-something, lives in the apartment building opposite. He is literally a peeping Tom.

The film explores the interrelated themes of watching, voyeurism, and the gaze generally. Indeed, at several points, the viewer is reminded, through camera angle and movement, that the director and viewer are also observers, also voyeurs.

At first glance, Tomek's spying is undeniably creepy, but Kieślowski, as he often does, overturns our expectations about his main character. We think we have Tomek worked out, pigeonholed, but the film subverts our assumptions by making him three-dimensional, fully human.

We find that, although Tomek is ashamed of his spying, he does not watch Magda out of voyeuristic lust. It may have started that way, but now (in the time frame of the film) he watches as a way of dealing with his own loneliness. In fact, whenever she is about to make love with one of her lovers, he turns away, unable to watch her cheapen herself. When he sees her get involved with a man he considers unworthy of her, he interferes, telephoning the gas company to report a phony gas leak coming from her apartment, interrupting the lovers.

What truly draws him is the details of her life, *her* loneliness. He cannot turn away when he sees her crying alone after a quarrel with another of her lovers. He comes away feeling deeply confused and sad. What we first

---

[7] Kieślowski started as a documentary filmmaker. He switched to dramatic film because the types of stories he wanted to tell were intimate. He didn't want to violate the privacy of real people.

take to be voyeurism for prurient sexual excitement is gradually revealed to be a caring, protective gaze (whether she wants the protection or not). Tomek loves her and cares deeply for her, in his own strange, broken, dysfunctional way.

Tomek intervenes in Magda's life in other ways as well. He calls her to hear her voice and then hangs up. He takes a second job to deliver milk to her building, just to get a glimpse of her. In his main job as a postal clerk, he sends her forged money orders so that he can see her when she comes to collect the (non-existent) cash. The second time she comes expecting money, the manager of the post office accuses her of attempted theft, and Magda leaves upset.

This is more than Tomek can stand. He runs after her and confesses that he is to blame for the fake money order, and he has been spying on her. At first she's confused, then angry. She dismisses him as a 'meddler'. But she is also intrigued.

The next evening, Madga calls one of her lovers, knowing that Tomek is spying on them. With a malicious delight, she seduces her lover, but before anything happens, she tells him that they are being watched. She even points out Tomek's window. Enraged, the man dresses and rushes to the front of Tomek's building, calling him out. Humiliated and frightened, Tomek emerges to meet him. The man knocks Tomek down with one punch, scolds him, and drives off.

The next day, Magda (who is catching on to the methods of her stalker) wakens early to confront Tomek as he delivers the morning milk. Now that she's taught him a lesson, she demands answers about why he spies on her.

> 'I love you,' he responds.
>
> 'What is it you want?' she demands. 'Do you want to kiss me? Sleep with me? Run away with me?'
>
> He responds simply, 'Nothing.'
>
> Incredulous, Magda presses, 'Nothing?'
>
> Tomek, resigned, responds flatly, 'Nothing.'

His face burning with shame, confused and overwhelmed, Tomek breaks away from the conversation and runs to the roof of her building to collect his thoughts. After a few moments, he has an idea. He returns to her door and asks her out for ice-cream. She accepts his invitation, and he responds by running with his milk cart in jubilant circles, round and round a man in a white coat who smiles back at him, a silent witness to his joy.[8]

On the date, Magda encourages Tomek to caress her. His hands tremble as he touches her hand. Here, Tomek experiences the immediacy of touch rather than the safe distance of sight. It is almost more than he can bear.

The conversation turns to the nature of love. Magda, the voice of cynical, world-weary experience, tries to instruct Tomek. There is no such thing as love. Love is simply sexual desire, nothing more. Tomek disagrees. Love does exist. After the date, they go to Magda's apartment where she seduces the sexually inexperienced Tomek by having him place his hands on her bare thighs (this is perhaps the most disturbing scene in the film). Tomek climaxes almost immediately and weeps quietly, overcome by shame.

Magda dismisses him with a curt, 'Already? That's all there is to love. Wash in the bathroom – there's a towel.' Unbeknown to them both, Tomek's landlady has found his telescope and is watching the scene unfold.

Tomek, confused and hurt, runs from Magda's apartment back to his own. Along the way, he passes the man in white, now a witness to his humiliation. Once he gets to his apartment, Tomek goes to the bathroom, finds a razor blade and slits his wrists.

Magda, unaware of the suicide attempt, tries to call Tomek back by placing a sign in her window saying that she is sorry and asking him to call. But the phone doesn't ring. Magda doesn't see the ambulance come and take him away.

Noticing a coat he'd left behind in his rush to escape, Magda decides to find Tomek's apartment and apologize. She is met by his landlady, who reluctantly tells her that he is in the hospital, but won't reveal which one. Magda later finds out from her postman that Tomek 'slit his wrists out of love'.

8 This mysterious figure appears briefly as a silent witness at significant moments in all the *Dekalog* films (save the last). In the credits, he is listed only as 'Young Man'. Perhaps he is an angelic stand-in for the watchful eye of God. Kieślowski leaves his role in the story ambiguous.

As Magda begins to put the pieces together, something inside her crumbles. Tomek's absence gnaws at her conscience, and she discovers that she has feelings for him, feelings she cannot convey because he is gone and she cannot find him. Magda visits every hospital in the vicinity, but to no avail; she doesn't know his last name. Overcome by guilt and worry, Magda the watched now becomes the watcher. She finds some old binoculars and spends her evenings watching Tomek's window, awaiting his return. When her old lover visits, she sends him away. She has no appetite for her old life now.

When Tomek finally returns home from the hospital, the watchful Magda sees this. Immediately, she goes to visit him at his apartment, where he lies sleeping, but the landlady will not let her waken him. So she sits and waits, longing to give him some comfort to make up for the pain she caused him. As she reaches out to touch his bandaged wrist, the landlady grabs her hand. Denied the chance to touch Tomek, instead Magda sits in a chair by his bed and peers through his telescope at her own apartment window (see page 7 in the plate section). As she does so, she has a vision: she sees herself through his eyes. She recollects her own weeping in solitude after the quarrel with her lover, but with one addition. She imagines that Tomek comes in and places a comforting hand on her shoulder. In her mind's eye, she reaches up and holds on to his hand. The film ends with Magda, eyes closed, smiling and imagining the scene, then the screen fades to black.[9]

A Short Film about Love and the Christian imagination: can you explore love, loneliness and voyeurism Christianly?

Why choose this film as a model oasis that exemplifies a distinctively Christian imagination? Christ is mentioned nowhere in the script. The film contains much that is dark and disturbing: voyeurism, an awkward sexual seduction scene, a suicide attempt – not your typical 'family fare'. Further, the film stubbornly avoids giving easy answers. No-one falls on

9 The original ending of *Dekalog 6* is brutally abrupt. Magda, after all her searching, finally catches up with him at the post office. Tomek looks up at her and says simply, 'I'm not peeping at you any more.' End of film. I personally prefer the longer ending, as it provides Magda with some consolation and hope that are denied in the original, shorter version.

their knees and professes their need for Christ.[10] How could we call this film Christian?

The answer to that question becomes clearer by understanding how and why Kieślowski made his films. He made them not to preach but to explore. Though his films feature compelling stories filled with beautifully lyrical and/or disturbing images, a Kieślowski film begins not with a story or an image but a question about the human condition. 'What is freedom?' (*Three Colours: Blue*, 1993) 'What is stealing?' (*Dekolog 7*, 1988). 'What is community?' (*Three Colours: Red*, 1994). The question for this film is, 'What is love, really? Merely sex, mechanical, chemical, biological? Or is there something more?' Kieślowski answers that question by exploring the themes woven into the film: isolation, loneliness, the gaze, touch, sex and love.

The way Kieślowski explores these themes resonates deeply with the Christian imagination. The story's structure propels the characters from isolation through spying and observation into real contact with each other, each step moving them with the subtle force of destiny. The first shot in *A Short Film about Love* is a close-up of a hand (Magda's) reaching out to touch Tomek's bandaged wrist, and being prevented from doing so by another hand (the landlady's). The film begins at the end, giving the whole story we are about to witness a momentum towards that conclusion. We are not watching random events – we are being guided, along with the characters, from a certain point (isolation) to a destination (human contact – or, at least, the promise of it). The mysterious man in white whom Tomek passes may be more than a passive witness. There may be a discrete agency hidden beneath his observation. In the film, one feels, almost unconsciously, the guiding hand of God, though the characters' choices matter a great deal – they are woven into that destiny.[11] The story's structure gestures beyond itself in a way that is distinctively Christian.

Further, as this story about gazing and voyeurism unfolds, we become aware of the extra dimension of Kieślowski's camera as another silent observer. At first, this is profoundly disturbing but, as the story progresses,

[10] We will discuss whether there are other sorts of repentance and conversion in the pages that follow.

[11] Recall Tolkien's interweaving of destiny and character choices in chapter 13.

we find the gaze deeply humane. There is an affection for his characters, flawed though they be, a yearning desire for their welfare.

This is completely unlike the impersonal, distancing lens of Stanley Kubrick in *2001: A Space Odyssey* (1968), *A Clockwork Orange* (1971) or *Barry Lyndon* (1975). Kieślowski's gaze does not distance, it embraces. One gets the feeling that his camera mimics the gaze of a loving God. And that affects how he deals with the voyeurism of characters like Tomek.

Film critic Annette Insdorf notes that Kieślowski's voyeurism is not the shameful, predatory gaze that characterized Alfred Hitchcock's lens.[12] Indeed, in *Psycho* (1960), one feels as though Norman Bates, in spying on the lovely Marion Crane, is pinning her down like an entomologist would an insect. The knife attack in the famous shower scene is simply the physical manifestation of what he has already done to her with his eyes, a visual dissection. Tomek's gaze is altogether different, stemming not from misogyny or grasping lust, but from the desire to enter into Magda's world and comfort someone who, like him, is very alone despite her foolish, unfulfilling romantic dalliances. Both Tomek and Kieślowski are best described as 'compassionate watchers'.

At the beginning of the story, we find both characters alone – Magda playing solitaire and Tomek eating a meal alone in his room. We are made aware of the weight of loneliness, the desire for contact. We feel the wrongness of their isolation – this is not what they are made for. Behind this is the distinctively Christian presupposition that people are made in God's image for *relationship*.[13] Further, through his depiction of their terrible isolation, and the clumsy and sinful ways in which the characters try to overcome their solitude (for Tomek, stealing a telescope and spying; for Magda, pursuing sexual encounters), Kieślowski reveals the messy brokenness of human life in a fallen world. The tenor of the film is melancholy and wistful. His imagination is acquainted with the darkness of creation, stunted and distorted, of a world gone wrong.

But Kieślowski also gives glimpses of hope that can pierce the darkness. The film is centred on an argument over the nature of love: *is* it merely

12 Annette Insdorf, *Double Lives, Second Chances: The cinema of Krzysztof Kieślowski* (New York: Hyperion, 1999), p. 100. See also her insightful introduction to the film on DVD (Artificial Eye, 2003). The same interview is available in region 1 on Kino Video's release (2004).

13 'It is not good that the man should be alone', God says in Genesis 2:18. See my book *Popologetics: Popular culture in Christian perspective* (Phillipsburg, NJ: P&R, 2012), pp. 51–53.

sex or is there something different, something more (for lack of a better word) *spiritual* at work? Magda is confronted with someone she thinks she understands (a voyeuristic kid looking for sexual excitement), but comes to realize by degrees that there is something different about Tomek. He presents her with an impenetrable mystery: selfless love. This is something that does not compute in Magda's world. His love is not about getting but giving – he wants 'nothing'. Or, more precisely, he wants nothing more than to comfort her, to alleviate her isolation.

Magda's seduction of Tomek, followed by her curt dismissal, has the feel of an argumentative victory: 'That's all love is. Now go clean yourself up. Point proven.' But her coolly calculated victory has a devastating (one could argue, a paradoxically eucatastrophic) aftermath for her and within her. As she investigates what happened to the young man who fled her apartment, she gradually realizes what she has done: she has betrayed love itself. By degrees, her cynicism unravels, leaving her aching and vulnerable. When she receives a night-time phone call from a silent caller days after Tomek's suicide attempt, she assumes that it is Tomek (it is, in fact, a bad connection). Seizing what she thinks is her first chance to communicate with him, she confesses that he was right and she was wrong. When the badly connected caller calls back, she simply hangs up. She wants to hear only from Tomek. She watches and waits for him to return from the hospital, turning away one of her old lovers who comes to call.

Magda is broken, but also sharpened – focused solely on restoring what she has damaged. The emotional power of the film emanates from Magda's slow repentance and, with it, her acknowledgement of the transcendent power of selfless love. By the end of the film (where we also began), we wait with Magda by Tomek's bedside, filled with expectation and hope that perhaps the relationship can be healed and made new. Magda has become, in a sense, a new creation, a spark of light reclaimed from the darkness.

In this way, Kieślowski's film expresses what I earlier called eschatological desire in all its subterranean power. He does not present to us a sanitized version of reality but, rather, a darkly twisted world. Nevertheless, light shines through and grows, turning what could be a disturbing film into a vehicle of beautiful, fragile hope. He is able to grasp both poles at once, and that gives his film a deeply Christian imaginative integrity.

A Short Film about Love affirms the Christian imagination, though indirectly, in all its aching tension and subversive power.

The Christian perspective is not shouted from the rooftops, not preached to the choir, but whispered in a clear, unmistakable tone. The final image, from Magda's vision, is Tomek standing over her, consoling hand on her shoulder, her hand grasping his in relief. We catch the unmistakable visual echo of Christ restoring the original Magda, Mary Magdalene. We understand, on some level, where the selfless love that moves us from isolation to loving connection comes from.

Conclusion: shifting our imaginative ground

As I said at the beginning of this chapter, this film will make some Christians uncomfortable, but perhaps the naked, evocative power of the Christian imagination *should* make us feel uncomfortable. The film does what all Christian culture should do: return us to reality with a deepened appreciation for both the darkness in which we are caught and the shattering light of grace. It places us in an oasis with room to explore, with room for Christ to beckon us to a completely different way of being.

For those sceptical that this film can have a deeply Christian impact on the imagination, let me share a story with you. My wife and I invite university students into our home for film nights. Years ago, the film up for discussion was *A Love Song for Bobby Long* (2004). In it, Pursy, a young woman, returns to New Orleans to claim property that her estranged, deceased mother left to her. She finds the dilapidated house occupied by squatters. One is Bobby Long, an ex-English professor who had taught at Auburn University. Pursy, unable or unwilling to evict the squatters, joins them, and they form a sort of odd family.

Eventually, Bobby tells Pursy how he ended up homeless. At Auburn he had been an alcoholic and a womanizer. One day, when he was supposed to be picking up his son from a Little League game, he was instead enjoying a tryst with a co-ed. The boy, tired of waiting for his father, attempted to walk home alone. He was struck by a car and killed. The resulting scandal cost Long his position and his marriage.

In our discussion after the film, I mentioned this sequence and asked the 15 to 20 students gathered in our living room, 'Can you see how Bobby Long's sexual choices led to bad consequences? Can you understand why the Christian tradition would want to preserve sex for marriage, why that might be wiser?' I could have tossed a grenade in the room and would have got a less violent reaction.

The students immediately defended their sexual freedom with an intense determination that surprised me, throwing out hostile questions with machinegun-like rapidity. 'Why should we wait? Aren't we adults?' 'What about sex with friends?' 'How could you believe something so outdated?' 'Shouldn't we be allowed pleasure any way we choose to receive it?'

The Christians in the audience shrank down in their seats as if to say, 'You dug yourself into this hole. You're on your own!' Needless to say, it wasn't what I'd call a helpful or constructive conversation. The common assumption coming from the non-Christians was that sex is simply a means of attaining fun and pleasure, and it can be used however consenting users see fit. Not the conclusion I was hoping for, but I filed that experience away for future reference.

The next year, we decided to host a fortnightly discussion series called, 'The meaning of . . .'. Each night explored a different aspect of human existence: work, art, death and so on. For 'The meaning of love and sex', I chose *A Short Film about Love*. The difference between that discussion and the one that had happened the previous year was stark and absolute.

The film moved us on to completely different imaginative ground. For perhaps the first time, some of my students saw sex and love as intertwined, fragile and absolutely brimming with spiritual meaning. They could see that sex is not something to use or abuse but has a depth they were just beginning to ponder. And perhaps, also, the key to unlocking its true significance has to do with the Christian faith.

Without even uttering his name, Christ the Lord of Creation and Salvation had been invoked in these students' imaginations in a way that was deeply moving. Through the film, he invited them to a deeper conversation within that oasis. That is all we can ask of great Christian art.

Even if Kieślowski himself had struggles with God, his imaginative vision opens up vistas of surprising, and ordinary, grace. Renowned critic Roger Ebert, in writing a memorial for Kieślowski, told of an interview he once gave.

In 1989, when his 'Decalogue' was first being seen in New York, Kieślowski was asked by *Village Voice* writer Samir Hachem to name the 10 words he would keep if all other words were taken from him. He said, 'Love. Hate. Loneliness. Fear. Coincidence. Pain. Anxiety. God. Responsibility.' Told that he had named only nine, he added, 'Innocence'. Those 10 qualities represented the building-blocks of his cinema.[14]

Postscript: when a non-Christian expresses a Christian imagination better than Christians

Now let me drop a bomb to complicate things: Kieślowski did not identify as a Christian. He called himself an 'agnostic mystic', a searcher who did not know.[15] Yet his films resonate with Christian imagination in a way that many films made by Christians do not.

Kieślowski's not the only one, either. I taught a class called 'Popular culture and Christian world view' for the Union School of Theology in Wales. On the course, the students watch a film that I feel expresses the Christian imagination well. In 2020, we watched John Michael McDonagh's *Calvary* (2014).

Father James is a priest to an Irish village. He has integrity and a deep compassion for the dysfunctional, cynical members of his parish. One tells him in confession that he's going to kill him in seven days' time. The film follows those seven days – his 'holy week' – during which Father James decides to keep caring for and ministering to his flock rather than run. He incarnates Christ's faithful love and wisdom throughout the film. Father James even pleads with his assailant *after* the parishioner has shot him, trying to save him from becoming a murderer.

While discussing the film, one of the students said, 'Does it matter that he's not a Christian?' I did an internal double take and said, 'Really?' He responded, 'Yeah, according to this interview, he left the Catholic Church

14 Roger Ebert, 'Krzysztof Kieślowski: In memoriam', *RogerEbert.com* (14 March 1996), <www.rogerebert.com/interviews/krzysztof-kieslowski-in-memoriam>, accessed February 2023.

15 Monica Maurer, *Krzysztof Kieślowski* (North Pomfret, VT: Trafalgar Square Publishing, 2000), p. 13, quoted in Jim Friedrich, 'Kieślowski's *Decalogue*: A masterpiece of religious cinema', *The Religious Imagineer* (28 January 2017), <https://jimfriedrich.com/2017/01/28/Kieslowskis-decalogue-a-masterpiece-of-religious-cinema/#_edn3>, accessed February 2023.

when he was 14.'[16] Flabbergasted, I said, 'Then why did he make the film?!' I said that because this film has such a deep admiration and affection for people of real faith. The faithful are the only ones who seem sane, grounded in hope beyond death and truly loving in the whole story.[17] Doesn't one need to have a living faith to express hope like that?

Another example: folk singer Gillian Welch's 'Orphan girl' is about a young woman bereft of parents who looks to her Saviour to be both mother and father to her, to give her patience until she can meet them again 'at God's table'.[18] By all accounts, Welch also is not a Christian (though she is an orphan).[19] Yet this and other songs she's written ache with a desire that is unmistakably born of faith.[20] What do we do with *that*?

Here are a couple of helpful ideas to keep in mind.[21]

Common grace runs deep and wide, and has some interesting wrinkles. Theologian John Murray defined common grace as widely as possible as being:

> every favour of whatever kind or degree, falling short of salvation, which this undeserving and sin-cursed world enjoys at the hand of God.[22]

Because God is generous, *any* joy, beauty, truth or justice we experience in this world should be recognized as a gift from God. Yet, Murray

---

16 Jason Di Rosso, 'Director John Michael McDonagh discusses *Calvary* and Catholicism', *Radio National* (3 July 2014), <https://discover.abc.net.au/index.html#/?configure%5BgetRankingInfo%5D=true&configure%5BclickAnalytics%5D=true&configure%5BuserToken%5D=anonymous-b5ddaebe-a873-4d21-ac61-c49d0d4ff376&configure%5BhitsPerPage%5D=10&query=john%20michael%20mcdonagh&page=1>, accessed February 2023. Thanks to my students, who started this conversation (I believe James Leverton dug up the interview).

17 Besides Father James there are other faithful (though struggling) Christians: his daughter, Fiona (Father James is a widower), and a grieving French woman, Teresa, whose husband was killed by drunk-driving teens.

18 Gillian Welch, 'Orphan girl', *Revival* (Acony Records, 1996), track 1.

19 Nick Ryerson, 'God and country music: Gillian Welch's soul journey', *Christ and Pop Culture* (20 March 2012), <https://christandpopculture.com/god-and-country-music-gillian-welchs-soul-journey>, accessed February 2023.

20 It's common for non-Christian folk musicians to cover traditional gospel songs. It's unusual for them to *write* them – Welch is the first one I've come across.

21 Many of these ideas were suggested by my insightful friend, Dan Strange.

22 John Murray, 'Common grace' in *Collected Writings of John Murray: Volume 2: Systematic theology* (Carlisle, PA, and Edinburgh: Banner of Truth, 1991 [1982]), <www.sounddoctrine.net/Modern_Day_Reform_Teaching/John%20Murray/Common_Grace.htm>, accessed February 2023 (italics in original).

carefully distinguishes *degrees* of common grace, from the most general (sunshine that makes the plants grow to feed us all) to the most pointed (someone brought up in the church, who has 'tasted' the gospel and been shaped morally by it, but has fallen away and is not saved, as in Hebrews 6:4–6). He insists that common grace serves as the necessary context for special, saving grace – it exists for that purpose! 'Common grace provides the sphere of operation of special grace and special grace therefore provides a rationale of common grace.'[23]

In other words, finding non-Christian artists whose works resonate with the gospel should not surprise us. There are, for instance, abundant cultural rivers, carved out for centuries, along which much gospel-shaped common grace now flows. As I mentioned in chapter 6, James K. A. Smith prefers the term 'craters of the gospel' to indicate the cultural heritage of Christianity's impact for liberal democracies. If such craters shape democratic values, why not art as well? Smith dislikes the term 'common grace', which he sees as an ahistorical stand-in for the historical and cultural inheritances due to special grace:

> Talk of common grace abounds where a theology of providence is lacking. Common grace invokes a deus ex machina operation to account for cultural realities that are, upon closer analysis . . . the historical legacy of special grace, the remnants of the specifically evangelical influence of Christology, ecclesiology, and the gospel.[24]

The more robust conception of common grace that Murray outlines includes within it the sorts of gifts of providence and history that Smith calls craters, but leaves open the possibility for more mysterious paths as well. Kieślowski's films are no doubt cratered with the heritage of being brought up in deeply Catholic Poland – the *Dekalog* is a series of cinematic meditations on the Ten Commandments, after all.

23 Murray, 'Common grace', p. 25. Murray adds that common grace may well have other purposes than simply as an entrée to the gospel, a point emphasized by Richard J. Mouw in *He Shines in All That's Fair: Culture and common grace* (Grand Rapids, MI, and Cambridge: Eerdmans, 2001). God also shows his generosity and care to those who will never know him in a saving way simply because he is kind and good.

24 James K. A. Smith, 'Excursus: Common grace versus providence' in *Awaiting the King: Reforming public theology*, Cultural Liturgies, Volume 3 (Grand Rapids, MI: Baker Academic, Kindle edn, 2017), in chapter 3, loc. 3385–3421.

As an established artist, Kieślowski was surrounded by prominent Christian thinkers and activists, including Nobel laureate poet Czesław Miłosz, who was brought up Catholic and eventually returned to Catholicism, and Karol Wojtyla, who would later become Pope John Paul II.[25] He was also influenced by his Christian screenwriting partner Krzysztof Piesiewicz. Kieślowski's imagination is permeated by Christian images, feelings and concepts. His cinematic imaginary worlds are, despite his own uncertainty, haunted by faith. The same might be said for John Michael McDonagh, brought up in the Catholic Church (even served as an altar boy).[26] The imaginations of both these men were shaped by deeply Christianized cultures.

But the gospel can shine even in the absence of such craters. Makoto Fujimura's writings have shown me many touchstones in Japanese culture that resonate and shimmer with a kind of ghostly gospel light. Consider *kintsugi* and the *wabi-sabi* aesthetic, where beauty is found in brokenness, in wounds. Both pre-date the introduction of the gospel to Japan, but they point unmistakably towards a hope past death, even when surrounded by death. As I mentioned in chapter 5, the Holy Spirit shapes imaginations far and wide, Christian and non-Christian. Perhaps we should *expect* to find artists and culture-makers who create better than they know. As Tolkien put it in his poem, 'Mythopoeia':

> The heart of Man is not compound of lies,
> but draws some wisdom from the only Wise,
> and still recalls him. Though now long estranged,
> Man is not wholly lost nor wholly changed.
> Dis-graced he may be, yet is not dethroned,
> and keeps the rags of lordship once he owned.[27]

---

25 Maria Elena de las Carreras Kuntz, 'Filming the 10 Commandments: Kieślowski as a Catholic director', *Crisis Magazine* (1 November 2000), <www.crisismagazine.com/vault/filming-the-10-commandments-kieslowski-as-a-catholic-director>, accessed February 2023. Carreras notes that many secular film critics ignore the Catholic themes of his work.

26 Cara Buckley, 'His turn with the past', *New York Times* (28 July 2014), <www.nytimes.com/2014/07/29/movies/john-michael-mcdonagh-carves-his-own-niche-with-calvary.html>, accessed February 2023.

27 J. R. R. Tolkien, 'Mythopoeia' in *Tree and Leaf* (London and New York: HarperCollins, 2001 [1964]), pp. 83–90. Reprinted by permission of HarperCollins Publishers Ltd © 1964, J.R.R. Tolkien.

We should *expect* to find gospel resonance in the works of those from outside the church community. In fact, the Christian community can place constraints on an artist that put a damper on the Christian imagination. When I told my wife about my student's discovery that McDonagh wasn't a Christian, it didn't surprise her. I asked her why not. 'Well, there's no way a film like that would have been funded by Christians. It uses language they would find objectionable and asks questions they'd find too disturbing.' That's quite an indictment.

Christian films, if they are made for adults, shouldn't shy away from the way people actually talk. And they *certainly* shouldn't shy away from difficult questions or flawed characters.[28] The communal addiction to niceness, kitsch, triumphalism that cannot admit weakness – this can make it *harder* for Christians to create imaginative works that plant oases.

This is not to say that an artist's personal faith doesn't matter. But in terms of Christian imaginative resonance, the shape and texture of the imaginary world of the work matters more. Or, to put it paradoxically, just because it's made by a Christian doesn't mean that it will reflect the Christian imagination. Common grace means that the Christian imagination can – and will – be found in unexpected places.[29]

Though the antithesis between faith and unbelief is stark and has dire consequences for every individual, in creative works that line can be blurred by common grace, especially in its more pointed, gospel-shaped forms. When dealing with art, beware tidy binaries.

Take the case of Kieślowski. Though he claimed to be agnostic, his work offers hints and clues that he longed for grace and saw glimpses of it here and there. We explored this in *A Short Film about Love*, but it is true also of his other films. He was a man calling out for God who knew something of his goodness. In episode 9 of the *Dekalog* (1988), a man lies immobile in a hospital bed after a bungled suicide attempt. His wife finds the suicide note and thinks him dead. A hospital nurse calls the wife and holds the phone to the man's ear. The wife, relieved, says, 'God, you're *there*.' Her husband answers, 'I am.' The ambiguity of the wife's

28 Recall the ban from a Christian film studio on presenting Christian characters with any flaws that I discussed in chapter 4, footnote 27.

29 I argue this in my book *Popologetics*, pp. 65–71 and 231–234.

sentence – she could be addressing either her husband or God or both – and his austere answer, 'I am', an echo of God at the burning bush, combine, subtly invoking the presence of God.[30]

Or consider this more direct piece of evidence from the first episode of the *Dekalog* (1988). Pawel, the young son of an atheist father, is curious about God. His father is no help, so he asks a devout Catholic aunt:

PAWEL: Do you believe that God exists?
IRENA: Yes.
PAWEL: What is God?

Irena puts her arms around Pawel and pulls him close.

IRENA: What do you feel now?
PAWEL: I love you.
IRENA: Exactly. That's what God is.[31]

Some readers might scoff: Kieślowski here has reduced the living God to a vague feeling. I disagree. Besides being completely biblical (1 John 4:18),[32] it reveals something of Kieślowski's own painful journey and how he related to God through his films. He felt the absence of God keenly – understandable for someone growing up in a repressive atheist regime who developed into a talented filmmaker and had to begin his career in constant fear of the censors.

For Kieślowski, God was an absentee father, much like his own biological father, who suffered from tuberculosis. Kieślowski's family spent his early years travelling from sanatorium to sanatorium. Because the family was poor, his mother sent him and his sister away to children's sanatoriums to take advantage of the free room and board. At the age of 16, Kieślowski was sent away again, this time to a military-style fireman's college. He did not stay there long. In his late teens, his father passed

30 Recounted in Friedrich, 'Kieślowski's *Decalogue*'.

31 This dialogue and the character description are also taken from Friedrich, 'Kieślowski's *Decalogue*'.

32 'Dear friends, let us love one another, for love comes from God. Everyone who loves has been born of God and knows God. Whoever does not love does not know God, because God is love.'

away, at the age of 47.[33] Kieślowski experienced life alone in the world. Of course, given that life-context, God *would* seem terribly distant. No doubt he wanted to be Pawel, to experience the embrace of a divine Father.

The scene between Pawel and his aunt shows something else about Kieślowski's understanding of God and divine love. Because God is far away, his love manifests, is incarnated, primarily through other human beings. Without knowing it, Magda longed for God's love and forgiveness, as she longed for Tomek's love and forgiveness. Just as the aunt was God's arms for Pawel, so we are to be the arms of God for one other. This, too, is wholly biblical.[34]

The dark side of this insight is that, for Kieślowski, God remained distant. Even Christ, Immanuel, God with us, appears in his films only as the occasional statue hung on a church wall, rumours of grace, brief reflections of his presence. This does not mean that Kieślowski did not believe in a personal God or God had been reduced to a human emotion. As I mentioned above, in all of the *Dekalog* films, there is a peculiar character, a man in white, who observes the characters at key moments in their stories – generally, in moments of joy or just as they are about to break God's law or are dealing with the consequences of having broken God's law. The man in white is present, silent, attentive, but does not intervene. Perhaps this is Kieślowski's view of God: the silent observer who acts only through ordinary humans in ordinary circumstances. God *is* there, but not close enough to embrace, unless we understand the human embrace as somehow gesturing beyond itself to the love of God.

For these reasons, although Kieślowski labelled himself an 'agnostic mystic', he knew more than he was willing to articulate, at least in an interview. His hope, though attenuated, was not altogether snuffed out. And, as we have seen, that hope has a distinctly Christian shape. I wouldn't

---

33 Biographical materials drawn from Doug Cummings, 'Great directors: Kieślowski, Krzysztof', *Senses of Cinema*, no. 27 (July 2003), <http://sensesofcinema.com/2003/great-directors/Kieslowski>, and the Editors of Encyclopaedia Britannica, 'Krzysztof Kieślowski', Britannica, <www.britannica.com/biography/Krzysztof-Kieslowski>, accessed February and March 2023.

34 Of course, the danger is that human connection can become a *substitute* for God's love rather than a gracious conduit for his love. That line, too, sometimes becomes blurred.

call him a Christian. His was a twilit spirituality, dwelling somewhere between the darkness and the light.[35]

Still, his films show us something that other films in post-Christian culture do not. As uneasy as Kieślowski was with the absence and presence of God, he had absolutely no patience with the facile denial of the spiritual, the blithe, one-dimensional materialism that pervades so much of our cultural life now. He is an antidote to those attitudes, for he raises questions that make philosophical materialists uneasy.[36] Indeed, this is what makes the imaginary worlds of his films such fertile ground for engaging post-Christian imaginations.

---

[35] This is not uncommon in Europe, particularly for post-communist countries. Scepticism runs deep, resisting a quick embrace of faith.

[36] Philosophical materialism is the assumption that reality is only physical, that which can be measured using scientific instruments.

Conclusion to part 4: what ties them together?

My argument thus far is that the Christian imagination can engage and enter into conversation with post-Christian culture in a productive, positive, inviting way by planting oases. Oases work best when they display the tension between the darkness and light, between the cross and empty tomb, by revealing an aching desire. They work best when they neither trumpet their perspective nor hide it entirely but, rather, whisper, resonate and raise questions.

We have considered seven artists (or groups of artists) who exemplify that kind of oasis-building: blues musician Blind Willie Johnson, rapper-activist Sho Baraka, jazz singer-photographer Ruth Naomi Floyd, game developers Ryan and Amy Green and Josh Larson, storyteller-mythmaker J. R. R. Tolkien and filmmakers Krzysztof Kieślowski and Krzysztof Piesiewicz. They are nothing if not diverse. Indeed, that's the point: there is no single pattern for Christian artistic creativity. It can be fantastic, sober and reflective, playful, lamenting, full of protest and everything in between.

What ties them together is the tensive vision that recognizes the dark and that God's light will scatter – and has started scattering – the darkness, plus the nuance to articulate that vision in a way which commands attention without cliché, without becoming trumpeting propaganda or simply conforming to the vox populi. Both the tension and the balance are essential ingredients of an authentic Christian cultural creativity. Much contemporary Christian popular culture lacks that tension and balance, in large part because entertainment companies find it easier to market overly simplistic 'inspirational' products than works that challenge, delight, disturb, raise questions and cause us to think.

If Christians want their voices to be taken seriously within the cultural arena, we shall have to rethink our approach to engaging and producing our cultural works. We need an aesthetic and imaginative vision that is hard to dismiss, hard to turn away from. We need creative visions that ache, resonate and plant oases.

We are in desperate need of these kinds of imagination right now, yet they are in seriously short supply. Why? Because they don't just happen. They depend on relationships, networks and institutions to nurture them into being. They need the church, and the church needs them. This interdependence, how artists and church communities can serve to resource one another, is the topic of part 5.

Part 5

REFORMING, REFRESHING AND SUSTAINING THE IMAGINATIVE LIFE OF THE CHRISTIAN COMMUNITY FOR THE COMMON GOOD

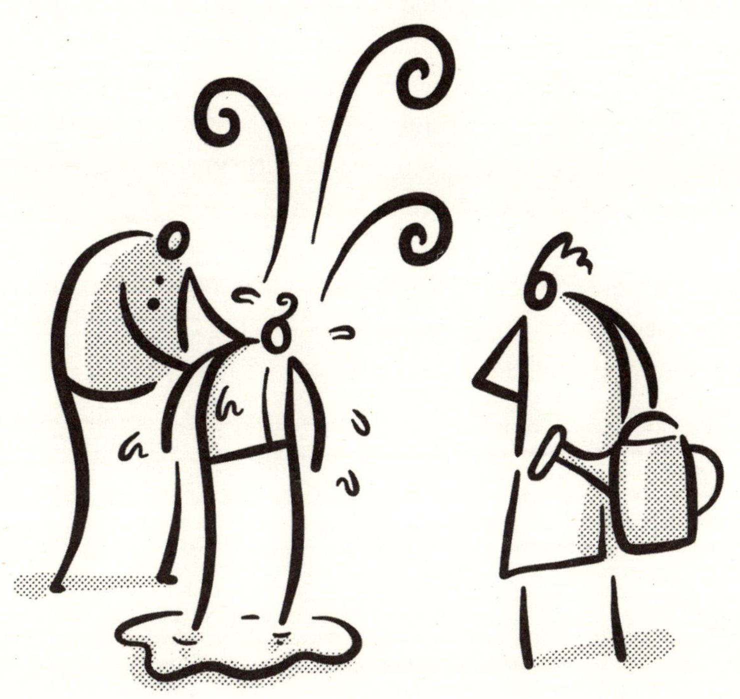

The argument thus far is, Christians should engage culture for God's glory and the common good, and they should start with the imaginary landscape.[1] We seek to set the imagination free.

That is no easy task. Christian creatives must swim against the stream, surrounded by strong currents that seek to confine imaginations by offering *false* freedoms. John Carpenter's 1988 film *They Live* portrays a world invaded by aliens who control humans through subliminal messages embedded in mass media. A homeless drifter finds a pair of sunglasses that expose these messages. Through the sunglasses, a computing ad on a billboard on a building transforms to the message 'obey'. Another billboard on the next building advertising a holiday featuring a bikini-clad model on a beach changes when viewed through the sunglasses to the message 'marry and reproduce'. He turns and, this time, through the sunglasses the sign for a men's apparel shop and a notice stuck in the window for a sale transform into the messages 'no independent thought' and 'consume'. Looking around, the sunglasses show him such messages everywhere. He sees magazine covers in front of another shop transform into many messages – 'buy', 'no thought' 'stay asleep', 'submit', 'obey'.[2]

The not-so-subtle point is that capitalism controls us all, puts us to sleep, makes us compliant.[3] Whether or not you agree with Carpenter (and Ray Nelson, whose short story inspired the film), it's an arresting image. What *feels* like normal life is guided, controlled, constrained by something; someone feeding our minds with messages of fulfilment, entertainment, enjoyment and contentment.

What if it wasn't merely a capitalist conspiracy but a *spiritual* conspiracy that engulfed everybody – *all* points of view along the political and economic spectrum? Neither the conservatives nor the liberals but simply

1 You may recall that the 'imaginary landscape' is my term for the fears, hopes and dreams shaped by creative works that we share as a cultural consciousness, our context for living.

2 The iconic 'Seeing the truth' scene can be found on YouTube: 'THEY LIVE Clip – Obey (1988)', JoBlo Movieclips, YouTube (26 August 2019), <www.youtube.com/watch?v=g4XiKChyK7A>, accessed February 2023.

3 This is a point made forcefully by the Frankfurt School theorists such as Theodor Adorno and Herbert Marcuse. See, for example, Herbert Marcuse, 'The new forms of control' in *One-Dimensional Man: Studies in the ideology of advanced industrial society* (London and New York: Routledge, 1991 [1964]), and Theodor Adorno, 'Culture industry reconsidered' in Paul Maris and Sue Thornham (eds), *Media Studies: A reader* (New York: New York University Press, 2nd edn, 2000 [1963]). I do not endorse all aspects of the Frankfurt School perspective, but they have some helpful and provocative insights.

all people living their lives, following false gods, paths that lead nowhere but away from God and towards death. Not the aliens among us but just us . . . with our built-in proclivity to reject the God who loves us.

Let's face it, both Christians and non-Christians need creative help to free our imaginations. We could all do with 'magic sunglasses' to give us a vision of something better, something more than what we have been fed up to now by the ad agencies, social media and the rest. It's too easy to go with the general flow – it seems so normal, so seductive, tugging our imagination in a not-so-Godward direction. We all need oases.

What can we do to promote long-lasting networks of creative oases that resonate and transform imaginations for the common good and God's glory?[4] How can we help to create an aesthetic and imaginative movement that will last? This doesn't happen automatically. The church has largely ignored the imagination, neglecting or exploiting creatives who work in the arts and entertainment industry, for generations. That damage will take generations to repair.

For a substantial change of direction, we need resources that will sustain both the creatives *and* those they serve. In this part, we will consider two such resources that we can draw on to reform, refresh and sustain our imagination: worship (the central focus of the Christian life and the place where imaginative transformation happens), and the relationship between creatives and the wider Christian community, how they can serve and support one another.

---

4 Oases are planted in other ways besides art and entertainment. Authentic, committed relationships, hospitality to the poor, standing against injustice, treating people with dignity in our business and work lives. See Philip Yancey's *Vanishing Grace: What ever happened to the good news?* (Grand Rapids, MI: Zondervan, 2014).

15

Worship as a resource for shaping imaginations

Introduction: worship as imagination training

Every act of creativity, if not done purely for pay, is an act of devotion.[1] Artists pour themselves into what they create. It's a struggle. It takes training. Even though it may be playful, it is not always or simply 'fun'. David Bowie, a fine painter as well as a songwriter and musician, said this about creating:

> It's the process, there's something in it that turns me to jelly, my heart and my mind . . . I can't explain it. It's a very strange feeling, and it's not particularly pleasant, either. I can't really say that I enjoy music or painting in quite that [way].[2]

Not every artist feels the same as Bowie. Some speak of great joy, even ecstasy. But for many (most?), it is exhausting, draining. Pouring oneself out in a risky, vulnerable act of devotion for all to see – like Mary breaking open her jar of nard to pour on her Master's feet – costs the artist something.[3] But doing so opens the imagination to what is most deeply true and beautiful.

How do artists keep going and avoid burnout? And what about the rest of us who aren't artists, but pour ourselves out in different ways? What

[1] Makoto Fujimura, *Art and Faith: A theology of making* (New Haven, CT, and London: Yale University Press, 2020), p. 117: 'Every act of creativity is an intuitive response to offer back to God what has been given to us.'

[2] David Bowie, interview with Charlie Rose, *The Charlie Rose Show*, PBS (31 March 1998). See clip on YouTube: 'David Bowie: To be an artist is to be "dysfunctional" (Mar. 31, 1998)', Charlie Rose, YouTube, <www.youtube.com/watch?v=t8CNhakfB7c>, accessed February 2023.

[3] Fujimura uses Mary's gesture recorded in Mark 14 as a model to understand the artist's role (*Art and Faith*, pp. 113–118). Given the costly, extravagant, repeated pouring out of oneself in creativity, it is no wonder that so many artists are prone to depression.

will renew, revive and reorientate the imagination in a way that leads to healthy and hopeful spirituality? If the imagination not only creates fictional worlds but also, in a sense, gives us the real world and makes it *our* world, then one cannot sustain a healthy faith without a healthy Christian imagination.

Christian imagination, the 'eyes of the heart', lets us see past the apparent reality of a world that proclaims (or simply assumes) God is dead, absent or irrelevant, and lets us see into what is truly real: that God is alive and active, redeeming a people for himself in this sin-twisted world, bringing healing and hope to the sick and hopeless. Suffering is real. Death is real. But because Christ lives and has triumphed on our behalf, they are not the final word. Christians are called to see the world, ourselves, one another, and God according to Reality. And that takes some imagination.

The imagination is an unruly beast that doesn't simply behave and obey our conscious commands. Ever found your imagination wandering where it ought not to go? How can we form it into something both God-honouring and healthy for us and those around us? The answer is worship. Not only is creativity an act of worship, but (paradoxically) worship is the primary resource for the imagination. Worship is where imagination is (and needs to be) repeatedly renewed and reformed.

What follows is not a guide for how to worship. Rather, it is a biblical meditation on and analysis of what worship is, and how it relates to developing and maintaining a healthy imagination.

The biblical paradigm for worship: Romans 12:1–2

The Bible's entire story arc has an irresistible momentum towards worship. Its purpose is to present God's being and character to us, which draws us into worship. From Genesis (creation sings God's glory) to Revelation (redeemed creation sings God's glory, but with added volume and beauty), and everything in between, it's all about God's glory. God's people and, eventually, all creation respond in worship.[4] Romans 12:1–2 helps us to

[4] Mike Cosper, *Rhythms of Grace: How the Church's worship tells the story of the gospel* (Wheaton, IL: Crossway, Kindle edn, 2013), loc. 294–150, chapters 1–4, present an overview of the Bible's story of worship initiated, corrupted and redeemed.

understand the relationship between worship and our imaginations, which need to undergo renewal and reformation in a fallen world.

> Therefore, I urge you brothers, in view of God's mercy, to offer your bodies as a living sacrifice, holy and pleasing to God – this is your spiritual [or reasonable] act of worship. Do not conform any longer to the pattern of this world, but be transformed by the renewing of your mind. Then you will be able to test and approve what God's will is – his good, pleasing and perfect will.

Here, Paul tells us four things about worship:

- worship's starting place: recalling God's grace to us;
- worship's mandate: a call to self-sacrifice;
- worship's struggle: it's a battle over the eyes of the heart;
- worship's result: renewed, discerning eyes of the heart.

Worship reorientates the imagination, recalibrates our seeing-as, setting us free from our slavery to self and refocusing our eyes on the God of grace. Let's look at each of these four things in turn.

Worship begins and is motivated by remembering the grace and excellence of God

> In view of God's mercy

Worship begins with the recollection that God has intervened to save his people. This is not something that we do naturally. Distracted by our daily routines, plans, meetings, what's for dinner – everyday stuff that forms the matrix we live in – we forget the bigger picture of who God is and what he has done for us.

But once we stop and dwell on the grace of God, we realize something: it doesn't make sense. It 'surpasses all understanding' (Philippians 4:7, NIV). Romans 12:1 refers us back to chapters 1–11: how the Father has shown grace to rebellious humanity through the sacrifice of his Son and the gift of the Spirit of adoption, confirming that we are now his children. Paul ends this recollection of grace with a doxology:

> Oh, the depth of the riches of the wisdom and knowledge
>   of God!
>   How unsearchable his judgments,
>   and his paths beyond tracing out.
> 'Who has known the mind of the Lord?
>   Or who has been his counsellor?'
> 'Who has ever given to God,
>   that God should repay them?'
> For from him and through him and for him are all things.
>   To him be the glory for ever! Amen.
> (Romans 11:33–36, NIV)

We tend to skip over such passages. 'Oh, Paul is getting excited again. Where does he calm down and start saying something interesting?' Do not miss his meaning here. As a conclusion to everything he has presented in Romans up to this point, he says: 'I don't get it. This is a mystery. God is a mystery. What did I do to deserve his overwhelming love?' The answer: 'Nothing.'

Dig deeper: it makes sense that it doesn't make sense. God is a being of a higher order than us. Surely we should expect him to do things that we find incomprehensible? Perfect wisdom might well look strange to us, but he *is* God – he does as he pleases. That is the gist of Isaiah 40 and Job 35 – 36, from which Paul takes his quote in Romans 11:33–36. Who has measured the mind of the Lord? Who really gets him? Not us, that's certain.

If you don't understand why God's grace doesn't make sense, try putting yourself in God's place. Imagine that you are the most excellent, dazzling being in existence. You have created all things as a reflection of that brilliance. Then the most wonderful parts of your creation turn against you, repeatedly doing stupid things that harm themselves and one another. They drag your name through the mud again and again and again. What would you do? I would say, 'Enough! I'll wipe out these annoying pests and start over.'

But God didn't do that.[5] Instead, he showed his perfect love and mercy by sending his Son, knowing full well unworthy scoundrels would kill him. But, in that act, he opened the door of life to unworthy scoundrels like us. That is astounding and confounding. As the English hymn says, 'What wondrous love is this? That caused the Lord of Bliss to bear the dreadful curse for my soul?'[6] The hymnwriter says, 'I just don't get it.' That recognition of unmerited grace is the beginning of worship – and the renovation of the imagination.

When confronted by the wild, inexplicable generosity of God, the imagination stretches. 'What sort of God would do something that overwhelming for an undeserving rebel like me?' Questions such as this are like opening a door on a sunny day after you've spent weeks in a dark room. Light floods in, enlightening the eyes of the heart. Those questions dazzle, and we were created to be dazzled.

Worship begins, then, by simply allowing reality – who God is and what he's done for us – to confront us, and praising God for it, letting gratitude and wonder feel the weight of his mercy. It sets the imagination free.

It also puts the next phrase of Romans 12:1–2 in a whole new light.

Worship is a call to sacrifice ourselves

> offer yourselves as a living sacrifice, holy and pleasing to God –
> that is your reasonable worship.

When we read 'offer yourselves as a sacrifice', we might say inwardly, 'OK, that's my Christian duty, so I guess I've got to do it. *Sigh*' Don't ignore the context: 'in view of God's mercy', in view of the fundamental 'it-doesn't-make-sense-that-God-is–so-ridiculously-gracious' that pours light into the eyes of our hearts. Once we understand the outrageous scope of God's mercy, we can respond, 'Well, *of course*, there is no appropriate response other than to glorify God and enjoy him for ever.'[7]

5 The flood didn't *completely* end us.
6 Lyrics by Alexander Means; traditional tune, circa 1811.
7 Answer to question 1 of the *Westminster Shorter Catechism*.

That is why Paul uses the word λογικήν (*logikēn*) or 'reasonable', the Greek root of the English word 'logical'. In the NIV and the ESV it is translated unhelpfully as 'spiritual').[8] God gave his only Son as a sacrifice of atonement (3:25) so that we, his enemies (5:8), might be cleansed and given the Spirit of adoption (8:15). *None* of that makes sense from a human perspective. It's too good to make sense. What *does* make sense (logically) is responding with a depth of gratitude whereby we give our whole selves back to him. Worship is the only reasonable response to dazzling mercy.

Let us examine Paul's phrase 'living sacrifice, holy and pleasing to God'. First, God's grace makes us 'holy,' (ἁγίαν, *hagian*), set apart, dedicated to God's service.[9] We are no longer our own; we have been set apart as God's special possession, people on a mission. We are like the tools used in temple service. You don't use the broom that sweeps up the ashes from the altar on your kitchen floor. It is special, reserved for a special task. Christians pursue moral purity because compromising with sin puts us fundamentally out of line with God's purposes for us. Repentance is realignment, turning away from sin to get back on task as his holy, set-apart instruments.

We are called not only to be holy but also to be 'pleasing' (εὐάρεστον, *euareston*) to God. Our motivation for everything we do should be, 'Does this please God?' rather than, 'Does this please me?' Not that we are called to a grey, joyless, ascetic existence, forbidden from enjoying ourselves. Paul affirms, 'For everything God created is good, and nothing is to be rejected if it is received with thanksgiving, because it is consecrated by the word of God and prayer' (1 Timothy 4:4–5).

God showers a great many gifts on his people: friendship, marriage, children, nature, art, music, films, video games and so on. But life isn't

---

[8] The phrase λογικήν λατρείαν (*logikēn latreian*) is hard to translate as both words carry multiple meanings. For a good discussion on why the ESV and NIV settled on 'spiritual worship' rather than 'reasonable service' (KJV), see a discussion thread hosted by Nate Eshelman, '"Spiritual worship" or "reasonable service" in Romans 12:1', *Puritan Board* (15 January 2010), <www.puritanboard.com/threads/spiritual-worship-or-reasonable-service-in-romans-12-1.57677>, accessed February 2023. My translation adopts the hybrid 'reasonable worship'.

[9] Walter Bauer, William F. Arndt and F. Wilbur Gingrich, *A Greek–English Lexicon of the New Testament and Other Early Christian Literature* (Chicago, IL: University of Chicago Press, 2nd edn, 1979), p. 9. It is similar to the Hebrew word קֹדֶשׁ (*qodesh*) that refers to sacred, set-apart things, places, persons and, supremely, God himself. See Francis Brown, S. R. Driver and Charles A. Briggs, *The New Brown–Driver–Briggs–Gesenius Hebrew and English Lexicon* (Peabody, MA: Hendrickson Publishers, 1979), pp. 871–872.

primarily or ultimately about them. The goodness and joy found in created things points to Someone greater who deserves our thanks and service. Each of us is set apart with a mission: living to please our Lord out of gratitude for the grace he has drenched us in. Given the fact that God has loved and continues to love us so lavishly, it shouldn't be a burden to live for his pleasure. It should be our joy.

Finally, we are called to be '*living* sacrifices'. Jesus offered himself for us as the sacrifice of atonement. His whole life was consumed on the cross, a full payment for our sin. God doesn't want or need sacrifices that die any more. He desires 'living sacrifices', but what does that mean? Consider the fate of a sacrificial lamb in the Old Testament. A priest would slit its throat and drain the blood. The lamb would be burnt or roasted on the altar. Its inner organs and bones would be burnt up and discarded. Its meat would be eaten by the priests and people. What remained? Nothing. The whole animal would be consumed, used up or dispersed.

In the same way, our lives, including our bodies,[10] are to be used for God, consumed completely by what is holy and pleasing to him. There should be no remainder, no private place where you say, 'Oh well, this part is for me – I don't have to please God *here*.' Given what God has done for us, we must offer all of our lives, every part, repeatedly.[11] *All* life is worship; nothing is to be held back.

Such worship frees us. It's strange, as burnt and consumed lambs aren't free. Are living sacrifices freer? Consider, however, that inevitably people will sacrifice themselves to something or someone. As the title of one of Bob Dylan's songs says, you 'Gotta serve somebody'.[12]

The real question is: in whose service is true freedom found? What will you spend yourself on? Raking in cash? Acquiring a hot partner? Establishing a shining reputation for your career? Bringing up perfect children?

---

10 John Murray notes that the force here is similar to Romans 6:13 – that is, to present our members as instruments of righteousness. A life dedicated to God is not ethereal or simply intellectual. It *must* include the body. See his *The Epistle to the Romans*, The New International Commentary on the New Testament (Grand Rapids, MI: Eerdmans, 1965), p. 111.

11 'Living' here may also mean 'permanent', as in 'ever-living', not a one-and-done offering. Murray, *The Epistle to the Romans*, p. 111.

12 Bob Dylan, 'Gotta serve somebody', *Slow Train Coming* (Columbia Records, CD, 1979), track 4.

No. Each of these will morph into a sort of slavery.[13] Rather, we are called to burn in the service of the one being in the cosmos actually worth burning up for, who has touched us and is transforming us with his everlasting love at the cost of his own Son's blood. *That* is freedom. We can be living sacrifices for him and, simultaneously, affirm that we have never been so free.

Not that we do this with perfect consistency. The tug of the world is insistent and it tugs hard. That is why ongoing repentance is a necessary ingredient for Christian life and worship. The freedom of being a living sacrifice is a freedom that must be repeatedly captured and recaptured. Only in this way do we become holy and pleasing to God.

However, worship isn't only about what you do with your body; it's also about what you do with your mind (that is, the imagination).

Worship is a battle for the believer's imagination, between being conformed and being transformed

> Do not conform any longer to the pattern of this world,
> but be transformed by the renewing of your mind.

The world keeps trying to pull us into conformity. 'World' (αἰῶνι, *aiōn*), here, does not mean planet earth, God's good creation.[14] Rather, Paul is referring to the organized system of rebellion against God's rule that has dominated and enslaved humans since Adam fell.[15] 'World' refers to the spiritual powers that dominate a fallen world.[16]

---

13 For explorations of how different aspects of 'secular' life take on sacred weight as idols we must satisfy (if we are to prove ourselves good enough), see David Zahl, *Seculosity: How career, parenting, technology, food, politics, and romance became our new religion and what to do about it* (Minneapolis, MN: Fortress Press, 2019). See also the excellent essay by Caleb Woodbridge, 'We are all worshippers', *Bigger on the Inside* (7 August 2022), <www.biggerinside.co.uk/p/we-are-all-worshippers>, accessed February 2023.

14 See chapter 1, under heading 'What is "the world"'.

15 See Ephesians 6:12: 'For our struggle is not against flesh and blood, but against the rulers, against the authorities, against the powers of this dark world (*aiōn*)'; and 2 Corinthians 4:4: 'The god of this age (*aiōn*) has blinded the minds of unbelievers'.

16 Murray (*The Epistle to the Romans*, pp. 113–140) interprets Paul's use of *aiōn* to mean temporal, in contrast to eternal. To be conformed to this *aiōn* is to be fixated on our own plans and projects to the exclusion of God's plan for eternity/the new creation.

Christ's incarnation, death, resurrection and giving of the Spirit has started something genuinely new: a 'new creation'. The world-age Paul refers to in verse 2 – the old world system – fights continually against what Christ has begun. Though Satan knows that defeat is inevitable and the new creation will eventually triumph, he wants to spoil as much as he can, while he can, starting with enslaving human beings who ought to be free.

Being 'conformed to the pattern of this world' means being integrated into that pattern (you can hear 'schema', or pattern, in the word). The Greek word συσχηματίζω (*syschēmatízō*) literally means to be pressed into a mould. Paul is referring here to how the world threatens to press us into its pattern of imagining that denies the relevance and reality of Christ's lordship.[17] The world pressures and seduces Christians into understanding reality and acting as though Jesus Christ doesn't matter – cookie-cutter imaginations, fitted with special glasses for the eyes of the heart that filter out the reality of God. Living out of a sense of godless reality kills godly worship at its roots, reshaping our imaginations so that we become enslaved to the pattern of this world.

Besides our sin-warped hearts, the pressure to conform comes from the imaginary landscapes that shape culture – the current against which we must swim. That is why we need a critical approach to popular culture (one of the more influential streams within culture). Left unchecked, these streams will press you into their moulds and reshape your imagination– and you will be none the wiser.

Paul tells us to 'stop being conformed to the pattern of this world' and, instead, 'be transformed by the renewing of your mind'. The verb (μεταμορφοῦσθε, *metamorphousthe*), 'be transformed', is passive. It is not something we do, but something that happens *to* us. We don't control our imaginations, but God can. Imaginative transformation is the Holy Spirit's work. Being connected to Christ through the Spirit makes us part of the new creation, the new order of things that is breaking into the old. With Spirit-awakened imaginations, we learn to see things anew, through a new lens (namely, verse 1, 'in view of God's mercy'). This, ultimately, is God's work.

---

17 J. B. Phillips translates this phrase as 'don't let the world squeeze you into its mould'. (Thanks to William Edgar for this.)

But we have a part to play. Else, why would Paul bother urging us to 'be transformed by the renewing of your mind'? We can and should actively seek imaginative renewal and transformation. Consider the parallel with 2 Corinthians 5:17: 'If anyone is in Christ, there is a new creation.' We don't re-create ourselves, but the new creation is something that we can pursue and participate in. It both happens to us *and* we need to go after it (in worship, broadly defined).

The verb tense of *metamorphousthe* is present continuous, so our transformation is not a 'one and done' deal; it must happen repeatedly, continually. The renewing of our minds and awakening of our imaginations by the Spirit is a *process* that we must pursue repeatedly, continually. We should seek transformation through the ongoing renewal of our minds through worship – offering our bodies as living sacrifices. To stop pursuing transformation is to be conformed to the pattern of this world. Drifting with the current is death; fighting against the flow – in tandem with and empowered by the Spirit – is life (cf. Romans 8:5–6).[18]

The imagination is the true arena of spiritual warfare, the tug of war between the world's power to mould us and God's power to renew us. This is a genuine 'battle for hearts and minds' – that is, for our imaginations, the way we see and feel reality. That battle is best fought through worship, the engine that renews our imaginations as we repeatedly apprehend the beauty and majesty of God.

The result of worship is discernment, an approval of the will of God

> Then you will be able to test and approve what God's will is – his good, pleasing and perfect will.

The result of worship is wisdom, discernment. The noun discernment, δοκιμάζειν (*dokimazein*), means 'to accept [something] as proved' after

18 Romans 8:5–6: 'Those who live according to the flesh have their minds set on what the flesh desires; but those who live in accordance with the Spirit have their minds set on what the Spirit desires. The mind governed by the flesh is death, but the mind governed by the Spirit is life and peace.'

testing.[19] The same word appears in Romans 1:28, in a negative form. There, the sinful mind considers the knowledge of God to be unworthy (as having failed the test), so it can be safely ignored.

Worship begins by recognizing God's dazzling mercy, responding in gratitude by laying your life open to God's service as a living sacrifice and renewing and reforming the eyes of the heart. Over time, that repeated renewal produces wisdom, discernment, a keenness of vision that harmonizes with *God's* imaginative vision of reality.[20] Through worship, Christians acquire a different outlook, a discerning seeing-as that perceives what God wants (for the world and our lives), and sees it as trustworthy, tested, 'good, pleasing, and perfect'. When we learn to see with our eyes of the heart, tuned to God's heart, the story God is writing seems right and good (even when it's hard).[21] Worship captures and recaptures our imaginations, reshaping them so we can wisely see what God desires.

God's desire is for us to live out lives of love for one another, and for the world. The process of worship – an awareness of grace that leads to sacrifice and an awakened imagination that leads to discernment – all of that flows outwards in love to those around us (see the rest of Romans 12). *True worship always flows out into the lives of others.* In this way, worship becomes an engine for the new creation, orientating God's people to love and serve others, becoming a healing force in a thousand different ways for this broken world.

This is a pattern throughout Paul's writings:

1 we recollect God's grace;
2 it awakens and renovates our imaginations (the way we feel and see the world);
3 from that awakening we move out into a life of love and service (see Table 15.1).[22]

---

19 Bauer, Arndt and Gingrich, *A Greek–English Lexicon of the New Testament and Other Early Christian Literature*, p. 202.

20 God has an imagination too. The difference between ours and his is that when he imagines, it is perfectly Real and True. God has ultimate authority – he calls the shots. Having imaginations that harmonize with his, approving his will as 'good and perfect' is simply 'seeing things the way they are'. Imaginations that agree with God's see Reality.

21 Hebrews 5:14 expresses a similar idea: through training we build up our ability to discern good and evil. Thanks to William Edgar for this connection.

22 All this applies both to individual private and corporate worship. For details on how to craft a worship service that engages the imagination, see Mike Cosper's *Rhythms of Grace*.

Table 15.1 The process of worship in Paul's writings

Passage	*We recall God's grace*	*God renews the imagination*	*Renewed imagination produces wisdom that discerns God's will and flows out into loving service of God and others*
Romans 12:1–2	'In view of God's mercy . . .' (see chapters 1–11)	'do not conform, but be transformed'	'Then you will test and approve God's will'; the rest of Romans (chapters 12–15)
Philippians 1:6, 9–10	'Being confident that he who began a good work in you will carry it on to completion'	'that your love may abound more and more in knowledge and depth of insight' (literally: 'every sensation')	'so that you may be able to discern what is best and may be pure and blameless for the day of Christ, filled with the fruit of righteousness' (see Galatians 5:22, fruit of the Spirit)
2 Corinthians 5:14–20	'For Christ's love compels us, because we are convinced that one died for all'	'So from now on, we regard no one from a worldly point of view . . . Therefore, if anyone is in Christ, there is a new creation'	God has given us the ministry of reconciliation and 'We are therefore Christ's ambassadors'
Titus 3:3–8	'At one time, we too were foolish, disobedient, deceived and enslaved by all kinds of passions and pleasures . . . But when the kindness and love of God our Saviour appeared, he saved us, not because of righteous things we had done, but because of his mercy'	'He saved us through the washing of rebirth and renewal by the Holy Spirit . . . so that we might become heirs having the hope of eternal life'	'I want you to stress these things, so that those who have trusted in God may be careful to devote themselves to doing what is good'

Worship as ritual: worship, body, imagination

Salmon subversively swimming upstream

Let us return to the idea of worship as a tug of war. Worship in a post-Christian world is *hard*, like salmon swimming upstream against the prevailing current of culture. The world threatens to press us into its mould, to standardize our imaginations to its dimensions. We resist precisely through worship. When we turn in hope to the living God, we necessarily turn away from all false gods, the fool's gold that the world calls treasure. Worship, in effect, is an act of dissent and subversion, a denial of the world's offered 'salvations'. Worship isn't simply a tug of war; it is a declaration of war.[23] Theologian John Witvliet asserts:

> Every time we sing praise to the triune God, we are asserting our opposition to anything that would attempt to stand in God's place. Every hymn of praise is a little anti-idolatry campaign . . . When we sing 'Praise God, from whom all blessings flow', we are also saying 'Down with the gods from whom no blessings flow.'[24]

The terrain on which this war is fought is the imagination, the seeing-as of God's people.

Worship is hard because *everybody* worships (only not the same things)

There is a good reason worship is a struggle: we aren't the only ones worshipping. James K. A. Smith calls us *homo liturgicus*, man the worshipper.[25] Not only Christians. Not only religious people. *Everybody* worships.

The modern word 'worship' derives from the Old English *weorthscipe*, 'to ascribe worth'.[26] 'To worship' means to ascribe worth, especially *ultimate* worth, to someone or something. Everyone does that: to ourselves,

---

23 Cosper brings this out beautifully in *Rhythms of Grace*, loc. 1522–1564.

24 John Witvliet, 'The opening of worship: Trinity' in Leanne Van Dyk, *A More Profound Alleluia: Theology and worship in harmony* (Grand Rapids, MI: Eerdmans, 2005), p. 12, quoted in Cosper, *Rhythms of Grace*, loc. 1930–1933.

25 See James K. A. Smith, *Desiring the Kingdom: Worship, worldview, and cultural formation*, Cultural Liturgies, Volume 1 (Grand Rapids, MI: Baker Academic, 2009), chapter 1.

26 Cosper, *Rhythms of Grace*, loc. 320.

to a lover, to a TV programme, to an ideal (science! humanity! freedom! the proletariat!), to family, to money and the things that it can buy, to career and reputation, to healthy living, to the Buddha, to spiritual transcendence. The list is endless. Everyone has something or someone they orbit around, like a planet orbits the sun – that thing (or things) which make life worth living, that get us out of bed in the morning. What makes Christians different is not *that* we worship, but *what* (or, rather, *who*) we worship. It is not the inclination but the orientation. All humans worship.

The reason worship is a tug of war over our imaginations is that we live in a world replete with competing objects of worship. It is like a coliseum full of burly gladiators, all pushing in different directions, vying for attention ('Are you not entertained?!').[27] Our world is awash with colourful, worshipful crosscurrents. Your pastor and worship leader have a lot of competition.

Advertisers steer worship in one direction, politicians in another, television and film writers and directors in yet another direction, the news in a further direction and academic celebrities such as Richard Dawkins or Neil deGrasse Tyson lead it in another still. Each direction invites you into its own worship-inscribed imaginary landscape, with visions of the way the world is and should be. Each has its own set of keys to salvation that will bring us to a brighter tomorrow, complete with aesthetics and specific worship ritual practices – watching television, listening to a podcast, scrolling through social media, playing a computer game, working a 60-hour week to secure that promotion and so on. It's chaos. How can the worshipping heart survive? How can the Christian imagination survive?

Worship is a thing of the body, of rhythm and repetition, not only the mind

The problem is even more complex than that: our imaginations and desires are stirred and shaped by repeated patterns of behaviour– what we do, not simply what we think. James K. A. Smith is emphatic that worship draws on imagination and habit.[28]

---

27 The reference is to Ridley Scott's film *Gladiator* (2000).

28 See his books *Desiring the Kingdom* and, especially, *Imagining the Kingdom: How worship works*, Cultural Liturgies, Volume 2 (Grand Rapids, MI: Baker Academic, Kindle edn, 2013). For a more accessible summary of these ideas, see his *You Are What You Love: The spiritual power of habit* (Grand Rapids, MI: Brazos Press, 2016).

Repeated behaviour (ritual) builds the 'muscle memory' that shapes the imagination. Buying the newest gadget at those modern cathedrals we call shopping centres; nationalistic 'worship' at a football game, standing for the national anthem as (in the USA) jets roar overhead, blessing us from the heavens; or Christian worship, singing hymns to God, reading Scripture, praying and sacraments – each of these ritual behaviours projects an imaginative vision of the world, both how it is and how it should be.[29] Thus, worship moulds our imaginations and desires à la Romans 12:2, steering our love, nurturing affection for certain objects, shaping our imaginary landscapes. Worship is a storyteller, weaving a web of narrative, a lived story that we participate in.

Smith asserts that worship largely bypasses conscious intellect: 'you might not love what you think'.[30] Hearts are formed not by a world view, what we think we know about the world, but by participation in 'liturgies', sacred or secular. Christians focus too much on knowing, not enough on ritual-formed devotion. We need to return to active, embodied, sense-filling worship.[31] We also desperately need the aesthetic resonance of artists and storytellers. Repeatedly inhabiting their imaginary worlds also shapes imaginations.[32] The eyes of the heart are formed through repetition and must be trained Godwards. Imagination needs practice.

But an account that locates the imagination (the seat of worship) in the body, largely bypassing the mind, concerns me.[33] Dead liturgy shows something of the dangers of worship that bypasses the mind. Yes, there is a virtue in going through the motions of worship, even when we don't feel like it or our minds are not particularly engaged.[34] When dead formal liturgy becomes the norm, however, when minds and intentional faith are bypassed, that can become toxic. Serbian priests baptized Kalashnikovs for ethnic cleansing *as worship*. Some American evangelical pastors have baptized nationalism and loyalty to a party that abuse the vulnerable *as*

29 See Smith, *Desiring the Kingdom*, chapter 3, and *You Are What You Love*, chapter 2.

30 Smith, *You Are What You Love*, p. 27.

31 The second half of Smith's *You Are What You Love* is filled with practical suggestions on building ritual-based worship environments in church, school, home and at work.

32 See Smith, *Imagining the Kingdom*, part 2.

33 See my 'Review article: *Imagining the Kingdom: How worship works* (James K. A. Smith)', *Foundations*, no. 65 (Autumn 2013), <www.affinity.org.uk/foundations-issues/issue-65-article-5-review-article-imagining-the-kingdom-how-worship-works--james-k-a-smith>, accessed February 2023.

34 See Smith, *Imagining the Kingdom*, section 'Redeeming repetition', chapter 4.

worship.[35] Christian ritual alone, apart from a mindful, intentional, biblical faith, cannot rightly form desire and imagination. Liturgy on its own does not lead to the kind of mercy-shaped imagination that should be formed within Christians.

Not that Smith ignores the need for intellectual intentionality (else, why write books that prescribe habits for the body to shape the imagination?),[36] but it remains underemphasized and underthematized. Smith is right: the repeated rituals and aesthetic forms we inhabit in worship *matter*, because they shape imagination. But this doesn't happen automatically, like exercise forming muscle. Rather, worship shapes the imagination, our 'seeing-as', through a two-way dynamic: it is a dialogue *between* body and mind, *between* preconscious desire and conscious reflection.[37] Yes, repeated behaviour shapes us (it pays to go to church when you don't feel like it). But we must add: no spiritual or imaginative formation happens unless the imagination engages intentional faith at some point.[38] The imagination is a bridge between mind and body, and we must attend to both.

One last thought on worship and its imagination-shaping power: expect to find God-honouring worship in unexpected places. Smith presents secular cultural liturgies as purely forces that *deform* the Christian imagination. That is, he rejects the theological concept of 'common grace'. Too often, it has served as an excuse to baptize a distorted status quo, to turn a blind eye to ungodly imagination-forming practices.[39] True enough, but let us now oversimplify – God's common grace still shines in his world.[40]

---

35 Smith's *Awaiting the King: Reforming public theology*, Cultural Liturgies, Volume 3 (Grand Rapids, MI: Baker Academic, Kindle edn, 2017) takes on the topic of distorted liturgies that support Christian nationalism.

36 Smith preserves a place for conscious intellectual reflection towards the end of *Imagining the Kingdom* (loc. 4036) but, after insisting for the whole book that conscious reflection serves little purpose other than to take stock of what the preconscious, embodied imagination has already given us, it's little more than an aside. Smith tries to counterbalance an unhealthy 'conceptualism' among Protestants, but perhaps the pendulum has swung too far the other way.

37 Recall chapter 6, under heading 'Imagination is the arena of dialogue between body and mind'.

38 See Matthew C. Bingham, 'Brains, bodies, and the task of discipleship: Re-aligning anthropology and ministry', *Themelios*, vol. 46, no. 1 (April 2021), <www.thegospelcoalition.org/themelios/article/brains-bodies-and-the-task-of-discipleship-re-aligning-anthropology-and-ministry>, accessed February 2023.

39 Smith, *Awaiting the King*, loc. 145–154, p. ix.

40 Recall our discussion at the end of chapter 16 on common grace in 'Christian' cultural works made by non-Christians, such as Kieślowski.

If we are to be Christ's ambassadors (2 Corinthians 5:20), shouldn't we engage secular 'liturgical' practices in a way that both appreciates their goodness *and* reveals their distortion, showing how the gospel subverts and fulfils what is good in their desires?[41] If secular culture is nothing but a collection of dangerous ritual seductions away from God, what is left but to retreat from culture into a monastery to try to preserve the purity of our own imaginations?[42] Rather than a strategy of spiritual self-protection, we need an holistic engagement with the world. We can and should involve ourselves with non-Christian culture without compromising our faith. Critical reflection – appreciating grace and letting it inspire worship, exposing the frailty of idols and letting that inspire worship – has an important role here.[43]

Worship wars: pushing back against the formative influence of the rage machine by learning to lament

Smith speaks of worship as a set of rituals, repeated acts that project a vision of the world that forms our imaginations and desires. They mould us either Godwards or away from God's heart. Confession time: here's what this looks like for me.

All my life, I have found the world a frustrating place. Not only does it not go the way I'd like, but often it doesn't even go the way it *should.* I write this during a pandemic, when hundreds of thousands of lives have been lost that shouldn't have been. A few months back, there were massive protests in the USA against yet another police killing of an unarmed black human being. The wrongness of it all makes me boil with anger, accompanied by a

41 On the gospel as the 'subversive fulfilment' of other religions, see Daniel Strange, '"For their rock is not as our rock"': The gospel as "subversive fulfilment" of the religious Other', *For Their Rock Is Not as Our Rock* (Nottingham: Apollos, 2014), chapter 7. For the subversive fulfilment of secular popular culture, see my book *Popologetics: Popular culture in Christian perspective* (Phillipsburg, NJ: P&R, 2012), chapters 10 and 11.

42 Though Smith seems to recommend a quasi-monastic withdrawal in the first and second books in his 'Cultural Liturgies' series, *Desiring the Kingdom* (pp. 91, 126 and 209–210) and *Imagining the Kingdom* (loc. 3307–3365), the third book, *Awaiting the King*, envisions a much more robust engagement with culture (especially political culture). See also his 'Reforming public theology: Two kingdoms, or two cities', *Calvin Theological Journal*, vol. 47 (2012), pp. 122–137, especially pp. 131 ff. He argues that Christians should work towards the common good, even finding common cause with secular allies, but always with a dose of suspicion. The 'peace' of the City of Man can never truly be called peace (as the City of God would know it) because it is linked to false worship.

43 See Arturo Azurdia's wonderful booklet, *Connected Christianity: Engaging culture without compromise* (Fearn, Ross-shire, Scotland and Bridgend, Wales: Christian Focus with Bryntirion Press, 2009), and my *Popologetics*, chapter 4, especially pp. 74–76.

deep sense of impotence in the face of problems too big for me to do much about. It's a mindset I've been training and massaging my whole life.

As a scrawny, hyperactive, not particularly athletic kid at primary school, I was deeply invested in kaiju (Japanese giant monster) films. I was/am especially fond of Godzilla. The way he (repeatedly) stomped Tokyo, defeated King Ghidorah or whoever challenged him, dazzled me. I didn't simply watch; I *inhabited* that world. I drew pictures, imagined scenarios, landscapes laid waste by the King of the Monsters. For a powerless kid, dreaming about stomping opponents and whole cities was nectar of the gods. My imagination learnt (without me being able to articulate it) that violence *is* catharsis, a release for pent-up rage that can change the world.

Now that I'm an adult, I still have a deep affection for kaiju films, and Godzilla in particular. I loved *Pacific Rim* (2013). I now find rage-release in other forms as well. We watch a lot of *shōnen* anime, with its depictions of unjust tyrants being trounced in single combat by righteously enraged heroes, the world repeatedly cleansed by violence. Social media seems designed to deliver a never-ending stream of anger-inducing news. Twitter is a rage-machine. The morning news is a rage-machine. In my unguarded moments, I daydream of Godzilla stomping injustice out of existence. If only these problems weren't so complex and ingrained. Surely, he could stomp on just a few of the more odious offenders and the world would become a better place, right? Why doesn't God act more like Godzilla and cleanse the world with holy violence? Where's the -zilla, God?

One day he will (tempered, thankfully, by mercy). But, until then, I find myself stuck, impotent, angry, depressed and alarmingly short on love for enemies (Matthew 5:44). If I allow myself to stay here, I know what will happen. I will conform to the world's mould. I will become a bitter person incapable of seeing God's hand anywhere or in anything. This is the power of repeated rituals like checking my Twitter feed or listening to the morning news again and again and again. It feels like an obligation, obeisance to FOMO. I need the feed to stay informed, engaged, involved.[44]

44 Lying behind FOMO are built-in 'persuasive technologies' that entice users to keep scrolling, posting, checking notifications, seeking the dopamine hits that come from other users' responses to my posts and so on. See child psychologist Richard Freed, 'The tech industry's war on kids: How psychology is being used as a weapon against children', *Medium* (12 March 2018), <https://medium.com/@richardnfreed/the-tech-industrys-psychological-war-on-kids-c452870464ce>, accessed February 2023. These technologies manipulate adults as well.

But that repeated ritual of feed-checking and staying in the loop comes at a price. It reinforces an imaginary landscape in which God remains distant, and outrage, injustice and schadenfreude rule. I can remind myself, intellectually, that the Bible affirms God is *still* in control, but my heart doesn't buy it. Sometimes I'm too entrenched in a land of rage and despair to rest in the peace of God.

What is to be done? Fight fire with fire, ritual against ritual. In this way, a new landscape can take shape – one formed by lament and hope rather than bitterness and despair. But how? I practise counter-rituals that remind me who's in charge even when I don't understand his ways or his timing.

- I use Scripture reading to 'frame' my day. I read and pray once in the morning (before I check my phone), and again as one of the last things I do before I sleep. I want the Bible to frame the way I experience life every day.
- Before we listen to the news at breakfast, we worship using a devotional called *Seeking God's Face* that draws from the Bible and Reformed confessions, as well as giving us topics to pray about.[45]
- Saturday mornings hold an important place in our weekly rhythm. We schedule nothing before noon, get up late and move slowly. One of us makes a special breakfast (pancakes, French toast, eggs Benedict) and we sit down as a family and take . . . our . . . time. It is an important moment of rest and enjoying being with one another.
- We look forward to attending our Czech church (we live in Prague). We deeply appreciate the experience of worshipping and taking the Lord's Supper with Christians who understand lament, having survived decades of communist rule. In post-communist times, Czech Christians comprise a tiny minority in a majority atheist country. We sing a number of songs together that express lament, tears, suffering and sorrow – not something most conservative Protestant American churches do (with the exception of the black church, which has a long history of lament songs).

[45] Philip F. Reinders, *Seeking God's Face: Praying with the Bible through the year* (Grand Rapids, MI: Baker Academic, 2013).

- Sunday is a day of rest, Sabbath, abstaining from work, not fretting about the week ahead. Instead, we use it for prayer and relaxation.
- On Sunday evenings, we set aside time to express gratitude to God for his gifts to us during the past week and ask him for what we need for the week to come.
- We try to make prayer a reflex throughout the week. When someone is upset by a turn of events, we ask, 'Can we pray about this now?' We may not have the power to change the thing that's bothering us directly, but we know someone who does.
- Occasionally, when the darkness of the world presses in too much, we will take a break from the news and social media. Instead, we listen to music to remind ourselves of what a beautiful place the world can be.
- We enjoy our evening entertainment and try to be intentional about finding the grace offered in each song, game or TV programme – as well as the idols involved. If we find compelling creative works by Christians, we share what we've found (currently the band half•alive and TV series *The Chosen*). Entertainment, properly understood, should lead to worship.[46]
- My wife and I try to take quarterly retreats to discuss our relationship, our spiritual health, our kids, our careers, the whole pattern of our lives together. And we pray over it all. No noise, no social media, just focus on God and each other. Being intentional about this helps us to stay sane.

These ritual interventions are meant to reshape our desires and imaginations. It is our way of living into an imaginary landscape that places God's love and power squarely at the centre, that spills out into empathy for others (even when we disagree with them) and learns how to lament.[47]

Lament is a tensive vision, of walking in the darkness while holding on to the hope that God knows what's going on, loves his people in the middle of it all and is active in accomplishing his purposes. A healthy dose of

46 See my book, *Popologetics*, pp. 74–76.

47 Makoto Fujimura calls us to 'comingle with Christ's tears' that he wept at the death of Lazarus (John 11:35). See Fujimura, *Art and Faith: A theology of making* (New Haven, CT, and London: Yale University Press, 2020), p. 112.

lament at intervals is a big part of walking by faith, not sight (2 Corinthians 5:7). In this way, my imagination is progressively being re-formed, weaned from flashes of hot anger and fantasies of cleansing violence. God *will* cleanse the world in his time, but it's not my job to invoke or provoke it. It's my job to grieve when there is pain, do what I can, pray and hope in God's power and love to change things for the better.

Conclusion: worship recharges and reorientates the imagination

Worship is the place where our wandering imaginations need to go to be re-centred, recalibrated and reorientated towards Reality. The Christian imagination needs times of private and corporate worship to counterbalance the tug of the world. Engaging the post-Christian world with integrity and creativity begins with worship.

One final thing. I began this chapter by talking about the exhausting life of an artist. Worship is the place where artists can come to recharge their imaginations in a Godwards direction. But artists, as workers in the fields of imagination, are also key resources for worship. Worship isn't solely about thinking; it should engage the senses and reshape stubborn or tired imaginations. Who better to enrich the service we render to God and one another in worship than creatives? Not only musicians but also visual artists, video creators, dancers and those talented in drama.[48]

This is not a recipe book on how to employ artists in worship. Pastors and worship leaders will need Spirit-guided wisdom to reflect on how patterns laid out in the Bible should apply today. Regardless, creatives should be encouraged to refresh the imagination of other creatives and the church as a whole. This is their distinctive offering to God.[49]

In the next chapter, we shall explore the special place that artists have in the life of the imagination in Christian communities. Beyond worship, they are essential for building bridges of imagination between church

---

[48] Sitcom writer James Cary recounts hearing Broadway actor Bruce Kuhn recite the Gospel of Luke by heart. Kuhn's training as an actor allowed him to bring out facets of meaning that are often missed when non-actors recite Scripture in worship. See Cary, *The Sacred Art of Joking* (London: SPCK, 2019), p. 90. Cary is an able (and funny) guide to humour's mystery and imaginative power in the life of faith.

[49] Wherever possible, creatives should be paid for their efforts, just as pastors should be (and normally are) paid to preach. Presenting a gift for God's service doesn't mean working for free.

and world. They are especially gifted at serving God's people and the wider community to focus imaginations, build oases. And the wider Christian community of non-artists has an essential role in supporting creatives, as they support us.

16

The artist as a resource for the church and the world: zookeeper of the imagination and loving cultural guerrilla

Introduction: why creatives matter to the Christian community

All God's people have imaginations, but not all imaginations are built the same. Some are bursting with ideas, some are unruly, some are flagging and tired, weak and unhealthy. In chapter 15, we explored worship as a means to revivify and re-form the imagination. This chapter considers another important resource for the Christian imagination: artists.[1]

Artists are specially gifted, trained and called to work in the territory of the imagination, shaping culture through various media. They engage the imaginations around them, coaxing, provoking, challenging, comforting, correcting and enlivening it. The church's cultural witness relies on them. We need to understand the role of artists as imaginative resources in both Christian communities and the wider world. When God calls Christians as cultural creatives, what is he calling them to?

But first we need to debunk certain popular myths about the role of the artist that are currently circulating in our society.

Myth-busting: not splendid isolation but community service

One dominant myth about the role of the artist is best summed up in Samuel Taylor Coleridge's famous opium-induced poem 'Kubla Khan'.

---

[1] By the terms 'artist' and 'creative' I mean anyone working in the fields of the arts and entertainment.

The poem describes an enchanted kingdom featuring a 'sunny pleasure-dome with caves of ice' floating in the air, while the earth below buckles as fountains force themselves through the frozen earth, hurling chunks of rock into the air. All in all, a place of serenity and chaotic torment paradoxically bound together. As the poem draws to a climax, the poet writes himself into the scene. He reminisces about an 'Abyssinian maid' playing a dulcimer (his muse perhaps), whose beautiful music entices him into his own ecstatic song as he tries to reconnect with her lost melody. At the end of the poem, the poet himself is transformed:

> Could I revive within me
> Her symphony and song,
> To such a deep delight 'twould win me
> That with music loud and long
> I would build that dome in air,
> That sunny dome! those caves of ice!
> And all who heard should see them there,
> And all should cry, Beware! Beware!
> His flashing eyes, his floating hair!
> Weave a circle round him thrice,
> And close your eyes with holy dread,
> For he on honey-dew hath fed,
> And drunk the milk of Paradise.[2]

That is the final image of the poem: the poet, eyes flashing and hair floating, surrounded by protective spells (perhaps protecting the poet from interruption by those outside the magic circle or protecting the audience from flashes of the poet's sacred energy) as he recites his prophetic vision of the sublime.

Nineteenth-century Romanticism installed this archetype in the Western psyche:[3] the artist as a breed apart, a blessed creature, a solitary

---

2 Samuel Taylor Coleridge, *Christabel; Kubla Khan, a Vision; The Pains of Sleep* (London: John Murray, 1816), <www.poetryfoundation.org/poems/43991/kubla-khan>, accessed February 2023.

3 Romanticism was/is an intellectual and artistic backlash against the Enlightenment's Cult of Reason, which they believed had drained the mystery and vitality from human life. The Romantics sought/seek to restore this lost element by focusing on passion and emotion through art and poetic inspiration.

visionary genius who has passed through the veil of appearances to naked Reality (or his creative vision of Reality). From thence the artist returns to us, bringing illumination and edification to us mere mortals. It is easy to see why, in European Romanticism, art effectively replaced religion as that which gives us access to Truth. Naturally, the poet or artist plays the starring role of the inspired prophet.

Though not always sketched as boldly as in 'Kubla Khan', this image of the artist still influences the way we think about creative culture-makers (both high art and popular) as solitary geniuses who have some privileged access to truth and wisdom. Artists might be eccentric and a little crazy, but inspired truth-seekers sometimes act in ways that we ordinary types cannot fathom or follow. That is why our culture treats famous musicians, actors, writers, directors or producers as special, as demigods. Consider how the graves of Elvis Presley, Kurt Cobain,[4] Jim Morrison, Stevie Ray Vaughan, Bruce Lee and James Dean have become shrines (Dean's gravestone, for example is covered with decades of lipstick kiss marks) to the sacred, holy places, for these artists captured the sublime and delivered it to us in song or on the silver screen. They had drunk the milk of paradise, and we drew a circle round them thrice and closed our eyes in holy dread.

The Christian artists I've talked to refuse to traffic in such pretence. They claim no such privileged access to the truth as we Christians all share the same revelation. Rather, they recognize that they are servants called to the community of other servants. They don't practise 'art for art's sake'.[5] Rather, they practise 'art for God's sake',[6] and for the sake of the imaginative life of their communities and beyond. Christian artists have gifts that they long to share with others – certain ways of encouraging, clarifying, challenging and healing through their chosen media. What they have, they share willingly.[7]

---

4 Cobain has no actual grave because he was cremated. Instead, he has his own memorial park in Aberdeen, Washington state.

5 French philosopher Victor Cousin coined the phrase to indicate that art needs no justification. It is its *own* justification. There's a grain of truth here – we must guard against 'instrumentalizing' art, enslaving it to serve as a go-between for our pet ideologies. Yet, in God's world, no-one and nothing is purely self-justified.

6 See Philip Ryken, *Art for God's Sake: A call to recover the arts* (Phillipsburg, NJ: P&R, 2006). For a survey of the freedom, pleasures and purposes of art, see Christian illustrator Seth T. Hahne, 'Art: What is it good for?' *Christ and Pop Culture* (13 May 2019), <https://christandpopculture.com/art-what-is-it-good-for>, accessed February 2023.

7 That is not to say they share it for *free*. We must remember that artists need to make a living. For practical advice about the relationship between churches and artists, see Philip Ryken,

Christian poet Wendell Berry wrote, 'The arts, traditionally, belong to the neighborhood. They are the means by which the neighborhood lives, works, remembers, worships, and enjoys itself.'[8] This is a singularly healthy way to view the arts and creativity. Christian art is not done in isolation, nor is it primarily about self-expression and self-focused. Rather, it is primarily other-focused, 'a service to fellow creatures and to God'.[9]

In contemporary culture where musicians, producers, directors, television and film stars are marketed as objects of worship, we have very nearly forgotten that. Christian artists aren't rock stars – or, rather, they shouldn't be. They are sinners, forgiven and redeemed, who are now beckoned by the Lord into a life of serving their communities (both Christian and non-Christian) through their art. Christian artists put on no airs. Their eyes don't flash. They live in a no honey-dew zone.

Technique is never neutral, or, 'mind your mannerisms'

That is not to say Christian art has nothing to do with self-expression. Christian art is incarnational, like Christ himself. Jesus had a specific human personality that was woven into everything he did, everything he was. So, too, are an artist's works. A major aspect of being an artist is finding your 'voice' by honing your craft.

But it is not meant to be a voice in the wilderness. Artists need communities. As Calvin Seerveld reminds us, artists can find inspiration and guidance in their artistic traditions rather than by isolating themselves.[10] Artists need not reinvent the wheel – they can find their voice *through* their specific artistic traditions, whether that tradition is the blues, abstract painting, science-fiction storytelling or film noir cinematography.

(note 7 *cont.*) 'How to discourage artists in the church', The Gospel Coalition (27 May 2013), <www.thegospelcoalition.org/article/how-to-discourage-artists-in-the-church>, and Sørina Higgins, 'The church's role in art', *Comment* (27 May 2011), <www.cardus.ca/comment/article/the-churchs-role-in-art>, both accessed February 2023.

8 Wendell Berry, 'Christianity and the survival of creation' in *Sex, Economy, Freedom and Community: Eight essays* (New York: Pantheon Books, 1993), p. 113.

9 Berry, 'Christianity and the survival of creation', p. 113.

10 Calvin Seerveld, 'Letter to a young artist' in Michael Card, *Scribbling in the Sand: Christ and creativity* (Downers Grove, IL: InterVarsity Press, 2002). Letter available online at the TECHNO-evangel, 'A letter to Christian artists', Venturopolis: <https://venturopolis.wordpress.com/2009/06/02/a-letter-to-christian-artists>, accessed February 2023.

Once artists feel reasonably confident in that voice, comfortable in their own artistic skin, they must pay attention to the consequences, the imaginary world projected by their art. Art projects a 'world of the work' for other people to visit and perhaps dwell in, at least for a little while.[11] Artists should reflect on questions such as what *sort* of world am I creating? How is grace woven into my imaginary world? Can people, Christian and non-Christian, connect with that grace or will it alienate them? Am I subtly establishing any idolatries or undermining them? Am I revealing truth or obscuring it? Am I honouring those made in his image or caricaturing them?[12]

Communications and media scholar Quentin Schultze has an apt name for this awareness: 'symbolic stewardship'.[13] Just as God has called humans to a place of authority over his world, to manage its physical resources creatively and wisely (Genesis 1:28–29), so he has also appointed us to manage the symbolic resources through which we communicate. Symbol shepherds are we, and we must be mindful of how we deploy and employ the symbols at our command as culture creators.

Whatever the medium, technique is never neutral. Artists can create in a way that speaks the truth in love and honours God by treating all image-bearers with compassion and dignity. If not, they may do it in ways that exploit, manipulate and lie. Of course, which techniques lead to truth and love, and which lead to manipulation and exploitation vary from medium to medium, from genre to genre and gesture to gesture.

This is a matter not only of craft but also Spirit-guided wisdom and keeping an open ear to the Christian community. Fellow Christians have wisdom to share if artists have the humility to hear it – another argument against the 'splendid isolation' view of how artists work. The artists and the Christian community need each other, though they often act as though they don't.

---

11 Paul Ricoeur, 'The hermeneutical function of distanciation' in *Hermeneutics and the Human Sciences*, ed. and tr. John B. Thompson (Cambridge and New York: Cambridge University Press, 1981), especially pp. 140–144.

12 This last question drives Eleanor Nickel's *Christian Popular Culture: From* The Chronicles of Narnia *to* Duck Dynasty (Eugene, OR: Wipf & Stock, 2021). Do the artists involved take the time and effort to create believable, three-dimensional characters or do their works fall prey to a whole host of racist and/or sexist stereotyping?

13 Quentin Schulze, 'Symbolic stewardship: The meaning and purpose of human communication' in *Communicating for Life: Christian stewardship in community and media* (Grand Rapids, MI: Baker Academic, 2000).

The Christian artist as zookeeper of the imagination

Why does the church need artists? How exactly can they serve the Christian community? Christian artists are, above all, workers in the field of the imagination. Through their chosen media, they present imaginary worlds, visions into which they invite others from their communities to come and bathe in this other reality. Artists invite others, quite literally, into their world views, their creative takes on reality. Artists provide oases, spaces for guided imaginative play and reflection. As Seerveld puts it:

> To become an artist means you become a professional imaginator in order to help your handicapped unimaginative neighbour. Our artistic profession is meant to give voice, eyes, ears, and tactile sense to those who are underdeveloped toward such rich nuances of meaning in God's creation.[14]

When I think of the role of the Christian artist, I think about zookeepers. Have you ever been to a poorly run zoo? Take note of the condition of the animals. They look scruffy, half-starved. Some pace restlessly in their cages. Others lie listlessly, worn-out eyes surveying the world beyond the bars.

I remember visiting a zoo and watching a lemur walking anxiously in a line that measured about 0.6 m (2 feet) in the corner of a much larger cage. Endlessly it paced, back and forth, back and forth, like a machine. I asked one of the staff about the animal's behaviour. He told me that, before the zoo acquired him, the lemur had been kept in a cage that was too small for it and so had developed this nervous condition. Now it paces endlessly as though it were still in the small space that it had become accustomed to. It cannot utilize the full scope of its new home.

Christian imaginations can be like that. They, too, can become scruffy and half-starved. They, too, can become restless, straying from God towards idols. Or they can become lazy and listless, unable to quite catch a glimpse of the beauty of their Saviour and his creation. They are, after

14 Seerveld, 'Letter to a young artist'.

all, surrounded by a secular culture that repeatedly insists God is simply an illusion that we must put behind us, an authoritarian myth from a bygone era. Christian imaginations can become hemmed in, told to pace these dimensions and go no further. In time, they become accustomed to their cages, unable to go beyond the boundaries imposed on them. Our imaginations are told by non-Christian popular culture to satisfy themselves with idols – sex, consumer goods, holidays, good times with friends. It is the best we can hope for.

The job of Christian artists, as world-weavers for the imagination, is to provide spacious habitats for these abused beasts, imaginary worlds that defy the limits imposed by post-Christian culture, worlds that show things as they are. These worlds underscore the bizarre ugliness of idolatry, the surprising beauty of grace suddenly unveiled, mercy found under the unlikeliest of rocks.

When all is said and done, the call to be a Christian artist is a pastoral one: to nourish and encourage their neighbours' animal imaginations to grow strong and healthy. Artists are called to expand habitats for the imaginations of those around them, enriching the diet of those imaginations with healthy doses of clear-eyed truth, arresting beauty, playfulness, poignant sorrows and hilarious joys. It need not always be gentle, but it does need to be *real*. Healthy imaginations, like healthy horses, run and jump and kick down the walls that our mainstream culture throws up against the knowledge of the wild beauty of God. Christian artists are called to exercise these imaginations until they are fit enough to glorify God and enjoy him as we were made to do.

The call to subversion, or, 'loving like a guerrilla'

Zookeeping for the imagination is an implicitly subversive activity. Christian artists, like all Christians, have a radically different first love: a different vision of what the world is and should be. We Christians celebrate or mourn different things from those mourned by the mainstream culture. Even when we celebrate or mourn the same things, it is for different reasons, stemming from different affections and loyalties. The Christian artistic imagination cannot help but be subversive.

Words such as 'subversion' often make conservative Christians nervous. Aren't we supposed to be good citizens, obeying the magistrate (see

Romans 13:1–6)? Doesn't 'subversion' mean sneaking around to plant bombs and sabotage the powers that be? In a word, *yes*. As theologian William Edgar puts it when he asks Christians what the aim of cultural engagement is: 'Is there not a place to undermine the dominant powers and exercise divine power to dismantle strongholds? (2 Corinthians 10:4)'[15]

Obviously, Christians have no business planting physical bombs that kill people, whether to cause terror or for other reasons. According to 2 Corinthians 10:3–5, our struggle isn't like that. Rather, the business of Christian artists is to plant *spiritual* bombs, not to terrorize people, but to jar them out of complacency, blast open new territories for the imagination. Christian artists are at their best when they are exploding myths, capturing eyes and ears and turning them towards the terrifying beauty of the God of glory, or towards the unsettling ugliness of sin and idolatry, or towards the gentle whisper of a rumoured redemption. From the perspective of a mainstream that is busy suppressing the knowledge of God (Romans 1:18–23), such work is annoying at best, dangerously subversive at worst. From the perspective of Christian artists, there is no other way to love the world *but* through subversion.

We must make an important distinction here. In chapter 2 I argued that a culture-war model only sows resentment in a post-Christian culture. When I use warlike words – subversive guerrillas, exploding myths, spiritual bombs and so forth – I am attempting to reflect and expand on what the Bible says about spiritual warfare in 2 Corinthians 10 and elsewhere. But make no mistake, this is *not* about 'winning the culture back for Christ'. Culture is not a thing to be 'won', like a trophy. Culture is not a war, but a conversation. It's a network of works, customs, souls and bodies that need to be loved and, sometimes, lovingly disrupted for their own good and for God's glory. Loving like a guerrilla means loving our neighbours and broader communities, entering into a cultural conversation in ways that subvert expectations, surprise through goodness and beauty, and end up overturning taken-for-granted destructive and degrading cultural patterns. Artists are called to be prophets, summoning a lethargic, wayward people back to God's truth. True prophets are always subversive.

15 William Edgar, 'The threat of culture', posted on the now defunct Gospel and Culture Project's website, March 2009.

Quentin Schultze distinguishes between priestly and prophetic media.[16] The media acts as a 'priest' when it affirms the status quo, politely blessing our normal life events and rhythms – birth, marriage, death and so on. A priestly media tells us that everything will turn out for the best, that our way of thinking is right and good. It exists to comfort us, to boost our self-esteem, to assure us that nothing need change for us to obtain the good life.

In a consumer-orientated culture, a priestly media predominates. A comforting myth sells better than a disturbing truth.[17] Kitsch prints with inspirational quasi-slogans still sell like hot cakes.[18] At best, priestly works inspire complacency. At worst, they justify demonizing people who are different from 'us' to bolster the group's own identity and sense of superiority.

Prophetic media is different. It exists to challenge the status quo, to make us feel *un*comfortable, question assumptions, point out what is disturbing, twisted and wrong in our world. Prophetic media proclaims that everything is definitely *not* OK. In a fallen world, Christian voices in the media and arts should be primarily prophetic.[19] Unfortunately, in practice, Christian media tends to be more priestly than prophetic. After all, Christians want their messages to sell too. Priests make better salespeople than prophets do.

An example of prophetic art is the work of photorealistic painter Lee Price, who spent two decades on a series of paintings called 'Women & food', in which she explored her relationship with her own body and with food as a source of comfort. Her paintings each feature a woman – mostly herself, sometimes other women – alone in private space – often in bed or a bath – surrounded by junk food. Sometimes, she is standing, looking straight ahead at the viewer while she indulges in an unhealthy snack, like a cinnamon bun. Other times, she is viewed directly from above, a

---

16 Schultze, 'Symbolic stewardship', pp. 126–134.

17 Christians do worship a 'God of all comfort' (2 Corinthians 1:3), so it is important to note that I am not discounting the need for real comfort. There is a difference between the comfort that God gives and becoming too comfortable with the way the world is. The comfort that God gives points forwards to a world healed and renewed. In a sense, true Christian comfort is indeed prophetic, even dangerously subversive to a distorted status quo.

18 See chapter 8, under 'Death by cute niceness: kitsch'.

19 Emphasis on 'primarily'. Of *course* there are times when Christian arts and media need to comfort and celebrate as well. The point is: complacency about the status quo is the chief enemy of the integrity of God's people. We *need* prophetic media.

God's-eye perspective, while she indulges her hunger.[20] Price struggled with an eating disorder, and what I love about her work is how she communicates the comfort *and* the shame of idolizing food.

But she hints at redemption as well. Late in the series she painted 'Sleeping with peaches', a triptych of herself sleeping next to a bowl of peach slices (see page 8 in the plate section). In the final picture, she has gone and the bowl of peaches remains, minus a few slices (she ate some and went on her way). At first, Price did not like this work because she wasn't sure what she was trying to say. Then she read a reviewer who said that it showed how far Price had come in her relationship with food.[21] The figure in the painting felt comfortable enough to sleep in the presence of food (healthy food, not junk food, as in earlier paintings). Then she leaves, having eaten some, but not all, of them. It's a picture of freedom from addiction.

The oasis that Price has built is one in which there is a recognition that all is *not* well in the world; there is pain, addiction and idolatry. But there is also the possibility of redemption. This is a prophetic imagination at work.[22]

The divergence between priestly and prophetic artistic paths presents artists with a hard decision to make: the path of subversive, uncomfortable love or the path of comfortable and palatable profitability. Around two decades ago, popular culture critic David Dark called this subversive path 'apocalyptic'.[23] Apocalyptic works overturn the money-changing tables of the powers that be. They expose the sinful, sentimental distortions tied up in the world of 'business as usual' by revealing the world as it should be, as it *will* be at the end of days: justice restored, creation renewed, love unleashed. Apocalyptic media 'highlights, exposes, or lampoons the moral bankruptcy of our imaginations while teasing us toward a better

20 Price has said that the God's-eye view is, in fact, her looking down on herself, judging her compulsive behaviour. See Heather Smith Stringer and Lee Price, 'Sleeping with peaches: An interview with painter Lee Price', *The Other Journal*, no. 19 (23 August 2011), <https://theotherjournal.com/2011/08/23/sleeping-with-peaches-an-interview-with-painter-lee-price>, accessed February 2023.

21 This story is recounted in Stringer and Price, 'Sleeping with peaches'.

22 Price hints at redemption, but not in explicitly Christian terms. She has made no claim to faith in her descriptions of herself or press statements. It is prophetic art, but not necessarily *Christian* prophetic art.

23 David Dark, *Everyday Apocalypse: The sacred revealed in Radiohead, The Simpsons and other pop icons* (Grand Rapids, MI: Brazos Press, 2002). If you're going to critique popular culture, David Dark is about the best name you can have. I almost expect him to have a superhero alter-ego.

way of looking at, and dwelling in, the world'.[24] I believe that Dark overstates his case in ways that mute the specificity of the gospel.[25] Nevertheless, his point is well observed.

While authentically Christian art and entertainment are more than simply subversive, they are never *less*. The gospel carries with it radical implications for how we live and move and have our being in the post-Christian world. Wherever it finds authentic cultural expression, true Christian creativity is never less than dangerously (and lovingly) subversive to the status quo. Why? Because it reveals something of the new creation, of creation as God intended it to be.[26]

Conclusion: creatives as imaginative servants in a post-Christian world

Creatives are vital in the life of the Christian community in a post-Christian world. They serve as zookeepers, nourishing and exercising imaginations beyond their accustomed confines. They serve as guerrillas, exploding expectations and opening our culture's vision to something genuinely new. They serve a prophetic role, overturning expectations and opening us to the wonder of God's grace. Along with worship, artists and creatives serve their communities by creating works that plant oases which expand and sharpen our imaginations. We owe them a debt of gratitude.

But how should the wider Christian community serve them? Too many artists and creatives are running on empty or find themselves fighting *against* their church communities for recognition. Chapter 17 will explore

---

24 Dark, *Everyday Apocalypse*, p. 19.

25 Dark seems so desperate to differentiate his approach from the standard evangelical model that he repeatedly baptizes any cultural voice that protests against the political powers that be as 'apocalyptic'. For him, such popular culture is always on the side of the angels. Radiohead, *The Simpsons* and Joel and Ethan Coen are genuinely Christian popular cultural agents because they are anti-establishment in the way that Jesus was. Though they have no interest in Jesus himself, they count as apocalyptic (that is, authentically Christian) because they follow Jesus' table-flipping cultural programme, even though they don't personally follow *him*. I address the confusion between common and special grace that turns popular culture (or a political attitude) into a sacrament in my book *Popologetics: Popular culture in Christian perspective* (Phillipsburg, NJ: P&R, 2012), chapter 9. I'm sympathetic, but surely Christian art and entertainment need some connection to Christ and his salvation – there is no other name given to us by which we must be saved (Acts 4:12). Protesting the status quo is important, but not sufficient in itself to create Christian oases.

26 Alastair Gordon describes the artist's job as cleaning the windows looking on to the new creation. See his *Why Art Matters* (London: IVP, 2021).

why creatives are too often estranged from the wider Christian community and what can be done to help. Artists need for their imaginations (and their livelihoods) to be resourced as well.

17

Bridging the chasm: the Christian community as a resource for creatives

Introduction: hearing from creatives

We have explored the calling of the artist as a resource for the imagination in the church. But what about the Christian community's calling regarding the artists in their midst?

Many (most?) creatives feel misunderstood and out of place in their churches. A chasm between artists and church communities exists, right where creatives should feel most at home. Instead, they feel isolated, marginalized, ignored and/or exploited. How can both the wider and local church communities better nurture and support artists in their calling, building bridges to support them on the paths of service (to the world and to us) that God has called them to?

I interviewed leaders from Morphē Arts, a UK-based artists' network – namely, Alastair (Ally) Gordon, David (Cully) McCulloch, Nate Orr and Sarah White.[1] They gave me insights into the causes and depth of the chasm . . . and the possibilities for bridge-building.

Chasm-creators: problems that alienate artists from churches

We need theological recalibration and reframing regarding the arts and imagination

One chasm-creator is incomplete, badly framed theology. The experience of these artists is that most in their churches understand neither the

[1] Ally is a painter and graphic designer. Cully is a printmaker and concept artist. He also organizes two alternative space gallery projects. Nate is a musician, songwriter and has sound production experience in the theatre. Sarah is a dancer, sculptor, writer and performance artist. She couldn't join the interview via Zoom, so she chimed in later via email. The interview was conducted on 12 March 2021. Comments have been lightly edited for grammar.

relevance nor the importance of the arts to human flourishing. Art and culture are seen as luxury add-ons to human existence, not integral parts of it. Creatives are seen as people without 'real jobs'. This attitude is not unique to the church. As Cully put it:

> Your local neighbour, if they say, 'Well, what do you do?' and you say you're an artist. Immediately they're going to say, 'Yeah, my aunt does landscape painting.' There's an expectation of what they think art is, and certainly most of the artists we work with, it's so far removed from that.

Nate added:

> It's systemic in the UK, culture-wide; art's a divide in a utilitarian/pragmatic sense. We've seen that more so during the coronavirus pandemic where you've had theatres across the whole nation crying out for financial support. Instead, in Parliament they're saying, 'Well, you should get a better job.' Or 'You should get a viable career', is the way they put it. So, there's a nationwide issue in regards to this, and I think, as the church, we pick up on that.

You expect this from a secular consumer culture focused solely on the bottom line and material concerns, but the church knows that we are more than material – we have non-material needs as well. As Cully remarked, echoing art scholar Dan Seidell's *Who's Afraid of Modern Art*, the church should know better:[2]

> It's not just a church issue – there's a disengagement with the value of art in the [wider] society as well. If there's a funding or economic crisis in the country, the arts are the first to go in terms of monetary

2 Dan Seidell, *Who's Afraid of Modern Art: Essays on modern art and theology in conversation* (Eugene, OR: Cascade Books, 2015). Seidell explores the deep suspicion with which the church views art, especially modern art. After being appointed curator of his home-town university's art museum, an elder in his church said, 'Now you can take down all the nudes on display in the museum.' He calls the remark 'an accurate indicator of the belief that art is more trouble than it's worth – it is something that has to be cleaned up and taken out, controlled, kept at arm's length; it's certainly not something to be embraced' (p. 3).

> priorities. What Dan Seidell was saying was that the church, of all people, should get the value of this. They should be saying, 'No, no. We're not going to put that down the list of priorities. We're going to raise it and recognize that it's so important for human flourishing.'

Most Christians do not recognize that the church has an aesthetic calling to the post-Christian world or to their own communities. They fail to comprehend the immense value of the arts for living a whole, rounded, beauty-enjoying existence in God's world (versus the 'cultural anorexia' many experience).[3]

There's no shortage of theological writing on the importance of art: Francis Schaeffer, Hans Rookmaker, Calvin Seerveld, as well as Dan Seidell, Alastair Gordon and a host of others have contributed. But, for whatever reason, their books either don't make it into the hands of seminarians or, if they do, they are ignored, so important theological ideas never make it to the pulpit, leaving the church largely uninformed about the ways of art and culture and how these relate to faith.

Further, conservative Protestant theologies of art and imagination are a mixed bag. Some tend to be *very* pessimistic about the current art world. Hans Rookmaker's landmark book *Modern Art and the Death of a Culture* links contemporary art to cultural decline and a broader loss of meaning, as though modern art existed simply to make philosophical and (a)theological statements.[4] But most art isn't propaganda for pet ideologies. Rather, it creates space for asking questions, groping for answers, wrestling with deeply human issues.

Jonathan Anderson, a writer, art critic and theologian, and William Dyrness, a cultural theologian, offer a more positive perspective in their *Modern Art and the Life of a Culture: The religious impulses of modern art.*[5] For them, art is more than a mere signifier of alienation – it's a searching conversation that can include aspects of faith as well.

---

[3] Brian Godawa, *Hollywood Worldviews: Watching films with wisdom and discernment* (Downers Grove, IL: InterVarsity Press, 2002), p. 13.

[4] Hans Rookmaker, *Modern Art and the Death of a Culture* (Wheaton, IL: Crossway, 1994 [1970]).

[5] Jonathan A. Anderson and William Dyrness, *Modern Art and the Life of a Culture: The religious impulses of modern art*, Studies in Theology and the Arts (Downers Grove, IL: InterVarsity Press, 2016).

When the church at large remains uninformed or misinformed about the arts and imagination, naturally it views creatives who move in that world with suspicion and disdain. This undermines the creatives' God-given calling.

On not speaking French: the 'language barrier' between pastors and creatives

Several times in our conversation, the artists brought up the issue of language. Cully, whose Master's dissertation was on the relationship between artists and the evangelical church in Scotland, told me about interviews that he did with church leaders about the arts:

> What I discovered was that . . . they kind of knew that they *shouldn't* really disregard the arts, but they just didn't know what to do with it. It was easier just to go, 'Yeah, we're not really going to include this in our church life or programme, because we don't really know how to do it.' Some of them are quite open to it; if an artist came along and said, 'Look, could I introduce these things in the context of church?', I think you'd need to prove its worth and so on, but a lot of them said they were open to that. But they just didn't know what to do, and they didn't know how to engage with it. It was like someone was speaking French to them, and they thought, 'I know French is an important and valid language, but I don't know how to speak it.'

On the one hand, many pastors are proficient in reading biblical texts, but functionally illiterate when it comes to reading art and entertainment. This is not a problem in itself, unless it is accompanied by an *unwillingness* to learn the new language, as though the arts and entertainment are somehow not worthy of consideration. Pastors who find it hard to navigate the arts may choose to delegate that task to artists. But it would be even better if they took 'language lessons' from their creatives, so that they could engage the arts properly and understand their power, as well as pastor the artists in their community. This requires humility and patience.

On the other hand, artists are sometimes impatient with church people who don't understand the language of art. Nate said that artists assume non-artists should be able to automatically understand art:

> [There is] an assumption that non-artists still have the language of contemporary art and *could* understand the French language … Artists are sometimes going, say, 'Well, why don't they understand it? Just understand it! This is obvious, isn't it?'

And, of course, the answer is *no,* it's *not* obvious. No-one is born knowing the language of contemporary art – it is a skill developed over time, requiring dedication and research. Artists need the humility to help translate for those who really do want to understand them and their world better.

But artists need to do their research as well. They can sometimes set themselves up to get hurt by failing to fully understand the context and sensitivities of the communities where they may be called to serve. For example, if an artist takes a commission to create a piece for a church group, doing this is a delicate thing. Ally pointed out that artists might feel at home, among family, and so might not do their research and end up violating a particular church's expectations.

For both the artists and the wider church, what is needed is intentionality, humility and a willingness to learn each other's languages. Otherwise, communication is short-circuited and the artists tend to get hurt, pushed away by the church, widening the chasm.

Too many church leaders have a narrow view of what counts as legitimate knowledge

Many church leaders do not understand or value the aesthetic and emotional dimensions of either the Christian faith or human existence. For them, only logical, rational, propositional knowledge counts as valid.

Nate told me the story of when he attended a training course on preaching and leading Bible studies for church leaders. The trainer focused solely on propositional theological statements, such as you find in Paul, and seemed to discount the rest. When Nate and some of his friends pointed out that the Bible contained poetry and songs, the trainer conceded that they could be helpful, but only because they were in the Bible. The idea that God could speak to someone through music or a sunset was dismissed by the leader and others at the seminar as quasi-heresy. In the end, Nate and others from his church had to leave the training course because they were being repeatedly shut down – told that God only speaks to people one way, and that's through logical theological statements from the Bible. Nate summed up this attitude as 'Head knowledge is the only knowledge.'[6]

This is, of course, unbiblical nonsense. The Bible communicates in multifaceted ways, using a variety of literary styles that address head, heart and imagination: 44 per cent of the Bible is narrative, 33 per cent poetry and 23 per cent rational propositional prose.[7] The Bible also affirms that God speaks to us *extra*-biblically through a whole host of aesthetic forms. Psalm 19:1–4 explicitly says that God's presence, character and excellence (his 'glory') is proclaimed *by the skies*. Romans 1:18 makes a similar point, although there it proclaims God's wrath. The nature imagery woven throughout the Psalms and other wisdom literature ('Go to the ant, you sluggard!'), as well as the parables, ought to be enough to convince us that God speaks to the whole person: emotions, imagination and aesthetics as well as logical mind.

The blinkers that people wear, so they see only logical/propositional knowledge as valid, come not from the Bible, but stem from the Enlightenment and the Cult of Reason.[8] It's a perspective that has done much damage to the Christian church, but it is so pervasive in society that many church leaders (and seminary professors) have absorbed it without question. The end result is that those gifted in seeing truth from other, more embodied, imaginative perspectives – creatives – are marginalized. It is assumed that creatives have nothing of real value to contribute.

Sarah pointed out that this attitude also degrades the church's ability to worship in an aesthetically rich, visually embodied way. This seems to be a particular problem for Protestants. It's no coincidence that many of

6 Nate was responding to my question, 'As creatives, what do you wish your Christian brothers and sisters understood about you as creatives that you don't think they get?' He replied, 'Head knowledge isn't the only knowledge.'

7 Ray Lubeck, *Read the Bible for a Change: Understanding and responding to God's word* (Eugene, OR: Wipf & Stock, 2005), p. 14. The Bible Project's video 'Literary styles in the Bible' illustrates this variety creatively; BibleProject, YouTube (22 July 2017), <www.youtube.com/watch?v=oUXJ8Owes8E>, accessed February 2023.

8 The 'Cult of Reason' was a short-lived atheist church that emerged (and perished) during the French Revolution. I mention it here to indicate a certain worshipful attitude towards autonomous Reason that persists and pervades the modern West, taking up residence, ironically, even in evangelical churches.

the leading filmmakers – Scorsese, Malick, Coppola, Kieślowski – come from Catholic backgrounds.[9]

Therefore, little is expected from artists in the life of the church

The narrowness of the vision of church leaders leads to a narrowing of the contributions expected of artists. The artists I spoke with all expressed frustration that typically they are pigeonholed by churches and pressured into volunteering their skills for a narrow range of activities – doing graphic design for a church advert, providing some decoration for the week's bulletin or playing music for worship services. They are reduced to minor functional roles, as though they had no other wisdom or gifting that might be valuable to the church family. In fact, artists excel at creative, lateral thinking and empathy. They are more than their skillsets, as we shall explore below.

Many artists have no theological training, so may struggle to integrate their faith and artistic calling

Most art schools provide no Christian theological training. Instead, typically, art students learn secular theories of art.[10] Christian perspectives have long been discarded and forgotten. As Ally put it:

> In the UK art world, we just live a long way downstream from where art had an alliance with theology ... particularly in Europe. I've seen in the UK, the art academies have aligned themselves with late modern sociopolitical positioning. So we'd read Derrida, Foucault, Barthes, Marx. We're not reading Augustine.

Reading Derrida, Foucault and the rest is not necessarily a bad thing – I teach about these thinkers in my classes. They are fundamental to

9 We need to be careful not to overstate this critique. The Reformed tradition gave rise to its own literary and visual cultures, often focused on celebrating the everyday. See William Dyrness, *Reformed Theology and Visual Culture: The Protestant imagination from Calvin to Edwards* (Cambridge: Cambridge University Press, 2004).

10 There are quite a few centres, institutes and universities that do seek to combine theology and art instruction. See this helpful list, 'Educational institutions', by ArtWay, a website that provides materials and resources for those wanting to link art and faith, <https://artway.eu/content.php?id=112&lang=en&action=show>, accessed March 2023.

understanding the contemporary world. But too often, these authors are taught in a way that celebrates their work uncritically, assuming that God is dead and only politics matters.

The results are threefold:

- the art world becomes ever more secular and cynical about the Christian faith;
- many art students yearn to be equipped in their churches with the kind of intellectual rigour that can match what they get in art school but, too often, they don't and are left to their own devices to find answers;
- young Christian artists remain confused about how to integrate their faith and creative gifts.

The church community is often no help at all because of the attitudes described above.

Too many artists are in desperate financial straits

When I asked, 'As creatives, what do you wish your Christian brothers and sisters understood about you that they don't?', Ally answered immediately, 'Money!'

Most in church communities don't understand the financial hardship that accompanies a life devoted to working in the arts. Attitudes that view art and creativity as unnecessary, impractical, a luxury, have material consequences on the lives of artists. They often lack funds and are always looking for patronage. The 'starving artist' stereotype comes from this reality. But if art is a legitimate calling from God, should they be starving? Shouldn't they be able to find support in the Christian community?

Sarah pointed out that the financial disparity between creatives and other members of the church can add to the mutual alienation felt because of differences in the lifestyles each can afford. The assumption that the church has no business supporting them contributes to the financial stress artists feel, and that widens the chasm further.

Many artists need spiritual and relational support, but too often receive neither

Creatives in the church endure not only material poverty but also relational poverty. Like the DJ in chapter 1, many artists feel isolated and alone. There's a yawning chasm between their spiritual home and their work life. Cully told me about another member of Morphē, an actress and dancer:

> She'd often go on tour for maybe three months with a dance company. And I remember one time there were maybe 21 of them in the company, and they were doing a programme [performance] about sexuality (a lot of dance stuff was dealing with that). And they had to go around and speak out their own sexual identity. It came to her, 'Well, I'm straight, but I'm also a Christian.' I think out of the whole company, there were maybe three people that were straight, and she was one of them, and she was also a Christian. Somebody said to her afterwards, 'Why are you even here?' They weren't saying, 'You don't *deserve* to be here.' They were just saying, 'I don't understand *why* you're here, in light of how different you are compared to everyone else.' And I remember her saying that, and then she was off with this company for three months. No Christian contact for three months, other than text or phone calls and so on. But she's away from her Christian community in terms of the church. It could be easy for the church to say, 'That's a really dangerous place to be. You're going to fall away. You're going to get tempted. You should come out of that world.'

But what if she is called precisely *into* that world? What if God gave her gifts and a heart *for* that world, for those people who need Jesus?

As Sarah explained, the art world often demands a massive time investment. To be known by the right people (and so get anywhere in your career), you are expected to be 'all in'. It is easy to succumb to those pressures and therefore have an unhealthy work–life balance. Artists need friendships and prayer to find a balance in the highly competitive art world.

But, according to Nate, some Christians refuse to pray for artists because they believe that God cannot be pleased with a life in the arts:

> We hear stories about this idea [from people in Morphē], like, 'I'm not going to pray for you in the art world because it's the wrong place to be', and that's their theological standpoint. 'So, actually, I'm not going to pray for that; I'm going to pray that you come to your senses and come out of the art world, because you're going to fall away there . . .'. Or 'I'm going to pray *against* your career.'

Can you imagine a Christian addressing a manager who works in a local business that way? 'There's greed in the business world, so I'm going to pray *against* your career.' That tends not to happen because Christians understand and value business more than art. Because Christians aren't taught to appreciate the arts and entertainment – except as sinful, worldly diversions – they turn their backs on artists. They refuse to engage them in lasting friendships and accountability relationships, which in turn sets creatives up to stumble. And then they blame the *creatives* for failing. It's a classic self-fulfilling prophecy, and it further widens the chasm.

Therefore, many artists give up on the church; some give up on the faith entirely

Because of the relational static and repeated discouragement received from fellow Christians, some artists step away and semi-excommunicate themselves. When I asked what is the biggest mistake that artists make concerning the wider Christian community, Cully replied:

> I think probably the mistake the artists make is that they just walk away from the church. And once you walk away from the community of believers, then you're missing one part of what helps you continue to sustain a life as a Christian. So, yeah, you can go on and say, 'Well, I'm not giving up on God. I'm Bible reading and praying', but you're missing a really big part: being part of the body of believers . . . What I've seen is inevitably it becomes harder [when you're] isolated, and it's harder to maintain your own walk with God without that sense of community. Then I see people falling away.

In other words, sometimes the chasm can be fatal to artists' faith.

Building (theological, relational, material, institutional and spiritual) bridges

How can we span the chasm that has developed in the church between creatives and the rest of the Christian community? What can we do to better support creatives?

Recalibrate our theology regarding art and the imagination

The first step is to recognize and reframe the imagination, arts and creativity in our theology so that Christians will understand its role in the Bible and in our lives. We have plenty of good theology to draw on, particularly from the Dutch Neo-Calvinist tradition (as I said, Seerveld is one of my heroes). I hope this book contributes to that discussion too.[11]

I use words such as 'recalibration' and 'reframe' advisedly. As I said earlier in this chapter, much of our theology of the arts in conservative Christian circles tends to see art and the imagination as 'the enemy' or at least as a sign of cultural decline, of descent into meaninglessness and rebellion, a danger to our very souls. Ally referred to this as an overly polemic approach to cultural imagination, 'church v. culture, a them and us kind of thing'.

We need a theology that acknowledges:

- the rich artistic imagination that runs throughout the Bible;
- God's common grace that shines even in non-Christian art and entertainment;
- the importance of the life of the imagination;
- the importance of *listening* to art in its explorations, laments, protests, confessions and celebrations without giving in to alarm and summary rejection in the name of self-protection.

The insights of artist-theologian Makoto Fujimura and others are helpful here. Art and entertainment are not the enemy. They are contributions to an ongoing conversation, seedlings planted in our shared cultural garden

11 Particularly chapters 5 to 8. If you skipped those, this might be a good time to read them.

that we have the honour, joy and duty to cultivate together.[12] Art must be seen as more than simply a place where the lost make gestures of seductive meaninglessness. Rather, it's a place where humans explore the meanings that *God* has given us – a way of being human. This theology needs to be widely preached and taught in churches. Everyday Christians need theological and biblical frameworks for understanding the arts and the people who create them.

Ground creatives in who they are in God

Theological recalibration is necessary not only for Christians to understand artists but also for artists to understand themselves. Christian artists often feel divided, as though they had two identities fighting against each other: Christian versus artist. Understanding who they are as *artists-in-Christ* can give them an integrated identity that helps them to cope with church people who sometimes don't understand or acknowledge them. Even if the church doesn't understand them, God does. Being grounded in that knowledge can help creatives to move towards openness vis-à-vis the church, from seeing themselves as victims to seeing themselves as gifted servants with something to share. As Cully put it, when working with art students for the Universities and Colleges Christian Fellowship (UCCF):

> I was really keen to distinguish between church as an institution – and what you may or may not like in that institution – and God and biblical theology, in terms of who you are as a person *and* an artist. If someone could think, 'Actually, I think the church might not get me, but God's really advocating this and values [my artistic calling]', then they might not throw away this belief in God. If someone's got to the point where they do believe and they're in a positive, affirming position, then it's easier to be more gracious towards the institution and what you don't like about the institution. So I always try to work on that, that God actually understands what they're doing and values it. And *then* say, 'OK, how can you contribute to this life, this church community life.'

12 This is the major thesis of Makoto Fujimura's *Culture Care: Reconnecting with beauty for our common life* (Downers Grove, IL: InterVarsity Press, 2017).

Understanding and believing that God values their creative calling integrates Christian creatives and helps them to relate in healthier ways to both the church and the art world.

Creatives need loyal friends in their churches – adopt one today!

One way to build bridges that is simple and full of joy (and sometimes difficult): be friends with an artist. I asked the artists from Morphē about what creatives wished other Christians understood that they don't presently. I added, 'If you had a megaphone and the license to use it', so that the message got through loud and clear. Cully's response surprised me:

> Actually, Ted . . . I would *not* use a megaphone, because I think it's about a slow burn in a relationship. I think if there's any kind of sense of, 'I'm going to shout this at you', people would be put off. I just think it needs to be about building relationships. And I know you're just using the megaphone as an analogy, but that's not the way I'm trying to do it. I think building relationships is key.

He's right. There is no quick fix, megaphone-delivered solution here. Bridge-building happens *through* relationships, through the church family acting like a family and loving their own, caring enough to understand one another across differences.

When I asked for their advice about how to walk alongside artists to encourage them, Ally got very practical:

> Go to their studio, sit down, and ask them about their art. Go to an art gallery with them, go to a concert. You know, *be in their world.* Experience it . . . learn the language [of their art]. Ask them about their finances. Ask them, 'What are the hardest things for you?' And artists don't mind talking about money – we actually talk about it all the time! Because none of us have it. It's sort of the small 1 per cent at the top who've got loads of it . . . Sit in the studio and talk about [art and the life of the artist]. Artists tend to play with really big ideas, and important ideas that the gospel has a lot to say about. You're never that far from talking about the gospel when you talk about art.

A church we attended encouraged families to 'adopt' a student from a nearby art school, to bring them home for lunch after church. One studied ballet. We learnt so much from her about hardships, both physical (the pressure to be anorexic, multiple leg fractures) and spiritual (dance teachers who believed that virgins couldn't really move fluidly, so they held a dismissive attitude towards chastity). But more than learning information, as she grew to be part of our family, we learnt how to pray for her. She became one of us – she was ours and we were hers. That is what relationships in church *should* be – mutual loyalty that cares enough to be in one another's worlds. Artists who are connected to a church through deep, loving relationships tend not to feel (or be) marginalized. Bridges are built over the chasm.

Creatives need this – maintaining Christian faith *and* being immersed in the art world or entertainment industry is *hard*. Artists can feel isolated. They swim in waters that often flow against faith. They rub shoulders with those who are sceptical of and, at times, hostile towards, the Christian faith. Yet these are the people they (and we) are called to love. Think of the Christian DJ, perhaps one of only a handful of Christians in the club. Think of the Christian dancer, perhaps the only Christian in her company, without Christian fellowship for three months. The US Marine Corps has a slogan: 'Never leave a man behind.' You never abandon a fellow soldier on the battlefield (or mission field). Surely, our Christian loyalty to one another should run *deeper* than that, for the battles we fight have eternal consequences, and they are fought not with bullets but love, service, prayer and the occasional text or phone call.

Recognize the multiple ways in which God shares truth with us that open up ways for creatives to contribute more to the life of the church

A deeper theological understanding of imagination and creativity should undermine attitudes that denigrate the emotional and aesthetic dimensions of knowing (Nate's 'Head knowledge isn't the only knowledge'). That could help churches see the *full* spectrum of ways in which creatives can serve.

One gift that creatives could give the church is renewed imagination. As imagination workers, they can put us in touch with new perspectives on experience – empathy, peace-making, lament and discovery. Ally put it this way:

> I think artists have so much to offer to a local church, and I just bang the drum on this, really. Sometimes churches reduce the artists to, 'Oh, they could do the music' or 'they could design the website' or they could have some sort of practical function in that way. But, in a way, it's a bit like asking the teacher to come and do the kids' work. This is our job nine to five, and on a weekend it's quite nice to offer something different. Artists are given training in creative thinking, lateral thinking, we flex that imaginative muscle on a daily basis. And that allows for all kinds of other involvements and inclusion in the church network. If one has the capacity to imagine, then you're probably really good at empathizing, because you sit down with someone you disagree with and you can see where they're coming from. You don't have to agree with them, but you can sit in that tension of disagreement and understand more. And that's a really great gift to bring into a leadership team, for example, home group leadership, to serve in a pastoral way in a church. I'd love to see artists more involved in leadership and home groups and preaching rotas and things like that, not just making advertising for the church as well. So, I think I'd probably want to chat with church leaders about their understanding the artistic mindset a little bit, and temperament and character, and seeing if there are ways that artists can serve that maybe haven't been considered before.

Artists stoke the imagination, and imagination, by its very nature, can hold us in its grip long enough to open us up to grieve over the brokenness of the world, resist injustice and imagine new possibilities, a new creation. Ally added:

> In [my new book][13] I talk about how art has the capacity to lament in a very unique way, to reflect on the brokenness of our world, how it can be a force of resistance and political action, and how it can hold

---

[13] Alastair Gordon, *Why Art Matters* (London: IVP, 2021).

> us, from the Latin 'to entertain', to hold. [The imagination] … is where you are held … And I think the artist has the capacity to create that space, that imaginative space that can open up possibilities …
>
> The artist has the unique capacity to envision and embody aspects of new creation. So my little catchphrase in the book is, 'The artist cleans the windows of the new creation.' The analogy being the new creation is closer than we think, and it is experienced today as well as anticipating for the future. It's so good it sort of leaks out into today. But we live in the now and not yet, and the artist has capacity just to wipe the dust off the windows, to look in so that we can see aspects of new creation that we haven't seen before.

Sarah added that the church is often critical of many aspects of post-Christian culture, including television, films, music and books: 'It is surprising that we are not doing more to support and build up the imagination of the artists who could contribute to changing this artistic output.' By supporting its creatives, the church can help introduce a measure of new creation ethos into post-Christian culture.

A second gift that creatives bring to the church, because they dwell on the cultural front lines, is that they are weathervanes. They detect shifts in cultural winds before the church notices them. Ally explained:

> artists tend to exist a little farther upstream culturally. You know, the ideas that exist in the arts, and not just in fine art, in films and popular culture, they work their way into the wider mindset of the population … Certainly we experience that at the moment in the UK, the creative arts have been discussing issues of gender, transgender, sexual identity for decades and decades and decades. But only more recently, the Church of England has produced a series of resources to help their congregations work through questions of transgender, in particular. It's a really well put together document, very thoughtful and sensitive, but it's like, 'Where have you been for the past 25 years?' … If the analogy is culture is like a river, that it's moving and there is a trajectory to it, artists are kind of surfing somewhere upstream but, broadly speaking, the church is still a wee bit downstream. Again, catching up, genuinely catching up, but

> not quite catching up fast enough. So, we can consider the artist, in that missional sense then, at least, has been able to resource the church to understand what's happening and what they might anticipate ten years down the line.[14]

Third, creatives befriend other (non-Christian) creatives, which are relationships that are normally out of reach for other Christians. For Cully, artists are cultural missionaries to the art world[15] and it flows naturally from their love of art, just being who they are. Of the artist's calling to the world and the church, he said:

> I like art so I'm going to be around artists. As an artist I want to develop and learn and engage with the art world because I love it. But as a Christian, I'm doing that partly because I love it, partly because it reveals to the world that I can connect with it on that level. So when you're talking about art [with other artists], then you start talking about other things, and those relationships are real. That's what I think an artist can bring to the world: they are who they are, and they can be in that world that others might not be able to. That's also their contribution to the church as well. I think that's why my church recognizes that, 'OK, it's not something we're interested in, but we see that you're engaging with the art world, and that's a good thing for us.'

Creatives have so much more potential to serve the church and world than Christians typically give them credit for. We can encourage them by giving them the chance to unleash all their gifts as imaginative thinkers, empathetic mediators, leaders in lament and resistance, cultural weather-vanes and emissaries.

Undermine the 'starving artist' cliché

Following God's call to a life as an imagination worker too often means a life of financial uncertainty. If the church values its creatives as its

---

14 Ruth Naomi Floyd (see chapter 12) said something similar about transgender issues back in 2015: 'I go into bars to sing and befriend people there who struggle with their gender identity. And, Ted, the church doesn't even know the language for this yet.'

15 They don't typically use that label, though, as it would cause problems with other artists.

cultural front-line ambassadors in the imaginary landscape, it should find ways to support them and release them to freely explore and create in their media. Here are a few ideas for how it could do this.

Ally mentioned a graduate residency programme at the Leith School of Art in Edinburgh. The school identifies its most talented students and, after they've graduated, supports them for a year with a stipend, materials and free studio space. It gives them lessons in how to build a website, put together a CV and approach galleries. The church could learn from such a model, not only for painters but also musicians, actors, filmmakers and others. In addition, they could equip talented young creatives with theological training that integrates faith and imaginative work. The church (or church-sponsored art colleges) could identify art students 'of Christian faith, with character and integrity'[16] and so raise up a generation of oasis planters. This is a long-term vision. The church will be 'sowing seeds for years to come, and we're not going to have . . . success stories for 10, 15, 20 years down the line'.[17]

Ally told me the story of the emergence of David Hockney, a gay British painter and photographer who has had a celebrated career. He rose to fame not simply because he was talented but also because, early on, patrons in the LGBTQI+ community invested in him.[18] Ally said that the same happened in the late eighteenth and early nineteenth century.

Lord Tate (of Tate Gallery fame) was a wealthy Christian who was friends with art critic John Ruskin. Ruskin alerted Tate to a promising young talent, William Turner. Turner became one of the most famous landscape painters of his day. This, in turn, produced a 'great legacy of painting that has an utterly creation ethos to it. And there's a nice model of art with critic and sponsor working together to create this legacy.'[19]

Christian artists need patrons of all sorts – from those who simply buy a single work to individuals who invest in whole careers and institutional sponsorship from the church itself.

Ally quickly added, though, that perhaps the smartest move would be to find mid-career artists and support them. By mid-career,

16 Ally Gordon, in interview with me.
17 Gordon, in interview with me.
18 Recall that chapter 4 started by focusing on how the LGBTQI+ community has done something similar in film and television.
19 Gordon, in interview with me.

> you're serious about your art, you know what you're doing, you've got a theological understanding, you're tried and tested, you're not flaky any more, you're in it for the long haul, *and* you've still got 20 to 30 years' painting ahead of you.[20] I think *that* would be an interesting place to run the programme.

Christians should invest in those who have proven that they can last in this difficult cultural work.

But churches are often strapped for cash. They need innovative funding plans to support artists. As a musician, Nate found himself frustrated by the current financial schemes for creative markets. The 'gatekeepers' (Spotify, Apple Music and others) keep most of the profits, leaving artists struggling to make ends meet. He shared an idea: find spaces that can be rehabbed into multidiscipline studios for music recording, dance practice, painting, film and so on. Part of the building could be rented to a well-financed company looking for office space and, with the rest, artists could, for free, practise their art and walk away with a product to sell to sustain themselves. 'We're basically making money *for* the arts as opposed to making money *from* the artist.'

The Christian church has a lot of people who know how to think creatively about finances. Surely there are other models that can help creatives to plant oases too.

The importance of mediating, educating institutions such as Morphē

To build bridges between creatives and the church, we need mediating institutions big and small.

When I lived in the USA, I was part of a small cadre of church members, most of whom were creatives (I wasn't), that formed a small group called Art and Soul. We existed to be a bridge between our church and a local secular art school. Our mission: to love art students. Likewise, Morphē was started by Christian artists who wanted to be a haven for confused and hurting artists. They wanted to pray for Christian artists, help them deepen their roots in the Christian faith so that they could return to their

20 The same applies to filmmaking, story-writing, music-making, game-developing and other forms of creativity.

careers refreshed and come to their churches encouraged and ready to serve. There are certain discussions that Christian artists need to have among themselves. Until the church learns to value and support its creatives more wisely and consistently, the need for these bridging communities will remain.

Fortunately, mediating institutions have emerged all over the place in the past several decades. In the UK, there are Morphē and Sputnik: Faith and Arts; in the USA, the Anselm Society, Renew the Arts and Rabbit Room. There is also the Christian Artists Network, which ties together arts groups spanning the globe. But we also need more art schools that value faith perspectives and can disciple younger artists so that they can raise up the next generation of oasis planters. There are reasons to be optimistic, but much remains to be done and it will take time.

Pray for your creatives – that means listening to them

We have discussed many practical ways to bridge the chasm. Cully was keen to remember prayer. It doesn't *seem* practical, but is perhaps the most practical of all. If you don't have money to support artists, you can still dedicate time and energy to praying for them. Pray for those whose careers take them on the road and away from church for long periods. Pray for their works to have an impact on the right people in the right way. Pray for wisdom and inspiration, against creative blocks. *Invest* in your artists by bringing them before the throne of God and asking him to bless them.

Conclusion: humility and the way forwards

Interviewing four artists who are part of an arts network is hardly a scientific survey. The insights they shared, however, come from more than a decade of hearing and responding to the frustrations of a wide range of Christian artists in the UK. Their insights have been hard won after years of wrestling through their own issues, bridging their identities as Christians and creatives. I learnt a lot from them and, even when they said things that surprised me, their remarks resonated with what I have heard over the years from other Christian artists.

The relational chasm between church and creatives is multifaceted. Bridging it will therefore require a multifaceted approach that includes:

- theological consciousness-raising, reframing the arts as less a threat and more an intrinsic part of being human that gives us an opportunity to take part in a cultural conversation for God's glory and loving those around us;
- relationships that are empathetic, supporting and sustaining creatives through tough times;
- a recognition of the whole spectrum of gifts that creatives bring to the church;
- financial and other forms of material support that free creatives to hone their crafts and explore their imaginative territory;
- building mediating institutions that bridge the gap between creatives and the church, and educational institutions that orientate artists towards a life of faith and imaginative integrity;
- praying to the One who can change things, heal wounds and renew all of creation.

That's a daunting list! It would be easy to throw our hands in the air and declare the chasm unbridgeable. Instead, we could consider the *benefits* of such a varied list: it's got something for everyone.

Choose one or two areas where you could make a contribution. If you're a pastor-theologian, you've got your work cut out for you. If you're a manager in a local business who is wise in the ways of finance and with access to material resources, you've got your work cut out for you. If you're an administrator who knows how to connect people and build institutions, you've got your work cut out for you. If you're an artist who has something to offer or if you're a prayer warrior who delights in bringing people before God or if you love creating new friendships and sustaining friends in times of trouble or weakness, you've got your work cut out for you. Essentially, if you name Christ as Lord and you've got a pulse, you've got your work cut out for you. But this is not a dry duty – bridge-building with the arts is a path full of joy and promise, a channel God can use to reconcile a deeply alienated world to himself.

The key to bridging the chasm between creatives and the wider Christian community is humility born of the gospel. As long as suspicions and resentments remain, stroked and nurtured like a pet dragon, the chasm will remain unbridged and the church will continue to flounder in its aesthetic witness before a watching world. The gospel teaches humility, that we are *all* screwed up and need help. For artists, that means having patience with those who don't get you and give you sideways glances. It means having a spirit of forgiveness for the thoughtless things that church people sometimes say. It means understanding that you might not be appreciated, but being willing to serve anyway because the Lord calls you to do so. For the rest of us, it means being willing to examine our preconceptions about creatives and those who don't quite fit the mould we're used to. It means loving across significant differences because we recognize a brother or sister, a son or daughter of the King. It means being willing to lay down your life for others who need you, even if (especially if) they're kind of strange and see the world differently from you.

The chasm is not equally wide and deep everywhere in the church. Sarah told me, 'I have experienced personally much support from my church in many ways; they really do take an interest in what I am doing and they turn up to exhibitions and pray for me. This is worth so much.' But, even so, 'I also see them wrestling with wanting to tell me to leave the art world because they are worried it is pulling me away from faith!' Even where churches *are* intentional about loving their creatives, there is still bridge-building work to do.

Building these bridges is where the rubber hits the road in the church's creative cultural engagement and aesthetic witness. If Christian creatives and the rest of the church can come together in humility, with an eager desire to love and serve the post-Christian world, God can bless that and create something genuinely new in our culture in the long term. And it will all be worth it.

Conclusion: endgame

In the Marvel films *Avengers: Infinity War* (2018) and *Avengers: Endgame* (2019), we are introduced to Thanos, a powerful villain with a powerful artefact: a glove that houses six 'Infinity Stones'. When combined, these stones could alter reality with a click of the fingers. Thanos planned to use them to restore balance in the universe in an instant. But for the church's aesthetic witness, it is the exact opposite. There are no Infinity Stones for oasis-building. It will require a slow, incremental process that remains perpetually unfinished – at least until Christ comes again. We need to take a long view and celebrate small changes.

Let me summarize the overall argument of this book.

- Part 1 argued that we are called by God to cultural engagement, to be involved in our shared cultural conversation. This is tricky in a post-Christian culture where many are inoculated against the gospel and many alternative paths seem to offer wholeness and significance.
  - The approaches Christians typically adopt – culture warring or withdrawal – both have significant shortcomings.
  - One often overlooked path for engaging with the post-Christian world is cultural creativity. The arts and entertainment address and shape our imaginary landscapes directly. We need to plant oases, spaces where imagination-shaping conversations can take place.
- To pursue this path, we need to understand the imagination. Part 2 explored the imagination in general and the image of God within us that both inflects our world and creates new ones.
- Part 3 examined more carefully what makes the Christian imagination distinctive and resonant in a post-Christian cultural context: the tension between the darkness of our fallen existence

and the light of our hope, and the balance between trumpeting our convictions and mumbling them to blend in. We also considered the pitfalls that Christian creative efforts too often fall into: kitsch, propaganda, triumphalism and a hopeless vision. This is not the fault of artists alone – there are institutional pressures that creators must reckon with.

- Part 4 looked at examples of the many and varied ways open to us to build oases using multiple media and genres – the blues, rap, jazz, photography, video games, storytelling and film. Authentic oasis-planting can take so many forms.
- Finally, part 5 explored resources for our shared imaginative life.
  - Worship is vital for reforming and refreshing us in a world of competing worship streams.
  - Creatives are zookeepers who exercise our imaginations, guerrillas who explode the expectations of the post-Christian status quo.
  - The church should, therefore, be intentional about nurturing, encouraging and supporting its creatives.
- Christians can thus re-enter and find a place in the ongoing cultural conversation in a way that gains a hearing.

But questions may remain. Let me address some of them.

Aren't you overselling the power of art and imagination to heal?

In other words, aren't I simply replicating the Romantics' mistake of confusing art and religion, seeing creativity as the saviour that will repair our damaged souls and society?

It's an understandable objection because I agree, in part, with the Romantics about art. It's no saviour, but it *is* powerful. The Bible itself testifies to this. How much poetry do you find there? How many stories? How many songs? How many word images? Not only in the Psalms and poetic books, but everywhere in Scripture. The Bible is infused with so much art, it is hard *not* to see it as put there to heal, persuade, comfort, encourage, chide, warn, brace, inspire hope. That is what art does, both in and outside the Bible.

However, art *alone* can do little of lasting (eternal) value.[1] I have focused on art and entertainment because they tend to be given short shrift in conservative Christian circles, ignored except as things to avoid. I want to raise the profile of the imagination and cultural creativity. But there is a whole host of other factors that influence the church's impact on the imaginary landscape. Are we good neighbours? Do our lives demonstrate love and integrity? Are we hospitable? Do we serve the least in our communities, drawing alongside the marginalized, the vulnerable, the suffering? Do we teach the whole Bible or only selected parts that don't challenge us? Do we preach the gospel – and its necessary impact on our personal and social lives – with consistency? Do we practise what we preach? Are we known for our humility and repentance or for our arrogance and defiance?

Art will have little impact if it is divorced from discipleship of both artists and audience.[2] But art is not to be neglected for that reason. The arts and entertainment together can play a powerful role in reaching the alienated and healing the broken. Art is not life; life is the proper context for art. If our art expresses a heart-message that we do not live out, then it is longhand for hypocrisy, and we need to repent. But if our lives reflect what our art expresses, that can have a powerful impact on the imaginary landscape of our friends, families and neighbours. As our own testimonies are often inconsistent, this requires a lifelong commitment to repentance, as well as a lifelong commitment to our imaginative life together.

Finally, we need to remember that transforming society and lives is God's work. He can use our efforts, but ultimately it depends on him. Cultural works can move the heart but cannot transform it by themselves. Transformation is the work of God's Spirit, through relationships, conversations, prayer and all the normal means of grace.

---

1 See David Covington, *A Redemptive Theology of Art: Restoring godly aesthetics to doctrine and culture* (Grand Rapids, MI: Zondervan, 2018), p. 182.

2 My friend Tony Watkins said, in a conversation about Christian culture-makers, 'Above any artistic outputs, we need to be concerned with the spiritual health of the artists.' He is absolutely right.

Aren't you simply instrumentalizing art, asking for the very propaganda you criticize?

This is a delicate subject. Artistic creativity is gratuitous, generous, not something to be reduced to its utility.[3] Something is lost when we instrumentalize (or weaponize) art. And yet, we are Christ's people, dedicated to his message – it is bound to emerge. There is always the risk that we reduce our art to a delivery system for that message.[4] That is a danger for all art and entertainment created by 'believers' of every stripe, Christian or not. Everyone is committed to some message, some faith or ideology and that will be expressed somehow. Everyone uses art to persuade, to ask questions, to stir things up.

The real question is whether art is *enslaved* to those uses or whether art, freely created, freely given, has an impact that honours or dishonours God and his creatures, brings life or death to our cultures, creates imaginary worlds that stretch us, telling the truth about our messy reality, expanding our love, or shrivel us into bitterness, oversimplifying reality. Great art and entertainment will always have an impact for good or ill; that doesn't mean it is merely useful.

It is my hope that art and entertainment, made with excellence and resonance, will feed imaginations and lead to a healthy imaginative life for those inside and outside the church. I hope that oases will be planted that can serve as shelters in the storm, in which friends can discuss things that matter. If someone chooses to call that 'instrumentalization', then guilty as charged, I guess. The alternative is 'Art for art's sake', art curved in on itself, which is illusion and idolatry.[5] Give art space to be art, give entertainment space to entertain, but let us not pretend that art and entertainment can ever be divorced from the things that make people tick, from their worshipping lives.

We need not be afraid of usefulness. Some of the most beautiful things in the world – jade combs, ancient and ornate wardrobes, Shaker chairs – were made to be useful. Are art and entertainment any different? If Christ

---

3 Makoto Fujimura makes this point repeatedly in both *Culture Care: Reconnecting with beauty for our common life* (Downers Grove, IL: InterVarsity Press, 2017) and *Art and Faith: A theology of making* (New Haven, CT, and London: Yale University Press, 2020).

4 Recall our discussion of propaganda in chapter 8.

5 Augustine called sinful humanity *incurvatis in se*, 'curved in on itself' rather than orientated outwards, towards God and neighbour. Art can fall prey to that same inwards curvature.

is Lord of all, can art be called to nobler service? Not as propaganda, not as a sermon dressed up artistically, but as a projector of imaginary worlds, a space for questioning and wrestling with deep human issues. Art can have a profound impact, even be useful, and still be generative and generous. It can still be art.

What does success look like? What's the endgame?

This is not a strategies guidebook for deploying art and entertainment to secure cultural victory to create a Christian safe zone or utopia. Rather, it offers a perspective on creating art and entertainment to love and serve those around us, both Christian and non-Christian. This book is about how to sustain a cultural conversation in which imaginations are stirred Godwards. 'Success' is not a Thanos click of the fingers. Rather, it is an ongoing and generous conversation, a blossoming relationship. Success is the church getting better and better at engaging, entering into the cultural conversation in love, nurturing and supporting its talented and creative imaginations, listening to and being heard instead of pushing people away. In other words, there is no finish line where we could definitively say 'We have succeeded', apart from the return of our King and hearing his, 'Well done, good and faithful servants.'

Our cultural works matter eternally. They may well be cleansed and brought into the new creation. Let us be faithful to being part of the cultural conversation through winsome witness and imaginative punch that will strengthen our church family and intrigue those alienated from Christ – that is, planting oases. Thus, we pursue faithfulness in the task of aesthetic cultural witness until Christ returns. May the Spirit draw us into integrity in our aesthetic, imaginative witness before a watching world.

Credits

I acknowledge with grateful thanks permission granted to include extracts or images from the following in this book.

Quotations

Sho Baraka, for permission to include lyrics from 'KJPJ'.

Wendell Berry, '2007, VI' ['It is hard to have hope']. Extract from the poem reprinted with the permission of The Permissions Company, LLC on behalf of Counterpoint Press.

Crosslands Foundation, for granting permission to expand on an earlier, shorter version of material published as a training curriculum on 'Christian imagination' in 2017.

Emily Dickinson, 'Tell all the truth but tell it slant', pp. 506–507 of THE POEMS OF EMILY DICKINSON, edited by Thomas H. Johnson, Cambridge, Mass.: The Belknap Press of Harvard University Press, Copyright © 1951, 1955 by the President and Fellows of Harvard College. Copyright © renewed 1979, 1983 by the President and Fellows of Harvard College. Copyright © 1914, 1918, 1919, 1924, 1929, 1930, 1932, 1935, 1937, 1942, by Martha Dickinson Bianchi. Copyright © 1952, 1957, 1958, 1963, 1965, by Mary L. Hampson. Used by permission. All rights reserved.

C. S. Lewis, *Prince Caspian*, The Chronicles of Narnia (New York: Scholastic, 1979); *An Experiment in Criticism* (Cambridge: Cambridge University Press, 1961); and 'The weight of glory', sermon delivered at the Church of St Mary the Virgin, Oxford (8 June 1942). With thanks to the C. S. Lewis Company for granting permission to reprint excerpts from these works (© copyright CS Lewis Pte Ltd, 1951, 1953 and 1961, respectively).

J. R. R. Tolkien, Letter to Robert Murray, S.J., dated 2 December 1953, in *The Letters of J. R. R. Tolkien* (New York: Houghton Mifflin, 2000).

Extract reprinted by permission of HarperCollins Publishers Ltd © 1981, J.R.R. Tolkien.

J. R. R. Tolkien, *The Lord of the Rings* (London: HarperCollins, 1995 [1954–55]). Extracts reprinted by permission of HarperCollins Publishers Ltd © 1954–55, J.R.R. Tolkien.

J. R. R. Tolkien, 'On fairy-stories' in *Tree and Leaf* (London and New York: HarperCollins, 2001 [1964]). Extracts reprinted by permission of HarperCollins Publishers Ltd © 1964, J.R.R. Tolkien.

Images

Ruth Naomi Floyd, for permission to reproduce her photographs 'Light, apples, and shadows' and 'Woman and the veil'.

Ryan Green, for permission to reproduce a still from the video game *That Dragon, Cancer*

Krzystof Kieślowski's *A Short Film about Love*. Thanks are due to the Wytwórnia Filmów Dokumentalnych i Fabularnych (the Polish national Documentary and Feature Film Studio) for granting permission to use a still from the film.

Pew Research Center, for permission to reproduce the chart 'Attitudes on same-sex marriage' (2019).

Dave Pike, *kintsugi* artist (<www.kintsugi.com/?page_id=8>), for permission to reproduce images of his work.

Lee Price, for permission to reproduce an image of her triptych 'Sleeping with peaches'.

Jason Ramasami, for permission to reproduce the line illustrations within the text and on page 3 of the plate section, <https://saamvisual.com>.

Claire Elise Turnau Ward, for permission to reproduce an image of her work 'The parable of the oasis that was really a portal to another universe'.

Bibliography

Adorno, Theodor, 'Culture industry reconsidered' in Paul Maris and Sue Thornham (eds), *Media Studies: A reader* (New York: New York University Press, 2nd edn, 2000 [1963]).

Alexander, Tim, 'Double entendre: A glimpse into the meanings of slave songs', *UC Merced Undergraduate Research Journal*, vol. 7, no. 1 (2014), pp. 114–120, especially pp. 116–117, <https://escholarship.org/content/qt4h3778q2/qt4h3778q2.pdf>, accessed February 2023.

Alexander, T. Desmond and Baker, David W. (eds), *Dictionary of the Old Testament: Pentateuch* (Downers Grove, IL: InterVarsity Press, 2003), pp. 137–138.

Allberry, Sam, *Is God Anti-Gay?* (Epsom, Surrey: The Good Book Company, 2013).

AND Campaign, <https://andcampaign.org>, accessed February 2023.

Anderson, Evan D. and Barbey, Aron K., 'Moral reasoning: A network neuroscience perspective' in Anna Abraham (ed.), *The Cambridge Handbook of the Imagination* (Cambridge: Cambridge University Press, 2020).

Anderson, Jonathan A. and Dyrness, William, *Modern Art and the Life of a Culture: The religious impulses of modern art*, Studies in Theology and the Arts (Downers Grove, IL: InterVarsity Press, 2016).

Armstrong, Thomas, *Multiple Intelligences in the Classroom* (Alexandria, VA: ASCD, 4th edn, 2018).

Arnheim, Rudolf, *Visual Thinking* (Berkeley, CA: University of California Press, 1969).

ArtWay, 'Educational institutions', *ArtWay*, <https://artway.eu/content.php?id=112&lang=en&action=show>, accessed March 2023.

Arveson, Paul, 'Calvin's role in the history of science', paper delivered on Calvin's 500th birthday, National Presbyterian Church,

Washington, DC (May 2009), <www.arveson.com/chr//resources/articles/Calvins_role.pdf>, accessed February 2023.

Asma, Steven, *Evolution of the Imagination* (Chicago, IL: University of Chicago Press, 2017).

Assayas, Mischka, *Bono on Bono: Conversations with Michka Assayas* (New York: Riverhead, 2005).

Association for Psychological Science, 'Imagination can influence perception', APS (16 June 2011), <www.psychologicalscience.org/news/releases/imagination-can-influence-perception.html>, accessed February 2023.

——, 'Imagination can influence perception', *ScienceDaily* (24 June 2011), <www.sciencedaily.com/releases/2011/06/110616193907.htm>, accessed February 2023.

Atra-Hasis, <www.livius.org/sources/content/anet/104-106-the-epic-of-atrahasis>, accessed February 2023.

Augustine, *City of God* in *St Augustine's* City of God *and* On Christian Doctrine, A Select Library of the Nicene and Post-Nicene Fathers of the Christian Church, tr. Marcus Dods, ed. Phillip Schaff (Edinburgh: T&T Clark and Grand Rapids, MI: Eerdmans, series I, vol. II, 1886), <https://ccel.org/ccel/s/schaff/npnf102/cache/npnf102.pdf>, accessed 2023.

——, Homily 7 on the First Epistle of John, paragraph 8, in H. Browne (tr.), Philip Schaff (ed.), *Nicene and Post-Nicene Fathers*, First Series, vol. 7 (Buffalo, NY: Christian Literature Publishing Co., 1888); Homily 7 also revised and edited for New Advent by Kevin Knight, <www.newadvent.org/fathers/170207.htm>, accessed February 2023.

Australian Bureau of Statistics, '1301.0 – Year Book Australia 2006: Religious affiliation', Australian Bureau of Statistics (20 January 2006), <www.abs.gov.au/ausstats/abs@.nsf/bb8db737e2af84b8ca2571780015701e/bfdda1ca506d6cfaca2570de0014496e!OpenDocument>, accessed February 2023.

——, 'Religion in Australia: 2016 census data summary', Australian Bureau of Statistics (28 June 2017), <www.abs.gov.au/ausstats/abs@.nsf/Lookup/by+Subject/2071.0~2016~Main+Features~Religion+Data+Summary~70>, accessed February 2023.

Azurdia, Arturo, *Connected Christianity: Engaging culture without compromise* (Fearn, Ross-shire, Scotland, and Bridgend, Wales: Christian Focus with Bryntirion Press, 2009).

Baker, Hunter, 'Can Christians change the world after *Obergefell*?' in Collin Hansen (ed.), *Revisiting 'Faithful Presence'*: To Change the World *five years later* (Deerfield, IL: Gospel Coalition Press, Kindle edn, 2015), e-book available online at <www.thegospelcoalition.org/article/revisiting-faithful-presence-to-change-the-world-five-years-later>, accessed February 2023, loc. 786.

Balmer, Randall, 'The Kinkade crusade', *Christianity Today* (4 December 2000), <www.christianitytoday.com/ct/2000/december4/6.48.html?start=2>, accessed February 2023.

Baraka, Sho, address given in Atlanta for Kulture City, an autism advocacy group, KULTURECITY, YouTube (3 March 2016), <www.youtube.com/watch?time_continue=988&v=iqiQR7qJoac>, accessed February 2023.

——, email correspondence with author (16 June 2019).

——, 'Epilogue 2: KJPJ', *Talented 10th* (Lions and Liars Music, 2013), track 16.

——, 'Sho Baraka: About', Humble Beast, <https://humblebeast.com/books/sho-baraka>, accessed May 2023.

——, 'Sho Baraka presents: Hello Rev – Kill Jesus, Praise Judas – Live Music Video (@hisocieties)', *Rapzilla*, YouTube (12 March 2012), 5:19, <www.youtube.com/watch?v=-NPemiiEVwA>, accessed February 2023.

——, 'Sho Baraka responds to the LifeWay decision', Forth District, YouTube (10 February 2017), 5:00, <www.youtube.com/watch?v=IlKxmkxZLoI>, accessed February 2023.

——, 'Words, 2006', *The Narrative* (Humble Beast, 2016), track 12; 'Words 2006', Sho Baraka, YouTube <www.youtube.com/watch?v=C_6ieBZkVlU>, accessed February 2023.

Barna, '51% of churchgoers do not know of the great commission', Barna (27 March 2018), <www.barna.com/research/half-churchgoers-not-heard-great-commission>, accessed February 2023.

Barr, Jerram, *Echoes of Eden: Reflections on Christianity, literature, and the arts* (Wheaton, IL: Crossway, 2013).

Barrett, Matthew, 'Reformed rap: Shai Linne', *Credo* (24 September 2011), <https://credomag.com/2011/09/reformed-rap-shai-linne>, accessed February 2023.

Basham, Megan, 'It's not about the dream', *World* (24 September 2011), <https://wng.org/articles/its-not-about-the-dream-1617330209>, accessed February 2023.

Bauer, Walter, Arndt, William F. and Gingrich, F. Wilbur, *A Greek–English Lexicon of the New Testament and Other Early Christian Literature* (Chicago, IL: University of Chicago Press, 2nd edn, 1979), pp. 9, 202.

Bauman, Neil, 'Apophenia, audio pareidolia and musical ear syndrome', Center for Hearing Loss Help (9 July 2015), <http://hearinglosshelp.com/blog/apophenia-audio-pareidolia-and-musical-ear-syndrome>, accessed February 2023.

Bavinck, Herman, 'Common grace', rectoral address, Theological University Kampen (December 1894), in R. C. Van Leeuwen (tr.), *Calvin Theological Journal*, vol. 24, no. 1 (April 1989), pp. 41, 51.

Baxter, Richard, *The Saint's Everlasting Rest* in *The Practical Works of Richard Baxter* (Ligonier, PA: Soli Deo Gloria, vol. 3, 1990), p. 293, cited in Eifion Evans, 'The Puritan use of the imagination', The Highway (n.d.), <www.the-highway.com/imagination_Evans.html>, accessed February 2023.

Bellah, Robert, 'Civil religion in America', *Daedalus*, vol. 96, no. 1 (Winter 1967), pp. 1–21, <www.robertbellah.com/articles_5.htm>, accessed February 2023.

Bennett, Jeff, 'Wars on Kinkade', *Deviant Art* (24 October 2013), <http://alienartisan.deviantart.com/gallery/46432162/Wars-on-Kinkade>, accessed February 2023.

Berger, Peter (ed.), *The Desecularization of the World: Resurgent religion and world politics* (Grand Rapids, MI: Eerdmans, 1999).

Berry, Wendell, 'Christianity and the survival of creation' in *Sex, Economy, Freedom and Community: Eight essays* (New York: Pantheon Books, 1993), p. 113.

——, 'It is hard to have hope. It is harder as you grow old' in *This Day: Collected and new Sabbath poems* (New York: Counterpoint Press,

2013), <https://wordsfortheyear.com/2019/01/20/2007-vi-it-is-hard-to-have-hope-by-wendell-berry>, accessed February 2023.

——, 'Wendell Berry reads a poem on hope', Moyers & Company, YouTube (3 October 2013), <www.youtube.com/watch?v=2j_r4jb9AYw&t=216s>, accessed February 2023.

Bible Project, The, 'Literary styles in the Bible', BibleProject, YouTube (22 July 2017), <www.youtube.com/watch?v=oUXJ8Owes8E>, accessed February 2023.

Biggin, Matthew, '*LOTR: The Rings of Power* show budget: Will cost more than $1 billion', *ScreenRant* (11 February 2022), <https://screenrant.com/lotr-rings-power-show-budget-billion-amazon-details>, accessed February 2023.

'big objections, The', Kings Church Eastbourne (n.d.), <www.kings.church/bigobjections.php>, accessed February 2023.

Bingham, Matthew C., 'Brains, bodies, and the task of discipleship: Re-aligning anthropology and ministry', *Themelios*, vol. 46, no. 1 (April 2021), <www.thegospelcoalition.org/themelios/article/brains-bodies-and-the-task-of-discipleship-re-aligning-anthropology-and-ministry>, accessed February 2023.

Blume, K. Allen/Biblical Recorder, '"Guilty as Charged," Cathy says of Chick-fil-A's stand on biblical and family values', *Baptist Press* (16 July 2012), <www.bpnews.net/38271>, accessed February 2023.

Boden, Margaret A., 'Creativity in a nutshell' in *The Creative Mind: Myths and mechanisms* (London: Routledge, 2004).

Bonhoeffer, Dietrich, *Letters and Papers from Prison*, tr. Reginald Fuller, Frank Clark, et. al., ed. Eberhard Bethge (New York: Touchstone, 1997), p. 382.

Bowie, David, interview with Charlie Rose, *The Charlie Rose Show*, PBS (31 March 1998); 'David Bowie: To be an artist is to be "dysfunctional" (Mar. 31, 1998)', Charlie Rose, YouTube, <www.youtube.com/watch?v=t8CNhakfB7c>, accessed February 2023.

Brigham Young University, 'Neuroscientists watch imagination happening in the brain', *ScienceDaily* (28 August 2014), <www.sciencedaily.com/releases/2014/08/140828110935.htm>, accessed February 2023.

Brown, Francis, Driver, S. R. and Briggs, Charles A., *The New Brown–Driver–Briggs–Gesenius Hebrew and English Lexicon* (Peabody, MA: Hendrickson Publishers, 1979), pp. 871–872.

Brown, Frank Burch, *Good Taste, Bad Taste, and Christian Taste: Aesthetics in religious life* (Oxford: Oxford University Press, 2000).

Browne, H. (tr.), Schaff, Philip (ed.), *Nicene and Post-Nicene Fathers*, First Series, Volume 7 (Buffalo, NY: Christian Literature Publishing Co., 1888).

Bruce, F. F., *The Epistles of John* (Grand Rapids, MI: Eerdmans, 1970), pp. 60–64.

Bruenig, Elizabeth, 'Why evangelicals aren't what they used to be', *New York Times* (6 November 2020), <www.nytimes.com/2020/11/06/opinion/evangelicals-republicans.html>, accessed February 2023.

Buckley, Cara, 'His turn with the past', *New York Times* (28 July 2014), <www.nytimes.com/2014/07/29/movies/john-michael-mcdonagh-carves-his-own-niche-with-calvary.html>, accessed February 2023.

Burnett, E. Stephen, 'Imagination: For God's glory and others' good, part 3', *Speculative Faith: Exploring epic stories for God's glory* (9 June 2011), <http://speculativefaith.lorehaven.com/imagination-for-gods-glory-and-others-good-part-3>, accessed February 2023.

Burton, Tara Isabella, *Strange Rites: New religions for a godless world* (New York: Public Affairs, 2020), especially chapters 2 and 3.

Byrne, Ruth M. J., 'The counterfactual imagination: The impact of alternatives to reality on morality' in Anna Abraham (ed.), *The Cambridge Handbook of the Imagination* (Cambridge: Cambridge University Press, 2020).

Cai, Zong-qi, 'Poetics of imagination: Wordsworth and Lui Xie on literary creation' in *Configurations of Comparative Poetics: Three perspectives on Western and Chinese literary criticism* (Honolulu, HI: University of Hawai'i Press, 2002), pp. 154–155.

Calvin, John, *Institutes of the Christian Religion,* ed. John T. MacNeill, tr. Ford Lewis Battles (Philadelphia, PA: Westminster Press, 1960), 2.2.15.

Carpenter, Humphrey (ed.), Letter to Robert Murray, S.J., dated 2 December 1953, in *The Letters of J. R. R. Tolkien* (New York: Houghton Mifflin, 2000), p. 172.

Carpenter, John, 'Seeing the truth' scene, 'THEY LIVE Clip – Obey (1988)', JoBlo Movieclips, YouTube (26 August 2019), <www.youtube.com/watch?v=g4XiKChyK7A>, accessed February 2023.

Carpenter, John, dir., *They Live*, Universal Pictures (1988).

Carruthers, Peter, 'Human creativity: Its cognitive basis, its evolution, and its connections with childhood pretence', *British Journal for the Philosophy of Science*, vol. 53, no. 2 (June 2002), pp. 225–249, <http://faculty.philosophy.umd.edu/pcarruthers/Creative-thinking.htm>, accessed February 2023.

Carter, Craig A., *Rethinking Christ and Culture: A post-Christendom perspective* (Grand Rapids, MI: Brazos, 2006), especially chapter 4.

Cary, James, *The Sacred Art of Joking* (London: SPCK, 2019), p. 90.

Cavicchi, Daniel, *Tramps Like Us: Music and meaning among Springsteen fans* (Oxford: Oxford University Press, 1998), pp. 41–57.

Chalmers, Thomas, sermon, 'The expulsive power of a new affection' (1855), <www.monergism.com/thethreshold/sdg/Chalmers,%20Thomas%20–%20The%20Exlpulsive%20Power%20of%20a%20New%20Af.pdf>, accessed January 2023.

Chesterton, G. K., 'The five deaths of the faith', *The Everlasting Man* (San Francisco, CA: Ignatius Press, 1993 [1925]), part 2, chapter 6, <www.worldinvisible.com/library/chesterton/everlasting/part2c6.htm>, accessed February 2023.

Chick, Jack T., Chick tracts, <www.chick.com>.

Chylińska, Monika, 'Counterfactual imagination as a mental tool for innovation', *AVANT*, vol. VIII, Special Issue (21 November 2017), pp. 241–251, <www.researchgate.net/publication/321223287_Counterfactual_Imagination_as_a_Mental_Tool_for_Innovation/fulltext/5a157c920f7e9b925cd5525f/Counterfactual-Imagination-as-a-Mental-Tool-for-Innovation.pdf>, accessed February 2023.

Clarke, Greg, 'Grace, karma and Bono', Center for Public Christianity (18 March 2008), <www.publicchristianity.org/grace-karma-and-bono>, accessed February 2023.

Clowney, Edmund P., 'Living art: Christian experience and the arts' in D. A. Carson and John D. Woodbridge (eds), *God and Culture*

(Grand Rapids, MI: Eerdmans, 1993), <https://biblicalworldview21.org/living-art-christian-experience-and-the-arts>, accessed February 2023.

Coleman, Dustin J., 'Derek Webb, wrestling with the category of "ex-Christian", and the nature of true saving faith', *Theology Along the Way* (10 April 2018), <https://theologyalongtheway.org/2018/04/10/derek-webb-wrestling-with-the-category-of-ex-christian-and-the-nature-of-true-saving-faith>, accessed February 2023.

Coleridge, Samuel Taylor, *Christabel; Kubla Khan, a Vision; The Pains of Sleep* (London: John Murray, 1816), <www.poetryfoundation.org/poems/43991/kubla-khan>, accessed February 2023.

Cooper, Betsy, Cox, Daniel, Lienesch, Rachel and Jones, Robert P., 'Exodus: Why Americans are leaving religion – and why they're unlikely to come back', PRRI.org (22 September 2016), <www.prri.org/research/prri-rns-poll-nones-atheist-leaving-religion>, accessed February 2023.

Cordova, Carlene (writer, director) and Broadway, Cliff (writer), *Ringers: Lord of the fans* (Sony Pictures Home Entertainment, 2005; DVD, Planet BB, 2005).

Cosper, Mike, 'Creation, culture, redemption, and hip hop: A response to the NCFIC panel', *Mike Cosper* (29 November 2013), <https://web.archive.org/web/20140203075613/http://www.mikedcosper.com/home/creation-culture-redemption-and-hip-hop-a-response-the-ncfic-panel>, accessed February 2023.

——, *Rhythms of Grace: How the Church's worship tells the story of the gospel* (Wheaton, IL: Crossway, Kindle edn, 2013) loc. 294–1050, 320, 1522–1564, 1930–1933, chapters 1–4.

——, *The Stories We Tell: How TV and movies long for and echo the truth* (Wheaton, IL: Crossway, 2014, Kindle edn), loc. 675–681.

Covington, David, *A Redemptive Theology of Art: Restoring godly aesthetics to doctrine and culture* (Grand Rapids, MI: Zondervan, 2018), pp. 92–93, 182, 185, 214–215.

Covington, Jesse, 'Cognition and embodiment: An ongoing conversation with Jamie Smith', *Civitas Peregrina* (1 February 2014), <http://civitasperegrina.wordpress.com/tag/james-k-a-smith>, accessed February 2023.

Covington, Jesse, Lee, Maurice, Skripsky, Sarah and Stern, Lesa, 'Irreducibly embodied: 4 questions on *Imagining the Kingdom*, *Books and Culture*, January/February 2014, <www.booksandculture.com/articles/2014/janfeb/irreducibly-embodied.html?paging=off>, accessed February 2023.

Crouch, Andy, *Culture Making: Recovering our creative calling* (Downers Grove, IL: InterVarsity Press, 2008), chapter 6.

Crowley, Aleister, *Liber AL vel Legis (The Book of the Law)*, III, The Law of Thelema, <https://lib.oto-usa.org/libri/liber0220.html>, accessed February 2023.

Cummings, Doug, 'Great directors: Kieślowski, Krzysztof', *Senses of Cinema*, no. 27 (July 2003), <http://sensesofcinema.com/2003/great-directors/Kieslowski>, accessed February 2023.

Daniels, David, 'Sho Baraka's "The Narrative" and Bizzle's "Crowns & Crosses" share several Billboard charts', *Rapzilla* (1 November 2016), <https://rapzilla.com/2016-11-sho-baraka-s-the-narrative-and-bizzle-s-crowns-crosses-share-several-billboard-charts>, accessed February 2023.

Dark, David, *Everyday Apocalypse: The sacred revealed in Radiohead, the Simpsons and other pop icons* (Grand Rapids, MI: Brazos Press, 2002), p. 19.

Davies, Jim, *Imagination: The science of your mind's greatest power* (New York: Pegasus Books, 2019), chapter 2.

Derrida, Jacques, 'Différance' in Richard Kearney and Mara Rainwater (eds), *The Continental Philosophy Reader* (London and New York: Routledge, 1996).

Detweiler, Craig, *Into the Dark: Seeing the sacred in the top films of the 21st century* (Grand Rapids, MI: Baker Academic, 2008), pp. 29–37.

Devi, Debra, 'The language of the blues: Griot', *American Blues Scene* (10 July 2014), <www.americanbluesscene.com/language-blues-griot>, accessed February 2023.

DeYoung, Kevin, 'Jesus, friend of sinners: But how?', The Gospel Coalition (4 March 2014), <https://blogs.thegospelcoalition.org/kevindeyoung/2014/03/04/jesus-friend-of-sinners-but-how>, accessed February 2023.

Dickerson, Matthew, *Following Gandalf: Epic battles and moral victory in* The Lord of the Rings (Grand Rapids, MI: Brazos Press, 2003), chapter 7 and pp. 96–100, 138–143, 204–206.

Dickinson, Emily, 'Tell all the truth but tell it slant' in Thomas H. Johnson (ed.), *The Complete Poems of Emily Dickinson* (Boston, MA, and Toronto, Ontario: Little Brown & Company, 1960), pp. 506–507, <www.poetryfoundation.org/poems/56824/tell-all-the-truth-but-tell-it-slant-1263>, accessed February 2023.

Di Rosso, Jason, 'Director John Michael McDonagh discusses *Calvary* and Catholicism', *Radio National* (3 July 2014), <https://discover.abc.net.au/index.html#/?configure%5BgetRankingInfo%5D=true&configure%5BclickAnalytics%5D=true&configure%5BuserToken%5D=anonymous-b5ddaebe-a873-4d21-ac61-c49d0d4ff376&configure%5BhitsPerPage%5D=10&query=john%20michael%20mcdonagh&page=1>, accessed February 2023.

Dooyeweerd, Herman, *A New Critique of Theoretical Thought*, Volume 1, tr. David H. Freeman and William S. Young (Jordan Station, Ontario: Paideia Press, 1984 [1953]), p. 4.

Dreher, Rod, 'The accidental Benedict option', *American Conservative* (19 April 2015), <www.theamericanconservative.com/dreher/accidental-benedict-option>, accessed February 2023.

——, *The Benedict Option: A strategy for Christians in a post-Christian nation* (New York: Sentinel, 2017), pp. 12–15, 101, chapters 5 and 6 and 'FAQ'.

——, 'Critics of the Benedict Option', *American Conservative* (8 July 2015), <www.theamericanconservative.com/dreher/critics-of-the-benedict-option>, accessed February 2023.

——, 'Head for higher ground', *American Conservative* (21 January 2016), <www.theamericanconservative.com/dreher/head-for-higher-ground>, accessed February 2023.

DuBoisopedia, 'Talented Tenth', *DuBoisopedia*, <https://web.archive.org/web/20160329212603/http://scua.library.umass.edu/duboisopedia/doku.php?id=about:talented_tenth>, accessed March 2023.

Dubs, Kathleen E., 'Providence, fate and chance: Boethian philosophy in *The Lord of the Rings*' in *Tolkien and the Invention of Myth: A reader*, ed. Jane Chance (Lexington, KY: University of Kentucky Press, 2004).

Duffet, Mark, *Understanding Fandom: An introduction to the study of media fan culture* (London and New York: Bloomsbury Academic, 2013), pp. 153 ff.

Dylan, Bob, 'Gotta serve somebody', *Slow Train Coming* (Columbia Records, CD, 1979), track 4.

Dyrness, William, *Reformed Theology and Visual Culture: The Protestant imagination from Calvin to Edwards* (Cambridge: Cambridge University Press, 2004).

Ebert, Roger, 'Krzysztof Kieślowski: In memoriam', *RogerEbert.com* (14 March 1996), <www.rogerebert.com/interviews/krzysztof-kieslowski-in-memoriam>, accessed February 2023.

——, 'Video games can never be art', *Roger Ebert.com* (16 April 2010), <www.rogerebert.com/rogers-journal/video-games-can-never-be-art>, accessed February 2023.

Edgar, William, 'Ain't it hard: Suffering and hope in the blues', *Modern Reformation*, vol. 14, no. 1 (January–February 2005), <https://issuu.com/modernreformation/docs/the-blue-note-january-february-2005>, pp. 3–39, accessed February 2023.

——, *Created and Creating: A biblical theology of culture* (Downers Grove, IL: InterVarsity Press, 2016), pp. 176–177.

——, 'The deep joy of jazz', *byFaith Online* (1 October 2006), <https://byfaithonline.com/the-deep-joy-of-jazz>, accessed February 2023.

——, 'How does music mean?' in *Taking Note of Music* (London: SPCK, 1986), pp. 57–58.

——, interview, *see under* Mathes, Glenda

——, *A Supreme Love: The music of jazz and the hope of the gospel* (Downers Grove, IL: InterVarsity Press, 2022).

——, 'The threat of culture', posted on the now defunct Gospel and Culture Project's website, March 2009.

Editors of Encyclopaedia Britannica, The, 'Krzysztof Kieślowski', Britannica, <www.britannica.com/biography/Krzysztof-Kieslowski>, accessed March 2023.

Enuma Elish, sixth tablet, <www.sacred-texts.com/ane/stc/stc09.htm>, accessed February 2023.

Eshelman, Nate, '"Spiritual worship" or "reasonable service" in Romans 12:1', *Puritan Board* (15 January 2010), <www.puritanboard.com/threads/spiritual-worship-or-reasonable-service-in-romans-12-1.57677>, accessed February 2023.

Facista, Kaitlyn, 'How Tolkien's Middle-earth introduced me to Catholicism', *Tea with Tolkien* (n.d.), <www.teawithtolkien.com/blog/2017/2/10/tolkien-my-conversion-to-catholicism>, accessed February 2023.

Fanlore, 'Frodo lives!', *Fanlore* (14 January 2022), <https://fanlore.org/wiki/Frodo_Lives!>, accessed February 2023.

Ferguson, Kirby, 'Everything is a remix remastered (2015 HD)', Kirby Ferguson, YouTube (17 May 2016), <www.youtube.com/watch?v=nJPERZDfyWc&t=4s>, accessed March 2023.

Ferguson, Sinclair, *The Holy Spirit,* Contours of Christian Theology, ed. Gerald Bray (Downers Grove, IL: InterVarsity Press, 1996), p. 246.

Ferris, William, 'Blues roots and development', *The Black Perspective in Music*, vol. 2, no. 2 (Autumn 1974), pp. 122–127.

Floyd, Ruth Naomi, recorded interview with author, 14 August 2015.

——, *Root to the Fruit* (Contour, 2007).

Frank, Jenn, 'He's still alive', *Unwinnable* (5 April 2013), <www.unwinnable.com/2013/04/05/that-dragon-cancer>, accessed February 2023.

Freed, Richard, 'The tech industry's war on kids: How psychology is being used as a weapon against children', *Medium* (12 March 2018), <https://medium.com/@richardnfreed/the-tech-industrys-psychological-war-on-kids-c452870464ce>, accessed February 2023.

Friedrich, Jim, 'Kieślowski's *Decalogue*: A masterpiece of religious cinema', *The Religious Imagineer* (28 January 2017), <https://jimfriedrich.com/2017/01/28/kieslowskis-decalogue-a-masterpiece-of-religious-cinema>, accessed February 2023.

Fujimura, Makoto, *Art and Faith: A theology of making* (New Haven, CT, and London: Yale University Press, 2020), pp. 12–14, 16–19, 34–35, 66–72, 92, 101–104, 112, 113–118.

——, *Culture Care: Reconnecting with beauty for our common life* (Downers Grove, IL: InterVarsity Press, Kindle edn, 2017), loc. 674, 1555.

——, *Silence and Beauty: Hidden faith born of suffering* (Downers Grove, IL: InterVarsity Press, 2016), especially chapter 3, plus chapter 2 and pp. 207–210.

Futter, Mike, 'Joel Green, inspiration for That Dragon, Cancer, passes away at age 5', *GameInformer* (13 March 2014), <www.gameinformer.com/b/news/archive/2014/03/13/joel-green-inspiration-for-that-dragon-cancer-passes-away-at-age-5.aspx>, accessed February 2023.

Gaffin Jr, Richard B., *Resurrection and Redemption: A study in Paul's soteriology* (Phillipsburg, NJ: P&R, 1987 [1978]).

Gardella, Peter, *American Civil Religion: What Americans hold sacred* (Oxford and New York: Oxford University Press, 2014), p. 3.

Gautam, Sandy, 'The faculty of imagination: Neural substrates and mechanisms', Science 2.0 (5 June 2007), <www.science20.com/sandygautam/the_faculty_of_imagination_neural_substrates_and_mechanisms>, accessed February 2023.

Gerson, Michael, 'The last temptation', *The Atlantic* (April 2018), <www.theatlantic.com/magazine/archive/2018/04/the-last-temptation/554066>, accessed February 2023.

Godawa, Brian, *Hollywood Worldviews: Watching films with wisdom and discernment* (Downers Grove, IL: InterVarsity Press, 2002), p. 13.

Goffman, Erving, *The Presentation of Self in Everyday Life* (New York: Doubleday, 1959).

Goldensohn, Barry, 'On kitsch', *Salmagundi: A quarterly of the humanities and social sciences*, vol. 85–86 (Winter–Spring, 1990), p. 248, cited in Tomas Kulka, *Kitsch and Art* (University Park, PA: Pennsylvania State University Press, 1996), pp. 94–95.

Gordon, Alastair, *Why Art Matters* (London: IVP, 2021).

Grant, Christan, 'Top ten most depressing music genres', The Top Tens (n.d.), <www.thetoptens.com/depressing-music-genres>, accessed February 2023.

Green, Amy, 'A video game to cope with grief', TEDNYC (February 2017), <www.ted.com/talks/amy_green_a_video_game_to_cope_with_grief>, accessed February 2023.

Green, Ryan and Amy and Larson, Josh, Skype interview with author (10 December 2015).

Green, Ryan and Amy and Larson, Josh, *That Dragon, Cancer* (Numinous Games, 2016).

Hahne, Seth T., 'Art: What is it good for?' *Christ and Pop Culture* (13 May 2019), <https://christandpopculture.com/art-what-is-it-good-for>, accessed February 2023.

Hainz, Michael, 'In favour, against and beyond secularization: Contemporary sociological disputes on a core concept of the sociology of religion', conference paper delivered at Eurojess, Lviv, Ukraine (August 2013), <www.researchgate.net/publication/271699405_In_Favour_Against_and_Beyond_Secularization_-_Contemporary_Sociological_Disputes_on_a_Core_Concept_of_the_Sociology_of_Religion>, accessed February 2023.

Hamlet, Janice D., 'Word! The African American oral tradition and its rhetorical impact on American popular culture', *Black History Bulletin*, vol. 74, no. 1 (Spring 2011), pp. 27–29, <https://docplayer.net/29619780-Word-the-african-american-oral-tradition-and-its-rhetorical-impact-on-american-popular-culture-by-janice-d-hamlet.html>, accessed February 2023.

Hansen, Collin (ed.), *Revisiting 'Faithful Presence'*: To Change the World *five years later* (Deerfield, IL: The Gospel Coalition Press, Kindle edn, 2015), e-book available online at <www.thegospelcoalition.org/article/revisiting-faithful-presence-to-change-the-world-five-years-later>, accessed February 2023, loc. 1177.

Hart, Trevor, 'A suspicion observed: Christian responses to the imagination', lecture delivered for the Billy Graham Center and Marion E. Wade Center Evangelism Roundtable V, 'Imagination and the gospel: Harnessing the imagination to engage contemporary culture and communicate the life-changing gospel', Wheaton College, Wheaton, IL (23–26 April 2008), pp. 4–5, 6–11, 15.

Haskins, James, *Black Music in America: A history through its people* (New York: HarperCollins, 1987), p. 45.

Hawkins, Ryan, 'Exchanging Christ's yoke: A response to Derek Webb, Josh Harris, and others leaving Christianity in search of freedom', *Looking at Christ* (2 September 2019), <www.lookingatchrist.com/exchanging-christs-yoke>, accessed February 2023.

Hedgehog Review, 'Research on evil: An annotated bibliography',

Hedgehog Review, vol. 2, no. 2 (Summer 2000), pp. 100–111, <https://hedgehogreview.com/issues/evil/articles/research-on-evil-an-annotated-bibliography>, accessed February 2023.

Heidegger, Martin, *Introduction to Metaphysics*, tr. Ralph Mannheim (New Haven, CT: Yale University Press, 1974), pp. 27–28, cited in Kathleen Lennon, 'Re-enchanting the world: The role of imagination in perception', *Philosophy*, vol. 85, no. 33 (July 2010), p. 378.

Higgins, Sørina, 'The church's role in art', *Comment* (27 May 2011), <www.cardus.ca/comment/article/the-churchs-role-in-art>, accessed February 2023.

Hobbs, Brent, 'Critiquing NCFIC arguments against Christian rap', *Deeper into Grace* (27 November 2013).

Hoekema, Anthony, *The Bible and the Future* (Grand Rapids, MI: Eerdmans, 1979), pp. 33, 38–40, 73–75 and 285–287.

Holland, Tom, *Dominion: How the Christian revolution remade the world* (New York: Basic Books, 2019, Kindle edn), loc. 13.

Hooker, Lee, quoted in Paul Oliver, *Conversations with the Blues* (New York: Horizon Press, 1965), pp. 160 and 168, quoted in Jon Michael Spencer, *Protest and Praise: Sacred music of black religion* (Minneapolis, MN: Fortress Press, 1990), p. 125.

House, Son, before a concert audience in Wabash, Indiana, in 1964, in Jon Michael Spencer, *Protest and Praise: Sacred music of black religion* (Minneapolis, MN: Fortress Press, 1990), p. 119.

House, Son (Eddie James Jr), 'Preachin' the blues, Part 1', *The Roots of Robert Johnson* (Shenachie Entertainment, 1989 [1930]), track 12.

Hume, David, *Treatise of Human Nature* (New York: Penguin Classics, 1986), book 1, part 3, section X, p. 170.

Hunter, James Davison, 'The challenge of faithfulness' in *To Change the World: The irony, tragedy, and possibility of Christianity in the late modern world* (Oxford and New York: Oxford University Press, 2010), pp. 20, 81–92, 200–210.

——, *Culture Wars: The struggle to define America* (New York: Basic Books, 1991).

Hunter, Robert, *The Greenpeace to Amchitka: An environmental odyssey* (Vancouver, British Columbia: Arsenal Pulp Press, 2004), p. 31, quoted in Doyle Irvin, 'The ent activist: Why "The Lord of the Rings" became a counterculture icon', American Forests (23 May 2017), <www.americanforests.org/blog/tolkien-lord-of-the-rings-became-counterculture-icon>, accessed February 2023.

Hurd, Seth Tower, 'Sho Baraka and Vanessa Hill speak out about their controversial new album', *Relevant* (20 March 2018), <https://relevantmagazine.com/culture/music/sho-baraka-vanessa-hill-speak-controversial-new-album>, accessed February 2023.

Hyde, Lewis, *The Gift: Creativity and the artist in the modern world* (New York: Vintage, 2007 [1983]).

Iacaboni, Marco and Lehrer, Jonah, 'The mirror neuron revolution: Explaining what makes humans social', *Scientific American* (1 July 2008), <www.scientificamerican.com/article/the-mirror-neuron-revolut>, accessed February 2023.

Idato, Michael, 'The true Doctor Who: Tom Baker', *Sydney Morning Herald* (15 November 2013), <www.smh.com.au/entertainment/tv-and-radio/the-true-doctor-who-tom-baker-20131115-2xks9.html>, accessed February 2023.

Imbert, Yannick, 'Covenantal faërie: A Reformed evaluation of Tolkien's theory of fantasy', *Westminster Theological Journal*, vol. 76 (2014), pp. 119–141.

Insdorf, Annette, *Double Lives, Second Chances: The cinema of Krzysztof Kieślowski* (New York: Hyperion, 1999), p. 100.

Irvin, Doyle, 'The ent activist: Why "The Lord of the Rings" became a counterculture icon', American Forests (23 May 2017), <www.americanforests.org/blog/tolkien-lord-of-the-rings-became-counterculture-icon>, accessed February 2023.

Iser, Wolfgang, *The Act of Reading: A theory of aesthetic response* (Baltimore, MD: Johns Hopkins University Press, 1978).

Jauss, Hans Robert, *Aesthetic Experience and Literary Hermeneutics,* tr. Michael Shaw (Minneapolis, MN: University of Minnesota Press, 1982), pp. 30–35.

Jefferson, Mark, 'What's wrong with sentimentality?' *Mind*, vol. XCII, no. 368 (October 1983), pp. 519–529, cited in Gregory Wolfe, *Intruding upon the Timeless: Meditations on art, faith, and mystery* (Baltimore, MD: Square Halo Books, Kindle edn, 2003), loc. 1579, 1612.

Johnson, Blind Willie, 'Dark was the night', *Dark Was the Night* (Columbia/Legacy, CK 65516, 1998 [this track originally recorded in 1927]), track 2; 'Dark was the night, cold was the ground', Blind Willie Johnson – Topic, YouTube, <https://www.youtube.com/watch?v=71Ti_TdpJHE>, accessed February 2023.

——, 'Motherless children'; Blind Willie Johnson, 'Mother's children have a hard time' [incorrectly titled], Traveler Into The Blue, YouTube, <www.youtube.com/watch?v=ywTC7yt7XZw>, accessed March 2023.

Johnson, Blind Willie/traditional, 'Let your light shine on me', *Dark Was the Night* (Columbia/Legacy, CK 65516, 1998 [this track originally recorded in 1929]), track 7; Blind Willie Johnson – 'Let your light shine on me', Traveler Into The Blue, YouTube, <www.youtube.com/watch?v=IcYKEGNQGJc>, accessed February 2023.

Johnson, Robert, 'Crossroad blues', *Robert Johnson: King of the Delta blues* (Columbia Records, 1997 [27 November 1936]), track 1.

Jones, Jeffrey M., 'US church membership falls below majority for first time', Gallup (29 March 2021), <https://news.gallup.com/poll/341963/church-membership-falls-below-majority-first-time.aspx>, accessed February 2023.

Jones, Jo and Mosher, William D., 'Fathers' involvement with their children: United States, 2006–2010', *National Health Statistics Reports*, no. 71 (20 December 2013), <www.cdc.gov/nchs/data/nhsr/nhsr071.pdf>, accessed February 2023.

Josephson-Storm, Jason A., *The Myth of Disenchantment: Magic, modernity, and the birth of the human sciences* (Chicago, IL: University of Chicago Press, 2017).

Jubalaires, The, 'Preacher and the bear', Soundie; The Jubalaires 'Preacher and the bear' (1941), vintage video clips, YouTube (1945), <www.youtube.com/watch?v=1mNP9f84Zk8&ab>, accessed February 2023. (Note that the YouTube recording mistakenly gives the date as 1941.)

K., Stephen, 'Is *Doctor Who* anti-religious?', *ArcadiaPod* (29 September 2011), <https://arcadiapod.com/2011/09/29/is-doctor-who-anti-religious>, accessed February 2023.

Kaag, John, 'The neurological dynamics of the imagination', *Phenomenology and the Cognitive Sciences*, vol. 8, no. 2 (2008), pp. 183–204, <https://citeseerx.ist.psu.edu/viewdoc/download?doi=10.1.1.471.2279&rep=rep1&type=pdf>, accessed February 2023.

Kearney, Richard, *The Wake of the Imagination* (New York: Routledge, 1988).

Kearney, Richard and Rainwater, Mara (eds), *The Continental Philosophy Reader* (London and New York: Routledge, 1996).

Keefe, Josh, 'Why Christian movies are BAD', Josh Keefe, YouTube (14 August 2017), 8:44, <www.youtube.com/watch?v=50_3J6Go5Ng>, accessed May 2023.

Keller, Timothy, 'A book review on the topic of Christian nationalism', Life in the Gospel (Spring 2021), <https://quarterly.gospelinlife.com/book-review-on-the-topic-of-christian-nationalism>, accessed February 2023.

——, *Center Church: Doing balanced, gospel-centered ministry in your city* (Grand Rapids, MI: Zondervan, 2012), especially part 3, 'Gospel contextualization'.

——, 'The dance of God', in *The Reason for God: Belief in an age of skepticism* (New York: Dutton, 2008).

——, *Every Good Endeavor* (New York: Dutton, 2012), p. 242.

——, *The Prodigal God: Recovering the heart of the Christian faith* (New York: Dutton, 2008), pp. 92–95.

——, 'Racism and corporate evil: A white guy's perspective', Desiring God, YouTube (26 August 2017), 26:05, <www.youtube.com/watch?v=EhJJcTKTVGo>, accessed February 2023.

——, 'Tim Keller – Center Church: What is contextualization?', Redeemer City to City, YouTube (28 February 2013), <www.youtube.com/watch?v=3eUvwzmV0P8>, accessed January 2023.

Kelley, Nancy, 'Over the rainbow?', NatCen Social Research (11 July 2019), <http://natcen.ac.uk/blog/over-the-rainbow>, accessed February 2023.

Kieślowski, Krzysztof (screenplay, director) and Piesiewicz, Krzysztof (screenplay), *A Short Film about Love* (*Krótki film o milosci*) (Zespol Filmowy 'Tor', 1988; DVD, Artificial Eye, 2002).

Kilby, Clyde, 'The aesthetic poverty of evangelicalism' in Leland Ryken (ed.), *The Christian Imagination: The practice of faith in literature and writing* (Colorado Springs, CO: Shaw Books, rev. exp. edn 2002), pp. 277–278.

Kind, Amy, 'Introduction: exploring imagination' in Amy Kind (ed.), *The Routledge Handbook of Philosophy of Imagination* (New York: Routledge, 2016), p. 3.

Kopp, Ed, 'A brief history of the blues', *All about Jazz* (16 August 2005).

Koyzis, David T., 'Two kingdoms and cultural obedience', *Comment* (1 March 2010), <https://comment.org/two-kingdoms-and-cultural-obedience>, accessed January 2023.

Kulka, Tomas, *Kitsch and Art* (University Park, PA: Pennsylvania State University Press, 1996), pp. 25–42.

Kundera, Milan, 'The Grand March', part 6 of *The Unbearable Lightness of Being*, tr. Michael Henry Heim (Cambridge, MA: Harper & Row, 1984).

Kuntz, Maria Elena de las Carreras, 'Filming the 10 Commandments: Kieślowski as a Catholic director', *Crisis Magazine* (1 November 2000), <www.crisismagazine.com/vault/filming-the-10-commandments-kieslowski-as-a-catholic-director>, accessed February 2023.

Kurosawa, Akira (director), *Rashomon* (Kadokawa Pictures, 1950; DVD, Criterion, 2012).

Laeng, Bruno and Teodorescu, Dinu-Stefan, 'Eye scanpaths during visual imagery reenact those of perception of the same visual scene', *Cognitive Science*, vol. 26, no. 2 (March–April 2002) pp. 207–231, cited in Colin Ware, *Visual Thinking for Design* (Burlington, MA: Morgan Kaufmann, 2008), p. 150.

Lakoff, George and Johnson, Mark, *Metaphors We Live By* (Chicago, IL: University of Chicago Press, 2003).

Langan, Janine, 'The Christian imagination' in Leland Ryken (ed.), *The Christian Imagination: The practice of faith in literature and writing* (Colorado Springs, CO: Shaw Books, rev. exp. edn, 2002), p. 64.

Layne, Joslyn, 'Blind Willie Johnson', *All Music*, <www.allmusic.com/artist/blind-willie-johnson-mn0000040137/biography>, accessed February 2023.

Leavis, F. R., 'Mass civilization and minority culture' in John Storey (ed.), *Cultural Theory and Popular Culture: A reader* (New York: Routledge, 4th edn, 2009 [1930]), p. 14.

Leithart, Peter, *Deep Comedy: Trinity, tragedy, and hope in Western literature* (Moscow, ID: Canon Press, 2006).

——, 'Introduction: The devil has no stories' in *Heroes of the City of Man: A Christian guide to select ancient literature* (Moscow, ID: Canon Press, 1999).

Lennon, Kathleen, 'Re-enchanting the world: The role of imagination in perception', *Philosophy*, vol. 85, no. 33 (July 2010), pp. 375–389.

Lewis, C. S., *An Experiment in Criticism* (Cambridge: Cambridge University Press, 1961), pp. 137–138.

——, *Prince Caspian*, The Chronicles of Narnia (New York: Scholastic, 1979), p. 116.

——, 'The weight of glory', sermon delivered at the Church of St Mary the Virgin, Oxford (8 June 1942), <www.wheelersburg.net/Downloads/Lewis%20Glory.pdf>, accessed February 2023.

Lindvall, Terry, *Sanctuary Cinema: Origins of the Christian film industry* (New York: NYU Press, 2011).

Loftus, Matthew, 'Curse your listeners: Making sense of Derek Webb's *Fingers Crossed*', *Christ and Pop Culture* (7 November 2017), <https://christandpopculture.com/curse-your-listeners-making-sense-derek-webb-fingers-crossed>, accessed January 2023.

Longman III, Tremper and Reid, Daniel L., 'God wars against the forces of chaos' in *God Is a Warrior*, Studies in Old Testament Biblical Theology (Grand Rapids, MI: Zondervan, 1995).

Lubeck, Ray, *Read the Bible for a Change: Understanding and responding to God's word* (Eugene, OR: Wipf & Stock, 2005), p. 14.

Lucas, E. C., 'Cosmology' in T. Desmond Alexander and David W. Baker (eds), *Dictionary of the Old Testament: Pentateuch* (Downers Grove, IL: InterVarsity Press, 2003), pp. 137–138.

McGee, J. Vernon, 'From the top of the Mount of Olives you can see forever', a pamphlet published by his Thru the Bible Radio Network, 1984, <www.ttb.org/resources/electronic-booklets>, see under 'Additional booklets', accessed January 2023.

McLeod, Jeff, 'Tolkien and Dungeons & Dragons', *The Artifice* (20 September 2019), <https://the-artifice.com/tolkien-dungeons-dragons>, accessed February 2023.

Magee, Rosemary M. (ed.), *Conversations with Flannery O'Connor*, (Jackson, MI, and London: University of Mississippi Press, 1987), p. 8.

Mănăstireanu, Dănuţ, 'Perichoresis and the early Christian doctrine of God', *Archæus*, vols XI–XII (2007–2008), pp. 61–63, <www.academia.edu/4794642/Perichoresis_and_the_Early_Christian_Doctrine_of_God>, accessed February 2023.

Marcuse, Herbert, 'The new forms of control' in *One-Dimensional Man: Studies in the ideology of advanced industrial society* (London and New York: Routledge, 1991 [1964]).

Maris, Paul and Thornham, Sue (eds), *Media Studies: A reader* (New York: New York University Press, 2nd edn, 2000 [1963]).

Marsden, George, *Understanding Fundamentalism and Evangelicalism* (Grand Rapids, MI: Eerdmans, 1991), p. 21.

Martin, David, *A General Theory of Secularization* (New York: Harper & Row, 1978).

Mathes, Glenda, interview with William Edgar for *Ascribelog* (6 October 2010), <https://ascribelog.blogspot.com/2010/10/william-edgar-theologian-and-jazz.html>, accessed February 2023.

Mathison, Keith, '2K or not 2K? That is the question: A review of David VanDrunen's *Living in God's Two Kingdoms*, part 1', Ligonier Ministries (9 December 2010), <www.ligonier.org/learn/articles/2k-or-not-2k-question-review-david-vandrunens-living-gods-two-kingdoms>, and part 2, <www.ligonier.org/learn/articles/2k-or-not-2k-question-review-david-vandrunens-living-gods-two-kingdoms-part-2>, both accessed January 2023.

Matis, Hannah, 'The Rings of Power', *Covenant* (10 November 2022), <https://covenant.livingchurch.org/2022/11/10/the-rings-of-power>, accessed February 2023.

Maurer, Monica, *Krzysztof Kieślowski* (North Pomfret, VT: Trafalgar Square Publishing, 2000), p. 13, quoted in Jim Friedrich, 'Kieślowski's *Decalogue*: A masterpiece of religious cinema', *The Religious Imagineer* (28 January 2017), <https://jimfriedrich.com/2017/01/28/Kieslowskis-decalogue-a-masterpiece-of-religious-cinema/#_edn3>, accessed February 2023.

Merleau-Ponty, Maurice, quoted in Kathleen Lennon, 'Re-enchanting the world: The role of imagination in perception', *Philosophy*, vol. 85, no. 33 (July 2010), pp. 375–389.

Middleton, Richard, *A New Heaven and a New Earth: Reclaiming biblical eschatology* (Grand Rapids, MI: Baker Academic, 2014), pp. 68–70, 161–162, 187–189, 190, 194–195, 197–199, 201–204, 218.

Milkowski, Bill, 'Ruth Naomi Floyd: Jazz mass', *JazzTimes* (1 April 2007 [updated 25 April 2019]), <https://jazztimes.com/archives/ruth-naomi-floyd-jazz-mass>, accessed February 2023.

Miller, Paul D. *The Religion of American Greatness: What's wrong with Christian nationalism* (Downers Grove, IL: IVP Academic, 2022), chapter 7.

Miller, Sharon Hodde, 'Evangelicals and the loss of prophetic imagination', *Mere Orthodoxy* (9 February 2017), <https://mereorthodoxy.com/evangelicals-loss-prophetic-imagination>, accessed February 2023.

Mills, Emily, 'Ascent into madness: The story of my personal conversion to fandom', *Whoosh*, vol. 53 (February 2001), <http://whoosh.org/issue53/mills1.html#pussycat>, accessed February 2023.

Milner, Richard, 'The truth about the Christian background of U2', Grunge (26 April 2022), <www.grunge.com/844162/the-truth-about-the-christian-background-of-u2>, accessed February 2023.

Moo, Douglas J., 'Nature in the new creation: New Testament eschatology and the environment', *Journal of the Evangelical Theological Society*, vol. 49, no. 3 (September 2006), p. 468.

Moody, Dwight L., quoted in George Marsden, *Understanding Fundamentalism and Evangelicalism* (Grand Rapids, MI: Eerdmans, 1991), pp. 21, 156–158 and 160–163.

Moore, Alan (writer), Gibbons, Dave (illustrator) and Higgins, John (colourist), *Watchmen* (New York: DC Comics, 1986–1987).

Mouw, Richard, *He Shines in All That's Fair: Culture and common grace* (Grand Rapids, MI, and Cambridge: Eerdmans, 2001).

——, *When the Kings Come Marching In: Isaiah and the new Jerusalem* (Grand Rapids, MI: Eerdmans, rev. edn, Kindle edn, 2002), loc. 430, 457–461.

Murphy, Sean Paul, 'Building the faith-based film ghetto', SeanPaulMurphyVille.com (29 September 2017), <https://seanpaulmurphyville.blogspot.com/2017/09/building-faith-based-film-ghetto.html>, accessed February 2023.

Murray, John, 'Common grace', *Collected Writings of John Murray: Volume 2: Systematic theology* (Edinburgh, Scotland, and Carlisle, PA: Banner of Truth, 1991 [1982]), pp. 25, 93–122, <www.sounddoctrine.net/Modern_Day_Reform_Teaching/John%20 Murray/Common_Grace.htm>, accessed February 2023.

——, *The Epistle to the Romans*, The New International Commentary on the New Testament (Grand Rapids, MI: Eerdmans, 1965), pp. 111, 113–140.

——, *Redemption Accomplished and Applied* (Grand Rapids, MI: Eerdmans, 1955).

Murray, S.J., Robert, Letter to, dated 2 December 1953, in Humphrey Carpenter (ed.), *The Letters of J. R. R. Tolkien* (New York: Houghton Mifflin, 2000), p. 172.

Naasel, Kenrya Rankin, 'It's a myth that black fathers are absent', *New York Times* (12 March 2014), <www.nytimes.com/roomfordebate/2014/03/12/the-assumptions-behind-obamas-initiative/its-a-myth-that-black-fathers-are-absent>, accessed February 2023.

Nakamura, Jeanne and Csikszentmihalyi, Mihaly, 'The concept of flow' in C. R. Snyder and Shane J. Lopez (eds), *Handbook of Positive Psychology* (Oxford: Oxford University Press, 2002), especially pp. 91–92.

Nickel, Eleanor, *Christian Popular Culture: From* The Chronicles of Narnia *to* Duck Dynasty (Eugene, OR: Wipf & Stock, 2021).

Nordqvist, Christian, 'Imagination: How and where does it occur in the brain?', *Medical News Today* (22 September 2013), <www.medicalnewstoday.com/articles/266426.php>, accessed February 2023.

Numbers, The, 'Movie franchises', The Numbers <www.the-numbers.com/movies/franchises#franchise_overview=od4>, accessed February 2023.

Nussbaum, Emily, 'Must-see metaphysics', *New York Times Magazine* (22 September 2002),<www.nytimes.com/2002/09/22/magazine/must-see-metaphysics.html.>, accessed February 2023.

Obrecht, Jas, liner notes for *Dark Was the Night* (Columbia/Legacy, CK 65516, 1998).

O'Connell, Michael and Pener, Degen, 'The 50 most powerful LGBTQ players in Hollywood', *The Hollywood Reporter* (3 June 2020), <www.hollywoodreporter.com/lists/pride-2020-50-powerful-lgbtq-players-hollywood-1295933>, accessed February 2023.

O'Connor, Flannery, *The Habit of Being: Letters of Flannery O'Connor*, ed. Sally Fitzgerald (New York: Vintage, 1980), p. 178.

——, 'Writing short stories' in Sally and Robert Fitzgerald (eds), *Mystery and Manners: Occasional Prose* (New York: Noonday Press, 1969), p. 96.

——, *see also* Magee, Rosemary M.

Oliver, Paul, *Conversations with the Blues* (New York: Horizon Press, 1965), pp. 52, 16, 160, 168, 169–170.

One Wiki to Rule Them All, The, 'One ring: Ring bearers', *The One Wiki to Rule Them All* <https://lotr.fandom.com/wiki/One_Ring#Ring-bearers>, accessed February 2023.

Onishi, Bradley, 'The rise of the #exvangelical', *Religion and Politics* (9 April 2019), <https://religionandpolitics.org/2019/04/09/the-rise-of-exvangelical>, accessed February 2023.

Osit, David and Zouhali-Worrall, Malika (writers and directors), *Thank You for Playing*, available to stream on AppleTV, Amazon Prime and other streaming sites.

Ostadan, 'From The Rings of Power to Poughkeepsie', *The OneRing.net* (26 September 2022), <www.theonering.net/torwp/2022/09/26/115304-from-the-rings-of-power-to-poughkeepsie/>, accessed February 2023.

Parker, Garrett, 'How much is the Lord of the Rings franchise worth?', *Moneyinc.* (14 June 2016 [updated 8 April 2020]), <https://moneyinc.com/lord-of-the-rings-franchise>, accessed February 2023.

Parkins, Larry, '182. The dance is not PERICHŌRĒSIS', *Internet Moments with God's Word* (2 December 2020), <https://moments.nbseminary.com/archives/182-the-dance-is-not-perichoresis>, accessed February 2023.

Parnell, Jonathan, 'Three tips on being a friend to sinners', Desiring God (22 March 2014) <www.desiringgod.org/articles/three-tips-on-being-a-friend-of-sinners>, accessed February 2023.

Peacock, Charlie, *At the Crossroads: An insider's look at the past, present, and future of contemporary Christian music* (Nashville, TN: Broadman & Holman, 1999), p. 17.

Pearce, Joseph, 'Is *The Lord of the Rings* an allegory?', *Faith and Culture: A Journal of the Augustine Institute* (4 May 2018), <www.faithandculture.com/home/2018/5/4/is-the-lord-of-the-rings-an-allegory>, accessed February 2023.

Perry, Samuel L. and Whitehead, Andrew, *Taking America Back for God: Christian nationalism in the United States* (Oxford: Oxford University Press, 2020).

Perry, Susan, 'Mirror neurons', BrainFacts.org (16 November 2008), <www.elegantbrain.com/edu4/classes/readings/depository/misc/mirror_neurons.pdf>, accessed February 2023.

Pew Research Center, 'Attitudes on same-sex marriage: Public opinion on same-sex marriage', Pew Research Center (14 May 2019), <www.pewresearch.org/religion/fact-sheet/changing-attitudes-on-gay-marriage>, accessed February 2023.

——, 'In US, decline of Christianity continues at rapid pace: An update on America's changing religious landscape', Pew Research Center (17 October 2019), <www.pewresearch.org/religion/2019/10/17/in-u-s-decline-of-christianity-continues-at-rapid-ace/#:~:text=The%20religious%20landscape%20of%20the,points%20over%20the%20past%20decade>, accessed February 2023.

——, 'US Religious Knowledge Survey: Executive summary', Pew Research Center (28 September 2010), <www.pewforum.org/2010/09/28/u-s-religious-knowledge-survey>, accessed February 2023.

Pezzulo, Giovanni, Donnarumma, Francesco, Iodice, Pierpaolo, Maisto, Domenico and Stoianov, Ivilin, 'Model-based approaches to active perception and control', *Entropy*, vol. 19 (9 June 2017), <www.mdpi.com/1099-4300/19/6/266/pdf-vor>, accessed February 2023.

Piedmont Renewal Network, 'Our city: the present', <https://renewalnetwork.org/the-present>, accessed February 2023.

Pierre, Vermon, 'Faithful presence needs prophets' in Collin Hansen (ed.), *Revisiting 'Faithful Presence'*: To Change the World *five years later* (Deerfield, IL: The Gospel Coalition Press, Kindle edn, 2015), e-book available online at <www.thegospelcoalition.org/article/revisiting-faithful-presence-to-change-the-world-five-years-later>, accessed February 2023, loc. 1177–1183.

——, interviewed by Collin Hansen, 'Faithful presence needs prophets', The Gospel Coalition (17 November 2015), <www.thegospelcoalition.org/podcasts/tgc-podcast/faithful-presence-needs-prophets>, accessed February 2023.

Popova, Maria, 'Neil Gaiman on how stories last', *The Marginalian* (16 June 2015), <www.brainpickings.org/2015/06/16/neil-gaiman-how-stories-last>, accessed February 2023.

Pound, Ezra, *Make It New: Essays by Ezra Pound* (London: Faber and Faber, 1934).

Powys Maurice, Emma, 'Russell T. Davies on queer representation on TV, time loop anomalies and homophobic folk dancers. Yes, really', *Pink News* (5 January 2020), <www.pinknews.co.uk/2020/01/05/russell-t-davies-john-barrowman-doctor-who-queer-as-folk-lgbt-television>, accessed February 2023.

Price, Lee, *see under* Stringer, Heather Smith

Prior, Karen Swallow, *On Reading Well: Finding the good life through great books* (Grand Rapids, MI: Brazos, 2018), especially pp. 19–22.

Public Religion Research Institute (PRRI), 'The 2020 Census of American Religion, PRRI (8 July 2021)', <www.prri.org/research/2020-census-of-american-religion>, accessed February 2023.

Ratliff, William E. and Flinn, Charles G., 'The hobbit and the hippie', *Modern Age*, vol. 12, no. 2 (Spring 1968), pp. 142–146, <https://isiorg.b-cdn.net/wp-content/uploads/2014/10/ratliff.pdf?x65817>, accessed February 2023.

Reformed-ish-Homeboy, 'Does reading Tolkien make you more interested in Christianity or Catholicism?', Tolkienfans subreddit, <www.reddit.com/r/tolkienfans/comments/9t03wl/does_reading_tolkien_make_you_more_interested_in>, accessed February 2023.

Reinders, Philip F., *Seeking God's Face: Praying with the Bible through the year* (Grand Rapids, MI: Baker Academic, 2013).

Ricoeur, Paul, 'The hermeneutical function of distanciation' in *Hermeneutics and the Human Sciences*, ed. and tr. John B. Thompson (Cambridge and New York: Cambridge University Press, 1981), especially pp. 140–144.

——, 'Life in quest of narrative' in David Wood (ed.), *On Paul Ricoeur: Narrative and Interpretation* (London: Routledge, 1991).

——, 'Metaphor and the central problem of hermeneutics' in *Hermeneutics and the Human Sciences*, tr. and ed. John B. Thompson (Cambridge: Cambridge University Press, 1982).

——, 'Narrative identity', tr. Mark S. Muldoon, *Philosophy Today*, vol. 35, no. 1 (Spring 1991), pp. 73–81, <www.scribd.com/doc/24868946/Paul-Ricoeur-Narrative-Identity>, accessed February 2023.

——, *The Rule of Metaphor: Multidisciplinary studies of the creation of meaning in language*, tr. Robert Czerny with Kathleen McLaughlin and John Costello (Toronto, Ontario: University of Toronto Press, 1977), chapters 6 and 7 and pp. 239–246.

——, *Time and Narrative*, Volume 1, tr. Kathleen McLaughlin and David Pellauer (Chicago, IL: University of Chicago Press, 1984), pp. 70–82.

——, *Time and Narrative*, Volume 3, tr. Kathleen Blamey and David Pellauer (Chicago, IL: University of Chicago Press, 1988), chapter 7 and pp. 160–179.

Ridderbos, Herman, *Paul: An outline of his theology* (Grand Rapids, MI: Eerdmans, 1975), p. 45.

Riess, Jana, 'Religious "nones" are gaining ground in America, and they're worried about the economy', Religion News Service (16 November 2016), <https://religionnews.com/2017/11/16/religious-nones-are-gaining-ground-in-america-and-theyre-worried-about-the-economy-says-new-study>, accessed February 2023.

——, 'Why millennials are really leaving religion (it's not just politics, folks)', *Religion and Ethics Newsweekly* (16 July 2018), <www.pbs.org/wnet/religionandethics/2018/07/16/millennials-really-leaving-religion-not-just-politics-folks/34880>, accessed February 2023.

Roberts, John R., 'Biblical cosmology: Implications for Bible translation', *Journal of Translation*, vol. 9, no. 2 (2013), pp. 1–53, especially

'Picture of biblical cosmology', p. 6, <www.sil.org/system/files/reapdata/12/43/41/124341128276351405827628859265062803872/siljot2013_2_01.pdf>, accessed January 2023.

Robertson, David G., interviewing Professor Linda Woodhead, 'The secularisation thesis', *The Religious Studies Project* (16 April 2012), <www.religiousstudiesproject.com/podcast/podcast-linda-woodhead-on-the-secularisation-thesis>, accessed February 2023.

Rolling Stone, 'Every Super Bowl halftime show, ranked from worst to best to worst', RollingStone.com (14 February 2022), <www.rollingstone.com/culture/culture-lists/super-bowl-halftime-shows-ranked-from-worst-to-best-14201/beyonce-2013-3-228225>, accessed February 2023.

Romanowski, William D., *Cinematic Faith: A Christian perspective on movies and meaning* (Grand Rapids, MI: Baker Academic, 2019), chapter 2.

——, *Eyes Wide Open: Looking for God in popular culture* (Grand Rapids, MI: Brazos Press, rev. exp. edn 2007 [2001]), chapter 7 and pp. 17, 93.

——, *Reforming Hollywood: How American Protestants fought for freedom at the movies* (Oxford and New York: Oxford University Press, 2012), chapter 3.

Rookmaker, Hans, *Modern Art and the Death of a Culture* (Wheaton, IL: Crossway, 1994 [1970]).

Rosencruft, Eli's answer to the question, 'Are the Rabbinic rules of hand washing before eating bread related to their ruling that the scriptures were unclean?', Biblical Hermeneutics Stack Exchange (6 August 2012), <https://hermeneutics.stackexchange.com/questions/2262/are-the-rabbinic-rules-of-hand-washing-before-eating-bread-related-to-their-uli>, accessed January 2023.

Roth, John D. (ed.), *Constantine Revisited: Leithart, Yoder, and the Constantinian debate* (Eugene, OR: Pickwick Publications, 2013).

Rothman, Joshua, 'The church of U2', *New Yorker* (16 September 2014), <www.newyorker.com/culture/cultural-comment/church-u2>, accessed February 2023.

Ryerson, Nick, 'God and country music: Gillian Welch's soul journey', *Christ and Pop Culture* (20 March 2012), <https://christandpopculture.com/god-and-country-music-gillian-welchs-soul-journey>, accessed February 2023.

Ryken, Leland (ed.), *The Christian Imagination: The practice of faith in literature and writing* (Colorado Springs, CO: Shaw Books, rev. exp. edn, 2002), pp. 277–278.

Ryken, Leland, Wilhoit, James C. and Longman III, Tremper (eds), entries 'Chaos', 'Creation', `Sea', 'Day, Day of the Lord', *Dictionary of Biblical Imagery* (Downers Grove, IL: InterVarsity Press, 1998).

Ryken, Philip, *Art for God's Sake: A call to recover the arts* (Phillipsburg, NJ: P&R, 2006).

——, 'How to discourage artists in the church', The Gospel Coalition (27 May 2013), <www.thegospelcoalition.org/article/how-to-discourage-artists-in-the-church>, accessed February 2023.

Sarachik, Justin, 'The Jubalaires were doing gospel rap back in the 1940s', *Rapzilla* (11 July 2016), <https://rapzilla.com/2016-07-the-jubalaires-were-doing-gospel-rap-back-in-the-1940s>, accessed February 2023.

——, 'Sho Baraka's "The Narrative" pulled from LifeWay bookstores for offensive language', *Rapzilla* (8 February 2017), <https://rapzilla.com/2017-02-sho-baraka-s-the-narrative-pulled-from-lifeway-bookstores-for-offensive-language>, accessed February 2023.

Schaeffer, Francis, *Art and the Bible* (Downers Grove, IL: InterVarsity Press, 2006 [1973]).

——, *The God Who Is There* (Downers Grove, IL: InterVarsity Press, 1968), p. 36.

Schlegel, Alexander, Kohler, Peter J., Fogelson, Sergey V., Alexander, Prescott, Konuthula, Dedeepya and Tse, Peter Ulric, 'Network structure and dynamics of the mental workspace', *Proceedings of the National Academy of Sciences*, vol. 110, no. 40 (16 September 2013), <www.pnas.org/content/110/40/16277.full>, accessed February 2023.

Schulze, Quentin, 'Symbolic stewardship: The meaning and purpose of human communication' in *Communicating for Life: Christian stewardship in community and media* (Grand Rapids, MI: Baker Academic, 2000), pp. 126–134.

Seerveld, Calvin, *Bearing Fresh Olive Leaves: Alternative steps in understanding art* (Carlisle and Toronto, Ontario: Toronto Tuppence Press/Piquant Press, 2000), pp. 8, 35–36, 126–127, 156, 181–182.

——, 'Letter to a young artist' in Michael Card, *Scribbling in the Sand: Christ and creativity* (Downers Grove, IL: InterVarsity Press, 2002). Letter available online at the TECHNO-evangel, 'A letter to Christian artists', Venturopolis: <https://venturopolis.wordpress.com/2009/06/02/a-letter-to-christian-artists>, accessed February 2023.

——, *Rainbows for the Fallen World* (Toronto, Ontario: Toronto Tuppence Press, 2005 [1980]), pp. 46–47.

Seidell, Dan, *Who's Afraid of Modern Art: Essays on modern art and theology in conversation* (Eugene, OR: Cascade Books, 2015), p. 3.

Shelley, Percy Bysshe, 'A defence of poetry' in Mary Wollstonecraft Shelley (ed.), *Essays, Letters from Abroad, Translations and Fragments* (London: Edward Moxton, 1840), <www.poetryfoundation.org/articles/69388/a-defence-of-poetry>, accessed February 2023.

Sherwood, Harriet, 'UK secularism on rise as more than half say they have no religion', *The Guardian* (11 July 2019), <www.theguardian.com/world/2019/jul/11/uk-secularism-on-rise-as-more-than-half-say-they-have-no-religion#:~:text=UK%20secularism%20on%20rise%20as%20more%20than%20half%20say%20they%20have%20no%20religion,-This%20article%20is&text=The%20growth%20of%20secularism%20in,religious%20to%20declare%20themselves%20atheist>, accessed January 2023.

Shippey, Tom, *J. R. R. Tolkien: Author of the century* (London: HarperCollins, 2000), pp. xx–xxi, 114, 119, 123–124, 124–125, 127, 128–143, 143–146, 207–208, 262.

Silva, Moisés, *Philippians*, Baker Exegetical Commentary on the New Testament (Grand Rapids, MI: Baker Academic, 2nd edn, 2005 [1992]), p. 197.

Sinha, Aishwarya, 'Is Joss Whedon heading towards retirement? Drink all the tea with us', *Film Daily* (7 December 2020), <https://filmdaily.co/news/joss-whedon-retirement/>, accessed February 2023.

Sinitiere, Phillip Luke, 'Derek Webb beyond belief', *Sacred Matters* (20 February 2020), <https://sacredmattersmagazine.com/derek-webb-beyond-belief>, both accessed February 2023.

Smith, James K. A., *Awaiting the King: Reforming public theology*, Cultural Liturgies, Volume 3 (Grand Rapids, MI: Baker Academic, Kindle edn, 2017), loc. 145–154, 2763–3796, 4036, 570–607 and 6004–6173, chapters 3 and 6 and pp. ix, 16–18, 213–221.

——, 'The Benedict option or the Augustinian call: Considering two ancient options for the contemporary church', *Comment* (16 March 2017), <www.cardus.ca/comment/article/the-benedict-option-or-the-augustinian-call>, accessed February 2023.

——, 'Continuing a conversation with the Westmont 4', at *Fors Clavigera* (23 January 2014), <https://forsclavigera.blogspot.com/2014/01/continuing-conversation-with-westmont.html>, accessed January 2023.

——, *Desiring the Kingdom: Worship, worldview, and cultural formation*, Cultural Liturgies, Volume 1 (Grand Rapids, MI: Baker Academic, 2009), chapter 3 and pp. 41, 46–71, 93–103, 209–213.

——, 'Excursus: Common grace versus providence' in *Awaiting the King*, chapter 3, loc. 3385–3421.

—— *Imagining the Kingdom: How worship works*, Cultural Liturgies, Volume 2 (Grand Rapids, MI: Baker Academic, Kindle edn, 2013), loc. 813–1719, 833, 1043–1064, 1660–1700, 1731–2246, 3307–3365, 4036, part 2, chapters 1, 2 and 4, and especially pp. 32, 43–44 and 70–72.

——, 'The new alarmism: How some Christians are stoking fear rather than hope', *Washington Post* (10 March 2017), <www.washingtonpost.com/news/acts-of-faith/wp/2017/03/10/the-new-alarmism-how-some-christians-are-stoking-fear-rather-than-hope>, accessed February 2023.

——, 'Reforming public theology: Two kingdoms, or two cities', *Calvin Theological Journal*, vol. 47 (2012), pp. 122–137, especially pp. 131 ff.

——, *You Are What You Love: The spiritual power of habit* (Grand Rapids, MI: Brazos Press, 2016), p. 27 and chapter 2.

Snow, Shane, 'Why commit?', TEDx Talks, YouTube (11 August 2014), 16:57, <www.youtube.com/watch?v=Asm2Ad49cyI>, accessed February 2023.

Snyder C. R. and Lopez, Shane J. (eds), *Handbook of Positive Psychology* (Oxford: Oxford University Press, 2002).

Spackman, Betty, *A Profound Weakness: Christians and kitsch* (Carlisle: Piquant Editions, 2005).

Spann, Otis in Paul Oliver, *Conversations with the Blues* (New York: Horizon Press, 1965), p. 52, quoted in Jon Michael Spencer, *Protest and Praise: Sacred music of black religion* (Minneapolis, MN: Fortress Press, 1990), p. 114.

Spencer, Jon Michael, *Protest and Praise: Sacred music of black religion* (Minneapolis, MN: Fortress Press, 1990), pp. 111, 112, 113, 114, 115, 120, 125, n. 64.

Steven, 'Sho Baraka "Talented 10th" debuts #1 gospel, #5 Christian and #12 rap on Billboard', *Rapzilla* (25 January 2013), <https://rapzilla.com/2013-01-sho-baraka-talented-10th-debuts-1-gospel-5-christian-a-12-rap-on-billboard>, accessed February 2023.

Stevens, Sufjan, 'Casimir Pulaski Day' is track 10 on Stevens' album *Come On, Feel the Illinoise* (Asthmatic Kitty, 2005).

Strange, Daniel, '"For their rock is not as our rock": The gospel as "subversive fulfilment" of the religious Other', *For Their Rock Is Not as Our Rock: An evangelical theology of religions* (Nottingham: Apollos, 2014), chapter 7.

——, 'I'm (not) getting sentimental over you', *Themelios*, vol. 42, no. 3 (December 2017), pp. 440–445.

Stringer, Heather Smith and Price, Lee, 'Sleeping with peaches: An interview with painter Lee Price', *The Other Journal*, no. 19 (23 August 2011), <https://theotherjournal.com/2011/08/23/sleeping-with-peaches-an-interview-with-painter-lee-price>, accessed February 2023.

Swain, Scott, *The Trinity: An introduction*, Short Studies in Systematic Theology, ed. Graham A. Cole and Oren R. Martin (Wheaton, IL: Crossway, 2020).

Szapołowska, Grażyna, interview on the American and Artificial Eye Region 2 DVD releases of *A Short Film about Love*, Tom Patson & Partners, YouTube (2003), <www.youtube.com/watch?v=5I5va4HmNAU>, February 2023.

Tanz, Jason, 'Playing for time: A father, a dying son, and the quest to build the most profound videogame ever', *Wired* (January 2016), <www.wired.com/2016/01/that-dragon-cancer>, accessed February 2023.

Taylor, Charles, *Modern Social Imaginaries* (Durham, NC, and London: Duke University Press, 2003), pp. 23–25.

Taylor, E. L. Hebden, 'The Reformation and the development of modern science', *Churchman*, vol. 82, no. 2 (1968), pp. 87–103, <www.alloflife redeemed.co.uk/reformation%20of%20modern%20science.pdf>, accessed February 2023.

Taylor, JohnMark, 'Mirror neurons after a quarter century: New light, new cracks', *Harvard University Science in the News Blog* (25 July 2016), <http://sitn.hms.harvard.edu/flash/2016/mirror-neurons-quarter-century-new-light-new-cracks>, accessed February 2023.

Temple, William, 'Lecture on church and state', in *Church and Nation: The Bishop Paddock Lectures for 1914–15* (London: Macmillan and Co., 1915), <www.gutenberg.org/ebooks/43896>, accessed January 2023.

Thomas, Nigel J. T., 'Are theories of imagery theories of imagination? An active perception approach to conscious mental content', *Cognitive Science*, vol. 23, issue 2 (11 February 1999), pp. 207–245, <www.academia.edu/3591301/Are_Theories_of_Imagery_Theories_of_Imagination_An_Active_Perception_Approach_to_Conscious_Mental_Content>, accessed January 2023.

——, 'The multidimensional spectrum of imagination: Images, dreams, hallucinations, and active, imaginative perception', *Humanities*, vol. 3 (15 April 2014), pp. 132–184, <www.mdpi.com/2076-0787/3/2/132/pdf>, accessed February 2023.

Thomas à Kempis, *The Imitation of Christ,* book 3, chapter 25.

Tisby, Jemar, 'The color of compromise', *The Color of Compromise: The truth about the American church's complicity in racism* (Grand Rapids, MI: Zondervan, 2019), chapter 1, especially pp. 16–17.

Tolkien, J. R. R., *The Hobbit, or There and Back Again* (New York: Ballantine Books, rev. edn 1973), pp. 92–93.

——, *The Lord of the Rings* (London: HarperCollins, 1995 [1954–55]), pp. xvi, 12, 32–34, 54–55, 58, 123–124, 260–262, 348, 366, 387–390, 394, 446, 503–504, 582, 600–601, 661, 666, 806, 832–839, 901, 923, 924–925, 930, 943, 996.

——, 'The music of Ainur', *The Silmarillion*, pp. 3–12.

——, 'Mythopoeia' in *Tree and Leaf* (London and New York: HarperCollins, 2001 [1964]), pp. 83–90.

——, 'Of the Rings of Power and the Third Age', *The Silmarillion*, ed. Christopher Tolkien (London: HarperCollins, 1999 [1977]), p. 346.

——, 'On fairy-stories' in *Tree and Leaf* (London and New York: HarperCollins, 2001 [1964]), p. 31, <https://archive.org/details/on-fairy-stories_202110>, accessed February 2023).

——, *The Silmarillion*, ed. Christopher Tolkien (London: HarperCollins, 1999 [1977]), pp. 3–12, 23, 346.

Townsend, Henry, quoted in Paul Oliver, *Conversations with the Blues* (New York: Horizon Press, 1965), pp. 169–170, quoted in Jon Michael Spencer, *Protest and Praise: Sacred music of black religion* (Minneapolis, MN: Fortress Press, 1990), p. 122.

Trent, John F., '"The Lord of the Rings: The Rings of Power" completely falls off Nielsen charts just two weeks after season finale', *Bounding into Comics* (30 November 2022), <https://boundingintocomics.com/2022/11/30/the-lord-of-the-rings-the-rings-of-power-completely-falls-off-nielsen-charts-just-two-weeks-after-season-finale>, accessed February 2023.

Turnau, Ted, 'Book reviews: The Benedict Option', *Foundations*, vol. 73 (Autumn 2017), <www.affinity.org.uk/foundations-issues/issue-73-book-review-4>, accessed February 2023.

——, 'Dialogues concerning cultural engagement', parts 1 and 2, *Foundations*, vol. 70 (Spring 2016), <www.affinity.org.uk/foundations/issue-70/issue-70-article-2-dialogues-concerning-cultural-engagement-part-one>, and vol. 71 (Autumn 2016), and <www.affinity.org.uk/foundations-issues/issue-71-article-1-dialogues-concerning-cultural-engagement-part-two>, respectively, accessed February 2023.

——, 'Inflecting the world: Popular culture and the perception of evil', *Journal of Popular Culture*, vol. 38, no. 2 (November 2004), pp. 391–392.

——, *Popologetics: Popular culture in Christian perspective* (Phillipsburg, NJ: P&R, 2012), chapters 3, 4, 8, 9, 10 and 11 and pp. 26–28, 51–53, 57–58, 65–72, 74–76, 231–234.

——, 'Popular culture, apologetics, and the discourse of desire – Introduction', *Cultural Encounters*, vol. 8, no. 2 (November 2012), pp. 25–46, <www.turnau.cz/content/popular-culture-apologetics-and-discourse-desire-introduction>, accessed February 2023.

——, 'Reflecting theologically on popular culture as meaningful: The role of sin, grace, and general revelation', *Calvin Theological Journal*, vol. 37, no. 2 (November 2002), pp. 270–296, <www.calvin.edu/library/database/crcpi/fulltext/ctj/88090.pdf>, accessed March 2023.

——, 'Review article: Imagining the Kingdom: How worship works (James K. A. Smith)', *Foundations*, no. 65 (Autumn 2013), <www.affinity.org.uk/foundations-issues/issue-65-article-5-review-article-imagining-the-kingdom-how-worship-works--james-k-a-smith>, accessed February 2023.

Turnau, Theodore, 'Re-imagining Ricoeur: Popular culture as discursive text, metaphor, and narrative', PhD thesis, Westminster Theological Seminary, Glenside, PA (1999), especially chapters 3 to 5.

Turnau, Ted and Floyd, Ruth Naomi, *Imagination Manifesto: A call to plant oases of imagination* (London: IVP, 2023).

Turnau, Ted, Burnett, E. Stephen and Moore, Jared, *The Pop Culture Parent: Helping kids engage their world for Christ* (Greensboro, NC: New Growth Press, 2020), pp. 44–45.

Turner, Victor, *The Ritual Process: Structure and anti-structure* (Hawthorne, NY: Aldine de Gruyter, 1969).

U2, 'U2's POWERFUL tribute to 9/11 victims', FreshVideos, YouTube, <www.youtube.com/watch?v=iBzdittT3c4>, accessed February 2023.

VanDrunen, David, *Living in God's Two Kingdoms: A biblical vision for Christianity and culture* (Wheaton, IL: Crossway, 2010), pp. 65–66.

Van Hunt, Mrs Zula, (b. 1902), oral history interview, by George McDaniel, Center for Southern Folklore, Memphis, Tennessee (5 January 1983), tape 3, p. 13, quoted in Spencer, *Protest and Praise: Sacred music of black religion* (Minneapolis, MN: Fortress Press, 1990), p. 111.

Van Til, Cornelius, *Essays on Christian Education* (Phillipsburg, NJ: P&R, 1979), part III, section 5.D.3.

Vezzali, Loris, Stathi, Sofia, Giovannini, Dino, Capozza, Dora and Trifiletti, Elena, 'The greatest magic of Harry Potter: Reducing prejudice', *Journal of Applied Psychology*, vol. 45, no. 2 (February 2015), pp. 105–121, <www.researchgate.net/publication/264162058_The_greatest_magic_of_Harry_Potter_Reducing_prejudice.>, accessed February 2023.

Vocal Group Harmony, 'Spotlight on J. C. Ginyard – Part One (The Jubalaires)', *Vocal Group Harmony*, no. 924 (25 May 2019), <www.vocalgroupharmony.com/6ROWNEW/BeforeThisTime.htm>, accessed February 2023.

Vos, Geerhardus, *The Pauline Eschatology*, tr. John Richard De Witt (Phillipsburg, NJ: P&R, 1986 [1930]).

Vyshedskiy, Andrey, 'The science of imagination', TED-Ed, YouTube (12 December 2016), <www.youtube.com/watch?v=e7uXAlXdTe4>, accessed February 2023.

Walker, Wyatt Tee, *Somebody's Calling My Name: Black sacred music and social change* (Valley Forge, PA: Judson Press, 1979), p. 46, 56–57.

Waltke, Bruce K., 'The literary genre of Genesis, chapter one', *Crux*, vol. 27 (December 1991), pp. 2–10.

Warnock, Mary, *Imagination* (Berkeley and Los Angeles, CA: University of California Press, 1976), parts I and II.

Wattercutter, Angela, 'How pop culture changed the face of the same-sex marriage debate', *Wired* (27 June 2013), <www.wired.com/2013/06/pop-culture-same-sex-marriage>, accessed February 2023.

Webb, Derek, 'What matters more' (track 6 on *Stockholm Syndrome*, 2009), Fair Trade Services, <www.youtube.com/watch?v=s5pBXY2AkeY>, accessed February 2023.

——, *see also under* Coleman, Dustin J.; Hawkins, Ryan; Loftus, Matthew; Sinitiere, Phillip Luke

Welch, Gillian, 'Orphan girl', *Revival* (Acony Records, 1996), track 1.

Whedon, Joss, quoted in Emily Nussbaum, 'Must-see metaphysics', *New York Times Magazine* (22 September 2002), <www.nytimes.com/2002/09/22/magazine/must-see-metaphysics.html.>, accessed February 2023.

Wieseltier, Leon, 'How voters' personal suffering overtook reason – and brought us Donald Trump', *Washington Post* (22 June 2016), <www.washingtonpost.com/posteverything/wp/2016/06/22/how-voters-personal-suffering-overtook-reason-and-brought-us-donald-trump/?utm_term=.dd65f67fef32>, accessed February 2023.

Windmeyer, Shane, 'Dan and me: My coming out as a friend of Dan Cathy and Chick-fil-A', *HuffPost* (28 January 2013; updated 6 December 2017), <www.huffpost.com/entry/dan-cathy-chick-fil-a_b_2564379>, accessed February 2023.

Winters, Clifford, 'A strange death: Cosmic conflagration as conceptual metaphor in 2 Peter 3:6–13', *Conversations with the Biblical World*, vol. 33 (2013), pp. 147–161, cited in Middleton, *A New Heaven and a New Earth*, pp. 197–199.

Witvliet, John, 'The opening of worship: Trinity' in Leanne Van Dyk, *A More Profound Alleluia: Theology and worship in harmony* (Grand Rapids, MI: Eerdmans, 2005), p. 12, quoted in Cosper, *Rhythms of Grace*, loc. 1930–1933.

Wolfe, Gregory, *Intruding upon the Timeless: Meditations on art, faith, and mystery* (Baltimore, MD: Square Halo Books, Kindle edn, 2003).

Wolters, Albert, 'Worldview and textual criticism in 2 Peter 3:10', *Westminster Theological Journal*, vol. 49 (1987), pp. 405–413, <www.allofliferedeemed.co.uk/Wolters/AMW2Peter3.pdf>, accessed January 2023.

Wood, David (ed.), *On Paul Ricoeur: Narrative and Interpretation* (London: Routledge, 1991).

Woodbridge, Caleb, 'We are all worshippers', *Bigger on the Inside* (7 August 2022), <www.biggerinside.co.uk/p/we-are-all-worshippers>, accessed February 2023.

Woodhead, Linda, *see under* Robertson, David G.

Wright, N. T., *Surprised by Hope: Rethinking heaven, the resurrection, and the mission of the church* (New York: HarperOne, 2008), p. 293.

Y2Karl, 'Dark was the night – cold was the ground', *Metafilter* (15 September 2005), <www.metafilter.com/45137/Dark-Was-The-NightCold-Was-The-Ground-by-Blind-Willie-Johnson>, accessed February 2023.

Yancey, Philip, *Vanishing Grace: What ever happened to the good news?* (Grand Rapids, MI: Zondervan, 2014), pp. 262–263.

Zahl, David, *Seculosity: How career, parenting, technology, food, politics, and romance became our new religion and what to do about it* (Minneapolis, MN: Fortress Press, 2019).

Zeidman, Peter and Maguire, Eleanor A., 'Anterior hippocampus: The anatomy of perception, imagination and episodic memory', *Nature Reviews Neuroscience*, vol. 17, no. 3 (March 2016), pp. 173–182 and Figure 2.j, <www.openacademyofmedicine.org/sites/default/files/pdf/Bibliografia/Anterior%20hippocampus%20the%20anatomy%20of%20perception,%20imagination%20and%20episodic%20memory.pdf>, all accessed February 2023.

Index of persons

Note: 'fn' indicates footnote.

Index of subjects

Note: 'fn' indicates footnote.

Index of Scripture references

Note: Primary discussions of a passage are often indicated in **bold.** 'Fn' indicates footnote.

ivp